Introduction to Foodservice

West's and Wood's

Introduction to Foodservice

Seventh Edition Prepared by

June Payne-Palacio, Ph.D., R.D.
Professor, Pepperdine University

Virginia Harger, M.S., R.D.
Professor Emeritus, Oregon State University

Grace Shugart, M.S.
Professor Emeritus, Kansas State University

Monica Theis, M.S., R.D.
Lecturer, University of Wisconsin–Madison

PRENTICE HALL
Englewood Cliffs, New Jersey 07632

Library of Congress Cataloging-in-Publication Data

West's and Wood's introduction to foodservice.—7th ed. / prepared
　by June Payne-Palacio . . . [et al.]
　　　p.　cm.
　　Rev. ed. of: Foodservice in institutions / Bessie B. West and
　LeVelle Wood.
　　Includes bibliographical references and index.
　　ISBN 0-02-390390-2
　　1. Food service management.　I. Payne-Palacio, June.　II. West,
　Bessie Brooks. Foodservice in institutions.　III. Title:
　Introduction to foodservice.
　TX911.3.M27W44　1994
　647.95'068—dc20

　　　　　　　　　　　　　　　　　　　　　　　　93-20467
　　　　　　　　　　　　　　　　　　　　　　　　CIP

Editor: Kevin Davis
Production Supervisor: Kelly Ricci
Production Manager: Aliza Greenblatt
Cover Designer: Proof Positive/Farrowlyne Associates
Cover photograph: Alain Choisnet/The Image Bank
Illustrations: Carlisle Communications

This book was set in Baskerville by Carlisle Communications.

Earlier editions entitled *Foodservice in Institutions* copyright © 1938, 1945, 1955, 1966, 1977 by
John Willey & Sons and copyright © 1986, 1988 by Macmillan Publishing Company

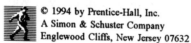

© 1994 by Prentice-Hall, Inc.
A Simon & Schuster Company
Englewood Cliffs, New Jersey 07632

Printed in the United States of America

10　9　8　7　6　5　4　3

ISBN　0-02-390390-2　NB2I

Prentice-Hall International (UK) Limited, *London*
Prentice-Hall of Australia Pty. Limited, *Sydney*
Prentice-Hall Canada Inc., *Toronto*
Prentice-Hall Hispanoamericana, S.A., *Mexico*
Prentice-Hall of India Private Limited, *New Delhi*
Prentice-Hall of Japan, Inc., *Tokyo*
Simon & Schuster Asia Pte. Ltd., *Singapore*
Editora Prentice-Hall do Brasil, Ltda., *Rio de Janeiro*

Preface

Ever since the first edition of *Foodservice in Institutions* (now entitled *Introduction to Foodservice*) was published in 1938, the authors have been committed to presenting the basic principles of foodservice management, which can be applied to *all* types of foodservice organizations. This new seventh edition is no exception. Consistent with previous editions, comprehensive coverage of all aspects of foodservice management is given. In the earlier years of this text, there was a distinct difference between commercial, or profit-seeking, organizations and noncommercial, or institutional, not-for-profit foodservice operations. Special emphasis then was given to institutional foodservices—schools and colleges, hospitals and health care facilities, and in-plant or industrial foodservices—hence the name, *Foodservice in Institutions*.

New Title and Scope

During the years, there has been a gradual change in the not-for-profit philosophy in the management of many institutional foodservices. With the rising health care costs of recent years, for example, many hospitals have become more financially competitive in order to succeed and remain in business. Today, most foodservices are striving for some margin of profit, making less of a distinction between the two classes of foodservices. Due to this, and to deemphasize the term *institutional,* the title of this edition has been changed to *Introduction to Foodservice*.

Basic, comprehensive coverage of the foodservice administration field, including principles applicable to *all* types of foodservice operations, is the focus of *Introduction to Foodservice*. This title change better reflects the major thrust of the text, and it is hoped that the new title will give a good connotation of the purpose, scope, and level of the subject matter.

Since no single text can cover all details of the management and operation of every type of foodservice organization, the authors have chosen examples and illustrations for this edition that primarily reflect the noncommercial foodservice field, although many commercial applications are included as well. As in the sixth edition, the subject matter is organized into four major sections, with a total of 16 chapters.

New in This Edition

The material presented in this edition is updated and revised according to current trends and practices. For example, the effects of the Americans with Disabilities Act (ADA) of 1990 on employment practices and foodservice management, as well as design of the facility, are discussed. Many new photographs and illustrations are included to help visually interpret the subject matter. In addition, some chapter titles have been renamed using new terminology to better reflect the subject matter.

New Chapter

In order to address an important aspect of successful management in today's competitive world, a new chapter has been added to *Introduction to Foodservice*. This addition, Chapter 15, "Marketing in Foodservice Organizations," discusses marketing concepts in foodservices. It points out the dual responsibility of foodservice managers: (1) to assure that good food is prepared, and (2) to present and promote the food more effectively than their competitors. This chapter includes the basic concept of marketing, outlines the steps for developing a marketing strategy and program, and gives some examples and illustrations of merchandising and marketing techniques that are suitable for use in foodservices. It should alert managers to the benefits of having a marketing program and the need for including a marketing strategy in their planning.

New Features in This Edition

Several new features are added to this edition that we believe will help students, instructors, and other users of the text by providing additional meaning. These include the following:

1. *Summary Questions* at the end of each chapter. These help pinpoint the important concepts of the subject matter and serve as a study review and test for the reader, ensuring that the more important information is learned.

2. A *Glossary* is included to help define and more clearly explain some of the terms peculiar to our field of study.

3. An *Appendix* has been added. In an attempt to streamline certain chapters, material not essential to understanding the basic concepts of the subject has been moved to the Appendix. The information serves as a ready-reference for the reader who seeks additional, detailed information. Teachers of foodservice management courses should find these additions helpful in guiding students' learning.

As with previous editions, each chapter concludes with a Summary and a Bibliography, with related references provided that will assist the reader in finding further sources of information on a particular topic. It is expected that users of this text will also supplement their reading with current journals, trade magazines, and research reports, as well as attend seminars and exhibits at conventions and trade shows to keep themselves up-to-date.

Expanded Coverage

The discussion of forecasting in foodservices (Chapter 3) is given in greater depth than in the previous edition. Likewise, more coverage is given to the receiving of purchases and to the newer legislation affecting the management of foodservices—especially the Americans with Disabilities Act (ADA) of 1990 and the Civil Rights Act of 1991. Greater emphasis is also given to food safety and protection, including the Hazard Analysis and Critical Control Points (HACCP). Overall, more coverage is given to the management of food production and less to the actual preparation of the food. These two topics are now covered in Chapter 5.

College Courses for Which Text is Suitable

Peer reviews of the manuscript for this edition, commissioned by Macmillan Publishing Company, provided many excellent suggestions and challenges for our revisions. One thing that became increasingly clear from the reviewers' comments is that no two teachers would organize the subject matter into specific courses in the same way. In fact, some of the reviewers would have preferred reorganization of the topics in our text. However, we believe that we present them in a logical sequence—first, a discussion of the technical operations of a foodservice so that students will have a basis for knowing what is to be managed and, then, the discussion of management techniques follows.

Not all schools and universities will use the material in the same sequence in which we have put it. However, the subject matter provided is appropriate for courses that include the following (with these or similar names):

Introduction to Foodservice Management
Quantity Food Production
Purchasing for Foodservices (Both food and equipment)
Organization and Management of Foodservices
Facility Design and Equipment Arrangement
Financial Management of Foodservices
Food Protection and Safety
Menu Planning for Foodservices
Foodservice Marketing and Merchandising

It is our hope that this newly revised edition of a classic text continues to meet the needs, as it has in the past, of the present generation of students who are preparing to become foodservice managers or qualified administrative dietitians. Also, we hope that teachers will find *Introduction to Foodservice* a helpful guide and that foodservice managers will use it as a ready-reference in their work.

Acknowledgments

Many people have assisted with the preparation of *Introduction to Foodservice*. Without the help of these persons, our task would have been impossible.

The current authors are deeply appreciative of the excellent work of the original authors, Bessie Brooks West and LeVelle Wood, in providing a text that has been so widely accepted for use in the United States and abroad for the past 55 years. The text has been recognized for its authenticity and accuracy, a standard that we have strived to maintain in the new edition. Mrs. West assisted with revisions through the fifth edition, before she passed away in 1984 at the age of 93. Miss Wood was active in all revisions through the sixth edition. Now, at the age of 93, she lives in a retirement home in Portland, Oregon, which is pictured in Chapter 8 (Fig. 8.3). Without the pioneering work and writing of these two women, then on the faculty of Kansas State University, this revision would not be a reality.

The continuing coauthors, Virginia Harger, Grace Shugart, and June Payne-Palacio, were pleased to welcome as a new coauthor, Monica Theis, Lecturer in the Department of Food Science, University of Wisconsin–Madison. She has brought a new, fresh perspective and an enthusiatic approach to revising the text. We are grateful to her for her many contributions.

We are grateful to the peer reviewers, commissioned by Macmillan, who challenged our thinking and made excellent suggestions for change or additions to the first drafts of the manuscript. Their comments were honest and open, and many of their ideas have been incorporated into the text. We believe their input will make the text even more meaningful to our readers. We thank them for their contributions to this revision.

The following individuals helped in special ways in the preparation of this edition. To each of them we are greatly indebted and give our thanks.

Mary Molt, Assistant Director, Housing and Dining Services, and Instructor, Department of Hotel, Restaurant, Institutional Management, and Dietetics, Kansas State University, who assisted with the chapter on quantity food production.

Jane Dunn, Director of Food and Nutrition Services, and members of her administrative staff at the University of Wisconsin Hospital and Clinics, for guidance, advice, and help in providing illustrations relating to purchasing, financial management, and marketing.

Dr. M. Eileen Matthews, Professor, Department of Food Science, University of Wisconsin–Madison, for critiquing the writing and content on food safety.

Dr. Ann Messersmith, Professor, Nutrition and Food Management Department, Oregon State University, for her encouragement and assistance with suggesting and locating references for several chapters of the book.

Dr. Zoe Ann Holmes, Professor, Nutrition and Food Management Department, Oregon State University, for assistance with the section on computer-aided design and other computer applications.

Wesley Smith, a resident at Willamette View Manor, Portland, Oregon, for obtaining pictures of that facility for our use as illustrations.

Gene Kelsey, free-lance photographer of Corvallis, Oregon, for taking many photographs for us.

Bob Honson, Director of Nutrition Services, Portland, Oregon Public School District, for allowing us use of their facilities for photos.

James L. Matthews, a free-lance writer in Chicago, for editing certain parts of this revision.

Christina Pyle, copyeditor of Corvallis, Oregon, who helped coordinate the illustrations and permissions section of the manuscript.

Secretarial staff of the Department of Food Science, University of Wisconsin–Madison, for their work on the manuscript.

We would like to express a special thank-you to our Macmillan editor, Kevin Davis, for his understanding of our subject matter and help in putting it in perspective, for his patience in working with us, and for giving encouragement for the completion of this revision. He has been outstanding. His assistants, Linda Cupp and Susan Wesner, have always been helpful and considerate with any concerns we have had.

The work of Kelly Ricci, Production Manager; Kathleen Riley-King, Editorial Manager; and the copy editor, all employees of Spectrum Publisher Services, Inc., deserves special recognition. They have been thorough and careful in handling the many details involved. We appreciate their friendly, helpful manner in working with us to produce a book of which we can be proud. Our thanks to them.

Finally, we wish to acknowledge the support and sympathetic encouragement of our families—in particular, Monica's husband, Craig Schiestl, and June's husband, Moki Palacio—as well as special friends who have endured the countless hours we have devoted to this work. We appreciate the committed efforts of all of these people.

June Payne-Palacio
Virginia Harger
Grace Shugart
Monica Theis

Brief Contents

x

Contents

CHAPTER 5

Production Management   131

CHAPTER 6

Delivery and Service   173

SECTION III

Physical Facilities   205

CHAPTER 7

Sanitation and Safety   207

CHAPTER 8

Facilities Planning and Design

253

CHAPTER 11
Staffing and Managing Human Resources   371

CHAPTER 12
Administrative Leadership   417

CHAPTER 16
Computer-Assisted Management   533

APPENDIX A
Basic Cooking Methods   571

Foodservice Organizations

The Foodservice Industry

More than 8 million people are employed in the foodservice industry in the United States, which is more than three times the number of persons who work in automobile and steel manufacturing companies. The number of jobs available for foodservice managers is expected to grow by 28% between 1988 and the year 2000. This is faster than the average growth rate for any other occupation in the country. The National Restaurant Association (NRA) projected $262 billion in sales for 1992, an increase of 1.8% from the previous year.

Today, the foodservice industry is defined in its broadest sense to mean all establishments where food is regularly served outside the home. Such establishments include formal restaurants, hotel or motel and department store dining rooms, coffee shops, family restaurants, specialty and ethnic restaurants, and fast-food outlets. In addition, foodservices that are operated in schools, colleges, and universities; in hospitals, nursing homes, and other health care settings; in recreational facilities; in transportation companies; in the military; in correctional facilities; in office buildings and plants; in convenience stores, supermarkets, and service delis; and in community centers and retirement residences are also included. The history and development of organizations within the foodservice industry presented in this chapter is intended to give the reader a perspective of, and an appreciation for, foodservices as they are today. This overview from early times to the present includes the many types of establishments that serve food to groups of people and are those that make up the foodservice industry. The background information should be of special interest to those who are or who are preparing to become managers of foodservice operations. The trends that are shown provide some basis for anticipating the future, and these trends should alert managers to the demands that new developments and changes in this field may bring, so that they can prepare to meet them. As George Santayana so wisely said, "Those who cannot remember the past are condemned to repeat it." History can not only provide people with an opportunity to learn from past mistakes, but also show which of the seeds that were sown blossomed into successes and why.

Information in the succeeding chapters is basic to the successful operation of all types of foodservices, whatever their philosophies and objectives. All are concerned with providing good food to meet specific needs of groups of people served outside the home.

Learning Objectives

After studying this chapter, the reader should be able to

1. trace the history and development of foodservice organizations from early times to the present
2. describe how the history and development of foodservice organizations has made an impact on present-day operations
3. discuss the role of religious orders and royal households in the development of institutional foodservice organizations
4. describe the trends in college and university foodservice
5. identify the legislation that has influenced school foodservice
6. describe the evolution of foodservice in hospitals, nursing homes, and other health care centers
7. trace the history of restaurants from early times to the present

Early-Day History

Foodservice organizations in operation in the United States today have become an accepted way of life, and we tend to regard them as relatively recent innovations. However, they have their roots in the habits and customs that characterize our civilization and pre-date the Middle Ages. Certain phases of foodservice operations reached a well-organized form as early as feudal times in countries that have exerted the most influence on the development of American food habits and customs. These countries are England, France, Germany, and Sweden. In each of those countries, partaking of food was a social event in which the entire family, and often guests, shared. There was no withdrawal for eating that characterizes the customs of certain peoples, no religious beliefs barring participation from meals with others. Their economic level and the type of food eaten also fostered serving food to groups. Instead of the few grains of parched wheat or corn, the bowl of rice, or a bit of raw fruit that satisfied some races, these people ate meat or a variety of other protein foods from various sources. Since these foods could not be transported without danger of spoilage, immediate food production in well-established kitchens and with good supervision was required. These countries, then, have contributed to the evolution of the foodservice industry.

Some of the types of foodservices that existed long ago are contrasted in this chapter with their present-day counterparts. Although in medieval times religious orders, royal households, colleges, and inns were the most prevalent types of organizations in which quantity food production was the rule, other types of foodservice organizations and their development are also considered. These include clubs and other social organizations, schools, the military, correctional facilities, hospitals and health care facilities, employee feeding in industrial plants or offices, retirement homes and residences for other groups of people, restaurants, and transportation companies.

Religious Orders

Religious orders and royal households were among the earliest practitioners of quantity food production, and although these foodservices were far different from those we know today, each has made a contribution to the evolvement of present-day foodservice.

Abbeys that dotted the countryside, particularly in England, served not only the numerous brethren of the order, but also thousands of pilgrims who flocked there to worship. The space provided for food preparation indicates the scope of their foodservice operations. At Canterbury Abbey, a favorite site of innumerable pilgrimages, the kitchen measures 45 feet in diameter.

Records show that the food preparation carried out by the brethren reached a much higher standard than food served in the inns at that time. The vows the brothers took did not diminish their appreciation for good food. Food was grown on the abbey's grounds, and lay contributions were provided liberally for the institution's table. The strong sense of stewardship in the abbeys led to the establishment of a detailed accounting system. These records showed that a specified per capita per diem food allowance was in effect. Thus, an effective, early-day cost accounting system came into existence.

Royal and Noble Households

The royal household, with its hundreds of retainers, and the households of nobles, often numbering as many as 150 to 250 persons, also necessitated an efficient foodservice. There was wide variance in rank and in the subsequent food allowances within these groups. In providing for the various needs, strict cost accounting was necessary, and here, perhaps, is the beginning of the present-day scientific foodservice cost accounting. The cost record most often cited is the *Northumberland Household Book*. For this household of more than 140 persons, 10 different breakfasts were recorded, the best for the earl and his lady, the poorest for the lowest workman or scullion. A similar range is presumed for the other meals.

The kitchens in these medieval households would appall the present-day foodservice manager by their disregard for sanitary standards in food storage, preparation, and handling. A clutter of supplies overflowing from inadequate table and shelf space to the wooden plank floors, handled by children and nosed by dogs, commonly composed the background for the preparation of elaborate creations for the table. A notable example is shown in Fig. 1.1. Since labor was cheap and readily available, a large staff of workers was employed to prepare the food. Rank was evident in the division of labor. The head cook might wear a gold chain over handsome clothing and present his culinary creations to his employer in person. The pastry cook and the meat cook did not rate as high, but were esteemed for their contributions. The average scullion often had scarcely a rag to wear and received broken bread and the privilege of sleeping on the hearth through the chilly winter nights as his wage.

As time passed, discovery of the causes of food spoilage led to improved practices in food storage and in food preparation in these noble households. Advances in the understanding of the laws of physics resulted in replacing open hearths with iron stoves and refining much of the kitchen equipment. A more convenient equipment arrangement led to a reduction in the number of workers required, helping to relieve disorder and confusion. Employees' dress changed to show some regard for the tasks they performed, by becoming more practical.

Figure 1.1.   The Kitchen, Windsor Castle at Christmas time. (Courtesy, Arnold Shircliffe.)

The United States has no equivalent of these royal households. However, the White House, as the president's residence, is one site of official entertainment in this country. Whereas the feasts of the royal households in the past were of "formidable proportions," observers have noted that the White House kitchen staff could prepare anything from "an egg to an ox." The White House kitchen of 100 years ago is shown in Fig. 1.2. An early-day state diplomatic dinner at the White House included seven courses, each with many accompaniments. The present trend is toward simplification of menu patterns even for more formal occasions, which is in harmony with current American food consumption habits. A photograph of the 1975 White House kitchen is shown in Fig. 1.3, and the White House State Dining Room is shown in Fig. 1.4. Both of these rooms are designed for efficient use of space. Equipment in the kitchen has been chosen and placed to maximize productivity.

Notable among the other early foodservices were the inns, taverns, and the hostels, which were established by European colleges. From these, the foodservices in schools and colleges, hospitals and other health care facilities, and

Figure 1.2.   1892 White House kitchen. (Reproduced from the Collections, Prints and Photograph Division, Library of Congress.)

Figure 1.3. 1975 White House kitchen. (Reproduced from the Collections, Prints and Photograph Division, Library of Congress.)

retirement communities, as well as the wide variety of commercial and industrial foodservices as we know them today, have evolved.

Development of Present-Day Foodservices

Colleges and Universities

Providing meals and rooms for college and university students has been the custom for many years. However, responsibility for the kinds of services offered and the administration of these living situations has changed considerably during the years.

From the twelfth century through the medieval ages, hostels were set up at European colleges and universities as the accepted arrangement for student living. On the continent, students managed these hostels. At Oxford, England, however, hostels were endowed to provide board and lodging for students unable to pay these costs for themselves. At least to some degree, the university managed these endowed hostels—a policy that continues today.

Figure 1.4. White House State Dining Room set for formal service. (Copyright © White House Historical Association. Photograph by George F. Mobley, National Geographic Society.)

Colonial colleges in the United States provided residence halls with dining rooms for all students. Administrators, generally clergymen, were responsible for their operation. They dispatched their duties prayerfully and thriftily—not always with student approval! Later, with a shift toward and an interest in German educational procedure, which did not include housing as a school responsibility, some colleges lost interest in student living situations. As a result, sororities and fraternities without faculty supervision assumed the feeding and housing of large groups of students. In many cases, this also led to the problem of providing adequate diets for all students.

The twentieth century has witnessed many changes in college and university foodservices in the United States. A shift occurred from the laissez-faire policy of early-day administrators to a very strict one in the late nineteenth century. Until World War II, colleges provided separate dining halls for men and women. Not only did students have their dietary needs satisfied, but they were also trained in the "social graces." Seated table service with students serving in rotation as hostess or host and as waiter or waitress was the accepted procedure in many residence hall dining rooms. Although this service may still be found in some colleges and universities today, it is the exception rather than the rule.

Gradually, with the influx of G.I. students into American schools of higher education during World War II, the more formal seated service and leisurely dining gave way to the speedy informality of cafeteria service. This service style makes it possible to meet student demands for greater menu variety and to cater to the food preferences of various ethnic groups that make up the student body. Also, with coeducational residences and dining halls now commonly found on the college campus, dietary requirements of both men and women in the same dining hall can be met by cafeteria or self-service. Student food habits have also changed as a result of today's concern for physical fitness and weight control. Foodservice managers have attempted to comply with this need through suitable menu selections. For example, salad bars, pasta bars, potato bars, and vegetarian bars are standard in most campus dining halls.

Other trends in residence hall dining are longer hours of service, fewer restrictions on the number of servings allowed, and greater flexibility in board plans, including a "pay as you eat" plan, rather than having to pay a set rate in advance.

In addition to residence hall dining, a diversity of other campus foodservices is a familiar pattern today. Student union buildings have, for example, set up creative and innovative units catering to students' changing food interests and demands. Commercial fast-food companies have been a major competitor for student patronage in many college towns. In some, therefore, the university has contracted with these companies to set up and operate one of their food units on campus.

Management of college and university foodservices is usually under the direction of well-qualified foodservice managers employed directly by the university or by a contract foodservice company. Both plans are found in colleges today.

The use of college and university dining facilities as laboratories for foodservice management classes is a common practice. Undoubtedly, this has helped establish high requirements for foodservice directors on such campuses. Directing the students' laboratory experiences and the work of numerous part-time student employees presents unique situations not common in other types of foodservice organizations.

School Foodservice

The history of school foodservice is inevitably a part of the larger story of the rapid development of public education. As reforms stemming from the Industrial Revolution began to free society from the supposed necessity of child labor, unemployment among children of school age increased and public concern with education soon became evident. To encourage school attendance, parents and civic-minded townspeople in some European countries banded together to provide low-cost school lunches. It is reported that canteens for schoolchildren were established in France in 1849 and that, in 1865, Victor Hugo started school feeding in England by providing children from a nearby school with hot lunches in his home. At some time between these dates, school foodservice began in the United States. The Children's Aid Society of New York City opened an industrial school in 1853 in an effort to persuade children from the slums to seek "instruction in industry and mental training," and offered food to all who came.

Beginning in the early 1900s, growing knowledge of nutrition placed emphasis on the importance of wise food selection and the need for nourishing school lunches at little or no cost. Under the notable leadership of Ellen H. Richards, the Boston school committee passed an order that "only such food as was approved by them should be sold in the city schoolhouses." Fig. 1.5 shows an early-day school lunchroom kitchen. At about this time, other men and women likewise concerned with child welfare sponsored similar developments in several urban centers, and the two decades that followed brought significant developments in the school lunchroom movement throughout the country. Although the program was implemented most rapidly in large cities where sustaining organizations and concerned leaders were prevalent, the cause of rural children was also championed by such groups as the Extension Service and PTA councils.

Figure 1.5.   Preparation for a school lunch in an early-day institutional kitchen in the U.S. (Reprinted by permission of *School Food Service Journal,* The American School Food Service Association, Denver, Colorado, 1986.)

Improving the nutrition of schoolchildren through adequate foodservices in schools was the goal.

World Wars I and II again brought into focus the need for improved nutrition among young people since so many were rejected from the military for reasons related to faulty nutrition. Concern was expressed for the future health of the nation if such a trend continued. As a direct result, the first federal legislation designed to assist and direct school foodservices was enacted in 1933. This provided loans enabling communities to pay labor costs for preparation and service of lunches in schools. In 1935, additional assistance came when the federal government was authorized to donate surplus farm commodities to schools. With these aids, a noon meal became a common part of school activities.

The *major* legislation governing the school lunch program, however, was the National School Lunch Act of 1946 (Public Law 79-396). Through this act, funds were appropriated "as may be necessary to safeguard the health and well-being of the nation's children, and to encourage the domestic consumption of nutritious agricultural commodities and other food by assisting the states through grants in aid and other means, in providing an adequate supply of funds and other facilities for the establishment, maintenance, operation and expansion of non-profit school lunch programs." States were required to supplement federal funding as set forth in Section 4 of the act, and lunches served by participating schools were obligated to meet the nutritional requirements prescribed. Although the National School Lunch Act allowed Types A, B, and C meals, the Type A lunch is the only one now served under the federal school foodservice program and is referred to as "the school meal pattern" (see Chapter 3 for specifics).

Other legislation and amendments have changed the funding policy and circumstances for offering free or reduced-price meals to students, revamped the commodity distribution plan, or provided for supplemental feeding programs. The Child Nutrition Act of 1966 authorized the School Breakfast Program and the Special Milk Program to further help alleviate inadequate nutrition. The Omnibus Reconciliation Act of 1980 reduced the reimbursement rate to schools for the first time and changed the income eligibility standard for students who would receive free or reduced-price meals. Further adjustments were made in 1981 and 1982 to help achieve reductions in federal spending. School foodservice managers work creatively to adjust to these changes while maintaining an attractive meal program to meet nutritional guidelines and appeal to students.

By the late 1980s, U.S. public school enrollments had dropped dramatically, but spending continued to climb. School foodservice directors had to switch from operating subsidized departments to self-supporting ones. Some of the changes that were made in an effort to make the switch include implementing centralized food production; raising prices for paying students; attracting more paying students to the program to offset the free and reduced-price lunches that are served; offering more high-profit fast-food–style à la carte items; and reaching out to service community programs, such as Meals-on-Wheels, senior citizen and day-care centers, and community "soup" kitchens.

School foodservice is most effective when dietitians, school administrators, food managers, and allied groups, such as the PTA, recognize its value in the child's mental and physical development. Then they can work together to make the foodservice not just a "feeding program," but rather a nutrition program for all students as part of their learning experience.

The type of organization and management found in school foodservices varies as much as the size and location of schools involved. Small independent schools may have simple on-premise food preparation and service supervised by a cook or manager with one or two employees and/or part-time student helpers. Large city school systems often use a centralized production kitchen and deliver meals for service to individual schools in the system. Centralized management with unit supervisors characterizes this system.

Clubs and Other Social Organizations

Clubs formed by people with a common interest have existed for decades. Member dues and assessments in some clubs provide funds to establish a "club house" or building that usually includes foodservice facilities. These clubs were especially prominent among the wealthy society class in England in the 1800s. As early as 1850, noted chef Alexis Soyer worked closely with the Reform Club of London to provide a sanitary and efficient foodservice setup that would utilize the then fairly recent innovations of stoves, water baths, and refrigeration (see Fig. 1.6).

Today, city clubs, athletic clubs, faculty clubs, country clubs, and others attempt to rival the settings of better hotels with a similar standard for foodservice. Few homes are spacious enough or adequately staffed to serve meals to 25 or more guests. Clubs provide these facilities and also cater to such

Figure 1.6. One of the early plans for an institutional kitchen made by Alexis Soyer for the Reform Club of London about 1850.

functions as receptions and banquets, in addition to providing regular meal service for their members. Sometimes the foodservice helps subsidize the cost of other services such as swimming pools or recreational rooms offered by the club. The number of meals served may be irregular and the stability of income somewhat uncertain, making club foodservice management a real challenge.

Hospitals

The evolution of foodservices in hospitals is as interesting as that of colleges and schools. The first hospital established in the United States was the Philadelphia General in 1751. Meals in early-day hospitals were simple to the point of monotony and no attempt was made to provide any special foods or therapeutic diets. Menus in an eighteenth-century American hospital, for example, included mush and molasses for breakfast on Monday, Wednesday, and Friday, varied by molasses and mush for supper on Monday, Wednesday, Thursday, and Saturday. Oxtail soup and black bread appeared on occasion.

Accounts of the Pennsylvania Hospital in the year 1804 stated that milk, butter, pork, and soap were produced on the hospital grounds for consumption in the hospital. Also, cows, calves, and pigs were sold for income. Salary for a husband and wife serving as steward and matron was $350 for 9 months of service.

Dietetics, as a hospital service, made its beginning at the time of the Crimean War (1854–1856). In 1855, Florence Nightingale, whom dietitians, as well as nurses, revere and honor as the pioneer of their profession, established a diet kitchen to provide clean, nourishing food for the ill and wounded soldiers in Scutari (now Uskudar), Turkey. Until then, foods of questionable quality were poorly cooked in insanitary conditions and served at irregular intervals.

Alexis Soyer (who, as noted earlier, was a chef who had worked with the Reform Club of London) contributed greatly to Nightingale's efforts when he offered to serve gratuitously as manager of the barracks hospital kitchen. Soyer's plan for operating it was as efficient as modern-day practice.

Changes during the next 100 years in hospital foodservice included introducing centralized tray service and mechanical dishwashing, establishing a separate kitchen for special diet preparation and later eliminating such kitchens, and the advent of frozen foods and their use in food preparation. Also, pay cafeterias for staff and employees and separate dining areas for these two groups were introduced during this period. Employing qualified dietitians to administer dietary departments and "therapeutic" dietitians for "special diet" supervision became the usual practice.

Today, hospitals comprise a large group of institutions operated and funded by various governing bodies (e.g., federal, state, county, and city governments) or by religious orders, or they are privately owned. Regardless of source of support, the main objective of hospital foodservice is to improve patient health and restore patients to normal activity and state of well-being. A secondary objective for most hospitals is to provide foodservice for staff, employees, and guests in order to maintain happy, well-nourished personnel and good public relations.

The past 30 years have brought more innovations and changes for greater operating efficiency and increased revenues to hospital dietary departments. Increasing nonpatient, in-house cafeteria volume; marketing catering services; use of professional chefs to improve menus; contracting professional and food production services to smaller operations; and creating new services, such as diet workshops for the public and take-home employee and patient meals, are just some of the innovations that have been implemented. Vended foods, used to supplement regular meal service, provide round-the-clock food availability. Many hospitals provide a dining room for ambulatory and wheelchair patients in recognition of the therapeutic value of mealtime social contact with others.

Technological advances have influenced foodservice systems, with the introduction of new methods of food production, holding, distribution, and service; computer use for many routine tasks; and use of robots in some hospital foodservices.

Federal policy has influenced trends in hospital procedures and budgeting, as is true with school foodservices. Medicare and Medicaid reimbursement payments for certain patients' hospital and nursing home costs constitute a major source of their income. In March 1983, Congress approved Medicare-mandated rates for reimbursement of Diagnosis Related Groups (DRGs) for illnesses and medical service for hospital inpatient services. This represents a strict set of cost controls for health care and has created financial incentives for hospitals to contain or reduce health care costs.

Ensuring quality care and service has been the focal point in hospitals and health care facilities in recent years. The Joint Commission on Accreditation of Healthcare Organizations has established standards to enforce quality assurance programs for accrediting its member facilities. One section is devoted to dietetic services to ensure that these services meet the nutritional needs of patients. Hospital foodservice today is unique and complex, requiring a well-qualified dietetic staff to coordinate activities that ensure optimum nutritional care.

Nursing Homes and Other Health Care Centers

Nursing homes and other health care facilities have come into prominence only relatively recently so their history is short compared with that of hospitals. However, the increase in demand for nursing home care has been phenomenal in the last 50 years due to several factors, among them population growth, longer life span, an increasing number of elderly persons in the population, urban living with condensed family housing units, increased incomes, and greater availability of health care insurance benefits.

The history of nursing homes tends to follow federal legislation enacted to help provide funds to care for individuals in such facilities. The modern nursing home era and the development of the nursing home as a distinct type of health care institution began in 1935 when federal funds to pay for nursing home care for the elderly were made available to the states by the passage of the Social Security Act.

In 1951, the Kerr-Mills Bill made federal matching funds for nursing home care available to states that were establishing satisfactory licensing and inspection programs. An amendment to the Hill-Burton program in 1954 provided financial aid to construct facilities for skilled nursing care in order to meet specified requirements. Many large nursing homes were built, while older smaller homes were forced to close or to modernize and expand to meet the standards of the new program.

Medicare and Medicaid legislation (1965) and its amendments (1967) established minimum standards and staff requirements for, as well as inspection of, nursing homes to permit the use of funds by their patients. Federal Conditions of Participation Regulations (1974) spell out, in detail, standards that skilled nursing facilities must meet.

General guidelines for all nursing homes include licensure and meeting standards of specific government programs in order to be certified, and one or more levels of care, such as nursing care and related medical services, personal care, and residential care.

Nursing homes provide different categories of nursing care and are classified as:

Skilled Nursing Facilities. Skilled nursing facilities offer 24-hour nursing care and provide other professional services as prescribed by the physician. Emphasis is on rehabilitation, and the facility is eligible for both Medicare and Medicaid reimbursement.

Intermediate Care Facilities. Intermediate care facilities provide basic medical, nursing, and social services in addition to room and board. Patients need some assistance but not intensive care. These facilities are eligible for the Medicaid program only.

Other Facilities. In contrast to skilled nursing and intermediate care facilities, which are certified under specific government programs, many nursing homes do not participate in these programs. Therefore, they are not classified as such, even though they may provide the same quality of care and categories of services. A facility may provide more than one category of care. The patients may be of any age. Many facilities specialize in child care or care of persons with mental illness or mental retardation.

Food plays a major part in the lives of most nursing home patients. For many, it may be the one thing they have to look forward to each day. The quality and amount of food offered as well as the care and supervision given to foodservice are important to any nursing home's success and effectiveness. Dining rooms are provided for patients who are ambulatory and able to participate in group dining. Others are served in their own rooms. Many require assistance with eating.

The 1974 federal Conditions of Participation Regulations, mentioned previously, stated these general "conditions" related to *dietary* services:

> Condition of participation dietetic services: The skilled nursing facility provides a hygienic dietetic service that meets the daily nutritional needs of patients, ensures that special dietary needs are met, and provides palatable and attractive meals. A facility that has a contract with an outside food management company may be found to be in compliance with this condition provided the facility and/or company meets the standards listed herein.

The services of registered dietitians (RDs) are required to ensure that dietary service regulations are adequately met and administered. Part-time or consultant RDs may be employed by small nursing homes. Full-time RDs are needed in the larger, skilled nursing homes.

Other Health Care Centers

Corrective institutions and homes for specialized groups such as persons with physical or mental disabilities, orphaned or runaway children; abused and battered women; and short-term residences for parolees, drug-abuse victims, or other groups during a rehabilitation period come under this category. These organizations usually serve low-income groups and may be supported by the state, county, private charities, or fraternal orders. Residents may or may not qualify for government assistance.

Trained foodservice supervisors are important to the success of these institutions in rehabilitating their residents to good health or for maintaining a healthy body. A well-balanced, nutritious diet that is acceptable to the group being served and that is within the constraints of the budget should be provided.

DAY-CARE CENTERS   Day-care centers for children of working parents, the underprivileged, and, more recently, for elderly persons who otherwise would be isolated and lonely offer an excellent opportunity for the foodservice to provide at least one nutritious meal a day in an attractive, friendly atmosphere. Facilities for special groups, such as camps for diabetics, combine social and recreational activities and proper nutrition.

SENIOR CITIZEN CENTERS   Many senior citizen centers employ trained supervisory personnel with leadership abilities to guide and assist volunteers who plan and carry out programs of value to the members. Primary among these is a limited meal service, usually a noon meal 5 days a week. In addition, a dietitian may give talks and advice on meal planning and good nutrition. Eating the noon meal together offers participants an opportunity to socialize. Often the meals served to senior citizen groups are subsidized in part by church, fraternal, or philanthropic organizations within the community. Free meals for those unable to pay is a common practice.

Meals-on-Wheels, a program for delivering meals (generally once a day, 5 days a week) to the homes of persons unable to go to a center or to prepare their own food, is usually funded through local charities. A large number of volunteer workers are involved in the program to help make it possible. Food for such meals may be prepared by contract with a senior citizen center, a school, a college, or a restaurant.

Health care of persons who are ill, disabled, and needy in the United States, whether at home, in hospitals, or in other health care facilities, holds unprecedented attention by legislative groups, patients, administrators, and the general public. Both recent government cuts in federal spending and the somewhat depressed state of the American economy for a period of time, together with the high cost of health care, have tended to slow the growth of and census in nursing homes and hospitals. Also, some of the available funds for long-term care have been diverted to home care or to newly organized, cost-containing alternate care delivery entities. Among the latter are Health Maintenance Organizations (HMOs), whose emphasis is on preventive care; immediate care centers for urgent situations; surgical centers for surgical procedures not requiring hospitalization; birthing stations; cardiac rehabilitation centers; and similar specialized units. Foodservice is a necessary part of such facilities. These developments have occurred during a short time and more changes are certain. On the part of all concerned, constant alertness to any pending or new legislation that may affect our present ways of health care is required.

Retirement Residences and Adult Communities

During the past few decades, many persons reaching retirement age expressed interest in an easier type of living than that required for total upkeep of their own homes. The result was the development of group living and dining facilities for retirees. These provide comfortable, congenial, independent living with minimal responsibility and offer freedom from coping with a large house, its taxes and maintenance problems, and little, if any, food preparation.

Many types of residences or adult communities are available at various price levels. Some are high-rise apartment-style buildings; others are on the cottage plan. Either type may have individual kitchenettes, central dining facilities, or both. Fig 8.3, Chapter 8, shows an attractive retirement home dining room. Other variations include purchase or rental units with full meal service, one meal a day, or no meals included in the monthly charge. Usually housekeeping, recreation and social activities, and medical and emergency nursing care units are provided. Access to public transportation is a factor, but adequate health care is considered the most important provision.

Foodservice for this older clientele should be directed by a well-qualified dietitian or foodservice manager who is knowledgeable about their dietary needs and food preferences and who can help contribute to the group's good health and relaxed, happy, gracious living.

Industrial and Business Foodservice

Providing food for employees at their workplace has been necessary since early times when labor was forced, or hired, to work in the fields or on the monuments of antiquity, such as the pyramids and the great walls of the world. The apprentices and journeymen in the guilds and manor houses of the Middle Ages had to be fed by their owners, like the slaves of ancient Greek and Roman households.

The Industrial Revolution brought great changes to social and economic systems. The plight of child laborers, in particular, resulted in legislation in England that forced managers to provide meal periods for the young workers.

Robert Owen, a Scottish mill owner near Glasgow during the early nineteenth century, is considered the "father of industrial catering." He so improved working conditions for his employees that his mill became a model throughout the industrial world. Among other things, it contained a large kitchen and eating room for employees and their families. Prices for meals were nominal, and so began the philosophy of subsidizing meal service for employees. In the United States in the 1800s, many employers provided free or below-cost meals to their employees, a practice that continues to some extent today.

The importance of industrial feeding was not fully realized, however, until the World War II period. A large percentage of workers in plants at that time were women who demanded facilities for obtaining a hot meal while at work. Since new plants were often in isolated locations and the competition for workers was intense, plant managers complied with worker demands and provided meal service facilities. Many plants have continued this service as an indispensable part of their operations, either under plant management or on a contract/concessionaire basis. Serving units within an industrial facility may include a central cafeteria, vending machines, and snack bars throughout the plant, and mobile carts to carry simple menu items to workers at their stations. Some also include a table-service dining room for executives and guests.

A newer segment of employee feeding, for office building workers, has mushroomed into existence since the 1970s. Enterprising contract foodservice caterers or companies have found this a ready market in larger cities. Many office workers enjoy the time-saving convenience of having meals delivered to them at their desks, eliminating the need to find an eating place during their brief meal period. This type of employee feeding appears to be increasing in popularity.

Today, the industrial and business foodservice manager faces challenges on many fronts. Their audiences are no longer quite as captive, and the employers can no longer be as benevolent as they were in the 1800s. No longer subsidized, in-plant foodservice must offer a variety of menu selections, at a reasonable price, and served in pleasant surroundings in order to successfully compete with the stiff competition provided by the myriad of fast-food outlets, mobile catering companies, sidewalk vendors, and "white tablecloth" restaurants that are in the neighborhood.

Restaurants

Historically, the evolution of public eating places was stimulated by people's desire to travel, for both spiritual enrichment and commercial gain. Religious pilgrimages played an important role in establishing the inns of France and England. Merchants traveling from country to country to buy or sell their wares also created the need for places to stop for food and rest. These early inns and taverns, providing for the needs of travelers, were perhaps the forerunners of our present restaurants. However, many of them were primitive and poorly organized and administered. The literature of the time describes unsanitary conditions under which food was prepared and served, monotonous menus, and poor service.

Stagecoach travel in colonial America, tedious at best, created the need for inns where travelers could rest and eat. They were much like those in England, but proprietors gave more attention to pleasing the guests. Many inns were largely family enterprises located in somewhat remote areas. The food offered was the same as for the family, plain, hearty, and ample. In urban centers during the early decades of the nineteenth century, hotels and inns presented extremely extensive and elaborate menus to attract guests to their facilities. Since revenues from these meals frequently did not cover preparation costs, the bar and lodging income was needed to make up the deficit.

Introducing the European hotel plan, which separated the charges for room and board, and later the à la carte foodservice were steps toward a rational foodservice in hotels. Through these measures, much of the waste that characterized their foodservice was abolished, opening the possibility that hotel and inn foodservice could be self-supporting. This led proprietors to establish foodservices separate and distinct from lodging facilities.

Origin of the restaurant concept, however, has been traced to the cook shops of France. They were licensed to prepare *ragouts*, or stews, to be eaten on the premises or taken to inns or homes for consumption. The shops had *ecriteurs*, or menus, posted on the wall or by the door to whet the interest of the passerby. The story goes that one Boulanger, a bouillon maker, added a meat dish with a sauce to his menu, contending that this was not a *ragout* and, therefore, did not violate the rights of the *traiteurs*. In the legal battle that followed, the French lawmakers sustained his point, and his new business was legalized as a restaurant. The word *restaurant* comes from the French verb *restaurer*, which means "to repair." It is said that the earliest restaurants had this Latin inscription over their doorway: *Venite ad me qui stomacho laoratis et ego restaurabo vos*—Come to me all whose stomachs cry out in anguish, and I shall restore you!

The cafeteria was a further step in the simplification of restaurant foodservices. This style of self-service came into being during the gold rush days of 1849 when the "forty-niners" demanded speedy service. Regarded as an American innovation, its popularity extended throughout the United States. Today, commercial cafeterias still represent an important part of the foodservice industry.

Another innovative foodservice was the automat, first opened in Philadelphia in 1902 by Horn and Hardart. Patterned after a "waiterless" restaurant in Berlin, it combined features of a cafeteria with those of vending. Individual food items were displayed in coin-operated window cases from which customers made their selections. This "nickel-in-a-slot" eatery provided good food and high standards of sanitation for nearly 50 years, drawing customers from every walk of life. For many people, it became a haven, especially during the Great Depression years beginning with the stock market crash in 1929, the years of the automat's greatest success. After World War II, the automat's popularity declined as a more affluent society sought greater sophistication in dining. Competition with other types of foodservices became intense.

The 1960s brought the advent of the "fast-food" concept when a midwestern chain of hamburger "drive-ups" went public. Competition in the fast-food field has brought many innovations and creative foodservice outlets throughout the United States, as well as around the world, many specializing in one particular food.

Perhaps the baby boom generation of World War II and the resulting population bulge have influenced the growth of the foodservice industry as much as any other factor in recent years. As this generation raised on "fast food" matures, it continues to seek more sophisticated fast-food dining. Many foodservice trends that seem to be new at the time are in reality "one more repeat in a cyclic phenomenon, wrapped up in a new language and viewed by a new generation."

This cycle is dramatically demonstrated in the uniforms worn by waiters, waitresses, and counter attendants throughout the years. The classic waiters' uniform of the 1900s, consisting of a white shirt, a black bow tie, a jacket, and pants (Fig. 1.7) is being seen more often in the fine dining establishments of the 1990s as a unisex garment with interchangeable elements (Fig. 1.8). The soda jerks' and waitresses' uniforms of the 1940s and 1950s (Fig. 1.9) have also given way to livelier, more durable, unisex uniforms as seen in today's fast-food operations.

The type of restaurant operations management ranges from the small, independent owners or managers to the complex franchises and chain operators to

Figure 1.7. Waiter's uniform borrowed from European fine dining tradition, 1906. (Reproduced from the Collections, Prints and Photograph Division, Library of Congress.)

executives of large corporations where mergers and acquisitions abound. Food-service managers in today's complex restaurant field must be highly motivated and knowledgeable in order to compete and survive.

Transportation Companies

A major segment of today's foodservice industry—titled "food on the move"—is provided by airlines, trains, and cruise ships. For all three, food and foodservice make up a marketing tool used to "sell" travel on a particular line. Both airlines and railroads face the unique problem of planning foods that will "go the distance"; the logistics of food they serve is a challenge. Management must test the market to determine who the travelers are and what they want or like to eat. Keeping up with changing fads and fluctuations in food preferences is an important aspect of meal service on trains and planes.

Figure 1.8. Modern-day unisex uniform. (Courtesy, Angelica Uniform Group, St. Louis.)

Most cruise ships offer such a variety of foods, styles of service, and presentations that their passengers can find their preferences well met. Usually, there is more good food available than any person can consume. Food storage and preparation facilities on these ships are adequate to make them self-sufficient for the length of the cruise or ocean voyage.

Career opportunities in foodservice management with transportation companies offer many possibilities for the future, especially for persons who have good business backgrounds in addition to their training in foodservice.

Figure 1.9. Uniforms of the 1940s and 1950s worn by soda jerks and waitresses at the "Palace of Sweets." (Reproduced from the Collections, Prints and Photograph Division, Library of Congress.)

Summary

This brief history of the development of the foodservice industry should give readers an appreciation of the industry as it is today. The present status of foodservice is impressive. NRA statistics indicate dramatic growth in the food-service industry: a sales volume of $262 billion was predicted for 1992. Individuals in the United States today eat 45% of their meals away from home, and one of four meals eaten at home was prepared outside the home. Foodservice is the number one employer among all retail business, with some 8 million persons employed, two-thirds of whom are women and one-fourth of whom are teenagers.

The large patronage given restaurant enterprises greatly exceeds any casual estimate. Statistics on the number of persons in the military services, in hospitals, in correctional facilities, and in other federal, state, or municipal institutions show the enormous scope of necessary foodservices. There are also the thousands of students whose nutrition the schools, colleges, and universities accept as a major responsibility. Industry, too, recognizes the importance of feeding its millions.

All U.S. citizens have direct personal contact with foodservices in institutions at some time during their lives. By paying taxes, they support federal, state, county, and municipal institutions that serve food to their residents. All persons probably have meals at school, some in college dining halls, and others at their workplaces. Some people enjoy dining at their clubs, while others may have meals "en route" as they travel. At some time, a large percentage of U.S. citizens may require the services of a hospital or nursing home; still others may choose retirement home living for later years. Whatever our involvement, we expect the food served to be of high quality, prepared to conserve its nutritive value, and served in the best condition and manner possible.

Essentials in attaining this goal are knowledge of menu planning, food purchasing, preparation, delivery service systems, successful personnel direction including delegation and supervision, wise planning and clear-cut organization, a good system of financial control, and efficient facility design and equipment arrangement. These are the responsibilities of the foodservice director and are discussed in the following chapters.

Summary Questions

1. Where did institutional foodservice get its start?
2. What are the trends in college and university foodservice? In hospital foodservice?
3. What major legislation established the National School Lunch Program?
4. Where did foodservice cost accounting get its start?
5. What sciences led to the improvements in methods used in institutional foodservice?
6. How have present-day life-styles made an impact on commercial and institutional foodservices?
7. Who is considered the pioneer of dietetics and why?
8. What are two main objectives of hospital foodservice today?

Bibliography

Barber, M.I.: History of the American Dietetic Association. Philadelphia: J. B. Lippincott, 1959.
Batty, J.: Uniforms through time. Natl. Rest. Assoc. 12(3):24, 1992.

Editorial. J. Am. Diet. Assoc. 9:405, 1934.

Feingold, S. N.: The futurist quiz. The Futurist 26(2):56, 1992.

Food Management: NRA projects growth in 1992. Food Mgmt. 27(3):49, 1992.

National Food Service Management Institute. Trends: School food service in the year 2000 and beyond. Natl. Food Serv. Mgmt. Institute Conference Proceedings, January 1992.

Social Security Administration: Skilled nursing facilities: Standards for certification and participation in Medicare and Medicaid programs. Federal Register 39:2241, 1974.

Schuster, K. and Staff, F. M.: Crossing the line. Food Mgmt. 23(1):94, 1988.

Woodman, J.: Twenty years of "400" translates into light years of change for foodservice. Restaurants and Institutions 94(15):98, 1984.

For More Information

Barber, E.: A culinary campaign. J. Am. Diet. Assoc. 11:89, 1935.

Boss, D. and Schecter, M.: Scene from the future. Food Mgmt. 24(10):164, 1989.

Chaudhry, R.: R & I report trends. Restaurants and Institutions 101(25):29, 1991.

Food Management: 1990 ideas catalog. Food Mgmt. 25(10):146, 1990.

Lundberg, D. E.: The Hotel and Restaurant Business, 5th ed. New York: Van Nostrand Reinhold, 1989.

National Restaurant Association (NRA): The foodservice manager in the year 2000. Natl. Rest. Assoc. 12(2):36, 1992.

Restaurant Business: Supermarkets market segment report. Rest. Bus. 91(3):136, 1992.

VonEgmond-Pannell, D.: School Foodservice Management, 4th ed. New York: Van Nostrand Reinhold, 1990.

Types of Foodservice Operations

The foodservice industry is complex, fast-growing, and ever-changing. Many factors affect its growth and status, including socioeconomic conditions, demographic shifts, and changing food habits and desires of the American people. Being alert to these changes will help foodservice managers adapt their operations to meet the demands of the times. This background information, together with a classification of the many types of foodservice markets, is provided in this chapter.

The systems approach to management is introduced. This concept is based on the idea that complex organizations are made up of interdependent parts (subsystems) that interact in ways to achieve common goals. Application of the systems concept is made to foodservice organizations.

Managers face decisions about how to organize foodservice departments for the efficient procurement and production of their food and meals. Many options are available based on the form of food purchased, where the food is prepared in relation to where it is served, the time span between preparation and service, and the amount and kind of personnel and equipment required.

Foodservices with similar characteristics are grouped together as particular types of production or operating systems. Each of the four types of foodservice operating systems found in the United States today is described with its identifying features, advantages, and disadvantages. The typical foodservice organizations that use each type are also identified. This description should provide a basis for managers to decide on the type of operation suitable for a particular situation.

Learning Objectives

After studying this chapter, the reader should be able to

1. list and briefly explain the factors that affect the growth of the foodservice industry
2. discuss the systems approach to management
3. describe how systems theory differs from earlier approaches to management
4. identify the five characteristics that differentiate the four major types of foodservice systems in use in the United States today
5. describe the identifying features, advantages, and disadvantages of the conventional, commissary, ready-prepared, and assembly/serve foodservice systems
6. identify the criteria that should be used to determine the most suitable system for a particular situation

Scope and Status of Foodservices

As described in Chapter 1, foodservice in the United States today is a complex and fast-changing industry, one that has expanded rapidly in the last half-century. It ranks as the number one retail employer with more than 8,000,000 workers. A conservative estimate is that one of every four meals consumed is planned, prepared, and served outside the home in a variety of establishments.

Factors Affecting Growth

The growth in patronage of foodservices may be attributed in part to socioeconomic trends and other demographic changes. For example, the *changing status of women* has had an influence on the work force. In 1970, approximately 43% of women over 16 years of age were working, and in 1982, 53% of women in that age group were in the work force. Today, two-thirds of the industry's employees are women. This may indicate a dual income for some families and may contribute toward the creation of a more affluent society. More people can afford to dine out; more women are lunchtime customers.

Another factor influencing the foodservice industry is the increasing number of *single-person households* and the potential for people living alone to eat out. They tend to spend a larger portion of their food budget on meals away from home than do family groups. Also, the population growth in the United States seems to be slowing. If this trend continues there will be fewer young people and an increasing number of older persons in our society. The *average age of the U.S. population*, now nearly 33 years, will continue to increase as the number of babies born remains low and the life span of adults continues to lengthen. These facts seem to indicate a need for more retirement and health care facilities, an older target market for restaurants, and a change in the age groups in the labor market. Recent *changes in the American workplace* also have had far-reaching effects on the foodservice market. With the shift toward high technology and the computer industry, there are more office-bound jobs and white collar workers. In-plant feeding is down and contract foodservice in business offices is increasing. The shortened work week of recent years has added leisure time and promoted the recreational foodservice segment of the industry.

The awakened *interest in the health and well-being* of people and a concern to improve the nutritional status of individuals has also had an impact on foodservice. In fact, much research is being conducted and reported by the media concerning the impact of nutrition on health. People are becoming generally more knowledgeable about nutrition and food safety. As a result, most types of foodservices, from schools and colleges to airline and commercial operations, are offering healthier choices on their menus.

All of these factors have helped shape the foodservice industry into what it is today. Managers must always be alert to societal trends and have the ability to adjust their operations to the changing situation in order to be competitive and successful in this market.

Classification of Foodservices

The foodservice industry is broad in scope and encompasses a wide range of establishments. *Restaurant Business* classifies them into three major groups:

- commercial/contract
- institutional/internal
- military (continental U.S. only)

Further, these three are described according to their various market segments.

MAJOR SEGMENTS OF THE FOODSERVICE MARKET

EATING AND DRINKING PLACES

- full menu restaurants and lunchrooms
- limited menu restaurants

- public cafeterias
- social caterers
- ice cream and frozen yogurt shops
- bars and taverns

HOTEL AND MOTEL DINING ROOMS
THE RETAIL MARKET

- department stores
- variety and general stores
- drugstores, supermarket dining
- convenience food stores
- other specialized retail stores (take-outs and gourmet foods as in shopping malls and kiosks)

BUSINESS/INDUSTRIAL MARKET (EMPLOYEE FEEDING)

- contract foodservices in plants
- contract foodservices in business offices
- internal (company-operated) foodservices—plants and business
- mobile on-street catering
- food vending machines
- U.S. defense personnel (military foodservices)
- meals furnished for foodservice employees

TRANSPORTATION MARKET

- in-transit air and rail
- terminal facilities
- passenger and cargo ships
- interstate highway foodservices

HEALTH CARE MARKET (INTERNAL AND CONTRACT)

- hospitals
- nursing homes
- specialized care homes (retirement homes, orphanages, etc.)

STUDENT MARKET (INTERNAL AND CONTRACT)

- schools—public and parochial, elementary and secondary
- colleges and universities

CORRECTIONAL FACILITIES
LEISURE MARKET

- theme parks, arenas, stadiums, tracks, and museums
- drive-in movie theaters
- bowling lanes
- summer camps and hunting facilities

Each of the establishments in these classifications has its own objectives, goals, and types of organization and management. Although they may seem widely divergent, each is concerned with providing a foodservice to some segment of the public. There is a commonality among them that can be identified for the purpose of grouping them into specific types of foodservice operations.

Foodservice Operations

The Systems Concept and Approach

Before discussing foodservice organizations as "systems," this section briefly reviews the systems *concept* and systems *approach* and how systems theory has evolved from other theories of management. This review will establish a common basis of understanding and make application of the systems concept to foodservice an easy transition.

The word *system* is used freely and in many different contexts. We read and speak of the solar system, defense system, transportation system, school system, and even of the human body as a system. A system has been defined in many ways and with so many different words that it may seem confusing. However, this commonality is found among systems: a system is a set of interdependent parts that work together to achieve a common goal. The interrelated parts are known as subsystems, each dependent on the others for achieving its goals. For example, a train cannot achieve its goal of transporting passengers from one destination to another if the wheels are off the track even though all parts of the train are in good working order. All elements must be coordinated to function together for success.

Organizations are systems. This concept has evolved gradually from earlier theories of management. Traditional views in prominence in the late nineteenth and early twentieth centuries included the scientific management theory, which puts emphasis on efficient work performance. Workers were trained to perform a task in what was perceived to be the *one* best way. If all performed efficiently, the goals could be reached.

In the late 1920s, research conducted by Elton Mayo and his associates at the Hawthorne Plant of the Western Electric Company led to the findings that social and psychological factors were critically important determinants of worker satisfaction and productivity. Thus, the human relations movement in industry began.

After World War II, quantitative methods began to be employed for the purposes of decision making. The application of computer technology and mathematical models were collectively called operations research or management science.

Each of these theories contributed to the development of systems theory as it is today; that is, viewing the organization as an entity composed or made up of interdependent parts—the subsystems. Each subsystem contributes to the whole and receives something from the whole while working to achieve common goals. Management's role is considered a "systematic endeavor," one that recognizes the needs of all of the parts. Decisions are made in light of the overall effect of management on the organization as a whole and its objectives. This type of leadership is the systems approach, that is, an acceptance of the systems theory of management and the use of it as a style of managing. The recognition that a change made in one part of the system has an impact on all parts of the system is an example of the use of the systems approach. Three areas of common usage of this approach are:

- systems philosophy, which is described as a way of thinking about phenomena in terms of wholes, including parts, components, or subsystems, with emphasis on their interrelationships
- subsystems analysis, as a method for problem solving or decision making
- systems management, as the application of the systems theory to managing organizational systems or subsystems

Money, materials, time, equipment, utilities, facilities, and personnel, together with the necessary information, are the *inputs* into the system. The work that is performed, known as *operations,* transforms the raw material into the finished product or services. These are the *outputs.* The outputs provide the information on how the operations worked or failed, or how they should be changed or modified. This information is known as *feedback* and provides management with data for decision making.

An organization is also an open system that interacts regularly with external forces in its surrounding environment. These forces include various regulatory

agencies, customers, competitors, and suppliers. Practices within the organization are affected by these external forces and, conversely, the organization has
an impact on the forces in its environment.

Various diagrams may be used to illustrate an organization as a system with
its inputs, subsystems performing the operations, and the outputs, together
with their interactions with the environment. One that is clear, simple, and
easily adaptable to specific organizations is given by Huse in Fig. 2.1.

The inputs in a foodservice system are food products, supplies, personnel
labor and skills, money, utilities, information, time, facilities, space, and
equipment. Transformation of these inputs into outputs takes place in the
functional subsystems shown in Fig. 2.2. The resulting outputs are
ready-to-serve foods, clientele and personnel satisfaction, and financial
accountability. Ideas generated from the results of operations are the
feedback for use in improving the operation as necessary. All parts of the
system are linked together by management functions, such as planning,
organizing, and staffing, which are discussed in Section IV. To accomplish
unification of the system, managers use various linking processes, such as
communicating and decision making. Surrounding the system are environmental factors, such as regulatory agencies, the economy, and social and
cultural aspects, and the various constituents of the operation, such as
customers and suppliers.

Of the three major subsystems—operations, management, and information,
named by Burch, Strater, and Grudnitski, only the organization of operations is

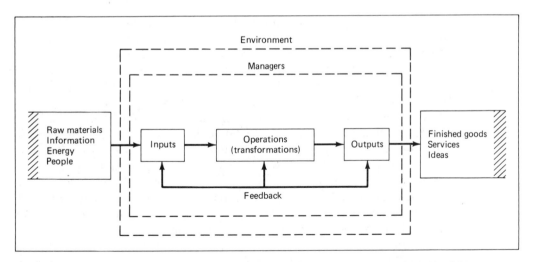

Figure 2.1.   The organization as a system. (Reprinted by permission from page 60 of *Management,*
Second Edition by Edgar Huse; Copyright © 1982 by West Publishing Company, St. Paul, Minnesota.
All rights reserved.)

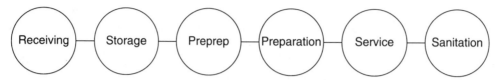

Figure 2.2.   The functional subsystems of a traditional foodservice operation.

considered in this chapter. Specific operations in the foodservice system, procurement, food preparation, delivery and service, and clean up are discussed in Chapters 4, 6, and 7 in Sections II and III. Management and information subsystems are discussed in Section IV.

Types of Foodservice Systems

Those foodservices that operate in a similar manner, or with common elements, give the basis for grouping them into specific types of systems. Four major types of foodservice systems are in operation in the United States today. The systems differ in *where* the food is *prepared* in relation to where it is served, the *time span* between preparation and service, the *forms of foods* purchased, *methods of holding* prepared foods, and the amount and kind of *labor and equipment required.* These four types of foodservice systems are: conventional, commissary (central production kitchen), ready-prepared (cook/chill or cook/freeze), and assembly/serve.

CONVENTIONAL   As the name implies, the conventional system has been used traditionally throughout the years. Menu items are prepared in an on-premise kitchen where the meals are served and held a short time, either hot or cold, until serving time. In earlier years, all preparation as well as cooking took place on-premise and foods were prepared from basic ingredients. Kitchens included a butcher shop, a bakery, and vegetable preparation units.

Over the years, a modified conventional system has evolved because of labor shortages, high labor costs, and the technological developments in the form of foods available. In order to reduce time and labor costs, foodservice managers began to purchase some foods with "built-in" labor. Butcher shops, in which meats were cut from prime cuts, and bake shops are gone from most "conventional" kitchens today. Meats are purchased ready-to-cook or portion-controlled; bread and many bakery items are purchased from a commercial bakery or prepared from mixes; and produce is available in prepeeled, cut, frozen, or canned forms, all of which reduce the amount of production and labor required on-premise. Foods with varying degrees of processing are now used in conventional foodservice systems.

This system is most effective in situations and locales where the labor supply is adequate and of relatively low cost, where sources of food supplies, especially raw foods, are readily available, and when adequate space is allocated for foodservice equipment and activities.

Typical users of the conventional system are smaller foodservice operations such as independent restaurants, schools, colleges, hospital and health care facilities, homes for specialized groups, and in-plant employee feeding.

Advantages: The conventional system has many advantages. Quality control is considered of primary importance. Through the menus, recipes, and quality of ingredients selected by the manager, the foodservice achieves its individuality and standard of quality desired. It is not dependent on the availability and variety of frozen entrées and other menu items commercially prepared. This system is more adaptable to regional, ethnic, and individual preferences of its customers than is possible with other systems. From an economic standpoint, greater flexibility is possible in making menu changes to take advantage of good market buys and seasonal fluctuations. Also, less freezer storage space is required than with the other systems and distribution costs are minimal, both of which save on energy use and costs.

Disadvantages: The conventional system produces an uneven, somewhat stressful workday caused by meal period demands. Since the menu differs each day, the workloads vary, making it difficult for workers to achieve high productivity. Skilled workers may be assigned tasks that could be completed by non-skilled employees just to fill their time between meal periods. When three meals a day are served, two shifts of employees are required to cover the 12 to 15 hour or more workday. Scheduling workers may be difficult with overlapping shifts.

COMMISSARY (CENTRAL PRODUCTION KITCHEN)   The commissary foodservice system is described as a large, central production kitchen with centralized food purchasing and delivery of prepared foods to service (satellite) units located in separate, remote areas for final preparation and service. This system came about with development of large, sophisticated equipment for preparing and cooking large quantities of food from the raw, unprocessed state that performs specialized processes, such as making sandwiches or cooking and turning pancakes. Most food items are completely processed from that raw state in the central kitchen. Foodservice organizations with many serving units, sometimes widely separated as in a large city school system, sought ways to consolidate operations and reduce costs. The commissary system is the result.

Prepared food may be stored frozen, chilled, or hot-held. Menu items may be distributed in any one of several forms: bulk hot, bulk cold, or frozen for reheating and portioning at the satellite serving units; or preportioned and plated for service and chilled or frozen before delivery.

Typical users of this system are airline caterers, large city school systems, and franchised or chain restaurant organizations that provide food for their various outlets and vending companies.

Advantages: The commissary foodservice system can realize cost savings due to large volume purchasing and reduced duplication of labor and equipment that would be required if each serving unit prepared its own food. Some facilities where food is served may not have adequate space for a production kitchen, or the space can be better utilized for some other purpose. Quality control may be more effective and consistent with only one unit to supervise than with many.

Disadvantages: Food safety and distribution of prepared foods may be concerns. There are many critical points in mass food production where contamination could occur. Employment of a food microbiologist or someone knowledgeable about safe techniques in mass food handling with specialized equipment is highly desirable yet often costly.

Food must be loaded and transported in such a manner that it maintains correct temperature for safety and is of good quality and appearance when received for service. This requires specialized equipment and trucks for delivery. Poor weather conditions, delivery truck breakdowns, or other such catastrophes can result in food arriving late, causing irritating delays in meal service.

Another disadvantage is the high cost of purchase, maintenance, and repair of the sophisticated and specialized equipment needed for this type of production and distribution.

READY-PREPARED (COOK/CHILL OR COOK/FREEZE) In the ready-prepared system, foods are prepared on-premise, then chilled or frozen and stored for use at some later time. Thus, foods are "ready," prepared well in advance of the time needed. This is the distinct feature of ready-prepared foodservice systems—the separation between time of preparation and service. In addition, the food is not for immediate use as in the conventional system. Foods *are* prepared on-premise, however, unlike the commissary system, where there is separation between place of preparation and of service.

The cook/chill method is accomplished in a variety of ways. Basic to all of the various methods is the fact that the food is prepared and cooked by conventional or other methods, then its temperature is brought down to 37° F in 90 minutes or less, and refrigerated for use at a later time. In one variation, prepared food is either preplated or put into bulk containers, such as hotel pans, chilled in a blast chiller, stored in a refrigerator for up to 5 days, rethermalized, and served. In another method, food items are prepared in kettles, pumped into special air- and water-tight plastic packages (Fig. 2.3) that hold 1.5 to 3 gallons, given an ice water bath in a tumble chiller (Fig. 2.4), and stored in the refrigerator. Food items prepared by this method may be held for up to 45 days. Meat is prepared in this method by putting it in a large tank that automatically cooks the meat and then chills it in ice water as

Figure 2.3.   Cooked food is pumped into bags in this cook/chill operation. (Courtesy, Nutrition Services, Portland Public Schools, Portland, Oregon.)

soon as the cooking cycle is over. Meats can then be held refrigerated for up to 60 days.

In the cook/freeze method, a blast freezer or cryogenic freezing system must be available to freeze foods quickly and so prevent cell damage. Foods for freezing may be preplated, but more often they are stored in bulk, which requires less freezer storage space.

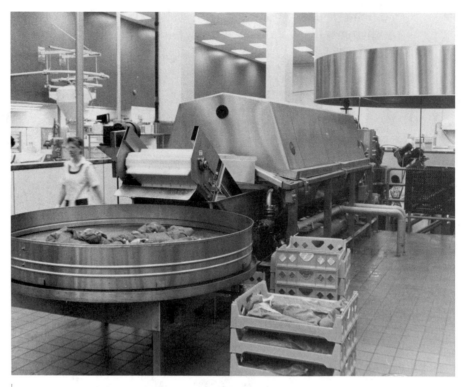

Figure 2.4.   Sealed bags of food are chilled quickly in an ice water bath in a tumble chiller. (Courtesy, Nutrition Services, Portland Public Schools, Portland, Oregon.)

It should be noted that the ready-prepared system entrées and vegetables undergo two heating periods: first, when foods are prepared and, second, after storage to reheat them for service to the consumer. Ready-prepared systems were developed to offset the critical shortage and high cost of skilled foodservice employees. Also, it was seen as a way of evening out the workload from day-to-day and during each day because only a large quantity of certain menu items are prepared on any given day to build up an inventory for future use.

Advantages: Ready-prepared system advantages are related to reducing the "peaks and valleys" of workloads that may be found in the conventional system. Production scheduling to build up the menu item inventory can be on a 40-hour week, 8-hour day, without early morning and late evening shifts. Employee turnover is decreased and recruitment of new employees is enhanced by offering staff a more normal work week and reasonable hours.

Other advantages are reductions in production labor costs, improved quality and quantity control by decreasing job stress related to production deadlines, and improved nutrient retention by decreasing time food is held within the serving temperature range. There can be more balanced use of equipment when preparation is spread over 8 hours, rather than at mealtime only.

Management has close control over menu selections, the quality of ingredients, and quantity and portion size. This is not always true in other systems, especially with the assembly/serve system. Menu variety is potentially greater with this system, as many items can be prepared and stored for future use.

One advantage that the ready-prepared system has over the commissary system is the lack of worry about delivery from the central production kitchen. When foods are prepared and stored on-premise, menu items are available on call and no waiting is involved.

Disadvantages: There is need for large cold storage and/or freezer units, which take space and add to energy costs. Depending on the method, a blast chiller or blast freezer is required and they are expensive to purchase and operate. Control for food safety is especially essential with the cook/freeze method. Longree (1980) warns that "the production of precooked frozen foods must not ever be handled in a haphazard fashion; unless the freezing operation can be a continuous, streamlined, bacteriologically controlled, short-time process, the bacteriological hazards could be formidable." (See Chapters 4 and 7 for more information on food safety.)

Since frozen foods are prone to structural and textural changes, extensive modifications in the recipe and ingredients usually are necessary to offset cell damage and to assure high-quality products.

Appropriate and adequate equipment for rethermalizing foods prior to service is essential and can be costly. Microwave and/or convection ovens are the equipment usually used in service units located near the consumers.

Although ready-prepared systems have been used primarily by large volume institutions and centralized commissary chain setups, such as health care units, employee feeding facilities, airlines, and correctional institutions, lower volume applications have begun to appear. Schools, supermarkets, and large restaurants are now utilizing this technology.

ASSEMBLY/SERVE   The assembly/serve system has no on-premise food production. This has led to the use of the term "kitchenless" kitchen. Fully prepared foods are purchased and require only storage, final assembling, heating, and serving. Assembly/serve systems evolved with the advances in food technology that led to development of high-quality frozen entrées and other food products, and the wide variety of such items that have appeared on the market in recent years. Also, foodservice managers confronted with high labor costs and few skilled employees available for food production turned to this system to relieve the labor situation. Often with this system, "single-use" disposable tableware is used, thus eliminating the need for a dishwashing unit.

With the introduction of frozen entrées with starch that are low in fat and sodium, hospitals have begun to purchase these retail-size commercially prepared frozen entrées for their patient foodservice. They are then "popped out" onto the service plate and rethermalized with IQF (individually quick frozen) vegetables and served. These pop-out food items have resulted in the system being characterized as "pick, pack, pop, and pitch!" In addition to the regular production line items, some companies are willing to produce items according to individual purchaser's recipes and specifications.

The primary users of this system are hospitals, yet some health care institutions and restaurants have also been known to use it. Although foodservices of all classifications can use prepared entrée items, few have adopted them exclusively. Hotels and restaurants that employ unionized chefs can be prohibited from using frozen entrées.

Advantages: The foremost advantage of the assembly/serve system is the reduction in labor cost that may be realized because of the built-in labor savings in the food items purchased. The reduced number of personnel that are required do not have to be highly skilled or experienced. Procurement costs are lower due to better portion control, less waste, reduced purchasing time required, and less pilferage. Equipment and space requirements are minimal as are operating costs for gas, electricity, and water.

Disadvantages: There is limited availability in some markets of a good selection of desired menu items or those that have regional appeal. However, more and better quality frozen entrées are becoming available. The higher cost of these prepared foods may not be offset by the labor savings realized. Managers must carefully weigh the overall cost effect of this system.

Another disadvantage may be the quality of available prepared products and customer acceptability. The proportion of protein food (meat, fish, seafood, etc.) to sauce or gravy in some menu items may not be adequate to meet nutritional requirements of the clientele. For example, 2 ounces of protein are required in the School Meal Pattern in school foodservice programs. Many frozen entrées may contain much less than that. Evaluation of products under consideration for use in the assembly/serve system is essential.

A manager considering a change from another system to the assembly/serve system should carefully evaluate the change in amount and kind of equipment needed. It may be excessively high in cost and in energy consummation to operate the duplicate pieces of heating equipment. Additional freezer space required for storage of the inventory of frozen entrées may not be available or may be too costly to install. Recycling or disposal of the large quantities of packaging materials and single-use tableware, if used, must be part of the total concern.

Each type of foodservice system has proved successful in providing acceptable quality food in specific organizations with the conditions described for each. However, foodservice managers attempting to decide on one system over another should undertake an extensive investigation and study before making any decision. Among the factors to consider are cost comparisons, availability of foods in all forms, quality, and nutritional value of fully prepared items, customer needs and acceptability, equipment and space requirements, energy use as estimated by the amount and kinds of equipment needed for each system, and availability and cost of labor.

A summary of the major characteristics of each system is given in Fig. 2.5. A flow chart of the processes, step by step, for the four foodservice systems is shown in Fig. 2.6.

Summary

Today's foodservice managers should view their organization as a system composed of various elements or subsystems that are united by a common goal and that are interdependent and interact so that the processes or functions involved produce outcomes to meet stated objectives.

An overall definition of foodservice systems is well stated by Livingston and Chang (1979): A food service system is an integrated program in which the procurement, storage, preparation and service of foods and beverages, and the equipment, methods (and personnel) required to accomplish these objectives are fully coordinated for minimum labor, optimum customer satisfaction, quality, and cost control.

The arrangement of subsystems, procurement, food preparation, delivery and service, and sanitation into varying ways is the basis for grouping foodservices into types of systems, each with common elements and procedures. Four major types of foodservice systems found in the United States are conventional, commissary, ready-prepared, and assembly/serve. An evaluation of the merits of each system based on its characteristics, advantages, and disadvantages should be made before any one is adopted for use in a specific foodservice organization. The North Central Regional research group (1977) has stated the rationale for each of the four systems, which should be helpful in this decision making:

> **Rationale for Conventional Foodservice Systems.** Traditionally, effective foodservice administrators with conventional foodservice systems have utilized a skilled labor force for food production 13-14 hours per day. Given adequate food production equipment and available skilled labor, foods may be procured with limited amounts of processing. However, with constantly rising labor costs within the foodservice industry, the current trend in conventional foodservice systems is to procure more extensively processed foods.

> **Rationale for Commissary Foodservice Systems.** The commissary foodservice principles have been adopted in systems where service areas are remote from, yet accessible to, the production center. This concept can be applied to reduce

Summary

	Conventional	Commissary	Ready Prepared		Assembly/Serve
			Cook/Chill	Cook/Freeze	
Location of Food Preparation Kitchen in Relation to Where Served:	On premises where food is served	Central production kitchen in building separate from service units. Food transported to satellite serving units.	On premises where food is served		Off premises (Commercially prepared foods are purchased)
Form of Food Purchased:	Raw; some convenience foods	Primarily raw ingredients	Raw; some convenience foods		All convenience and prepared foods-frozen, canned dehydrated, or prepeeled fresh
Food Procurement:	Purchase for its own unit	Centralized purchasing for all service units	Purchase for its own unit		Purchase for own use
Time span between preparation and service, and method of holding:	Food prepared for immediate service (may be held hot, or chilled for a few hours)	Food prepared and may be: a) distributed to satellite units for immediate service b) chilled and either pre-plated or put into bulk c) chilled and frozen and stored for later use either pre-plated or in bulk	Food prepared & cooked then chilled and held for 1-3 days, or 45-60 days depending on the system.	Food prepared and fast frozen; held for later use up to 3-4 months	No on-premises preparation. Foods purchased pre-prepared are stored and ready for reheating and service at any time needed
Amount and kind of equipment required:	All pre-preparation, cooking and serving equipment needed. Both	Large, sophisticated equipment for pre-preparation and cooking. Some robots may be	All pre-preparation, and cooking and serving equipment.		Equipment for reheating as steamers, steam jacketed kettles, convection or microwave

	Conventional	Commissary	Ready-prepared	Assembly-serve
	skilled and unskilled employees needed	used—can be reprogrammed for various tasks. Suitable containers for packaging and delivery; trucks to deliver prepared foods to service units; reheating equipment if foods frozen or chilled	A "blast" or cryogenic freezer—large amounts of freezer holding space.	ovens. Equipment for setting up and serving Reheating equipment as convection or microwave ovens and kettles for immersion heating
Labor Needs:	Skilled cooks and preparation workers as well as less skilled for pre-preparation and serving	Highly trained in technological aspects of food production in mass quantities. Food microbiologists to assure food safety. Employees must be able to operate highly specialized equipment used for food production	Fewer highly skilled cooks needed compared with conventional because of "production line" type of work and only one or two items prepared per day; workers needed to reheat foods, operate that equipment, and to assemble & serve meals	No skilled cooks nor other pre-preparation employees needed. Workers for assembling salads, and desserts, etc. Workers for reheating and serving foods must be able to operate equipment.
Typical Foodservices Using This:	Independent restaurants and cafeterias; hospitals and health care facilities; homes for specialized groups; in-plant foodservices; colleges and universities; schools	Airlines; chain restaurants; large school districts; commercial caterers and vending companies	Large hospitals, some large colleges and universities	Hospitals and nursing homes. Some commercial foodservices and colleges

Figure 2.5. Summary: Characteristics of four types of foodservice systems.

Conventional	Commissary	Ready-Prepared	Assembly/Serve
Purchase raw basic foods and limited convenience items	Purchase raw basic foods for all units	Purchase raw basic foods and limited convenience items	Purchase fully prepared foods in frozen, canned, dehydrated form; salad ingredients pre-prepared
Receive goods			
Store foods: Refrigerator at 40° or lower Drystores 65–70° F.			Store in freezer, 0° F. or refrigerator 40°F or lower until serving time.
Prepreparation: washing, sorting peeling, cutting, etc.			(none required)
Preparation and cooking: small to large batch & short order	Large batch cookery	Large batch cookery	(none required)

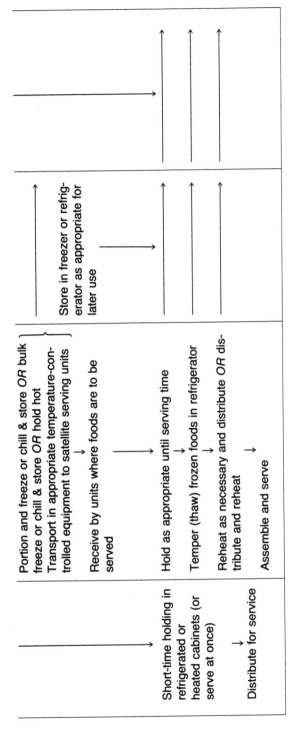

Figure 2.6. Flowchart: Processes, step by step, of the four foodservice systems.

the duplication of production labor and equipment which occurs if production centers are located at each foodservice site. Space requirements at the service sites are minimized because limited production equipment is required. By centralizing food procurement and production, the economies of volume purchasing may be realized. Commissary foodservice concepts are employed to meet various operational objectives related to effect use of resources.

Rationale for Ready-Prepared Foodservice Systems. Mass producing and freezing food may reduce labor expenditures by more effective use of labor in selected situations. Peak demands for labor may be removed because production is designed to meet future rather than daily needs. Furthermore, fewer skilled employees can be trained to heat and serve menu items, thus reducing the number of highly skilled workers required by the system. Food procurement in volume may decrease food costs for the system. A foodservice system based on ready-prepared products is contraindicated if additional expenditures for storage facilities, equipment, and food inventory cannot be absorbed by the organization.

Rationale for Assembly/Serve Foodservice Systems. Assuming a lack of skilled food production employees, and an available supply of highly processed, quality food products, an assembly/serve foodservice operation may achieve operational objectives to provide client satisfaction. Managerial decisions to adopt this form of foodservice system should consider the availability of these resources to the foodservice operation.

Recent research studies on foodservice systems in relation to time and temperature effects on food quality have been summarized and reported in another North Central Research bulletin. These microbiological safety, nutrient retention, and sensory quality studies provide specific data useful to persons deciding on a system to install or to those contemplating a change in systems. Further investigations are needed to advance understanding of the interrelationships among food products, resources, processes, and management in foodservices and so improve food quality in foodservice establishments.

The vast and ever-changing foodservice industry continues to be shaped by socioeconomic changes, demographic shifts, and the varying food habits and desires of the American people. Foodservice managers must keep abreast of these conditions and adapt their operations to the changing times in order to be competitive and successful.

Summary Questions

1. What are the socioeconomic conditions and demographic changes that have influenced the foodservice industry, and how have they had an impact on foodservices?

2. Define the systems concept.

3. Compare and contrast the systems theory to the scientific management theory.

4. Diagram a foodservice organization as a system.

5. Compare and contrast the four major types of foodservice systems described.

6. Which foodservice system(s) should be considered in each of the following situations:

    a. high labor cost in the area

    b. very low equipment budget

    c. close quality control is desired

    d. high food cost in the area

Bibliography

FoodService Director: Berkman installs 1st 'kitchenless' kitchen. FoodService Director 4(8):1, 1991.

FoodService Director: Rising food and labor costs top "worry list." FoodService Director 4(8):71, 1991.

FoodService Director: Soap box. FoodService Director 5(1):34, 1992.

Foodservice Systems: Product Flow and Microbial Quality and Safety of Foods. North Central Regional Research Publication No. 245. Columbia: University of Missouri Agriculture Experiment Station Research Bulletin 1018, 1977.

Hitt, M. A., Middlemist, R. D., and Mathis, R. L.: Management Concepts and Effective Practice, 3rd ed. Saint Paul: West Publishing Co., 1989.

Livingston, G. E. and Chang, C. M., eds.: Food Service Systems: Analysis, Design and Implementation. New York: Academic Press, 1979.

Schuster, K. and Staff, F. M.: Crossing the line. Food Mgmt. 23(1):94, 1988.

U.S. Bureau of Census: Statistical Abstract of the United States: 1991, 111th ed. Washington, DC: U.S. Bureau of Census, 1991.

Ward, B.: Cold facts on quick chillers. Foodservice Equipment & Supplies 44(9):65, 1991.

For More Information

Food Mgmt.: What is sous vide? Food Mgmt. 25(10):96, 1990.

King, P.: A system with room to grow. Food Mgmt. 23(3):61, 1988.

King, P.: Back to the future. Food Mgmt. 24(11):63, 1989.

King, P.: Food production on a grand scale. Food Mgmt. 23(4):60, 1988.

King, P.: Meeting a need efficiently. Food Mgmt. 24(3):52, 1989.

King, P.: Producing a less costly foodservice. Food Mgmt. 24(5):88, 1989.

King, P.: Production for profit. Food Mgmt. 22(3):68, 1987.

King, P.: System on a shoestring. Food Mgmt. 24(4):62, 1989.

King, P.: The future of central production? Food Mgmt. 24(2):52, 1989.

Morris, W. V.: Correctional farming programs provide food and cash. Corrections 1(1):20, 1991.

Quantity Food Production and Service

Menu Planning, Development, and Implementation

Production and service of food is determined by the menu. A *menu* is a detailed list of foods to be served at a meal or, in a broader sense, it is a total list of items offered by a foodservice. The term "menu" also applies to the printed list given to the patron.

The menu is the basic control tool used to design and manage all functions of a foodservice system. It determines the foods to be purchased, the personnel and equipment needed for production and service, and the employees' work schedules. The menu generates information needed for the financial management of the foodservice and is used as a basis for marketing functions. In a new foodservice, the menu influences the design of the kitchen and the equipment to be selected. To a large extent, the menu determines customer satisfaction and, thus, the success of the foodservice operation.

This chapter reviews factors that must be considered in menu planning to successfully achieve the goals of the foodservice. The most important influence is the customer. Other key considerations are organizational goals and production or service capabilities.

Menu development procedures are also discussed. Guidelines are presented on how to develop a month-to-month timetable for menu planning. Types of menu and patterns are defined. A step-by-step menu planning procedure is outlined and menu evaluation techniques are reviewed.

Finally, guidance is offered on how the newly planned menu can be implemented into the foodservice. Suggestions on printed menu design and on adapting the general (or master) menu to comply with diet modifications in a health care facility are offered.

Learning Objectives

After studying this chapter, the reader should be able to

1. apply preliminary planning considerations to the menu planning process
2. design a menu planning timetable to assure that new or revised menus are implemented on a timely basis
3. identify various types of menus and select the appropriate type for specific foodservice organizations
4. plan a menu for a specific foodservice operation
5. evaluate a planned menu to assure appropriateness for the customer and organizational capabilities
6. implement menu management strategies to assure proper documentation of master and therapeutic menus

Preliminary Planning

The major goal of most foodservices is to serve food that is acceptable to its clientele. It is important to be familiar with the target market: who the consumers are, their characteristics, and their food preferences. They may be located in a variety of settings, such as schools, hospitals, restaurants, or extended care facilities. The menus for each type of organization and its patrons will be different.

Certain management factors must be considered. Allowing adequate time to complete the menu planning process is essential to smooth implementation of the menu. The menu planner should aim for the best menu and service, with optional use of personnel and equipment. Often, a compromise must be made between what a foodservice would like to offer and what it is capable of producing and serving. The following is a more detailed description of preplanning considerations.

Organizational Goals

The planned menu must be appropriate for the foodservice and consistent with its organizational goals. Whether the major goal is to provide nutritionally adequate meals at a reasonable cost, as in school foodservice, or whether profit is the major goal, the menus must reflect the organization's stated purpose. Whatever the specific goals, most foodservices are offering food choices that reflect the current emphasis on nutrition and that meet the quality and service expectations of the customer.

The Customer

The menu planner should study the population to be served to determine their nutritional needs, eating habits, and food preferences. A profile of the clientele for which menus are being planned may include

- age range and average age
- estimated number of males and females
- state of health and activity levels
- social, cultural, and economic background
- nutritional requirements, food habits, and preferences

NUTRITIONAL REQUIREMENTS   Meeting the nutritional requirements of individuals in the group to be served is important in meal planning. This is especially true in foodservices that are responsible for providing the total daily nutritive requirements such as in long-term care facilities. These menus should fulfill the most recent recommended dietary allowances (RDA) defined by the National Research Council, which specify nutrient needs for various age groups by sex. Schools participating in the National School Lunch Program are required to meet certain nutrition requirements, as are many hospitals and government-sponsored nutrition programs (see Figs. 3.1a and 3.1b). Before planning menus for a government-funded operation, it is recommended that the menu planner contact an appropriate government agency to verify regulatory requirements for menu composition. For example, one may wish to contact a state health department to acquire regulatory information applicable to health care facilities, such as hospitals or long-term care facilities.

The general public is increasingly concerned about health and more interested in nutrition than ever before. In response to this changing attitude, restaurants and other foodservices are featuring foods that comply with today's definition of healthful eating. Many people are observing the dietary guidelines issued by the United States Department of Agriculture (USDA) and the United States Department of Health and Human Services. The guidelines were revised in 1990 and include the following recommendations:

1. Eat a variety of foods.
2. Maintain a healthy weight.
3. Choose a diet low in fat, saturated fat, and cholesterol.
4. Choose a diet with plenty of vegetables, fruits, and grain products.

SCHOOL LUNCH PATTERNS

COMPONENTS		MINIMUM QUANTITIES		RECOMMENDED QUANTITIES
		GRADES K – 3 ages 5 – 8 (Group III)	GRADES 4 – 12 age 9 & over (Group IV)	GRADES 7 – 12 age 12 & over (Group V)
MEAT OR MEAT ALTERNATE	A serving of one of the following or a combination to give an equivalent quantity:			
	Lean meat, poultry, or fish (edible portion as served)	1½ oz	2 oz	3 oz
	Cheese	1½ oz	2 oz	3 oz
	Large egg(s)	¾	1	1½
	Cooked dry beans or peas	⅜ cup	½ cup	¾ cup
	Peanut butter	3 Tbsp	4 Tbsp	6 Tbsp
	Nuts/seeds	¾ oz = 50%	1 oz = 50%	1½ oz = 50%
VEGETABLE AND/OR FRUIT	Two or more servings of vegetable or fruit or both to total	½ cup	¾ cup	¾ cup
BREAD OR BREAD ALTERNATE	Servings of bread or bread alternate	8 per week	8 per week	10 per week
MILK	A serving of fluid milk	½ pint (8 fl oz)	½ pint (8 fl oz)	½ pint (8 fl oz)

Figure 3.1a. National School Lunch patterns. (Source: *Supplement to 1984 Food Buying Guide for Child Nutrition Programs,* PA-1331, USDA.)

SCHOOL BREAKFAST PATTERNS

FOOD COMPONENTS/ITEMS	MINIMUM REQUIRED SERVING SIZE		
	AGES 1 and 2	GRADES 3, 4, 5	GRADES K – 12
MILK (Fluid) As a beverage, on cereal, or both:	½ cup	¾ cup	½ pint
JUICE/FRUIT/ VEGETABLE* Fruit and/or vegetable OR full-strength fruit juice or vegetable juice	¼ cup	½ cup	½ cup
Select one serving from each of the following components/items or two servings from one component/item.			
BREAD/ BREAD ALTERNATES** One of the following or an equivalent combination:			
Cereal (whole-grain or enriched or fortified)	¼ cup vol or ⅓ oz wt	⅓ cup vol or ½ oz wt	¾ cup vol or 1oz wt
Bread (whole-grain or enriched)	½ slice	½ slice	1 slice
Biscuit, roll, muffin, cornbread, etc. (whole-grain or enriched meal or flour)	½ serving	½ serving	1 serving
MEAT OR MEAT ALTERNATE One of the following or an equivalent combination:			
Lean meat, poultry, or fish	½ oz	½ oz	1 oz
Cheese	½ oz	½ oz	1 oz
Egg (large)	½	½	½
Peanut butter or other nut or seed butters	1 Tbsp	1 Tbsp	2 Tbsp
Nuts and/or seeds*** (as listed in program guidance)	½ oz	½ oz	1 oz
Cooked dry beans and peas	2 Tbsp	2 Tbsp	4 Tbsp

* Recommended daily: Citrus juice or fruit or a fruit or vegetable that is a good source of vitamin C (See *Menu Planning Guide for School Food Service*, PA-1260).
** For serving sizes of breads and bread alternates, see *Food Buying Guide for Child Nutrition Programs*, PA-1331 (1984).
*** No more than one ounce of nuts and/or seeds may be served in any one meal.

Figure 3.1b. National School Breakfast patterns. (Source: Supplement to *1984 Food Buying Guide for Child Nutrition Programs*, PA-1331, USDA.)

5. Use sugars only in moderation.

6. Use salt and sodium only in moderation.

7. If you drink alcoholic beverages, do so in moderation.

FOOD HABITS AND PREFERENCES   The clientele of a foodservice operation is generally composed of individuals from different cultural, ethnic, and economic backgrounds, most of whom have definite food likes and dislikes. The menu planner must keep this in mind when selecting foods that satisfy this diverse group.

Food habits are based on many influences, the most direct being the attitude of the parents in the home about food and eating. The family's ethnic and cultural backgrounds, as well as its economic level, all combine to determine the foods served and enjoyed. These habits are passed down from generation to generation, and when several different cultural or ethnic backgrounds are represented in one group for which a menu is to be made, the task of planning presents a challenge.

In today's mobile society, however, people are becoming more knowledgeable about ethnic and regional foods. Interest in Mexican, Oriental, Italian, and other international foods is evident from the number of specialty restaurants. Many health care facilities, schools, colleges, and similar foodservices include these foods in their menus to add variety and to contribute to the cultural education of the clientele. The menu planner should be aware of local and regional food customs and religious restrictions. For example, a menu planner should be well aware of kosher and Muslim dietary restrictions.

In addition, the traditional three-meals-a-day pattern, with the entire family eating together, has changed. People are eating fewer meals at home. They are eating more frequently and at less regular hours. To accommodate this change in eating habits, a more flexible meal schedule is evident in most institutional foodservices, and continuous service is available in many restaurants. Breakfast or lunch have, in many cases, replaced the luncheon as a business meal. In spite of the desire for fast-paced services, some experts predict that with the variety of prepared foods available today, many people will eat frozen and other easily prepared foods at home and will seek a restaurant with interesting decor and atmosphere when they dine away from home. The person planning menus for any type of foodservice should monitor such trends.

Production and Service Capabilities

FINANCIAL RESOURCES   Before any menu is planned, the amount of money that can be spent on food must be known. In commercial operations, the amount to be budgeted for the foodservice department is based on projected income from the sale of food. This income must generate adequate revenue to cover the cost of the raw food used and the cost of labor and operating expenses, and must allow for reasonable profit. Management determines the percentage of the income to be spent for each of these items. Food, a costly and variable expense, must be closely controlled. (Menu pricing is further discussed in Chapter 14.)

In a school, college, health care facility, or other nonprofit organization, a raw food-cost allowance per person, per meal, or per day may be determined. This does not mean that the cost of every item must fall below the budgeted figure. The planner looks at the total week's or month's food cost. This cumulative average can be readily available in a computer-assisted system. By balancing more costly items with less expensive foods, a more interesting variety can be offered and the budget can still be maintained. For example, the raw food cost of rib roast or beef tenderloin steak may be offset by low-cost poultry or ground beef items. On selective menus that offer a choice of 2 or more entrées, a well-liked lower cost item should be offered with a more expensive food. For example, tacos or burritos are popular and relatively low-cost entrées that could be offered as alternatives to more costly baked pork chops. Costs, then, may determine the choices, but it is important to remember that variety in the menu may be enhanced by balancing high- and low-cost items.

EQUIPMENT AND PHYSICAL FACILITIES   The menu plan for the day must be one that can be produced in the available work space and with the number and capacity of large and small equipment. Care should be taken to distribute the workload evenly for ovens, ranges, mixers, and other large pieces of equipment. The ovens are especially vulnerable to overuse. The inclusion of too many foods at one meal that require oven use may cause an overload or complicate production schedules. For example, it may not be possible to bake Swiss steak, potatoes, and a vegetable casserole at the same meal. If equipment must be shared, the menu should not include items that will cause a conflict. For example, unless separate ovens are available to the bakery unit, it may not be possible to bake hot breads if other menu items must be baked just prior to serving. Equipment usage errors can be alleviated by involving the production staff in the menu planning process.

The planner should be aware of restrictions on equipment and space, and be familiar with the methods of preparation, the equipment used, and the pans or other utensils needed before choosing the menu items. Refrigerator and freezer space must be considered. A chilled dessert, molded gelatin salad, and individual cold plates may be difficult to refrigerate if planned on the same day's menu. If the refrigerator and freezer space are inadequate, the frequency of delivery becomes a determining factor in the planning of the menu.

The amount of china, glassware, or silverware available may prevent the serving of certain menu items at the same meal. For example, fruit cobbler and a creamed vegetable may both require sauce dishes. Foods such as parfaits or shrimp cocktail should not be placed on the menu unless there is appropriate glassware for serving. For hospital patients and other tray service, the type and number of dishes required for service of the menu must fit on the tray.

PERSONNEL   The number and skill of employees are factors to consider when determining the variety and complexity of a menu. Understanding the relationship between menu and personnel helps the planner to develop menus that can be prepared with the available staff. Work schedules must be considered for all days because some foods require advance preparation, whereas others are prepared just prior to service. Menu items should be planned that enable employees' workloads to be spread evenly throughout the day and that do not result in too much last-minute preparation.

AVAILABILITY OF FOODS   The location of the market or other sources of food may have a limiting effect on the menu. This is especially true of fresh foods. A knowledge of fruits and vegetables and their seasons enables a planner to include them on the menu while they are at their peak of quality and at an affordable price. Whether the menu planner is responsible for ordering or purchasing the food, it is important to keep abreast of new items on the market and to be alert to foods that would add interest to the menu or that would improve variety and quality of menu items offered.

SERVICE   The style of service influences food item selection and the number of choices on the menu. Some foods are more adaptable to seated service than to cafeteria service; for example, cherries jubilee requires tableside preparation. Baked Alaska would be difficult to manage in cafeteria service because of last-minute preparation and the need for immediate service. Tray design may limit the number or form of foods offered. For example, a layered cake with whipped topping may not work if a covered, insulated tray is being used.

The distance between the point of preparation and the point of distribution should be considered, as well as the time elapsing between the completion of preparation and service. If the food is prepared in a central kitchen and sent to service areas in remote locations, the menu should not include foods, such as soufflés, that change during transportation. Foods transferred in bulk to a service unit must be of a type that will hold up well and still be appetizing when served.

Menu Development

An inherent liking for good food, a lack of prejudice, a flair for planning based on creativity and imagination, and the ability to merchandise food attractively are traits that aid the menu planner. If one individual is responsible for menu planning, it is helpful to have input from purchasing, production, and service personnel. Many foodservices assign this responsibility to a committee rather than to one individual, a practice that is especially appropriate for a multi-unit foodservice. Input from the public through marketing research, food preference studies, test marketing, and participation of food or menu committees can be of assistance. The planner should be alert to new products and to trends in consumer preferences and aware of menu items that are offered successfully by the competition, whether it is a nonprofit or commercial situation. Menu planning should be ongoing, current, and flexible enough to respond to changing conditions.

Information on consumer preference is important in menu planning. The relative popularity of a food may serve as a guide to the frequency by which a given item appears on the menu. A file of previous menus with comments concerning the reactions of guests, the difficulty or ease of preparation, and the cost helps prevent repetition and indicates combinations found satisfactory and profitable.

Types of Menus

A *selective menu* includes two or more choices in each menu category, the exact number of options varying with different types of foodservices. The menu mix, or the selection of food items to be offered in each category, is important to the success of a selective menu.

EXTENT OF SELECTION   The menu may take different forms, each written for the needs of the particular market it serves. Patrons may be offered an extensive list of items from which to select a meal or they may be given a menu that offers little, if any, choice.

Limited or semiselective refers to menus that allow one or more selections in some of the menu categories. For example, a long-term care facility may offer two entrée and two dessert selections at lunch and dinner, but only one choice in the vegetable and salad categories.

A *nonselective menu* offers no choices, but in many schools and health care facilities where these are used there may be two or three options in certain items, such as salads, desserts, and beverages. A single entrée may be offered, with a choice of tossed salad or molded fruit salad, and fresh fruit or ice cream may be available as an alternative to a baked or other prepared dessert. In some cases, the choice may be between a full meal and a soup and salad combination. Some foodservices that have a nonselective menu provide certain items daily, in addition to the planned menu; for example, cottage cheese, tossed salad, ice cream, and fresh or canned fruit. Table 3.1 illustrates the variations of selective menus.

Menus may be *static* or *set;* that is, the same menus are used each day. This type of menu is found in restaurants and other foodservices where the clientele changes daily or where there are enough items listed on the menu to offer

TABLE 3.1. Extent of Selections—Sample Menus.

Selective	Limited Selective	Nonselective

Appetizers
  Chilled tomato juice
  Cream of mushroom soup
	Appetizers
	  Chilled tomato juice	

Entrées
  Roast beef with gravy
  Grilled tuna steak with dill
    sauce
  Chicken salad on croissant
    with relishes
  Fresh fruit and cottage cheese
    plate with muffin
	Entrées
	  Roast beef with gravy
	  Chicken salad on croissant
	    with relishes
		Entrées
		  Roast beef with gravy

Vegetables
  Mashed potatoes with gravy
  Boiled red potatoes
  Steamed broccoli spears
  Creamed carrots
	Vegetables
	  Mashed potatoes with gravy
	  Steamed broccoli spears
		Vegetables
		  Mashed potatoes with gravy
		  Steamed broccoli spears

Salads
  Garden salad with French
    dressing
  Mandarin orange gelatin salad
	Salads
	  Garden salad with French
	    dressing
		Salads
		  Garden salad with French
		    dressing

Desserts
  Pecan pie with whipped
    topping
  German chocolate cake with
    coconut icing
  Butter brickle ice cream
  Fresh fruit
	Desserts
	  Pecan pie with whipped
	    topping
	  Butter brickle ice cream
	  Fresh fruit
		Desserts
		  Pecan pie with whipped
		    topping

Breads
  Dinner roll
  White bread
  Whole wheat bread
  Bread sticks
	Breads
	  Dinner rolls
	  Whole wheat bread
		Breads
		  Dinner roll

Beverages
  Coffee   2% milk
  Tea   Skim milk
  Hot cocoa   Chocolate milk
	Beverages
	  Coffee
	  Tea
	  2% milk
		Beverages
		  Coffee
		  2% milk

sufficient variety. Some flexibility may be built into the menu by changing an item or two daily or offering daily specials. The static menu may be quite limited in choice, as in most fast-food restaurants. Changes in these menus are made only after careful development of a new product and extensive market research and testing. With a set menu, the purchasing, production, and service can be simplified.

A *single-use menu* is one in which the menu is planned for a certain day and is not repeated again in exactly the same form, although some food combinations may be used again in future meals. This type of menu is often used for special functions, holidays, or catering events.

The *cycle menu* is a carefully planned set of menus that is rotated at definite intervals—the length of cycle depending on the type of foodservice. With a 3-day average patient stay, hospitals could have a 7-day cycle, but may prefer 8- or 12-day cycles to avoid repetition of foods on the same day each week. A 3-week cycle, however, would accommodate a wider variety of foods and result in greater patient satisfaction. Most hospitals add additional choices for the employees' cafeterias and may use a longer cycle for that service. An extended care facility normally has a longer cycle because of length of stay of the residents.

There are many advantages in using a cycle menu. After the initial planning has been completed, time is freed for the planner to review and revise the menus to meet changing needs such as holidays, vacations, changes in personnel, or unavailability of a food item. Repetition of the same menu aids in standardizing preparation procedures and in efficient use of equipment. Forecasting and purchasing are simplified and, with repeated use of the menus and needed adjustments, employee workloads can be equalized and distributed fairly.

There are some potential disadvantages in using cycle menus. They may become monotonous if the cycle is too short or if the same food is offered on the same day each week. The cycle menu may not include well-liked foods often enough, or it may include unpopular items too frequently. Some variety may be added by specifying certain changes in the second and third rotations. For example, spice cake may be substituted for a white layer cake in the second week, or pot roast with vegetables may be substituted for beef stew. The cycle menu may not provide for foods that come into the market at varying times of the year, but many foodservices solve this problem by developing summer, fall, winter, and spring cycles; others note the seasonal alternatives on the menu. If these disadvantages can be resolved and the menu properly developed to meet the needs of a particular foodservice system, the cycle menu can become an effective management tool.

Whatever the length of the cycle, the menus must be carefully planned and evaluated after each use. A cycle menu should be flexible enough to handle emergencies, to utilize leftover food, and to accommodate new ideas and menu items.

Menus may also be categorized by the method of pricing. In the *à la carte menu*, food items are priced separately. This type of menu allows the patron to select only the food wanted. The *table d'hote menu* offers a complete meal at a fixed price, usually with a choice of some items. The *du jour menu* means menu of the day. It must be planned and written daily. This is a good way to utilize leftover foods and food bargains.

Timetable for Planning, Development, and Implementation

How far in advance of actual production and service should menus be planned? The answer depends greatly on the type of menu used, the extent of selections offered, and the size and complexity of the foodservice system. For example, a single-use menu for a holiday meal in a restaurant may require as little as a week of planning time assuming recipes are tested and standardized. A selective, cycle menu with several selections and never-before-tried items for a large hospital can take several weeks of advanced planning to assure proper implementation (see Table 3.2).

Menu Patterns

The menu pattern is an outline of food to be included in each meal, and the extent of this choice must be decided before menus are planned. For years, the traditional schedule has been three meals a day, including breakfast, lunch, and

TABLE 3.2.   Suggested Timetable for Menu Planning, Development, and Implementation.

Time Period	Recommended Activities
6 months in advance	• Gather menu planning information: recipes, customer, survey summaries, etc. • Review budget • Organize menu planning team
5 months in advance	• Meet with menu planning team • Establish goals of menu plan • Assign responsibility
4 months in advance	• Begin writing master menu • Have menu planning team evaluate menu • Review availability of equipment and china needed to produce menu
3 months equipment in advance	• Allow production staff to review master menu for utilization and work load • Have purchasing agent review new menu items and write specifications
2 months in advance	• Develop production sheets and update forecasting methods • Design menus to be distributed to customers • Send first draft to printers
1 month before implementation date	• Proofread printed menus • Return to printers for final revisions • Conduct final implementation procedures

dinner, served within a certain time span. In some cases, the larger meal has been served at noon, resulting in a pattern of breakfast, dinner, and supper. In foodservice, the trend is moving away from this traditionally structured plan because of the desire of many patrons for fast food and instant service and because many people prefer to eat at different times of the day.

To accommodate this trend, some cafeterias are offering snack-type foods as part of their regular menu and lengthening their service hours. Some hospitals offer light evening meals as an alternative to the traditional dinner menu. Many foodservices with multiple choice menus have essentially the same menu for the noon and evening meals, and some give patrons not only a choice of food items but of menu structure as well. Brunch, the combination of breakfast and lunch, is becoming an increasingly popular choice.

A traditional basic menu pattern is as follows:

Breakfast—Fruit or juice
          Cereal, hot or cold
          Eggs and breakfast meat
          Toast or hot bread
          Choice of beverages
Lunch— Soup (optional)
          Entrée or sandwich
          Salad or vegetable
          Bread with margarine or butter
          Fruit or light dessert
          Choice of beverages
Dinner— Soup (optional)
          Entrée (meat, fish, poultry, or vegetarian)
          Two vegetables (one may be potato or pasta)
          Salad
          Bread with margarine or butter
          Dessert
          Choice of beverages

Menus for most institutions that serve three meals a day are based on this pattern. The number of choices offered varies with the type of foodservice; with the type of service or method of delivery of the food; and with the personnel, equipment, and money available.

Special Considerations

COMMERCIAL FOODSERVICES   For the commercial restaurant, profit is a major objective, but customer satisfaction is also an important consideration. Merchandising and competition have become important factors in this type of foodservice. Goals in commercial foodservices may differ, too, with some featuring service in a relaxed atmosphere and others stressing convenience and speed of service. Many industrial organizations believe in quality, low-cost food as a means of maintaining a healthy work force whose morale is high. To assure this fringe benefit to employees, the foodservice may be partially or wholly subsidized by the company.

Menu planning for commercial foodservices is influenced by many factors including the size and type of operation, its goals, and its financial objectives. Menus range from the fast-food chain's limited menu for high volume and speedy service to the elaborate table d'hote menu of a formal seated-service restaurant.

In addition to the basic rules of successful meal planning and food combinations, special emphasis must be placed on choosing menu items that will sell and be profitable. With the exact number of patrons from day-to-day unknown, the menu must be flexible enough to accommodate any excess in food production. As in any other foodservice, labor is one of the largest items of expense and one of the most difficult to control. The use of preportioned foods, portion-ready entrées, ready-to-cook foods, and other labor-saving items is of major importance in affecting the economies of time and cost.

Some restaurants have a set menu that does not vary from day-to-day; others have found the use of cycle menus to be valuable in reducing planning time and equalizing labor. The menu may be planned and presented as a listing of à la carte items rather than complete meals, or may include both. Some restaurants having a set menu that features daily specials to add interest to the menu, to enable them to take advantage of seasonal foods, and to incorporate foods on hand. In national restaurant chains, the same menu may be offered in all units and generally is limited to a few items that have been carefully developed and standardized. In commercial cafeterias, the noon and evening meals may be essentially the same with a wide selection of entrées, sandwiches, and desserts. It is not uncommon to have 5 to 6 entrées, 8 to 10 salads, and 8 to 10 desserts. Cafeteria operations may offer special food items on individual days or may serve a unique soup, salad, or dessert as their specialty.

INDUSTRIAL OR EMPLOYEE FOODSERVICES Many industrial organizations offer meal service as an employee benefit. Reasonably priced food with convenient service may contribute to maintaining a healthy work force and high morale. Companies have various options in offering employee meals, from free meals subsidized by the company to reduced price meals in the organization's cafeteria.

Menu planning for employee feeding is similar to other operations. One unique factor to consider would be timing of service. Service lines must move along quickly to prevent the employee from spending limited break time standing in line.

INSTITUTIONS   Institutions provide services including food to a defined population. For example, long-term facilities provide care to the elderly (Fig. 3.2). Schools and colleges cater to the young, healthy population. Special menu planning considerations for institutions are summarized in Table 3.3.

FOOD CHARACTERISTICS AND COMBINATIONS   When planning menus, one must visualize how the food will look on the plate, tray, or cafeteria counter and sense the combinations of foods presented. This is referred to as presentation. Consider how the flavors will combine, whether there is contrast in texture, shape, and consistency; in other words, an overview of the final menu as it is served.

Color gives eye appeal and helps to merchandise the food. At least one or two colorful foods should be included on each menu. A green vegetable adds color to an otherwise colorless combination of broiled fish and creamed potatoes, or buttered parsley potatoes and glazed carrots also improve the appearance of a plate. Other green vegetables, tomatoes, and beets also add color, as do garnishes of fruit, watercress, or radishes. It is just as important to have pleasing color combinations on the cafeteria counter as on the individual plate.

Texture refers to the structure of foods and can best be detected by the feel of foods in the mouth. Crisp, soft, smooth, and chewy are adjectives describing

Figure 3.2.   Residents enjoying mealtime. (Courtesy, Willamette View, Inc., Portland, Oregon.)

TABLE 3.3.   Menu Considerations for Institutions.

Colleges/Universities	Hospitals	Extended Care/Retirement Home	Schools
Offer ethnic and cultural food choices to meet multicultural preferences and contribute to the social and cultural education of the student	Meet total nutritional needs of patients within budgetary allowance	Meet total nutritional needs of residents within budgetary allowance	Provide one-third of the child's daily nutritive requirement
Offer a variety of meal plans along with à la carte selections	Adapt menu to therapeutic or modified diets	Consider smaller portions of nutrient dense foods in recognition of low activity level and energy expenditure	Offer additional foods to improve student acceptability of meals
Offer a variety of dining atmospheres	Plan for therapeutic nourishment	Offer appropriate texture modifications for those residents with chewing difficulty	Implement "offer vs. serve" strategy
Implement merchandising strategies to attract and retain customers	Consider a 1- to 2-week cycle of selective menus based on average patient stay	Consider a 4- to 6-week cycle menu of limited selections	Consider alternatives, such as salad bars and selective menus
Meet total daily nutrition needs of the students	Comply with regulatory agencies; federal, state, and Joint Commission on Accreditation for Healthcare Organizations (JCAHO)	Comply with regulatory agencies; federal and state	Consider theme days and special menus to pique interest

food texture. A variety of textures should be included in a meal. A crisp vegetable salad accompanying a chicken and rice casserole, along with fruit cobbler or other fruit dessert, would offer more contrast in texture than would a gelatin salad and a chocolate pudding served with the casserole meal. For cafeterias, contrasts in texture are usually offered in each menu category.

Consistency is the way foods adhere together—their degree of firmness, density, or viscosity—and may be described as firm, thin, thick, or gelatinous. Serving two creamed foods on the plate would be unattractive. A menu including baked ham with cherry sauce, escalloped potatoes, and creamed peas would be unappetizing because the foods would intermingle on the plate.

Shape of food plays a big part in eye appeal, and interest can be created through variety in the form in which foods are presented. One way to add interest to the menu is to vary the way in which vegetables are cut; for example, carrots cut into julienne strips or circles, cubed, or shredded; or green beans served whole, cut, or French cut. Dicing and cutting machines provide an easy method for obtaining different forms and sizes. Variation in height of food also aids in eye appeal for the customer.

Flavor combinations are important in menu planning. In addition to the basic flavors of sweet, sour, bitter, and salty, vegetables may be thought of as strong and mild flavored, while chili or other foods may be thought of as spicy or highly seasoned. A variety of flavors in the meal is more enjoyable than duplication of any one flavor. Foods with the same basic flavors, such as spaghetti with tomato sauce and sliced tomato salad, should be avoided in the same meal.

Certain food combinations complement each other, such as turkey and cranberries, roast beef and horseradish sauce, or pork and applesauce. The planner should avoid exclusive use of stereotyped combinations, however, and explore other accompaniments to make menus more interesting. Red currant jelly instead of mint with lamb is an example.

Variety in preparation should be considered in menu planning, and two foods prepared in the same way should not be included in the same meal. Variety may be introduced by marinating or stir-frying foods in addition to the traditional fried, broiled, baked, braised, or steamed. Foods can be varied further by serving them creamed, buttered, or escalloped, or by adding a variety of sauces.

Steps in Menu Development

A planning worksheet on which to record menu items is shown in Figure 3.3. For a selective menu offering certain items daily, time is saved by having the names of these foods printed on the worksheet. A suggested step-by-step procedure for planning menus follows.

1. **Entrées.**   Plan the meats and other entrées for the entire period or cycle. If planning 1 week at a time, select entrées for a month or longer, then complete the menus weekly or as needed. Since entrées are the most expensive items on the menu, costs can be controlled to a great extent through careful planning at this point.

Menus				
Week of _____				
	Monday	Tuesday	Wednesday	Thursday
Breakfast Fruit Fruit juice Cereal Entree Bread Beverages	1. 1. 2. 1. 2. Assorted dry 1. 1. Toast 2. C.T.M.	 Assorted dry Toast C.T.M.	 Assorted dry Toast C.T.M.	 Assorted dry Toast C.T.M.
Lunch Soup Entrees Vegetable Bread Salads Desserts Beverages	1. 1. 2. 1. 1. Assorted 1. Salad bar 2. 1. 2. 1. C.T.M. 2.	 Assorted Salad bar C.T.M.	 Assorted Salad bar C.T.M.	 Assorted Salad bar C.T.M.
Dinner Soup Entrees Potato or pasta Vegetables Salads Desserts Beverages	1. 1. 2. 1. 1. 2. 1. Salad bar 2. 1. 2. 3. 1. C.T.M.	 Salad bar C.T.M.	 Salad bar C.T.M.	 Salad bar C.T.M.

Figure 3.3.   Suggested worksheet for menu planning.

If the menu pattern provides entrée choices, the selection should include at least one meat and a vegetarian entrée, along with poultry, fish, and meat extenders to complete the number of items required. Fewer luncheon entrées may be offered than for the dinner meal, depending on the type of foodservice.

2. **Soups and sandwiches.** If a soup and sandwich combination is to be an entrée choice, it should be planned with the other entrées. In a cafeteria, a variety of sandwiches may be offered, and these may not change from day-to-day. If more than one soup is included, one should be a cream or hearty soup and one a stock soup.

3. **Vegetables.** Decide on the vegetables appropriate to serve with the entrées. Potatoes, rice, or pasta may be included as one choice. On a selective menu, pair a less popular vegetable with one that is well-accepted.

4. **Salads.** Select salads that are compatible with the entrées and vegetables. If a protein-type salad, such as chicken, tuna, or deviled egg, is planned as an entrée choice, it should be coordinated with the other entrée selections. If only one salad is to be offered, choose one that complements or is a contrast in texture to the other menu items.

    On a selective menu, include a green salad plus fruit, vegetable, and gelatin salads to complete the desired number. Certain salads, such as tossed salad, cottage cheese, deviled egg, or cabbage slaw, can be offered daily. A salad bar that includes a variety of salads and relishes may also be a standard feature.

5. **Desserts.** If no choice is to be offered, plan a light dessert with a hearty meal and a richer dessert when the rest of the meal is not too filling. On a selective menu, the number of choices may be limited to two or three plus a daily offering of fruit, ice cream or sherbet, and yogurt. For a commercial cafeteria, it may be quite extensive and include a two-crust pie, a creme pie, cake or cookies, pudding, fruit, ice cream or sherbet, and gelatin dessert.

6. **Garnishes.** To maximize plate appearance, it is recommended that a planned garnish be considered for each meal. The garnishes should be part of the master menu or a separate cycle. The planned garnishes eliminate last-minute decision making and allow adequate time to assure that proper ingredients are available to assemble garnishes for each meal. Menu planning books and trade publications are excellent resources for garnish ideas.

7. **Breads.** Vary the kinds of breads offered or provide a choice of white or whole grain bread and a hot bread. Many foodservices use homemade breads as one of their specialties. Vary shape and ingredients of bread selections to maximize variety.

8. **Breakfast items.** Certain breakfast foods are standard and generally include fruit juices, hot and cold cereals, and toast. It is customary to offer eggs in some form and to introduce variety through the addition of other entrées, hot breads, and fresh fruits.

9. **Beverages.** A choice of beverages that include coffee, tea, whole milk, and lowfat milk is offered in most foodservices. Decaffeinated coffee and tea are generally provided, and soft drinks and a variety of juices also may be included. Some hospitals now offer wine selections to their patients when approved by the attending physician.

Menu Evaluation

Menu evaluation is an important part of menu planning and should be an ongoing process. The menu as planned should be reviewed prior to its use and again after it has been served. A foodservice manager can best evaluate menus by looking at the entire planned menu and responding to the following questions. The use of a checklist helps to make certain that all factors of good menu planning have been met. (Figs. 3.4 and 3.5 are examples of menu evaluation tools.)

CHECKLIST FOR MENU EVALUATION

1. Does the menu meet nutritional guidelines and organizational objectives?
2. Are the in-season foods that are offered available and within an acceptable price range?
3. Do foods on each menu offer contrasts of color? texture? flavor? consistency? shape or form? type of preparation? temperature?
4. Can these foods be prepared with the personnel and equipment available?
5. Are the workloads balanced for personnel and equipment?
6. Is any one food item or flavor repeated too frequently during this menu period?
7. Are the meals made attractive with suitable garnishes and accompaniments?
8. Do the combinations make a pleasing whole, and will they be acceptable to the clientele?

The Printed Menu

As indicated at the beginning of this chapter, the menu is an itemized list of foods served at a meal. From it, a working menu and production schedules evolve. The term also refers to the medium on which the menu is printed, which presents the food selection to the restaurant customer, the hospital patient, or other clientele. The menu may also be posted on a menu board, as is the custom in most cafeterias and fast-food restaurants.

MENU DESIGN   A menu card must be designed and worded to appeal to the guest, to stimulate sales, and often to influence clientele to select items that the foodservice wants to sell. The menu card should be of a size that can be easily handled. It should also be spotlessly clean, simple in format with appropriate print size and type, and have ample margin space. The menu should be highly legible and interesting in color and design, harmonizing with the decor of the foodservice. The printed menu is a form of merchandising and an important

MENU EVALUATION FORM

CYCLE _____   DATES _____   EVALUATOR _____

Place a check mark on days when a problem is noted for any characteristic. Comment on the problem.

CHARACTERISTICS	DAYS							COMMENTS
	S	M	T	W	T	F	S	
MENU PATTERN–NUTRITIONAL ADEQUACY Each meal is consistent with the menu pattern. All food components specified met the nutritional needs of the clientele.								
COLOR AND EYE APPEAL A variety of colors is used in each meal. Color combinations do not clash. Colorless or one-color meals are avoided. Attractive garnishes are used.								
TEXTURE AND CONSISTENCY A contrast of soft, creamy, crisp, chewy, and firm-textured foods are included in each meal, as much as possible, for clientele served.								
FLAVOR COMBINATIONS Foods with compatible, varied flavors are offered. Two or more foods with strong flavors are avoided in the same meal. For example, onions, broccoli, turnips, cabbage, or cauliflower; tomato juice and tomato base casserole; and macaroni and cheese and pineapple-cheese salad, are not served together.								
SIZES AND SHAPES Pleasing contrasts of food sizes and shapes appear in each meal. Many chopped or mixed items are avoided in the same meal. For example, cubed meat, diced potatoes, mixed vegetables, and fruit cocktail are not served together.								

Figure 3.4. Menu evaluation form.

MENU REPEAT FORM

DIRECTIONS: List each food item from the menu only once and then check off the meals and days on which each item appears. (B, breakfast; L, lunch; D, dinner)

Item Served	Monday B	L	D	Tuesday B	L	D	Wednesday B	L	D	Thursday B	L	D	Friday B	L	D	Saturday B	L	D	Sunday B	L	D
Scrambled eggs	X			X							X					X			X		
Mashed potatoes			X			X						X									X
Carrots					X																X
Gelatin		X			X						X	X									X

Figure 3.5. Menu repeat form.

marketing tool. It should not be thought of as a price sheet alone, but as a selling and public relations device.

DESCRIPTIVE WORDING Menu items are listed in the sequence in which they are eaten and should present an accurate word picture of the foods available so that the patron can properly visualize the menu items. It is disappointing for the guest to imagine one thing and be served something entirely different.

Giving misleading names to menu items is unfair to the customer and is illegal where truth in menu legislation has been enacted. In general, these laws require that the menu accurately describe the foods to be served. If baked Idaho potatoes are listed on the menu, they must indeed be Idaho potatoes. The same is true when listing Maine lobster, or the point of origin for other foods. "Fresh" foods listed on the menu must be fresh, not frozen or canned. If the word "homemade" is used on the menu, it means that the food was made on the premises. If a menu lists a grade such as U.S. Choice beef and indicates portion size, the meat must be of that grade and size.

Descriptive words do enhance the menu and, if accurate, may influence the customers' selections. Examples are slices of red ripe tomato on Bibb lettuce, fresh spinach salad with bacon-mayonnaise dressing, old-fashioned beef stew with fresh vegetables, chilled melon wedge, and warm peach cobbler with fluffy hard sauce. The menu should not include recipe names that are unknown to the customer or that do not indicate the contents. Even where truth in menu legislation is not in effect, accuracy in menu wording helps to ensure customer satisfaction.

Menu Management

PLANNING MODIFIED DIETS   In many foodservice operations, especially those affiliated with health care, the foodservice department is responsible for assuring that physician-ordered diets are provided accurately. A qualified dietetics professional, such as a registered dietitian or dietetic technician, works with the foodservice manager to implement these special menus. Modified menu extensions are an excellent management tool for monitoring this responsibility. The modified menu extensions are generated from the master menu and a diet manual that defines the modified diets for a particular facility. Many dietetic associations and hospitals have written diet manuals that are available for sale. It is important to select a diet manual that best represents the diets needed in a given situation. For example, a manual developed for a hospital may not be the best choice for an extended care facility.

Once diets are defined, the foodservice administrator should meet with a dietitian knowledgeable in modified diets and develop the menu extensions (Fig. 3.6). A menu extension should be planned for each day. The extended portion of the menu illustrates how the modified diet, as defined in the manual, can be adapted from the master.

Extended menus have several advantages. These menus serve as a tool for menu analysis to assure that modified diets are prepared and served according to physicians' written diet orders. The extensions also serve as a reference for the foodservice employees so they can be certain that diets are prepared and served accurately. Finally, the extensions are a useful purchasing tool, clearly identifying the need for special dietary foods (i.e., low sodium items).

MENUS AS DOCUMENTS   Printed master menus for both general and modified diets are excellent documents for department evaluation and budget planning

Walnut Grove Health Care Center
General and Therapeutic Diets
Cycle _____ **Day** _____
Dietitian _____

	General Menu	Portion	Therapeutic Diets				
			Mechan	Puree	2 gm Na$^+$	1500 ADA	1200 ADA
B							
L							
D							
H S							

Figure 3.6.   Therapeutic menu extension form.

functions. Any changes made from the master should be noted on the master menu for future evaluation. Master menus should be signed and dated by the person responsible for menu content.

Summary

The menu is the focal point from which many functions and activities in a foodservice organization begin. It determines the foods to be purchased, it is the basis for planning production and employee schedules, and it is an important factor in controlling costs.

In planning foodservice menus, many factors must be considered: (1) the nutritional requirements, food habits, and preferences of the individuals in the group for which menus are being planned; (2) the goals of the organization; (3) the amount of money available; (4) limitations on equipment and physical facilities; (5) the number and skill of employees; and (6) the type of service. The menu must offer a selection of foods that is satisfying to the clientele, but it must be one that can be produced within the constraints of the physical facility and limitations dictated by management policies.

The menu can take different forms, each written for the needs of a particular type of foodservice. The static or set menu, in which the same menu items are offered each day, is found mainly in commercial foodservices. A selective menu offers two or more choices in each menu category and is widely used in various types of foodservices. A nonselective menu offers no choice, but in schools and health care facilities where this type of menu is often used, there may be limited choices in some categories. A cycle menu is a carefully planned set of menus that are rotated at definite intervals. The single-use menu is planned for a certain day and is not repeated in the same form.

Systematic planning procedures that include continuous evaluation of the menus as served should be followed. The menu planner should keep abreast of new products on the market and should be alert to the preferences of the clientele and the need for changes in the menu. Innovation is a key word in today's menu planning. New menu ideas and marketing techniques must be developed if the foodservice is to satisfy a clientele that is becoming increasingly sophisticated about food.

Summary Questions

1. What are the preliminary planning factors to consider in a menu planning process?
2. How might these factors vary between menus for a hospital and those for an extended care facility?

3. What are the various types of menus from which to choose? What might be an appropriate type of menu for a school lunch program?

4. Plan a 1-week, limited, select menu for a psychiatric facility—age range is 18 to 85 years. What factors did you consider in planning this menu?

5. Obtain a menu from a local organization (i.e., hospital, restaurant, school, nursing home). Evaluate the menu on food characteristics and combinations. What changes would you recommend?

For More Information

Drummond, K. E.: Nutrition for the Foodservice Professional. New York: Van Nostrand Reinhold, 1989.

Eckstein, E. F.: Menu Planning, 3rd ed. Westport, CT: AVI Publishing Co., 1983.

Fanelli, M. T. and Stevenhagen, K. J.: Characterizing consumption patterns by food frequency methods: Core foods and variety of foods in diets of older Americans. J. Am. Diet. Assoc. 85:1570, 1985.

Food and Nutrition Service, USDA: Menu Planning Guide for School Food Service, PA No. 1250. Washington, DC: U.S. Government Printing Office, 1980.

Hodges, C. A.: Culinary Nutrition for Foodservice Professionals. New York: Van Nostrand Reinhold, 1989.

Kirks, B. A. and Wolff, H. K.: A comparison of methods for plate waste determinations. J. Am. Diet. Assoc. 85:329, 1985.

Menu census: A 15-year retrospective. Restaurant and Institutions 96:4, 1986.

National Research Council: Recommended Dietary Allowances, 10th ed. Washington, DC: National Academy of Sciences, 1989.

Puckett R. P. and Miller, B. B.: Food Service Manual for Health Care Institutions. Chicago: American Hospital Publishing, Inc., 1988.

Reid, R. D.: Foodservice and Restaurant Marketing. Ch. 7 Planning and designing the menu. Boston: CBI Publishing Co., 1983.

Shugart, G. and Molt, M.: Food for Fifty, 9th ed. Part 3 Menu planning. New York: John Wiley & Sons, 1993

Tastes of America. Restaurants and Institutions 95:97, 1985.

U.S. Department of Agriculture and U.S. Department of Health and Human Services: Nutrition and Your Health: Dietary Guidelines for Americans. Washington, DC: Office of Governmental and Public Affairs, 1990.

VonEgmond-Pannell, D.: School Foodservice Management, 4th ed. New York: Van Nostrand Reinhold, 1990.

Purchasing and Storage

Purchasing is an essential function in the foodservice system and is the first step in the production and service of quality food. Although the procurement process for an institutional or commercial foodservice involves food, supplies, and equipment, major emphasis in this chapter is on the buying of food.

Today's market offers a large variety of products from which selections must be made in order to meet the needs of a particular foodservice. Whether the buying decisions are made by the administrative dietitian, a chef, a purchasing agent, or other qualified personnel, they must be based on quality standards, the economic structure of the organization, and a thorough knowledge of the marketing system.

Procedures for the selection of vendors, determining food needs, and writing specifications are discussed, as are the methods of purchasing. Emphasis is on information that will assist the buyer in making purchasing decisions rather than an in-depth discussion of individual food items.

An important part of the purchasing process is the receiving, storage, and issuing of food and supplies. Requirements for storage facilities and records needed for inventory control are included here.

Learning Objectives

After studying this chapter, the reader should be able to

1. understand the market and market regulations
2. identify the knowledge requirements of a food purchaser
3. explain the two principal methods of food purchasing that are used by organizations

4. describe procedures that may be used to select vendors, determine food needs, and write specifications

5. identify characteristics of quality food

6. understand the receiving process and its importance in cost and quality control

7. list the different types of storage and briefly describe the requirements of each

8. discuss inventory control, including records that may be used

9. describe the role of governmental regulatory agencies in assuring food quality

What Is Purchasing?

Purchasing is the process of getting the right product into a facility and to the consumer at the right time and in a form that meets preestablished standards for quantity, quality, and price. Other related terms used include procurement, buying, or shopping. Regardless of the term used, purchasing as a process involves several key functions:

- identification of a need to be filled by an outside source
- development of specifications or detailed descriptions of desired products
- determination of quantity needed
- market research for product availability
- negotiation with sellers and placing orders
- receiving items and transfer into proper storage
- issuing

The purchasing process begins with a well-planned menu and a thorough understanding of the market and current market conditions.

The Market

The market is the medium through which commodities are moved from the producer to the consumer—an exchange of ownership takes place. Markets are classified as **primary, secondary,** and **local.** A market is classified depending on the type of food sold, the location of the market, and the marketing channels involved.

In the food industry, a **primary** market is the basic source of supply. Examples include roasted coffee from New York City, meats from Chicago stockyards, and fruits and vegetables from the growing areas of California. Primary markets influence the sales and distribution of their goods through various activities, such as setting prices and quality standards. Raw agricultural products are delivered to primary markets where they are processed or prepared for distribution to secondary markets.

The **secondary** market is the physical, functional unit of the market system where products are accepted from the primary markets and distributed to local buyers. Secondary markets greatly influence activities in primary markets and have gradually assumed many of the functions traditionally performed in the primary markets.

The third type of market available to the food buyer is the **local** market. Farmers' markets may offer savings on seasonal products, and local supermarkets may be a good source of supply for the restaurant or small foodservice operator who only has money and storage space to buy what is currently needed.

Food is distributed through marketing channels with the aid of numerous marketing agents often referred to as middlemen. For example, wholesalers in secondary markets purchase products in large quantities from primary markets and redistribute in smaller quantities to local buyers. Full service wholesalers handle all items typically required by their customers, whereas specialty wholesalers restrict their sales to only three or four items within a particular line, such as fresh and frozen meats, fresh produce, or canned foods and groceries. Food also may be distributed through brokers and commissioned agents. (See Fig. 4.1.)

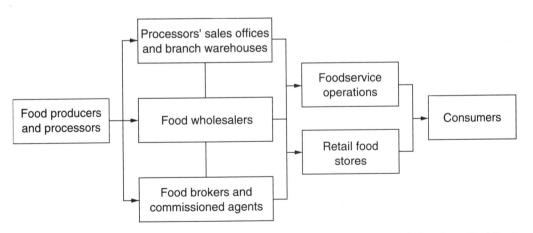

Figure 4.1. Structure of the food distribution system. (Reprinted with permission from *Food Service Manual for Health Care Institutions*, 1988 Edition, published by American Hospital Publishing, Inc., copyright © 1988.)

A broker is a sales representative for a manufacturer or a group of manufacturers, but is in business for himself. Food brokers do not buy or own any merchandise, they find buyers for the manufacturers' products. A commissioned agent is similar to a broker except that the commissioned agent takes ownership of the merchandise from the manufacturer, and then seeks interested buyers.

The marketing system involves the growing, harvesting, transporting, processing, packaging, storing, selling, financing, and supplying of market information for the many foods and food products available. Each process and transfer of ownership adds to the cost of the end product so that the final consumer cost is far in excess of the amount paid to the original producer of the commodity. The tendency today is to bypass as many individual marketing agents as possible and, thus, reduce the marketing cost contributed by these agents' charges. For example, large volume buyers may be able to purchase directly from the food processor, thus saving the middleman's charges for handling, storing, and selling the product.

The market is dynamic and ever-changing and the food buyer must be alert to trends and conditions that affect it. Government policy, economic trends, and adverse weather conditions are but a few of the factors that demand the attention of the buyer. Exchange of information between seller and buyer is an important function of the market and is made possible through various channels, such as trade association newsletters, local and federal market reports, and the press. Other sources of market information are technical and trade association meetings and magazines, research reports, talks with sales representatives, and visits to the produce markets and wholesale distributors.

Adverse growing conditions can affect food prices, as can unusual consumer demands and seasonal variations. Some foods are relatively stable in price and follow general economic conditions. Others are more perishable and have greater price fluctuations during the year. Most fresh fruits and vegetables are considered best at the height of the production season, particularly those grown within a given market area. However, treatment of fresh foods and improved transportation, refrigeration, and storage facilities have greatly reduced the so-called seasonability of foods. Stocks of processed foods may be high or depleted at times, which will affect both price and availability.

Market Regulation

Food Safety and Inspection Programs

The safety and wholesomeness of our food supply is assured through government safety and inspection programs. Quality is defined and assured through grading services, which are not to be confused with the inspection programs. Grading is discussed later in this chapter.

Government safety and inspection programs are used to evaluate foods for signs of disease, bacteria, chemicals, infestation, filth, or any other factor that may render the food item unfit for human consumption. All foods shipped in interstate commerce must meet the requirements of one or more federal laws and regulations. Foods sold intrastate must meet state and local regulations that are *at least equal to* the federal requirements.

The major responsibility for ensuring safe, wholesome food is that of the U.S. Department of Agriculture (USDA) and the Food and Drug Administration (FDA). Numerous other government departments and agencies are also involved in specific aspects of food safety regulation. The following is a summary, by both government department and enforcement agency, of food safety programs in the United States.

U.S. DEPARTMENT OF AGRICULTURE (USDA)   Within the USDA, the Agricultural Marketing Service is responsible for enforcing the Meat Inspection Act, Poultry Products Inspection Act, and Egg Products Inspection Act. Inspection of commodities for wholesomeness is *mandatory* for meats, poultry, and other processed foods. An official stamp affixed to the product indicates that it is a high-quality product and processed under sanitary conditions. Fig. 4.2 illustrates examples of federal food inspection stamps.

Federal Inspection Stamp for Meat

Federal Inspection Stamp for Fish

USDA Poultry Inspection Mark

USDA Egg Products Inspection Mark

Figure 4.2.   Federal inspection stamps for meats, poultry, seafood, and eggs.

Food and Drug Administration (FDA)　The FDA is an enforcement agency within the Department of Health and Human Services. The FDA is responsible for the enforcement of the Federal Food, Drug, and Cosmetic Act; Fair Packaging and Labeling Act; and Nutritional Labeling and Education Act, and it covers the production, manufacture, and distribution of all food involved in interstate commerce except meat, poultry, and eggs.

Under the Food, Drug, and Cosmetic Act no food may enter interstate commerce that is deemed adulterated or misbranded. A food is **adulterated** if

- it contains substances that are injurious to health
- any part is filthy or decomposed
- it has been prepared or held under unsanitary conditions
- contains portions of diseased animals

A food is **misbranded** if the label does not include the information mandated by law or if it gives misleading information.

The FDA also determines and enforces standards of identity, quality, and fill. **Standards of identity** define what a food product must contain to be called by a certain name. For example, percent butterfat is defined for the different types of fluid milk (i.e., whole, 2% lowfat, skim). **Standards of quality** apply chiefly to canned fruits and vegetables, describing the ingredients that go into those products. These standards limit and define the number and kinds of defects permitted. They do not provide a basis for comparing foods as do grades, but they do establish minimum quality requirements. **Standards of fill** regulate the quantity of food in the container. They tell the packer how full the container must be to avoid deceiving the consumer. All of these standards are mandatory for foods in interstate commerce and may be used voluntarily for others.

The FDA is responsible for enforcing federal labeling requirements. Such requirements were first made mandatory with the passage of the Pure Food and Drug Act of 1906. Since then, several laws have been passed by Congress to further define these labeling requirements. Table 4.1 provides an historical review of this legislation.

National Marine and Fisheries Service　A voluntary inspection system for fish, fish products, and grade standards for some products are controlled by the National Marine and Fisheries Service, an agency of the Department of Commerce. If the product carries a U.S. grade designation, the purchaser is assured of continuous in-plant inspection during processing by federal inspectors. An ungraded product may or may not have been inspected during processing.

United States Public Health Service　The U.S. Public Health Service (PHS) is concerned primarily with control of infectious and contagious disease but is

TABLE 4.1. Federal Labeling Requirements.

Legislation	Pure Food and Drug Act	Food and Drug Cosmetic Act (FDCA)	Fair Packaging and Labeling Act (FPLA)	Nutrition Labeling Regulations	Nutritional Labeling and Education Act (NLEA)
Passed by Congress	1906	1938	1966	1973	1990
Intent	• Protects the public • Defines misbranding and adulteration • Prohibits foods that *are* injurious to a person's health	• Establishes standards of identity • States specific labeling requirements • Prohibits foods that *may be* injurious to a person's health	• Provides consumer with accurate information for value comparison • Prevents use of unfair or deceptive methods of packaging or labeling of consumer products	• Educates the consumer about the nutrient content of foods	• Provides extensive nutrient information of packaged foods • Improves nutritional content of packaged foods
Key requirements	• Authorized food processing plant inspections to assure sanitary conditions	• Name and address of the manufacturer or distributor • Name of the food • Quantity of content • Statement of ingredients listed by common or usual name in decreasing predominance	• Same information as the FDCA • Defines a food label in terms of format and information • Name of food/net quantity must appear on "principle display panel" • Net content must be in legible type and in distinct color contrast • Defines type size and location	• *Voluntary* except for foods fortified with vitamins, minerals, or protein, or in situations where a nutritional claim is made	• *Mandatory* for all packaged food • Includes provisions for the nutritional labeling of the 20 most common produce and seafood items • Serving sizes are stated in household units • Regulates nutrient content and health claims

also responsible for the safety of some foods. This agency is responsible for the inspection of some shellfish, and they advise state and local governments on sanitation standards for production, processing, and distribution of milk. The PHS standard for Grade A fresh milk is a standard of wholesomeness, which means that it has met state or local requirements that equal or exceed federal requirements.

ENVIRONMENTAL PROTECTION AGENCY (EPA) The EPA regulates pesticides. Responsibilities include: setting tolerance levels for pesticide residues in foods, establishing the safety of new pesticides, and providing education materials on the safe use of pesticides. The EPA also determines quality standards for water.

DEPARTMENT OF THE TREASURY The Bureau of Alcohol, Tobacco, and Firearms (BATF) in the Department of the Treasury is responsible for monitoring the production, distribution, and labeling of alcoholic beverages. This includes all alcoholic beverages except those that contain less than 7% alcohol, which are monitored by the FDA.

The Buyer

Food and supplies for a foodservice organization may be purchased by an individual, by a purchasing department, or through a cooperative arrangement with other institutions, depending on the size and ownership of the organization and its procurement policies. In a small operation, the buying can be done by the manager or dietitian as part of his or her responsibilities.

Whatever the arrangement, it is the responsibility of the foodservice or the individual units of a foodservice to communicate its needs to the buyer to assure delivery of the needed amount of food and supplies at an appropriate time and of the desired quality. This requires cooperation on the part of the buyer, as well as the foodservice personnel, and a willingness to honor the quality standards set by the foodservice.

To purchase the amount and quality of food required for the foodservice within the limitations imposed by the budget and financial policies of the organization requires knowledge of internal and external factors. Internal factors include the customers, the menus, recipes, labor availability and skills, equipment, storage facilities, and quantities of foods needed. External factors include the marketing system, food standards and quality, what is available on the market, and purchasing methods.

The buyer represents the institution in negotiations with market representatives and should have some knowledge and understanding of legal requirements, especially as they relate to orders and contracts. There should be a clear understanding as to the extent of the buyer's decision-making authority and of the institutional policies within which the buyer must operate.

Ethics in Purchasing

Buying demands integrity, maturity, bargaining skills, and maintenance of a high standard of ethics. Acting as an agent for the institution, the buyer is entrusted with making decisions concerning quality, prices, and amounts to purchase, and cannot afford to compromise either money or position. Buyers may be subjected to bribes and other kinds of inducements to influence a buying decision, but no gifts or other favors should be accepted that might obligate the buyer.

A buyer must be able to deal successfully with sales representatives, purveyors, and other marketing agents. Courtesy and fair treatment contribute to establishing a satisfactory working relationship with these agents who can be valuable sources of information on new products and the availability of foods on the market. If orders are placed through a salesperson, scheduling regular office appointments or a specific time for telephoning saves time for both the buyer and seller.

Products should be evaluated objectively and buying decisions made on the basis of quality, price, and service. Information received in confidence from one company should not be used to obtain an unfair advantage in competitive negotiations.

Types of Purchasing

CENTRALIZED PURCHASING   Centralized buying, in which a purchasing department is responsible for obtaining needed supplies and equipment for all units in the organization, is used in many universities, schools, multiunit restaurants, and hospitals. By relieving the individual units of responsibility for interviewing sales representatives, negotiating contracts, and placing orders, this system has proven to be cost-effective and time-saving for the foodservice, especially if the system also has central storage. Where centralized purchasing is used, the authority to buy fresh produce or other perishables can be delegated to the foodservice, or in multiunit organizations to the individual units.

One disadvantage of centralized purchasing is that excessive paper work can result. In addition, friction can develop between the purchasing department and the foodservice unit if there is not a clear understanding of decision-making authority, especially on quality standards. This possibility for friction exists in all large-scale purchasing unless the limits of authority are well-defined and the lines of communication kept open.

GROUP OR COOPERATIVE PURCHASING   It is obvious that buyers must increase volume and/or lower service requirements to improve leverage with suppliers and, thus, buy at lower prices. The efforts to increase volume have led some foodservice directors to consolidate their buying with that of other organizations in cooperative purchasing arrangements. For example, several hospitals in a metropolitan area may combine their purchases to obtain lower prices and possibly more favorable service arrangements; or in smaller communities, two or more dissimilar foodservices, such as a school, hospital, and nursing home, may join in a group purchasing agreement. Central warehousing may or may not be part of a group purchasing plan and, if the volume is large enough, vendors may agree to deliver merchandise to the individual units.

Group buying differs from central purchasing in that members of the group are independent organizations and are not under the same management. In central purchasing, the members are usually units of a larger system, such as schools in a city or countywide school system. Obviously, the main advantage of group buying is the price advantage gained by increased volume, which in turn may attract more prospective vendors.

The buyer is selected by the group and usually maintains an office independent of the participating organizations. The purchasing service generally is supported by a fee paid by each institution determined by the percentage of its orders. To be effective, all members of the group must commit their time and the majority of their purchase orders to the group's efforts. Participating agencies must agree on common specifications and establish a bid schedule. Food preferences may differ from system to system so members must occasionally be willing to compromise their requirements for the benefit of the group.

The Vendor

The selection of suppliers is one of the most important decisions that must be made in a purchasing program. Management and the buyer should work together to establish quality standards for food and supplies to be purchased, and to conduct a market search for reliable vendors that are able to furnish the desired products.

A buyer new to a foodservice operation can locate vendors through numerous resources. These resources include

- the phone book
- other foodservice operators in the area
- trade journals and publications
- local trade shows

A key responsibility of the buyer in initiating a professional working relationship with a vendor is to carefully evaluate the vendor's scope of products and services. To accomplish this, the buyer must make the necessary inquiries into the vendor's product line, available services, and reliability in meeting contract specifications.

The buyer should carefully evaluate the product line of the potential vendor to assess availability of needed products and to assure that the products meet the quality standards of the organization. Details of delivery schedules, payment policies, and contingency plans for when standards are not met should be known by the buyer. For example, a buyer would want to know the vendor's policy to correct billing when a damaged or spoiled product is delivered. Policies on emergency deliveries should also be reviewed. Some vendors carry policies on how to deliver food supplies in the event of a disaster such as a tornado, snowstorm, or earthquake. It is very important to review discount policies on early payments, rebates, and volume purchasing discounts. Visits to the vendors' local headquarters and talks with other buyers can supply much of this information.

Many vendors provide support equipment or service programs with the purchase of certain food products. For example, a vendor may offer to give coffee-making equipment at no extra cost with the purchase of their coffee products or a popcorn popper with the purchase of the vendor's popcorn line. It is important for the buyer to inquire about the technical assistance provided by the vendor for service and maintenance of these programs. Necessary information would include service availability in the event of equipment failure and scheduling of routine maintenance on the equipment.

The location and size of the foodservice are important factors in the selection of a supplier. If the operation is located in or near a large metropolitan area, there may be several suppliers that could meet quantity and quality needs and whose delivery schedules are satisfactory for the foodservice.

For an operation in a small or remote location, part or all of its supplies may be purchased locally. In this situation, the buyer should be sure that the vendors carry adequate stocks and are able to obtain replenishment quickly. If there are not enough local suppliers to offer competitive prices, the buyer may prefer to purchase only certain products locally, such as dairy products, bakery items, and fresh produce, and place less frequent orders for canned goods and groceries with a larger wholesaler that will break, or split, cases of food or supplies into quantities that the foodservice can use.

In some situations, large-volume operators may be able to purchase canned foods or other nonperishable items directly from the processor and work out satisfactory arrangements for delivery of their products. Since the quantity of foods purchased would be large, the amount and kind of storage space and the financial resources can be determining factors in whether direct buying is possible.

Methods of Purchasing

The two principal methods of buying are **informal or open market** and **formal competitive bid** buying. Both may be used at various times for different commodities. Variations of these methods or alternative buying arrangements may be preferred by some foodservices or may be used during uncertain market conditions.

Purchasing is a management function and, as such, the foodservice administrator will have policies and procedures to guide him or her in setting up a course of action. The method of buying that is selected depends on these institutional policies, on the size of the organization, the amount of money available, location of the vendors, and the frequency of deliveries.

Informal or Open-Market Buying

Informal purchasing is probably the most commonly used method of buying, especially in smaller foodservice operations. The system involves ordering needed food supplies from a selected list of dealers based on daily, weekly, or monthly quotations. These prices are based on a set of specifications furnished to interested dealers. The buyer may request daily prices for fresh fruits and vegetables but may use a monthly quotation list for grocery items. The order is placed after consideration of price in relation to quality, delivery, and other services offered.

Contact between the buyer and vendor is made by telephone, a visit to the market, or through sales representatives who call on the buyer. The use of price quotation and order forms on which to record the prices submitted by each seller (Fig. 4.3) is an aid to the buyer. If the quotations are given by telephone, the prices should be recorded. For large orders of canned goods or groceries, or where the time lapse between quotations and ordering is not important, requests for written quotations can be made by mail, as shown in Fig. 4.4.

Informal buying requires less lead time than formal competitive buying and is appropriate for foodservices that are too small to justify more formal procedures or when immediate delivery is required. It does have some disadvantages, however. Prices often are not compared with two or more vendors, and because the procedure usually is completed in 1 day, the buyer does not have an opportunity to negotiate or take advantage of seasonal trends.

Introducing new dealers from time to time and visiting the market when possible enables the buyer to examine what is available from other vendors and note the prices for the current week. When using informal purchasing, the buyer and vendor must agree on quantities and prices before delivery. Only vendors who give reliable service and competitive prices should be considered for open-market buying.

					Price Quotes			
						Vendors		
	Specs	Amount Needed	Amount on Hand	Amount to Order	A	B	C	D
Name of Food Service								

Name of Food Service
Fruit and Vegetable Quotation and Order Sheet

For Use on_____   Delivery Date_____

	Specs	Amount Needed	Amount on Hand	Amount to Order	A	B	C	D
Fruits:								
Vegetables:								

Figure 4.3.   A suggested form for recording telephoned price quotations for fresh produce. Combines a listing of total needs, the inventory on hand, and the resulting quantities to order. When order is placed, the vendor's price quotation is circled.

————————————— **University**
Food Stores Department

—————————————————
(Date)

INQUIRY NO.

To: ┌   ┐

Quote on this sheet your net price f.o.b.
for the items specified below. We reserve
the right to accept or reject all or part of
this proposal.
Quotations received
until 4:00 P.M. ————————

└   ┘

Important: Read instructions on reverse side before preparing bid.

Quantity	Unit	REQUEST FOR QUOTATIONS–This is NOT an order	Price Unit	Total Price
		Return—TWO COPIES—To: Food Stores Department		

We quote you f.o.b. ————————————

Delivery can be made { immediately

———————————— days.

————————————————
Sign Firm Name Here

Cash Discount: ————————————

———————— Per ————————————
Date

Figure 4.4.   Suggested form for requesting price quotations by mail.

Formal Competitive Bid Buying

In formal competitive bid buying, written specifications and quantities needed are submitted to vendors with an invitation for them to quote prices, within a stated time, for the items listed. The request for bids can be quite formal and advertised in the newspaper, copies may be printed and widely distributed, or less formal with single copies supplied to interested sellers. Bids are opened on a designated date, and the contract generally is awarded to the lowest responsible bidder.

Purchasing agents for local, state, or federal government-controlled institutions are usually required to submit bids to all qualified vendors, especially those bids over a certain dollar limit. Buyers for private organizations, however, may select the companies whom they wish to invite to bid and the buyer may include on the list only those vendors whose performance and reliability are known. The procedure for competitive bid buying is discussed in more detail later in this chapter under "Purchasing Procedures."

ADVANTAGES AND DISADVANTAGES OF FORMAL BID BUYING Bid buying is usually required by government procurement systems and is found to be advantageous by large foodservices or multiple unit organizations. The formal bid, if written clearly, minimizes the possibility of misunderstanding as to quality, price, and delivery. The bid system is satisfactory for canned goods, frozen products, staples, and other nonperishable foods. Food that is purchased by standing order, such as milk and bread, is appropriate also for this type of buying, but it may not be practical for perishable items because of the day-to-day fluctuation in market prices.

There are two main disadvantages to formal competitive bidding. The system is time-consuming, and the planning and requests for bids must be made well in advance so that the buyer has time to distribute the bid forms and the suppliers have time to check availability of supplies and determine a fair price. Although this type of buying was designed to ensure honesty, it does lend itself to manipulation when large amounts of money are involved, especially if the buyers and the purchasing department are open to political pressure.

COMPETITIVE BIDDING VARIATIONS Many variations and techniques are found in formal competitive bidding, depending on the type of institution, financial resources of both vendor and buyer, and storage facilities of the foodservice and delivery capabilities of the vendor. Bids can be written for a supply of merchandise over a period of time at prices that fluctuate with the market; for example, a 6-month supply of flour may be required, with 500 pounds delivered each month, at a price compatible with current market conditions.

In a firm fixed price contract (FFP), the price is not subject to adjustment during the period of the contract, which places maximum risk on the vendor and is used when definite specifications are available and when fair and reasonable prices can be established at the outset. A buyer may request bids for a month's supply of dairy products, to be delivered daily as needed. Another variation involves the purchase of a specific quantity of merchandise, such as a year's supply of canned goods, but because of inadequate storage the foodservice may wish to withdraw portions of the order as needed within the year.

Many different forms are used in the written bidding system and the terms may differ in various parts of the country, but all of them basically are invitations to bid with the conditions of the bid clearly specified. Attached to the invitation is a listing of the merchandise needed, specifications and quantities involved, and any conditions related to supply and fluctuations in the market. (See the example of a bid request later in this chapter in Fig. 4.10)

A bid can be written so that the buyer pays for the entire order at the time of purchase, or the merchandise can be paid for as it is withdrawn, with a suitable arrangement to cover the cost of storage and the cost of placing the inventory in storage.

Other Types of Purchasing

COST-PLUS PURCHASING   In cost-plus purchasing, a buyer agrees to buy certain items from a purveyor for an agreed-upon period of time based on a fixed markup over the dealer's cost. The time period may vary and could be open for bid among different dealers. Such a plan is most effective with large volume buying and when deliveries are restricted, preferably to one location.

The dealer's cost generally is based on the cost of material to the purveyor plus any costs incurred in changes in packaging, fabrication of products, loss of required trim, or shrinkage from aging. The markup, which must cover overhead, cost of billing or deliveries, or other expenses that are borne by the vendor, may vary with the type of food being purchased. When negotiating a cost-plus purchasing agreement, there should be a clear understanding of what is included in the cost and what is considered part of the dealer's markup. Some way of verifying the dealer's cost should also be part of the agreement.

PRIME VENDOR OR ONE-STOP PURCHASING   A system of purchasing that is gaining acceptance among restaurant and institutional buyers is prime vendor buying, which is based on an agreement to purchase the majority of specified supply categories from one vendor at an agreed-upon price. For example, a vendor may bid on supplying the foodservice with meats, frozen foods, canned goods, cheese, and prepared entrées, to be delivered as needed at regularly scheduled times. A prime vendor agreement usually is for a definite period and, normally, covers a specified quantity of items.

Prime vendor purchasing saves time for the buyer, and the overhead, delivery costs, and selling and billing costs can be less than when dealing with several purveyors. One disadvantage is the loss of a reliable backup vendor; another could be an increase in prices due to less competition. This type of purchasing is similar to cost-plus buying except that the buyer is dealing with fewer vendors.

BLANKET PURCHASE AGREEMENT (BPA)   The BPA is sometimes used when a wide variety of items are purchased from local suppliers, but the exact items, quantities, and delivery requirements are not known in advance and may vary. Vendors agree to furnish—on a "charge account" basis—such supplies as may be ordered during a stated period of time. BPAs should be established with more than one vendor so that delivery orders can be placed with the firm offering the best price. Use of more than one vendor also allows the buyer to identify a "price creep," which is possible if only one vendor is involved.

Product Selection

Market Forms of Foods

Deciding on the form in which food is to be purchased is a major decision that requires careful study. Several different products may be available, all of which will produce an acceptable menu item. Costs involved in purchase and use of fresh or natural forms of food versus partially prepared or ready-to-eat foods and the acceptability of such items by the consumer are major factors to consider.

Due to a lack of space, equipment, or personnel, some foodservices are faced with a decision to convert to a convenience system in which all prepared foods are purchased. Before making this decision, the cost, quality, and acceptability to patrons of the purchased prepared food should be compared with the same menu item made on the premises. Table 4.2 lists the factors to consider in a make-or-buy decision. If the decision is to buy the prepared product, the administrative dietitian or manager and the buyer must establish quality standards for these foods. Standards of identity have been developed for some, but there is wide variation in quality.

For foodservices preferring the preparation of products in their own kitchens, there are alternatives in purchasing that save preparation time. The market offers a variety of processed ingredients from which to choose. Dehydrated chopped onions, frozen lemon juice, cooked chicken and turkey, and the various baking, soup, sauce, and pudding mixes are examples. Casserole-type entrées, often requiring time-consuming processes, may be made by combining several convenience items, such as frozen diced chicken, sauce made from a mix or from canned soups, and pasta or vegetables.

Choices among fresh, frozen, and canned foods depend on the amount of labor available for preparation, comparative portion costs, and acceptability by

TABLE 4.2.   Make-or-Buy Decisions.

Factor	Considerations
Quality	Evaluate whether quality standard, as defined by and for the organization, can be achieved.
Equipment	Assess availability, capacity, and batch turnover time to assure that product demand can be met.
Labor	Evaluate availability, current skills, and training needs.
Time	Evaluate product setup, production, and service time based on forecasted demand for the product.
Inventory	Gauge needed storage and holding space.
Total cost	Conduct complete cost analysis of all resources expended to make or buy product. Use cost as decision basis after other factors have been carefully analyzed.

patrons. The high cost of labor has caused many foodservices to limit the use of fresh fruits and vegetables except for salads or during times of plentiful supply when costs are lower. There may be times when a menu change must be made because of the price differential among fresh, frozen, and canned food items.

Keeping in mind the quality standard established for the finished product, the administrative dietitian or manager must find the right combination of available foods in a form that will keep preparation to a minimum yet yield a product of the desired quality.

Food Quality

Before food can be purchased, the quality of foods most appropriate to the foodservice operation and their use on the menu must be decided. The top grade may not always be necessary for all purposes. Foods sold under the lower grades are wholesome and have essentially the same nutritional value, but they differ mainly in appearance and, to a lesser degree, in flavor.

Foods that have been downgraded because of lack of uniformity in size or that have broken or have irregular pieces can be used in soups, casseroles, fruit gelatin, or fruit cobblers. Also, more than one style or pack in some food items may be needed. Unsweetened or pie pack canned peaches can be satisfactory for making pies, but peaches in heavy syrup would be preferable for serving in a dish as a dessert.

QUALITY STANDARDS   Quality may refer to wholesomeness, cleanliness, or freedom from undesirable substances. It may denote a degree of perfection in shape, uniformity of size, or freedom from blemishes. It may also describe the extent of desirable characteristics of color, flavor, aroma, texture, tenderness, and maturity. Assessment of quality may be denoted by grade, brand, or condition.

GRADES Grades are market classifications of quality. They reflect the relationship of quality to the standard established for the product, and they indicate the degree of variation from that standard. Grades have been established by the United States Department of Agriculture for most agricultural products, but their use is voluntary.

Grading and Acceptance Services: The Agricultural Marketing Service, in cooperation with state agencies, offers official grading or inspection for quality of meat and meat products, fresh and processed fruits and vegetables, poultry and eggs, and manufactured dairy products. Grading is based on U.S. grade standards developed by the USDA for these products.

Included in the grading and inspection programs is an **Acceptance Service** available to institutional food buyers on request. This service provides verification of the quality specified in a purchase contract. The product is examined at the processing or packing plant or at the supplier's warehouse by an official of the Agricultural Marketing Service or a cooperating state agency. If the product meets the specifications as stated in the contract, the grader stamps it with an official stamp and issues a certificate indicating compliance. If the purchases are to be certified, this provision should be specified in contracts with vendors. The inspection fee is then the responsibility of the supplier.

USDA grades are based on scoring factors, with the total score determining the grade. The grades vary with different categories of food as noted in the following list.

- *Meats:* U.S. Prime, U.S. Choice, U.S. Select, and U.S. Standard. Quality grades are assigned according to marbling, maturity of the animal, and color, firmness, and texture of the muscle. Yield grades of 1, 2, 3, 4, or 5 are used for beef and lamb to indicate the proportion of usable meat to fat and bone, with 1 having the lowest fat content. Veal and pork are not graded separately for yield and quality. (See "Additional Resources" at end of the chapter for guidance or specifications.)

- *Poultry:* Consumer grades are U.S. Grades A, B, and C, based on conformation, fleshing, fat covering, and freedom from defects. Grades often used in institutional purchasing are U.S. Procurement Grades 1 and 2. The procurement grades place more emphasis on meat yield than on appearance.

- *Eggs:* U.S. Grades AA, A, and B. Quality in shell eggs is based on exterior factors (cleanliness, soundness, shape of shell, and texture) and interior factors (condition of the yolk and white and the size of the air cell, as determined by candling). Shell eggs are classified according to size, as Extra Large, Large, Medium, and Small. (Due to recent detection of salmonella in whole, fresh eggs, it is recommended that the buyer contact the local health department for guidance on egg selection and preparation.)

- *Cheddar cheese:* U.S. Grades AA, A, B, and C. Scores are on the basis of flavor, aroma, body and texture, finish and appearance, and color.
- *Butter:* U.S. Grades AA (93 score), A (92 score), B (90 score), and C (89 score), based on flavor, body and texture, color, and salt.
- *Fresh produce:* U.S. Fancy, U.S. Extra No. 1, U.S. No. 1, U.S. Combination, and U.S. No. 2. Fresh fruits and vegetables are graded according to the qualities deemed desirable for the individual type of commodity, but may include uniformity of size, cleanliness, color, or lack of damage or defects. Grades are designated by name or by number. Because of the wide variation in quality and the perishable nature of fresh fruits and vegetables, visual inspection may be as important as grade; or a buyer might specify that the condition of the product at the time of delivery should equal the grade requested.
- *Canned fruits and vegetables:* U.S. Grade A (or Fancy), U.S. Grade B (or Choice for fruits and Extra Standard for vegetables), U.S. Grade C (or Standard), and U.S. Grade D (or Substandard). The factors for canned fruits and vegetables include color, uniformity of size, absence of defects, character, flavor, consistency, finish, size, symmetry, clearness of liquor, maturity, texture, wholeness, and cut. In addition to these factors, general requirements must be met, such as fill of container, drained weight, and syrup density. The grading factors vary with individual canned fruits and vegetables, but the scoring range is the same. Fig. 4.5 shows suggested standards for canned foods. Following is a summary of the total scoring ranges for grades of canned fruits and vegetables:

Grades	Scores
A (Fancy)	90–100
B (Choice, Extra Standard)	75–89
C (Standard)	60–74
Substandard	0–59

- *Frozen fruits and vegetables:* U.S. grade standards are available for many frozen fruits and vegetables but not standards of identity, quality, or fill of container. Fruit can be packed with sugar in varying proportions such as four or five parts of fruit to one part of sugar by weight or without sugar. Fruits or vegetables can be individually quick frozen (IQF) or frozen in solid blocks.

Designation of U.S. grades and marking in the form of a shield are permitted only on foods officially graded under the supervision of the Agricultural Marketing Service of the USDA. Fig. 4.6 shows examples of grade stamps.

BRANDS   Brands are assigned by private organizations. Producers, processors, or distributors attempt to establish a commodity as a standard product and to develop demand specifically for their own brands. The reliability of these trade

Standards for Canned Foods

Fruits

Grade	Quality of Fruit	Syrup
U.S. Grade A or Fancy	Excellent quality, high color, ripe, firm, free from blemishes, uniform in size, and very symmetrical	Heavy, about 55%. May vary from 40 to 70%, depending on acidity of fruit
U.S. Grade B or Choice or Extra-Standard	Fine quality, high color, ripe, firm, free from serious blemishes, uniform in size, and symmetrical	About 40%. Usually contains 10 to 15% less sugar than in Fancy grade.
U.S. Grade C or Standard	Good quality, reasonably good color, reasonably free from blemishes, reasonably uniform in size, color, and degree of ripeness, and reasonably symmetrical	About 25%. Contains 10 to 15% less sugar than in Choice grades
Substandard	Lower than the minimum grade for Standard.	Often water-packed. If packed in syrup, it is not over 10%.

Vegetables

Grade	Quality of Vegetable
U.S. Grade A or Fancy	Best flavored, most tender and succulent, uniform in size, shape, color, tenderness; represents choice of crop.
U.S. Grade B or Extra-Standard (sometimes called Choice)	Flavor fine; tender and succulent; may be slightly more mature, more firm in texture, and sometimes less uniform than Fancy grade.
U.S. Grade C or Standard	Flavor less delicate; more firm in texture, often less uniform in size, shape, color; more mature.
Substandard	Lower than the minimum grade for Standard.

Figure 4.5. Suggested standards for USDA grades of canned fruits and vegetables.

names depends on the reliability of the company. Brand names may represent products that are higher or lower in quality than the corresponding government grade. However, some brand name products are not consistent in quality. Private companies may set up their own grading system, but such ranking may show variation from season to season.

Some knowledge of brand names is essential in today's marketing system. USDA grades are used for most fresh meats and for fresh fruits and vegetables,

Federal Grade Stamp for Meat   USDA Poultry Grade Mark   USDA Shell Egg Grade Mark

Figure 4.6. Federal grade stamps for meat, poultry, and eggs.

but very few canners use them, preferring instead to develop their own brands. If USDA grades are specified and bidders submit prices on brand products, the buyer should be familiar with USDA grades and scores in order to evaluate the products. The buyer may wish to request samples or, if the order is large enough to justify it, request a USDA grading certificate.

Purchasing Procedures

The complexity of the purchasing system depends on the size and type of an organization, whether the buying is centralized or decentralized, and established management policies. Procedures should be as simple as possible, with record keeping and paper work limited to those essential for control and communication.

Good purchasing practices include the use of appropriate buying methods, a systematic ordering schedule, maintenance of an adequate flow of goods to meet production requirements, and a systematic receiving procedure and inventory control.

The process of purchasing, using the informal and formal methods of buying, is shown in Fig. 4.7 and discussed in the following sections.

IDENTIFYING NEEDS   Quantities of food needed for production of the planned menus are identified from the menus and from recipes used to prepare them. Added to this are staples and other supplies needed in the various departments or production and service areas. Ingredients that are in stock are requisitioned from the storeroom, as explained in more detail later in this chapter under "Storeroom Issues."

Inventory Stock Level: A system of communicating needs from the production areas and the storeroom to the buyer is essential. Establishing a minimum and maximum stock level provides a means of alerting the buyer to needs. The minimum level is the point, established for each item, below which the

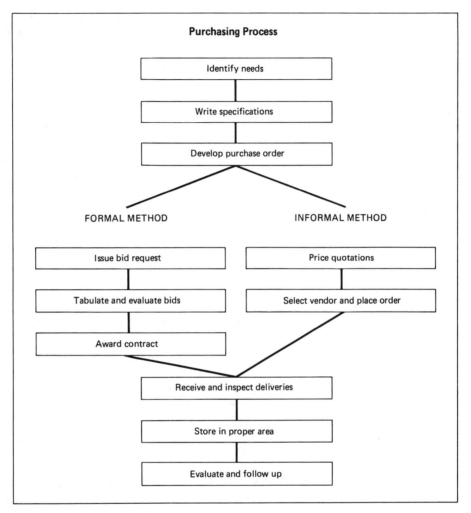

Figure 4.7.   The process of purchasing, using the informal and formal methods of buying.

inventory should not fall. This amount depends on the usage and time required for ordering and delivery. If canned fruits and vegetables, for example, are purchased every 3 months through the formal bidding procedure, the time lapse would be longer than for fresh produce that is ordered daily or weekly through informal buying.

The **minimum stock level,** then, includes a safety factor for replenishing the stock. The **maximum inventory level** is equal to the safety stock plus the estimated usage, which is determined by past experience and forecasts. From this information, a reorder point is established.

Another factor to be considered in the amount to reorder is the quantity most feasible economically. For example, if 5 cases of a food are needed to bring the stock to the desired level, but a price advantage can be gained by buying 10 cases, the buyer may consider purchasing the larger quantity. The buyer is encouraged to carefully weigh the true economic advantages of these price incentives. Stored food ties up cash, and unused food that spoils is literally money down the drain.

Quantity to Buy: The amount of food and supplies purchased at one time and the frequency of ordering depend on the amount of money on hand, the method of buying, the frequency of deliveries, and storage space. With adequate and suitable storage, the purchase of staples may vary from a 2- to 6-month supply, with perishables weekly and/or daily.

Meat, poultry, fish, fresh fruits and vegetables, and other perishable foods may be purchased for immediate use on the day's menu or more likely are calculated for 2 or more days, depending on delivery schedules, storage facilities, and preparation requirements. Quantities are based on the portion size and projected number of servings needed, taking into consideration the preparation and cooking losses. If the recipes are stored in a computer, it is a simple task to calculate the amount needed for the desired number of servings.

Some products, such as milk and bread, are delivered daily or several times a week, and the orders are based on the amount needed to keep the inventory up to a desired level. The price can be determined by a contract to furnish certain items as needed for a period of a month or longer. A stock level of butter and margarine, cheese, eggs, lettuce, celery, onions, and certain other fruits and vegetables can be established and maintained, whereas other produce is ordered as needed from the menu. Fig. 4.8 is a suggested form for recording supplies on hand and the amounts to order.

Canned foods and groceries are generally purchased less often than are perishable foods, the frequency depending on storage space and money available. Assuming adequate storage is available, a year's supply of canned goods can be purchased at one time if bought on competitive bid or if growing conditions indicate a possible shortage or a rise in prices. In some cases, an arrangement can be made for the supplier to store the food and deliver as needed. A projection is made of the quantity that will be needed for the designated period, based on past purchases. That amount less the inventory is the quantity to purchase.

WRITING SPECIFICATIONS   Many foodservice operations have a set of specifications that have been developed as different food and supply items have been purchased. If specifications do not exist for the items being purchased, they should be written before bids or quotations are sought.

A specification is a detailed description of a product, stated in terms that are clearly understood by both buyer and seller. Specifications should be brief and

Daily Purchase Order

Date _____

ON HAND		ORDER	ON HAND		ORDER

Dairy:

_____ gal whole milk _____   **Fresh Vegetables:**

_____ cs ½ pt whole _____   _____ Cabbage _____

_____ cs ½ pt choc _____   _____ Carrots _____

_____ cs ½ pt B. milk _____   _____ Cauliflower _____

_____ cs ½ pt skim _____   _____ Celery _____

_____ lb cot. cheese _____   _____ Celery cabbage _____

_____ Ice cream _____   _____ Cucumbers _____

Bread: _____ Egg plant _____

_____ White bread _____   _____ Head lettuce _____

_____ Wheat bread _____   _____ Leaf lettuce _____

_____ Rye _____   _____ Onions _____

_____ Sandwich white _____   _____ Parsley _____

_____ Sandwich wheat _____   _____ Peppers _____

_____ Sandwich rye _____   _____ Potatoes _____

_____ Crumbs _____   _____ Spinach _____

Sweet Rolls: _____ Squash _____

_____ Raisin bread _____   _____ Tomatoes _____

_____ Cinnamon _____   **Frozen Vegetables:**

_____ Butterscotch _____   _____ Asparagus _____

_____ Raised donuts _____   _____ Green beans _____

_____ Bismark _____   _____ Lima beans _____

_____ Twist _____   _____ Broccoli _____

_____ Pecan strip _____   _____ Brussel sprouts _____

_____ Stick donuts _____   _____ Cauliflower _____

_____ Jelly donuts _____   _____ Peas _____

Meats: **Fresh Fruits:**

_____   _____ Apples _____

_____   _____ Bananas _____

_____   _____ Berries _____

_____   _____ Cantaloupe _____

_____   _____ Grapefruit _____

_____   _____ Grapes _____

_____   _____ Lemons _____

_____   _____ Oranges _____

_____   _____ Peaches _____

_____   _____ Pineapple _____

_____   _____ Plums _____

Fish: _____ Watermelon _____

_____   **Poultry:**

_____   _____ Chicken _____

_____   _____ Turkey _____

Miscellaneous: _____ Eggs _____

_____   **Frozen Fruits and Juices:**

_____   _____ Apples _____

_____   _____ Cherries _____

_____   _____ G. fruit sections _____

Potato Chips: _____ Lemon juice _____

_____   _____ Orange juice _____

_____   _____ Peaches _____

_____   _____ Rhubarb _____

   _____ Strawberries _____

Figure 4.8. Daily purchase order form.

concise but should contain enough information so that there can be no misunderstanding. Certain information is included in all specifications for food products:

- **Name of the product.** The common, or trade, name of an item generally is simple, but the name of some products may vary in different parts of the country.
- **Federal grade or brand.** As already noted, the USDA has established federal grades for most agricultural products, but many packers or food processors have developed their own brands or trade names for canned, frozen, or other processed foods. If a bidder submits a quotation on a brand name product in lieu of a federal grade, buyers may request verification of quality by the USDA Acceptance Service; see "Grading and Acceptance Services" earlier in this chapter under "Food Quality."
- **Unit on which price is quoted.** This refers to the size and type of unit, such as pound, gallon, can, bunch, or other unit in common use.
- **Name and size of container.** Examples of container size are: a case holding 6 no. 10 cans, a 30-pound can of frozen cherries, or a 30-pound lug of tomatoes.
- **Count per container or approximate number per pound.** Examples are: 30/35 count canned peach halves per no. 10 can; 8 per pound frankfurters; size 36 grapefruit, which indicates the number of fruit in a 4/5 bushel box. Sizes 27 through 40 are acceptable for half grapefruit servings. Oranges and apples also are sized according to the number in the box. Apples 80 to 100 are large, 113 to 138 medium, and 150 to 175 small.

Additional information may be included for different categories of food:

- **Fresh fruits and vegetables:** variety, weight, degree of maturity, geographical location; for example, Jonathan apples, Indian River grapefruit, or bananas turning ripe, pale yellow with green tips; if needed immediately, specify fully ripe, bright yellow flecked with brown, and no green.
- **Canned foods:** type or style, pack, size, syrup type, drained weight, specific gravity. Examples are: cream style corn; whole vertical pack green beans; no. 4 sieve peas; apricot halves in heavy syrup or 21 to 25 degrees brix (syrup density); diced beets, drained weight 72 ounces (per no. 10 can); tomato catsup with total solids content of at least 33%.
- **Frozen foods:** variety, sugar ratio, temperature during delivery and upon receipt; for example, sliced strawberries, sugar ratio of 4:1, or delivered frozen, 0°F or less.
- **Meats and meat products:** age, market class, cut of meat, exact cutting instructions, weight range, fat content, condition upon receipt.

- **Dairy products:** milk fat content, milk solids, bacteria count, temperature during delivery and upon receipt.

A well-written specification includes all of the information needed to identify the food item and to assure the buyer of getting exactly the quality desired. It should be identifiable with products or grades currently on the market and capable of being checked by label statements or USDA grades. Information for use in writing specifications is available from the USDA and from material published by industry such as the National Association of Meat Purveyors. See the section entitled "Additional Resources" at the end of this chapter.

DEVELOPING PURCHASE ORDERS   The procedure for authorizing purchases differs in various foodservices. The process may begin with a purchase request, to be used along with quality specifications, as the basis for a purchase order and bid request to be issued by an authorized purchasing agent. A foodservice director, who is also the buyer, may develop a market order or purchase order that has been compiled from requisitions from the various production and service units or from individual units in a school system or other multi-unit organization. In central purchasing for these operations, the requisitions originating in individual units do not necessarily need to include specifications, since the quality is determined at a central point and is uniform throughout the system.

Regardless of the method used, there should be a clear understanding of who is authorized to issue purchase requests or orders and the vendors should be aware of the name, or names, of authorized purchasing personnel. Authorization to sign for goods received and to requisition supplies from the storage areas should also be understood.

The purchase order specifies the quantity of each item needed for the bid period, quality specifications, and required date of delivery. The order must include the name of the organization, the individual making the request, and the signature of the person officially authorized to sign the order. Purchase order forms can be prenumbered or the number can be added at the time of final approval, but a number, as well as the date of issue, is essential for identification. Fig. 4.9 is a suggested purchase order form.

ISSUING BID REQUESTS   An invitation to bid provides vendors with an opportunity to submit bids for specific items advertised. Bid requests originate in the office of the purchasing agent or the person authorized to purchase for the foodservice. A bid request includes quantities required and purchase specifications for each item. In addition, the general conditions of acceptance are outlined, including the date and method of delivery, terms of payment, willingness to accept all or part of the bid, discounts, the date of closing bids, and other terms of the negotiations. Fig. 4.10 is a sample bid request that includes general requirements and that would be used with Fig. 4.11, which would list needed items and specifications.

Purchase Order

Name of Institution _____

_____
Address

_____
Address

Department _____

To _____

_____

_____

_____

Date _____

Purchase Order # _____
*(Please refer to above number
on all invoices)*

Requisition No. _____

Date Required _____

*Instruction for Completing Order. Prepare in triplicate for the
vendor, business office, and the manager.*

Shipped to: _____ FOB _____ Via _____ Terms _____

Unit	Total Quantity	Specification	Price per unit	Total cost

Approved by _____

Figure 4.9. Suggested purchase order form.

The bid request may also ask for samples to be tested. This is especially important when large quantities are involved and often is requested when purchasing canned foods. Testing of canned foods is done by "can cutting," which involves opening of the sample cans and evaluating the products

Bid Request for Frozen Fruits and Vegetables

Issued By _____   Date _____

_____   Date to be Delivered _____

Address _____

_____

Bid Request for _____

Notice is hereby given that the Board of Education of _____ County,
_____ State (hereinafter referred to as the Board) requests written and sealed bids
on the following items to be submitted to said Board on or before 10:30 a.m. on _____, 19__ and
on each subsequent bidding period date indicated in the bid specifications. Sealed bids will not be opened
until 10:30 a.m. _____, 19__ if the outside is marked: Do not open until _____.
Respond on attached bid form.

Contract Period: The bid covers the period from date of award through _____, 19__, inclusive and
vendors receiving awards shall be the sole suppliers to all schools for items for the period.

Samples: Bidders will be required to submit samples of the items bid upon. Samples are to be furnished
without cost to _____ and are to be sent to _____
on _____ by _____.

Quality: Successful bidders must furnish United States Department of Agriculture Grade Certificates indicating
each fruit and vegetable item to be U.S. Grade __.

Grade Certificates: A U.S. Grade Certificate shall be submitted for required items prior to delivery. These
certificates must cover the specific brand name of items being delivered. The code numbers on the item being
delivered shall be the same as the codes listed on the certificate.

Estimated Quantities: Quantities indicated on Bid Proposal Forms are estimated total requirements based on
anticipated use. They will provide the basis for determining the total low bid complying with specifications for
each group of items and are submitted as information.

Actual Quantities: Quantities on attached Bid Sheet are estimated to cover the period from date of award
to _____, 19__, inclusive. The School Food Service Department will furnish the successful
bidder with actual quantities as are needed. Purchaser guarantees to purchase during contract period only,
the actual requirements needed.

Delivery (Equipment): Carrier shall utilize only properly insulated, mechanical or thermostatic temperature
control refrigeration equipment. Such equipment must be capable of maintaining temperature to protect the
product. All products must be delivered in a hard frozen state, 0°F. or below.

The Board of Public Education reserves the right to reject the use of any equipment by a carrier if it is not in a
clean, sanitary condition and suitable for hauling of all goods.

Each carrier shall furnish a Certificate of Insurance issued by an insurance company showing that the Board of
Public Education will be protected from loss or damage to property of third persons or to the carriers' own
property, loss or damage to Board of Public Education commodities, and injury or death to third persons or to
the carrier's employees. Carrier will assume full common liability for all shipments.

Figure 4.10. Sample bid request. (From *Food Buying Guide for School Food Service,* PA 1257, USDA.) (*continued*)

Orders: All orders will be placed directly with awardees by telephone by the individual qualified purchasing official who in some cases may be the individual lunchroom manager. They may order fractional cases. Regular orders should be placed at least seventy-two (72) hours (3 work days) before the delivery time requested; but each emergency order should be filled within two (2) hours after the order is placed. ALL VENDORS MUST SUBMIT SEPARATE DELIVERY TICKETS AND/OR INVOICES FOR NONBID ITEMS.

Deliveries: Deliveries shall be made to the receiving area of individual schools between the hours of 7:00 a.m. and 2:15 p.m. These deliveries must be made in mechanically refrigerated trucks maintaining a temperature below freezing at all times.

Invoices & Statements: Invoices for the purchases of food and miscellaneous supplies made by schools are paid by the central accounting department. In order to facilitate the handling of these invoices, ALL VENDORS MUST ADHERE TO THE FOLLOWING INSTRUCTIONS:

Code number for each school listed on each invoice. (A list of schools with code number is attached.)

All items on delivery tickets MUST be billed according to description of item quoted on bid. Unit prices for all items shall be recorded and invoices shall be accurately extended. SEPARATE DELIVERY TICKETS AND/OR INVOICES SHALL BE MADE FOR ALL NONBID ITEMS.

All vendors must issue delivery tickets and credit memos in QUADRUPLICATE, and all four (4) copies must be signed by qualified purchasing official.

    2 copies (original and 1 carbon) left with proper person at time of delivery.

    2 copies to be returned to vendor.

The vendor shall forward as per attached list, weekly statements, with one signed delivery ticket attached, directly to the School Food Service Department.

All delivery tickets supporting weekly statements must be in exact agreement with copy of delivery tickets left with manager. If for any reason it is necessary to make a change on the delivery ticket, MAKE AN ADDITIONAL CHARGE OR CREDIT MEMO.

All cancellations or merchandise returns must be recorded by driver on all FOUR COPIES of delivery tickets, or "pick-up tickets."

    2 copies left with manager at time of pick-up.

    2 copies to be returned to vendor.

    Do not mail statement to individual schools.

A monthly statement for each school should be sent to the official responsible for paying bills by the 10th working day or by the 10th calendar day of every month, following date of purchase.

Figure 4.10.   (*continued*)

according to USDA scoring factors. If samples from more than one company are being tested, the labels on the cans should be covered so the test will be impartial.

Copies of USDA specifications and score sheets are available from the Government Printing Office. An example of a score sheet for canned foods is shown in Fig. 4.12. Scores from different samples would be summarized on a form similar to Fig. 4.13. Product evaluation forms may be developed for testing of other foods and should include specific qualities to be judged. A panel composed of persons who are involved in foodservice quality control should participate.

A bid schedule outlining the bid periods and delivery frequency should be established and, when possible, planned so that new packs of processed fruits and vegetables, usually available in October and January, can be used. This step is omitted in informal buying. Quotations are requested from two or more vendors, usually by telephone or from price sheets.

TABULATING AND EVALUATING BIDS   Bids should be kept sealed and confidential until the designated time for opening. Sealed envelopes containing the bids

Bid Form

Name of School District _____   Date _____

Item no.	Quantity	Unit size	Item and specification	Brand quoted	Quantity quoted	Unit price	Total price

Figure 4.11.   Bid form to be used with Fig. 4.10 to list items and specifications.

should be stamped to indicate the date, time, and place of receipt. Bids received after the time and date specified for bid opening must be rejected and returned unopened to the bidder.

The opening and tabulation of bids should be under the control of an appropriate official. When schools and other public institutions are involved, the quotations and contents of bids should be open to the public. The bids and low bids should be carefully examined. In most instances, public purchasing laws specify that the award be made to the lowest responsible bidder. The following points should be considered, however, before accepting bids:

1. ability and capacity of the bidder to perform the contract and provide the service
2. ability of the bidder to provide the service promptly and within the time specified
3. integrity and reputation of the bidder
4. quality of bidder's performance on previous contracts or services
5. bidder's compliance with laws and with specifications relating to contracts or service
6. bidder's financial resources

When the award is not given to the lowest bidder, a full and complete statement of the reasons should be prepared and filed with other papers relating to the transaction.

Score Sheet for Canned Tomatoes

Number, Size, and Kind of Container

Label

Container Mark or Identification	Cans/Glass		
	Cases		
Net Weight (oz)			
Vacuum (in.)			
Drained Weight (oz)			

Factors		*Score Points*		
I. DRAINED WEIGHT	20	(A) 18–20 (B) 15–17 (C) 12–14 (SStd) 0–11		
II. WHOLENESS	20	(A) 18–20 (B) 15–17 (C) 12–14		
III. COLOR	30	(A) 27–30 (B) 23–36 (C) 19–22 (SStd) 0–18		
IV. ABSENCE OF DEFECTS	30	(A) 27–30 (B) 22–26 (C) 17–21 (SStd) 0–16		
TOTAL SCORE	100			
NORMAL FLAVOR AND ODOR				
GRADE				

Figure 4.12.   Government score sheet for grading canned tomatoes.

Kind	Code	Label Net Weight	Actual Weight	Sp. Gr. or Drained Weight	Brix	Count	Remarks and Ratings (Defects, Color, etc.)	Price Per Dozen	Price Per Can	Price Per Piece

Figure 4.13.   Suggested form for recording data on samples of canned products.

AWARDING CONTRACTS   The contract should be awarded to the most responsive and responsible bidder with the price most advantageous to the purchaser. Buying on the basis of price alone can result in the delivery of products that are below the expectations of the foodservice. Purchasing should be on the basis of price, quality, and service.

The general conditions of the contract should include services to be rendered, dates and method of deliveries, inspection requests, grade certificates required, procedure for substitutions, and conditions for payment. The following information should also be provided: name and address of the foodservice, a contract number, type of items the contract covers, contract period, date of contract issue, point of delivery, quantities to be purchased, and the signature of an authorized representative of the firm submitting the bid. The terms of sale must be clearly stated in the contract. Table 4.3 is a summary of the various FOB (Free on Board) terms of sale methods used in formal purchasing. Point of origin is defined as the manufacturer's loading dock.

A contract that is issued represents the legal acceptance of the offer made by the successful bidder, and it is binding. All bidders, both successful and unsuccessful, should be notified of the action. When the contract is made by a purchasing agent, the foodservice should receive a copy of the contract award and specifications.

This step is omitted when using informal purchasing.

Receiving

Receiving is the point at which foodservice operations inspect the products, and take legal ownership and physical possession of the items ordered. The purpose of receiving is to ensure that the food and supplies delivered match established quality and quantity specifications. The receiving process also offers an opportunity to verify price.

A well-designed receiving process is important to cost and to quality control and, therefore, warrants careful planning and implementation. Minimally, a

TABLE 4.3.   Terms of Sale and Freight Charges.

Terms of Sale	Responsibilities			
	Pays Freight Charges	Bears Freight Charges	Owns Product During Transit	Files Damage Claims (if necessary)
FOB origin freight collect	Buyer	Buyer	Buyer	Buyer
FOB origin freight prepaid	Seller	Seller	Buyer	Buyer
FOB origin freight prepaid and charged back	Seller	Buyer	Buyer	Buyer
FOB destination freight collect	Buyer	Buyer	Seller	Seller
FOB destination freight prepaid	Seller	Seller	Seller	Seller
FOB destination freight collect and allowed	Buyer	Seller	Seller	Seller

FOB = Free on Board

good receiving program should include clearly written policies and procedures on each of the following components:

- coordination with other departments (i.e., production and accounting)
- training for receiving personnel
- facility and equipment needs
- written specifications
- authority and supervision
- scheduled receiving hours
- security measures
- documentation procedures

Consequences of a poorly planned receiving program include

- short weights
- substandard quality
- double billing
- inflated prices

- mislabeled merchandise
- inappropriate substitutions
- spoiled or damaged merchandise
- pilferage or theft

In simple terms, a poorly planned and executed receiving process results in financial loss for the operation.

Coordination with Other Departments

The receiving function needs to be coordinated with other departments in the foodservice organization. Production and accounting are two key departments that need a well-defined working relationship with receiving personnel.

The production department needs in-house food and supply products to meet the demands of the menu and service centers. Many operations are evaluating the feasibility of implementing a receiving and production method referred to as "just in time," in which food items are brought into inventory and production just prior to production of needed menu items. The goal of this approach is to reduce inventory of food items and to minimize the amount of time that prepared food is held prior to service. Obviously, a well-orchestrated receiving process is essential to the success of this approach.

In many organizations, the accounting department is responsible for processing the billing of food and supply purchases. Receiving records must be completed and submitted to accounting in a timely fashion to assure that payments are made on time. Prompt billing allows the organization to take advantage of early payment discounts and avoids late payment penalties.

Personnel

The responsibility of receiving should be assigned to a specific, competent, well-trained person. However, in reality this job is often not assigned to all, but simply handled by the person working closest to the dock. During training, this individual must learn to appreciate the importance of the receiving function in cost and quality control. Qualifications of the receiving clerk should include knowledge of food quality standards and awareness of written specifications, the ability to evaluate product quality and recognize unacceptable product, and an understanding of the proper documentation procedures. The receiver's authority must be well-defined by policy, which should clarify the scope of the receiver's authority and to whom he or she reports. Even though the receiver is well-trained and trustworthy, consistent and routine supervision of the receiving area is recommended to assure that procedures are followed and that the area is kept secure.

Facilities, Equipment, and Sanitation

A well-planned receiving area should be as close to the delivery docks as possible, with easy access to the storage facilities of the operation. This arrangement helps to minimize traffic through the production area and reinforces good security measures.

The area itself should be large enough to accommodate an entire delivery at one time. If a receiving office is in the area, it should have large glass windows so receiving personnel can easily monitor the activities of the area.

The amount and capacity of receiving equipment depends on the size and frequency of deliveries. Large deliveries may require a forklift for pallet deliveries. A hand truck may be adequate in medium to small operations. Scales, ranging from platform models to countertop designs, are needed to weigh goods as they arrive. A policy should be in place to assure that the scales are calibrated on a regular basis to ensure accuracy.

Some small equipment is also needed, including thermometers for checking refrigerated food temperatures and various opening devices, such as shortblade knives and crate hammers. Specifications, purchase orders, and documentation records need to be readily available and the receiving office should carry an ample supply of pens, paper, tape, and markers. Filing cabinets to house documents are recommended.

Cleaning and sanitation procedures for the receiving should be defined by policy. Plans for pest control need to be determined and some cleaning supplies should be readily available to keep the area clean during the daily activities.

Scheduled Hours for Receiving

Hours of receiving should be defined by policy and vendors should be instructed to deliver within a specific time range. The purpose of defined receiving times is to avoid too many deliveries at one time and the busiest production times in the operation. Thus, many operations instruct vendors to deliver mid-morning or mid-afternoon to avoid high food production and service times.

Security

The receiving components already discussed contribute to the security of the receiving process. There are, however, a few additional practices that can contribute to a secure receiving program. Deliveries should be checked immediately upon arrival. After the receiving personnel is confident that the order meets specifications, he or she can sign the invoice and the delivery should be moved immediately to proper storage. This practice minimizes the time the product sits in the receiving area and, in turn, minimizes quality deterioration and opportunity for theft.

Doors to the receiving area should be kept locked. Some facilities keep doors locked at all times and use a doorbell system for the delivery personnel to use when they arrive. Finally, all unauthorized personnel should be kept out of the receiving area. This is particularly difficult in facilities where the area is used for other purposes, such as trash removal. More frequent supervision is recommended in these situations.

The Receiving Process

Once the components of a receiving program are planned and implemented an organization is ready to receive goods. The receiving process involves five key steps:

1. Inspect the delivery and check it against the purchase order.
2. Inspect the delivery against the invoice.
3. Accept order only if all quantities and quality specifications are met.
4. Complete receiving records.
5. Immediately place goods in appropriate storage.

Methods

There are two main methods of receiving: the blind method and invoice receiving method. The *blind method* involves providing an invoice or purchase order, one in which the quantities have been erased or blacked out, to the receiving clerk. The clerk must then quantify each item by weighing, measuring, or counting and recording it on the blind purchase order. The blind document is then compared with the original order. This method offers an unbiased approach by the receiving clerk but is time-consuming and, therefore, more labor intensive.

A frequently used and more traditional method is *invoice receiving*. Using this method, the receiving clerk checks the delivered items against the original purchase order and notes any deviations. This method is efficient but requires careful evaluation by the clerk to assure that the delivery is accurate and quality standards are met.

Tips for Inspecting Deliveries

The following are some additional tips that the receiver should keep in mind when evaluating food and supply deliveries:

- Inspect foods immediately upon arrival for quality and quantity ordered.
- Anticipate arrival and be prepared.
- Check adequacy of storage space.
- Have purchase orders and specifications ready.
- Make certain the receiving personnel are well-trained.
- Check temperatures of refrigerated items upon arrival.
- Check frozen items for evidence of thawing or burn.
- Check perishable items first.
- Randomly open cases or crates of product to assure container includes entire order.

Numerous resources are available for use in evaluating food quality and several of these are listed at the end of this chapter.

Evaluating and Following Up

Evaluation of products should be continued as they are issued for use because some discrepancies may not be detected until the item is in use. When products are found to be defective, some type of adjustment should be made. If the products are usable but do not meet the specifications, the buyer may request a price adjustment. The manager may refuse to accept the shipment or, if some of the food or supplies are used but found to be unsatisfactory, the buyer may arrange to return the remaining merchandise or request some type of compensation. The purchasing agent or other proper official should be notified of deficiencies in quality, service, or delivery.

Storage

The flow of materials through a foodservice operation begins in the receiving and storage areas. Careful consideration should be given to procedures for receiving and storage, as well as to the construction and physical needs of both areas. In planning, there should be a straight line from the receiving dock to the storeroom and/or refrigerators and, preferably, on the same level as the kitchen. A short distance between receiving and storage reduces the amount of labor required, lessens pilferage, and causes the least amount of deterioration in food products.

The proper storage of food immediately after it has been received and checked is an important factor in the prevention and control of loss or waste. When food is left unguarded in the receiving area or exposed to the elements or extremes of temperature for even a short time, its safekeeping and quality are jeopardized.

Adequate space for dry, refrigerator, and freezer storage should be provided in locations that are convenient to receiving and preparation areas. Temperature and humidity controls and provision for circulation of air are necessary to retain the various quality factors of the stored foods. The length of time foods can be held satisfactorily and without appreciable deterioration depends on the product and its quality when stored as well as the conditions of storage. Suggested maximum temperatures and storage times for a few typical foods are given in Fig. 4.14. The condition of stored food and the temperature of the storage units should be checked frequently.

Security measures in the receiving and storage areas include the employment and training of qualified reliable personnel, immediate moving of products from receiving to storage, and scheduled hours for receiving. Storage areas should be kept locked, and daily stores and refrigerator areas should also be locked when responsible personnel are not present.

Dry Storage

The main requisites of a food dry-storage area are that it be dry, cool, and properly ventilated. If possible, it should be in a convenient location to the receiving and preparation areas.

Dry storage is intended for nonperishable foods that do not require refrigeration. Paper supplies often are stored with foods, but a separate room should be provided for cleaning supplies, as required in many health codes. The separation of food and cleaning materials that could be toxic prevents a possible error in identification or a mix-up in filling requisitions.

TEMPERATURE AND VENTILATION   The storage area should be dry and the temperature not over 70°F. A dark, damp atmosphere is conducive to the growth of certain organisms, such as molds, and to the development of unpleasant odors. Dry staples such as flour, sugar, rice, condiments, and canned foods are more apt to deteriorate in a damp storage area. The storeroom is more easily kept dry if located at or above ground level, although it need not have outside windows unless required by code. All plumbing pipes should be insulated and well-protected to prevent condensation and leakage onto food stores. If the storage area does have windows, they should be equipped with security-type sash and screens and painted opaque to protect foods from direct sunlight.

Food	Suggested Maximum Temperature (°F)	Recommended Maximum Storage
Canned products	70	12 months
Cooked dishes with eggs, meat, milk, fish, poultry	36	Serve day prepared
Cream filled pastries	36	Serve day prepared
Dairy products		
Milk (fluid)	40	3 days In original container, tightly covered
Milk (dried)	70	3 months In original container
Butter	40	2 weeks In waxed cartons
Cheese (hard)	40	6 months Tightly wrapped
Cheese (soft)	40	7 days In tightly covered container
Ice cream and ices	10	3 months In original container, covered
Eggs	45	7 days Unwashed, not in cardboard
Fish (fresh)	36	2 days Loosely wrapped
Shellfish	36	5 days In covered container
Frozen products	0 (to −20)	
Fruits and vegetables		1 growing season to another Original container
Beef, poultry, eggs		6–12 months Original container
Fresh pork (not ground)		3–6 months Original container
Lamb and veal		6–9 months Original container
Sausage, ground meat, fish		1–3 months Original container
Fruits		
Peaches, plums, berries	50	7 days Unwashed
Apples, pears, citrus	50 (to 70)	2 weeks Original container
Leftovers	36	2 days In covered container
Poultry	36	1–2 days Loosely wrapped
Meat		
Ground	38	2 days Loosely wrapped
Fresh meat cuts	38	3–5 days Loosely wrapped
Liver and variety meats	38	2 days Loosely wrapped
Cold cuts (sliced)	38	3–5 days Wrapped in semi-moisture-proof paper
Cured bacon	38	1–4 weeks May wrap tightly
Ham (tender cured)	38	1–6 weeks May wrap tightly
Ham (canned)	38	6 weeks Original container, unopened
Dried beef	38	6 weeks May wrap tightly
Vegetables		
Leafy	45	7 days Unwashed
Potatoes, onions, root vegetables	70	7–30 days Dry in ventilated container or bags

Figure 4.14.   Suggested maximum storage temperatures and times.

Ventilation is one of the most important factors in dry storage. The use of wall vents, as shown in Fig. 4.15, is the most efficient method of obtaining circulation of air, but other methods are possible. The circulation of air around bags and cartons of food is necessary to aid in the removal of moisture, reduction of temperature, and elimination of odors. For this reason, containers of food are often cross-stacked for better air circulation.

STOREROOM ARRANGEMENT Foods and supplies should be stored in an orderly and systematic arrangement. A definite place should be assigned to each item with similar products grouped together. The containers are dated and usually left in the original package or placed in tightly covered containers if the lots are broken. All items should be stored on racks or shelves instead of directly on the floor or against walls.

Cases and bags of food can be stacked on slatted floor racks, pallets, or wheeled metal platforms. Hand or power lifts are useful for moving loaded pallets from one location to another, but the aisles between shelves and platforms should be wide enough for the use of such mobile equipment.

Shelving, preferably metal and adjustable, is required for canned goods or other items that have been removed from cases. Shelves should be at least 10 inches above the floor and 2 inches away from the wall to permit a free flow of air. Broken lots of dry foods, such as sugar and flour, should be stored in metal containers with tightly fitted lids. The items can be arranged according to

Figure 4.15. Suggestions of possible ways to provide circulation of air in a dry storage area. (Courtesy, Ohio Department of Health.)

groups, and foods in each group can be placed on the shelves in alphabetical order—for example, *canned fruits:* apples, apricots, etc. Food should also be stored using the FIFO method, (first-in, first-out). New shipments should be placed in back to ensure use of the oldest stock first. Alphabetical arrangement facilitates counting when the physical inventory is taken and locating items when filling storeroom requisitions. A chart showing the arrangement of supplies is helpful to storeroom personnel. It should be posted near the door or other place where it can be easily seen.

SANITATION   Food in dry storage must be protected from insects and rodents by preventive measures, such as the use of proper insecticides and rodenticides, the latter under the direction of persons qualified for this type of work. Many operators contract with a pest control service to assure routine monitoring. Floors in the dry storage area should be slip resistant and easily cleaned. A regular cleaning schedule designed according to the volume of traffic and other activity in this area is vital to the maintenance of clean and orderly storage rooms. No trash should be left on the shelves or floor, and spilled food should be wiped up immediately.

Refrigerated and Freezer Storage

The storage of perishable foods is an important factor in their safety and retention of quality. Fresh and frozen foods should be placed in refrigerated or frozen storage immediately after delivery and kept at these temperatures until ready to use. Recommended holding temperatures for fresh fruits and vegetables are 40° to 45°F and 32° to 40°F for meat, poultry, dairy products, and eggs. Frozen products should be stored at 0° to −20°F.

In some foodservices, separate refrigerators are available for fruits and vegetables, dairy products and eggs, and for meats, fish, and poultry. Fruits and vegetables, due to their high moisture content, are susceptible to freezing and, therefore, should be kept at a slightly higher temperature than meats or dairy products. As in dry storage, foods under refrigeration should be rotated so that the oldest is used first. Fruits and vegetables should be checked periodically for ripeness and decaying pieces removed to prevent further spoilage. Some vegetables, like potatoes, onions, and squash, can be kept at temperatures up to 60°F and, in some foodservices, are placed in dry storage. Foods that absorb odors must be stored away from those that give off odors.

In many operations, walk-in refrigerators are used for general and long-term storage, with reach-in units located near workstations for storage of daily perishables and foods in preparation and storage. All refrigeration and freezer units should be provided with thermometers, preferably the recording type. Walk-in refrigerators can have remote thermometers mounted outside the door so that temperatures can be read without opening the door, as shown in Fig. 4.16. Temperatures should be checked twice daily and any irregularity reported to the appropriate supervisor. Prompt action can result in saving food as well as money. Employees should be aware of the correct temperatures for the refrigerators and should be encouraged to open the doors as infrequently as possible.

Cleanliness is vital to food safety. Refrigerators should be thoroughly cleaned at least weekly and any spillage wiped up immediately. Hot food should be placed in shallow pans to chill as soon as possible after preparation unless it is to be served immediately. Cooked foods and meat should be covered to reduce

Figure 4.16. Individual refrigerator units in a large foodservice, grouped together to provide convenience to receiving and preparation areas and for servicing. Separate cooling equipment makes it possible to control and maintain the proper temperature for the food stored in each unit. Floors on the same level as the corridor, easily visible temperature indicators outside the unit, and tight-fitting, well-hinged doors with locks that release from the inside are only a few of the built-in features of a refrigerated walk-in storage area. (Courtesy, Kent State University.)

evaporation losses and to limit odor absorption and damage from possible overhead leakage or dripping. Cooked meats should be stored above raw meats in the refrigerator to assure that cooked foods are protected from raw meat drippings. Daily checks on the contents of refrigerators is advisable so that leftover and broken package foods are incorporated into the menu without delay.

Self-contained refrigeration units are used for ice makers, water dispensers, counter sections for display of salads, and storage for individual milk cartons. Each is adjusted to maintain the temperature needed. Freezer storage generally is in walk-in units, which may open from a walk-in refrigerator or the dry storage area. Ice cream and other frozen desserts may be kept in separate freezer cabinets.

The maintenance of refrigeration equipment requires the regular inspection by and services of a competent engineer to keep it in good working order. However, the manager and other employees must be able to detect and report any noticeable irregularities, since a breakdown in the system could result in heavy loss of food and damage to equipment. In most installations, the refrigerator system is divided into several units so that failure in one will not disrupt the operation of the others.

Inventory Records and Control

Accurate records are essential to inventory control and provide a basis for purchasing and for cost analysis. The exact procedure and forms used will vary according to policies of the institution, but an adequate control system requires that a record be made of all food products and supplies as they are received and stored, and again as they are issued for use in production or other areas of the foodservice.

Receiving

All incoming supplies should be inspected, as explained earlier under "Receiving," and recorded on a receiving record form such as the one shown in Fig. 4.17. A journal in which to list the items received, with date of receipt, can also be used as a receiving record. Whatever form is used, the information should be checked with the purchase order, the delivery slip, and the invoice to be sure that the merchandise has been received as ordered and that the price is correct.

Storeroom Issues

Control of goods received cannot be effective unless storerooms are kept locked and authority and control over the merchandise is delegated to one person. Even if the foodservice is too small to justify the employment of a full-time

Quantity	Unit	Description of item	Name of vendor	Inspected and quantity verified by	Unit price	Total cost	Distribution	
							To kitchen	To store room

Receiving Record Date _____

Figure 4.17. Sample receiving record form.

storekeeper, an employee may be made responsible for receiving, putting away, and issuing goods from the storeroom in addition to other assigned duties.

No food or other supplies should be removed from the storeroom without authorization, usually in the form of a written requisition. An exception may be perishable foods that are to be used the same day they are received and are sent directly to the production units. In that case, they are treated as direct issues and are charged to the food cost for that day. All foods that are stored after delivery are considered storeroom purchases and in most operations can be removed only by requisition.

A list of supplies needed for production and service of the day's menu is compiled by the cook or other person responsible for assembling ingredients. If the foodservice uses an ingredient room for weighing and measuring ingredients for all recipes, the personnel in this unit are responsible for requesting supplies. (The ingredient room is discussed in more detail in Chapter 5.) The list of needed supplies is then submitted to the storekeeper, who completes the requisition. The order is filled and delivered to the appropriate department or section. The exact procedure for issuing supplies varies with the size of the operation and whether there is a full-time storekeeper.

Requisitions should be numbered and made out in duplicate or triplicate as the situation requires. Prenumbering of the requisitions makes it possible to trace missing or duplicate requisitions. An example of a storeroom requisition is shown in Fig. 4.18. Columns should be included for unit price and total cost unless a computer-assisted program is used, in which case the data will be available from the stored information in the computer. An inventory number is needed for each item on the requisition if a computer is used in calculating costs.

The requisition should be signed by a person authorized to request supplies and should be signed or initialed by the individual who fills the order. The requisitioning of food and supplies is an important factor in controlling costs

Figure 4.18.   Requisition for storeroom issues.

and in preventing loss from pilferage, and it should be practiced in some form even in a small foodservice.

Perpetual Inventory

The perpetual inventory is a running record of the balance on hand for each item in the storeroom. The use of computers has simplified the process of maintaining the perpetual inventory and is used by many foodservices. In organizations where data processing is not used, the inventory information is usually recorded on cards. Standard forms for perpetual inventory are available from suppliers, or the foodservice manager can design forms that will work best for an individual operation. An example is given in Fig. 4.19.

The perpetual inventory provides a continuing record of food and supplies purchased, in storage, and used. Items received are recorded on the inventory from the invoices, and the amounts are added to the previous balance on hand. Storeroom issues are recorded from the requisitions and subtracted from the balance. Additional information usually includes the date of purchase, the vendor, the brand purchased, and the price paid.

If minimum and maximum stock levels have been established, as discussed earlier under "Identifying Needs—Inventory Stock Level," these figures should be indicated on the inventory. When computers are used, the reorder point is included in the program. If cards are used, a colored marker or some other method of flagging will alert the storekeeper or manager to reorder the item when the inventory reaches that level.

These inventory records are recommended for all items except perishable foods that are delivered and stored in the production area. A physical inventory taken at the time perishable foods are ordered is more realistic. However, if there is a need for purchasing information on prices or total amounts of these foods used during a certain period of time, a purchase record as illustrated in Fig. 4.20 may be used to record the date of purchase, amounts, prices, and vendors. In Fig. 4.21, a purchase record and summary of purchases are combined with a perpetual inventory.

Time and strict supervision are required if the perpetual inventory is to be an effective tool, but it is a useful guide for purchasing and serves as a check on irregularities, such as pilferage or displacement of stock. It also provides useful information on fast-moving, slow-moving, or unusable items.

Physical Inventory

An actual count of items in all storage areas should be taken periodically, usually to coincide with an accounting period. In some organizations, an inventory is taken at the end of each month, in others two or three times a year. The inventory is simplified if two people work together, one in a supervisory position

Figure 4.19. Perpetual inventory form.

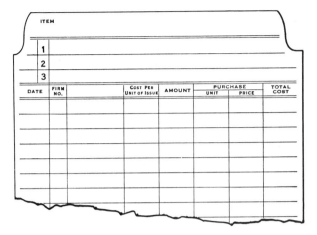

Figure 4.20. Purchase record form.

or not directly involved with the storeroom operation. As one person counts the number of each item on hand, the other enters it on the inventory.

The procedure for taking a physical inventory is simplified by developing a printed form on which are listed the items normally carried in stock and their unit sizes, as shown in Fig. 4.22. For convenience and efficiency in recording, the items on the inventory form can be classified and then arranged alphabetically within the group or listed in the same order as they are arranged in the storeroom and in the perpetual inventory. Space should be left on the form between each grouping to allow for new items to be added.

After the physical inventory is completed, the value of each item is calculated and the total value of the inventory determined. Inventory figures are used to calculate food costs by adding the total food purchases to the beginning inventory and subtracting the ending inventory. The physical count also serves as a check against perpetual inventory records. Minor differences are expected, but major discrepancies should be investigated. Carelessness in filling requisitions or in record keeping is the most common reason for these errors, which may indicate a need for tighter storeroom controls or more accurate record keeping.

Both perpetual and physical inventories should be kept of china, glassware, and silverware. These items should be revalued at least once a year on the basis of physical inventory, although it may be desirable to revalue them at more frequent intervals. An inventory of other kitchen and dining room equipment and furniture normally is taken once a year.

Management of inventory is practiced both to determine quantities to keep on hand and to determine the security methods used to control how the stock influences overall foodservice costs. Each organization should decide on maximum and minimum quantities desirable to maintain in the storeroom. This

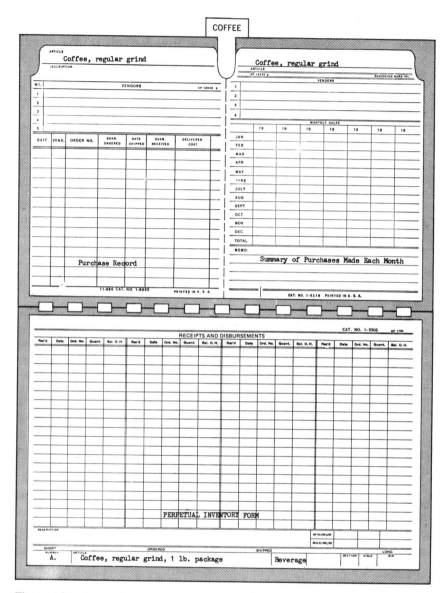

Figure 4.21. Form for purchase and summary records combined with perpetual inventory.

decision is based on storage facilities and capacities, delivery patterns, and the volume of business. Established standards for quantities desirable to keep on hand aid in purchasing—both as to quantity to order and when to order.

Carrying an inventory is costly, and some thought should be given to the total value of such an investment. Carrying costs normally range from 15% to 35% of

The Student Union Food Division

Physical Inventory _____ 19 _____   Page 1

Classification	Item	Unit	Quantity	Unit Price	Total Cost
Beverages:					
	Coffee	14 oz pkg			
	Tea, iced	1 gal			
	Tea, individual	100/Box			
Cereals:					
	Assorted individual	50/carton			
	Corn Flakes	100/cs			
	Cream of Wheat	1# 12 oz box			
	Hominy grits	1# 8 oz box			
	Oats, Rolled	3# box			
	Ralstons	1# 6 oz box			
	Rice, white	1# box			
Cereal Products and Flour: Cornmeal		Bulk/lb			

TOTAL PAGE 1 _____

Figure 4.22.   A sample page from a physical inventory form.

the inventory value, but can be as high as 50%, and fast-food operations with a minimum of inventory and rapid turnover may be as low as 2% to 4% of the inventory value. This percentage includes capital invested in inventory that prevents the use of money for other purposes; storage costs of space, personnel, materials handling, records, and utilities; deterioration and spoilages; obsolescence of items no longer in use; and insurance on this asset.

Summary

Purchasing is an essential function in the operation of a foodservice organization and is vital to maintaining an adequate flow of food and supplies to meet production and service requirements.

Informal or formal methods of buying may be used, sometimes varying for different commodities. The buyer should be knowledgeable about the market and should understand the legal implications of contracts and bid buying. Purchasing may be the responsibility of the foodservice administrator or may be done centrally through a purchasing department. Group buying, in which several organizations combine their purchasing volume, has been successful in many cases.

The safety of food products is protected by several federal agencies, and quality grades have been established for many products. Detailed specifications should be used to ensure the purchase and delivery of products of the desired quality. Decisions must be made by the foodservice on the market form preferred, the quality to buy, and whether to make or buy prepared foods.

Good purchasing procedures include the use of appropriate buying methods, establishment of ordering schedules, and a system of communicating needs from production and service areas to the buyer. Foods and supplies should be received and checked by trained personnel and properly stored at appropriate temperatures. A storeroom control system that includes authorized issuing of supplies and complete inventory records is essential, but the procedures and paper work should be limited to those necessary for control and communications.

Summary Questions

1. What are the most recent trends and changes in the food market? How have these changes influenced the purchasing function of the foodservice organization?

2. Read a local newspaper for several consecutive days. What events (economic, political, environmental, social) might have an impact on purchasing decisions made in a foodservice department?

3. How does the marketing channel have an impact on the price paid for a food product by the consumer?

4. Which food products are under the regulatory control of one or more government agencies?

5. What qualities should a foodservice buyer possess?

6. What are the advantages and disadvantages of group and centralized purchasing?

7. What are the advantages and disadvantages of the two principal methods of buying? What are some alternative methods of purchasing?

8. Explain the following recommendation—"level of quality purchased should match intended use."

9. Compare and contrast a perpetual and physical inventory.

10. How does a well-planned receiving program contribute to cost and quality control?

11. What are some potential consequences of a poorly planned and monitored receiving process?

For More Information

Food and Nutrition Service, USDA: Food Buying Guide for School Food Service. PA No. 1331. Washington, DC: U.S. Government Printing Office, 1984.

Knight, J. B. and Kotschevar, L. H.: Quantity Food Production, Planning and Management. Ch. 6 Purchasing and receiving. Boston: CBI Publishing Co., 1989.

Kotschevar, L. H.: Quantity Food Purchasing, 3rd ed. New York: Macmillan, 1988.

Levine, A. S., Labuza, T. P., and Morley, J. E.: Food technology: A primer for physicians. New Engl. J. Med. 312:628, 1985.

Livestock Division, Agricultural Marketing Service, USDA: Institutional Meat Purchase Specifications. Washington, DC, 1975.

Livingston, G. E.: Prepared food. Part 2: Make or buy? Hospitals 46:95, 1972.

Longree, K.: Quantity Food Sanitation, 4th ed. New York: Wiley-Interscience, 1987.

Mahaffey, M. J., Mennes, M. E., and Miller, B. B.: Food Service Manual for Health Care Institutions. Chicago: American Hospital Association, 1981.

National Association of Meat Purveyors: The Meat Buyers Guide, 7th ed. McLean, VA: National Association of Meat Purveyors, 1984.

National Live Stock and Meat Board: Meat in the Foodservice Industry. Chicago: National Live Stock and Meat Board, 1975.

National Restaurant Association, The Education Foundation. Applied Foodservice Sanitation, 4th ed. John Wiley & Sons, 1992.

Ninemeier, J. D.: Purchasing, Receiving, and Storage: A Systems Manual for Restaurants, Hotels, and Clubs. Boston: CBI Publishing Co., 1983.

Nix, M.: Purchasing, purchasing, purchasing! School Food Serv. J. 37:161, 1983.

Oakley, H., ed.: The Buying Guide, 7th ed. Hagerstown, MD: Blue Goose, 1980.

Peddersen, R. B.: SPECS: The Comprehensive Foodservice Purchasing and Specification Manual. Boston: Cahners Book International, 1977.

Peddersen, R. B.: Foodservice and Hotel Purchasing. Boston: Cahners Books International, 1981.

Puckett, R. P. and Miller, B. B.: Food service manual for health care institutions. Chicago: American Hospital Association, 1988.

Spears, M. C. and Vaden, A. G.: Foodservice Organizations: A Managerial and Systems Approach. New York: John Wiley & Sons, 1985.

Stefanelli, J. M.: Purchasing Selection and Procurement for the Hospitality Industry. New York: John Wiley & Sons, 1984.

Warfel, M. C. and Cremer, M. L.: Purchasing for Food Service Managers, 2nd ed. Berkeley, CA: McCutchan Publishing Corp., 1990.

Zenz, G. J.: Purchasing and the Management of Materials, 5th ed. New York: John Wiley & Sons, 1981.

Additional Resources

Food Buying Guide for School Food Service
U.S. Government Printing Office
Washington, DC 20402

Food Service Directory and Buyer's Guide for Fresh Produce
Produce Marketing Association
700 Barksdale Road
Newark, DE 19711

Grade Standards for Fresh and Processed Fruits and Vegetables
USDA Fruit and Vegetable Division
Washington, DC 20250

Grade Standards for Poultry, Rabbits, and Shell Eggs
USDA Poultry and Dairy Division
Washington, DC 20250

National Association of Meat Purveyors
Meat Buyer's Guide
8365B Greensboro Dr.
McLean, VA 22101

National Dairy Council
6300 N. River Road
Rosemont, IL 60018

National Livestock and Meat Board
36 S. Wabash Avenue
Chicago, IL 60603

Quality and Yields Grades for Beef, Veal, . . . and Hog Carcasses
USDA Livestock Meat, Grain, and Seed Division
Washington, DC 20250

Production Management

Production of high-quality food involves a number of interrelated steps, each dependent on the other. The transformation of raw or processed foods into an acceptable finished product ready for service is an essential operation in the overall foodservice system. It requires the purchase of food products of good quality, initial storage and "holding" at optimum temperatures at various points in its production, and, generally, one or more processing procedures under controlled conditions.

Traditionally, these procedures have been carried out in the individual foodservice, and menu items were prepared "from scratch." Today, however, there are alternatives to this conventional system. Foodservice organizations composed of several individual units may centralize all or part of their food production in a commissary or central production kitchen. Preparation in these facilities can range from controlled production of items such as desserts and baked goods; preparation of meats ready for cooking; preparation of fruits and vegetables for salads or for final cooking in the individual foodservice units; or complete preparation and cooking of menu items, packaged in individual or bulk containers, and chilled or frozen for delivery to serving units.

Many foodservices prepare either all or part of the food for immediate service or hot-holding, but in some, food is cooked then chilled or frozen for later service. Others purchase certain menu items in ready-to-cook or ready-to-serve forms, and most use some type of convenience ingredients or components. These foodservice systems—conventional, commissary (central production kitchen), ready prepared (cook/chill or cook/freeze), and assembly/serve—are discussed in detail in Chapter 2.

Regardless of the system used, production planning and control are vital to the successful production of high-quality food. Forecasting the quantities to prepare and scheduling of production are discussed in this chapter, as are the various elements of production and quality control.

Learning Objectives

After studying this chapter, the reader should be able to

1. list the steps required to transform raw food into acceptable finished products
2. calculate the quantity of food to be produced when the portion size, number to be served, and yield percentage are known
3. list and briefly explain the preparation steps undergone by most menu items
4. discuss the factors that should be considered when scheduling food production
5. describe management's responsibility in the area of food quality production controls
6. apply HACCP concepts to food production
7. identify the advantages of using standardized recipes
8. adjust recipes to yield desired quantities using both the factor and percent methods
9. list and briefly discuss the advantages and disadvantages of an ingredient room

Production Planning

Forecasting

The goal of forecasting is to estimate future needs using past data. Applied to foodservice, *forecasting* is a prediction of food needs for a day or other specific time period. Forecasting differs from tallying, which is a simple count of menu items actually requested or selected by the customers. Production planning begins with the menu and the production forecast. Other foodservice functions, such as purchasing, are triggered by the forecast. Sound forecasting is vital to financial management; it facilitates efficient scheduling of labor, use of equipment, and space.

REASONS FOR FORECASTING   A great deal of time (i.e., lead time) is needed to complete all phases of menu item preparation: purchasing, storage, thawing, prepreparation, production, distribution, and final service. Forecasting serves as a means of communication with purchasing and food production staff to assure that all of these stages are completed in a timely manner and that the final product meets standards of quality.

The purchasing representative needs to know how much food to order and when it needs to be available for use in the foodservice production area. The hot and cold food production staff(s) need to know how many servings of each menu item are needed, and in what form and for which service unit (e.g., cafeteria, vending, patients, catering) they are needed.

Accurate forecasting minimizes the chance of over- or underproduction—both of which have serious consequences. Without proper guidelines, production employees have a tendency to overproduce food for fear of running short of actual need. This can be a costly comfort measure. Leftover food is often held for later service or redirected to an alternate service unit within the department such as the cafeteria or vending or catering services. Each choice is risky in that the food may not meet minimum quality standards at point-of-service, ultimately ending up in the garbage disposal.

Underproduction can be costly as well, and may result in customer dissatisfaction. To compensate for shortages, managers often substitute expensive heat-and-serve items, such as ready-prepared chicken cordon bleu. More serious than increased raw food costs, however, is the risk of upsetting a customer by providing him or her with a substitute menu item that was not ordered. Foodservice employees may get frustrated if food shortages occur too frequently, resulting in rushed, last-minute food preparation or delayed service.

In small health care organizations, such as long-term care facilities or hospitals, amounts to be produced could be determined by simple tally, especially if the patient census is stable and a nonselective menu is used. In large organizations with multiple service units, a more sophisticated forecasting may be beneficial if there is wide variation in menu item demand. A simple tally system would be far too time-consuming for these larger organizations. Regardless of the size and complexity of the foodservice organization, a good forecasting system is based on sound historical data that reflects the pattern of actual menu item demand in the foodservice operation.

HISTORICAL DATA   Historical data is used to determine needs and to establish trends in all forecasting methods. To be of value, this data must be consistently and accurately recorded. Categories of data to collect vary depending on the type of foodservice organization, scope of services provided, and whether customers are allowed to select menu items. The following are a few examples of data categories for various organizations:

Restaurants/cafeterias
- Customers served per meal
- Menu items selected per meal
- Beverage sales (types and amounts)

Schools
- Student enrollment
- Students purchasing full USDA meal
- À la carte items sold per lunch period
- Teachers and staff purchasing meals

Hospitals
- Daily patient census
- Patients on therapeutic diets
- Daily patient admissions and discharges

Vending services
- Product placed in machine at each fill
- Total cash removed
- Food remaining in machine at each refill

Fig. 5.1 is an example of a form designed to document meal participation in a school lunch program. During a period of time, a pattern of menu item demand or total meals served will emerge from this recorded data. This pattern, along with knowledge of pattern variance, will assist the production planner in making a valid estimate of future menu item needs. Factors influencing pattern variance include holidays, weather conditions, and special events.

CRITERIA FOR SELECTING A FORECASTING PROCESS Careful planning and evaluation are essential in selection of the best forecasting method for a given foodservice operation. Numerous computer forecasting models have been developed during the past several years that have been a great aid to the foodservice manager. However, regardless of whether a manual or computer-assisted method is chosen, several factors should be considered before deciding on a forecasting system. These factors include cost, accuracy, relevancy, lead time, pattern of food selection, ease of use, responsiveness to changes, and stability. Table 5.1 is a summary of the considerations related to each of these factors.

FORECAST MODELS Types of forecasting models for use with manual or electronic systems include: moving average, exponential smoothing, regression, and auto regressive moving average (Box-Jenkins). These models are mathematical descriptions of meals served or of menu item selection behavior. The information for the mathematical models is based on historical data and is expressed as an average of past service or selection behavior.

The moving average and exponential smoothing models are commonly used in foodservices for production forecasting. Fig. 5.2 illustrates the calculations for each of these methods and gives an example of how each method is used with past data from a small hospital. The number of customers served from a foodservice is generally different on each day of the week. For this reason, forecasts are calculated for intervals of 7 days. For example, in a hospital, data collected on Mondays is used to forecast needs for future Mondays.

The *moving average* model is referred to as a time series method of forecasting and is easy to use. Using records from the past, a group of data are averaged and used as the first forecast. The next forecast is calculated by dropping the first number and adding the next. This process continues for all data available.

DAILY PARTICIPATION RECORD
LUNCH PROGRAM

SCHOOL _____   MONTH _____

Days of operation	STUDENTS				ADULTS		2nd lunches	Absences (excluding kindergarten)
	Paid (1)	Reduced (3)	Free (2)	TOTAL	Program*	Nonprogram**		
1								
2								
3								
4								
5								
6								
7								
8								
9								
10								
11								
12								
13								
14								
15								
16								
17								
18								
19								
20								
21								
22								
23								
24								
25								
26								
27								
28								
29								
30								
31								
MONTHLY TOTAL								

Average enrollment this month _____
 (minus kindergarten)

Average enrollment − Average absences = Average daily attendance   Total absences ÷ Days in session = Average absences

_____ − _____ = _____   _____ ÷ _____ = _____

* Program adults: all foodservice workers. Adult meals are not reimbursable.

** Nonprogram adults: teachers, administrators, office workers, janitors, and any occasional visitors.
 Adult meals are not reimbursable.

Figure 5.1. Sample form for lunch participation in a school lunch program. (Courtesy, Beth Mincemoyer Egan, Manager–Food Services, Sun Prairie Public Schools, Sun Prairie, Wisconsin.)

TABLE 5.1. Criteria for Selecting a Forecasting System.

Factor	Considerations
Costs	• Development, implementation, and system operational costs (i.e., data collection, analysis) are reasonable; that is, within budgetary guidelines • Training and education for staff
Accuracy/relevancy	• Past data and food selection patterns are relevant and accurately reflect current demand
Lead time	• System allows adequate time for purchasing, delivery, and production • Accounts for perishability of food items
Pattern of behavior	• System can be adjusted for changes in menu item demand as a result of seasonality and consumer preference
Ease of use	• Use of system is easily understood • What knowledge and skills are required to operate system?
Level of detail	• System can generate desired forecasts • What is to be forecasted?
Responsiveness	• System generates accurate information on a timely basis

The *exponential smoothing* model is another time series model, similar to the moving average technique except that it accounts for seasonality of data and adjusts for forecast error. This results in a higher level of forecast accuracy. The simple exponential smoothing model predicts the next demand by weighting the data; more recent data is weighted more heavily than older data. The factor used to weight the data is referred to as *alpha*. Alpha is determined statistically and, in foodservice forecasting, is generally valued at 0.3. The purpose of alpha is to adjust for any errors in previous forecasts.

Regression and *auto regressive moving average* models are sophisticated, statistical methods by which past data is analyzed to determine the best mathematical approach to forecasting. These methods generally require the assistance of a statistician and are used with computer-assisted forecasting systems. These two methods are beyond the scope of this textbook. For more information refer to "For More Information" at the end of this chapter.

Quantities to Produce

The forecast is the basis for determining quantities of menu items to be prepared and foods to be purchased or requisitioned from the storerooms. An

Examples of Forecasting Using Actual Data

Type of Model	Mathematics		Examples of Forecasting Using Actual Data

Moving average

$$F = \dfrac{\sum\limits_{i=1}^{N} A_i}{N}$$

F = Next forecast
Σ = Summation
i = Time unit of forecast (i.e., Mondays, Tuesdays, etc.)
N = Number of observations
A = Actual demand

Actual demand data

Week #	S	M	T	W	R	F	S
1	104	112	128	142	133	133	117
2	107	125	134	147	137	159	145
3	137	155	155	150	150	153	134
4	122	134	142	135	123	125	116
5	108	128	134	140	147	146	121

Week #5 forecast (N = 4)

Week #	S	M	T	W	R	F	S
5	118	132	140	144	136	143	128

Forecast error

Week #	S	M	T	W	R	F	S
5	10	4	6	4	-11	-4	7

Exponential smoothing

$$F_{t+1} = \alpha A_t + (1 - \alpha)\, F_t$$

F = Next forecast
t = Time point
t+1 = Next forecast time point
α = Judgment factor to weight data
A = Actual demand

Actual demand data

Week #	S	M	T	W	R	F	S
1	104	112	128	142	133	133	117
2	107	125	134	147	137	159	145
3	137	155	155	150	150	153	134
4	122	134	142	135	123	125	116
5	108	128	134	140	147	146	121

Week #5 forecast

Week #	S	M	T	W	R	F	S
5	117	130	139	142	134	139	124

Forecast error

Week #	S	M	T	W	R	F	S
5	9	2	5	2	-13	-7	3

Figure 5.2. Commonly used forecasting models in foodservice. (Adapted from Messersmith, A. M. and Miller, J. L.: Forecasting in Foodservice. Copyright © 1992. New York: John Wiley & Sons, Inc. Reprinted by permission of John Wiley & Sons, Inc.)

estimate at the time the major food orders are placed is later adjusted, 1 to 2 days prior to the day of production, for more accurate decisions on amounts of food to be prepared. The amount of food needed is based on the number of persons to be served, portion size, and the amount of waste and shrinkage loss in the preparation of foods.

Recipes adjusted to the predicted number of portions needed provide much of this information. Most quantity recipes for noncomputer systems are calculated in modules of 50 or 100 or, in foods such as cakes or casserole-type entrées, to pan sizes and equipment capacity. For example, if a recipe produces two sheet cakes, which can be cut into 30 or 32 servings each, three cakes (or one and one-half times the recipe) would be required for 75 portions. When very large quantities are produced, the amount to prepare in one batch is limited to the capacity of the production equipment.

In foodservices that use a computer, recipes are printed daily and, when appropriate, provide recipes for the exact number of individual portions, or are adjusted to the number of pans or other modules required to serve the predicted numbers. To be effective, computer-assisted programs include recipes for all menu items offered, including fresh vegetables and fruits, salads, relishes, and meats, such as roast beef or baked pork chops. Quantities to purchase or requisition are readily available from these computer-generated recipes. In foodservices not having a computer-assisted system, standardizing and calculating recipes for more than one amount lessens the need for refiguring the quantities for each day's forecast.

A general procedure for determining amounts of meats, poultry, fruits, and vegetables follows.

1. Determine the portion size in ounces.

2. Multiply portion size by the estimated number to be served and convert to pounds. This is the edible portion (EP) required. EP may also be given in the standardized recipe.

$$\frac{\text{ounces} \times \text{number of portions}}{16 \text{ oz}} = \begin{array}{l}\text{number of pounds edible} \\ \text{portion (EP) required}\end{array}$$

3. To determine the amount to order, divide the EP weight by the yield percentage (or the weight in decimal parts of a pound of ready-to-eat or ready-to-cook product from 1 pound of the commodity as purchased). The *USDA Food Buying Guide for School Food Service*, PA 1257 is a good source for yield information.

$$\frac{\text{EP weight}}{\text{yield}} = \text{amount to order}$$

4. For foods to be purchased, convert the amount needed to the most appropriate purchase unit (e.g., case, crate, or roast). If the food is to be

used for other menu items, combine the amounts and then convert to purchase units.

As an example, if 3-ounce portions of fresh asparagus are needed for 50 people, you would calculate the amount to purchase in the following way:

1. $\dfrac{3 \text{ oz} \times 50 \text{ portions}}{} = \dfrac{150 \text{ oz}}{16 \text{ oz}} = 9.375 \text{ lbs of EP needed}$

2. $\dfrac{9.375 \text{ lbs needed}}{0.53 \text{ lb yield from 1 lb as purchased}} = 17.68 \text{ lbs to purchase}$

3. Convert to purchase unit, 18 lbs to 20 lbs

In a computer system, these figures would be calculated automatically from the forecast, portion size, and yield data.

Scheduling

Once the needed quantity of food is known and recipes are obtained from the file or from the computer, supplies are requisitioned or ordered, as previously discussed. The next step in production planning is scheduling of food preparation. Careful planning ensures the efficient use of employee time and equipment, and a minimum of production problems. Foods that are ready for service at the scheduled time without undue holding are superior in quality to those prepared too early.

Production planning and scheduling require a knowledge of the steps through which a product must go and the time required for each, as well as the steps that can be completed early without affecting the quality of the food. Most menu items go through part or all of the following steps:

• Storage—dry, refrigerated, freezer
• Thaw time
• Assembly—weighing or measuring ingredients
• Prepreparation—vegetable cleaning, peeling, cutting, chopping, preparing pans
• Preparation—mixing, combining ingredients, panning
• Cooking—baking, frying, broiling, steaming, simmering
• Finishing—setting up salads, portioning desserts, slicing meats, packaging food for freezing
• Storage prior to serving—heated, refrigerated, frozen

Up to the point of final cooking, many steps can and should be scheduled early, possibly the day before. Each recipe should be broken down into production stages to determine which steps can be done in advance. Preparation of casserole-type entrées should be scheduled so that the cooking of all recipe components is completed in time for final assembling and baking; for example, browning the beef cubes, dicing and cooking the vegetables, and preparing the topping for beef pot pie; or cooking ground beef, tomato sauce, and pasta for a casserole.

For some foods, it may be better to assemble the product in batches as needed for final cooking and serving. Combining the entire amount may reduce the flexibility of the individual ingredients if there is an overproduction. For example, the ground beef could be used for tacos, the pasta for a salad, and the tomato sauce in chili. These would be "new" menu items rather than "leftovers." In commercial cooking, where food may be prepared in relatively small quantities because of the uncertain number of portions needed or if the menu includes a large selection of items, the finished product may be cooked to order or in amounts compatible with the anticipated patronage.

Cheese balls, croquettes, and similar foods must be shaped and chilled for several hours before deep-fat frying. Other procedures, such as breading of chicken, cutlets, or fish prior to cooking; shaping of meat balls; and filling of deviled eggs are examples of time-consuming procedures that can be scheduled early. Some menu items or ingredients can be prepared 2 to 3 days ahead, but care must be taken not to schedule early preparation if the quality or safety of the food is endangered. If frozen foods are to be defrosted, time must be allowed for thawing in the refrigerator.

When scheduling the cooking of foods in quantity, allowances must be made for the time required for heat to penetrate. For example, it will take longer for heat to reach the center of a pan with 50 servings of scalloped potatoes than a casserole serving six. Sheet cake baked in an 18×26-inch pan needs more cooking time than the same amount of batter baked in 9-inch layer cake pans. Four beef roasts in an oven require more cooking time than just one. Size of container, then, and oven load affect the total cooking time.

Final cooking should be scheduled so that only food needed for immediate service is cooked at one time. Batch cooking of vegetables in small amounts, baking of pans of entrées at intervals, and continuous deep-fat frying "to the line" or "to order" are examples. Some cooks are more comfortable if all food is cooked at once, but batch cooking should be scheduled and employees encouraged to recognize that the quality of the prepared food is better when it has not been held for long periods.

Due to the variation in complexity of menu items from day-to-day, production should be planned several days ahead to distribute the work load evenly. An increasing number of foodservices are using advance production to equalize work loads. Food preparation is scheduled during slack periods, and the food is frozen for later use. Such a program should not be attempted, however, without adequate freezing and refrigeration equipment and without some knowledge of foods that freeze well and the effect of storage length on different foods. Proper cooling, packaging, and freezing are especially important to the quality and safety of the finished products. The foods, of course, should be prepared under close supervision so that adequate sanitation and processing precautions are observed. If the product will be stored for any length of time, a system of inventory control of the frozen prepared foods should be implemented.

PRODUCTION SCHEDULES   A production schedule, sometimes called a production sheet or work sheet, lists in detail the items to be produced for the current day's menu plus any advance preparation needed. This schedule should include, as a minimum, the menu items, amounts to prepare, cooking times, special instructions for preparation and serving, and the name of the employee assigned to prepare each item. Some production schedules include space for recording quantities of food prepared and amounts left after the serving is completed. This information is important to the menu planner or production supervisor who must plan for incorporating these foods into the menu for the next meal or the next day, or to freeze for later use. Also added on some production schedules is information concerning weather, holidays, or special events that might assist in explaining the quantities prepared and served.

A single schedule for a small foodservice may include preparation and cleaning assignments for all employees, with production times set for specific times of the day to assist employees in planning their work. In a large, more complex operation, schedules are made for each department and usually are quite detailed. Fig. 5.3 is an example of a production schedule that also serves as a production record. If cycle menus are used, time is saved by setting up orders and production schedules for each cycle as a "package" to be used with the cycle. Adjustments, of course, may be needed if there are changes in menus or the numbers to be served.

PRODUCTION MEETINGS   A meeting with appropriate staff and employees to discuss the menu and production plans heightens the effectiveness of the written production schedule. Such meetings generally do not need to be long, but they should be held regularly and at a time when activity in the production area is at a minimum. At meeting time, the menu can be explained and special instructions given for the items as needed. Employees also have an opportunity to discuss the schedule and any production problems they may anticipate.

No amount of "paper work" can replace the human element in food production. Food must be prepared by people, and no matter how carefully plans are made and how many instructions are written, there must be "follow through" to be sure that the menu as served measures up to the menu as planned.

PRODUCTION SCHEDULE

DATE _____ AREA _____

Meal Count _____

Weather _____

Special Events _____

PERSON	MENU ITEM	QUANTITY TO PREPARE	ACTUAL YIELD	DIRECTIONS	TIME SCHEDULE	LEFT OVER AMOUNT	RUN OUT TIME	SUBSTITUTION	CLEANING ASSIGNMENT

PRE-PREPARATION:

PERSON	MENU ITEM	QUANTITY	PERSON	MENU ITEM	QUANTITY

Form 4.1

F.S. Form 60

Figure 5.3. Production schedule for a large residence hall food center. Information useful for production forecasting is also recorded on this form. (Courtesy, Kansas State University Residence Halls.)

Food Production

Production planning and scheduling, as discussed earlier in this chapter, are vital to the production of good quality food and are important management responsibilities. The true test of the planning, however, is the production of food that is appealing to the clientele, prepared in the appropriate quantity, microbiologically safe, and within budgetary constraints. A knowledge of basic food preparation techniques and equipment usage will assist the foodservice manager in planning and achieving these goals.

The extent of actual preparation and cooking done on-premise depends on the type of foodservice system (conventional, commissary, ready-prepared, or assembly/serve), as explained in Chapter 2. Even in the conventional system, in which all or most of the food is prepared, the production methods and equipment needs vary with the type and size of the foodservice. For example, in some retirement homes in which all residents are served at the same, set time, it is necessary to prepare larger amounts of food at one time and with different equipment than in a restaurant where much of the food is prepared "to order" during an extended service period.

Quantity is the element that introduces complexity to food preparation in the foodservice system. Therefore, the foodservice manager should not only be knowledgeable about basic cooking methods but should understand the time-temperature relationships and quality control challenges inherent in quantity food production. The principles of food preparation in large quantity are much the same as in small quantity except that there are differences in procedures because of the larger amounts of food involved. Mechanized equipment is essential for heavy processes and for time-consuming procedures, especially in the larger operations. Pie rollers, automatic bread and roll shaping equipment, steam-jacketed kettles with stirring paddles, timers on steam-cooking equipment, metering devices for measuring water, and high-speed vegetable cutters are examples of labor-saving equipment in use. Convection ovens and compartment steamers used in many foodservices reduce the time required for cooking. Nontransfer cooking, in which foods are cooked in the same pans used for serving, saves time and possible damage to the food quality through additional handling.

As discussed previously, a list of steps required in the transformation of raw food into acceptable finished products includes: storage, thaw time, assembly, prepreparation, preparation, cooking, finishing, and storage prior to serving. The extent of ingredient assembly, prepreparation, and preparation of the food before being delivered to the cooking area depends on the size and physical layout of the foodservice operation. With some foods, such as fresh fruit and certain salads and sandwiches, the cooking procedure is omitted. However, most foods do require cooking and, at this point, quality control becomes increasingly important. It requires constant vigilance to see that food is cooked properly, that it is well-seasoned, and that cooking is scheduled so that food will not be held too long before service.

OBJECTIVES OF COOKING   The basic objectives of cooking are to enhance the flavor and attractiveness of the original color, form, and texture; to destroy harmful organisms and substances to ensure food that is safe for human consumption; and to improve digestibility.

HEAT TRANSFER   Cooking is accomplished by the transfer of heat from an energy source to and through the food by one of three methods: conduction, convection, or radiation.

Conduction is the transfer of heat through direct contact from one item or substance to another. The heat is first transferred from a heat source, usually gas or electricity, through a cooking vessel to the food. Conduction is the principal means of heat transfer in grilling, frying, boiling, and, to some extent, in roasting and baking. In pan broiling or grilling, for example, the heat is transferred from the source to the pan or grill and then directly to the food. In panfrying, fat is the transfer agent between the pan and the food.

Convection, in which heat is spread by the movement of air, steam or liquid, or *radiation,* in which energy is transferred by waves from the source to the food are additional means of heat transfer. These methods usually involve some intermediary, such as the air in the oven; the water, steam, or fat that may surround the food and/or container; or the metal, glass, or ceramic of which the food container is composed. In convection ovens, for example, heat is circulated by fans, thus transferring the heat more quickly to the food. In a microwave, radiation is used in food production. The radiation waves do not possess energy, but upon entering the food induce heat by molecular movement.

COOKING METHODS   Cooking methods are classified as dry heat or moist heat. *Dry heat* methods are those in which the heat is conducted to the food by dry air, hot metal, radiation, or in a minimum amount of fat. Roasting, baking, broiling, grilling, griddling, and frying are examples of dry heat methods. *Moist heat* methods are those in which the heat is conducted to the food product by water or steam. Examples are boiling or simmering, stewing, blanching, poaching, braising, and steaming.

The method used depends on the type and quality of the food and availability of equipment. Different cooking methods are suitable for different kinds of food. For example, tender cuts of meat usually are prepared using a dry heat method, and a less tender cut should be cooked using moist heat. Basic cooking processes, with suggested equipment and types of products cooked by these methods, are presented in Appendix A. In Appendix C, information on the application of cooking methods to quantity production of different types of foods is provided.

Production Controls

Quality Standards and Control

Food quality is a primary objective of foodservice systems and its control is a major function of management. Quality is closely related to consumer acceptability, which can vary with the expectations and needs of customers, patients, students, or other patrons in different types of foodservices. Each person has his or her own perception of what constitutes quality food based in part on personal likes and dislikes.

Traditionally, quality has referred to sensory characteristics, such as flavor, texture, appearance, and temperature, and is measured by the response of the clientele to the food. Assurance of quality food has been provided through purchase of quality ingredients, use of standardized recipes, continuous supervision of food production, and critical tasting of the finished product. In addition, many foodservices have established quality standards for each product to use in evaluating the purchased ingredients and/or the cooked product.

Although sensory characteristics are vital to consumer acceptance of food, a broader definition of quality includes nutritional and microbiological attributes, according to Bobeng and David; in other words, food that is nutritious and safe, as well as satisfying to the consumer. The Hazard Analysis and Critical Control Points (HACCP), used successfully by the food processing industry, has been recommended as a preventative approach to quality control in foodservice systems.

Hazard Analysis and Critical Control Points (HACCP)

The HACCP concept has recently been recommended for use by the foodservice industry, although it has been used in other industries since the 1960s. An HACCP process was developed in 1971 by the Pillsbury Company for the National Aeronautics and Space Administration (NASA) to ensure that food served to the astronauts in outerspace would be absolutely safe.

The original HACCP model was modified by Bobeng and David to include nutritive and sensory quality. A critical control point (CCP) is an operational procedure whereby proper prevention or control measures will eliminate or minimize hazards. Four CCPs in the production of entrées in conventional, cook/chill, and cook/freeze hospital foodservice systems were identified. These are ingredient control and storage, equipment sanitation, personnel sanitation, and time-temperature relationships.

HACCP is a systematic process that ensures food safety through the identification and control of any point or procedure in a specific food system in which loss of control may result in an unacceptable health risk. This process is used to monitor food preparation. The goal is to identify errors in preparation and correct them before they affect the product rather than wait for error detection in the end-product.

To identify CCPs, the food manager must first have a clear understanding of the flow of food through his or her operation. The flow of food begins with the placement of the food item on the menu and proceeds through the following stages: purchasing and receiving, storage, prepreparation, preparation, holding or display, and service. If leftovers are saved for future service the process includes additional stages of cooling, storage, and reheating.

Each of these stages carries risk for contamination. The chance that conditions will lead to contamination is referred to as *risk*. A *hazard* is defined as an unacceptable contamination, microbial growth, or survival of microorganisms or toxins that may pose a health risk. Once risks are identified, the foodservice manager can proceed by identifying CCPs in the food preparation process.

It is the responsibility of management to provide for inspection of food at the CCPs. Management must establish quality standards for the finished product and then monitor its production at critical points during procurement, storage, preparation, heating, holding (hot, chilled, or frozen), thawing when necessary, portioning, distribution, and service.

The complexity of the HACCP process depends on the scope and complexity of the foodservice operation. For example, a small foodservice operation using a nonselective menu may be able to design and implement a simple HACCP model. However, it may be impractical for a large foodservice with a wide scope of services and selective menus to implement a comprehensive HACCP process all at once. In this situation, it may be best for the operation to start planning the HACCP system by focusing on the menu items that are prepared using any one of the potentially hazardous foods as defined in Chapter 7.

It is important for the foodservice manager to recognize that the HACCP concept is new to the foodservice industry. The reader, as well, is encouraged to seek additional information on this timely topic. Several resources are included at the end of the chapter that further describe the HACCP process and offer specific guidelines on implementation procedures (FDA, 1991; NRA, 1992; NSFI, 1992).

Product Evaluation

One useful tool for quality control is product evaluation. Products generally are evaluated when a new product or recipe is being tested, but product evaluation should be a continuing process to make certain that the original high quality is maintained. Responsibility for this important part of quality control should be assigned to a person or a committee, but staff, employees, and consumers often participate. Many large foodservices and most commissaries have facilities for product development and laboratories for product evaluation.

Subjective or **sensory** methods are used most often to evaluate menu items or new products for such qualities as flavor, odor, texture, tenderness, and color. Foods are evaluated by a panel, composed of several persons who are knowledgeable about product standards and who have been trained to judge quality characteristics and differences among food items. The evaluations should be made in an area that is quiet and free from distractions, well-lighted, and ventilated. Each panel member should, if possible, be provided with an individual booth or table. Samples to be tested are coded, and a score card, such as that illustrated in Fig. 5.4, is provided.

Standardized Recipes

An important tool for production control is the standardized recipe sometimes referred to as a *recipe formulation.* It enables the manager to predict quality, quantity, and portion cost of the finished product, and it simplifies purchasing. Use of standardized recipes is helpful in training new or substitute production employees and makes management less dependent on the whims of and changes in personnel. Accuracy in the use of standardized recipes and in weighing and measuring ingredients takes the guesswork out of quantity food production. Clientele expect to and should be able to depend on having a food item be the same each time it is selected.

Standardized recipes are required if ingredients are assembled in a central area and are essential in a computer-assisted production system because the recipe is the starting point for many procedures. Each recipe and each ingredient has an identification number that is essential for purchasing, inventory, and cost records. Production scheduling is simplified if recipes include all essential information needed to produce the menu item.

The standardized recipes must be **used** by the employees, too, if the system is to be effective. For example, if the daily cost report is calculated on the basis of standardized recipes provided by the production personnel, but employees change the amounts and ingredients, there will be a discrepancy in figures that will not give a true financial picture.

Format   A suitable recipe form or format that provides all information needed for production of the menu item should be selected. An orderly arrangement of this information should be developed and the same general pattern followed for all recipes in the file. Each foodservice should decide on the format best suited to its operation and use this form consistently.

In most recipes, the ingredients are listed in the order in which they are used. A block arrangement, in which ingredients that are to be combined are grouped together, is helpful, and separating these groups with space or lines above or below them makes following recipes easier and faster. Listing the procedures directly across from the ingredients involved simplifies preparation and enables clear

Score Card for Cake

Date _____

Factor	Qualities	Standard	Sample No. 1	2	3	Comments
I. External appearance	Shape, symmetrical, slightly rounded top, free from cracks or peaks	10				
	Volume, light in weight in proportion to size	10				
	Crust, smooth uniform golden brown	10				
II. Internal appearance	Texture, tender, slightly moist, velvety feel to tongue and finger	10				
	Grain, fine, round, evenly distributed cells with thin cell walls, free from tunnels	10				
	Color, crumb even and rich looking	10				
III. Flavor	Delicate, well-blended flavor of ingredients. Free from unpleasant odors or taste	10				

Directions for use of score card for plain cake:

Standard	10	No detectable fault, highest possible score
Excellent	8–9	Of unusual excellence but not perfect
Good	6–7	Average good quality
Fair	4–5	Below average, slightly objectionable
Poor	2–3	Objectionable, but edible
Bad	0–1	Highly objectionable, inedible

Signature of evaluator

Figure 5.4. Suggested score card for evaluating cakes or muffins.

directions to be written in a minimum number of words. Fig. 5.5 illustrates this suggested format. Some recipe writers like to number the steps in the procedure.

Certain information is essential, regardless of the form in which the recipe is written. Following are suggestions for material that should be included.

PASTA WITH VEGETABLE SAUCE

Yield: 50 portions or 2½ gal sauce   *Portion:* 6 oz sauce + 4 oz pasta

Ingredient	Amount	Procedure
Onions, chopped	2 lb	Sauté onion in oil until tender, using a steam-jacketed or other large kettle.
Olive oil	1 cup	
Oregano, dried, crumbled	¼ cup	Add spices to onion. Mix well.
Basil, dried, crumbled	½ oz (½ cup)	
Pepper, black	1 Tbsp	
Garlic powder	1 Tbsp	
Salt	1 oz (1½ Tbsp)	
Bay leaves	2	
Tomato juice	5 46-oz cans	Add tomato juice and paste to spices and onion. Heat to boiling. Reduce heat and simmer uncovered for 15–20 minutes. Remove bay leaves.
Tomato paste	1 lb 12 oz	
Zucchini, sliced	2 lb 8 oz	Add zucchini and mushrooms just before serving. Cook only until zucchini is tender.
Mushrooms, sliced	1 lb 8 oz	
Pasta	5 lb	Cook pasta according to directions. Serve 6 oz sauce over 4 oz pasta.
Water, boiling	5 gal	
Salt	5 oz	
Vegetable oil (optional)	3 Tbsp	

Approximate nutritive values per portion

Calories (kcal)	Protein (grams)	Carbohydrate (grams)	Fat (grams)	Cholesterol (mg)	Sodium (mg)	Iron (mg)	Calcium (mg)
265	8.2 (12%)	46.8 (69%)	5.7 (19%)	0	1023	3.4	47

Notes
- 2 cups finely chopped fresh basil may be substituted for dried basil.
- 4 oz (2 cups) dehydrated onions, rehydrated in 3 cups water, may be substituted for fresh onions.

Variations
- **Italian Sausage Pasta.** Delete olive oil, salt, and zucchini. Brown 5 lb bulk Italian sausage in steam-jacketed kettle. Drain. Add onions to sausage and continue to cook until onions are tender. Add spices, tomato juice, and tomato paste. Simmer for 15–20 minutes. Add meat sauce to 6 lb 8 oz cooked pasta (approximately 3 lb AP) and mix gently. Be careful not to overcook pasta. Scale 12 lb per 12 x 20 x 2 inch pan. Sprinkle 1 lb shredded mozzarella cheese over each pan and place in low oven until cheese is melted. Suggested pasta combination: 1 lb (AP) rotini, 1 lb (AP) bow ties, 1 lb (AP) rigatoni.
- **Pizza Sauce.** Reduce olive oil to 4 oz. Delete zucchini and mushrooms. Increase tomato paste to 5 lb 8 oz and decrease tomato juice to 5¼ qt. Add 1 tsp fennel seed, 2 Tbsp sugar, 1 tsp paprika, and ¼ tsp cayenne. Spread 1 qt sauce on top of 18 x 26-inch pizza dough before adding toppings.
- **Sandwich Tomato Sauce.** Delete salt, zucchini, and mushrooms. Add 1 Tbsp sugar. Reduce olive oil to 1 Tbsp, onions to ½ cup, oregano to 1 tsp, basil to 1 Tbsp, pepper to ½ tsp, garlic powder to ½ tsp, bay leaf to 1, tomato juice to 1¼ qt, and tomato paste to 1½ cups. Yield: 50 1-oz servings.

Figure 5.5. Recipe format showing block arrangement. Nutritive value, notes, and variations are given at the end of the recipe. Reprinted with the permission of Macmillan Publishing Company from FOOD FOR FIFTY, Ninth Edition by Grace Shugart and Mary Molt. Copyright © 1993 by Macmillan Publishing Company.

Recipe Title.   The title should be printed in large type and either centered on the page or placed on the left or right side at the top of the page as shown in Fig. 5.5. The recipe identification code for ease in filing is also placed here.

Yield and Portion Size.   The total yield may be given in measure, weight, number of pans, or number of portions. The portion size may be in weight, measure, or count.

Baking Time and Temperature.   This information is listed at the top of the page so the preheating of the oven and the scheduling of baking can be determined without reading the entire recipe. Some recipe writers repeat the baking time and temperature in the instructions so the cooks can see them while working with the ingredients.

Ingredients and Quantities.   The amounts of ingredients may be listed first followed by the names of ingredients, as in Fig. 5.5, or the ingredients may be given first with the quantities arranged in one or more columns to accommodate different yields (Fig. 5.6) For the sake of accuracy, however, there should not be more than three ingredient amount columns on one card. Too many columns increase the chances of error in reading amounts and crowd the space needed to give complete directions for preparation.

Names of ingredients should be consistent. Descriptive terms are used to define clearly the kind and form of each ingredient. In some recipes, the term *before* the name of the ingredient designates the form as purchased or that the ingredient has been cooked or heated before using in the product. Examples are *canned* tomatoes, *frozen chopped* broccoli, *hot* milk, *boiling* water, and *cooked* turkey. The descriptive term is placed *after* the ingredient to indicate processing after the ingredient is weighed or measured—onions, *chopped;* eggs, *beaten;* or raw potato, *grated.* It is important in some recipes to designate AP (as purchased) or EP (edible portion). For example, 15 pounds (AP) of fresh broccoli would be 10 pounds (EP) or less. Whatever system is used, it should be consistent and understood by those using the recipes. Abbreviations should be consistent and easily understood, as qt for quart or lb for pound.

Procedures.   Directions for preparation of the product should be divided into logical steps and are most effective when placed directly across from the ingredients involved. Procedures should be clear and concise so that employees can easily read and understand them. It is helpful if basic procedures are uniform in all recipes for similar products. For example, white sauce is basic to many other sauces and is an ingredient in many menu items. The procedures on the recipe should be worded the same in each recipe. Likewise, there are several basic procedures in baked products, such as those of creaming fat and sugar or of combining dry and liquid ingredients, that should be the same on all recipes using them.

Timing should be given for procedures in which mixers, steamers, or other mechanical equipment is used. For example, "cream shortening and sugar on medium speed for 10 minutes," or "cook on low heat until rice is tender and all water is absorbed, about 15 to 20 minutes."

Applesauce Cake

Desserts No. Ck-3
Portion: 2 x 2¾ in.
Cut 6 x 8

Oven temperature: 350 °F
Time: 30–35 minutes

Ingredients	2 pans	3 pans	Procedure
Shortening	1 lb 7 oz	2 lb 3 oz	Cream 5 min. on
Sugar	2 lb 14 oz	4 lb 5 oz	medium speed, with paddle.
Eggs	2 cups	3 cups	Add and beat 5 min. on medium speed.
Applesauce	2 qt +½ c	3¼ qt	Add gradually on low speed. Beat 1 min. on medium speed after last addition. Scrape down.
Cake flour	2 lb 14 oz	4 lb 5 oz	Sift dry ingredients
Salt	4 tsp	2 Tbsp	together and mix
Soda	1 oz	1½ oz	with raisins.
Cinnamon	1 Tbsp	4½ tsp	Add to creamed
Nutmeg	1½ tsp	2¼ tsp	mixture gradually
Cloves	1½ tsp	2½ tsp	on low speed.
Raisins	12 oz	1 lb 2 oz	Beat 2 min., medium speed, after last addition. Scrape down once.
Total wt	13 lb 6 oz	20 lb 2 oz	Weigh into greased baking pans, 12 x 22 x 2 in., 6 lb 8 oz / pan.

Figure 5.6. Recipe format with columns for two quantities. Total weight of batter is helpful in adjusting recipes. Preparation steps may be numbered, if space permits.

Panning instructions should include the weight per pan to help in dividing the product equally into the required number of pans. For example: "Scale batter into two prepared 12 × 18 × 2-inch baking pans, 4 lb 10 oz per pan." When layering ingredients in baking pans for a casserole-type entrée, it is helpful if the weight or measure of each layer is given. For example: "Place dressing, sauce, and chicken in two 12 × 20 × 2-inch counter pans, layered in each pan as follows: 4 lb 8 oz dressing, 1½ qt sauce, 3 lb chicken, 1¼ qt sauce."

The size dipper to use in portioning meatballs and similar foods ensures uniform portions. Instructions for serving are needed in many recipes, too. Such directions are especially important in baked products that are cut into portions or when a ladle is used for serving soups, sauces, or puddings.

Additional information not essential to the recipe but that may be helpful in substituting ingredients, alternate methods of preparation, or comments about the appearance of the product, such as "These cookies puff up at first, then flatten out with crinkled tops," can be added as footnotes. Variations of a basic recipe usually are included at the end of the recipe, and may include tips on how to plate or garnish the product.

The size and form of the recipe card or sheet, the format to be followed, and the manner of filing the recipes are optional. Cards 4″ × 6″ and 5″ × 8″ are popular sizes, and heavy typing paper, 8½″ × 11″, is used in some operations. In deciding on a size and format, keep in mind that the recipes will be used by cooks and other employees who will be busy weighing and mixing ingredients and may not be able to read a small crowded card easily. Recipes should be typed or printed and should be readable at a distance of 18 to 20 inches. Recipes that are used in the production or ingredient assembly areas should be placed in clear plastic covers to keep the copy clean.

In foodservices using a computer-assisted system, recipes are printed as needed and for the quantities required for the day's production. Since the printout is generated each time the recipe is used, it is considered a working copy and does not need a protective covering. An example of a computer-generated recipe is shown in Fig. 5.7. The format for recipes in this type of system depends on the software purchased, so the format should be considered when comparing different software packages.

RECIPE FILES   A master file of all recipes used by the foodservice should be maintained, with at least two complete sets available, one to be kept on permanent file in the office of the dietitian or foodservice manager and the other to be available for production employees. Additional sets may be needed by other key personnel.

A system of classification and filing enables recipes to be located easily. Recipes can be coded by number or filed alphabetically under appropriate headings, such as appetizers, beverages, breads, desserts, eggs and cheese, fish, meat, pasta, poultry, salads, sandwiches, sauces, soups, and vegetables.

STANDARDIZING RECIPES   A recipe is considered **standardized** only when it has been tried and adapted for use by a given foodservice operation. **Tested** quantity recipes are available from many sources, such as cookbooks, trade journals, materials distributed by commercial food companies from their own experimental kitchens, and from other foodservice managers. Regardless of the

Figure 5.7. Example of computer-generated recipe. (Courtesy, Kansas State University Residence Halls.)

CHILI CON CARNE

RECIPE CODE — 14-01-0-023-7   STATUS — STANDARDIZED   1

EQUIPMENT-STEAM KETTLE
COUNTER PANS-LIDS

RECIPE SOURCE-

04/16/86 10.20 AM   751124

*** NUMBER OF PORTIONS	68	
PORTION SIZE / COST	.560 LBS. / $0.3044	
MEAL PATTERN ALLOWANCE		
SUGGESTED SERVING UTENSIL	1 PORTION	6 OZ LADLE
PAN SIZE	10X12X6	
NUMBER OF PANS		
WEIGHT PER PAN	LBS.	
HANDLING LOSS	6.00 PERCENT	
MINIMUM BATCH		
MAXIMUM BATCH		
FORECAST UNIT		
*TOTAL RECIPE WEIGHT / COST	40.5 LBS. / $20.6992	
TOTAL RECIPE VOLUME		

CODE	PERCENT	INGREDIENT	WEIGHTS AND MEASURES	AP/EP	STEP	PROCEDURE
0012113719	22.49	GROUND BEEF CHILI BULK	9.1 LBS	EP	A	1. COOK MEAT IN KETTLE UNTIL
			13.6 LBS	AP		IT LOSES ITS COLOR. STIR
						OFTEN TO PREVENT LUMPS
						FROM FORMING. DRAIN OFF FAT.
0052001211	1.68	ONIONS CHOPPED FRESH	0.68 LBS		B	2. COMBINE WITH MEAT.
0082000826	0.02	GARLIC MINCED FRESH	1.0 TSP			
0082054100	0.34	SALT	0.14 LBS			
0082060401	0.57	CHILI POWDER	0.23 LBS			
0082093008	0.34	SUGAR GRANULATED	0.14 LBS			
0082060801	0.08	CUMIN GROUND	0.03 LBS			
0082063109	0.02	PEPPER BLACK GROUND	1.8 TSP			
0072011602	17.12	TOMATOES DICED CND	6.9 LBS		C	3. ADD TO MEAT MIXTURE.
0072011751	15.40	TOMATO PUREE CND	6.2 LBS			4. SIMMER 1 HOUR OR MORE. STIR
0072010363	33.90	BEANS RED CND	13.7 LBS			FREQUENTLY.
0000000001	8.05	WATER	3.3 LBS			5. TAKE UP IN SOUP PANS. COVER.

153

source, each recipe should be tested and evaluated, then standardized for use in a particular situation.

The first step in standardizing a new recipe is to analyze the proportion of ingredients and clarity of instructions, and to determine whether the recipe can be produced with the equipment and personnel available. The recipe should then be tested, being sure ingredients are weighed and measured accurately and that procedures are followed exactly. The yield, number, and size of portions as well as problems with preparation should be recorded, and the finished product should be evaluated for acceptability. A suggested evaluation form is shown in Fig. 5.8. If the product is judged suitable for use, the recipe is then adjusted to the quantities needed and tested again. If other changes are needed, they are made and the recipe retested, but only one change should be made at a time. When the testing is completed, the recipe is ready to be set up in finished form for the permanent file. Some foodservice managers use cards of one color for recipes during testing and standardizing and a different color for the final completed copy.

Recipe standardization need not be used entirely for new recipes. There may be recipes in the file that produce food of satisfactory quality but that yield more or less food than is needed. The product may lack proper seasoning or the consistency may need improvement. In some cases, an ingredient change is made that necessitates some adjustment in the recipe; for example, catsup may be substituted for tomato puree or cream of mushroom soup for white sauce and mushrooms. The manager may wish to implement a program for standardizing these recipes by testing each time the item is on the menu until the recipe is satisfactory.

ADJUSTING RECIPES   Three methods commonly used to adjust recipes are the factor method, the percentage method, and direct-reading measurement tables.

Factor Method: In the factor method, the quantities of ingredients in the original recipe are multiplied by a conversion factor, as explained in the following steps.

1. Convert all volume measurements to weights, when possible. For example, 3 cups of water would weigh 1 pound 8 ounces. For ease in figuring, weights should be expressed in pounds and decimal components of pounds; 1 pound 8 ounces would be 1.5 pounds. Add together the weights of all ingredients.

2. Divide the desired yield by the known yield of the original recipe to obtain the conversion factor. For example, if you have a recipe for pie crust for 12 two-crust pies that you wish to change to 66 two-crust pies, as shown in Table 5.2, divide the desired yield (66) by the known yield (11) to obtain the factor of 5.5.

3. Multiply the amount of each ingredient in the original recipe by the factor, which in the example would be 5.5.

Recipe Evaluation Card

Please Return This Card to the Test Kitchen as Promptly as Possible.

Product _____   Residence Hall _____
                                     Date _____

Quantity prepared _____
Did you obtain yield as stated in recipe? _____
If not, what quantity was obtained? _____
Do you consider size of portion adequate? _____
If not, what change would you suggest? _____
_____

Was product generally well accepted? _____
_____

Further comments on recipe—for example—ease of using recipe; problems encountered; suggestions for changes in procedure, kind and/or amount of ingredients, etc.:
   (Consult cooks for suggestions) _____
_____
_____
_____
_____
_____

                                        _____
                                                 Reporting Supervisor

---

Figure 5.8.   Recipe evaluation card. (Courtesy, Central Food Stores, University of
Illinois.)

4. A check on the accuracy of the figures can be made by multiplying the total
   weight of ingredients in the original recipe by the factor and comparing with
   the total weight of ingredients in the new recipe. If the two are not the same,
   check the calculations before preparing the product.

5. Change weights back to pounds and ounces and convert to quarts, cups, or
   other volume measures for ingredients that are more easily measured than
   weighed.

6. Round off unnecessary or awkward fractions that would be difficult to
   measure or weigh as far as accuracy permits.

Percentage Method: In the percentage method, the percentage of the total
weight of the product is calculated for each ingredient, and once this percentage has been established, it remains constant for all future adjustments. Recipe

TABLE 5.2.   Pastry—Adjusting Yield *from* 12 2-Crust Pies *to* 66 2-Crust Pies.

Ingredients	Original Recipe 12 2-Crust Pies	Step 1 Original Recipe in Weight	Step 2 Original Recipe in Ounces	Step 4 Each Amount in Step 2 Multiplied by Factor	New Recipe in Weight	Step 5 New Recipe Rounded Weight and Measure
Pastry flour	5 lb	5 lb	80	440.0	27 lb 8 oz	27 lb 8 oz
Salt	1¼ oz	1¼ oz	1¼	6.9	6.9 oz	7 oz
Shortening	3 lb	3 lb	48	264.0	16 lb 8 oz	16 lb 8 oz
Water	3 c	1 lb 8 oz	24	132.0	8 lb 4 oz	1 gal ½ c
Total weight		9 lb 9¼ oz	153¼	842.9	52 lb 9 oz	52 lb 11 oz

Step 3: Conversion Factor

$$\frac{66 \text{ (new)}}{12 \text{ (original)}} = \frac{11}{2} = 5\tfrac{1}{2} = 5.5$$

Essential information needed:

Water: 1 c = 8 oz
          4 c = 1 qt   = 2 lb
          4 qt = 1 gal = 8 lb

          1 lb = 16 oz

Total Weight in Step 2 × Factor
153¼ oz × 5.5 =
     153.25 × 5.5 = 842.875 = 842.9 oz

SOURCE: Procedure for Adjusting Recipe Yield, Department of Institution Administration, Michigan State University.

increases and decreases are made by multiplying the total weight desired by the percentage of each ingredient.

The percentage method is based on weights expressed in pounds and decimal parts of a pound. The total quantity to be prepared is based on the weight of each portion multiplied by the number of servings needed. The constant number used in calculating a recipe is the weight of each individual serving. Following is a step-by-step procedure, as used at Kansas State University and reported by McManis and Molt (NACUFS J. 35, 1978), for adjusting a recipe by the percentage method.

Step 1.   Convert all ingredients in the original recipe from measure or pounds and ounces to pounds and tenths of a pound. Make desired equivalent ingredient substitutions, such as frozen whole eggs for fresh eggs and powdered milk for liquid milk.

Step 2.   Total the weight of ingredients in the recipe. Use edible portion (EP) weights when a difference exists between EP and as purchased (AP) weights. For example, the weight of onions or celery should be the weight after the foods have been cleaned, peeled, and are ready for use. The recipe may show both AP and EP weights, but the edible portion is used in determining the total weight.

Step 3.   Calculate the percentage of each ingredient in relation to the total weight. Repeat for each ingredient.

Formula:

$$\frac{\text{Individual ingredient weight}}{\text{Total weight of ingredients}} = \text{percentage of each ingredient}$$

Sum of percentages should total 100%.

Step 4. Check the ratio of ingredients, which should be in proper balance before going further. Standards have been established for ingredient proportions of many items.

Step 5. Determine the total weight of the product needed by multiplying the portion weight expressed in decimal parts of a pound by the number of servings to be prepared. To convert a portion weight to a decimal part of a pound, divide the number of ounces by 16 or refer to a decimal equivalent table (Table 5.3). For example, a 2-ounce portion would be 0.125 pound. This figure multiplied by the number of portions desired gives the total weight of product needed. The weight is then adjusted, as necessary, to pan size and equipment capacity. For example, the total weight must be divisible by the optimum weight for each pan. The capacity of mixing bowls, steam-jacketed kettles, and other equipment must be considered in determining the total weight. Use the established portions, modular pan charts, or known capacity equipment guides to determine batch sizes to be written.

Step 6. Add estimated handling loss to the weight needed. An example of handling loss is the batter left in bowls or on equipment. This loss will vary according to the product being made and preparation techniques of the worker. Similar recipes, however, produce predictable losses, which with some experimentation can be accurately assigned. The formula for adding handling loss to a recipe follows.

$$(100\% - \text{Assigned Handling Loss }\%)\ X = \text{Desired Yield}$$
$$X = \frac{\text{Desired Yield}}{100\% - \text{Handling Loss }\%}$$

Example: Butter cake has a 1% handling loss. Desired yield is 80 lbs (or 600 servings).

$$(100\% - 1\%)X = 80 \text{ lbs}$$
$$.99\ X = 80$$
$$X = 80/.99$$
$$X = 80.80 \text{ total lbs of ingredients to}$$
produce 80 lbs of batter

Step 7. Multiply each percentage number by the total weight to give the exact amount of each ingredient needed. Once the percentages of a recipe have been established, any number of servings can be calculated and the ratio of ingredients to the total will be the same. One decimal place on a recipe is shown (e.g., 8.3 lbs) unless it is less than one pound, then two places are shown (e.g., 0.15 lb).

TABLE 5.3.   Ounces and Decimal Equivalents of a Pound.

Ounces	Decimal Part of a Pound	Ounces	Decimal Part of a Pound
¼	0.016	8¼	0.516
½	0.031	8½	0.531
¾	0.047	8¾	0.547
1	0.063	9	0.563
1¼	0.078	9¼	0.578
1½	0.094	9½	0.594
1¾	0.109	9¾	0.609
2	0.125	10	0.625
2¼	0.141	10¼	0.641
2½	0.156	10½	0.656
2¾	0.172	10¾	0.672
3	0.188	11	0.688
3¼	0.203	11¼	0.703
3½	0.219	11½	0.719
3¾	0.234	11¾	0.734
4	0.250	12	0.750
4¼	0.266	12¼	0.766
4½	0.281	12½	0.781
4¾	0.297	12¾	0.797
5	0.313	13	0.813
5¼	0.328	13¼	0.828
5½	0.344	13½	0.844
5¾	0.359	13¾	0.859
6	0.375	14	0.875
6¼	0.391	14¼	0.891
6½	0.406	14½	0.906
6¾	0.422	14¾	0.922
7	0.438	15	0.938
7¼	0.453	15¼	0.953
7½	0.469	15½	0.969
7¾	0.484	15¾	0.984
8	0.500	16	1.000

NOTE: This table is useful when increasing or decreasing recipes. The multiplication or division of pounds and ounces is simplified if the ounces are converted to decimal parts of a pound. For example, when multiplying 1 lb 9 oz by 3, first change the 9 oz to 0.563, by using the table. Thus, the 1 lb 9 oz becomes 1.563 lbs, which multiplied by 3 is 4.683 lbs or 4 lbs 11 oz.

Tables 5.4 to 5.6 illustrate the expansion of a recipe for muffins from 60 to 340 servings.

Direct Reading Measurement Tables: The use of tables showing ingredient amounts for different numbers of portions saves time and simplifies recipe adjustment. Conversion charts have been developed that give amounts in weight

TABLE 5.4.   Original Recipe for Muffins. *Yield: 60 muffins*

Ingredients	Amount
Flour, all-purpose	2 lbs 8 oz
Baking powder	2 oz
Salt	1 Tbsp
Sugar	6 oz
Eggs, beaten	4
Milk	1½ qt
Shortening	8 oz

and measure in increments of 25 for 25 to 500 portions. Measurement tables are included in *Quantity Food Preparation: Standardizing Recipes and Controlling Ingredients* by Buchanan, and *Food for Fifty* by Shugart and Molt.

ADAPTING HOME-SIZE RECIPES   Many quantity recipes can be successfully expanded from home-size recipes, but their development involves a number of carefully planned steps. Before attempting to enlarge a small recipe, be sure that it is appropriate to the foodservice and that the same quality can be achieved when prepared in large quantity and possibly held for a time before serving. Procedures should be checked because many home recipes are lacking in detailed directions for their preparation. Before preparing the product, the extent of mixing, time, and temperature used in cooking or baking, and special precautions that should be observed and any other details that may have been omitted should be known.

Enlarging the recipe in steps is more likely to be successful than increasing from a small quantity to a large quantity without the intermediate steps.

TABLE 5.5.   Percentage Calculated on Original Recipe. *Yield: 60 muffins*

Percentage	Ingredients	Measure	Pounds
35.79	Flour	2 lbs 8 oz	2.500
1.79	Baking powder	2 oz	0.125
0.67	Salt	1 T	0.047
5.37	Sugar	6 oz	0.375
6.27	Eggs	4	0.438
42.95	Milk	1½ qt	3.000
7.16	Shortening	8 oz	0.500
100.00	Total		6.985

6.985 lbs divided by 60 = .116 lb per muffin

Following are suggestions for a step-by-step approach for expanding home-size recipes.

Step 1. Prepare the product in the amount of the original recipe, following exactly the quantities and procedures, noting any procedures that are unclear or any problems with the preparation.

Step 2. Evaluate the product, using a written form such as shown in Fig. 5.8, and decide if it has the potential for the foodservice. If adjustments are necessary, revise the recipe and make the product again. Work with the original amount until the product is satisfactory.

Step 3. Double the recipe or expand to appropriate amount for the pan size that will be used and prepare the product, making notations on the recipe of any changes you make. For example, additional cooking time may be needed for the larger amount. Evaluate the product and record the yield, portion size, and acceptability.

Step 4. Double the recipe again, or if the product is to be baked, calculate the quantities needed to prepare one baking pan that will be used by the foodservice. If ingredients are to be weighed, home-size measures should be converted to pounds and ounces or to pounds and tenths of a pound before proceeding further. Prepare and evaluate the product as before.

Step 5. If the product is satisfactory, continue to enlarge by increments of 25 portions or by pans. When the recipe has been expanded to 100 or a specific amount that would be used in the foodservice, adjustments should be made for handling or cooking losses. Handling loss refers to losses that occur in making and panning batters. About 3% to 5% more batter, sauces, and puddings are required to compensate for the

TABLE 5.6.   Expanded Recipe for Muffins. *Yield: 340 muffins*

Percentage	Ingredients	Pounds
35.79	Flour	14.26
1.79	Baking powder	0.713
0.67	Salt	0.267
5.37	Sugar	2.14
6.27	Eggs	2.50
42.95	Milk	17.11
7.16	Shortening	2.85
100.00	Total	39.84

.116 lb per muffin × 340 = 39.44 lbs with 1% handling loss, 39.84 lbs batter needed 39.84 lbs × % each ingredient = weight of ingredient

If using pounds and ounces, change decimal parts of pounds to ounces by using Table 5.3. If using measures for some ingredients, adjust to measurable amounts.

handling loss. Cooking losses result from evaporation of water from the food during cooking. Soups, stews, and casseroles can lose from 10% to 30% of their water during cooking. The actual yield of the recipe should be checked carefully. Mixing, preparation, and cooking times should be noted because these may increase when the product is prepared in large quantity. Preparation methods should be checked to see if they are consistent with methods used for similar products. An evaluation of the product should be made and its acceptance by the clientele determined before it becomes a part of the permanent recipe file.

Ingredient Assembly

Central assembly of ingredients for food production has been found to be cost-effective in many operations. In this system, the ingredients needed for recipes for the day's production and for advance preparation are weighed, measured, and assembled in a central ingredient room or area. If prepreparation equipment and low temperature storage are available, certain other procedures, such as peeling, dicing, and chopping of vegetables; breading and panning of meats; opening of canned goods; and thawing of frozen foods, can be completed in the ingredient room. The extent of responsibilities depends on the space, equipment, and personnel available.

After ingredients have been weighed or measured and the prepreparation completed, each ingredient is packaged in a plastic bag or other container and labeled. The ingredients for each recipe are assembled and delivered, with a copy of the recipe, to the appropriate production unit. In some operations, the assembled ingredients are distributed when needed according to a predetermined schedule.

There are many advantages to an ingredient room, the term used most often for this production facility. Increased production control, improved security, more consistent quality control, and more efficient use of equipment, especially if prepreparation is included in this area, are possible with central ingredient assembly. Since cooks are not involved in the time-consuming job of weighing and measuring ingredients, their time and skills can be more effectively used in production.

There are some disadvantages, the main one being the lack of flexibility. For example, the ingredients must be weighed the day before, or earlier in some cases, which does not provide for last-minute changes in menus or quantities needed. Cooks may feel restricted by not being able to add their own touches to the food they are preparing. This attitude usually changes when they are satisfied that the recipes as written will result in a product of the desired quality and once the cooks have confidence in the person who weighs the ingredients.

PERSONNEL AND EQUIPMENT   Accuracy in measuring ingredients contributes to the acceptability of the finished product, so it is important that the ingredient room personnel be well-qualified and that they be provided with adequate equipment.

Personnel assigned to the ingredient room must be able to read and write and perform simple arithmetic with at least minimal ease and accuracy. These traits, as well as honesty and dependability, are desirable for this person or persons to have. Safety precautions and sanitation standards should be stressed in their training.

Weighing is the quickest, easiest, and most accurate means of measure in most cases, so good scales are essential. A scale that accurately weighs up to 25 pounds is usually adequate and, if more than that is required, the ingredients are divided in two or three lots for easier handling. Some foodservices have separate scales for very small amounts such as spices. If scales that accurately weigh small amounts are not available, volume measurement may be preferable for those foods. Scales that are calibrated to pounds and tenths of a pound instead of pounds and ounces are useful with a system that uses a computer for calculating recipes.

The equipment needed depends on the functions performed in this area. Suggested minimum equipment for weighing and measuring includes

- Worktable, 6 to 8 feet long, with one or two drawers
- Counter scales, with gradations of 1 ounce minimum to 25 pounds
- Mobile storage bins for sugar, flour, and other large volume staples
- Shelving for bulk staples and spices
- Mobile racks for delivery of foods to production areas
- Refrigeration (and freezer if frozen foods are distributed)
- Sink and water supply
- Can opener
- Trash containers
- Counter pans with lids if canned foods are opened
- Trays for assembling ingredients
- Rubber spatulas
- Measuring utensils (gallon, quart, pint, cup measures; measuring spoons)
- Scoops for dipping flour and sugar
- Packaging materials (paper and plastic bags, paper cups)
- Masking tape and marking pens to label ingredients

If vegetable preparation is part of the ingredient room responsibilities, the following additional equipment is needed:

- Double or triple sink
- Waste disposal

- Peeling, slicing, and/or dicing equipment
- Cutting board
- Assorted knives and sharpening equipment
- Plastic tubs or bags for cleaned products

Portion Control

An early step in recipe standardization is making a decision on the size of portions to be offered. Standardized portions are important not only in the control of costs, but also in creating and maintaining consumer satisfaction and good will. No one likes to receive a smaller serving than other customers for the same price.

Food is portioned by weight, measure, or count and really begins with the purchase of foods according to definite specifications so that known yields can be obtained from each food. Portioned meats, fish, and poultry; fresh fruits ordered by size (count per shipping box); canned peaches, pears, pineapple slices, and other foods in which the number of pieces is specified are examples. Also helpful in portion control is the purchase of individual butter and margarine pats and individually packaged crackers, cereals, and condiments.

During food production, portions are measured by scoop or dipper or are weighed on portion scales. For example, the recipe for meatballs may call for dipping the mixture with a size 16 dipper (or scoop), which means ¼ cup or 2 ounces. The numbering system for scoop sizes is based on the number of scoops per quart. Table 5.7 shows approximate dipper and ladle sizes. Dippers range from size 6 (10 tablespoons/6 ounces) to size 100, which holds a scant 2 teaspoons. Muffins are also measured by dippers, but bread and roll doughs are weighed. A roll cutter provides equal portions without the necessity of weighing each roll. Each recipe should indicate the yield expected in number of portions, total weight or measure, and the size in weight or measure of each serving.

The appropriate utensil and its size for serving the product should be indicated. Ladles, which are used for serving sauces, soups, and similar foods, are sized according to capacity (1 ounce/⅛ cup to 8 ounces/1 cup). Although spoons are used for serving some foods, they are not as accurate as ladles unless the employees have been instructed in their use and know how full to make the spoon. For cakes and other desserts baked in a pan, instructions for cutting should be included. Many foodservices have pie markers or other marking devices to ensure equal portions of baked products.

Employees should know the number of servings expected from a certain batch size and should be familiar with the size of the portion. In addition to the information included on recipes, a list of portion sizes for all foods should be made available to employees either in an employees' manual or posted in a convenient location (see Fig. 5.9 on page 165).

TABLE 5.7. Dipper (or Scoop) Equivalents.

Dipper No.*	Approximate Measure	Approximate Weight	Suggested Use
6	10 T (⅔ c)	6 oz	Entrée salads
8	8 T (½ c)	4–5 oz	Entrées
10	6 T (⅜ c)	3–4 oz	Desserts
12	5 T (⅓ c)	2½–3 oz	Muffins, salads, desserts
16	4 T (¼ c)	2–2¼ oz	Muffins, desserts
20	3⅕ T	1¾–2 oz	Sandwich fillings, muffins, cup cakes
24	2⅔ T	1½–1¾ oz	Cream puffs
30	2⅕ T	1–1½ oz	Large drop cookies
40	1½ T	¾ oz	Drop cookies
60	1 T	½ oz	Small drop cookies, garnishes
Ladles	⅛ c	1 oz	Sauces, salad dressings
	¼ c	2 oz	Gravies, sauces
	½ c	4 oz	Stews, creamed foods
	⅔ c	6 oz	Stews, creamed foods
	1 c	8 oz	Soup

These measurements are based on level dippers and ladles.

*Portions per quart.

Guidelines for Food Production Employees

Efficient Work Habits

Efficient work habits and organization of the preparation area simplifies the job for employees and contributes to the attainment of high standards in food production. Observance of certain basic rules for foodservice workers also greatly aids in the promotion of efficient work habits.

- Check assignment to be sure that there is no question as to what is to be done or how it is to be accomplished.
- Plan work so that everything can be done within the time limit. Often, several preparation procedures can be carried on simultaneously, but those that are preliminary or require the longest time should be started first.
- Assemble any equipment or ingredients not at hand and arrange them conveniently for use before beginning work. If ingredients are weighed and measured in a central ingredient area, ingredients will not need to be assembled, but they should be checked with the recipe to be sure all items have been delivered.
- Prepare equipment (preheat oven, line baking sheets).

Portion Guide

Breakfast Items		
Bacon	2 strips	1 oz
Cereal, hot	1 portion	4-oz ladle
Eggs, scrambled	No. 8 dipper	4 oz
Fruit, canned, frozen, or dried	No. 12 dipper	2½ oz
Juices	1 glass	8 oz

Luncheon Entrees		
Bacon, lettuce, tomato sandwich	1 sandwich	2 slices bread, 2 slices tomato, 3 strips bacon, 1 lettuce leaf
Barbecued meat sandwich	No. 16 dipper	1½ oz on 4-in. bun
Casserole entree	1 portion	cut 24 per 12 x 20-in. pan or 4 oz ladle meat on No. 12 dipper of rice or pasta
Chili	1 dipper	6-oz ladle
Soup or chowder	1 dipper	4-oz ladle
Tacos	1 portion	2 shells, No. 12 dipper meat, 2 oz salad mixture

Dinner Entrees		
Beef roast	1 slice	2½ oz E.P.
Fried chicken	2 pieces	1 breast and 1 wing OR 1 thigh and 1 leg
Fish	1 portion	5 oz A.P.
Meat loaf	1 slice	cut 10 per 5 x 9-in. pan
Pork chops	1 chop	6 oz A.P.
Roast pork, dressing	1 portion	2 oz meat, No. 16 dipper dressing

Vegetables and Pasta		
Broccoli spears	3–4 spears	3 oz
French fries	1 portion	3 oz
Noodles or spaghetti	Tongs	2½ oz lunch; 4 oz dinner
Whipped potatoes	No. 12 dipper	3½ oz

Desserts		
Bar cookies	1 portion	18 x 26-in. pan cut 6 x 10
Cake, sheet	1 piece	cut 6 x 10, 18 x 26-in. pan
Ice cream	1 scoop	No. 12 dipper
Pies	1 piece	9-in. pies cut in 6

Figure 5.9.   Portion guide for use by production and service employees. This is a partial listing but includes portion sizes for some typical food.

- If prepreparation has not been done in another area, wash, trim, cut, prepare, and measure raw materials.
- Use proper equipment for the job. Employees should master the technique of using a French knife and should be aware of time-saving equipment available.
- Use power equipment whenever possible. Economy of effort and time can soon pay for additional conveniences.
- Arrange equipment and materials in the work area so that tasks can be accomplished in logical sequence with minimum movement of the worker. For example, for efficiency in breading chops, arrange pans containing the chops and dipping mixtures on the worktable from left to right.
- Use of smooth, continuous motions will keep fatigue to a minimum. Use both hands simultaneously whenever possible. Comfortable working heights and good lighting also reduce fatigue.
- Make each motion rhythmic. For example, portion meat balls by dipping and placing on baking sheets at regular intervals (count if necessary); stir mixtures evenly, taking each stroke in the same direction.
- Carry through one step in a procedure before beginning the next for speed in accomplishing a task.
- Accomplish something each time you pass from one part of the kitchen to another. For example, when soiled dishes are taken to the sink for washing, clean mixing bowls can be brought back on the return trip.
- Keep the work area clean and orderly. Use of a tray on which to work or to place soiled equipment simplifies the cleaning of the table or counter. For example, place a cutting board on the tray when peeling citrus or other juicy fruits. If responsible for measuring ingredients, place soiled measuring cups and spoons on a tray as soon as the ingredients for a recipe have been weighed or measured.

Precautions for Safe Food Production

Proper handling throughout the purchasing, storage, production, and service of food is critical in safeguarding the food against contamination. As discussed in Chapter 4, legal safeguards are provided by federal, state, and local regulatory agencies, which are responsible for setting and enforcing standards for raw and processed foods. Minimum standards for sanitation in foodservice establishments are monitored by city and state agencies, but managers and dietitians are responsible for the maintenance of sanitation standards in their respective foodservices.

Numerous factors can contribute to the outbreak of foodborne illness. Factors associated with food production include: improper holding temperatures, inadequate cooking, contaminated equipment, food from an unsafe source, and poor personal hygiene. Personnel must be made aware of these critical points in the production and service of food through thorough and consistent training in safe food handling procedures.

Temperature is another important factor in the control of harmful organisms. Their growth can be slowed by refrigeration or freezing, and they can be destroyed by sufficient heat. As shown in Fig. 5.10, the danger zone favoring bacterial growth is the temperature range of 45° to 140°F, and the period of time that food is allowed to remain in this critical temperature zone largely determines the rate and extent of bacterial growth. It is imperative, therefore, that the internal temperature of potentially hazardous food be kept **below** 45°F or **above** 140°F to ensure safety. This means that the temperature of the refrigerator should be colder or the holding equipment hotter to maintain the proper internal temperature in the food. Temperature controls on walk-in and other refrigerators should be in good working order and checked and documented daily to make certain that temperatures are maintained below 45°F, as appropriate for the specific foods stored in them.

POTENTIAL HAZARDS IN FOOD PRODUCTION   Foods that are potentially hazardous include meat, poultry, and fish. These products are frequently contaminated with foodborne pathogens, which can be spread to surfaces of equipment, to the hands of workers, and to other foods. If frozen turkeys are to be cooked whole, they should be thawed completely in the refrigerator before being cooked, and if cooked the day before, they should not be refrigerated without first reducing their bulk. The practice of cooking, chilling, and then reheating beef roasts is also potentially hazardous because reheating may not produce a temperature high enough (165°F) to destroy any bacteria that may have survived in the meat.

Food requiring preliminary preparation, which may include cooking prior to the final steps in their preparation, should be refrigerated following the preliminary steps. This includes items such as sandwich and salad mixtures; sliced, chopped, cut, and boned poultry and meats; ground, mixed, and shaped cooked meats; cream pie fillings and puddings; and sliced ham and similar items.

Cream pie fillings, puddings, and other products made with eggs, if not served hot, should be refrigerated as soon as possible after cooking. Attempting to cool at room temperature to save refrigeration is a practice to be discouraged. Masses of hot food cool slowly, even in large walk-in refrigerators. To be cooled quickly, the food should be poured into shallow containers to a depth of no more than two inches and refrigerated, as shown in Fig. 5.11. Other suggestions for cooling large amounts of food quickly include stirring the food and placing the pan of food into an ice bath or vat of cold running water.

Mishandling of food by cooks and other production workers also constitutes a hazard. Cooked ingredients in potato salad, for instance, can be contaminated

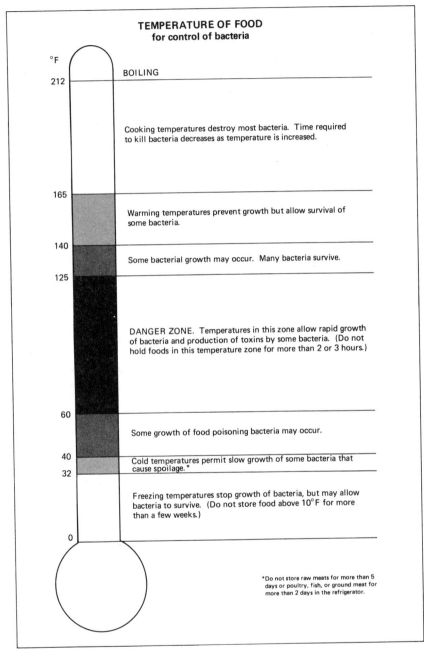

Figure 5.10. Temperature guide for food safety. (From Keeping Food Safe, *Home and Garden Bulletin*, No. 162, USDA.)

Figure 5.11. Portable wire racks facilitate rapid cooling of food in shallow pans. (Courtesy, Metropolitan Wire Goods Corporation.)

by persons during peeling, slicing, chopping, or mixing operations in its preparation. Cross-contamination by a worker or equipment that has been in contact with raw meat or poultry, and then with the cooked product, is to be avoided.

Following is a summary of basic standards for safeguarding the preparation and storage of food:

- Select clean, wholesome food from sources approved or considered satisfactory by the health authority.
- Specify that frozen products be maintained at 0°F or lower during delivery.
- Wash thoroughly all raw fruits and vegetables before using.
- Scour and sanitize all cutting boards, knives, and electric slicers immediately after use with raw or cooked meats, fish, or poultry.
- Cook food to recommended temperatures.
- Maintain all potentially hazardous foods at **safe** temperatures; 45°F or below, or 140°F or above, except for brief periods necessary for preparation.
- Check internal temperatures of cooked food to be held on a serving counter or in a holding cabinet; should be 165° to 170°F before taking to the serving unit in order to maintain 140°F during the serving period.

- Refrigerate immediately any cooked foods to be used later; refrigerate in shallow containers; center of food mass should reach 45°F within 4 hours. Place pans in refrigerators so that air circulation is not blocked.
- Discard any questionable food.
- Protect food from contamination or cross-contamination during preparation, service, and storage through precautionary measures such as use of clean, properly sanitized equipment; optimum refrigerator temperatures; proper handling of food by healthy personnel who wash hands thoroughly after touching any food or objects that may be contaminated; and storage and use of poisonous or toxic materials away from the food.

FOOD HANDLING PROCEDURES   Correct work habits of employees and sanitary food handling procedures to be followed by the foodservice personnel include

- Wash hands with soap and water on reporting for work and after handling raw poultry and meat, smoking, sneezing, and using a handkerchief, and, above all, after each visit to the toilet.
- Keep work surfaces clean and the work area well-organized and orderly.
- Refrigerate unused foods and clean up any spillage promptly.
- Use only clean utensils in preparing, cooking, and serving food.
- Keep fingers and hands out of food as much as possible. Use spoons, forks, tongs, or other appropriate utensils. Wear disposable gloves for handling food that will not be further cooked before serving.
- Always grasp utensils such as spoons, spatulas, tongs, and forks by the handles.
- Use a clean spoon each time for tasting food.

Summary

Basic to production planning and scheduling is the forecast, which is a prediction of the number of persons to be served for a meal or a day and, for a selective menu, an estimate of the number who will choose each menu item. Quantities of food to prepare are based on the predicted number of servings needed and the portion size to be offered. This information, plus special instructions for preparation and work assignments, are included in a production schedule.

Management's responsibility for serving high-quality food starts with the setting of standards and ensuring that employees are aware of them. The use of standardized recipes, good quality ingredients, and proper supervision of food production are vital to quality control. The dietitian or manager must also be aware of the critical points in food production that affect food safety and insist on personal and work habits of employees that will minimize the danger of food contamination.

Summary Questions

1. Discuss the use of historical data in the process of forecasting.
2. Calculate the quantity of lettuce to purchase when 1 pound AP equals 0.76 EP and 100-¾ oz servings are required.
3. What should be included on a production sheet?
4. What is HACCP? Why must a manager have a clear understanding of the flow of food through a foodservice operation?
5. Describe the difference between the heat transfer methods of convection and radiation.
6. Why is it important for a foodservice to develop and implement standardized recipes as a means of production control?
7. What are the advantages of an ingredient assembly center in a foodservice operation?

Bibliography

Bean, N. H. and Griffin, P. M.: Foodborne disease outbreaks in the United States, 1973–1987: Pathogens, vehicles, and trends. J. Food Protec. 53:804–817, 1990.
Bobeng, B. J. and David, B. D.: HACCP models for quality control of entree production in foodservice systems. I. Development of Hazard Analysis Critical Point models. II. Quality assessment of beef loaves utilizing HACCP models. J. Am. Diet. Assoc. 73:526, 1978.
Food and Drug Administration (FDA). Hazard Analysis and Critical Control Points. Division of Federal-State Relations State Training and Information Branch. Department of Health and Human Services. Public Health Service. Minneapolis, MN, May 1991.
National Restaurant Association (NRA): Applied Foodservice Sanitation, 4th ed. New York: John Wiley & Sons, 1992.

For More Information

Chandler, S. J., Norton, L. C., Hoover, L. W., and Moore, A. N.: Analysis of meal census patterns for forecasting menu item demand. J. Am. Diet. Assoc. 80:317–323, 1982.
Kavulla, T. A.: Developing forecasting systems. Food Mgmt. 21:19, 1986.

McManis, H. and Molt, M.: Recipe standardization and percentage method of adjustment. NACUFS J. 35, 1978.

Messersmith, A. M. and Miller, J. L.: Forecasting in Foodservice. New York: John Wiley & Sons, 1992.

Miller, J. L. and Shanklin, C. W.: Status of menu item forecasting in dietetic education. J. Am. Diet. Assoc. 88:443–449, 1988.

Repko, C. J. and Miller, J. L. Survey of foodservice production forecasting. J. Am. Diet. Assoc. 90:1067–1071, 1990.

Rose, J. C.: Forecasting: Parts I, II, and III. Hospital Food and Nutrition Focus. Gaithersburg, MD: Aspen Publishing Co., 1986.

Shugart, G. and Molt, M.: Food for Fifty, 9th ed. New York: Macmillan Publishing Co., 1993.

Delivery and Service

Foodservice managers have the responsibility of making certain that after food is prepared, it is safely held, transported, delivered, and served to consumers. Therefore, the goals of a delivery and service system should be to

- maintain quality food characteristics
- assure microbial safety of food
- serve food that is attractive and satisfying to the consumer

In addition, the system should be designed and selected for optimal use of available resources: labor, time, money, and space.

This chapter provides information for the foodservice manager so that he or she can make sound decisions about delivery and service systems. The information is appropriate whether the manager is evaluating a currently existing system or preparing to select a new system for a particular situation. Chapter content includes factors that affect selection of a system, equipment needs for delivery-service functions, and a review of various styles of service.

Learning Objectives

After studying this chapter, the reader should be able to

1. name the three major goals of the delivery and service subsystems
2. identify three additional secondary goals of these subsystems
3. compare and contrast the two major on-premise delivery systems
4. list and briefly explain the factors that affect a foodservice's choice of a delivery system

5. discuss the general classification of delivery-service equipment
6. describe the equipment that is employed in the rethermalization of frozen and chilled foods
7. list and briefly explain five types of table service

Methods of Delivery and Service

Modern technological research and development related to foodservice have brought many advances in methods of delivery and service of food and in the equipment used for those processes. These developments resulted in large part from the production systems discussed in Chapter 2 and from the complexity of modern-day foodservice operations. With the increased time and distance between production and service, the potential for loss of food quality has also increased. Newer delivery and service methods are designed to protect against such loss.

Most menu items are at their peak of goodness at the time production and cooking are completed. It is not possible to serve food at that precise time in many foodservice systems because of the need to assemble, transport, and deliver meals for service. Equipment that maintains foods at proper temperatures for best quality and ensures safety of the foods in transit is a necessity. Methods of delivery and service that involve the shortest possible time and distance are best able to help achieve the desired goal. It is assumed that the foods as prepared were of good quality before delivery and service begin.

Methods—Delivery and Service as Subsystems

The term *delivery* is used to mean transporting ready-prepared foods from production to place of service; *service* involves assembling prepared menu items and distributing them to the consumer. The equipment required for both delivery and service is an essential part of these subsystems. Whereas delivery and service *are* subsystems in the overall foodservice system, they are small systems within themselves and are referred to here as "systems."

Basically, there are two major *on-premise* delivery-service systems: centralized and decentralized. Although some people think of these two terms only in relation to tray service to hospital patients, they are used in relation to other types of foodservices as well.

CENTRALIZED DELIVERY-SERVICE SYSTEM   In the centralized method, prepared foods are portioned for individual service and meals assembled at a central area in or adjacent to the main kitchen. The completed orders are then transported and distributed to the customer. This is typical of over-the-counter service in fast-food restaurants, of table or counter service in restaurants that utilize waiters or waitresses to transport and deliver meals to the patrons of room service in hotels or motels, and of banquet service where plates are filled in a central location and transported by various means to the dining areas for service. This method is used also in many hospitals and health care facilities. Foods are portioned and plated, and trays for individual patients are assembled in the central serving room. Completed trays are then transported by various means to the patients throughout the facility. Soiled trays and dishes are returned to the central area for washing.

Kotschevar and Terrell (1985) note a modification of the centralized service called "*centralized bulk,* in which food is sent in trucks for dispensing in corridors near patients' rooms or from a floor pantry." Trucks may have microwave ovens attached for rapid reheating of food just prior to service.

Centralized delivery-service systems are prevalent today because of the close supervision and control of food quality, portion size, assurance of correct menu items on each tray or order, and correct food temperatures at point of service that this system affords. Also, it requires less equipment and labor time than does the decentralized method. If the number of people to be served is large, however, the total time span required for service may be excessively long.

Decentralized Delivery-Service System In the decentralized system, bulk quantities of prepared foods are sent hot and/or cold to serving pantries or ward kitchens located throughout the facility, where the reheating (if needed), portioning, and meal assembly take place. Thus, instead of one central serving area, there are several smaller ones close to the consumers. Often, these pantries have facilities for limited short-order cooking for eggs, toast, coffee, and for broiling certain items. Refrigerators, ovens for reheating, temperature-holding cabinets, and a counter or conveyor belt for tray assembly are a part of the equipment provided in these serving pantries. Dishwashers can also be provided for warewashing in the ward kitchens; or soiled dishes and trays can be returned to the central area for washing, which eliminates the need for duplication of dishwashing equipment for each pantry. If dishes are washed in the central area, the clean dishes must be returned to the pantries for use for the next meal. It is time- and energy-consuming to transport dishes twice each meal, soiled and clean, from and to the pantries. Over a period of time, this may be more expensive than providing dishwashing facilities for each serving unit.

Decentralized service is considered most desirable for use in facilities that are low and spread out in design or in any facility where there are great distances from the main kitchen to the consumers. It is expected that foods will be of better quality and retain desired temperatures more effectively if served near the consumer rather than plated in a central location and transported to distant locations within the facility. Also, with many serving units rather than one, meals for all consumers can be distributed within a reasonable time span.

Types of foodservice that utilize the decentralized system include large hospitals and medical centers; industrial plants with several serving units or with mobile carts that are used to travel throughout the plant to serve workers at their workstations; hotels providing room service from serving pantries on various floors, and banquets from serving kitchens within the facility.

Costs and values of centralized versus decentralized methods should be studied and carefully weighed before deciding on which one to adopt. Both can be successfully utilized in specific situations and with given conditions.

Factors Affecting Choice of Delivery Systems

Every organization has its own requirements for delivery and service based on the type of foodservice system, the kind of foodservice, the size and physical layout of the facility, style of service used, skill level of available personnel, economic factors related to labor and equipment costs, quality standards for food and microbial safety desired, timing necessary for meal service, space requirements versus space available for foodservice activities, and the energy use involved.

No one factor can alone be considered when deciding on a delivery-service system, for most of the factors interact with, and have an influence on, the others. They must be regarded as a whole when a choice is made.

Type of Foodservice System

The system used determines to some extent its own needs for delivery and service. Of the four types of foodservice systems discussed in Chapter 2, the commissary system, for example, is the only one requiring delivery trucks to take prepared foods to satellite serving units. In both the conventional and ready-prepared systems, foods are prepared on-premise, and the assembly/serve system has meals that are purchased and delivered by the vendor to the service facility. Table 6.1 illustrates the assembly, delivery, and service components of each type of foodservice.

As noted previously, menu items processed in the commissary are either held in bulk or portioned before storage. Three alternatives for storage following food production are frozen, chilled, or hot-held. Each method requires different equipment.

Bulk foods may be placed in 12″ × 20″ counter-size pans for freezing so that they may be reheated and served from the same pan. Or, if they are to be transferred to serving units in the chilled or hot state instead of frozen, they are placed in heavy containers with lids that clamp on securely. Otherwise, spillage may result during transport to the foodservice facility.

TABLE 6.1.   Sequence of Process Steps for Entrée Menu Items Using Alternate Food Production and Storage Methods in Foodservice Systems.

	Food Production and Storage Methods			
Process Steps	Cook/Freeze[AB]	Cook/Chill[AB]	Cook/Hot-Hold[AC]	Heat/Serve[D]
Ingredient and menu item storage	Ingredients enter foodservice	Ingredients enter foodservice	Ingredients enter foodservice	Commercially prepared shelf-stable menu item enter foodservice
Preparation Heating Postheating storage	Preparation Initial heating Freezing and frozen storage Thawing	Preparation Initial heating Chilling and chilled storage	Preparation Final heating Hot-holding storage	Room temperature storage
Portioning and assembly Storage during distribution	Portioning and assembly Cold-holding and distribution	Portioning and assembly Cold-holding and distribution	Portioning and assembly Hot-holding and distribution	Portioning and assembly Cold-holding and distribution
Final heating Service	Final heating Service	Final heating Service	Service	Final heating Service

SOURCE: Adapted with permission from M. E. Matthews: *Microbiological Safety of Foods in Feeding Systems.* Published by the National Academy Press, Washington, DC, 1982.

[A] Used in commissary foodservice systems.
[B] Used in ready-prepared foodservice systems.
[C] Used in conventional foodservice systems.
[D] Used in assembly/service foodservice systems.

Carriers (Fig. 6.1a and b, for example) to hold the portioned food in their containers are filled at the commissary. At scheduled times each day, carriers are loaded onto a truck for transfer to the service unit. In many cases, the driver is responsible for unloading the truck and taking the food carriers to the storage or service area as required. Empty carriers from the previous delivery are collected and returned to the commissary on the delivery truck.

The fleet of trucks required by the commissary depends on geographic distances to be traveled and number of deliveries to be made by each truck driver. Timing can be crucial, especially in those situations where the food is delivered hot just at meal times. School foodservices or college residence hall service may utilize the hot food delivery system to a greater extent than other foodservices since they may not have finishing kitchens. Distances for hot foods to be transported should be short. Timing is also essential for delivery of meals to airports for loading onto planes before take-off. Heavy penalties are imposed for deliveries not meeting airline schedules.

(a)   (b)

Figure 6.1.   (a) An example of a carrier for transporting prepared hot food. This
model has two snap-in Heat Packs for efficient heat distribution that extends holding
time at a desired temperature. NSFI approved. (b) Cutaway shot of same insulated
carrier. Note the one-piece polyethylene, double-wall construction; thick polyurethane
insulation; and the design features for heat retention. (Courtesy, Cambro
Manufacturing Company, Huntington Beach, California.)

Delivery of frozen foods requires well-insulated carriers to maintain food in
the frozen state during the time it is being transported. If the service facility has
adequate space for holding frozen food, there is little problem with delivery
time, since meals can be sent a day or two ahead. If there is no such storage
space, delivery timing must be correlated with meal periods and time for
rethermalizing and assembling the menu items.

At this point, foods are on-premise, and the procedures for delivery and
service within the facility may be the same for all four systems.

Kind of Foodservice Organization

The type of organization determines to a large extent the delivery and service
system requirements. Those where large numbers of people must be served
quickly, such as schools, colleges, and industrial plants, usually provide cafeterias for meal service. Fast-food restaurants serve foods as quickly as possible, too,
but with over-the-counter service or drive-thru windows or drive-in service by car
hops.

Hospitals and nursing homes cater to the foodservice needs not only of their
patients but also of the employees, professional staff, and visitors. This calls for
tray service for patients who are bedfast, perhaps dining room service for
ambulatory patients in some care centers, cafeteria service for staff, employees,

and visitors, and often vending machines provided as a supplemental service for between-meal hours.

Airlines have special delivery-service needs also. Food must be transported by delivery truck from commissary to airport for loading onto the planes for service after take-off (see Fig. 6.2). Meals may be transported preplated hot or cold for reheating in the galley of the plane. Passengers are served meals or snacks on trays at their seats by flight attendants.

Table service restaurants may use differing styles of service (see later in this chapter under "Style of Service"), but all employ servers to carry meals from kitchen to dining area for service to the guests. In restaurants in which customers serve themselves, buffet service is used in some restaurants. Employees replenish the food and usually serve beverages to the guests' tables.

The large hotel or motel may have several types of service within its facility, including a counter or coffee shop for fast meals and table service dining

Figure 6.2. Marriott In-Flite Service supplies more than 150 carriers and is typical of foodservice delivery to airlines. (Courtesy, H. H. Gill, president, Gladieux Corporation, Toledo, Ohio [now merged with Marriott Corporation].)

rooms, some more "exclusive" and expensive than others, and so may use more formal types of service. Since many hotels cater to conventions and group meetings, banquet service is also offered. Room service is available in most hotels, which calls for a different means of delivery and service, such as servers using trays or tables on wheels to take meals to guests in their rooms.

Meal service aboard cruise ships parallels that of hotels or motels, except that there is no banquet service. In the main dining room, guests are served at one or two sittings, depending on facilities and number of guests aboard. In addition to regular meals, specialty foods such as pizza and short-order menu items may be served in snack bars, around the pool, or in a lounge. Mid-morning coffee or bouillon, afternoon tea, and elaborate midnight buffets necessitate various delivery-service methods. Foodservice is provided almost around the clock.

Size and Physical Layout of Facility

The size and building arrangement of the facility are other factors to consider when determining a delivery system. Some restaurants, for example, may be in a high-priced downtown location and, thus, are generally narrow and several stories in height in order to utilize valuable land to its best advantage. In this case, the bakery may be on one level, preparation and cooking units on another, and dishwashing on still another, all being on different levels from the dining room. This calls for a well-coordinated system of mechanized conveyors, subveyors, and elevators to deliver food quickly to the place of service.

Hospitals and health care facilities can be constructed as high-rise buildings or low, rambling facilities with miles of corridors. Different systems are required for each to ensure tray delivery to the patient within a reasonable time. The distance and the routing from production to service areas are points for consideration.

Style of Service

Whether or not the style is *self-service* as cafeteria, buffet, vended, or pick-up by the consumer; *tray service*, either centralized or decentralized; *waiter or waitress service* for table, counter, or drive-in facilities; or *portable meal service* with meals delivered to home or office throughout an industrial plant, each has different equipment and delivery needs. (See later in this chapter under "Equipment Needs" and "Styles of Service.")

Skill Level of Available Personnel

Labor needs and required skills vary for different types of delivery systems and for the equipment used in each type of system. When planning to alter the current delivery system or select a new one, the foodservice manager must assess the current skills and availability of the foodservice employees. Judgment must be made on the skills needed to operate a new system and on the learning ability of the employees. A training program should then be designed to ensure that employees are well-trained in the use, care, and safety features of all equipment and delivery procedures.

Economic Factors

Labor and equipment required in the various delivery-service systems must be costed and evaluated in relation to budgeted allocations. Unless adequate funding is available, the foodservice would not, for example, be able to install automated electronic delivery equipment. Economic factors play a part in deciding where and how frozen or chilled foods should be reheated, assembled, and served. Decentralized service requires duplication of assembling and serving and, sometimes, dishwashing equipment, as well as personnel for the many pantries or ward kitchens throughout the facility, and so may be more expensive to install and operate than the centralized service. Cost comparisons of the numerous types of carts and trucks for transporting food should precede the selection of a specific delivery and serving system.

Quality Standard for Food and Microbial Safety

Management establishes standards for food quality and safety, then selects equipment for heating, holding, and transporting food to achieve those standards. How hot should the food be when served to the consumer? How can that temperature be maintained through delivery and service? How hot must foods be at the time of serving and portioning to aid in achieving the desired standards?

Considerable research has been conducted to find answers for these questions; a summary is reported by a group of North Central Regional Researchers. Studies relate to the four foodservice systems, microbial safety, nutrient retention, and sensory qualities. Microbial quality of menu items studied is dependent on the type of food, quality of raw ingredients, batch size, type of equipment used for cooking, and position of menu items in foodservice equipment, among others. The management of time and temperature relationships throughout all stages of product flow in every foodservice system is considered of major importance. (See Chapter 9 for more on microbial safety.) Time and temperature relationships are also important in nutrient retention and on sensory qualities of food products. Managers should be knowledgeable about these factors to improve their foodservice.

Timing Required for Meal Service

The time of day desired or established for meals is another factor influencing the choice of a delivery-service system. For example, if 1,200 people are to be served at a 7 P.M. seated banquet, all food must be ready at once and served within a few minutes to all of the guests. Many serving stations and adequate personnel for each station are prerequisites for achieving the time objective. Preheated electric carts can be loaded with the preplated meals a short time before service and then taken to various locations in the dining room for service from the carts to guests. An alternate method is to place the plates as they are served on trays and carried by servers to the dining room. This will require several trips from serving area to dining room, thus, it takes more time than when carts are used.

If only a few people need to be served at one time, as in a restaurant where customer orders come to the kitchen over a period of a few hours, food is cooked to order, or in small batches, and held for short periods of time.

In school foodservice, many children are ready for lunch at the same time. To avoid long waits in a cafeteria line, however, a staggered meal period can be scheduled, which allows various grades to be dismissed for lunch at 5- or 10-minute intervals. Another option, if space allows, would be multiple serving lines.

Large hospitals have the problem of serving their many patients within a reasonable meal period time span. Should all be served at approximately the same time as may be possible with decentralized service? Or is a 1- to 2-hour time span acceptable as may be required with centralized service? Various systems meet specific needs. The dietitian must work with nursing staff to assure that patient care is not disrupted and that quality food and service are provided.

Space Requirements or Space Available

Allocation of space for departments and their activities is determined at the time of building construction. The delivery-service system preferred should be stated early in the facility planning process so adequate space will be available for those foodservice activities. Any later remodeling to change to a different system can be disruptive and expensive, if possible at all.

Decentralized systems require less space in the main kitchen area but more throughout the facility for the serving pantries than do centralized systems. In hospitals with centralized service, tray assembly equipment, as well as trucks or carts, take up considerable space. Based on the number and size of the transport carts or trucks, the space needed for their storage when not in use can be calculated. Added spaced must be allocated for moving the carts through the facility with ease.

Energy Usage

A concern for energy use and its conservation plays a role in deciding on a delivery-service system. Systems that utilize a large number of pieces of electrically powered or heated equipment are more costly to operate than those that use the "passive" temperature retention equipment, such as insulated trays or pellet-heated plates.

A report of a research study by Franzese (1984) in 66 New York City hospitals showed that 30% of the hospitals changed their meal delivery systems during the period between 1979 and 1983. There was a trend toward a decrease in decentralized and microwave systems and an increase in insulated tray meal delivery systems that use hot food assembly at a central tray line and transport portioned food in trays designed to maintain food temperatures during transport to the patient. The "active" hot food systems, using hot/cold carts and rethermalizing food previously prepared, decreased in use. Reasons given for this "switch" to centralized from decentralized service and to the hot food assembly with "passive" temperature retention equipment were to decrease electrical energy consumption, to decrease labor costs and increase manager's control of food and supplies, and to improve the quality of patient food.

Concern for energy conservation diminished during the 1980s when management was focused on a labor shortage in many parts of the United States. Labor savings seemed to be the most marketable equipment feature during these lean labor years. Today, energy awareness is on the increase again and energy savings are an important consideration in delivery system and equipment selection.

Equipment Needs

Delivery and service of food in institutions necessitates the use of specialized equipment for each step of the procedure: reheat if necessary, assemble, transport, distribute, and serve. Every foodservice system has its own requirements. Manufacturers work closely with foodservice directors to design pieces of equipment that best fills those specific needs. Equipment for delivery and service may be classified in several ways:

- In general: fixed or built-in, mobile, and portable
- According to a specific use: reheating, assembling, temperature maintenance, transporting, and serving
- For each of the four foodservice systems: conventional, commissary, ready-prepared, and assembly/serve

A brief description of general and specific classification follows for an understanding of the various delivery-service systems in their entirety. For more detailed information about this equipment, see Chapter 11.

General Classification of Delivery-Service Equipment

FIXED OR BUILT-IN   Equipment that is fixed or built-in should be planned as an integral part of the structure at the time a facility is being built.

One such system is the automated cart transport or monorail. This has its own specially built corridor for rapid transit, out of the way of other traffic in the building. It is intended for use by all departments since it is so expensive to install. It can transport items in a few seconds from one part of the building to another and is desirable because of its speed. The carts are not seen while in transit and do not interfere with other traffic in the building. An alternate plan for tray delivery may be needed in case of power failures that could incapacitate the automated tray delivery system.

Other fixed equipment includes: elevators; manual or power-driven conveyors for horizontal movement as for tray assembly; and subveyors and lifts (dumb waiters) to move trays, food, or soiled and clean dishes to another level within the facility.

MOBILE EQUIPMENT   Mobile equipment is equipment that is moved on wheels or casters. This includes *delivery trucks* for off-premise use to transport food from commissary or central kitchen to the meal sites, and for "meals-on-wheels" delivery to home or offices.

Another type is *movable carts and trucks,* either hand-pushed or mechanized, for on-premise transport of either bulk food for decentralized service or preplated meals for centralized service. Such carts are available in many models, open or closed, insulated or not, temperature controlled for heated or refrigerated units, or combinations of both (see Fig. 6.3 for an example). Some movable carts are designed to accommodate the served plates of hot food for banquet service, others are designed for entire meals assembled on trays for service in hospitals, and still others for bulk quantities of food. Assembly equipment and galley units are also mobile, instead of built-in, which permits flexibility of arrangement. An example of a galley is shown in Fig. 6.4.

PORTABLE EQUIPMENT   Included in this category are items that may be *carried,* as opposed to mobile equipment that is moved on wheels or casters. For delivery and service, equipment such as pans of all sizes and shapes, many with clamp-on lids to prevent spillage in transit, and hand carriers (also called totes) are commonly used. Totes may be insulated to retain temperature of foods for short-time transport or delivery (see Fig. 6.5).

Figure 6.3. Crimsco hot/cold tray cart designed with two convection ovens and two refrigerated units to keep foods above 140°F and below 40°F for service. (Courtesy, Crimsco, Inc., Kansas City, Missouri.)

Also, a variety of plates and trays can keep preplated foods at proper temperatures for service. When these are used, unheated carts can be employed for transporting meals to consumers. Types of these plates and trays include unitized pellet disc, insulated trays, and dish reheat.

Unitized Pellet Disc: A metal disc (pellet) is preheated and at mealtime is placed in a metal base. Individual portions of hot food are plated and placed over the base and then covered. Either china or disposable dishes can be used. The hot metal pellet generates heat and keeps the meal at serving temperature for approximately 40 to 45 minutes (Fig. 6.6).

Insulated Trays with Insulated Covers: Insulated trays are designed with a variety of configurations for the differing types of dishes used for the menu of

DOUBLE COMPARTMENT REFRIG-ERATOR/FREEZER. Ideal for storing in-between meal nourishments, sandwiches, drinks, milk and entrees. Located for easy access to work area. Keeps ice cream frozen.

ICE MAKER/DISPENSER. Produces up to 500 lbs. of ice or more per day with 35-lb. storage bin. Bin easily removable for cleaning. Meets or exceeds all requirements for the sanitary storage and dispensing of patient ice.

STAINLESS STEEL. All work surfaces are made of heavy-duty 16- or 20-gauge lifetime stainless steel. Easy to clean and will withstand years of heavy service.

3 DUPLEX 115/208 VOLT OUTLETS. No special wiring needed. Outlets conveniently located to serve auxiliary appliance needs.

OVERCOUNTER WORK-SHELF. Well lighted, conveniently located for toasters, coffee dispenser and other appliances. Saves time and labor.

SINK and FIXTURES. This deep sink is located at the end of counter leaving a large unobstructed work area. High quality fixtures are built to take heavy use.

INSTANT HOT WATER. This optional feature provides up to 60 cups of steaming hot (190°F) water per hour for soups, tea, coffee and instant cereals.

WORKCOUNTER. Wide and deep enough to hold 6 patient trays. Clear unobstructed work surface provides for excellent workflow when preparing meals or nourishments.

OPTIONAL MICROWAVE OVEN. Perfect for quick heating of unscheduled meals, hold trays and late trays.

STORAGE COMPARTMENT. Contains 2 adjustable shelves.

Figure 6.4.   CYBEX Model 8430 Galley Station, a 5' × 7' unit for patient meal services. (Courtesy, Crimsco, Inc., Kansas City, Missouri.)

the day. Thermal, china, or disposable dishes can be used. After the food is served, the dishes are placed on the tray and covered with the insulated cover. No special carts are needed to transport these trays as they are nesting and stackable, and, of course, no temperature-controlled units are necessary. Some insulated tray systems are designed to create "synergism"; that is, when stacked properly, the cold and hot sections of each tray work together in a column to maintain proper temperatures. The combined temperatures of the individual sections exceed the sum of the individual temperatures. Meals in these insulated trays retain heat quite well for short periods of time, as during transport and distribution. It should be noted that many foods retain heat much better than others under any circumstances. For example, a hearty entrée such as beef stew retains heat much better than a single serving of green beans. Portion size also

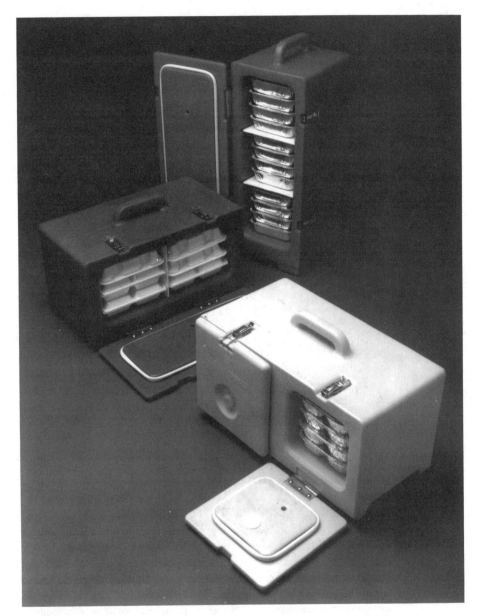

Figure 6.5.   Portable totes are insulated for holding temperatures for short-time delivery. (Courtesy, Cambro Manufacturing Co., Huntington Beach, California.)

(a)

(b)

Figure 6.6.   (a) Unitized base of pellet system is constructed of two 20-gauge stainless steel shells that are hermetically sealed. Bases are heated in specially designed heater/dispenser before filled dinner plate is set in and covered. (b) Cover for unitized pellet. (Courtesy, Seco Products, St. Louis, Missouri.)

influences how well and for how long a food item will maintain desirable temperature. Figures 6.7 and 6.8 illustrate two types of tray systems designed to maximize food quality and heat retention.

Equipment for Specific Uses

REHEATING FROZEN OR CHILLED FOODS Foods prepared, cooked, and then frozen or chilled for later service must be reheated at serving time. This may be done in the central serving area or in serving pantries throughout the facility. Equipment used for reheating in both cases is the same. This includes: convection ovens, conduction (conventional) ovens, microwave ovens, infrared ovens, and the integral cabinets described in the previous section. Also used are immersion equipment (for food in pouches) such as steam-jacketed kettles or tilting frypans. Microwave ovens are the fastest for single portions, but unless a fleet of these ovens or a tunnel-type microwave is available, reheating a large number of meals can take a long time. Convection ovens with the forced air heat can reheat many meals at one time, the number depending on size model selected. Frozen foods usually are tempered in the refrigerator before reheating to reduce time for bringing foods to serving temperature. With any rethermal-

Figure 6.7. Aladdin Temp-Rite II Excel™ System rethermalization cart. Meals are assembled cold; assembled trays are placed in carts, on specially designed conduction heating elements. Carts are held in walk-in refrigerators until 36 minutes before meal service, when meals are heated within the cart. (Courtesy, Aladdin Synergetics, Inc., Nashville, Tennessee.)

ization system, the objective is to heat the food product to service temperature and to retain nutrient content, microbial safety, and sensory quality.

MEAL ASSEMBLY The assembling of meals for service is an important step in the delivery-service system. Methods vary for various types of establishments and the activities involved must be suited to the specific needs of each.

Meal assembly requires that the various menu items that make up a meal are collected and put in one place. This may require equipment as simple as a

Figure 6.8. Cutaway section of Aladdin Temp-Rite II Excel™ Meal System tray servers. They are stacked for delivery and designed for natural thermal retention—hot foods on trays are stacked above hot food, cold foods above cold. Insulated cover protects top and bottom of stack, and the system assures proper serving temperatures. Lightweight stacks are easy to carry for delivery on-premise or off. (Courtesy, Aladdin Synergetics, Inc., Nashville, Tennessee.)

convenient table or counter for bagging or plating the foods cooked behind the counter in a fast-food restaurant. In a table service restaurant, servers may pick up the cold foods at one or more stations and hot foods from the chef's station and assemble them all on a tray for service.

The most complex assembly is for tray service for many patients or other consumers. Trays, dishes, silverware, and food are prepositioned along a conveyor belt. Employees are stationed to place a specific item or items on the tray as it passes along. A patient menu or diet card precedes the tray and indicates which menu items should be placed on the tray. Conveyors of various types are commonly used for this purpose. All must be sized to the width of the trays used. The simplest is a manual or self-propelling conveyor with rollers that move trays when they are pushed from one station to the next. Others are motor-driven. Power-operated conveyors can be set at varying speeds for moving trays along the belt automatically (see Fig. 6.9). Conveyors may be mobile or built-in.

TEMPERATURE MAINTENANCE AND HOLDING   Foods prepared and ready for service often must be held for short periods until needed, while being transported to another area for service, or during the serving period itself. Equipment for this short-time holding includes refrigerated and heated storage units of many types.

Figure 6.9.   (a) Roller-type conveyor; (b) skate wheel conveyor. Both are mobile, stainless steel construction, adjustable in height, and NSFI approved. (Courtesy, Precision Industries, Inc., Miami, Florida.)

It should be noted that heated storage cabinets will *not* heat the food, but will, when preheated, maintain for short periods the temperature of the food as it was when it was placed in them.

Heated or refrigerated cabinets may be built in, pass through from kitchen to serving area, or from mobile carts and trucks of all types, some designed with both refrigerated and heated sections. Movable refrigerated units are often used for banquet service. Salads and desserts can be preportioned and placed in them in the production area and held until moved to the banquet hall at service time. Likewise, hot foods for large groups can be portioned and placed in preheated carts close to serving time but held until all plates are ready to be served at the same time.

Infrared lamps are also used to keep certain foods hot on a serving counter during the serving period.

TRANSPORTING AND DELIVERY   Equipment for transporting and delivery is described earlier in this chapter under "Mobile Equipment" and "Portable Equipment." Open or closed noninsulated carts, including monorail, are used to transport meals served on pellet- or capsule-heated dishes, or placed on insulated trays with covers. Temperature maintenance carts with heated and refrigerated sections or insulated nonheated carts are used to transport meals preplated on regular dishes and placed on noninsulated trays. Other carts are designed with heated wells and compartments for bulk amounts of soup, vegetables, meats, and so forth, as well as for cold ingredients and other food items for meal assembly in another location.

Roll-in refrigerator units serve as transport equipment also with preplated salads and desserts set up in the production area and moved later to the dining areas. Similarly, other mobile serving equipment, such as banquet carts and buffet or catering tables, can serve the dual functions of transporting and serving. Some catering carts for snack items, soups, sandwiches, and beverages are used to take foodservice to workers in plants or office buildings. Insulated totes are inexpensive yet effective means for home delivery of meals.

Many methods and pieces of equipment are available for transporting food from the kitchen to the consumer. The manager must identify the specific needs of the organization when choosing among them. Consideration must be given to the total number to be served; the distance to be traveled between production and service areas; layout of the building with routes including doors, ramps, and elevators involved; and the form of food to be transported: hot, cold, bulk, or preplated.

SERVING   Cafeteria counters of varying configurations and with sections for hot and cold foods, buffet tables with temperature-controlled sections and sneeze guards, and vending machines all provide a means for self-service. Various methods for tray service have been described. The diagram of alternate plans for tray service shown in Fig. 6.10 provides a summary of them.

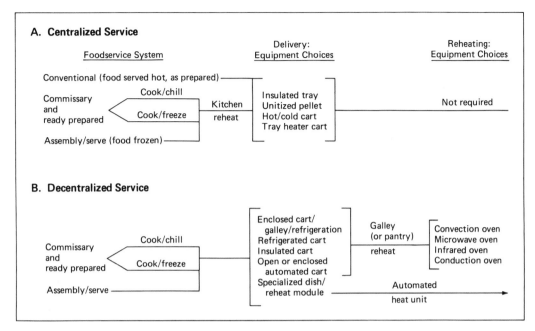

Figure 6.10.   Alternative systems for food service to patients. (Adapted from Herz et al. *Analysis of Alternative Patient Tray Delivery Concepts.* Natick, MA: U.S. Army Natick Research & Development Command, 1977.)

For dining room table service, trays or carts are used to carry the assembled menu items ordered to the guests. Serving stations, small cabinets often located in or near the dining room, are equipped with table setup items such as silverware, napkins, and perhaps water, ice, glasses, coffee, and cups. This speeds service and reduces the distance traveled to serve guests. Other specialized serving equipment is noted under "Styles of Service."

Styles of Service

There are many styles of services, differing widely among institutions, but all with the common objective of satisfying the consumer with food of good quality, correct temperature for palatability and microbial safety, and attractively served.

The style of service selected, appropriate for a particular type of foodservice operation, should contribute toward reaching those objectives. Also, the style must be economically compatible with the goals and standards of the organization. The basic types or styles of service discussed are

1. Self-service: cafeteria—traditional, free flow, or scramble; machine vended; buffet, smorgasbord, salad bar; and drive-thru pick-up

2. Tray service: centralized or decentralized

3. Waiter-waitress service: counter, table—American, French, Russian, family, banquet; and drive-in

4. Portable meals: off-premise or on-premise delivery

Self-Service

The simplest provisions for foodservices involve guests or customers carrying their own food selection from place of display or assembly to a dining spot. The best-known example of self-service is the cafeteria, although buffet service with its variations, smorgasbord and salad bars, and vending are also popular.

CAFETERIA   Cafeterias are of two types. The *traditional* is where employees are stationed behind the counter to serve the guests and encourage them with selections as they move along a counter displaying the food choices. There are many configurations for counter arrangement, from the straight line to parallel or double line, zigzag, and U-shaped. In each case, however, the patrons follow each other in line to make their selections.

The traditional self-service is used in colleges and other residences, cafeterias open to the public, school lunchrooms, in-plant foodservices, and commercial operations. The emphasis is on standardized portions and speedy yet courteous service. The rate of flow of people through the cafeteria line varies according to the number of choices offered and patron familiarity with the setup.

The second type of cafeteria is known variously as the *hollow square, free flow,* or *scramble system.* In this, separate sections of counter are provided for various menu groups, such as hot foods, sandwiches and salads, and desserts. The sections are usually placed along three sides of the serving room, and customers flow from the center to any section desired. This may seem confusing for the first-timer, but it does provide speed and flexibility by eliminating the need to wait in line for customers ahead to be served. Also, it relieves the pressure on those who do not wish to hurry in making decisions. In order to be successful, it is necessary to have repeat business and a mechanism for controlling the number of people who enter at one time. Fig. 8.20 in Chapter 8 shows a diagram of a free flow cafeteria.

MACHINE VENDED   The history of vending dates back as far as 215 B.C. in Greece, but *food* vending began in this country centuries later with penny candy and gum machines. Other items such as cold drinks and coffee soon were dispensed from vending machines. Today, a complexity of menu items, including complete meals, are available through vending machines. Some contain heating elements to cook or reheat foods before dispensing them. Others are refrigerated, some low temperature-controlled for holding frozen foods, such as ice cream.

Machine-vending foodservice skyrocketed in use and popularity in the 1950s and 1960s as it met a demand for speedy service and for having foodservice available 24 hours a day, 7 days a week. Its popularity continues, and today vending is accepted as an important component of the foodservice industry, especially as a means for supplementing other styles of service. Schools, residence halls, hospitals, industrial plants, office buildings, and transportation terminals especially have used this mode of service for coffee breaks, after-meal-hour snacks, and, in some, as the sole means of providing meals.

Food for the vending machines can be prepared by the institutions using them, or by an outside vending company that delivers fresh foods at frequent intervals and keeps the machines supplied and in good working order. Fast turnover of the food and good supply service are requisites for safety and success of vended foods. Also, the foods offered must be fresh and displayed attractively. Glass-front display cases are far superior to metal-front machines for this purpose. Cleanliness and adherence to city health and sanitation codes are essential. Cooperative efforts by those concerned with packaging, production, merchandising, transportation, storage, and sanitation have brought about improvements in the quality and variety of the food offered and will continue to do so in the future. Another innovation is the "talking" machine, which "communicates" some brief statement to the customer.

BUFFET   Buffet service, such as the smorgasbord and the popular salad bar, is a means for dramatically displaying foods on a large serving table. Guests move around the table to help themselves to foods of their choice. Selections usually are numerous, and eye appeal is an important factor in the foods offered. Foods that hold up during the meal hour and the proper equipment to keep this food hot or cold as desired are essential to the success of this type of service. For aesthetic appeal and to comply with health regulations, displayed food must be protected against patron contamination. Portable sneeze guards placed around the foods give some protection as customers serve themselves. Fig. 6.11 is an example of one type of mobile salad bar with sneeze guard.

DRIVE-THRU PICK-UP   This type of service, popular with fast-food establishments to speed customer service, is a variation of the drive-in service. Customers drive through the restaurant grounds in a specially designated lane, make their food selection from a large menu board posted outside, and call their order in through a speaker box (usually next to the menu board). By the time they reach the dispensing window, their order has been assembled and packaged for pick-up.

Figure 6.11.   Portable food bar with sneeze guard, adaptable for many uses. (Courtesy, Atlas Metal Industries, Inc., Miami, Florida.)

Tray Service

Meals or snacks that are assembled and carried on a tray to individual consumers by an employee is a type of service provided for those unable to utilize other dining facilities. Airlines, hospitals, nursing homes, and other health care facilities use this method. For persons who are ill or infirm, attractively appointed trays served by pleasant-mannered employees do much to tempt their appetites and help restore health. Airline travelers also appreciate attractive meals served to them in flight and often judge the airline company by the quality of its food and service.

The two types of tray delivery service in hospitals, centralized and decentralized, are described earlier in this chapter. After trays have been transported to serving pantries, they are carried to patients by an employee either of the nursing or dietary department. Good cooperation between the two departments is a prerequisite to coordinate timing for prompt delivery. Delays in getting trays to patients can cause loss of temperature and quality of the food; thus, a major objective of foodservice will not be attained.

Meals for airline foodservice are supplied by the airline's own commissary or on contract from caterers. Foods generally are preplated at the commissary and loaded, either hot or cold, into insulated holding cabinets that are delivered to planes at flight time. Meals loaded hot must be served soon after take-off; those chilled are reheated on the plane in either small convection or microwave ovens. The length of the flight may determine the method to be used for there must be adequate time for reheating all meals. Flight attendants assemble the meals in the galley, placing the hot entrée (if one is served) on a tray with cold foods, and hand carry the trays or wheel them down the aisle on carts to serve passengers where they sit. Beverages are distributed in a similar manner. Many airlines have expanded the use of cold plates, sandwiches, and snacks on shorter flights, but all continue to use good merchandising techniques to make food attractive and satisfying and so help meet the competition for business among airlines.

Waiter-Waitress Service

COUNTER   Lunch counter and fountain service are perhaps the next thing to self-service in informality. Guests sit at a counter table that makes for ease and speed of service and permits one or two attendants to handle a sizable volume of trade. Covers are laid and cleared by the waiter or waitress from the back of the counter, and the proximity of the location of food preparation to the serving unit facilitates easy handling of food. The U-shaped counter design utilizes space to the maximum, and personnel can serve many customers with few steps to travel.

TABLE SERVICE   Most restaurants and hotel or motel dining rooms use more formal patterns of service in addition to the counter service, although both employ service personnel. Many degrees of formality (or informality) can be observed as one dines in commercial foodservice establishments around the world. Generally, there are four major styles of service classified under table service: American, French, Russian, and banquet.

American service is the one generally used in the United States, although all styles are employed to some degree. A maitre d', host, or hostess greets and seats the guests and provides them with a menu card for the meal. Waitresses or waiters place fresh table covers, take the orders, bring in food from the kitchen serving area, serve the guests, and may also remove soiled dishes from the tables. Busers may be employed to set up tables, fill water glasses, serve bread and butter, and remove soiled dishes from the dining room. Checkers see that the food taken to the dining room corresponds with the order and also verify prices on the bill before it is presented to the guest. Characteristic of this type of service is that food is portioned and served onto dinner plates in the kitchen.

French service (synonymous with "fine dining") is often used in exclusive, elegant restaurants. In this style, portions of food are brought to the dining room on serving platters and placed on a small heater (*rechaud*) that is on a small portable table (*gueridon*). This table is wheeled up beside the guests' table and here the chief waiter (*chef de rang*) completes preparation, for example, boning, carving, flaming, or making a sauce. The chief waiter then serves the plates, which are carried by an assistant waiter (*commis de rang*) to each guest in turn. This style is expensive, since two professionally trained waiters are needed to serve properly and service is paced slowly. The atmosphere is gracious, leisurely, and much enjoyed by patrons because of the individual attention they receive.

Russian service is the most popular style used in all of the better restaurants and motel dining rooms of the world. Due to its simplicity, it has replaced, to a high degree, the French style that seems cumbersome to many. In Russian service, the food is completely prepared and portioned in the kitchen. An adequate number of portions for the number of guests at the table are arranged on serving platters by the chef. A waiter or waitress brings the platters, usually silver, with food to the dining room along with heated dinner plates and places them on a tray stand near the guests' table. A dinner plate is placed in front of each guest. The waiter then carries the platter of food to each guest in turn and serves each a portion, using a spoon and a fork as tongs in the right hand and serving from the left side. This is repeated until all items on the menu have been served. Although this service is speedy, only requires one waiter, and needs little space in the dining room, it has the possible disadvantage that the last person served may see a disarrayed unappetizing serving platter. Also, if every guest orders a different entrée, many serving platters would be required.

Family style is often used in restaurants or residences of various types. Quantities of the various menu items, appropriate for the number of guests at the table, are served in bowls or platters and placed on the dining table. Guests serve themselves and pass the serving dishes to the others. This is an informal method that is popular for Sunday "fried chicken dinner specials" and in Chinese restaurants for foods that are to be shared, family style. Family-style service is used in some long-term care facilities in an effort to create a home-like atmosphere.

Banquet service, unlike other types discussed, is a preset service and menu for a given number of people for a specific time of day. Some items, such as salads, salad dressings, butter, or appetizers, may be on the table before guests are seated. Either the American style or the Russian style of service is used.

For American style, dinner plates filled in the kitchen are transported to the guests in one of several different ways: preheated carts are filled with numerous plates and taken to the dining room before guests arrive. Service personnel remove plates from these carts to serve their guests. Another way is for each server to obtain two dinner plates from the serving station, and with one in each hand, go, as a group, to the dining room and serve one table completely. Several trips back and forth are required to finish this service. Still another method is to use busers to carry trays of dinner plates to the dining room, place them on tray stands, and return for another load. Service personnel, working as a team in the dining room, serve the plates as busers bring them in. The head table is served first; then the table farthest from the serving area is served next, so that each succeeding trip is shorter. All guests at one table are served before proceeding to the next table.

The Russian style is used at banquets as described for restaurant service. Sixteen to 20 guests per server is a good estimate for banquet service.

DRIVE-IN   Drive-in service requires waiters or waitresses (carhops) to serve patrons who drive up to the restaurant and remain in their parked cars. The service was most popular in the 1950s and 1960s. Today patrons seem to prefer going into a restaurant instead of eating in their cars. Most drive-ins provide dining space inside. Although many still enjoy good business as they were, others have changed to the drive-thru customer pick-up method described earlier.

Table Settings and Serving Procedures

Many foodservice operations including restaurants, catering services, long-term care facilities, and hospitals are emphasizing formal or fine dining in at least some of their service options. For example, a nursing home may offer formal dinners for special events such as birthdays, holidays, or anniversaries. A catering service may offer formal sit-down dining, family-style dining, or a buffet. Proper table settings are defined for each type of service.

According to *Emily Post's Etiquette* (1984) few absolute rules apply to table setting but the end result must achieve geometrical balance; the centerpiece should be in the center, places should be set at equal distances, and utensils should be balanced.

The amount of space allotted to each guest or customer is referred to as the cover. Amounts vary but 24 to 36 inches of table edge space should be allowed for each guest. Dinner plates and the handles of flatware should be placed 1 inch from the edge of the table. This is referred to as the set line. Figure 6.12 illustrates a correct place setting for a luncheon.

Figure 6.12.   Luncheon place setting.

Waitress/waiter training manuals are excellent resources in which to find proper serving techniques. The following are a few of the traditional service rules used in formal dining:

1. Using his or her left hand, the waitperson serves the food from the left-hand side of the guest.
2. The dinner plate is placed directly in front of the guest.
3. The waitperson uses his or her right hand to serve beverages from the right-hand side of the guest.
4. Dishes and beverage containers are removed from the left.

Portable Meal

OFF-PREMISE DELIVERY   One example of off-premise service is delivering meals to the homes of elderly, chronically ill, or infirm individuals not requiring hospitalization. This plan, sometimes called Meals-on-Wheels, attempts to meet the need for nutritious meals for those persons who are temporarily disabled, or for the elderly who may live alone and are unable to cook for themselves. In communities where such a plan is in operation, meals are contracted and paid for by the individual in need of the service or by some federal or community agency or volunteer organization for persons unable to pay. Desirably, the menus are planned by a dietitian working cooperatively with the organization providing the meals. Food may be prepared by restaurants, hospitals, colleges, or other foodservices and delivered by volunteer workers. Preplated meals are covered and loaded into some type of insulated carrier (see Fig. 6.5) to ensure food safety while in transit and to maintain desired temperatures until delivered to the home.

A similar service is provided by caterers for workers in office buildings or to customers in their homes by pizza restaurants or others, but on a profit-making basis.

ON-PREMISE DELIVERY   Another example of portable meals often used in some industrial plants is the distribution of foods to workers at their workplace by mobile carts that move throughout the plant. Carts are equipped with heated and refrigerated sections for simple menu items such as soup, hot beverages, sandwiches, snack items, fruits, and pastries. Workers pay the cart attendant as selections are made. This provides a time-saving service for employees who might have long distances to go to a central cafeteria in a large plant during a short meal period.

An alternate-type portable service is utilized by some companies not having foodservice facilities. That is the mobile canteen provided by a catering firm and driven each day to the yard of the plant. Workers go outside to buy their meals from the canteen truck.

Although variations of these basic styles of service can be found in today's innovative foodservice systems, the types discussed here should provide understanding of the most commonly used service systems.

Summary

The delivery and service of food after it has been prepared are important aspects of the total foodservice system. Consumer satisfaction depends in large part on the pleasing presentation of carefully prepared, assembled, and transported food in every type of foodservice operation.

Foodservice managers should be cognizant of the major goals of delivery and service systems. These goals are to maintain quality food characteristics including desirable temperatures, ensure microbial safety, and present food attractively. In addition, the system selected should save worker steps and energy, reduce labor time and costs, and lessen worker fatigue.

Factors affecting the selection of a particular delivery system, either centralized or decentralized, as well as the appropriate equipment needed include: the type of foodservice system (conventional, commissary, ready-prepared, or assembly/serve); the type of organization, such as school, hospital, commercial, or other; the size of physical facilities and amount of space available; the style of service to be used; the skill level of personnel; the labor and equipment costs involved; the quality standards required and desired; the timing for meal service; and the energy usage involved.

The style of service used whether self-serve, tray, or waiter/waitress service must be appropriate for the type of operation and for attaining its goals. Training the workers to use correct serving procedures and to present the food to the consumers in a pleasing and courteous manner are also essential elements in achieving a successful foodservice operation.

Summary Questions

1. Define the terms "delivery" and "service" as they relate to foodservice in institutions.

2. Discuss the advantages and disadvantages of centralized and decentralized delivery-service systems.

3. Describe the impact of the skill level of available personnel on the choice of delivery-service systems.

4. What is the difference between energy usage of "passive" and "active" temperature retention equipment?

5. Describe the various equipment options that can be employed for heat retention in a centralized hospital delivery system.

Bibliography

Kotschevar, L. and Terrell, M. E.: Foodservice Planning: Layout and Equipment, 3rd ed. New York: John Wiley & Sons, 1985, p. 205.

Foodservice Systems: Time and Temperature Effects on Food Quality. North Central Regional Research Publication No. 293. Urbana-Champaign, IL: Agricultural Experiment Station (Illinois Bulletin 779), 1984.

Franzese, Rita: Food services survey shows delivery shift. Hospitals 58:61, August 16, 1984.

Post, E. L.: Emily Post's Etiquette: A Guide to Modern Manners, 14th ed. (pp. 689–706). New York: Harper & Row Publishers, 1984.

For More Information

Dowling, R. A. and Cotner, C. G.: Monitor of tray error rates for quality control. J. Am. Diet. Assoc. 88:450–453, 1988.

Khan, M.: Concepts of Foodservice Operations and Management, 2nd ed. New York: Van Nostrand Reinhold, 1991.

Khan, M.: Foodservice Operations. Westport, CT: AVI Publishing Company, Inc., 1987.

Knight, J. B. and Kotschevar, L. H.: Quantity Food Production, Planning, and Management, 2nd ed. New York: Van Nostrand Reinhold, 1989.

Kotschevar, L. H.: Management by Menu, 2nd ed. Wm. C. Brown Publishers, 1987.

Puckett, R. P. and Miller B. B.: Food Service Manual for Health Care Institutions, 1988 Edition. Chicago: American Hospital Publishing Incorporated, 1988.

Puckett, R. P., Boe, D. G., and Medved, C. K.: Management engineering principles applied to foodservice operations. J. Am. Diet. Assoc. 87:770–774, 1987.

Snyder, P. O. and Matthews, M. E.: Effect of hot-holding on the nutritious quality of menu items in food service systems: A review. School Food Service Research Review 8:6, 1984.

Physical Facilities

Sanitation and Safety

Providing a clean, safe foodservice facility is basic to achieving a successful operation and assuring the health and well-being of both employees and customers. Also, it contributes to the aesthetic satisfaction that guests derive from dining and gives a feeling of personal security to all.

Sanitation and safety are closely related environmental factors, to be considered when planning a facility and followed in its daily operations. Maintaining high standards of cleanliness, making sure that the food served is safe for consumption and that the workplace is free from hazards are management responsibilities.

To help maintain minimum sanitation and safety standards, certain regulations have been established and enforced by city, state, and federal law. Agencies such as the United States Public Health Service (USPHS) and state and city health departments, and organizations such as the National Sanitation Foundation International (NSFI), Occupational Safety and Health Association (OSHA), and the National Safety Council recommend standards. Results of research conducted at universities, hospitals, food, chemical, and equipment manufacturing companies provide data for recommending or setting standards. These groups, individually or cooperatively, work with the foodservice industry to prepare, distribute, and interpret pertinent information in publications and exhibits. Some present seminars, classes, and programs for various foodservice groups and the public. All are aimed at informing concerned persons of the rules, regulations, and standards to be met and how to achieve them.

Food safety, as an integral part of food purchasing, preparation, and service, is discussed previously in Chapters 4, 5, and 6. A brief review of microbiology involved with food safety and cleanliness, together with sanitation of the facility and its equipment, and the personal safety of workers and guests are discussed in this chapter.

Learning Objectives

After studying this chapter, the reader should be able to

1. discuss how bacterial growth occurs in food
2. describe how a food handler might contaminate food
3. explain the difference between foodborne infection and intoxication
4. identify features of physical plant and equipment that contribute to achieving high standards of safety and sanitation
5. describe how a high standard of sanitation for foodservice personnel may be best achieved and maintained
6. list and briefly explain what should be included on a job breakdown for cleaning tasks
7. discuss the three basic phases of detergency and the agents required for each phase
8. name and briefly describe the "three Es" of safety

Sanitation

Students majoring in food-related programs will have had a course in microbiology. The application of the microbiological principles involved in the operation of a foodservice department cannot be overemphasized. Too many establishments receive poor ratings by health department inspectors because of lack of cleanliness or improper food handling procedures. Reports of outbreaks of foodborne illnesses due to contaminated food or workers continue to occur. Such outbreaks have devastating effects on the reputation of an establishment and possibly on its success or failure. Also, the economic loss associated with foodborne disease outbreaks can be much more startling than most foodservice directors realize. Todd (1989) reports that in the United States the preliminary cost estimates are $1,000 per reported case. Loss of business for the foodservice and lawsuits contribute the most to the cost, but loss of income for victims and infected food handlers is also considerable.

The Centers for Disease Control and Prevention in Atlanta, Georgia, an agency of the USPHS, is the clearinghouse for receiving reports of foodborne illness outbreaks. These food poisoning incidents are published each week in *Morbidity and Mortality Weekly Report* (see the section entitled "For More Information" at the end of this chapter).

Foodservice managers should have an understanding of the microbiological aspects involved in such outbreaks and be able to implement procedures to prevent their occurrence.

Microbiology and Food

Certain organisms such as bacteria, which are microscopic in size, are able to invade the human body causing illness and hazard to life. Since food and contaminated workers are major sources for transmitting the organisms to people, it is essential that foodservice managers understand the conditions involved and insist that employees follow correct procedures to prevent such illnesses from occurring.

Bacteria whose forms are recognizable under the microscope are *cocci*, round in shape; *bacilli*, rod-shaped; and *spirilla*, corkscrew-like. The conditions necessary for bacterial growth are food, moisture, favorable temperatures, and time. Most bacteria grow best in low acid food; a few in acid food. Some grow best if sugar is present in the food, others if proteins are present. Some need air for growth, and others thrive in its absence. The temperature most favorable to the growth of pathogenic bacteria is body temperature of about 98°F; temperatures below 45°F inhibit their growth markedly, and temperatures above 140°F for a period of time are lethal to many varieties of organisms. Time required for growth and multiplication depends on the other conditions present and the type of food.

Any food can be a vehicle for foodborne illness, but some are more hazardous than others. The USPHS defines *potentially hazardous foods* as

> any food that consists in whole or in part of milk or milk products, shell eggs, meats, poultry, fish, shellfish, edible crustacea (shrimp, lobster, crab, etc.), baked or boiled potatoes, tofu and other soy-protein foods, plant foods that have been heat-treated, raw seed sprouts, or synthetic ingredients. (*National Restaurant Association*, 1992, pp. 6–7)

One means of transport or channel by which bacteria are transmitted from person to person is through *direct contact*. This direct contact either by carriers or infected persons who harbor the disease-causing bacteria and convey them to other individuals accounts for a large part of the spread of communicable disease. According to the USPHS, there are some 62 different communicable diseases, each caused by a specific kind of organism. A *carrier* is a person who, without symptoms of a communicable disease, harbors and gives off from his or her body the specific bacteria of a disease, usually without being aware of it. An *infected* person is one in whose body the specific bacteria of a disease are lodged and have produced symptoms of illness. Thus, others are aware of the possible danger of contamination.

Consumers can become infected through water, milk, and other food products that have been contaminated with the fecal material of an infected person. Still another path of infection is through drinking raw milk drawn from cows with infected udders. A now rare source of infection is from muscle tissues of hogs infected with the parasitic organism *Trichinella spiralis.*

An infectious disorder of the respiratory system such as the common cold can be spread by the droplet spray of infected discharges of coughing and sneezing without safeguard. An *indirect route* of infection spread through respiratory discharges is the used handkerchief, the contaminated hand, and the subsequent handling of food or plates and cups in serving a patron.

The modes of transmission or locomotion for pathogens are diagrammed in Fig. 7.1. It should be noted that human wastes, particularly fecal material, are especially hazardous. An individual who has used the toilet is certain to have contaminated hands. If careful and thorough handwashing is ignored, the worker's hands can be a dangerous "tool" in the kitchen.

Common foodborne diseases are caused either by bacterial *infections* or by food *intoxication* or poisoning. The term "foodborne infections" means an illness caused by the ingestion of harmful living organisms into the body, usually on the food consumed. With "food intoxication or poisoning," however, the bacteria grow on the food prior to its ingestion and produce toxins or poisonous substances that cause the illness. In this case, the microorganisms themselves are not harmful, but the toxins they produce are. Illness occurs more quickly from toxins than from infection from living bacteria. In both cases, however, cramps, nausea, diarrhea, and sometimes vomiting can occur.

MICROORGANISMS CAUSING FOODBORNE INFECTIONS   Primary organisms that cause foodborne infections are salmonellae, pathogenic *Escherichia coli, Vibrio parahaemolyticus,* and *Campylobacter jejuni.* The first two are especially prevalent and require special care in food handling.

Salmonellae infections account for numerous cases of gastrointestinal disorders. The causative organism may be any one of the 2,300 known serotypes of salmonellae, of which the three most common are *S. enteritidis, S. typhimurium,* and *S. heidelberg* (Cliver, 1990). The intestinal tract of animals and humans is the principal reservoir of salmonellae. It is excreted in the feces and can contaminate food and water if personal hygiene and proper food handling are not practiced. Primary food sources of salmonellae infections include poultry, poultry products, beef, and pork.

S. enteritidis infections accounted for 25% of all reported cases of salmonellosis in 1985. Infections have been a particular concern in the Northeast portion of the United States where there has been a five-fold increase since 1975. This increase has been associated with raw and undercooked commercial Grade A shell eggs. Many states have adopted various guidelines regarding the preparation and service of eggs. The food manager is encouraged to contact the local

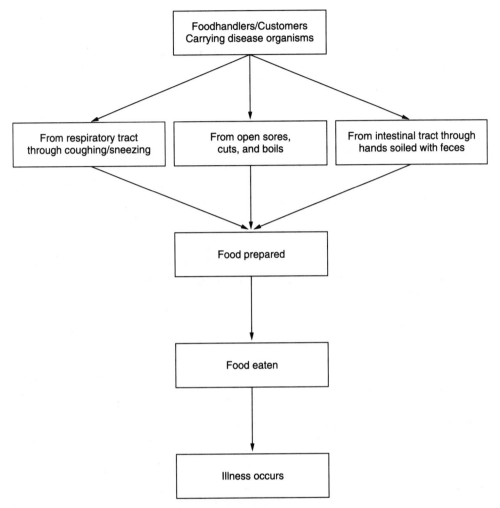

Figure 7.1. Transmission of a foodborne illness from infected human beings to food and back to other human beings. (From *Applied Foodservice Sanitation,* 4th ed., Copyright © 1992 by the Educational Foundation of the National Restaurant Association. Reprinted by permission of John Wiley & Sons, Inc.)

health department for regional guidelines. The following are general egg handling recommendations:

- purchase Grade A or better eggs from a reliable source
- check eggs upon delivery to assure that they have been kept refrigerated during transport
- keep eggs refrigerated, pulling eggs from such storage only as needed

- raw eggs should not be used as an ingredient in the preparation of foods that will not be thoroughly cooked
- individually prepared eggs and pooled eggs should be cooked to assure that all parts reach a temperature of at least 140°F
- cooked eggs should be held at an internal temperature of at least 140°F

Pathogenic *Escherichia coli* has been responsible for a number of foodborne illness outbreaks in this country. Imported soft cheese was the cause of the first identified outbreak, occurring in 1971. This organism is found in feces of humans and other animals, and so may contaminate soil, water, and food plants. It is considered a moderate hazard but with potential for extensive spread. The organism is easily killed by heat, but foods that have been heat-processed can be contaminated after heating, due especially to improper refrigeration and temperature control. In addition to cheese, both raw and processed shellfish, raw ground beef, and inadequately cooked ground beef have caused some outbreaks of gastrointestinal illness due to the presence of pathogenic *E. coli*.

Vibrio parahaemolyticus has been the cause of the majority of foodborne illnesses in Japan, but only in recent years has been recognized as the cause in other countries. Since this microorganism lives in salt water, contamination of fish and shellfish can occur, especially in those from warm waters. Most outbreaks have resulted from eating raw or undercooked seafood or cooked seafood that has come into contact with raw products or contaminated containers. At present, *V. parahaemolyticus* gastroenteritis has not been considered a serious health problem in the United States. But if seafood, especially crustaceans, are mishandled during storage, cooking, and holding, the organism will multiply and cause mild abdominal pain, diarrhea, and often nausea and vomiting—all symptoms of various foodborne illnesses in varying degrees of severity.

Another organism, long known as an animal pathogen, has only recently been recognized for its importance and prevalence in human gastroenteritis. It is *Campylobacter jejuni* and is transmitted by the consumption of raw milk, contaminated water, undercooked chicken, beef, pork, and raw clams. Poultry has an especially high carriage rate of this contamination. Cross-contamination from knives or cutting boards may be another source of contamination. Evidence of the importance of *C. jejuni* is that it is now isolated from human diarrheal stools more frequently in the United States than are salmonella and shigella *spp.*

MICROORGANISMS CAUSING FOOD INTOXICATION OR POISONING   Major organisms that cause food intoxication or poisoning are *Staphylococcus aureus*, *Clostridium botulinum*, and *Clostridium perfringens*.

Staphylococcal food intoxication, the most frequent type of food poisoning, results from the contamination with *Staphylococcus aureus* of menu items high in protein, meat, eggs, and milk, as well as cream pie. This organism is commonly found on the human skin and is abundantly present in pimples and suppurating wounds. Major points of control of this food hazard are to exclude from work any employee with pimples, pus pockets, or suppurating wounds so that gross contamination of food may be avoided, and to keep foods potentially susceptible to the organism under refrigeration.

General estimates are that a majority of the cases of "food poisoning" are due to staphylococcal organisms. The illness is not fatal, but causes extreme pain and nausea to its victims for several hours. Usually the symptoms are evident within 1 to 7 hours after the ingestion of the infected food, which may have shown no visible indications of the contamination at the time of consumption.

Clostridium botulinum is a spore-forming organism that causes a far more serious food poisoning, known as botulism. The toxin produced in various media under anaerobic conditions is highly poisonous and usually fatal. Commonly, food contaminated with botulism shows more or less marked changes from normal. The toxin can be destroyed by boiling vigorously for 20 minutes. Fortunately, botulinum poisoning is an uncommon occurrence in foodservice operations. Commercially processed foods are usually fully sterilized at high temperatures under pressure. However, the hazard is great enough to stimulate constant watchfulness of food condition and quality.

Clostridium perfringens, which is an anaerobic, spore-forming bacteria, is often also placed in the group of organisms causing food poisoning. However, the toxin, instead of being present in the food, is produced in the intestinal tract. The incubation period varies between 8 and 20 hours, when illness then occurs.

Clostridium perfringens is found widely distributed in the soil, water, dust, sewage, and manure, and is also found in the intestinal tracts of humans and healthy animals. Many foods purchased by foodservices, especially meats, are probably contaminated with this organism. Also, foodservice workers may carry this organism into the kitchen on their hands. Extreme care must be taken to keep hands and equipment clean, especially meat slicers. Meats to be sliced should never be left to be "cut as needed" over a long serving period, and slicers must be thoroughly cleaned after each use. *Clostridium perfringens* grow rapidly, faster than almost any other of the bacteria discussed here. Gravy, a frequent offender, should be held above 140°F. Table 7.1 summarizes the most common of the foodborne diseases.

Some agents are increasingly identified as causing foodborne illness. These agents are referred to as emerging pathogens and cause diseases such as listeriosis, campylobacteriosis, gastroenteritis, and Norwalk virus. Table 7.2 summarizes the emerging pathogens.

One other type of poisoning that should be included here is chemical poisoning. This results from eating food to which toxic chemicals have been added accidentally. Reports from the Centers for Disease Control for 1987 showed that 29% of all foodborne outbreaks were of chemical etiology.

Chemical poisoning may result from contamination of food with foodservice chemicals such as cleaning and sanitizing compounds, excessive use of additives

TABLE 7.1. Major Foodborne Diseases.

Disease	Salmonellosis Infection	Staphylococcal Intoxication	Clostridium Perfringens Toxin Medicated Infection	Bacillus Cereus Intoxication	Botulism Intoxication
Foods implicated	Poultry, poultry salads, meat and meat products, milk, shell eggs, egg custards and sauces, other protein foods	Reheated foods, ham and other meats, dairy products, custards, potato salad, cream-filled pastries, and other protein foods	Meat that has been cooked at low temperature for long period of time or cooled slowly	Rice and rice dishes, custards, seasonings, dry food mixes, puddings, cereal products, sauces, vegetable dishes, meat loaf	Improperly processed canned goods of low acid foods, garlic-in-oil products, grilled onions, stews, meat/poultry, leaves
Incubation period	6 to 72 hours	1 to 6 hours	8 to 22 hours	1/2 to 5 hours	12 to 36 hours
Symptoms	Abdominal pain, headache, nausea, vomiting, fever, diarrhea	Nausea, vomiting, diarrhea, dehydration	Abdominal pain, diarrhea	Nausea and vomiting, diarrhea, abdominal cramps	Vertigo, visual disturbances, inability to swallow, respiratory paralysis
Duration	2 to 3 days	24 to 48 hours	24 hours	6 to 24 hours	Several days to a year
Precautionary measures	Avoid cross-contamination, refrigerate food, cool cooked meats and meat products properly, avoid fecal contamination from food handlers by practicing good personal hygiene	Avoid contamination from bare hands, exclude sick food handlers from food preparation and serving, practice sanitary habits, proper heating and refrigeration of food	Use careful time and temperature control in cooling and reheating cooked meat dishes and products	Use careful time and temperature control and quick chilling methods to cool foods, hold hot foods above 140°F (60°C), reheat leftovers to 165°F (74°C)	Do not use home-canned products, use careful time and temperature control for sous-vide items and all large, bulky foods, keep sous-vide packages refrigerated, purchase garlic-in-oil in small quantities for immediate use, cook onions only on request

SOURCE: Adapted from National Restaurant Association: *Applied Foodservice Sanitation*, 4th ed., New York: John Wiley & Sons, Inc., 1992, p. 35.

TABLE 7.2. Emerging Pathogens that are Increasingly Identified as Causing Foodborne Illness.

Disease	Campylobacteriosis Infection	E. Coli 0157:H7 Infection	Listeriosis Infection	Norwalk Virus Illness
Pathogen	Campylobacter jejuni	Escherichia coli	Listeria monocytogenes	Norwalk and Norwalk-like viral agent
Foods implicated	Raw vegetables, unpasteurized milk and dairy products, poultry, pork, beef, and lamb	Raw and undercooked beef and other red meats, imported cheeses, unpasteurized milk, raw finfish, cream pies, mashed potatoes, and other prepared foods	Unpasteurized milk and cheese, vegetables, poultry and meats, seafood, and prepared, chilled, ready-to-eat foods	Raw vegetables, prepared salads, raw shellfish, and water contaminated from human feces
Incubation	3 to 5 days	12 to 72 hours	1 day to 3 weeks	24 to 48 hours
Duration of illness	1 to 4 days	1 to 3 days	Depends on treatment—high mortality in those with compromised immune system	24 to 48 hours
Symptoms	Diarrhea, fever, nausea, abdominal pain, headache	Bloody diarrhea; severe abdominal pain, nausea, vomiting, diarrhea, and occasionally fever	Nausea, vomiting, headache, fever, chills, backache, meningitis	Nausea, vomiting, diarrhea, abdominal pain, headache, and low-grade fever
Precautionary measures	Avoid cross-contamination, cook foods thoroughly	Cook beef and red meats thoroughly, avoid cross-contamination, use safe food and water supplies, avoid fecal contamination from food handlers by practicing good personal hygiene	Use pasteurized milk and milk products, cook food to proper temperatures, avoid cross-contamination	Use safe food and water supplies, avoid fecal contamination from food handlers by practicing good personal hygiene, thoroughly cook foods

SOURCE: Adapted from National Restaurant Association: Applied Foodservice Sanitation, 4th ed., New York: John Wiley & Sons, Inc., 1992, p. 48.

and preservatives, or contamination of food with toxic metals. The foodservice manager is responsible for implementing the necessary precautionary measures to ensure that food is protected from these hazards. Minimum precautions include proper labeling and storage of all chemicals and frequent inservice training for employees on the hazards and proper use of chemicals.

Achieving Good Sanitation Standards

Many elements are involved in establishing and achieving high standards of sanitation and safety in foodservices. These include

- the physical plant
- availability of supplies and services
- the skill level of the employees
- type and design of equipment
- type of warewashing system

These elements contribute to achieving a high degree of success in meeting the standards desired by the organization and its manager.

THE PHYSICAL PLANT

Built-in Features: Many features that facilitate easy cleaning and maintenance of the foodservice should be built in at the time of construction. Refer to Chapter 8 for further details on built-in sanitation features.

Water Supply: The adequacy and quality of the water supply available to the institution is of prime concern in the operation of a sanitary foodservice. It is relatively easy to check on the water and its safeness from the reports of the department of health.

The relative hardness of the water will have a bearing on the detergents selected and perhaps on the predicted time span of useful service of necessary equipment such as that in the dishwashing area, most of which is expensive to replace. If there is an unpleasant taste or odor, the quality of coffee and other foods may be impaired. If iron and manganese are present in excess, staining and discoloration will occur, with probable alteration in the flavors of food. Any organic matter present should be cause for questioning the safety of the water.

Trash and Waste Removal: Provision for the daily removal of trash and any other wastes not eliminated by mechanical means is essential for good sanitation. Until such disposal is made, garbage should be stored temporarily in garbage cans with tight-fitting lids, in a well-ventilated area. The containers should be scrubbed daily, rinsed, and sanitized.

Sanitary Facilities: Rest Rooms and Locker Rooms: Adequate sanitary facilities for employees are basic requirements that must be provided in the physical plant of any food or related service. Most states have laws specifying the kind and number of facilities to be provided.

Hand-washing facilities must be provided in an area adjacent to the toilet rooms and be supplied with running hot and cold water, soap, paper towels, or air-drying blowers. The hot water supply for hand washing should not exceed 120°F (lower than required for dishwashing), otherwise persons could be burned. Toilet and wash rooms should have self-closing doors and completely screened outside windows or built-in ventilating fan(s).

Another provision for employee cleanliness and comfort are locker rooms, one for each sex, with ample space for changing clothes. Minimal equipment includes individual lockers with locks for storage of uniforms and benches to sit on while changing.

In the kitchen work areas, drinking fountains and additional hand-washing facilities, separate and apart from food preparation sinks, are required. They should be placed so that they are readily available to employees in various parts of the kitchen. Only if a lavatory is close to the workstation will most employees wash their hands frequently. Otherwise, they tend to use food preparation or pot washing sinks, or go without washing soiled hands, both unsanitary practices. Sinks that are used for washing equipment or utensils should not be used for hand washing.

EQUIPMENT: DESIGN AND PLACEMENT   Each piece of equipment that will come in contact with food should be so designed and constructed that the food contact surfaces are nonabsorbent (i.e., stainless steel), continuous, smooth, free from open seams, cracks, chipped places, exposed junctions, and sharp corners. All junctions should be rounded or coved. The food contact surface should not only be readily cleanable, but also readily accessible for cleaning.

The NSFI has been instrumental in establishing definite acceptable sanitation standards for materials used in foodservice equipment and for equipment design, construction, installation, and maintenance. These standards, based on scientific research, are agreed on by joint committees made up of qualified representatives from research, industry, education, and the public health profession. Publications are available from the foundation in which minimum standards are clearly and specifically defined and are adaptable to various geographical areas. Attention will be called to some of the standards in this text, but each foodservice director should request specific standards as needed from the NSFI.

Manufacturers who meet the standards are privileged to use the seal of approval of the NSFI (see Fig. 7.2) on their products, and the purchaser is

Figure 7.2. National Sanitation Foundation International's (NSFI) seal of approval.

assured of acceptable design, materials, construction, and performance if the equipment is properly installed and operated. Recommended standards give much attention to the proper conditions for installation and use of equipment as well as construction in the factory.

Publicity of the recommended standards is given through publication and distribution of booklets and posters. Local and state public health departments make wide use of the standards in formulating and enforcing codes for physical facilities and the operation of foodservices under their jurisdictions. Emphasis in the work of the NSFI is on the positive approach to good health in the prevention of disease through knowledge and practice of high standards of sanitation for the community, especially in the foodservice industry.

The placement of the pieces of large fixed equipment should be determined thoughtfully to allow the worker space for necessary activity and to avoid such things as accident and spillage. Adequate space beneath and behind heavy equipment is necessary for mopping and cleaning if such items are not built into the floor or wall with proper fittings and joinings. Fig. 7.3 is an illustration of equipment of simple design and good arrangement of work to ensure that high sanitation can be maintained.

PERSONNEL   Foodservice workers carry a heavy responsibility for the health and well-being of the people they serve. The importance of their own good personal habits and of using correct food handling techniques cannot be overemphasized. An outbreak of foodborne illness among those who eat at a foodservice establishment may result from carelessness of its employees.

Food should be handled only by healthy individuals. Physical and medical examinations may or may not be a requirement in the selection of foodservice workers, although most health authorities require at least tuberculin tests, chest X-rays, and blood tests before issuing any food handlers' permits, if and where required. Additional checks depend on the local health service regulations and the individual food operation. Constant observation of the health of employees and attention to their work habits are important functions in supervision. Those who have symptoms of colds, flu, or other communicable illness, such as sore throat, diarrhea, fever, or similar conditions, and those who have acne, boils, "running sores," or any pus-containing lesions should not be allowed to work in food preparation or service areas. Infection control measures should be established to minimize the possibility of contamination. The measures should

Figure 7.3. Simple design and good construction of equipment facilitate ease of maintenance and contribute to beauty of a modern foodservice. Note: equipment is built into the floor or is mounted on wheels.

include procedures for monitoring staff to assure that they are free from communicable diseases and open skin lesions.

Standards of cleanliness and sanitation will be only as high as those established and enforced by the foodservice director. That person must create the philosophy of good sanitation and impart a sense of urgency about the matter to the employees. This is best accomplished through an intense, ongoing training program for the foodservice workers, organized and led by the foodservice administrators. This assumes that foodservice directors themselves have had some training and are knowledgeable about sanitary procedures and practices advocated in legislative measures and why they are important. In many cities, a formal training program in food protection and safety is mandatory before restaurant operators can obtain a required food sanitation certificate. In other cities, voluntary or mandatory certification programs for managers, as well as workers, have been initiated by state restaurant associations or by the state health department. A large number of foodservice directors have had college courses that teach safe and sanitary food handling procedures. Although not all foodservice directors may feel capable of conducting an employee training program in this area, they can plan for and initiate one.

A *continuous* educational program for foodservice personnel is obligatory if a high standard of sanitation is to be maintained. This program should keep the employees aware of sanitary procedures and practices and why they are important. Also, employees must continually realize the heavy responsibilities that they, as foodservice personnel, assume for the health and well-being of the people to whom they serve food. Keen awareness of the importance of their own good health, personal hygiene, and work habits, and the inherent dangers in improper care and handling of food should be emphasized. The educational program that combines the "why" with the "how to do" is usually a well-organized, systematic, and functioning program.

There are many visual aids available in the form of videos, films, slides, and posters that may be used to add interest and emphasis. The National Restaurant Association (NRA) distributes many such materials. Also, training materials can be obtained from the Centers for Disease Control and Prevention and from the NSFI.

Topics to be included in a training program or class in sanitation for foodservice workers are those required by regulatory agencies and desired by the organization. These topics include but are not limited to

- *Dress standards:* The wearing of hair restraints by women and men is a protective measure to be observed by all food personnel. Clean aprons, clean uniforms, and comfortable, well-fitted shoes are essential; elimination of jewelry and nail polish and avoidance of excessive makeup are common requirements of the worker.

- *Personal hygiene and cleanliness:* General good appearance includes clean, well-kept nails; clear skin with no pimples, boils, or blemishes; clean teeth; nonoffensive breath; lack of body odors; and freedom from colds or other respiratory difficulties. Hands and the exposed portion of the arms should be washed with soap and warm water on reporting for work and after handling raw poultry and meat, smoking, sneezing, and use of handkerchief, and, above all, after each visit to the toilet (see the handwashing guide in Fig. 7.4).

- *Proper food handling and work habits:* Keep work surfaces clean and the work area well-organized and orderly so that each part of the work may be carried through to completion without hazard.

- Use only clean utensils in preparing, cooking, and serving food.

- Keep fingers and hands out of food as much as possible. Use spoons, forks, tongs, or other appropriate utensils. Wear disposable gloves for handling food that will not be further cooked before serving.

- Always grasp utensils, such as spoons, spatulas, tongs, and forks, by the handles.

- Pick up and convey glasses by the bases, cups by their handles, and plates by their rims, being careful to avoid possible contamination of the serving surface.

1. Use water as hot as the hands can comfortably stand.

2. Moisten hands, soap thoroughly, and lather to elbow.

3. Scrub thoroughly, using brush for nails.

4. Rub hands together, using friction for 20 seconds.

5. Rinse thoroughly under running water.

6. Dry hands, using single-service towels or hot-air dryer.

Figure 7.4. Proper handwashing techniques. (From *Applied Foodservice Sanitation*, 4th ed., Copyright © 1992 by the Educational Foundation of the National Restaurant Association. Reprinted by permission of John Wiley & Sons, Inc.)

- Use a clean spoon each time for tasting food; never put a tasting spoon back into a pan of food nor use a stirring spoon for tasting the product.
- Observe "no smoking" rules in all food preparation and serving areas.
- Consume food in designated dining areas only.

After the training sessions, frequent follow-up supervision on the job is necessary to ensure that workers actually understand and observe the procedures taught. Only then will the desired high standards be maintained from day-to-day.

CLEANING AND MAINTENANCE   The total housekeeping and maintenance program of a foodservice department must be planned to reflect concern for sanitation as "a way of life" if this philosophy phrased by the NSFI is to pass from words to reality. Good sanitation results can be obtained through establishing high standards, rigid scheduling of assignments that are clearly understood by the workers, ongoing training, proper use of cleaning supplies, provision of proper materials and equipment to accomplish tasks, and frequent meaningful inspections and performance reviews.

Organization and Scheduling: The organization of a plan for housekeeping and maintenance begins with a list of duties to be performed daily, weekly, and monthly. Most organizations believe that "sanitation is a part of every person's job," and that daily cleaning of the equipment and utensils used by each person is that person's responsibility. General cleaning of floors, windows, walls, lighting fixtures, and certain equipment should be assigned to personnel as needed. Do not implement a policy of "clean if you have time." These tasks can be scheduled in rotation so a few of them are performed each day; at the end of the week or month, all will have been completed and the workers then repeat the schedule. Fig. 7.5 gives an example of such a schedule. Each of the duties on the schedule list must be explained in detail on a written work sheet or "job breakdown" for the employee to follow. This description is the procedure that management requires to be used in performing each task. The job breakdown includes the name of the task, tools, equipment, and materials to be used, and the step-by-step list of *what to do* and *how to do it.* Fig. 7.6 is an example of such a job breakdown.

In addition to establishing procedures, a time standard for accomplishing each task is important. Based on studies of the actual time required for performing the same tasks by several different workers, an average time standard can be set. This is used to determine labor-hour requirements for each department within the foodservice and also provides management with data to establish a realistic daily workload.

Equipment: Heavy-duty power equipment is available to foodservice managers to aid in keeping the facility clean and properly maintained. Mechanical food waste disposals indispensable in most foodservices, eliminate the need for garbage cans, which may become unsightly and difficult to keep clean. Disposals are located where food waste originates in quantities such as in vegetable and salad preparation units, main cooking areas, and the dishwashing room. In the latter, a disposal can be incorporated as a part of the scraping and prewash units of the dishwashing machine.

Compactors and can and bottle crushers (Fig. 7.7) reduce appreciably the volume of trash, including items such as disposable dishes and tableware, food cartons, bags, and crates. (See Chapter 9 for details of this equipment.)

Scrubbing/waxing machines are used for cleaning both kitchen and dining room floors and are available in many sizes and models. Adequate drains in the kitchen floor are essential for proper sanitizing, and should be cleaned regularly.

Care of equipment used in food preparation, storage, and service is an essential part of the maintenance program to ensure good sanitation. All

---

Typical Job Assignments for Heavy-duty Cleaner

MONDAY
Filter grease in snack bar
Clean left side of cafeteria hot-food pass-through
Clean all kitchen windows
Clean all kitchen table legs
Vacuum air-conditioner filters; wipe exterior of air conditioner
Wash all walls around garbage cans
Complete high dusting around cooking areas
Clean outside of steam kettles
Wash kitchen carts
Clean cart-washing area

TUESDAY
Snack bar: Wash inside of hood exhaust
Clean all corners, walls, and behind refrigerator
Empty and clean grease can
Wash garbage cans
Main range area: Clean sides of ovens, deep-fat fryers, grills, drip pans, and hood over ovens

WEDNESDAY
Clean two refrigerators in cooks' area
Clean right side of cafeteria hot-food pass-through
Clean kettles, backs of steamers, and behind steamers
Clean walls around assembly line and pot room

THURSDAY
Clean all ovens in cooks' area, bottoms of ovens, and between ovens and stoves
Clean long tables in cooks' area, including legs and underneath
Clean and mop storage area

FRIDAY
Clean stainless steel behind kettles and steamers
Clean main range and tops of ovens
Clean legs of assembly line tables
Clean vents in all refrigeration equipment
Clean cart-washing area

Figure 7.5. Certain weekly or monthly tasks are scheduled, a few each day, for balanced workload and completion of all such tasks within the time frame of the rotation period.

containers and utensils must be cleaned thoroughly after *each* use. This is especially true of meat grinders and slicers, cutting boards, and knives in order to prevent any cross-contamination and ensure safety against *Clostridium perfringens, Campylobacter jejuni,* and salmonellae.

The thorough cleaning and sanitizing of stationary equipment are more difficult but quite as necessary as is the cleaning of dishes and small portable equipment. No piece of large equipment should be purchased unless the

---

How to Clean a Food Slicer

Equipment and supplies needed:
  Three cloths:
    One to wash
    One to dry
    One to apply rust preventative
  One-gal container for detergent
  One container with sanitizer
  One table knife

Cleaning products needed:
  Hand detergent
    In amount needed to make one gal of solution
    Usual proportion: 1 oz to 1 gal of water
  Sanitizer:
    Usual proportion: 2 oz chlorine to 1 gal water
  Rust preventative:
    In amount needed to moisten cloth for application of thin film to specified metal surfaces

Approximate time: 20 min
Frequency of cleaning: Daily, after each use.
Approximate cost: Labor _____
                  Supplies _____

What To Do	How To Do It
1. Remove parts	1. a. Remove electric cord from socket. b. Set blade control indicator at zero. c. Loosen knurled screw to release; remove meat holder and chute. d. Grasp scrap tray by handle; pull away from blade; remove. e. Loosen bolt at top of knife guard in front of sharpening device; remove bolt at bottom of guard; remove guard. f. Remove two knurled screw nuts under receiving tray; remove tray.

Figure 7.6. A Job Breakdown is prepared by managers detailing correct procedures, one for each task performed, and is used as a tool for training employees.

operating parts can be disassembled easily for cleaning purposes. Dishwashing machines, mixers, peelers, slicing machines, and stationary can openers are also examples of equipment that should be cleaned after each use. The standard practices for hand dishwashing should be followed in the routine cleaning of such equipment. An example of the detailed daily care necessary for one piece of equipment is shown in Fig. 7.6.

Detergents: The selection of a compound to aid in cleaning the many types of soil and food residues is a complex one because so many compounds are

What To Do	How To Do It
2. Clean knife	2. *a.* Wash circular surface with hot hand-detergent solution; rinse; dip in sanitizing solution; dry. DANGER: Keep clear of knife edge. *b.* Wring out cloth dipped in hot detergent solution, bunch thickly and wipe entire circumference of blade, wiping from center toward edge of blade; rinse; dip in sanitizing solution; dry with bunched cloth.
3. Clean and replace guard	3. *a.* Wash knife guard in hot detergent solution; rinse; sanitize; dry. *b.* Replace knife guard. *c.* Tighten bolt at top; insert and tighten bolt at bottom. DANGER: Replace knife guard as quickly as possible to prevent injury.
4. Clean other parts	4. *a.* Immerse in hot detergent solution: 1. Meat holder and chute. 2. Receiving tray. *b.* Wash; rinse, sanitize; dry.
5. Clean beneath receiving tray	5. *a.* Wash surface below receiving tray with hot detergent solution; rinse; dry. *b.* Apply *very thin* film of rust preventative to any exposed metal *under* receiving tray.
6. Clean frame and base	6. *a.* Wash frame with hot detergent solution, rinse, dry. *b.* With table knife, push damp cloth under knife of slicer; pull cloth through to remove food particles.
7. Replace parts	7. *a.* Replace meat holder and chute; tighten knurled screw. *b.* Replace scrap tray. *c.* Replace receiving tray; replace and tighten two screw nuts under tray.

Figure 7.6. *(continued)*

available from which to choose. An understanding of the basic principles involved in cleaning will assist the foodservice manager in making this decision.

Detergents are defined as cleansing agents, solvents, or any substances that will remove foreign or soiling material from surfaces. Specifically listed are water, soap, soap powders, cleansers, acids, volatile solvents, and abrasives. Water alone has some detergency value, but most often it is the carrier of the cleansing agent to the soiled surface. Its efficiency for removing soil is increased when combined with certain chemical cleaning agents.

The three basic phases of detergency are penetration, suspension, and rinsing. Following are the actions and agents required for each phase.

Figure 7.7.   Waste equipment system. (Reprinted, courtesy of Hobart Corporation, Troy, Ohio.)

1. **Penetration:** The cleaning agent must penetrate between the particles of soil and between the layers of soil and the surface to which it adheres. This action, known as *wetting,* reduces surface tension and makes penetration possible. Agents are water, soaps, and synthetic detergents, which are rather fragile suds formers.

2. **Suspension:** An agent is required to hold the loosened soil in the washing solution so it can be flushed away and not redeposited. Agents (vary according to type of soil) are: *For sugars and salts,* water is the agent since these are water-soluble and are easily converted into solutions. *For fat* particles, an emulsifying action is required to saponify the fat and carry it away. Soap, highly alkaline salts, and nonionic synthetics may be used. *For protein* particles, colloidal solutions must be formed by *peptizing* (known also as sequestering or deflocculating). This action prevents curd formation in hard water, solvents, and sometimes abrasives are needed.

3. **Rinsing:** The agent used must remove and flush away soils and cleaners so they are not redeposited on the surfaces being washed. Agents: clean, clear,

hot water is usually effective alone. With some types of water, a *drying* agent may be needed to speed drying by helping the rinse water drain off surfaces quickly. This eliminates alkaline and hard water spotting, films, and streaks on the tableware or other items being cleaned.

The development of polyphosphate detergents has provided a wide variety of highly satisfactory cleaning compounds. Film deposit from precipitation, poor rinsability, and harshness to hands no longer are problems, and the selection of cleaners can be made to meet the needs for particular uses in the institution foodservices: for instance, a suds-producing hand wash with high wetting action would be satisfactory as such but entirely unsatisfactory for machine dishwashing where a nonsuds-producing detergent is needed.

Selection of the right detergent for the job of cleaning in any situation is determined in large measure by the hardness of the water. The sequestering of the lime and magnesia of hard water by the polyphosphates produces a clear, not muddy, solution with insoluble precipitates, as is the case when some of the phosphates and silicates are used.

Foodservice sanitation is concerned mainly with china, crockery, glass, and metal surfaces. Common soils to be removed are saliva, lipstick, grease, and carbohydrate and protein food particles that may adhere to dishes, glassware, silverware, cooking utensils, worktable tops, floors, or other surfaces. Some types of food soils such as sugars, starches, and certain salts are water soluble. The addition of a wetting agent to hot water will readily remove most of these simple soils. The soils that are insoluble in water, such as animal and vegetable fats and proteins, organic fiber or carbon residues, and mineral oil, are more difficult to remove. Abrasives or solvents may be necessary in some cases to effect complete cleanliness.

The use of a "balanced" detergent or one with a carefully adjusted formula of ingredients suitable for the hardness of the water and the characteristics of the soil is advised in order to produce the best results. The properties of the detergent must cause complete removal of the soil without deposition of any substance or deleterious effect on surfaces washed.

Detergents for *dishwashing machines* must be a complex combination of chemicals that will completely remove the soil in a single pass through a high-speed machine. It must soften the water, solubilize and emulsify greases, break down proteins, suspend soil, protect the metal of the machine, increase wetting action, and counteract minerals in the wash water. Other characteristics desired in some situations are defoaming action where excess sudsing is a problem, and chlorination action where a chlorine-type detergent is used to remove stains and discolorations.

It is the phosphate in dishwashing compounds that reacts with the minerals in the water. Many different types of phosphates are used, from the crude ones, such as trisodium phosphate, and the more refined, such as pyrophosphates; but the most efficient is the highly refined polyphosphate ingredient that completely cancels out the mineralization of the water and "conditions" water in the wash tank for the cleansing task.

Managers responsible for purchasing dishwashing and other cleaning compounds should be aware of the chemicals they contain and the suitability for use in a particular situation. The effectiveness of the product instead of the price should be the primary factor in the selection of any cleaning compound. In evaluating the cost of a rinse agent, for example, consider the concentration required (parts per million) for effective drying in relation to the price to get a true usage cost.

The quality of service offered by the company selling detergents is an important factor in selecting a particular brand. Sales representatives know their products' capabilities and can give good assistance in selection of items for the foodservice's specific needs. For example, the salesperson should know as much or more about the operation of various dishwashing machines than do the managers. Since the company representative is accustomed to making quantitative and qualitative tests under differing circumstances and conditions, that person can wisely recommend the amounts of a compound to use. Since it is to the company's advantage to have its products do the best job possible, the representative will not want to recommend using too much as it may be as ineffective as too little.

Dishwashing machines should be equipped with automatic detergent dispensers. Also, a water softener more than pays for itself and is recommended for use in hard water areas.

Pest Control: The importance of rodent and insect control cannot be minimized. Rats, mice, flies, roaches, grain insects, fruit flies, and gnats all facilitate the transmission of communicable disease; therefore, it is essential for any foodservice to try to effect complete elimination of resident pest infestations and then to correct conditions within the establishment so that such pests cannot gain entrance in the future.

Two conditions, food and a place to "harbor" or hide and live, are required for these pests to survive. Adherence to strict rules for proper food storage and maintenance of high standards for cleaning the nooks and corners, such as drawers in cooks' tables, around sink pipes and drains, as well as the general overall sanitation and cleaning program, provides good preventive maintenance against pests.

Many roaches and insects gain entrance to a building on incoming foodstuffs and packages, which makes their control difficult. Their reproduction is rapid, and they thrive in the warm, damp hiding places afforded in many foodservices. Screens to help keep out flies, covered trash and garbage cans, closed cracks and crevices in walls and around equipment and areas around pipes, and clean storerooms are preventive measures to try to block the entrance and reduce the hiding places of such pests. The use of certain residual insecticides is effective treatment when there is no danger of polluting food, whereas the use of less toxic insecticides is recommended for contact spraying.

Ratproofing the building to make it impossible for rodents to gain entrance is the best preventive measure for making it free of the rodents. This means the closing of openings as small as one-half inch in diameter, placing rat guards on all wires both inside and outside of pipes leading into the building, and careful joining of the cement walls and foundations of the building. Trapping and the use of rodenticides are part of a rodent-control program and are used either inside or outside the building. However, the most effective rodenticides are also the most dangerous to humans and pets; therefore, they must be used with care and caution.

Constant attention and alertness to signs of pests and an effective program for their destruction by a trained person within the organization or an outside agency are usually required. Specialized entomological services can be scheduled, as often as once a month. The effectiveness of such an effort depends on its scope, regularity, and intelligent administration of a cleaning program and proper care of foodstuffs to eliminate the environmental factors conducive to the harboring of pests.

DISHWASHING/WAREWASHING   Dishwashing requires a two-part operation, that is, the cleaning procedure to free dishes and utensils of visible soil by scraping or a water flow method, and the sanitizing or bactericidal treatment to eliminate the health hazard. Dishwashing for public eating places is subject to rigid regulations.

The two groups of equipment and utensils that are commonly considered for discussion under dishwashing are: kitchen utensils, such as pots, pans, strainers, skillets, and kettles soiled in the process of food preparation; and eating and drinking utensils, such as dishes, glassware, spoons, forks, and knives.

Kitchen Utensils: Mechanical pot and pan washing equipment is relatively expensive; therefore, in many foodservices this activity remains a hand operation. A three-compartment sink is recommended for any hand dishwashing setup (see Fig. 7.8). Public health authorities recommend that sinks used for manual washing and sanitizing operations be of adequate length, width, and depth to permit the complete immersion of the equipment and utensils.

The soil may be loosened from the utensils by scraping and then soaking them in one compartment of the sink, well filled with hot water, previous to the time of washing. A forced-flow pump system unit, such as shown in Fig. 7.9, facilitates the cleaning of pots and pans. It can be installed onto the end of any sink and is relatively inexpensive to install and operate, and highly effective in the loosening and removing of cooked-on food.

After the surface soil has been removed from the utensils, the sink is drained and refilled with hot water to which a washing compound is added. The utensils are washed in the hot detergent solution in the first compartment; rinsed in the second compartment, the outlet and inlet of which are so adjusted as to keep

Figure 7.8. Three-compartment stainless steel pot and pan sink with sliding platform. Note the rounded corners for ease of cleaning and good sanitation. (Courtesy, S. Blickman.)

Figure 7.9. Pump-forced flow of water loosens food particles from cooking utensils in a pot and pan sink. Easily installed on end of sink. (Courtesy, Kewanee Washer Corporation.)

the water level constant if hot water is kept running throughout the process; and sanitized in the third compartment.

There are several methods for sanitizing both dishes and utensils. One recommended method is by immersing them for at least 1 minute in a lukewarm (at least 75°F) chlorine bath containing a minimum of 50 ppm available chlorine. Dishes and utensils must be thoroughly clean for a chlorine rinse to be an effective germicidal treatment. Another method of sanitizing hand-washed dishes or utensils is immersion in clean soft water of at least 170° for 1 minute (see Fig. 7.9). Fig. 7.10 illustrates a sink arrangement for the wash, rinse, and sanitize phases of hand dishwashing. (Note that some states require a "prewash" phase in addition to the standard three phases.) Utensils also may be successfully sanitized by subjecting them to live steam in an enclosed cabinet after washing and rinsing. The hot, clean utensils should be air-dried before stacking upside down on racks or hanging for storage.

Dishes, Glassware, Silverware: Washing of these items can be accomplished by hand or by use of mechanical dishwashers. Steps for these are outlined in Figs. 7.11 and 7.12. In either case, *prewashing* or *preflushing*, which applies to any type of water scrapping of dishes before washing, is recommended to prevent food soil in the wash water. The usual types of water scrapping equipment include: (1) a combination forced water stream and food waste collection unit built into the scrapping table, by use of which dishes are rinsed under the stream of water before racking, (2) a hose and nozzle arrangement over a sink for spraying the dishes after they are in racks, and (3) a prewash cabinet through which the racks of soiled dishes pass and are jet-sprayed to remove food particles prior to their entering the wash section of the dishwashing machine (see Fig. 8.18 in Chapter 8). The prewash cabinet can be built in as a part of the large model machines or, in small installations, may be a separate unit attached

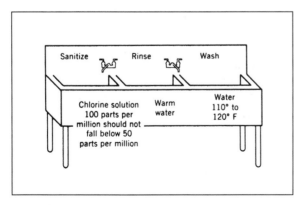

Figure 7.10.   Sink arrangement and U.S. Public Health Service (USPHS) recommended temperature and sanitizing method for hand dish- or panwashing.

HAND DISHWASHING

Important Steps (in Doing the Job)	Key Points [a]
1. Get ready (materials and equipment)	Sinks Hot water Washing powders (chlorine, or other bactericidal treatment, if used) Scraper Garbage can Drying racks
2. Scrape dishes and prewash	Use scraper Garbage in can or disposer
3. Wash dishes	Each piece separately Hot water, 110–120° F Use detergent (washing powder)
4. Rinse	Place in basket Set in hot rinse water
5. Sanitize	Place basket in vat In hot water (170° F for one min or 212° F for 30 sec) [b] 2 min in chemical solution (chlorine of approved strength)
6. Dry	Lift out basket Place on drain board Air dry
7. Store	Cups and glasses bottoms up Stack dishes on mobile carts In clean protected place
8. Clean vats	Stiff brush Washing powder
9. Use separate baskets for dishes, cups, and glasses	
10. Silver may be air-dried or by use of clean towel	
11. Fingers should not touch surfaces which come in contact with food or drink	
12. All multiservice eating and drinking utensils must be thoroughly cleaned after each usage	
13. Single-service containers must be used only once	

[a] Key points are those things which will make or break the job, injure the worker, or make the job easier to do.
[b] This standard may vary with local or area regulations.

Figure 7.11. Job breakdown details procedure for hand dishwashing.

MACHINE DISHWASHING

Important Steps (in Doing the Job)	Key Points [a]
1. Get ready (materials and equipment)	Sort dishes, cups, glassware, and silver Water temperature: 140° F wash, 170° F rinse [b] Check washing powder and dispenser, wash and rinse sprays
2. Scrape and prerinse	Use brush to scrape off garbage
3. Rack dishes, etc.	Place in separate racks Do not pile dishes, cups, etc. Cups and glassware bottoms up One kind at a time, separately
4. Place racks in machine	Every dish, etc., under spray
5. Wash	Start machine Turn on wash spray 140° to 160° F Do not hurry machine if it is manually operated Keep washtank water clean
6. Rinse	10 sec 170° F [b]
7. Dry	Remove racks Allow dishes, etc., to dry in racks on drain table or if flight type machine, do not remove dishes before they reach end of conveyer
8. Store	Fingers should not touch surfaces which come in contact with food In a clean, dry place above floor Away from dust and flies Dishes stacked Cups and glasses bottoms up—leave in racks in which they are washed
9. Clean machine	Take out scrap trays and clean Clean wash sprays Use clean water Add new washing powder as required

[a] *Key points are those things which will make or break the job, injure the worker, or make the job easier to do.*
[b] *This means temperature of 170° F at the dish, and requires 180° F water in the line. This standard may vary with local or area regulations.*

Figure 7.12. Job breakdown details procedure for machine dishwashing.

to the wash machine in such a way that the water used is the overflow from the wash tank. The prewash water should be at a temperature of 110° to 140°F to provide for the liquefying of fat and the noncoagulation of protein food particles adhering to dish surfaces. The installation and use of a prewash system lessens the amount of organic waste and the number of microorganisms entering the wash tank, removes fat that might otherwise result in suds formation, reduces the number of washwater changes, cuts the costs for detergents, and results in cleaner dishes.

There are many dishwashing machines on the market. Various types are discussed in Chapter 9, but Fig. 7.13 illustrates the general principles of *how* dishes are washed in a single-tank, spray-type machine. Large machines have divided tanks (Fig. 7.14) so that the wash and rinse waters are kept separate and the dilution of the wash water is less rapid.

After the prerinse, the dishes are loaded into racks or on conveyor belts in a way that food-contact surfaces will be exposed to direct application of the wash water with detergent and to the clean rinse waters. Cups, bowls, and glasses must be inverted and overcrowding or nesting of pieces avoided if dishwashing is to be effective. Wash water shall not be less than 120°F, and if hot water is the sanitizing agent, the rinse water shall be 180°F. The pressure of the rinse water must be maintained at a minimum of 15 pounds per square inch (psi) but not more than 25 psi to make the sanitizing effective.

China, glassware, and silver can be washed in the same machine, but it is preferred wherever possible to subject glasses to friction by brushes so that all parts of the glass are thoroughly cleaned, which means the use of a special machine designed for that purpose (Fig. 7.15). This is especially important in soda fountains, bars, and similar establishments where glasses are the primary utensils used. To prevent water spotting, it is advisable to use a suitable detergent for the washing of silver and also a drying agent with high wetting property in the final rinse water to facilitate air drying. The introduction of a drying agent with low foam characteristics into the sanitizing rinse promotes rapid drying of all types of tableware.

Provision for the storage of clean glasses and cups in the racks or containers in which they have been washed reduces the possibility of hand contamination.

Some machines are designed for a chemical solution rinse rather than the high-energy use of the 180°F temperature water. In this case, the rinse water used with the chemical sanitizer shall not be less than 75°F or less than that specified by the manufacturer. Chemicals used for sanitizing should be dispensed automatically to make sure that the proper amount and concentration are used.

Dishes can be dried by hot air blast within the machine or allowed to air dry. If the hot water rinse is used, dishes should be hot enough to air dry within 45 seconds before they are removed for storage.

All steps require energy except air drying. For this reason, the low-temperature models are preferred by many operators. To minimize energy use, only fully loaded racks or conveyors should be put through the machine.

Figure 7.13.   Design and identification of parts of a single-tank dishwashing machine. (Reprinted, courtesy of Hobart Corporation, Troy, Ohio.)

The NSFI (see section entitled "For More Information" at the end of this chapter) offers acceptable standards for wash and rinse cycles of three types of dishwashing machines: (1) single tank, stationary rack, hood, and door types, (2) single tank, conveyor type, and (3) multiple-tank conveyor type with dishes in inclined position on conveyor or in rack. These standards can be obtained and used as a check on specifications of various makes of dishwashers and by managers for ensuring that the specified conditions such as water temperature and pressure are met. Employees, too, should be trained to follow proper

Figure 7.14. Phantom view of a two-tank dishwashing machine and identification of ports. (Reprinted, courtesy of Hobart Corporation, Troy, Ohio.)

procedures in the use and care of the dishwashing machine, or hand washing of dishes if no machine is available.

Any machine can fail in its function if it is not kept clean and properly maintained, and dishwashing equipment is no exception. Corrosion or lime deposits in nozzles can alter the jet or spray materially. Also, detergent sanitizers can be inactivated by contact with soiled surfaces and lose their power of penetration. The removal of microbial contamination is necessary; otherwise, the washed surfaces of dishes will have deposited on them bacterial populations and soil proportionate to that in the washing solution.

Figure 7.15. Glasswasher installed for convenient use in a back-counter unit.

Good maintenance includes frequent examination and lubrication where needed by a qualified maintenance person to ensure the continuing satisfactory operation of motors, nozzles, pumps, thermostats, thermometers, and all moving parts of a dishwashing machine.

The installation of elaborate equipment, however, offers no real security for good sanitation, since the efficiency of the machines depends almost entirely on the operator, the availability of an adequate supply of hot water at the proper temperature and pressure, the selection and concentration of detergent used for the hardness of the water, and the length of time the dishes are subjected to treatment. In the small, hand-operated, single-tank machines, the process and length of washing time are under the control of the operator and are followed by the rinsing process, also under manual control. Other machines have automatic controls that regulate the length of times for washing and rinsing. Thermometers that record the temperatures of both wash and rinse waters and thermostatic controls, except for the final rinse, are included as standard parts of dishwashing machines. Booster heaters with temperature controls are available and necessary to provide the sanitizing rinse temperature, because 180°F water in the pipe lines of a building would be a hazard to personnel safety. The installation of electronic detergent dispensers makes it possible to maintain optimum detergent concentration in the wash water and sanitizing chemical rinse in low-temperature machines. Each of these mechanical aids is most helpful in reducing the variables due to the human element and ensures clean, properly sanitized dishes and pots and pans.

CHECKS AND INSPECTIONS   Maintaining high standards of sanitation is essential in *all* foodservice establishments regardless of type or size. Consumers expect and demand a clean facility. In fact, it is one of the first criteria they use for judging an eating place. The best means to ensure that proper sanitation procedures and high standards of sanitation are followed and achieved is to develop a departmental sanitation program. A cooperative effort is necessary to carry out an effective program. By setting high departmental standards and conducting routine self-inspections, management can be assured that sanitation regulations are met. It is critical that management take corrective action on sanitation deficiencies in order for the program to be fully effective.

All foodservice operations are regulated by local, state, or federal agencies. The purpose of these agencies is to administer and enforce regulations and standards for food protection. The major federal agency involved in setting and enforcing standards is the Food and Drug Administration (FDA). The FDA had the responsibility for developing model codes to be adopted by state and local health departments. The Model Food Service Sanitation Ordinance developed in 1976 is used as the basis for setting standards and codes. Official inspections are conducted on a periodic, monthly, or an annual basis depending on the type of foodservice and size of foodservice operation. Fig. 7.16 is an example of a health department's inspection form.

Safety

Physical safety of workers and customers alike is a major concern of foodservice administrators. A work environment free from hazards that cause accidents and a dining facility in which customers are safe and secure should be aims of all managers.

The Occupational Safety and Health Act (OSHA), which became effective April 28, 1971, makes it illegal *not* to have a safe establishment. It is administered by the U.S. Department of Labor (see section entitled "For More Information" at the end of this chapter). The act mandates action on the part of management to ensure safe and healthful working conditions for all of the nation's wage earners. It states, among other things, that each employer has a duty to furnish the employees with a place of employment that is safe and free from any hazards that can cause serious physical harm or death. The organization set up to enforce this act has the authority to inspect any place of business and to penalize those who do not comply with the provisions of the law. Managers must strictly comply with correcting specific potential hazards and furnish written records of any accidents that have occurred.

Two OSHA standards of particular concern to foodservice operators are the Hazard Communication Standard (HCS) and the bloodborne pathogens standards. The HCS also recognized as the "right-to-know" requires that employers

State of Oregon
OREGON STATE HEALTH DIVISION
Department of Human Resources
Environmental Health Services
FOOD INSPECTION REPORT

| FAC. TYPE | CTY NO. | ESTAB. NO. | INSPECT TIME |
| TRAVEL TIME |

ESTABLISHMENT NAME:

STREET ADDRESS:

CITY/COUNTY:

NAME OF LICENSEE:

INSPECTION DATE
MO.   DAY   YR.

Semi-Annual _____ Complaints _____

Critical Items _____ Reinspection _____

SCORE: _____

Public Notice of Restaurant Sanitation

☐ EXCEEDED THE SANITATION STANDARDS

☐ MET THE SANITATION STANDARDS

☐ FAILED TO MEET THE SANITATION STANDARDS

AN EVALUATION OF SANITATION ON YOUR PREMISES HAS THIS DAY BEEN MADE AND YOU ARE HEREBY NOTIFIED OF THE VIOLATIONS FOUND. SUCH VIOLATIONS MAY RESULT IN DENIAL, SUSPENSION, OR REVOCATION OF YOUR LICENSE; OR CLOSURE OF THE RESTAURANT MAY RESULT FROM UNCORRECTED CRITICAL VIOLATIONS OR FAILURE TO MAINTAIN THE MINIMUM ACCEPTABLE SCORE. YOU MAY OBTAIN A CONTESTED CASE HEARING FOR ANY DENIAL, SUSPENSION, REVOCATION OR CLOSURE BY CONTACTING THE LICENSING AGENCY. SUCH HEARINGS ARE IN ACCORDANCE WITH ORS CHAPTER 183.

ITEM NO./PT. OAR/ORS	SPECIFIC PROBLEM	REQUIRED CORRECTION & TIME LIMIT

OPERATOR _____   SANITARIAN _____

Figure 7.16. An example of one state's sanitation inspection report form for foodservice establishments. (Courtesy, Oregon State Health Division.)

(*continued*)

FOOD SOURCE

No.	Item	Pts
01	Approved source; unadulterated; no spoilage (OAR 32-026)	5
02	Approved milk dispensing; original container for shellfish (OAR 32-026)	1

FOOD PROTECTION

No.	Item	Pts
03	Potentially hazardous food meets temperature requirements during storage, preparation, display, service, transportation (OAR 32-024, -026, -028)	5
04	Dependable, spirit stem thermometers provided and located (OAR 32-024)	1
05	Potentially hazardous food properly thawed, cooked, preheated before hot-holding, rapidly reheated and cooled (OAR 32-024, -026)	4
06	Unwrapped and potentially hazardous food hot not reserved; self-service foods effectively protected (OAR 32-026, -028)	4
07	Food protection during storage, preparation, display, service, transportation (OAR 32-028)	2
08	Handling of food (ice) minimized (OAR 32-026, -024)	2
09	In use, food (ice) dispensing utensils properly stored (OAR 32-022)	1

PERSONNEL

No.	Item	Pts
10	Personnel with infections and sores restricted (ORS 624.080)	5
11	Hands washed and clean, good hygienic practices, no smoking in food preparation and service areas (OAR 32-030)	5
12	Clean clothes, hair restraints, no unauthorized personnel (OAR 32-030, -028)	1

FOOD EQUIPMENT AND UTENSILS – SANITIZING

No.	Item	Pts
13	Food (ice) contact surfaces of equipment; designed, constructed, maintained, installed, located (OAR 32-018)	2
14	Non-food contact surfaces of equipment; designed, constructed, maintained, installed, located (OAR-018)	1
15	Dishwashing facilities; designed, constructed, maintained, installed, located, operated (OAR 32-020)	2
16	Accurate thermometers, chemical test kits provided (OAR 32-020)	1
17	Pre-scrape, soak, wash, rinse water; clean, proper temperature (OAR 32-020)	2
18	Sanitization rinse; clean, temperature, concentration, exposure time; equipment, utensils sanitized (OAR 32-020)	4
19	Wiping cloths; clean, use restricted, stored in sanitizing solution (OAR 32-020)	1
20	Food contact surfaces of equipment and utensils clean, free of abrasives, detergents (OAR 32-020)	4
21	Non-food contact surfaces of equipment and utensils clean (OAR 32-020)	2
22	Protected storage, handling of clean equipment/utensils (OAR 32-022)	1
23	Single-service articles, storage, display, no re-use (OAR 32-022)	1

WATER, SEWAGE AND PLUMBING

No.	Item	Pts
24	Water source approved, safe, at least 20 P.S.I. (OAR 32-014)	5
25	Approved sewage and waste disposal (OAR 32-023)	4
26	Sewage disposal violations which do not directly or indirectly effect food service operations inside the restaurant (OAR 32-023)	2
27	Plumbing installed, maintained (OAR 32-023)	1
28	Cross-connection, back siphonage, backflow (OAR 32-023)	5

TOILET AND HANDWASHING FACILITIES

No.	Item	Pts
29	Number, convenient, accessible, designed, installed (OAR 32-012, -16)	2
30	Clean, enclosed, self-closing doors, fixtures good repair, hot and cold water, hand cleanser, sanitary towels/hand drying devices, provided, proper waste receptacles, handwashing signs posted (OAR 32-023, -012, -016)	2

GARBAGE AND REFUSE DISPOSAL

No.	Item	Pts
31	Containers or receptacles, covered; adequate number insect/rodent proof, frequency, clean (OAR 32-023)	1
32	Outside storage area enclosures properly constructed, clean (OAR 32-023)	1

INSECT AND RODENT, ANIMAL CONTROL

No.	Item	Pts
33	Approved and effective control of insects/rodents, outer openings protected, no birds, turtles, other animals (OAR 32-006, -028)	4

FLOORS, WALLS AND CEILINGS

No.	Item	Pts
34	Floors; installed, constructed with sealed junctures, smooth, easily cleanable, good repair (OAR 32-002)	1
35	Walls and ceilings; installed, constructed; washable up to splash level in food preparation, utensil washing and toilet areas (OAR 32-004)	1
36	Floors and junctures; clean, dustless cleaning methods (OAR 32-002)	2
37	Walls, attached equipment, ceilings; clean (OAR 32-004)	2

LIGHTING AND VENTILATION

No.	Item	Pts
38	Uniform lighting provided in food preparation and storage areas (OAR 32-008)	1
39	Adequate, designed ventilation systems in food preparation, dishwashing and restroom areas; filters cleaned (OAR 32-010)	1

HOUSEKEEPING

No.	Item	Pts
40	Toxic items properly stored, labeled, used (OAR 32-028, -032)	5
41	Premises maintained free of litter, unnecessary articles, cleaning/maintenance equipment properly stored (OAR 32-032)	1
42	Complete separation from living/sleeping quarters, personal items separate (OAR 32-032)	1
43	Clean, soiled linen properly stored (OAR 32-032)	1

Other Areas (do not affect grade)
____ Employes certified in First-aid for choking victims (ORS 624.130)
____ Smoking area comply with ORS 433.845 (effective July 1, 1983)
____ Food Sanitation Training ____

100% - 92% and no uncorrected critical violations:
EXCEEDED THE SANITATION STANDARDS

91% - 60% and no uncorrected critical violations:
MET THE SANITATION STANDARDS

59% or below:
FAILED TO MEET THE SANITATION STANDARDS

All 4 and 5 point critical violations must be rectified immediately with an approved alternative procedure and must be corrected within the designated time period. Previously cited 1 and 2 point items which have not been corrected are considered repeat violations and will accumulate 1 or 2 penalty points respectively each time they are observed on semi-annual inspections. Failure to correct critical violations as described above or two consecutive complete inspection sanitation scores below 60% may result in the closure of the restaurant or the revocation, suspension or denial of the license.

Figure 7.16. *(continued)*

develop and implement a program to communicate chemical hazards to all employees. An inventory of all chemicals used by the operation must be maintained, and they must be properly labeled. The manufacturer must supply, for each chemical, a Material Safety Data Sheet (MSDS) that identifies the chemical and includes a hazard warning. Fig. 7.17 is a sample of an MSDS

Material Safety Data Sheet

May be used to comply with
OSHA's Hazard Communication Standard,
29 CFR 1910.1200. Standard must be
consulted for specific requirements.

U.S. Department of Labor

Occupational Safety and Health Administration
(Non-Mandatory Form)
Form Approved
OMB No. 1218–0072

IDENTITY *(As Used on Label and List)*

Note: *Blank spaces are not permitted. If any item is not applicable, or no information is available, the space must be marked to indicate that.*

Section I

Manufacturer's Name	Emergency Telephone Number
Address *(Number, Street, City, State, and ZIP Code)*	Telephone Number for Information
	Date Prepared
	Signature of Preparer *(optional)*

Section II — Hazardous Ingredients/Identity Information

Hazardous Components (Specific Chemical Identity; Common Name(s))	OSHA PEL	ACGIH TLV	Other Limits Recommended	% *(optional)*

Section III — Physical/Chemical Characteristics

Boiling Point		Specific Gravity (H$_2$O = 1)	
Vapor Pressure (mm Hg.)		Melting Point	
Vapor Density (AIR = 1)		Evaporation Rate (Butyl Acetate = 1)	
Solubility in Water			
Appearance and Odor			

Section IV — Fire and Explosion Hazard Data

Flash Point (Method Used)	Flammable Limits	LEL	UEL
Extinguishing Media			
Special Fire Fighting Procedures			
Unusual Fire and Explosion Hazards			

(Reproduce locally)   OSHA 174, Sept. 1985

Figure 7.17.   Sample of a Material Safety Data Sheet (MSDS).

form. The bloodborne pathogen standard requires that all employees be made aware of potentially infectious materials that they may be exposed to while on duty. Examples of pathogens include the hepatitis B virus and the human immunodeficiency virus (HIV). For the foodservice manager, this means educating employees on risks of and proper procedures for entering patient rooms or cleaning food trays in the dishroom that may be contaminated with hazardous matter.

The National Safety Council, although not a regulatory agency but a nonprofit service organization, is devoted to safety education. Through its research, reports, and printed materials available to the public, the council provides valuable assistance to managers of numerous types of businesses, including foodservice.

Worker Safety

The provision of a safe workplace through a well-designed facility (see Chapter 8) with equipment facilities that meet federal, state, and local standards is a first step in ensuring worker safety. However, safety is more than a building with built-in safe features. Safety can never be *assumed,* for accidents can and do occur. Managers and employees must work together on a safety awareness program to attain a good safety record.

"Accidents don't happen; they are caused"—and they can be prevented. The National Safety Council has defined an accident as any suddenly occurring, unintentional event that causes injury or property damage. An accident has become a symbol of inefficiency, either human or mechanical, and usually represents a monetary loss to the organization. The injured individual loses not only time at work and wages, but also incurs indirect costs such as medical and insurance expenses, cost of training new workers, waste production resulting from inexperienced substitute workers, administrative costs for investigating and taking care of accidents, and cost of repair or replacement of broken or damaged equipment. Not only from the humanitarian standpoint, but also from the economic, should dietitians and other foodservice managers be aware of the advantages of good safety measures. All should seek ways to improve working conditions and employee performance that will reduce accidents with their resulting waste, and maintain low accident frequency and severity rates. *Severity rate* is computed by the number of working days lost because of accidents, and *frequency rate* by the number of lost-time accidents during any selected period, each multiplied by 1,000,000 and the result divided by the total number of hours worked during the same period. National Safety Council statistics rank the food industry about midway among all industry classifications in terms of severity rates. However, in terms of frequency rate, it is nearly twice as high as the average for all industries reporting.

Foodservice managers must organize for safety and develop a wholesome regard for safe procedures among the entire staff.

Safety Program

Specific topics for a safety campaign may be centered around the "three Es" of safety: engineering, education, and enforcement.

The *engineering* aspect refers to the built-in safety features of the building and equipment, and the manner in which the equipment is installed to make it safe to use. Encased motors, safety valves on pressure steamers, easily manipulated spigots on urns, and guards on slicing and chopping machines are examples of safety features. A maintenance program to keep equipment in good working order is the responsibility of management, as are all other phases of providing a safe environment.

A study of traffic patterns in kitchen and dining areas and the placement of equipment and supplies in locations to avoid as much cross traffic as possible, and the arrangement of equipment within a work unit to provide for logical sequence of movement without backtracking are a part of the engineering phase of the safety program.

Education for safety is a never-ending process. It begins with the establishment of firm policies regarding safety, which then should be discussed with each new employee during the orientation period. "Safety from the first day" is an appropriate slogan for any organization.

Since safety is an integrated part of every activity, it should be taught as a component of all skills and procedures. Written procedures for tasks to be performed by each employee must include the safe way of doing each task, and the written outline then used to train the employee in the correct steps to follow. These written, step-by-step procedures provide a follow-up, on-the-job reference for the employee, and can be used by managers as a check against employee performance.

Safety education, however, is more than training each employee in the procedures for a particular job. An ongoing group program based on *facts* about safe and unsafe practices keeps employees aware of safety. The National Safety Council, the Bureau of Vital Statistics, and various community safety councils, as well as trade and professional organizations, can provide statistics and materials for planning such a program. Data obtained from records kept on accidents *within* the organization are invaluable and more meaningful than general statistics.

A form for reporting accidents should be provided by management (see Fig. 7.18 as an example). These written records should include the type of accident, kind of injury that has occurred and to whom, when it occurred, the day and hour, and where it took place. In foodservices, most accidents occur at rush hours when it is especially difficult to take care of the injured, find replacement help, and continue efficient customer service. This fact alone should provide incentive enough for the manager to do all that is possible to promote safety.

Board of Education
Office of Assistant Supervisor of Home Economics
in Charge of Cafeterias

Department Report of Personal Injury Involving
the Employees of the City Schools

School _____   Date _____
Name _____   Title _____
Address _____   Date of accident _____
Sex _____   Time of accident _____
State fully in your own words how accident occurred: _____
_____
_____

Exact part of person injured and extent of injuries: _____
_____
_____

Probable period of disability _____
Was medical attention necessary? _____
Name and address of Physician _____
_____

Give location where accident occurred _____
Will employee lose any time? _____
If not able to work, give probable date of recovery _____
Are there any indications of permanent injury? _____
State monthly salary of employee _____
How long in our employ? _____

IMPORTANT: Fill out report in *duplicate* on day of accident and mail immediately
            to above office.

                                    _____
                                              Employee

Figure 7.18.   Example of a typical accident report form; to be filled in and filed immediately.

An analysis of the causes of accidents provides further data for preventing them. Causes may be classified into "unsafe acts" and "unsafe conditions." Usually it is found that unsafe acts outnumber unsafe conditions three to one. From this, there is an immediate indication of the need for proper training to reduce accidents.

In the foodservice industry, falls cause the largest number of food-handling accidents, usually due to greasy or wet floors, with cuts second, and burns and strains from lifting next in order. Falls and strains result in the greatest loss of time from the job and monetary loss to the institution.

It is management's responsibility to ferret out the reasons, remove the hazards, and then train the employees to prevent recurrence of the same accident. Good housekeeping procedures, such as storing tools and materials in proper places and keeping aisles and pathways clear, optimum lighting of work areas, prompt repair of broken tools and equipment, replacement of worn electrical cords, and proper care and removal of broken china and glassware, are only a few of the things that can be done to correct unsafe conditions. Employees should be encouraged to report to the manager any unsafe conditions they may notice. A simple form could be developed and made available to the employees for such reporting. Having the information in writing is helpful to the manager who must then follow-up to correct the situation.

The possibility of fires is an ever-present threat in foodservice establishments, making it essential that all employees follow good procedures in use of equipment and cooking techniques. Further, they should know the location of fire extinguishing equipment and how to use it. Directions for and practice in the use of fire extinguishers, fire blankets, and other first aid equipment, necessities in every institution kitchen, are included in training meetings, for supervisory personnel particularly. Information about the various types of fire extinguishers and which should be used for grease, paper and wood, and other types of fires is important. Fig. 7.19 gives this information. Group training in precautionary procedures to be followed in everyday work and instructions in what to do in case of an accident should be part of the overall safety program. Be certain that all employees know where and to whom to report an accident and that the phone numbers to use for emergencies are posted on or near the telephone.

Many aids are available to foodservice managers to use in setting up a training program. The National Restaurant Association's *Safety Operations Manual* is an excellent resource. The National Safety Council has posters, pamphlets, and other materials available for use in training sessions. These are invaluable sources of information and illustration for foodservice managers. Clear eye-catching posters that create favorable impressions and serve as reminders of good, safe practices are effective supplements to other types of training. The safety rules given in Fig. 7.20 may be used as topics for training sessions. However, each foodservice organization should establish its own similar list of safety rules to be adhered to in its own department.

The third "E" in the overall safety campaign is *enforcement*. This represents the follow-up or constant vigilance required to prevent carelessness and to make certain that the rules and prescribed procedures are observed. Enforcement can be accomplished in many ways. In some organizations, safety committees are set up among the employees, who observe and report unsafe conditions and practices. Membership on this committee may be rotated so that everyone will be personally involved in a campaign against accidents. In other places, contests among departments serve as incentives for keeping accident rates low. Honor rolls for accident-free days or months help call attention to safety records. If

KNOW YOUR FIRE EXTINGUISHERS

	WATER TYPE				FOAM	CARBON DIOXIDE	DRY CHEMICAL		MULTI-PURPOSE ABC	
							SODIUM OR POTASSIUM BICARBONATE			
	STORED PRESSURE	CARTRIDGE OPERATED	WATER PUMP TANK	SODA ACID	FOAM	CO2	CARTRIDGE OPERATED	STORED PRESSURE	STORED PRESSURE	CARTRIDGE OPERATED
CLASS A FIRES — ORDINARY COMBUSTIBLES — WOOD, PAPER, TRASH HAVING GLOWING EMBERS	YES	YES	YES	YES	YES	NO (BUT WILL CONTROL SMALL SURFACE FIRES)	NO (BUT WILL CONTROL SMALL SURFACE FIRES)	NO (BUT WILL CONTROL SMALL SURFACE FIRES)	YES	YES
CLASS B FIRES — FLAMMABLE LIQUIDS — FLAMMABLE LIQUIDS, GASOLINE, OIL, PAINTS, GREASE, ETC.	NO	NO	NO	NO	YES	YES	YES	YES	YES	YES
CLASS C FIRES — ELECTRICAL EQUIPMENT — ELECTRICAL EQUIPMENT	NO	NO	NO	NO	NO	YES	YES	YES	YES	YES
CLASS D FIRES — COMBUSTIBLE METALS	SPECIAL EXTINGUISHING AGENTS APPROVED BY RECOGNIZED TESTING LABORATORIES									
METHOD OF OPERATION	PULL PIN-SQUEEZE HANDLE	TURN UPSIDE DOWN AND BUMP	PUMP HANDLE	TURN UPSIDE DOWN	TURN UPSIDE DOWN	PULL PIN-SQUEEZE LEVER	RUPTURE CARTRIDGE-SQUEEZE LEVER	PULL PIN-SQUEEZE HANDLE	PULL PIN-SQUEEZE HANDLE	RUPTURE CARTRIDGE-SQUEEZE LEVER
RANGE	30'-40'	30'-40'	30'-40'	30'-40'	30'-40'	3'-8'	5'-20'	5'-20'	5'-20'	5'-20'
MAINTENANCE	CHECK AIR PRESSURE GAUGE MONTHLY	WEIGH GAS CARTRIDGE ADD WATER IF REQUIRED ANNUALLY	DISCHARGE AND FILL WITH WATER ANNUALLY	DISCHARGE ANNUALLY -RECHARGE	DISCHARGE ANNUALLY -RECHARGE	WEIGH SEMI-ANNUALLY	WEIGH GAS CARTRIDGE-CHECK CONDITION OF DRY CHEMICAL ANNUALLY	CHECK PRESSURE GAUGE AND CONDITION OF DRY CHEMICAL ANNUALLY	CHECK PRESSURE GAUGE AND CONDITION OF DRY CHEMICAL ANNUALLY	WEIGH GAS CARTRIDGE-CHECK CONDITION OF DRY CHEMICAL ANNUALLY

Class symbols: A — ORDINARY COMBUSTIBLES; B — FLAMMABLE LIQUIDS; C — ELECTRICAL EQUIPMENT; D — COMBUSTIBLE METALS

Figure 7.19. Types of fire extinguishers.

General Restaurant Safety Rules

(please post)

- Report *every* injury *at once,* regardless of severity, to your Supervisor for first aid. *Avoid delay.*

- Report all *unsafe conditions,* broken or splintered chairs or tables, defective equipment, leaking radiators, torn carpeting, uneven floors, loose rails, unsafe tools or knives, broken china and glass, etc.

- Understand the *safe way* to perform any task assigned to you. If in doubt, see your Supervisor. Never take unnecessary chances.

- If you have to move over-heavy objects, ask for help. *Do not overlift.* When lifting any heavy object, keep your back straight, bend your knees and *use your leg muscles.* Your back has weak muscles and can easily be strained.

- Wear safe, sensible clothes for your work. Wear safe, comfortable shoes, with good soles. Never wear thin-soled or broken-down shoes. *Do not wear high-heeled shoes for work.* Ragged or over-long sleeves or ragged clothing may result in an injury.

- If you have to reach for a high object, use a ladder, not a chair or table or a makeshift. There is no substitute of any kind of a good ladder. *Never overreach.* Be careful when you have to reach high to fill coffee urns, milk tanks, etc.

- Horseplay or practical jokes on the job are forbidden.

- Do not argue or fight with fellow employees. The results are usually unpleasant and dangerous.

- Keep floors clean and dry. Pick up any loose object from the floor immediately to prevent someone from falling.

- Do not overload your trays. Trays should be loaded so as to give good balance. An improperly loaded tray can become dangerous.

- Aisles, passageways, stairways must be kept clean and free from obstructions. Do not permit brooms, pails, mops, cans, boxes, etc., to remain where someone can fall over them. Wipe up any grease or wet spots from stairs or floors or ramps *at once.* These are serious falling hazards.

- Walk, do not run, in halls, down ramps or stairs, or around work areas. Be careful when passing through swinging doors.

- Keep your locker clean and the locker top free from all loose or discarded materials, such as: newspapers, old boxes, bottles, broken equipment, etc.

- Dispose of all broken glass and china immediately. Never serve a guest with a cracked or chipped glass or piece of china. Check all silverware.

- Take sufficient time to serve your guests properly. Too much haste is liable to cause accidents to your guests and to yourself. *Haste makes waste.*

- Remove from service any chair, table or other equipment that is loose, broken or splintered so as to prevent injury.

- *Cashiers.* Close cash registers with back of hand. Do not permit fingers to hang over edge of drawer.

- Money is germ-laden. Keep your fingers out of your hair, eyes, and mouth after handling. Wash hands carefully before eating. Report the slightest cut or sore *at once* for treatment.

- Help *new employees* to work safely on the job. Show them the right way to do the job—the safe way.

Figure 7.20. Safety rules—a basis for safety training programs.

possible, one person in each organization should have the overall responsibility for developing and supervising the safety program, after being specifically trained for the task.

Probably the most effective overall enforcement plan, however, is a periodic inspection of the department by someone on the supervisory staff. The use of a checklist as a reminder of all points to be observed is helpful. Any foodservice manager could develop a form for use in a specific operation. The comprehensive checklist illustrated in Fig. 7.21 includes both food safety and sanitation and may serve as a model for developing a checklist for a specific department.

Customer Protection

Customers of foodservices deserve the same careful concern given employees in regard to safety. They expect and should have assurance that the food served will be safe for consumption and that the facility for dining is also safe. This includes everything from a safe parking area that is well-lighted and free of any stumbling "blocks" to furniture that is in good condition and will not cause snags or splinters. The flooring must be kept in good repair to prevent tripping and falls, and any spillage should be wiped up at once so that no one will slip and fall.

Dining rooms should be adequately lighted and ample aisle space provided between tables so that diners can see to make their way through the room without tripping.

Servers must be well-trained in correct serving procedures so they will not spill any hot food on the customers or anything on the floor that could cause accidents. Any spillage must be cleaned up at once.

Managers are liable for accidents that may occur on the premises. Lawsuits could result that are costly as well as detrimental to the reputation of the establishment. Therefore, extreme care should be taken so that none will occur.

Summary

In summary, the steps to safety in any foodservice include awareness, involvement, and control. The first step is *awareness* on the part of managers for the need to provide a safe environment for employees and patrons, and to assume the responsibility for and positive attitude toward accident prevention. *Involvement* includes initiating a safety education program or campaign that keeps employees safety conscious. A training program that indoctrinates employees with the philosophy of working safely and instructs them in how to do so is a major part of being involved. Seeking employee suggestions about safe procedures and forming safety committees in which employees participate are other forms of involvement. *Control* is insisting on safety, checking on safety codes and

Check Sheet
Safety in the Kitchen

(Rating Scale: 5—1; 5 points is highest and 1 point the lowest.)

Burns
1. Are handles of pans on the stove turned so the pans cannot be knocked off? _____
2. Are flames turned off when removing pans from stove? _____
3. Are dry pot holders used for lifting hot pans? _____
4. Are fellow workers warned when pans are hot? When pans of hot food are to be moved? _____
5. Is steam equipment in proper working order to avoid burns from leaks? _____
6. Is hot water regulated at proper temperature so it will not scald? _____
7. Are lids lifted cautiously and steamer doors opened slowly to avoid steam burns? _____

Cuts
1. Are broken dishes and glasses promptly cleaned up and disposed of in special container provided? _____
2. Are knives stored in the slotted case provided for them? _____
3. Are knives left on the drain board to be washed, and not dropped into the sink? _____
4. Is the safety hood put over the slicer after each use and cleaning? _____
5. Is the can opener in good repair so it cuts sharply and leaves no ragged edges? _____
6. Are safety devices provided on slicers and choppers? _____

Electricity
1. Are electric cords in good repair? _____
2. Are sufficient outlets provided for the equipment in use? _____
3. Are hands always dry before touching electrical equipment? _____
4. Are there extra fuses in the fuse box? _____

Falls
1. Are spilled foods cleaned up immediately? _____
2. Are corridors and stairways free from debris? _____
3. Are articles placed on shelves securely so they will not jar off? _____
4. Are step ladders sturdy and in good repair? _____
5. Are brooms and mops put away properly after use and not left out against a wall or table to trip someone? _____
6. Are hallways well lighted and steps well marked so no one will trip? _____

Fires and Explosions
1. Are gas pipes free from leaks? Have they been checked by the gas company? _____
2. Are matches kept in a covered metal container? _____
3. Are fire blankets and extinguishers provided? _____
4. Has the fire extinguisher been checked in the last month? _____
5. Is the first-aid box fully supplied? _____
6. Is hot fat watched carefully, and is cold fat stored away from flame? _____

Please Report Immediately Any Fires or Accidents to the Food Manager
or Dial _____ to Report a Fire

Figure 7.21. Example of a kitchen safety check sheet to be used by managers to help identify unsafe practices.

meeting them, analyzing accident records as a basis for improvement, and, above all, good consistent supervision of employees' work. This assumes that the institution has established safety policies, written procedures for job performance, and adopted a procedure for reporting and handling accidents that are known to all in the organization.

Benefits of a safety program include: a reduction in accidents, improvement in employee morale, patron satisfaction and feeling of security, and fewer workers' compensation claims, resulting in reduced costs and better financial performance for the foodservice. The objective is to keep injuries to a minimum and the working force at maximum efficiency.

Summary Questions

1. Which organizations establish and enforce sanitation and safety standards?
2. How does the USPHS define potentially hazardous foods?
3. Other than food handlers, what are six other sources and routes of transmission of pathogens through food?
4. Which is the most frequent type of food poisoning and why?
5. What is the NSFI? Its purposes?
6. List some relevant topics for employee inservice training in the area of sanitation.
7. Describe the recommended procedure for manual pot and pan washing.
8. What is OSHA? What is its influence on foodservice operations?

Bibliography

Cliver, D. O.: Foodborne Diseases. San Diego: Academic Press, Inc., 1990.

National Restaurant Association (NRA): Applied Foodservice Sanitation, 4th ed. John Wiley & Sons, Inc., 1992.

National Restaurant Association (NRA): Safety Operations Manual. Washington, DC: Author, 1989.

Todd, E. C. D.: Preliminary estimates of costs of foodborne disease in the United States. J. Food Protec. 52:595–601.

Additional Resources

Centers for Disease Control and Prevention: Morbidity and Mortality Weekly Report. Atlanta, GA: U.S. Dept. of Health, Education, and Welfare, Public Health Service.

National Restaurant Association Education Foundation, 250 S. Wacker Dr., Suite 1400, Chicago, IL 60606.

NSF International, P.O. Box 130140, Ann Arbor, MI 48113-0140.

Occupational Safety and Health Act. Office of Assistant Secretary of Labor for OSHA, 200 Constitution Ave., NW, Washington, DC 20210. For publications: OSHA Publication Distribution, Room S 4203, Washington, DC 20210.

U.S. Department of Health, Education, and Welfare, Public Health Service, Food and Drug Administration: Food Service Sanitation Manual, Publ. No. (FDA) 78-2081, 1976.

Facilities Planning and Design

Facility planning and design are among the responsibilities of foodservice managers. Their involvement can range from planning a new foodservice facility to remodeling or making minor changes within an existing facility.

The concepts presented in this chapter apply to all planning projects regardless of size or scope. However, managers must identify their own goals and needs, work to maximize the project's attributes, and plan for and around any constraints that exist. Providing an appropriate, efficient facility for the production and service of high-quality, attractive food is the desired outcome of all foodservices.

Learning Objectives

After studying this chapter, the reader should be able to

1. explain the preliminary preparation necessary before undertaking a facility design project

2. make appropriate, simple data collection studies required for the preliminary planning

3. develop a prospectus (written plan) for a simple remodeling or building project

4. list the members of a project-planning team and state their roles and expected contributions to the project plan

5. list the legal considerations relating to a building project and where to obtain information about state and local regulations

6. prepare a floor plan to scale that reflects the goals and procedures of the prospectus

7. arrange on the floor plan the various work units and required equipment for greatest work efficiency

Definitions and Goals

To thoroughly understand the planning process, foodservice managers and others involved in a design project need to know certain definitions and examples of terminology used in this chapter and, also, the goals to be achieved. Definitions include

- *Physical*—pertaining to material existence measured by weight, motion, and resistance. Thus, anything taking up space in a facility must be accounted for and fit the available space.
- *Design*—refers to the broad function of developing the facility, including site selection, menu, equipment requirements, and other planning functions that will guide the project into reality.
- *Layout*—the process of arranging the physical facilities, including equipment, that dictates operational efficiency. This involves a design drawn on paper to show walls, windows, doors, and other structural components. After this outline drawing is complete, required work areas are designated on the plan, then the equipment and other facilities are arranged and drawn onto the plan.

Foodservice managers must be involved with the development of all aspects of the design plan to assure that the facility is properly coordinated and functional. Although other professionals will design the electrical, water, and plumbing systems, as well as lighting, heating, ventilation, and structural components of the building, the foodservice manager must give input on the specific needs of the foodservice facility. The finished project plan results in either success or failure for the organization involved!

Preliminary Preparation for Facility Planning

Before attempting to develop a final design, foodservice managers need to prepare themselves for the task ahead. This may include

- studying trends that affect foodservice design
- learning what is new in design and equipment

- obtaining and reading copies of regulatory codes and required operating licenses that have a bearing on foodservice design and operation
- becoming knowledgeable about special requirements for specific types of foodservices

Thus, they will have the information needed for making a worthwhile contribution to the overall planning team and the background to make sound decisions as the project progresses.

Trends Affecting Foodservice Design

DINING OUT CHANGES   More people are eating meals away from home than ever before. Depending on the economy, however, the types of foodservices patronized will be affected. The foodservice industry is responding to this trend by making changes in the style of foodservices, types of food served, and prices charged. All these factors, in turn, influence a facility's design.

CHANGE IN DESIRED MENU ITEMS   Continuing changes in customer preferences for types of foods and meals eaten away from home also affect design requirements of a foodservice facility. A concern for physical fitness and well-being, for example, changed the menus of most foodservices. Menus now offer lighter, more healthful food selections and limited desserts. This changes the equipment needed and the space requirements and, thus, affects the remodeling or new construction to accommodate preparation of foods customers prefer.

ECONOMIC FACTORS   Costs of wages, food, and utilities can influence selection of a type of foodservice and its design. For example, as employees' wages increase, automation of equipment (e.g., robots) and the purchase of convenience foods are more common. In addition, as costs for food and the energy to prepare it continue to rise, the foodservice design must provide for efficient operation. Managers must strive to maximize the operation's efficiency through the best possible design and layout of work centers; for example, minimizing the number of steps a worker must take, as well as the distances necessary to transport and distribute food.

FLEXIBILITY OF USE   One trend in facility design is to make the existing space adaptable either for multiple uses or for meeting future demands. This may be accomplished in part by selecting wheel-mounted and modular equipment or by using portable units. The key is to choose equipment that is uniform in size, movable, and adaptable for numerous work activities.

ENERGY CONSERVATION   With the ever-rising energy costs, trends are to design and equip foodservice facilities to save energy to the greatest extent possible.

Equipment manufacturers are producing equipment that gives a high yield of energy for the work accomplished. The energy used by specific pieces of equipment is stated in the specifications, and comparisons should be made by the foodservice manager before selecting a particular make or model.

Other energy conservation trends are toward better insulation, heat recapture for other uses, and recirculation of heat. Solar heat designs are used in some areas, especially for restaurants, and may be a future trend of other types of foodservices. (See Chapter 9 for details on energy-conserving equipment.)

BUILT-IN SAFETY, SANITATION, AND NOISE REDUCTION   In planning the total facility, the safety of the employees, safety of food, and overall sanitary conditions are considerations in new designs. These may be achieved by the type of floor covering, ventilation, building materials, lighting, and equipment selected, and the method of their installation. Ease of cleaning reduces labor costs, and materials and designs chosen for safety features help reduce accidents. Both make for an attractive, safe working environment for the employees. Many of these features reduce noise and worker fatigue, and so, result in greater productivity.

Information on Developments in Design and Equipment

Visits to new or remodeled facilities of the same type to be planned and talks with managers of those facilities may garner new ideas and serve as a means to obtain first-hand information. Those with recent building experience usually are pleased to share workable ideas, mistakes that are made, and suggestions for improvement.

Obtaining catalogs and specification sheets from various equipment companies for comparative purposes and determining equipment space needs is essential. A file of such reference materials will be invaluable during work on the project. Equipment company representatives can be excellent sources of information for learning what is new and workable in various situations. Design consultants can also be contacted with any specific questions that arise.

Trade journals should be reviewed for articles on planning and design. Information gained can contribute new ideas and helpful suggestions to the planner. If the project is to remodel a facility, present staff and employees may have excellent suggestions resulting from their own work experience. Giving them an opportunity to express opinions is a valuable resource and should be mutually beneficial.

Regulatory Considerations

Foodservice managers need to know which federal, state, and local laws, codes, and regulations will affect their building or remodeling project. These regulations have to do with zoning restrictions; building standards, including those to accommodate persons with disabilities; electrical wiring and outlets; gas outlets and installations; health, fire, and safety codes; sanitation standards that govern water pollution and waste disposal systems; and installation of heavy-duty equipment.

Regulations have been established by agencies and organizations such as state, county, and local health and engineering departments; the American Gas Association, Underwriters' Laboratories, and the National Sanitation Foundation International; by federal legislation such as the Occupational Safety and Health Act (OSHA) and the Americans with Disabilities Act (ADA). Copies of these codes may be obtained by writing to or visiting the appropriate agency. Usually, major libraries also have copies of the codes and regulations.

Other professional persons will assist in the identification and application of regulatory codes and standards. These people make up a part of the planning team discussed later in this chapter.

Building permits are required but, in most instances, will not be issued for foodservice projects until health department officials have reviewed and approved the plans. Breit notes that it is expedient, therefore, to contact a local health department official and work closely with that person as plans are developed, so that approval is assured.

Special Considerations for Specific Types of Foodservices

Following is a brief review of some special considerations to keep in mind when planning a specific type of foodservice.

COMMERCIAL FACILITIES   Restaurants catering to downtown shoppers and businesspeople prefer a location near a busy intersection. Their customers, who often have a limited lunch period, may be those within a 10-minute walk of the restaurant. Since rents for prime downtown sites are likely to be high, effective use of every square inch of space is a top planning priority. Many such restaurants are built vertically with several levels for their various functions. Coordinating these activities with a good transport system between floors is a unique planning challenge. Suburban restaurants typically draw patrons from a larger area, making adequate parking the first essential. In addition, the location should be easily accessible and highly visible to approaching motorists. Shopping centers, which not only attract large numbers of customers but also provide ample parking, are considered desirable locations for commercial foodservices.

Hotels and motels usually have coffee shops located in visible locations, with entrances from both the street and the lobby. However, the main dining, party, and banquet rooms are frequently less visible, with access only through the lobby. For these facilities, basic food items are often prepared in a central kitchen. Finishing or banquet kitchens should then be located adjacent to the various serving areas.

SCHOOLS AND UNIVERSITIES   School foodservices are preferably located on the first floor, convenient to the central hallway. The area should be well-ventilated to allow cooking odors to dissipate rather than to permeate classrooms. Dining areas in some schools may have to double as a study hall or gymnasium, which would present a different planning situation.

Many large city school systems utilize a central production kitchen, or commissary, for food production for all schools in the system. Often, these are cook/chill or cook/freeze systems, which require specialized cooking equipment and good transporting systems and schedules. With this system, individual schools need only limited equipment for finishing off baking, reheating certain items, and serving the food.

Colleges and universities provide many and varied types of foodservices to accommodate the needs of the entire campus community. Residence halls may have their own kitchen and dining rooms or, if there are several halls on campus, may have a central production unit for certain items, such as baked goods, or for preparation of produce or meats. The trend is to have a choice of menu items, usually served cafeteria-style.

Peak work loads at the three meal periods may necessitate duplicate pieces of large equipment and adequate work space for personnel. Student unions usually offer a variety of types of foodservices, including large banquet halls for seated service, short-order units, cafeterias, and possibly small dining rooms for special meals. Some colleges and universities have invited various fast-food companies to operate one of their units on campus to satisfy students' requests for that type of food. Each type of foodservice requires different space and equipment, making planning for these facilities a challenge.

IN-PLANT FACILITIES   The *in-plant* or *industrial foodservice* should be central in location, allowing for ready access from as many areas in the plant as possible. Every provision should be made to expedite service so that all workers can be accommodated quickly during a fairly short lunch break. Mobile units and vending operations can be used in remote areas of large plants or in those too small to justify the space and expenditure for kitchen equipment, management, and labor. Adequate passageways for such carts are essential.

HOMES FOR CHILDREN AND ADULT COMMUNITIES   Homes for children and retired persons make use of the residence hall and cottage-type of plan. Because a quiet, home-like atmosphere is desirable for this type of situation, they often are located away from the busy streets of the city and surrounded by private grounds.

HOSPITALS AND HEALTH CARE CENTERS   Facility planning for hospitals and other health care centers must provide for the needs of staff, employees, visitors, and guests, as well as the patients. The decision as to type of **service** to use, centralized or decentralized, has to be made at the outset of planning, as space and equipment requirements differ greatly for each. A central kitchen ordinarily provides food for these groups with one dining room/cafeteria that serves everyone except bed patients. Sometimes small, private dining rooms can be planned for official catering functions. For after hours, vending machines can be installed to supplement regular meal service. Adequate passageways for transporting patients' meals on carts and trucks, as well as space for cart storage, are other special considerations. Elevators or lifts designated solely for foodservice use will expedite meal service to patients. Office space for clinical dietitians in large hospitals is another planning consideration. If off-premise catering, Meals-on-Wheels, or other services are to be provided, adequate space for them must also be included in the facility plan.

CORRECTIONAL FACILITIES   Kitchen and dining rooms for correctional facilities present a planning challenge different from most other types of foodservices. Since inmates often serve as foodservice workers, the basic design consideration is to provide for personal safety, security, and protection against sabotage. The foodservice manager should have a full view of all operations. Therefore, the office should be centrally located in the kitchen, raised above the floor level, and safety glass windows should be in place on all four sides. For security, all cabinets should be open with no drawers, and secure locks should be provided for all storage areas. Hall (1989), a registered dietitian, recommends a storage warehouse built outside but adjacent to the kitchen so deliveries for daily use can be made easily, thus eliminating the need for large storage areas in the kitchen and reducing chances of theft. She also suggests that the serving area be designed to prevent face-to-face interaction between servers and inmate "customers" that could create confrontations. A partitioning wall from the ceiling down to within approximately 24 inches of the front of the serving counter achieves this objective while still allowing easy viewing for selection of foods. The dining area is best divided into small units seating 100 to 125 persons for control of potential riots.

Other planning considerations may include the delivery of food to some inmates in their cells. The choice of centralized service with food portioned and served onto trays in the kitchen for distribution or decentralized service with bulk food delivery to serving areas throughout the facility for service is one to be made by the planning team.

Generally, kitchens and dining areas in any type of foodservice facility should provide maximum convenience and accessibility for customers. For efficiency's sake, locating dining rooms adjacent to kitchens is preferable. Foodservices are best located on the first floor to obtain the best lighting, ventilation, and outdoor views. Basement-level locations can have a poor psychological effect on both patrons and employees if the area is dark and unattractive. The disadvantages of foodservices that are located above the first floor are inaccessibility to patrons and problems related to bringing in supplies and removing trash and waste. The physical environment has much to do with the success of any foodservice design.

Steps in the Planning Procedure

After preliminary study to prepare for the facility design project, completing the following developmental steps will lead to a completed layout design:

- Prepare a prospectus (a program or planning guide).
- Organize a planning team.
- Conduct a feasibility study.
- Make a menu analysis.
- Consider the desired architectural features: building materials, floors, walls, lighting, heating, cooling, ventilation, refrigeration, plumbing.
- Adjust costs and money available relationships.

Upon completion of these preliminaries, the design development process can proceed.

The Prospectus

The prospectus is a written description that details all aspects of the situation under consideration and helps other professionals on the planning team understand the exact needs of the foodservice department. It should contain the elements that will affect and guide the proposed design, as well as present a clear picture of the physical and operational aspects of the proposed facility or remodeling project. Usually, it is based on questions such as

- What type of foodservice is planned?
- What is the foodservice to accomplish?
- Which major type of food production system will be used?
- How many people and what age groups are to be served? How many must be served at one time?
- What will be the hours of service? style of service?
- What is the menu pattern?
- In what form will food be purchased? how often?

- What storage facilities will be needed? amount of refrigerated and amount of freezer space?
- What equipment and what capacity for each piece will be required to prepare and serve the menu items?
- What are desirable space relationships?
- How will safety precautions be incorporated in the plan? sanitary measures?
- What facilities must be planned for persons with disabilities?
- What energy sources are most economical? available?
- What activities will be computerized?

The prospectus usually contains three major sections:

1. The *rationale* includes title, reason or need for project, and its goal, objectives, policies, and procedures.
2. *Physical and operational characteristics* include architectural designs and features, all details about the menu, food preparation and service, employee and customer profiles, and anticipated volume of business.
3. *Regulatory information* includes built-in sanitation, safety, and noise control features, and energy and type of utility usage desired.

RATIONALE   The title, goal, objectives, policies and procedures, and a statement of need for the project are, perhaps, the most difficult components to define. The following definitions and examples should help make the exercise easier.

- *Title.* Description of the plan. Narrow the title to reflect the actual scope of the design that is proposed. Example: Design for a warewashing area of the Coastal Restaurant Foodservice.
- *Goal.* State the single outcome of the project. Example: To develop a central warewashing area that will process all dishes, utensils, and pans of the foodservice.
- *Objective.* Specific statements that indicate what is necessary to achieve the goal. Example: The warehouse area will: (1) utilize no more than 36 square feet of floor space, (2) be operated with no more than four persons, and (3) operate with minimum energy usage.
- *Policy.* A definite course or method of action selected from among alternatives and in light of given conditions to guide and determine present and future decisions. Example: All dishes, utensils, and pans will be washed and stored within 45 minutes of use.
- *Procedure.* A particular way of accomplishing something. Example: Conveyor belts will be used to carry dirty dishes to the warewashing area, or scrap-

ping, racking, and washing of dirty utensils and pans and storing clean ones should be accomplished with 80% automation.

The statement of need for the project may be simple or complex, depending on the project; for example: "The foodservice dry and refrigerated storage areas need to be expanded 60% to accommodate an increase in meal census from 500 per day to 1,200 per day as a result of a recent building addition."

PHYSICAL AND OPERATIONAL CHARACTERISTICS   Physical characteristics relate to architectural or design features, such as building style appropriate to the type of food to be served. Mexican foods, for example, often call for Mexican or Spanish architecture. A necessary design feature to identify in a remodeling project could be an existing support pillar, an elevator shaft that cannot be moved, or a desired solar heating system. These must be identified at this stage because they could affect other considerations, such as the style of the roof and types of windows.

Operational data refer to activities that take place in the foodservice department. The type of foods on the menu is the key concern in the planning stage. Further, the form in which food will be purchased—fresh, canned, and/or frozen—and the approximate quantities of each must be estimated with some accuracy. This information helps planners determine the amount and kind of storage space required. Food preparation methods to be used, including on-premise preparation, tell the planners what equipment is needed and the amount of space that is required to accommodate the equipment.

The major operational characteristic, or type of foodservice system, is basic to all design planning. Space requirements for an assembly/serve system are quite different from those of a conventional system. Other decisions to make in advance are whether to use centralized or decentralized service and the method of delivery and service to be employed.

Other operational characteristics are the hours of service, anticipated volume of business (both total and per meal period), and the number of diners to be seated at any one time. These data help determine the required size for the dining area.

A **customer profile,** including age, size of group, and mobility, helps determine the probable dining space required per person. An **employee profile** includes the number of employees, the number of shifts and employees on duty per shift, the employees' sex (to plan locker and rest room space), and each work position as it relates to standing, sitting, walking, pushing carts, and so forth. Special considerations to meet the needs of persons with disabilities are included as well. This information is essential so that adequate space for work and movement of people and equipment will be allocated.

REGULATORY INFORMATION   This section identifies the standards of safety, sanitation and cleanliness, noise control, and waste disposal that the design must meet. Also included are standards established by the Americans with Disabilities Act (ADA), to provide for employees and patrons with disabilities. (See Appendix B for more information on the ADA and a partial compliance checklist for meeting building accommodation regulations.) Guidelines for selection of the type of utilities to be used and energy constraints are also stated.

Since every project is unique, the various sections of a prospectus will not always include all of the same data. Just those that pertain to the situation are necessary. For example, a dry and refrigerated storage design does not need a customer profile. Instead, employee and equipment characteristics would be the focus, in addition to information regarding the menu, food items, and safety and sanitation regulations.

The key in writing the plan is to include all pertinent technical data and to always comment on how the data presented will affect the proposed design. The seating space in a cocktail lounge, for example, will depend on the size of the tables and chairs selected. The person who writes the prospectus and later helps to develop the design should be a professional foodservice manager with the knowledge and authority to make decisions about the anticipated menu, space, and equipment needs. That person must also be able to provide other operational data required by planning team members.

The Planning Team

When the project plan is complete, it is time to organize a team to develop the design plan. The expertise required of those on the team will vary depending on the extent of the project, its objectives, and its size. Typical planning team members include a(n)

1. owner or administrator (the person with authority to spend money for the project and give final approval to carry it out)
2. foodservice manager
3. architect
4. foodservice design consultant
5. equipment representative
6. business manager
7. builder/contractor
8. maintenance engineer/mechanical engineer

Not all team members are involved in all planning stages. Certain members are included at intervals throughout the design development. Generally, the owner or administrator and foodservice manager will co-plan the initial design and bring in other team members for planning meetings at appropriate times during the project's development.

The planning team chooses a floor plan, selects materials, and writes specifications cooperatively. However, team members need to check the plans many times before submitting final proposals to builders and to equipment vendors for bids. It is essential to include every detail and be so specific that no part of the architectural features, equipment layout, and specifications is left to chance or misinterpretation.

Feasibility Study

A feasibility study—the collection of data about the market and other factors relating to the operation of the proposed facility—justifies the proposed project, helping to ensure that the project is worth pursuing. This study follows the prospectus outline, with data being collected for each major category. Since each project is unique, categories vary according to need. For instance, the feasibility study for a new restaurant would include research on the proposed site, potential customer profiles and community growth, building trends, competition in the area, and possible revenue-generating sources, such as catering. For a small remodeling project in an existing building, the feasibility study would focus more on operational details than on community and competitive information.

Because the financial commitment for most projects is so large, cost information for the building or for remodeling, and for equipping it is an essential part of the feasibility study. Many people can assist in this effort, but one person should be the coordinator. This person may be the business or financial manager who also interprets the cost data for the planning team.

Data sources for the feasibility study may include

1. payroll, production, cash register, and inventory records
2. city, county, state, and national regulations, obtained from the respective agencies involved or from library copies of those documents
3. statistics regarding trends, average costs, and customer information obtained from trade journals and independent studies

The feasibility study is a critical component of a project plan. If done well, funds are more likely to be made available, allowing the project to proceed. (See Appendix B for a list of Feasibility Study Resources.)

Menu Analysis

An important step in preliminary planning is identifying the type of menu to be served (see Chapter 3 for menu types) and the various food preparation methods required for that menu type. This is the key to equipment needs, which in turn determines the space requirements for the equipment.

TABLE 8.1. Menu Analysis.

Menu Item	Storage Type	Portion Size	Table Portions	Batch Size	Process Required	Utensils	Work Surface	Large Equipment	Holding Equipment
Spinach salad	Refrigerated	1 ounce	350	100	Wash Trim Drain	Knife Drain pan	Sink Counter	Sink Counter	Refrigerator
Beef patty	Freezer	4 ounces	300	50	Grill	Spatula	Counter Utility cart	Grill	Warming oven

A sample of a menu analysis to be made for all menu categories. When similar menu items are used, such as several salad dressings that require the same production and service treatment, only one analysis need be made. This information is the basis for determining equipment and space needs for designing a foodservice facility.

Menu, foodservice system, and style-of-service decisions are the major food-service planning components. The menu affects equipment design and layout, as well as personnel skills and staffing levels required. For example, if the menu and menu pattern contain no fried foods, frying equipment need not be included in the design and no cooks will be needed to perform this task.

The prospectus should include a sample of several days' menus and a menu pattern. The pattern specifies meal categories or courses, while the menu identifies the respective preparation methods required. From this sample menu, the foodservice manager analyzes the variables involved in producing menu items, such as type of storage needed, portion size, total number of portions, batch size, processing required, utensils needed, necessary work surfaces, and type of equipment required (see Table 8.1). The estimated time when a batch is needed and when preparation is complete are also helpful in deciding whether equipment could be shared or whether duplication is necessary. The manager also evaluates the menu for production, service, acceptability, and feasibility. At this point, menu changes can be made to balance equipment use, workload, and acceptability.

Architectural Features

During a project's planning phase, the planning team considers certain architectural features such as building style and materials; types of floors, walls, ceilings, and noise reduction components; lighting; heating and cooling; ventilation; built-in refrigeration; and plumbing. Not only is making a decision on these features essential for determining project cost, but also for ensuring ease of cleaning, good sanitation, safety, adequate type and amount of lighting and temperature control for high productivity, and noise reduction methods for a more pleasant work environment. Because certain refrigeration units are usually built-in, the number and location of such units must be determined before construction or remodeling begins.

Some of the components previously mentioned are included here as a basic information review.

BUILDING STYLE AND MATERIALS   Type of foodservice operation, its geographic location, and its menu markedly influence the type of architecture and materials used. Material selection for any building depends largely on the type of architecture planned, the permanence desired, the location, and the effect of local weather conditions on the materials. The building engineer and the architect will know the characteristics of the various building materials and help select the most suitable in relation to cost.

The restaurant in Fig. 8.1 (a, b) is a fine example of modern design. It is built of local stone and situated to take advantage of a scenic location and provide diners with an outstanding view.

FLOORS   Floors have to meet certain utility, durability, and resiliency requirements. They should be impervious to moisture, grease, and food stains, as well as nonslippery and resistant to scratches and acids, alkali, and organic solvents. Floors should be durable enough to withstand the wear from heavy traffic characteristic of large food units and, in kitchens, to support the weight of heavy-duty equipment.

What is the best flooring material for a foodservice unit? Opinions vary. Hard surfaces tire employees and may cause accidents by causing persons to slip or fall when the floor is wet. However, this type of flooring is highly resistant to wear and soil, comparatively easy to maintain, and permanent. Rough or abrasive slip-resistant tile is safer but more difficult to clean and, therefore, less hygienic. Norwich reported that some flooring manufacturers are now producing specially constructed resilient sheet vinyl that is smooth on the surface, easy to clean, and seems more slip resistant than hard tiles (i.e., quarry). Sheet vinyl flooring is easier to stand on than tile and has no grouting to clean. Although this type of flooring has potential for future use in foodservice installations, at present, it seems too soft to support the weight of heavy-duty equipment. Quarry tile seems to be the preferred flooring in most institutional kitchens today. Any floor surface that is to comply with health department requirements must be coved 6 inches up at all walls and equipment bases. In addition, floors must be installed so that they are sloped to drain at various parts of the kitchen for ease in cleaning.

WALLS, CEILINGS, AND NOISE REDUCTION   The type of wall and ceiling materials selected for kitchen and dining areas can contribute to the overall aesthetic value and sanitary conditions, as well as help to reduce the noise level. As with floors, wall and ceiling materials that are durable and easily cleaned will meet health department regulations and reduce labor time required for cleaning. In addition to wall and floor joinings being coved, all other corners and angles

(a)

(b)

Figure 8.1.   (*a*) The curved facade of the Top of the Falls Restaurant overlooks the whole Niagara Falls panorama. (*b*) The multilevel design of the restaurant interior offers every customer a spectacular view. (Courtesy, Herbert H. Gill, President, Gladieux Corp., Toledo, Ohio.)

used in installations should be rounded to make cleaning easier and prevent chipping. All pipes and wiring conduits should be concealed in walls.

The amount of natural and artificial light available helps determine the wall finish for a given room. Various colors and textures of materials reflect and absorb different amounts of light. This is one aspect to consider in relation to the amount of light desired in the room.

Several materials are suitable for walls in foodservice kitchens. Ceramic tile is probably the most suitable material because of its durability and cleanability, although it is expensive to install. However, over its expected life span, the cost of ceramic tile is comparable with other materials.

Fiberglass reinforced panels (FRP), a plastic-like paneling, is quite durable, available in several colors, and less expensive to install than ceramic tile. A minimum-quality material for kitchen wall surfaces is wallboard painted with washable enamel. Since it lacks durability, it is not suitable for use in wet areas, such as around sinks and in warewashing rooms.

A desirable arrangement is to cover walls with ceramic or other glazed tile to a height of 5 to 8 feet where food and water splashes occur. The remainder of the wall may be smooth-finished washable enamel or semi-gloss paint.

Stainless steel is another material highly suited for kitchen walls; however, due to its very high cost, its use is often limited to cooking areas. It is also quite reflective and may cause glares from the lighting.

Ceiling heights vary widely, with kitchens typically averaging 14 to 18 feet. Kitchen and dining room ceilings should be acoustically treated and lighter in color than the walls. Using sound-absorbing materials, such as draperies and carpeting, tends to minimize local noises in dining rooms. There are many acoustical ceiling materials to chose from for kitchen use. They must resist deterioration from rapid temperature and humidity changes and from corrosive cooking fumes. In addition, those that have a low reflectance value, are resistant to fire, and are washable are most suited for new or remodeled foodservice kitchens.

Sound-absorbing materials are used not only as surface finishes in construction but also as insulators. Vents, radiator pipes, and water pipes may act as carriers of sound, and the most effective means of noise prevention is their careful and thorough insulation with sound-absorbing material. Because of later inaccessibility and prohibitive costs, it is most important that this precaution be taken in the original construction.

Fig. 8.2 (a, b) shows an example of sound reduction treatment in a noisy area. Features such as automatic lubrication of the so-called noiseless power equipment that keeps it in quiet working condition, rubber-tired carts, rubber collars on openings in dish-scrapping tables, and ball-bearing glide table drawers help to minimize noise in the kitchen.

LIGHTING   The amount and kind of lighting required for a foodservice represents a long-term investment and merits the assistance of technical experts in

Figure 8.2.   Special sound-absorbing ceiling treatments above dishwashing area.
(*a*) Removable perforated acoustical panels hung from ceiling. (*b*) Box-like corrugated
aluminum sheets filled with 1 inch of fiberglass insulation suspended from ceiling in
metal frame.

the field. However, the lighting's adequacy, efficiency, and suitability are far more important concerns than its installation cost.

The design should allow for as much natural light as possible. Natural light not only makes food look more appealing, but it can also reduce operating expenses. In addition, natural light exerts a positive psychological effect on workers and guests. Because it is not possible to rely totally on natural light, it is desirable for foodservice managers to have some knowledge of lighting and its requirements when working with lighting experts.

The amount or intensity of light, the kind and color of light, and type of fixtures and their placement combine to create good lighting. Reflective values of walls, ceilings, and other surfaces also affect lighting. Light intensity is measured in footcandles obtained from light meter readings, and the number of required footcandles per square foot depends on the work to be done. The following general guidelines are helpful for planning:

Light Intensity (in footcandles)	Activity
10 to 20	Walkways (halls and corridors)
15 to 20	Dining
15 to 35	Rough work
35 to 70	General work or food display area
70 to 150	Reading recipes, weighing and measuring ingredients, inspecting, checking, and record keeping

Planners should choose the light fixtures and their placement during the project's design phase so outlet and switch locations can be identified. Fixtures should harmonize with the architectural plan and be placed to provide the recommended illumination level and balance for dining areas as well as for food storage, preparation, and serving areas. Studies have shown that proper workplace lighting can increase employee productivity by 3% to 4%, a significant amount in overall efficiency.

Lighting systems may be either indirect, direct, or a combination of the two. In indirect systems, about 90% to 100% of the light is directed upward, while in direct systems, a corresponding amount is directed downward. Luminous ceiling lighting gives an evenly dispersed light that creates the effect of natural sunlight and is desirable in kitchen areas. Brightness, though, should be low enough to prevent glare or cause reflections on shiny surfaces that may affect workers' eyes. Light fixtures should be positioned to prevent employees from standing in their own shadows while working. Good lighting reduces eye strain and general worker fatigue, and is conducive to accuracy in work, as well as to good sanitation and safety in the workplace (Kotschevar & Terrell).

HEATING, VENTILATION, & AIR CONDITIONING (HVAC)   The HVAC system provides comfortable temperatures for employees and guests. An architect, working with an HVAC specialist, is best qualified to specify a system of sufficient capacity for the facility in question. Foodservice presents a somewhat different problem from other building uses because cooking processes generate heat, moisture, and food odors.

Air conditioning means more than air cooling. It includes heating, humidity control, and circulating, cleaning, and cooling of the air. Systems are available with controls for all features in one unit. The system may be set up to filter, warm, humidify, and circulate the air in winter and, by adding cooling coils and refrigeration, maintain a comfortable summer temperature. Dehumidification may be necessary in some climates.

The placement of air ducts is important to prevent direct blasts of cold air onto those in the room. Fig. 8.3, which shows a retirement home dining room that seats 400 people, illustrates several points. The ceiling is designed with wood slats backed by sound absorption material. This permits enough sound to create a friendly atmosphere, but reduces the sound level enough to allow people with hearing aids to be comfortable. The lighting is excellent, with natural light on three sides and adequate, well-spaced ceiling lights. Ducts located beside the right-hand row of lights supply conditioned air. The suspended umbrellas add an aesthetic touch.

Satisfactory kitchen ventilation typically consists of an exhaust fan system, built into a hood placed over cooking equipment, to eliminate cooking odors, as well as fumes, moisture, and grease-laden vapors. In the absence of direct air conditioning, cool outdoor air may be drawn into the kitchen by fans to reduce the temperature and increase circulation of air, making body surfaces feel cooler.

Although air conditioning may be considered expensive to install and operate, employee productivity is estimated to increase 5% to 15% in such a controlled environment. As a result, planners should carefully consider what type of temperature control system is most appropriate for their climate and facility.

BUILT-IN REFRIGERATION   The smooth, efficient operation of foodservice departments will be enhanced by planning the adequate kind and amount of refrigeration. The foodservice manager should have some knowledge of the principles of refrigeration, types of systems used, and how to determine space needs for the facility being planned. Walk-in, built-in, and reach-in refrigerators and freezers are essential. At this stage of planning, however, only the permanent built-in types need to be considered. Reach-in and portable types are discussed in Chapter 9.

Mechanical refrigeration is the removal of heat from food and other products stored in an enclosed area. The system includes the use of a *refrigerant* (chemical) that circulates through a series of coils known as the *evaporator.* It begins as a liquid in the coils then is vaporized and pressure is built up by the heat it absorbs from the food. This starts a *compressor,* which pumps the heat-laden gas out of the evaporator and compresses it to a high pressure. The compressed gas flows to a *condenser,* which is air- or water-cooled, the heat is

Figure 8.3. (*a*) LeVelle Wood, one of the two original authors of this text, lives in the retirement community shown. (*b*) Distinctive treatment of the retirement residence dining room. (Courtesy, Willamette View, Inc., Portland, Oregon.)

(*a*)

(*b*)

released, the gas is reliquified, and the cycle is ready to repeat when the temperature in the refrigerator or freezer becomes higher than desired.

It is desirable for a refrigerant to have a low boiling point, an inoffensive odor, high latent heat, and a reasonable cost, as well as to be nontoxic, nonexplosive, nonflammable, noncorrosive, stable, and not harmful to foods. Most important, with today's concern over the depletion of the ozone layer in our atmosphere, refrigerants used must be ozone "friendly." Many of the old, standard refrigerants, such as Freon (F12 and F22), are the harmful chlorofluorocarbons (CFCs) that are responsible for the depleting ozone layer. They are therefore being phased out of use. Less harmful are the hydrochlorofluorocarbons (HCFCs) that are now being used by compressor manufacturers for refrigerants in their compressors. According to Richardson, HCFC 22 is 90% safer than CFC 12. He estimates that by the year 2000, all CFCs will be entirely eliminated for use in any foodservice. Thus, the foodservice industry is doing its share to help alleviate the worldwide concern for stress on the ozone layer.

Refrigerator systems may be central, multiple unit, and single unit. In a *central* system, one machine supplies refrigeration in adequate amount for all cooling units throughout the building. This system is rarely used because of the problem of trying to maintain desirable refrigeration in all the different units and because, in case of a breakdown, *all* refrigeration is gone. In a *multiple* or parallel system of refrigeration, there is a compressor for a series of coolers, the compressor being of proper capacity to carry the load required to maintain the desired temperature in the series of coolers. A *single* unit is the self-contained refrigerating system used in the reach-in types.

The location and space allocations for built-in units require careful planning. Generally, they are placed close to the delivery area to minimize distance to transport items received into refrigerated storage. They also need to be close to the preparation units that most frequently use the products stored in them. Three separate walk-in refrigerators are recommended as a minimum, one for fresh produce, one for dairy products and eggs, and one for meat and poultry. Each food group requires a different temperature for optimum storage. Walk-in freezer or freezers may also be planned.

Many factors influence the amount of refrigerated and freezer space needed:

1. *The size of the establishment.* Since permanent walk-in units that are smaller than about 8 × 10 feet are uneconomical to install, small facilities may use reach-in rather than walk-in units.

2. *The kind of foodservice system used.* Systems with cook/chill methods require a large amount of refrigerated space while cook/freeze and assembly/serve systems require primarily freezer space.

3. *The frequency of deliveries.* Establishments that are close to markets and receive daily deliveries would require less storage space than those foodservices located in remote areas where deliveries are infrequent.

4. *The form in which food is purchased.* If primarily frozen foods are purchased, naturally more freezer space will be required than if all fresh or canned goods are used.

Figure 8.4. Overhead electrical raceways to accommodate 10 patient food carts. Connection plates are equipped with receptacles and point-of-use circuit breakers. (Courtesy, Louisiana State University Medical Center Hospital, Shreveport.)

Total space required may be estimated by measuring the size of units of purchase (i.e., cases, bags, crates) and multiplying each by the number of units to be stored at one time. This will give the total cubic feet of space required, which will be divided into the separate food items to be stored together. Most walk-in units are 7 or 8 feet high. Aisle space in the refrigerator must be wide enough for trucks or carts to enter. Width of shelving is based on the items to be stored; 2 to 3 feet is the usual width. Space for the insulation of the walk-ins also has to be included, a minimum of 3 inches on all sides for built-in refrigerators and 5 to 8 inches for built-in freezers.

Floors of walk-ins should be made of strong, durable, easily cleaned tile that is flush with the adjoining floor to permit easy entry and exit of food on trucks or carts. Wall surfaces should be washable and moisture resistant. Each unit should be equipped with an internal door-opening device and a bell as a safety measure. An exterior wall-mounted recorder to show the box's inside temperature saves energy by eliminating the need to open the door to check temperatures as shown in Fig. 4.19. (See the "Schematic Drawing" section in this chapter for more information on location of refrigerated storage space.)

PLUMBING   Although architects and engineers plan the plumbing for a facility, foodservice managers must be aware of and able to describe the foodservice's need for kitchen and dishroom floor drains and proper drains around steam equipment; the desired location for water and steam inlets and for hand-washing sinks in work areas and rest rooms; the water and steam pressure needs for equipment to be installed; and adequate drains to sewer lines for waste disposal equipment.

ELECTRICITY   Food managers are responsible for providing information on the needed location of electrical outlets and the voltage requirements of all equipment to be used in the facility. Equipment manufacturers' specifications list power requirements for their equipment. These must be compatible with the building's power supply or else the equipment will not operate at peak efficiency or will overload the wiring.

The mechanical engineer on the planning team details the electrical specifications, based on the foodservice's requirements, including the wattage and horsepower of the facility's equipment. Hospitals and health care facilities may require special electrical receptacles for food carts used to deliver patients' meals. Because these carts will be moved to various locations, compatible receptacles must be installed at all points of use. Fig. 8.4 shows an overhead electrical raceway installation of receptacles for carts in a hospital kitchen.

All pipes and wiring going into a kitchen should be enclosed and out of sight. A modular utility distribution and control system offers many advantages compared with fixed and permanent installations. The entrance of and controls for all utilities are centered in one end-support column or panel of the system. All pipes and wiring are enclosed, but controls for both operation and quick-disconnect are on the outside of the panel within easy reach. Water, steam, gas, and electrical outlets may be installed as desired in panels extending from the one-point control column along a wall; to a center room unit, directly behind equipment; or from above as shown in Fig. 8.5. Utility distribution systems are usually custom designed. A wall-type unit may house electrical wiring, plumbing assemblies, gas piping, and contain controls for water-wash cleaning for the exhaust ventilator. A fire control system for protection of cooking equipment may be located in the exhaust ventilator, which is located above the utility distribution system.

Budget/Cost Relationship

Because unlimited budgets are rare, studying the costs involved in any facility design project is inevitable. Planners usually establish a predetermined budget, which the project's total cost cannot exceed. Yet, the quality and features that foodservice managers select for a facility may well affect its operating costs. A detailed financial analysis may reveal that a higher initial expenditure for top-quality design and fixtures will result in lower operating costs during the project's anticipated life—its life cycle cost—than a less expensive design.

Figure 8.5.   An overhead modular utility distribution and control system facilitates flexibility in arrangement, as well as ease of maintenance. (Courtesy, Avtec Industries, Inc.)

Building and construction costs are affected by many interrelated factors, including the prevailing prices for labor and materials, quality and quantity of items selected, and the building's overall design. It may be helpful to think of these three factors—cost, quality, and quantity—as a triangle. If the project's budget is a fixed amount, it may be necessary to restrict quantity, quality, or both. However, if a predetermined amount of space is the top priority for the facility, planners must anticipate financing a building or site large enough to accommodate the required size. Alternatively, if planners assign top priority to the quality of fixtures and equipment, they must be flexible regarding the project's cost and quantity factors.

The particular design selected for the building or foodservice department will impose certain operating costs, especially those for labor. A well-planned arrangement on one floor minimizes the distance food and people must travel and permits good supervision. Compact work units, with the proper equipment easily accessible to workers, tend to reduce steps, motion, and fatigue, helping to minimize labor and operating costs. In poorly planned facilities, it is not uncommon for employees to spend at least 10% of their time locating and assembling utensils and supplies. Some assessments indicate that in an efficiently planned department, only the dietitian or foodservice supervisor, storeroom clerk, dishroom supervisor, pot and pan washer, and janitor would need to leave their work areas.

It is also important to include the total costs for cleaning materials, utilities, building and equipment depreciation, and the amount of equipment needed. Such costs will vary directly with the amount of space allocated to the foodservice department.

Furnishings and other equipment should contribute to efficient operation and reflect the best design, materials, and workmanship to conform to established sanitary standards. The degree of comfort for both guests and employees depends on the provisions made for them during the project's planning phase. They are particularly sensitive to amenities such as air conditioning, type of lighting, sound deadening, artistic incorporation of color and design, comfortable chair and work surface heights, and clean, well-ventilated rest rooms.

The facility's cost directly influences what can be done with a fixed budget. However, the material in the remainder of this chapter assumes that adequate funds are available for foodservice planning on a moderate scale.

Design Development

After completing preliminary preparations, the feasibility study, menu analysis, prospectus writing, and cost considerations, the foodservice manager needs to develop a design and layout plan. Providing adequate facilities for all anticipated activities, incorporating the ideas that planning members generate, and considering the facility's future growth are important aspects involved in design development.

A logical sequence for developing a design and for completing a foodservice facility follows:

1. Determine space allowances. Draw a flow diagram showing space relationships of the work units and routes for supplies and workers.
2. Prepare a schematic design to scale, to show space allowances and relationships and placement of equipment, for consideration by the planning team before the architect begins preparing blueprints. Revise as needed.
3. Prepare and submit the architect's complete set of blueprints and contract documents, including specifications, to reliable interested contractors, builders, engineers, and equipment representatives for competitive bids.
4. Formulate contracts with accepted bidders.
5. Inspect construction, wiring, plumbing, finishing, and the equipment and its installation, as specified in blueprints and contracts. This is the responsibility of the architect and contractor.

Space Allowances and Relationships

Determining the amount of floor space and how to divide it for foodservice activities varies with every operation. Each needs adequate space to prepare and serve the planned number of meals. Yet, allowing too much space can result in inefficiency and lost time and effort.

The prospectus and menu analysis specify the number and kind of activities to be performed. For each activity, such as vegetable preparation, cooking specific menu items, and service methods to be used, the required equipment is listed. From the manufacturers' equipment catalogs, the size and, thus, the space requirements for each model to be purchased can be found. The space for equipment plus adequate aisle space represents a fair estimate of the total area required.

One commonly used procedure to determine kitchen space requirements begins by calculating the amount of space needed for the dining room. Fairly accurate estimates for dining areas can be calculated if the type of service and number of persons to be seated at one time are known. Likewise, seating capacity can be determined by using the generally accepted number of square feet per seat for different kinds of foodservices. Variations from the following suggestions will depend on the sizes of tables and chairs and whether spacious arrangement is desired.

School lunchrooms	9 to 12 sq ft per seat
Hotel and club banquet rooms	10 to 11 sq ft per seat
Commercial cafeterias	16 to 18 sq ft per seat
Industrial and university cafeterias	12 to 15 sq ft per seat
Residence halls	12 to 15 sq ft per seat
Restaurants and hotels (table service)	15 to 18 sq ft per seat
Lunch counters	12 to 20 sq ft per seat

The kitchen size is often about one-third to one-fourth of the dining room area. This is a rough estimate at best because so many variables are involved. For example, dining room and kitchen space requirements are entirely different for a fast-food restaurant and a school cafeteria serving the same number of persons per meal period. The restaurant's turnover rate may be three customers per hour for each seat during a 3-hour meal period; thus, the restaurant would need to prepare food in small batches. In the school cafeteria, one-half of the group may be seated at one time with the total number served during a 50-minute period; therefore, larger quantities of food would be prepared and ready to serve the students. As a result, the restaurant kitchen would most likely be considerably smaller than the school kitchen with its larger capacity equipment.

Hospital foodservices confront a unique situation for space determination because only one-third to one-half of the total number of meals served are eaten in the dining room; patients are usually served in bed. Consequently, hospital kitchen space requirements are large, relative to dining areas, so the quantity and variety of food needed for patients, staff, employees, and guests can be prepared and assembled.

FLOW DIAGRAM OF SPACE RELATIONSHIPS   Designing the floor plan begins with a diagram showing the flow of work, food, and supplies from one procedure to the next in logical sequence. To find the shortest, most direct route is the goal. The assembly-line concept provides for efficient operations by creating a continuous work flow from receiving, storing, issuing, preparing, cooking, and serving the food, while minimizing traffic lines, backtracking, and cross traffic. After food has been served and consumed, the direction reverses to remove soiled dishes and trash. Fig. 8.6 shows a typical foodservice flow diagram with desirable work area relationships. Only those work units required in a specific planning project need be shown. Because many foods are now purchased ready-to-cook, certain preparation units may be unnecessary in some kitchens. For example, since most foodservices no longer purchase carcass meat or wholesale cuts of meat, the meat preparation unit has been eliminated entirely in those facilities.

The relationship of one work unit to another is also a consideration; that is, deciding on which work units need to be close to each other, which ones adjacent to other areas of the building, and which must be located near an outside door. Fig. 8.7 shows the relationship of areas in a medium-size facility using the conventional foodservice system. As can be noted, the main cooking unit is the central area of most kitchens with supporting units feeding to or from it. Further discussion of desirable relationship of units is given under the "Work Areas" section that follows.

Schematic Drawing

Translating a flow diagram into a preliminary floor plan is the next step in design development. The floor plan is a sketch or sketches of possible arrangements of the work units, with equipment drawn to scale within the allocated space. The required traffic aisles and work space also have to be included. Some general guidelines and a brief description of various work areas and their basic equipment needs are given on the following pages.

GENERAL GUIDELINES   Several considerations should be noted when planning a foodservice facility. The main traffic aisles should be a minimum of 5 feet wide, or wide enough to permit carts or hand trucks to pass without interfering with each other or with the workers in a unit. Aisles between equipment and work tables must have at least a 3-foot clearance; 3.5 to 4 feet are required if oven doors are to be opened or contents from tilting kettles must be removed in the

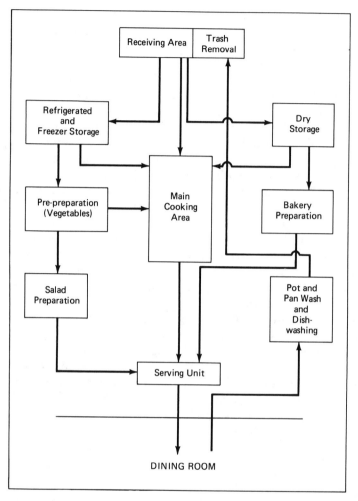

Figure 8.6. Flowchart diagram showing desirable work area relationships and progression of work from receiving goods to serving without backtracking and with little cross traffic.

aisle space. Usually one or two main aisles go through a kitchen with aisles into work areas that are parallel or perpendicular to the main aisle but are separate from them. (See Fig. 8.8 for one efficient cook's unit.)

The Americans with Disabilities Act (ADA), which went into effect July 26, 1992, for companies with 25 or more employees (July 26, 1994, for companies with 15 or more), mandates some general guidelines for implementing "reasonable accommodation" to make the workplace and dining area accessible to persons with disabilities. The ADA applies to almost every public facility, and to new construction and alterations in existing facilities. Accommodations may

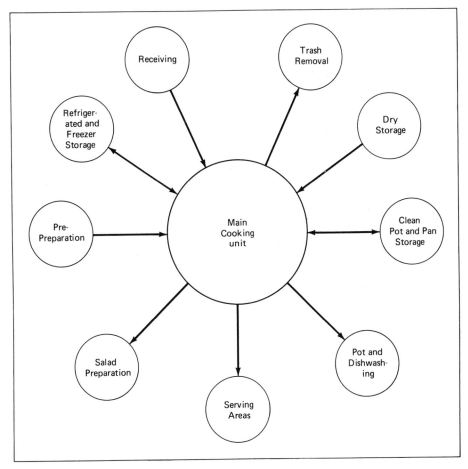

Figure 8.7. Relationship of main cooking unit to other work areas in a conventional foodservice system.

include installing ramps, widening doors, and lowering shelves and counters. Aisles must be at least 36 inches wide (preferably 42 inches) to accommodate persons with wheelchairs. Fig. 8.9 gives dimensions of dining and serving room space requirements for wheelchair accommodation in order to comply with the ADA regulations. A checklist for determining compliance with some of these regulations may be found in Appendix A. This list is intended to serve as an aid in assessing a facility for compliance and for future building programs. Refer to the act itself for complete regulations.

A minimum of 4 linear feet of work table space is recommended for each preparation employee, but 6 feet is preferable. Work heights are generally 36 to 41 inches for standing and 28 to 30 inches for sitting positions (see Fig. 8.10).

Figure 8.8.   Compact, efficient kitchen arrangement with serving and dishwashing units in one room. A power-driven conveyor for soiled dish return is on the right.

Tools and equipment require adequate storage space that is located at the place of use. Sinks, reach-in refrigerators, and space for short-term storage of supplies should be located in or near each of the work areas so employees at one location will have everything needed to perform their work. This includes space for racks to store clean pots and pans. Hand-washing facilities and drinking water should also be in a convenient location for all personnel.

Rectangular or square kitchens are considered the most convenient. The length of a rectangular-shaped kitchen should be no more than twice its width for best efficiency. Employees will save steps if the dining room entrance is on the longer side of a rectangular kitchen. Fig. 8.11 shows another efficient arrangement for some restaurants, with a square dining space and the kitchen occupying a smaller space in one corner. The dining area is on two sides, and entrances to the kitchen can be located on each side. During slow periods of service, one section or side of the dining room can be closed off with a folding partition. When there is sufficient business, both sides can be used.

Routing servers counterclockwise through the kitchen or patrons through a cafeteria line is more efficient than a clockwise arrangement, at least for right-handed people. This way the right hand of the patron or employee is closest to the food to be selected.

RESTAURANT AND CAFETERIA REQUIREMENTS

Foodservice lines

Tableware areas

SIDE REACH

High and low side reach limits

Maximum side reach over an obstruction

FORWARD REACH

High forward reach limit

Maximum forward reach over an obstruction

Figure 8.9. The Americans with Disabilities Act (ADA) requirements for space to accommodate wheelchair patrons in foodservice facilities. (Courtesy, Liberty Northwest Insurance Corporation, Portland, Oregon.)

Figure 8.10. Optimum heights for worktable and for working area. (Courtesy, Arthur C. Avery.)

Large kitchens usually have specialized work areas, each with its own equipment and short-term storage facilities. For efficiency in work and to reduce the noise level in the kitchen, these work areas may be divided with semipartitions, walls 5 to 5.5 feet high. Thus, there is separation of work but air circulation in the kitchen is not blocked by ceiling-high partitions.

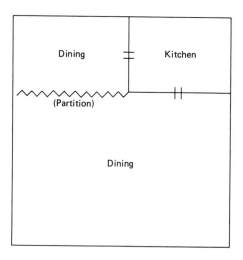

Figure 8.11. Efficient kitchen/dining room arrangement.

In smaller kitchens, the work areas may merge together and so equipment can be shared by employees. For example, the cook and the salad worker may share an electric mixer that could be located at the end of the cook's table but close to the salad preparation area. This requires careful planning of work schedules so both workers will not need to use the equipment at the same time.

Work Areas

Seven major types of work may occur in foodservice departments: (1) receiving; (2) storing and issuing of dry and refrigerated foods; (3) prepreparation; (4) preparation/cooking; (5) food assembly/serving; (6) warewashing (e.g., dishes, pots and pans); (7) supporting services such as administration, janitorial work, locker and rest rooms for employees, and storage for extra china, linens, paper goods, and supplies. The number of work areas to plan for a specific foodservice depends on the type of operating system to be used (see Chapter 2), the volume of business, types of menu items to be prepared, and the form in which food will be purchased.

The *receiving area* includes an outside platform or loading dock, preferably covered, and adjacent floor space, large enough to check in, examine, weigh, and count food, and to check invoices when they are delivered. The floor of the platform should be equal to the height of a standard delivery truck bed and on the same level as the building's entrance. The suggested minimum width is 8 feet, while the platform's length is dictated by the number of trucks that are to be unloaded at any one time.

Space should also be allowed for hand trucks, platform scales, and a desk or work space for the receiving clerk for checking off items delivered. Large institutions that process their own meat need to include an overhead track with hooks for carcass meat. This track would extend from the loading platform through to the meat department's refrigerators.

The exterior door must be wide enough (6 feet is common) to accommodate hand trucks, large cartons, and any large pieces of equipment that are to be installed in the kitchen. A glass-walled office facing the loading dock and with a double-faced platform scale is efficient for a clerk in the office to check weights of goods being delivered and received.

The *storage areas* should be close to the delivery entrance so goods will not have to be moved far to be stored. Space needed for canned foods, staples, and grocery items is known as "dry stores." This area should be easily accessible to the bakery and the cook's units in particular. Dry storerooms must be cool and well-ventilated. Other requirements are moisture-proof floors, screened windows, metal-slatted shelves for case goods, and tightly covered storage bins for items such as cereals, rice, and condiments. Wooden, or polypropylene, mobile pallets should be provided for stacking sacks of flour, sugar, and similar products to keep them off the floor. These pallets should be mobile for ease in cleaning the floor. Space should be arranged to accommodate carts and hand trucks. A desk and files should be included for keeping inventory records, either by computer or manually. Scales are a necessity. Lockable double doors or a wide single door should open to the preparation areas.

Walk-in refrigerators and freezers must be provided for perishable foods. Reach-in refrigerators located in the work units used for daily supplies and leftovers are usually not considered as storage. Refrigerated storage areas should be as close as possible to the receiving platform and accessible to the work unit that will use it most frequently.

The amount of storage required depends on the frequency of deliveries, daily or less frequent, and the form of food purchased. Also, the extent of the menu and the variety of foods offered will influence the amount and kind of storage required. Restaurants may also require space for storing wines and liquor.

Cleaning supplies must be stored separate and apart from all foods, helping to ensure that none of those poisonous chemicals will be mistakenly issued as a food product. Also, additional space must be allocated for extra stocks of paper goods and reserves of china, glassware, linens, towels, uniforms, and aprons.

A *central ingredient room,* if used, will be located adjacent yet connected to the storage areas. Adequate table or counter space for weighing, measuring, and counting ingredients and ample aisle space for carts carrying assembled ingredients to the production units are basic requirements for this room.

The *prepreparation area* for meat, fish, and poultry includes butcher blocks, an electric saw and grinder, sinks, storage trays, and refrigerators. The overhead tracks for bringing in carcass meat from the delivery area that were mentioned earlier would lead to this unit.

For many foodservices, however, this unit is almost a thing of the past except in very large facilities. The trend to buy prefabricated and pan-ready meats, poultry, and fish decreases the need for this once necessary work unit.

The *vegetable preparation area* should be located near the refrigerated storage and the cooking and salad areas (see Fig. 8.7). The usual vegetable preparation area is equipped with a chopper, a cutter, a two-compartment sink, worktables, a cart, knives, and cutting boards. If a peeler is needed, it may be either a pedestal or a table model, placed to empty directly into a sink. Fig. 8.12 shows three possible arrangements for this unit.

Two separate sinks should be provided to permit unhampered use. Food waste disposals are placed in the drainboard to the sink or on a worktable near the end of the sink, or space for a garbage can may be provided, often under an opening cut in the worktable or drainboard.

Because the vegetable preparation area is often responsible for prepreparing some items for the salad unit, ample space for many workers may be needed.

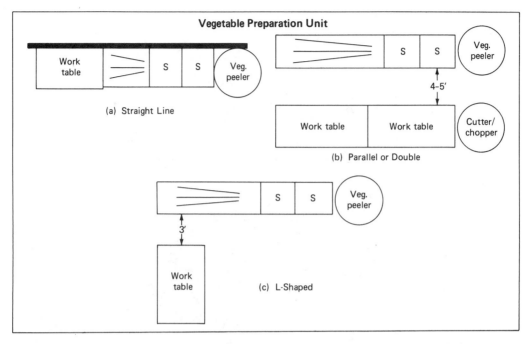

Figure 8.12.   Three possible arrangements for vegetable preparation unit: (*a*) straight-line, (*b*) parallel, (*c*) L-shaped.

Tables that are 30 to 36 inches wide and 6 to 8 feet long are adequate, permitting employees to work on either side for most types of preparation. Providing at least one table low enough for employees to sit comfortably to perform certain tasks is advisable. Fig. 8.13 shows a close-up view of part of a vegetable preparation unit in a large, central production kitchen. Workers are slicing potatoes for use by the cook's unit. Note the electrical circuit posts on the left side, to accommodate heavy-duty equipment requirements.

The main *cooking area* is the hub of the kitchen, which is usually located in or near the center of the kitchen. It is most efficient when adjacent to the vegetable preparation area, the storage rooms, and behind or near the serving area (see Figs. 8.7 and 8.8). The equipment needs are entirely dependent on the amount and type of foods to be cooked on-premise. The usual for conventional type of production would include ovens, broilers, fryers, steam equipment, mixers with attachments, and cook's tables with sink, pot and pan storage racks, and overhead utensil racks. Ranges may also be used although, in many cases, they have been replaced with specialized pieces of equipment such as pressure steam cookers for batch cookery, tilting fry pans, meat roasting ovens, convection ovens, and grills. These may be more energy efficient and allow less heat to be generated into the room than the ranges.

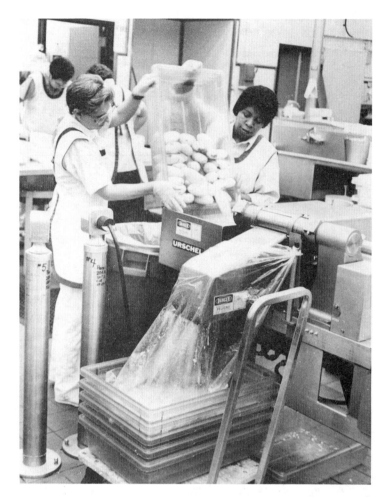

Figure 8.13.   Vegetable prepreparation for the cook's unit in a large, central production kitchen. (Courtesy, Bob Honson, Director, Nutrition Services, Portland, Oregon Public Schools.)

The grouping of equipment varies according to the size and shape of the kitchen. However, steam equipment is usually installed together in a row with the appropriate floor drains in front. Grills and broilers for short-order cooking should be closest of all equipment to the serving unit but not next to deep-fat fryers. Fire danger is great when the intense heat from grills and broilers is close

Figure 8.14.   Four suggested arrangements for a main cooking area: (*a*) straight-line, (*b*) back-to-back or double, (*c*) L-shaped, (*d*) U-shaped. Note the amount of aisle space and total floor space required for each.

to hot fat that may splatter. Fig. 8.14 illustrates four possible arrangements for the cook's unit. Note the amount of space required for each arrangement, including a 12- to 18-inch cleaning space between back-to-back rows of cooking equipment.

Ceiling-mounted hoods with separately vented exhaust fans, which extend 1 foot down over all cooking equipment, help ventilate the kitchen by removing odors, smoke, moisture, and fumes. Hoods also facilitate the installation of direct lighting fixtures to illuminate cooking surfaces.

Water outlets at each point of use, such as a swing-arm faucet between each pair of steam-jacketed kettles, above or beside a tilting frypan, or over the range area are a great convenience and a timesaver for the cooks. A cook's table, located directly in front of the cooking equipment, may contain a small hand sink at one end and an overhead rack for small utensils. A rack for storing clean pots and pans should be easily accessible to the cook's unit, the pot and pan sink, and the power washer, if one is used. Much of the equipment in the cook's area can be wall- or wheel-mounted for ease in cleaning.

The *salad area* is generally located at one side or at the end of the kitchen, as close as possible to the serving unit and to the produce walk-in refrigerators. This unit requires a liberal amount of worktable space and refrigeration for set-up salads. In cafeterias, it is most efficient to have the salad preparation area located directly behind the salad counter on the cafeteria line. A pass-through refrigerator allows kitchen workers to place the trays of set-up salads in the refrigerator from their side, and the counter workers remove them as needed.

Mobile refrigerated units are available for banquet or special party use so that set-up salads may be refrigerated in them until meal time, and then moved directly to the dining area for service. For short-order salad making, a refrigerated table is a convenience for storing salad ingredients between times of use. In a hospital, nursing home, or restaurant that is built on more than one floor, easy access to service elevators, subveyors, or dumb waiters enables made-up salads to be delivered in good condition. Fig. 8.15 shows some possible arrangements for the salad unit.

The *bakery and dessert preparation area* operates as a fairly independent unit. Having little direct association with the other preparation areas, it may be separated from them. Because the quality of the products from this unit is not as dependent on time and temperature as are meats, vegetables, and salads, the bakery need not be as close to the serving area as the other units.

Equipment for a typical bakeshop unit includes baker's table with roll-out bins, ovens, pan storage and cooling racks, mixers, steam-jacketed kettle, dough divider and roller, pie crust roller, and reach-in or small walk-in refrigerator. Large bakery units may include dough mixer, proof box, dough troughs, and reel ovens. Small operations may not have a separate bakery unit, but placing a baker's table near the cooking unit allows the equipment to be shared.

Routing of work and placement of equipment should be in a counterclockwise arrangement for greatest efficiency. The finished product should be on the side closest to the serving unit for shortest transport distance. Performance of tasks should proceed in a direct line from one function to the next without any backtracking or crisscrossing of workers.

If frozen desserts such as ice cream and ices are to be made on the premises rather than purchased, a separate room with specialized equipment to handle these products will have to be provided. It must meet strict sanitation codes and requirements established for production of frozen dessert items.

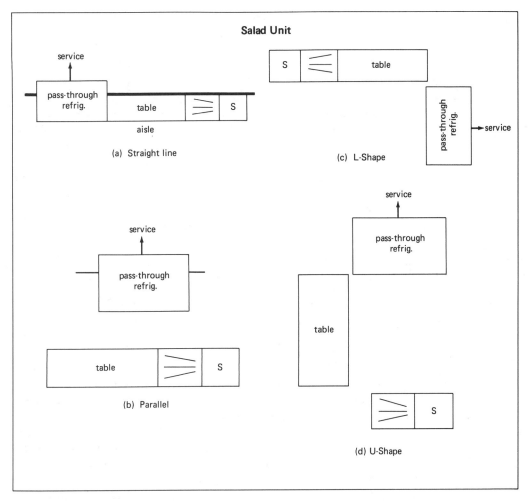

Figure 8.15.   Four suggested arrangements for a salad unit: (*a*) straight-line, (*b*) parallel, (*c*) L-shaped, (*d*) U-shaped. Note: Equipment is arranged so work progresses from right to left (preferred progression) in all except (*c*).

The *assembly/serve area* may be at various preparation centers in the kitchen where servers pick up their orders for table service or for assembling trays for hospital tray service. The latter requires a tray line as described in Chapter 6. Separate serving rooms may adjoin the kitchen and, in some facilities, serving pantries may be located throughout the building. Cafeteria counters located between the kitchen and dining room can be of many different configurations. The length and number of counters needed depends on the number of persons to be served, the number of menu items offered, and the desired speed of service. Speed of service can be increased if the counter is designed for customer movement from right to left or counterclockwise, making it easier for right-handed persons to pick up and put food on their trays.

Serving counter designs depend on the amount of available space. Counters can be arranged in a straight line, in a parallel or double-line with a serving station in-between, in zigzag sections, or are in a hollow square. Whatever configuration is selected, the design should permit speedy service and prevent long waits for patrons, as well as keep labor at a minimum. To speed the flow, silverware, napkins, condiment bars, and beverage dispensers are often placed in the dining room area, encouraging patrons to move away from the serving area more rapidly. A revolving counter section, placed near the wall to the kitchen, is ideal for displaying cold items, such as salads, sandwiches, and desserts.

The hollow square arrangement (sometimes called the "scramble" or "supermarket" system) may be constructed with a center island for trays, silverware, and napkins, and with serving counters on three sides. With this design, patrons enter the square, pick up a tray and utensils, and move to any section of the counter that they desire without standing in line to wait for others to make their choices. A typical arrangement is illustrated in Fig. 8.16.

Cafeteria counters are usually custom-made so that the desired length and design can be obtained. Sections for hot food, once heated with steam, are now mostly electrically heated and have thermostat-controlled units. Hot foods may be placed on the counter in the pans in which they were cooked, if the counter openings are the same size as the pans. This hot unit should be located as close as possible to the kitchen cooking area. Heated, pass-through holding cabinets can be installed into the wall between the kitchen and serving room close to the hot-food section to facilitate supplying foods to the counter.

The arrangement of food items on a cafeteria line may be in a logical sequence; that is, in the order that the food would be eaten. Schools usually prefer this arrangement so that students will choose the most nourishing items first and desserts last. For commercial cafeterias, however, a psychological arrangement might be more profitable; for example, the most eye-appealing items, such as salads and desserts, are placed first for greater selection, and hot foods placed near the end of the counter. Counter units can be mobile to provide flexibility in arrangement.

The size of serving pantries, such as those in hospitals, depends on whether centralized or decentralized service is used. Refer to Chapter 6 for details of the equipment and space requirements for these two service systems.

Warewashing includes dishes, silverware, glassware, trays, and pots and pans. Each of these is discussed individually. The *pot and pan* washing area should be located near the cooking and bakery units as most of the soiled pots and pans come from those units. The area should not be in any main aisle or traffic lane. It is often at the end or back of the cook's unit or in an alcove allocated for this purpose.

Equipment needs include a three-compartment sink: one for soaking and washing, one for rinsing, and one for sanitizing (with drainboards). Racks for

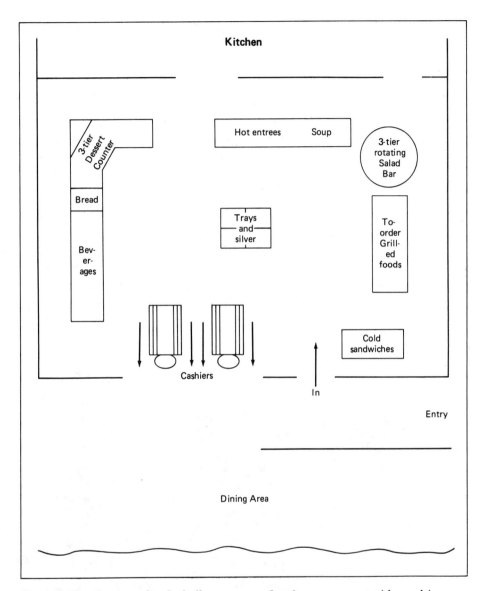

Figure 8.16.   An example of a hollow square cafeteria arrangement with revolving three-tiered salad display.

clean pots and pans are also needed and, in some facilities, a mechanical pot and pan washer. Hand washing of pots and pans may be aided by a manually guided power scrubber or a pump-forced flow of water to loosen food from pans as shown in Chapter 7, Figs. 7.8 and 7.9. After hand washing, pots and pans may be sanitized in a steam cabinet or run through the dish machine.

Large foodservices, particularly hospitals with serving carts for meal delivery to patients, may need space for a room-sized cart and pan washer as shown in Fig. 8.17.

Dishwashing areas should be compact, well-lit, and well-ventilated. It is desirable to locate this unit away from the dining room because of the noise. If this is not possible, surrounding the area with acoustical material will help muffle the sounds. Two examples of such installations are shown in Fig. 8.2 (a, b). Mechanical conveyors save time and money by transporting soiled dishes from the dining area to the dishwashing room. The location of the dishwashing area should be such that the return of soiled dishes will not interfere with the routine of service or cross through work units.

The process of dishwashing is described in Chapter 7. The design of, and space for, the dishwashing area must allow for the smooth flow of dishes through the processes of sorting, scrapping, washing, rinsing, drying, and storage. The overall arrangement of the area and the size and type of dishwashing machine to be selected depends on the number of pieces to be washed, the speed with which they must be returned for reuse, and the shape of the available space. Arrangements for a dishwashing area may be straight-line, L-shaped, U-shaped, open square, platform, or closed circle. The straight-line

Figure 8.17. (*a*) Insulated rack, cart, and pan washer with "drip off" area in front of the door. (*b*) Mechanical pot and pan washer for corner installation. (Courtesy, Alvey Washing Equipment, Division of Alvey Industries, Cincinnati, Ohio.)

type is often installed near a side wall in small operations. The U-shaped arrangement is compact and efficient for small spaces, while the open square might be preferable for a larger facility and could easily accommodate a glass washer. Machines are designed for either right- or left-hand operation, although the usual flow direction is from right to left. Fig. 8.18 shows one layout plan for a small space. Fig. 8.19 shows a closed-circle, or fast-rack conveyor, arrangement that mechanically moves racks continuously to the soiled dish end of the machine. Although this arrangement requires about the same amount of floor space as a straight-line type, it is more compact and can be operated by fewer employees.

Any dishwashing layout should be arranged far enough away from the walls to permit workers to have easy access. At least a 4-foot aisle is desirable on either side of the dishwasher.

Equipment for the dishwashing unit may include a prewash arrangement, the dish machine, possibly a glasswashing machine, soiled and clean dish tables, waste disposals, storage carts, and carts or conveyors to transport dishes to and from this area. Fig. 8.20 shows a well-arranged unit. The usual division of space allocated to dish tables is 60% for soiled dishes and 40% for clean. (See Appendix C for further details on dishwashers.)

Prewashing or preflushing equipment includes a unit built into the dish machine, a hose and nozzle, or a forced water spray as illustrated in Fig. 8.21. It should be noted that the forced water spray method utilizes more water than the other methods; therefore, it is not a desirable choice if water conservation is a concern. The hose and nozzle can be near the machine, but the forced spray should be far enough away so that dishes can be easily racked following the preflush. Food waste disposals can be installed with either type. A method for returning emptied racks to the soiled dish table for reuse should also be provided. (See the power-driven conveyor in Fig. 8.8.)

A booster heater to increase the temperature of the usual 120° to 140°F water used throughout the building to 180°F required for the sanitizing rinse water for the dish machine should be installed near the machine. Some dishroom layouts may include an oversized sink for washing serving trays that are too large to go through the dish machine. If many trays are to be washed (as in hospitals serving patients in bed), a special machine designed especially for washing trays would be desirable. Such a machine is shown in Appendix C.

Proper ventilation of the dishwashing area is essential. A hood-mounted exhaust fan should be installed over the unit, or rustproof, watertight exhaust ducts, which are vented directly to the outside, may be attached directly to the machines to remove steam and hot air.

Supporting/auxiliary services must not be forgotten when planning a facility. Space for *employees'* rest rooms, lockers, showers, and hand-washing facilities are to be included. The number of toilets and other amenities is determined by the number of workers of each sex on duty at any one time and by the Health Department's standards and codes. Requirements of the ADA must be met when planning these facilities as well. (See the ADA compliance checklist in Appendix B.)

Figure 8.18. A dishroom layout plan for a small space. This company's power loader and unloader enables many facilities to use larger dish machines in a small area. The unloaders eject dish racks at a right angle to the machine, which is a space-saving feature. (Courtesy, Insinger Machine Co., Philadelphia.)

Figure 8.19. Fast-rack conveyor warewashing system can be custom designed to fit the space and needs of the situation. (Reprinted courtesy of Hobart Corporation, Troy, Ohio.)

Figure 8.20. Dishwashing room shows incoming conveyor belts on left that merge on a double scrapping table with integral silver soak sink and waste disposal; convenient dish rack return. (Courtesy, S. Blickman, Inc.)

Office space for the foodservice management staff is preferably located so the staff has a view of the kitchen and the work going on. This may be accomplished in part by using glass walls or large windows for the office. The number of persons who will need desks, files, chairs for visitors, and aisle space will

Figure 8.21.   Three arrangements for preflushing soiled dishes. (*a*) Forced water spray. (*b*) Hose and nozzle. (*c*) Water scrapping unit on dish machine.

determine the size of the offices. Those staff members not directly supervising food production may have offices in an area adjacent to the kitchen.

Janitors' closets for storage of mops, brooms, and cleaning materials, as well as a large low sink for washing mops, require consideration in planning a foodservice facility. An area equipped with a steam hose, often located near the back door, may be required for sanitizing food carts and trucks, especially in hospitals that have many such items to clean. This should be a separate area with curbing around it and equipped with floor drains.

Trash and food waste storage and removal space is necessary if disposal facilities are not available in the building. Many buildings have their own incinerator for burning trash, central compactors to compress trash and cans, and preparation unit waste disposals. When such facilities are not available, both garbage and trash must be collected and held for frequent pick-up removal. A cooled room near the back entrance may be provided for the daily storage of garbage, but when feasible, unit or central disposers incorporated into the system are more desirable and efficient.

The *dining area* is generally a part of the total foodservice design plan. For greatest efficiency, it is located adjacent to the kitchen or serving area, sometimes opening off the cafeteria. Dining rooms that are quiet, well-lighted, and well-ventilated are conducive to the enjoyment of good food and hospitality. The size of the dining room was discussed in the "Space Allowances and Relationships" section.

Equipment for dining areas includes the tables, chairs, and small serving stations. Two- and four-seat tables that can be combined to accommodate larger groups are typical of most public dining rooms. Tables in school foodservices are larger to conserve space, but difficult for waiter or waitress service and less satisfactory for socializing. The size of the tables to be used, the type and size of chairs, and the number of people to be seated at one time are basic to determining space needs. Also, space between tables and aisle space must be added; minimum space between chair backs is 18 inches after guests are seated. Main traffic aisles of 4.5 to 5 feet are recommended. Public dining rooms should accommodate patrons who may be in wheelchairs or who use walkers, and so may need wider aisles. (See Figure 8.9 for details.)

Folding partitions that are decorative as well as functional may be used to close off part of the dining room for special groups or when all of the room is not in use. Customer rest rooms are located close to the dining area for convenience and security. See Chapter 9 for more on dining room furnishings.

The planning team, supplied with this information, should now have a conference to discuss ideas, rejecting or discarding features and/or components of the plan until agreement is reached on what shall be included and the boundaries for the project. If it is a remodeling project, the team decides how much can be done and, perhaps, what has to be left undone. Decisions on quantity and quality within the confines of the budget will be made. Only with this agreement among all team members will each be fully committed to the project and continue to devote work time and provide the expertise needed to bring the project to a successful conclusion—to bring the menu and customers together through a planned system of time and motion.

Mechanics of Drawing

The actual drawing of a plan to scale requires certain tools and techniques. The use of quarter-inch squared paper provides a good sized scale to visually depict the entire plan, yet is a convenient size with which to work. A pen and India ink, or a heavy black ink pen, a good ruler, preferably an architect's ruler with various scales marked on it, and some tracing paper and masking tape are other needed supplies.

An outline of the size and shape of the space allocated is first drawn to scale with pencil on the squared paper. (If a one-eighth-inch scale is used, buy one-eighth-inch squared paper and so on.) When the location of doors and windows has been decided on, these are marked off on the outline. Then, the outline of the space is inked in, using proper architectural symbols for walls, doors, and windows as illustrated in Fig. 8.22.

The next step is to obtain a set of templates, to-scale model drawings, of each piece of equipment to be used. They must be to the same scale as the floor plan. Label each template with the name and dimensions of the piece of equipment it represents; see Fig. 8.23. Sometimes a different color is used for each work unit. Templates should include overall measurements of features that require space, such as the swing of door openings, control boxes or fittings, and any installation needs as specified in equipment catalogs. The templates are then cut out, placed on the floor plan, and moved about until a good arrangement is found. Templates may then be secured to the plan with a bit of rubber cement (for easy removal if changes are made).

A sheet of thin tracing paper is taped over the floor plan, and lines are drawn on it to show the route used in the preparation of several menu items. Drawing lines tracing the movements of food and workers from one key work point to the next within a unit, as well as from one work area or department to the next, is a good check on the efficiency of the arrangement. Actual measurement of the distances can be made by passing a string over pintacks at each key point as the preparation of a menu item progresses and then measuring the string (usual scale is ¼ inch to 1 foot). At this time, a check on width of aisles, work area space, location of hand-washing sinks for employees, storage space for carts and trucks, and similar details is made.

The above procedures afford good checks of the adequacy of the tentative floor plan, for necessary equipment, and of working areas before the final plan is made. The space allowances for passageways between working areas, between tables, between ranges and cook's table, and between other major pieces of equipment should also be checked for adequacy. Changes and adjustments should be made on paper instead of after construction has begun, because it is costly to make revisions at that time.

Separate drawings are made by the architect for plumbing, electric, and gas installations in addition to those for the building construction. All must be coordinated and checked carefully to ensure that gas, water, and waste outlets and vents will be in the correct positions for the equipment planned. Also, the electrical wiring with convenient switch control boxes, power and regular outlets and turn-on switches, and locations and kinds of light fixtures must be noted. Telephone conduits and outlets, wiring for computers, and intercom, public address, or TV system as decided on are indicated.

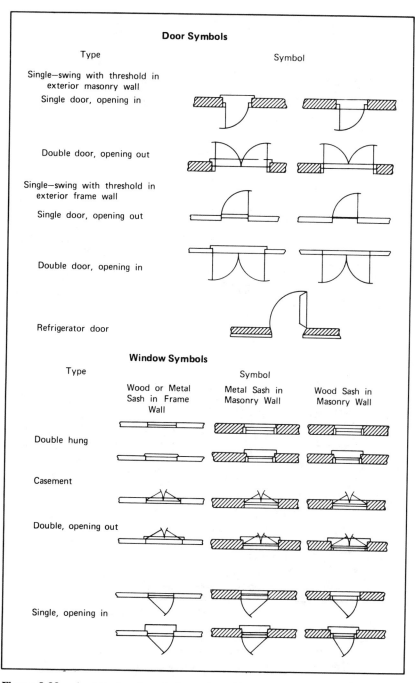

Figure 8.22. Architectural symbols used on blueprints to show placement and arrangement of various types of doors and windows.

Figure 8.23. Templates of sample pieces of equipment drawn to 1/4-inch scale. Cut-out templates may be moved about on the floor plan of same scale to determine floor space needs, and to find most efficient arrangement of equipment.

Designing by Computer

Computer-assisted design (CAD) planning began in the early 1960s (Riggs) and has grown and expanded rapidly during the past 3 decades. Computer capability for graphically designing a floor plan and equipment layout can replace the method just described in the "Mechanics of Drawing" section. However, all of the preliminary studies, analyses, and team input remain as necessary steps to obtain data for computer input for designing by computer.

CAD for foodservices is based on an interactive graphic concept; that is, the software programs are developed to assist with schematic planning. Software programs use variables that must be identified by the foodservice manager and the planning team.

Today, programs are sophisticated and technologies that have been developed led to the use of the terms, "before CAD" and "after CAD." *Before CAD* is computer-modeling software meant to replace the use of "sketching on napkins and tissues" as the starting point for conceptual design. *After CAD* refers to computer-aided facilities management (CAFM), which provides a greater range of services for managing the building project beyond the designing function.

CAD software systems have been adapted and expanded by many companies. An update of the most recent systems is best obtained by reviewing trade journals and contacting companies. Many software programs can be used on personal computers, as well as on more powerful, network workstations. CAD systems run on a variety of platforms, such as UNIX, DOS, MAC, and VAX.

Many add-on packages are available today to make floor plan designing faster and easier. These range from instant viewing and zooming devices, capabilities to display several views simultaneously, cutting and pasting drawings to create new ones, and marking drawings for modifications and easier version control. The output devices may include high-end digital plotters, interactive video displays, or virtual reality programs.

Foodservice managers or planning teams wishing to design facilities by computer will want to search the market carefully for appropriate software and add-ons. New developments appear almost daily and any listing of components today may soon be outmoded or obsolete. Some resources for keeping abreast of developments are listed at the end of this chapter under "Resources for CAD Programs."

Architect's Blueprints

After the dietitian, foodservice manager, and others thoroughly check the preliminary plans, the architect prepares a complete set of drawings that are reproduced as blueprints. Blueprints always include the name and address of the facility, the scale used, and the date the plan was prepared. Details of construction, materials, plumbing, and electrical wiring, connections, and fixtures are indicated and coded. Side elevation drawings are included for door and window finishings, stairways, and built-in or attached equipment.

When reading and checking blueprints, one must constantly consider the scale to which they are drawn. The scale should be sufficiently large to permit detailed study. The heavy, solid lines indicate walls; the space between lines indicates the wall thickness; and the markings in-between denote the kind of materials, such as stone, brick, and concrete blocks. Three or four parallel lines at a break in the wall denote the position and size of windows. The direction in which doors will open appears in blueprints as an arc extending from the door hinge to the door's fully open position (see Fig. 8.22). Steps are shown as parallel lines with an arrow and the words "up" or "down." Dimensions of all spaces are indicated, and rooms and equipment are labeled. Architects use a variety of symbols to identify special features; for example, some electrical symbols are shown in Fig. 8.24. All the symbols the architect uses are explained in a legend on the drawing.

Specifications and Contract Documents

The architect must also prepare a set of written documents to accompany the blueprints when presented to contractors for bid. These documents include: a statement of general conditions and scope of the work to be done; a schedule of operations, which includes a timetable for contractors to complete their work and details of penalties resulting from failure to meet deadlines; who has the responsibility for installations and inspections; and specifications for all aspects of the work and for the equipment required.

Figure 8.24. Electrical symbols used on blueprints to indicate type and location of wiring and outlets.

Specifications include details such as the location of the building; type of base construction; mix of cement; size and kinds of conduits, drains, and vents; type and installation of roofing and flooring; wall finishes and colors; hardware; doors and windows; and all other construction features. Equipment specifications generally include the brand name and model number, material to be used, size or capacity, and the number required (see Chapter 9 for details). In large installations, separate contract documents may be prepared for bids on the electrical or HVAC system. All specifications must meet applicable building and installation codes, and all the documents must be clearly worded to avoid misinterpretations.

Bids, Contracts, Construction, and Inspection

When the contract documents are completed, they are advertised and made available to interested bidders. Certain reputable contractors and equipment dealers may be notified that the plans are complete and are invited to bid on the project.

The contract is generally awarded to the low bidder, who then works closely with the architect until construction is complete. The foodservice manager closely monitors developments during the construction phase of the project, checking frequently with the architect. Conditions of the contract, as well as the individuals concerned, will determine what adjustments can be made after the contract is signed.

The actual construction time will vary, depending on the type and size of the building and the availability of labor, materials, and equipment. During construction, the architect will frequently check the progress and quality of work to be sure that both meet contract specifications. In addition, the architect must inspect and approve all construction, equipment, and installations before the sponsoring organization accepts the facility. Each item of equipment is performance-tested to see that it meets specifications and claims and that it has been installed correctly. These performance tests, usually conducted by the vendor's representative to demonstrate proper operation, care, and maintenance of the equipment, should be attended by the dietitian, foodservice manager and assistants, the kitchen supervisor, maintenance personnel, and the architect. The demonstrations may be videotaped, too, for use in training future employees and for later review sessions for present personnel.

Usually, the various contractors guarantee necessary adjustments and some service for a specified period following the project's completion. After some predetermined date, all repairs and full maintenance become the foodservice management's responsibility. Any warranty contract forms supplied should be completed and returned promptly to the manufacturer.

Summary

The principles and guidelines for facility design planning presented in this chapter apply to all types of foodservice building projects. In fact, the general considerations for making and checking floor plans are similar for different kinds of institutions, regardless of the type of service, menu, clientele, and other governing conditions. Parts of a project that were originally eliminated can possibly be included at lower cost in the future if basic plans for them are incorporated during the construction period. For example, if a monorail system for transporting supplies and food is anticipated in the future, the necessary overhead rails and other requirements could be incorporated into the original construction.

During the project's planning phase, foodservice managers would have been collecting a list of items that should be included in the proposed plans. These could range from a telephone jack in the dining room to storage space for banquet tables, high chairs, reserve china, and utensils. A written list of such details is an excellent way to ensure that these items are included in the final plans.

A balance of beauty and utility in the structure, furnishings, and equipment is helpful for successful foodservice planning. Colorful walls and floor coverings; modern lighting; streamlined, modular kitchen equipment made of well-finished metals; machines with mechanical parts and motors enclosed; and the use of attractive woods and metals in dining room furniture are but a few of the many features contributing to the functionality of modern foodservice areas. Sanitation, ease of maintenance, noise reduction, and controlled environmental temperatures for comfort are built-in features that contribute to making a facility successful and help to achieve the objectives outlined in the prospectus for the foodservice operation.

Summary Questions

1. What does facilities planning and design encompass?

2. What preliminary studies and data collection are essential to prepare for a facilities planning project and why?

3. How can a foodservice manager learn what new developments there are in foodservice design and equipment?

4. What are some of the sources of information on the regulatory considerations that must be observed in planning a new foodservice facility?

5. Generally, who are the members of the team that cooperatively plan a foodservice facility? What contributions does each make? What information must the foodservice manager be prepared to provide for the other team members?

6. Why is a prospectus an important document in a planning project? What are the three parts of a prospectus?

7. Point out some ways that energy conservation, sanitation, safety, and noise control can be built in to a facility plan?

8. For greatest efficiency, what is the recommended flow of work and people, and the space relationships for a foodservice facility?

9. What determines the number and kind of work units that are to be included in any given floor plan design?

10. What are the mechanics of drawing a floor plan and arranging the equipment layout by hand? by computer-aided facility design?

11. What contract agreements and specifications must be prepared and included in the documents sent out for bid for the facility construction?

12. After construction is complete, what inspections and performance tests should be made before the sponsoring organization formally and finally accepts the facility?

Bibliography

Breit, A.: Satisfying the health department. Food Management 26(8):60, 1991.

Hall, L.: Design considerations for correctional facilities. The Consultant 22(3): 45, 1989.

Kotschevar, L. and Terrell, M. E.: Foodservice Planning: Layout and Equipment, 3rd ed. New York: John Wiley & Sons, 1985.

Norwich, R.: Safe and hygienic floors in food preparation areas. The Consultant 24(3):59, 1991.

Richardson, J. K., Jr.: CFC's and the foodservice industry. The Consultant 23(2):27, 1990.

Riggs, J. L.: Production Systems: Planning, Analysis and Control. New York: John Wiley & Sons, 1981.

For More Information

Accommodating Disabilities—Business Management Guide. 1992. (Contact: Commerce Clearing House, Inc., P.O. Box 5490, Chicago, IL 60680-9882)

Bean, N. R.: Planning for catastrophe: Fast track to recovery. Cornell HRA Quarterly 32(2):64, 1992.

Borsenik, F. D. and Stutts, A. T.: The Management of Maintenance and Engineering Systems in the Hospitality Industry, 2nd ed. New York: John Wiley & Sons, 1987.

Haasis, J., Jr.: Design and chlorofluorocarbons (CFC's). The Consultant 23(3):31, 1990.

Kaye, R. E.: The food storage area—Just another closet? The Consultant 23(2):54, 1990.

Kazarian, E. A.: Food Service Facilities Planning, 3rd ed. New York: Van Nostrand Reinhold, 1989.

Kohl, J. P. and Greenlaw, P. S.: Here comes the Americans with Disabilities Act. Part II. Implications for managers. Cornell HRA Quarterly 33(1):33, 1992.

Lundberg, D. E.: The Restaurant From Concept to Operation. New York: John Wiley & Sons, 1985.

Markham, J. E.: The blueprint for success. (About feasibility studies). The Consultant 23(3):34, 1990.

Norton, L. C.: Planning for the 90's. Food Management 25(10):75, 1990.

Rethmeyer, A.: Evaluating a planned renovation. Food Management 24(4):48, 1989.

Unklesbay, N. and Unklesbay, K.: Energy Management in Foodservice. Westport, CT: AVI Publishing Co., 1981.

Von Egmond-Pannell, D. V.: School Foodservice, 3rd ed. Westport, CT: AVI Publishing Co., 1985.

Woods, R. H. and Kavanaugh, R. R.: Here comes the Americans with Disabilities Act. Part I. Are you ready? Cornell HRA Quarterly 33(1):24, 1992.

Resources for CAD Programs

Architectural Record. Each issue has a section on computers: Product review. Subscription address: P.O. Box 564, Hightstown, NJ 08520-9885.

Gen CADD Architecular. (A general drafting program for laying out space, drawing walls, footings, doors, windows, stairs, and elevations. IBM PC compatible.) DCA Softdesk, Henniker, NH.

Stover, R. N.: An Analysis of CAD/CAM Applications. Englewood Cliffs, NJ: Prentice Hall, Inc., 1984.

Versa CAD. (For MacIntosh 4.0; compatible with Systems & Support.) One of the fastest project managers available for microcomputers—For large projects. Computervision, Inc., 100 Crosby Drive, Bedford, MA 01730.

Zawacki, G.: A review of CAD—Past, present, and future in the foodservice industry. The Consultant 22(3):42, 1989.

Equipment and Furnishings

Complete coverage of this broad subject area is impossible in a general textbook, but an effort is made here to include pertinent basic information that can be supplemented by current literature from the manufacturers and from observations of equipment in use.

The selection and purchase of furnishings and equipment for any foodservice are major responsibilities of the director and the staff, and the wisdom with which selection is made determines in large measure the attainment of lasting satisfaction. Employee and customer safety, the efficiency of work units, and the beauty of environment may be marred by poor selection and placement of furnishings and equipment, and the quality of service that an organization may render is influenced, if not limited, by these features.

The wise selection of equipment for any foodservice can be made only after a thorough study of all factors affecting the particular situation has been made. Items are available in many designs, materials, sizes, and within a wide cost range, but only those items that will help to meet the specific needs of the foodservice and contribute to its efficient operation should be purchased.

The problem of selection is so important and errors so costly that major characteristics to consider in the selection of certain basic pieces of equipment are included in Appendix C. This chapter includes a discussion of energy conservation as it relates to the selection and operation of foodservice equipment.

A section devoted to dining room furnishings concludes this chapter. Basic information needed for the wise selection of dinnerware, tableware, glassware, and table covers is presented in Appendix C.

Learning Objectives

After studying this chapter, the reader should be able to

1. list the many factors that affect decisions regarding equipment selection
2. discuss the advantages of modular equipment
3. discuss the factors that determine the size and capacity of equipment chosen
4. describe how gauge of metals is determined in the United States
5. list and briefly explain the desired characteristics of a metal chosen for foodservice equipment
6. identify what should be included in a specification for a piece of foodservice equipment
7. discuss the role of the National Sanitation Foundation International (NSFI) regarding foodservice equipment and furnishings

Factors Affecting Selection of Equipment

Equipment for any foodservice should be selected on the basis of a thorough study of all major considerations. Important among these are

1. the menu
2. number and type of patrons to be served
3. form in which the food will be purchased
4. style of service and length of serving period
5. number of labor hours available
6. abilities of employees to do the work
7. accessibility and cost of utilities
8. budget and amount of money allotted for equipment
9. floor plan and space allotments

Most foodservices include one or more of each of the following: oven, range, tilting frypan, fryer, broiler, steam-jacked kettle, pressure steam cooker, coffee maker, refrigerator, freezer, ice maker, mixer with attachments, food cutter, sinks, tables, and carts. A wide variety of additional equipment may be purchased as necessity demands and money permits.

Before final decisions are made, individual pieces of equipment should be considered as to design, materials in relation to suitability for the purpose, durability and cleanability, construction and safety, size and capacity, installation, operation, and performance, maintenance, and replacement of parts. Cost and method of purchase are also major considerations in the selection of equipment.

Sound generalizations concerning equipment needs are difficult to formulate because each foodservice presents an individual problem with an interplay of factors not exactly duplicated elsewhere. The determination of these needs, therefore, should be one of the first and most important considerations of the foodservice manager as a basis for deciding what equipment should be purchased. Each item selected must accomplish those definite tasks peculiar to the specific situation. If the installation is new, information concerning the demands to be made of the facility and the ways in which the furnishings and equipment may help to meet these demands is of primary importance in planning the layout and selecting the equipment. If the installation is already in operation and has been found to be inefficient, an analysis should be made of the layout and equipment as it exists. This study can be used as a basis to rearrange the floor plan and include any additional furnishings and equipment needed.

The Menu

The menu pattern and typical foods to be served must be known in order to determine the extent and complexity of the required food preparation. Detailed analysis of the preparation requirements of several typical menus provides the best basis for estimating foodservice equipment needs for a particular situation.

Standardized recipes that include AP and EP (as purchased and edible portion, see Chapter 5), weights of ingredients, yields, pan sizes, and portion size are invaluable aids to planning for efficient equipment. Batch size and how often a procedure is repeated are important considerations for determining equipment needs. A large mixer and both large capacity and duplicate steam-jacketed kettles or tilting frypans might be advisable, since they are used in the preparation of many menu items. An increase in the lengths of time required for certain processes for 500 over that needed for 100 portions would be necessary but not always proportional to the increase in quantities. In general, little difference in time is required for chopping various amounts of food in less than machine-capacity quantities or for mixing or cooking an increased amount of food in larger equipment. Repetitive processes such as hand rolling of pastry or batch cooking vegetables in a small pressure steamer requires almost proportional quantity, time, and space increases.

Once the equipment has been installed, care must be taken that menus are planned with consideration for its balanced use. This means that the person responsible for planning menus must be familiar with the facilities at hand and know the capacities of the equipment and the timing of processes for the amounts of food to be prepared. Demands for oven cooking beyond the capacity load may lead to much unhappiness between manager and cook and may also encourage the production of inferior quality food or too-early preparation. Preparation timetables, equipment capacity charts, and standardized recipes that indicate AP and EP weights of ingredients, yield, and pan size for the particular setup can contribute much to effective planning for the efficient use of equipment.

Number and Type of Patrons

The number and type of patrons are important factors in selecting the appropriate amount and kind of equipment for a foodservice. The equipment needs for the preparation and serving of a plate lunch to 500 children in a school dining room are quite different from those of a service restaurant offering a diversified menu to approximately the same number of people three times daily. In the school foodservice there probably would not be more than two hot entrées on the menu for any one day, but all food would have to be ready to serve within a short period of time. In the restaurant, a variety of items would be ready for final preparation over extended serving periods; also, some items would be cooked in small quantities at spaced intervals according to the peak hours of service. Obviously, smaller and more varied types of equipment would be needed in the restaurant than in the school dining room. Production schedules in a short-order operation would require duplicates of such items as griddles, broilers, and fryers, whereas a residence hall foodservice would need steam-jacketed kettles, steamers, and ovens to produce a large volume of food within a specified time period.

The number of people to be fed determines to a great extent the total volume of food that must be prepared, but numbers in themselves cannot be used to evaluate equipment needs. Estimates of numbers of persons to be served during each 15-minute interval of the serving period will provide a guide to food and equipment needs. Amount and capacity of equipment to select is based on the number served at the interval of greatest demand in relation to cooking time required for specific items.

Form of Food Purchased and Styles of Service

The form in which the food is to be purchased will greatly influence equipment needs. The selection of fabricated meats and poultry, frozen portioned fish, frozen juices and vegetables, juice concentrates, ready-to-bake pies, and some cooked entrées, chilled citrus fruit sections, washed spinach and other greens, and processed potatoes, carrots, and apples eliminates the need for space and equipment usually required for preparation and disposal of waste. Adequate facilities for short and long storage at the proper temperatures must be provided, but other equipment needs would be limited primarily to those pieces required in the final stages of production and the serving of the finished products.

Various styles of service, such as self-service in a cafeteria, table or buffet service in a public dining room, or vended service, require particular kinds of equipment for their efficient functioning. Length of serving period is another factor.

Labor Hours and Worker Abilities

The labor hours available and the skill of the workers cannot be overlooked in considering the equipment needs of any foodservice. If the labor budget or local labor market is limited, usually the selection of as much labor-saving equipment as possible is warranted. Judgment must be exercised in deciding what equipment will provide for the smooth functioning of the organization and also give the best return on the investment. Will the increased productivity of employees with automated equipment compensate for the possible increased payroll costs, initial costs, and maintenance costs? With the rising pay rates for employees at all levels, managers must weigh values carefully in selecting equipment they can operate successfully, efficiently, and economically to accomplish the job to be done.

Utilities

The adequacy of utilities for the successful installation and performance of commercial cooking and warming or power-driven equipment must be checked before the final decision is made on selections. Often the choice between gas, electric, or steam-heated cooking equipment demands considerable investigation of the continuing supply of the source of heat, replaceability of parts, relative costs of operation and maintenance, and the probable satisfaction received from use in the particular situation. High-pressure steam is not always available, thus, self-generating steam units would be a necessary choice. Power-driven equipment is equipped with motors of the proper size for the capacity of the machine, but cycle and current would have to be designated so that the machine would operate properly for the wiring and power in the building.

The Budget

The budgetary allowance must cover not only the initial cost of the equipment but often the additional cost of installation. Available funds determine to a great extent the possible amount and quality of equipment that can be purchased at any given time. If the initial equipment budget is adequate, the choice among various pieces becomes mere determination of the superior and preferred qualities for each article desired. Sometimes the equipment budget is so limited that the food director is forced to decide between certain desirable articles and to weigh with serious thought the relative points in quality grades of the pieces believed to be essential. It is advisable then to list all the needed equipment so that unbalanced expenditure will not result. Lack of such thought or insistence on the best may lead to disastrous spending.

Consensus is that equipment of good quality is the most economical. Generally, if the amount of money is limited, it is better to buy a few well-chosen pieces of equipment that will meet basic needs and make additions as funds are available than to purchase many pieces of inferior quality that will need to be replaced in a short time. In contrast, some consultants warn that because of the rapid change in the trend toward the use of prepared foods, it may be preferable in some installations to plan equipment for a short life span and early replacement until such developments are stabilized. The initial cost of equipment is influenced by the size; materials used; quality of workmanship; construction, including special mechanical features; and finish of the article. The limitation of funds may lead to the necessity of a choice as to which one or more of these points may be sacrificed with least jeopardy to the permanence of the article and satisfaction in its use.

Estimates of cost for foodservice equipment are difficult to ascertain as each operation must be considered individually. It is advisable to learn the costs of comparable situations before making tentative estimates for a new or remodeled setup.

The Floor Plan

Space allocation for the foodservice may restrict the amount and type of equipment and its placement, especially in old buildings where architectural changes are limited and in new ones where the original planning may have been ill-advised regarding the functions and needs. The size and shape of the space allotted to food preparation and its relation to receiving, storage, and dining areas greatly influence the efficiency of operation and, ultimately, customer satisfaction, as discussed in the preceding chapter. Floor space either too small or too large to accommodate the equipment suitable and desirable for the volume of food production anticipated creates an unsatisfactory situation. In the first instance, the overcrowding of work makes for confusion and frustration, limits the amount and type of preparation that can be done, and slows production. When the space is too large, much time and effort can be wasted by workers in transporting food long distances. Also, there can be a tendency to overequip with needless items simply because ample space is available. In any case, a complete analysis of the real needs is necessary before an equipment investment is made.

Features of Equipment

General objectives and trends in current equipment developments include an increase in the number and kind of specialized items, many of which are adaptable to multiple use; function and attractiveness in appearance; compactness and efficient utilization of space to reduce labor hours and time requirements to a minimum; speed output of quality products; modular planning of matched units as shown in Fig. 9.1, mobility and flexibility of arrangement; exact engineering tolerances, effective insulation, computerized and solid-state controls (Fig. 9.2) for even temperatures and operation; built-in sanitation; and fuel efficiency. With the change in the type and amount of food preparation in the individual units has come a corresponding change in equipment to meet the particular production needs.

Design and Function

The design of equipment and furnishings for the foodservice should be in close harmony with the general plan of the building, especially in the decorative features and items such as table appointments. This is particularly noticeable in summer resorts, children's hospitals, and certain types of restaurants, where not only the modern trend of foodservice planning and interior decoration has been followed, but also some specialized idea or theme has been expressed through the design and type of furnishings selected. Sensitivity to the artistic design of foodservice furnishings and equipment is often more acute than to the design of similar items for the home, because of the larger size of items

Figure 9.1. A compact arrangement of modular cooking units can be fitted into a continuous framework for beauty, space saving, operational efficiency, and maintenance of sanitation. This one includes cabinet-mounted steamers, kettles, and a tilting braising pan. (Courtesy, Groen Division, Dover Corporation.)

Figure 9.2. This computerized convection oven utilizes solid-state temperature devices accurate to within one degree (± 1°F). A digital control panel replaces conventional control knobs and allows entry of exact cooking temperatures and times. (Courtesy, Lang Manufacturing Company, Redmond, Washington.)

required and duplication in number, as in dining room tables and chairs. Generally speaking, heavy-duty equipment is designed to give a streamlined effect.

Beauty and utility may be combined in foodservice equipment through the application of art principles and consideration of the functions of the various items by the designer. The gadget or piece of equipment may be beautiful in line and design, but it is of little value if it serves no real purpose or if an unreasonable amount of time is required for its operation or care. The design of cutlery such as a chef's knife with a heavy wide blade shaped for cutting on a board and a long-handled cook's fork are examples of how closely design is related to use of an article. Also, the design may influence the timing, efficiency, and comfort of operation, such as the utensils shown in Fig. 9.3. These spoodles, or combination spoon and ladle, are not only color coded for portion control, but feature a handle that is designed for control and comfort.

Simplicity of design is pleasing and restful and usually means a minimum amount of care. The maintenance of high sanitation standards in a foodservice is aided if equipment selected is designed so that sharp corners, cracks, and crevices are eliminated and all surfaces are within easy access for cleaning. The Joint Committee on Food Equipment Standards has stressed the sanitation

(a)

(b)

Figure 9.3. Spoodles are designed to give the portion control of a ladle with the ease and balance of a spoon. Made of either (*a*) stainless steel with plastic handles or (*b*) entirely of high-impact plastic in a variety of capacities with perforated or solid bowls. (Courtesy, Vollrath Company.)

aspect of kitchen equipment design and construction as exemplified in the following statement:

> Food service equipment and appurtenances shall be fabricated to exclude vermin, dust, dirt, splash, or spillage as may be encountered under normal use, and shall be easily cleaned, maintained, and serviced.

All equipment mounted on legs or casters, such as the tray unit in Fig. 9.4, should be designed to have a minimum clearance of 6 inches, but preferably 8 inches, between the floor and the bottom surfaces of equipment, shelves, pipes, drains, or traps, to permit ease of cleaning. Heavy stationary equipment such as ranges and cabinets can be mounted successfully on a raised masonry, tile, or metal platform at least 2 inches high, sealed to the floor at all edges. Usually, this type of island base is recessed to allow for toe space beneath the equipment.

Specially designed mountings on wheels for specific purposes have become an important feature of foodservice planning for convenience, sanitation, and economical use of space and labor. Portable back-of-the-counter breakfast service units, including toaster, waffle irons, and egg cookers, can be transported out of the way during the remainder of the day. Dispenser units can be filled with clean trays in the dishwashing room and wheeled into position at the counter with minimum handling (see Fig. 9.4). Portable bins for flour and sugar are more convenient to use and easier to keep clean than built-in bins. Sections of shelves in walk-in refrigerators and dry-storage rooms mounted on wheels make for convenience in cleaning and rearrangement of storage. The importance of designing general utility trucks and dollies to fit into the places in which they are to be used cannot be overestimated.

Heavy-duty wheeled equipment, such as range sections, tilting frypans, fryers, ovens, reach-in refrigerators, and the many mobile work and serving units, make rearrangement possible in order to adapt to changing needs at minimum cost. Often the conversion of certain spaces from limited- to multiple-use areas can

Figure 9.4. Mobile self-leveling tray unit, filled at dish machine and transported to the point of use. (Courtesy, Precision Metal Products, Inc.)

be effected through the inclusion of mobile designed equipment. Also, thorough cleaning in back of and underneath equipment is made easier when it is movable and accessible from all sides.

One of the outstanding improvements in serving equipment has been effected through a change in the design and construction of heated serving counters. This change from the old pattern of a given number of rectangular and round openings, far apart, in an elongated steam-table arrangement with limited fixed storage, to a condensed type with fractional size containers, has been estimated to permit up to 50% greater food capacity in the same amount of space. This arrangement also makes possible almost unlimited flexibility in service through the close arrangement of a few regular 18- by 12-inch rectangular top openings into which full-size or combinations of fractional-size pans of different depths may be fitted with or without the aid of adaptor bars. Hot food serving counters may be designed and constructed for two or more openings, moist or dry heat, gas or electricity, separate heat controls for individual sections or for the unit, and space below enclosed or fitted for dish storage.

The selection of inserts for this type of counter should be made to meet the demands at peak times for the best service of all the usual types of hot foods included on a menu. The number of each size and depth of pans to purchase can be determined easily by careful analysis of several sample menus, the quantities of each type of food required, and the most satisfactory size and depth of pans for their preparation and service. In most instances, this will mean a relatively small number of sizes with ample duplication of those for which there will be the greatest need.

Common depths of the counter pans are 2½, 4, and 6 inches with some sizes available 1 and 8 inches deep. Capacities are listed for each size as, for example, in the accompanying table. All inserts fit flush with top openings, except the 8-inch deep pans, which have a 2-inch shoulder extending above the opening. Pans of one size and depth are designed to nest together for convenient storage. Since these pans are made of noncorrosive well-finished metal, certain types of menu items may be cooked in and served directly from them, whereas other foods will need to be transferred to them for serving. Recipes can be standardized for a specific number of pans of suitable size and depth for a product and with the exact number of portions predetermined. The pan shown in Fig. 9.5 is designed with reinforced corners to add strength and prevent vacuum-sticking of stacked pans. As with most hotel pans, they are available in full, half, one-third, one-fourth, and one-sixth sizes.

One-Half Size		One-Fourth Size	
Depth (in)	Capacity (qt)	Depth (in)	Capacity (qt)
1	1¾		
2½	4½	2½	2⅛
4	7⅛	4	3⅜
6	10⅞	6	4¾
8	15		

Figure 9.5. A hotel pan designed to last longer, not stick together when stacked, be more comfortable to carry, provide a better steamtable seal, and be easier to clean. (Courtesy, Vollrath Company.)

Size or Capacity

The size or capacity of equipment to select for a given situation is determined largely by the type of menu and service offered and the quantities of different types of foods to be prepared at one time. More pieces of heavy-duty equipment of larger capacities are required for the preparation of food for a college residence hall serving a nonselective menu at a set hour than for the preparation and service for a short-order lunch counter serving comparable or even greater numbers throughout an extended meal hour. Batch cooking, the cooking of vegetables in not more than 5-pound lots, timed at intervals to provide for a continuous supply to meet the demands of the service, is far preferable to cooking the entire amount at one time and holding the cooked product through the serving period. The latter would require one or two large steam-jacketed kettles instead of a battery of small ones and would mean less effort and time for the cook, but at the sacrifice of eye appeal, flavor, crispness, nutritive value of the food served, and the satisfaction of the guests.

Large equipment, such as ranges, ovens, tilting frypans, mixers, and dishwashers, may be obtained in more or less standard sizes, with slight variations in the articles produced by different manufacturers. For example, range sections may vary a few inches in the overall measurements and the inside dimensions of ovens may differ, whereas the capacities of mixers made by most firms are comparable.

Charts are available from most manufacturers that show the capacity or output per hour for each size of machine. For example, the capacity of a dishwasher is measured by the number of dishes that can be washed in an hour. The size of mixer to purchase would be determined by the volume of a product to be prepared each mixing, the time required for mixing or mashing each batch, and the total quantity of the produce needed within a given period of time. Obviously, the size and number of pieces of each item of equipment required will depend on the needs of the particular institution.

The articles most often fabricated or built to individual specifications are those that must conform to a given size or are desired because of special material. Special orders make the equipment more expensive and often delay delivery; however, to most people, the satisfaction of having a piece of equipment that exactly fits usually more than compensates for the disadvantages.

Standards of uniformity in size of both small and large equipment have become fairly well-established through the experience of users and their work with designers, manufacturers, and consultants. Many kitchens of the past have had a multiplicity of sizes of cooking utensils, baking pans, and trays that may or may not have made economical use of range, oven, refrigerator, cabinet, or truck spaces in the particular situation. An example is the large oval serving tray that would never fit on a rack, shelf, or truck. Alert foodservice directors and planning experts have come to recognize some of these problems and to note the advantages that are gained by simplification of the whole setup through improved planning for the efficient and interrelated use of the items selected.

The selection of certain modular items of equipment, or those of uniform size, has proven advantageous in quantity food operations. When a specified size pan, tray, or rack fits easily in the refrigerator, storage cabinet, serving counter, or on racks or carts, great adaptability in and economical utilization of space are made possible. Also, manpower efficiency is increased and labor hours are reduced; less floor area is required with improved use of vertical space; the use of pans and trays of the same size or in their multiple units reduces the total number and kind to buy, their cost, and the storage space needed; the number of shelves in refrigerators, cabinets, and carts can be reduced when trays and pans can be inserted at close intervals on angle runners or glides; the rehandling or transfer of foods or dishes is reduced, since the tray rack fits into any unit, either on a shelf, on glides, or in the counter; sanitation is improved through reduced handling of food or dishes, low spillage, and machine washing of trays and pans.

Common modules are the 12- by 18-inch and 18- by 26-inch trays, which are easily accessible in several materials and convenient to use. The 12- by 18-inch trays fit into standard dishwashing racks of conveyor-type machines. Cabinets, shelves, refrigerators, and carts are readily available to accommodate one or a combination of such trays. Some spaces could be sized so that either one 18- by 26-inch bun pan or two 12- by 18-inch trays could be used. Another common module is space into which 20- by 20-inch dishracks would fit, for storage of cups and glasses in the racks in which they were washed.

This system merits careful consideration in planning equipment for simplified operation with maximum efficiency and economy. Each unit will continue to need a certain amount of its equipment custom built according to specification, but certainly there should be uniformity within each operation.

Materials

Materials for the various pieces of foodservice equipment should be suitable for the purpose and give the best satisfaction possible. The materials used in the equipment influence price, wearing qualities, sanitation, satisfaction, and usefulness. The weight, finish, and workmanship of the materials are important factors in determining their suitability and wearing qualities.

The Joint Committee on Food Equipment Standards has established minimum requirements for materials and construction of certain foodservice equipment items as follows:

Materials shall withstand normal wear, penetration of vermin, corrosive action of refrigerants, foods, cleaning and sanitizing compounds, and other elements in the intended end use environment.

The committee further specifies that surface materials in the food zone

shall not impart toxic substances, odor, color, or taste to food. Exposed surfaces shall be smooth and easily cleanable.

Nonfood zone materials shall be smooth and corrosion resistant or rendered corrosion resistant. Coatings, if used, shall be noncracking and nonchipping.

Solder in food zones shall be formulated to be nontoxic and corrosion resistant under use conditions. Lead based solder shall not be used.

METALS   Metals have become increasingly important in foodservice planning. Today, we depend on them for nearly everything, from structural features such as doors, flooring under steam units, and walk-in refrigerators to tables, sinks, dishwashers, and cooking equipment. A wide variety of old and well-known metals and alloys, such as copper, tin, chromium, iron, steel, and aluminum, were used in the foodservices of the past, but have been outmoded by the chromium and chromium-nickel stainless steels. At one time, copper cooking utensils and dishwashers were commonly found in institutional foodservices. Their care and upkeep were high because they required frequent polishing and replacement of nickel or tin linings to prevent the reaction of foodstuffs with the copper. Such utensils were heavy to handle and were used mostly in hotels and the military where male cooks were employed. Nickel was used considerably as a plating for equipment trim, rails of cafeteria counters, and inexpensive tableware.

Aluminum lends itself to fabrication of numerous kinds and will take a satin, frosted, or chrome-plated finish. It can be painted, etched, or engraved. It is relatively light in weight, has high thermal and electrical conductivity, does not corrode readily, and if cold-rolled, is relatively hard and durable. It is capable of withstanding pressure at high temperature, which makes it particularly well-suited for cooking and baking utensils and steam-jacketed kettles. Aluminum cooking utensils often become discolored by food or water containing alkali, certain acids, and iron. Many items are manufactured from anodized aluminum that has been subjected to electrolytic action to coat and harden the surface and increase its resistance to oxidation, discoloration, marring, and scratching. Anodized aluminum is often used for items such as dry-storage cabinets and service carts and trays. Its strength and light weight are factors in its favor for mobile equipment. Aluminum may be combined with other metals to produce alloys of higher tensile strength than aluminum alone.

Cast iron is used in institution equipment as braces and castings for stands and supports, for pipes, and for large pieces of equipment such as ranges. Its use in small equipment is restricted to skillets, Dutch ovens, and griddles.

Galvanized steel and iron were long used for such equipment as sinks, dishwashers, and tables. In the process of galvanizing, a coating of zinc, deposited on the base metal, protects it to a certain extent from corrosion. The initial cost of equipment made of galvanized material is comparatively low, but the length of life is short, repair and replacement expenses are high, sanitation is low, contamination is likely, and the general appearance is undesirable and unattractive in comparison to equipment made of noncorrosive metal.

The use of *noncorrosive metals,* mainly the alloys of iron, nickel, and chromium, for equipment in food-processing plants such as bakeries, dairies, canneries, and in-home and institution-size kitchens has increased tremendously within recent years until at present all such units are planned with widespread usage of this material. These materials are available in forms suitable for fabrication into any desired types of equipment. If the sheets are too small for the particular item, they may be joined and welded most satisfactorily. The price is not prohibitive, so that this type of material functions in many and varied instances from decorative effects in or on public buildings to heavy-duty equipment, cooking utensils, and tableware. Improved methods of fabrication and the unprecedented emphasis on sanitation have been important factors in the high utilization of noncorrosive metals in items of equipment.

The outstanding characteristics of noncorrosive metals for foodservice equipment include permanence, resistance to ordinary stains and corrosion, lack of chemical reaction with food, attractive appearance, ease of cleaning and fabrication, and nonprohibitive price. Tests show that with proper construction and care noncorrosive metals wear indefinitely, and equipment made from them may be considered permanent investments. The strength and toughness are so high that even a comparatively lightweight metal may be used for heavy-duty items. These metals do not chip or crack. High ductility and weldability also make for permanence of the equipment made from them; thus, the upkeep costs are reduced to a minimum.

Resistance to stains and corrosion is a major feature in foodservice equipment where cleanliness, appearance, and sanitation are of utmost importance. The freedom from chemical reactions of the noncorrosive metals with foodstuffs at any temperature makes their use safe in food preparation. Tests show few or no traces of metals or metallic salts present after different foods have been heated and chilled for varying periods of time in containers made of these metals.

The appearance of noncorrosive metal equipment when well-made and carefully finished is satisfying and conducive to the maintenance of excellent standards of cleanliness and order. The smooth, hard surface is not easily scratched or marred, and simple cleaning methods are all that are required. There are special metal cleaners on the market, but a good cleaner and water and the usual polishing should be enough to keep the equipment in good condition. Common steel wool, scouring pads, scrapers, or wire brushes may mar the surface or leave small particles of iron imbedded in the stainless steel to cause rust stains. Darkened areas are caused usually by heat applied either in fabrication or in use and may be removed by vigorous rubbing with stainless steel wool, a stainless steel pad and powder, or a commercial heat-tint remover. To avoid heat tinting of cooking utensils, they should be subjected to no more heat than required to do the job effectively, never heated empty or with heat concentrated on a small area.

The noncorrosive alloys manufactured most often into institutional equipment are nickel-copper and the stainless steels. Monel metal is a natural alloy that contains approximately two-thirds nickel and one-third copper, with a small amount of iron. The supply is fairly limited so it is seldom selected for fabrication into foodservice equipment.

By far the greatest amount of foodservice equipment is made of some type of stainless steel. Each company producing stainless steel under its own trade name may use a slightly different formula, but the important elements are practically the same. A relatively low carbon content in the stainless steels gives high resistance to attack by corrosive agents. A chromium-nickel stainless steel alloy commonly called "18-8" (number 302) is a favorite material for foodservice equipment. As its name indicates, it contains approximately 18% chromium and 8% nickel with no copper present. Observations of equipment made of the noncorrosive alloys in satisfactory use and their appearance and sanitary qualities prove the value of these materials for heavy-duty equipment.

Standard Gauge: The gauge of thickness of metals is an important consideration in selecting materials for equipment. The adoption of the micrometer caliber to indicate the thickness of sheet metal in decimal parts of an inch and the abolition of gauge numbers are strongly recommended. However, the United States standard gauge is used by most manufacturers of iron and steel sheets. This system is a weight, not a thickness, gauge. For instance, number 20 United States gauge weighs 1.5 pounds per square foot, subject to the standard allowable variation. Weight always is the determining factor. That this gauge is 0.037-inch thick is secondary in the system. Numbers 10 to 14 gauge galvanized steel or 12 to 16 noncorrosive metals are most generally used for foodservice equipment. Metal lighter than 16 gauge is commonly used for sides or parts where the wear is light (see Fig. 9.6).

Finish of Metals: The surface or finish of metals may be dull or bright; the higher the polish, the more susceptible the surface is to scratches. The degree of metal finish is indicated by a gradation in number, the larger numbers indicating finer finish and a higher degree of polish. Standard finishes for the steels in sheet form are listed in this table.

Finish	*Description*
No. 1	Hot-rolled, annealed, and pickled
No. 2B	Full finish—bright cold-rolled
No. 2D	Full finish—dull cold-rolled
No. 4	Standard polish, one or both sides
No. 6	Standard polish, tampico brushed one or both sides
No. 7	High-luster polish on one or both sides

Numbers 4, 6, and 7 are produced by grinding and polishing the sheets of metal with different grades of abrasives. These original surface finishes are

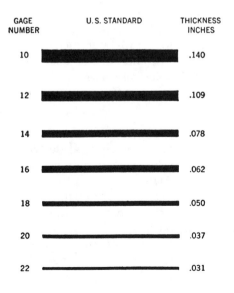

GAGE NUMBER	U.S. STANDARD	THICKNESS INCHES
10		.140
12		.109
14		.078
16		.062
18		.050
20		.037
22		.031

Figure 9.6.   A diagram showing actual thickness of commonly used gauges of metals.

capable of being retained in the usual fabrication of equipment, which requires only local forming. Materials with a number 4 grind surface are more often selected for such items as table tops, sinks, and counters than are those with shiny or mirror-like finishes.

GLASS   Glass and ceramic-lined equipment, such as drip coffee pots, are most satisfactory for certain purposes. They protect against metallic contamination, corrosion, and absorption. Glass-lined equipment is highly acid resistant and will withstand heat shock. This last quality is due to the fact that the coefficient of expansion of the glass enamel is similar to that of the steel shell. Most ceramics will break readily when exposed to extreme heat or mechanical shock.

OTHER MATERIALS   Items such as counter fronts and ends and food tray delivery carts made of mirror-finish *fiberglass* with stainless steel structural trim are available in many beautiful colors. The interior and exterior walls of the food delivery carts are molded in one piece, then insulated with polyurethane foam. The surfaces are strong, dent and scratch resistant, and light in weight. *Porcelain* (glass on steel) or *vinyl* covered galvanized steel may be used satisfactorily on outside walls of refrigerators and on counter fronts at less cost than stainless steel. The above materials contribute to a colorful and pleasing decor, reduce reflected glare of light, and are easily maintained. Detached well-laminated and sealed *hardwood* cutting boards are permissible in some cities and states, although for purposes of sanitation, an increasing number of operators are choosing to use cutting boards made of reversible nontoxic, nonabsorbent polyethylene or hard rubber.

Carts, racks, stands, and dollies made of *polycarbonate* are light in weight, but capable of carrying heavy loads; they resist stains, dents, and scratches, will not rust or crack, and are easily disassembled for cleaning in a conveyor-type dishwashing machine. Side panels may be of a solid color or transparent, and most models are designed to accommodate 18- by 26-inch food boxes with fitted lids, trays, and bunpans (see Fig. 9.7a and b). All items can be fitted with nonmarking neoprene brake wheels and ball bearings.

Construction

The construction of and workmanship on equipment determines whether or not it is durable, attractive, and sanitary. High-quality material and a perfect design for the purpose do not ensure good construction, although they contribute to it. Accurate dimensions, careful and well-finished joinings, solidarity, pleasing appearance, and ease of cleaning are important factors. Sinks, drainboards, and dishtables sloped to drain; tables and chairs properly braced; hinges and fasteners of heavy-duty materials and drawers constructed to function properly; adequate insulation where needed; and safety features are a

(a)   (b)

Figure 9.7.   A selection of food storage containers that stack or nest easily and are available with snap-tight covers facilitate sanitary and efficient storage and transportation of food. Boxes made from (*a*) clear polycarbonate and (*b*) white high-density polyethylene are shown. (Courtesy, Cambro Manufacturing Company.)

few of the points to consider under construction. It is a necessity that all parts are easily cleanable.

Welding has replaced riveting, bolting, and soldering of both surface and understructure joinings in metal foodservice equipment. Great emphasis is placed on the importance of grinding, polishing, and finishing of the surfaces and welded joints for smoothness and to ensure against possible progressive corrosion. Mitered corners (shown in Fig. 9.8) properly welded and finished smooth, in items such as dishtables and sinks are superior to deep square corners or those filled with solder. The construction recommended for items of equipment used for unpackaged food is for rounded internal angles with a minimum continuous and smooth radius of ⅛ inch and internal rounded corners with a minimum continuous and a smooth radius of ¼ inch for vertical and horizontal intersections and ⅛-inch radius for the alternate intersection.

The bull-nosed corner construction is used most often in finishing off the corners of horizontal surfaces such as worktables. The corner section of the top material is rounded off and made smooth both horizontally and vertically as an

Figure 9.8.   A mitered corner, welded and finished smooth. (Courtesy, National Sanitation Foundation International.)

integral part of the horizontal surface. If the edge is flanged down and turned back, a minimum of ¾ inch should be allowed between the top and the flange, and the same distance should be allowed between the sheared edge and the frame angle or cabinet body to provide easy access for cleaning. (See Fig. 9.9.)

To simplify construction and eliminate some of the hazards to good sanitation, fittings and parts have been combined into single forgings and castings wherever possible, and tubular supports sealed off smooth or fitted with adjustable screw-in solid pear-shaped feet have replaced open angular bracings with flange bases. In many instances, mobile, self-supporting, or wall-hung structures have replaced external framing. Several items welded or fitted together into a continuous unit may need to be brought into the facility and positioned before construction of the building is complete and while there is ample space for transporting the unit into the area.

The Joint Committee on Food Equipment Standards outlines in detail permissible methods for construction of such general parts as angles, seams, finishes of joinings, openings, rims, framing and reinforcement, and body construction. Specifically, they give construction features for special items such as hoods, water-cooling units, counter guards, doors, hardware, sinks, refrigerators, power-driven machines and their installation. Many health departments use the recommended standards as a basis for approving equipment and its installation. An example of such a standard follows. Fig. 9.10 gives the diagram.

Food Shields   Display stands for unpackaged foods are to be effectively shielded so as to intercept the direct line between the average customer's mouth and the food being displayed and shall be designed to minimize contamination by the customer.

Shields shall be mounted so as to intercept a direct line between the customer's mouth and the food display area at the customer-use position. The vertical distance from the average customer's mouth to the floor shall be considered to be 4 feet 6 inches (1.4 meters) to 5 feet (1.5 meters) for public eating establishments. Special consideration must be given to use location conditions such as tray rails and average customer's mouth height in educational institutions and other special installations. Such shields are to be fabricated of easy-to-clean, sanitary materials conforming to materials specifications.

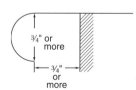

Figure 9.9.   A bull-nosed corner, rounded off and finished smooth. (Courtesy, National Sanitation Foundation International.)

(a) TYPICAL BUFFET TABLE

Customer's average mouth heights on a line perpendicular to the horizontal edge of the buffet table

Exposed edges of glass shelves or shields shall have a safety edge of parent material, or be trimmed with stainless steel channels.

5'0" (1.5 m)

4'6" (1.4 m)

Food shields are to intercept the direct line between the customer's mouth and the food being displayed and to minimize contamination by the customer

food display area

4'6" (1.4 m)

5'0" (1.5 m)

(b) TYPICAL CAFETERIA COUNTER

Customer's average mouth heights on a line perpendicular to the horizontal edge of the tray slide

Exposed edges of glass shelves or shields shall have a safety edge of parent material, or be trimmed with stainless steel channels

5'0" (1.5 m)

4'6" (1.4 m)

Food shields are to intercept the direct line between the customer's mouth and the food being displayed and to minimize contamination by the customer

food display

Figure 9.10. Standards for food shields. (Courtesy, National Sanitation Foundation International.)

SAFETY FEATURES   Safety features for the protection of workers in the use and care of equipment and for the production of safe food are important factors in the design, choice of materials, and construction of kitchen equipment. There is also a close relationship between these and the standards and controls for sanitation in a foodservice operation. Smooth, rounded corners on work surfaces, table drawers with stops and recessed pulls, automatic steam shut-off when cooker doors are opened, temperature controls, guards on slicers and chopping machines, brakes on mixers, recessed manifold control knobs on ranges and ovens, smooth, polished, welded seams, rounded corners, and knee-lever drain controls on sinks are a few examples of built-in safety in heavy-duty kitchen equipment.

Installation, Operation, and Performance

Proper installation is a necessity for the successful operation of all equipment. The best design and construction would be worthless if electrical, gas, or water connections were inadequate or poorly done. The dealer from whom the equipment was purchased may not be responsible for its installation by contract but will usually deliver, uncrate, assemble, and position the item ready for steam fitting or electrical and plumbing connections. In many cases, the dealer will supervise the installation and test it out to be certain that the equipment will function properly and instruct personnel in its operation and maintenance.

Architects, contractors, and engineers are responsible for providing proper and adequate plumbing, electrical wiring, and venting facilities for the satisfactory installation of kitchen equipment according to the standards of the local building, plumbing, electrical, and sanitation codes. Water, steam, gas, and waste pipe lines and electrical conduits must be planned for each piece of equipment so that proper joinings can be made at the time of installation to avoid the necessity of extra pipe or wiring that might interfere with cleaning or placement of other equipment items.

The sanitation and safety aspects of equipment installation are important to the convenience and safety of its use and care. Sinks that drain well, wall-hung or mobile equipment that permits easy cleaning under and around it, equipment sealed to the wall, and adequate aisle clearance so that food and supplies can be transported easily and safely on carts are but a few of the considerations to make in planning installations. Refer to Fig. 9.1 for an example of combining related pieces of equipment into a single continuous unit.

The operation of each piece of equipment must be checked many times by both the contractors and service engineers before it is ready for actual use. Full instruction for the proper operation and satisfactory performance of each piece of equipment should be given to all persons who work with it. They must know the danger signals, such as the sound of a defective motor, so that preventive measures can be taken early.

Maintenance and Replacement

The cost of care and upkeep on a piece of equipment may determine whether or not its purchase and use are justified. The annual repair and replacement of equipment should be made with consideration of the unit as a whole, and labor and operating costs should be checked constantly. If these are too high, they limit other expenditures that might promote greater efficiency in the organization. The dispersion of outlay between care and repair is important in more ways than one. Money, attention, and effort spent on care assume the continuance of the necessary equipment in use; money and the effort spent on repair are often attended by a disrupted work schedule, unpleasant stresses and strains on personnel, and sometimes definite fire hazards.

Many questions arise in regard to care and upkeep costs when equipment is selected. Are parts readily available, easily replaced, and relatively inexpensive? Does the replacement require the services of a specialist, or can a regular employee be trained to do the work? Should some piece of equipment fail to operate when needed, has provision been made in planning so that operations may be carried on? Are special cleaning materials needed in caring for the equipment?

The care and repair of electrical equipment represents a major item in the maintenance cost of many foodservices. The adequate care of electric motors requires expert attention by technically trained and responsible engineers. Arrangements for such care are commonly made with the maintenance department on a contract basis, covering weekly inspection and other checkups necessary for good maintenance. Competent maintenance personnel will have a record card for every motor in the plant. All repair work, with its cost, and every inspection can be entered on the record. If this system is used, excessive amounts of attention or expense will show up, and the causes can be determined and corrected. Inspection records will also serve as a guide to indicate when motors should be replaced because of the high cost of keeping them in operating condition.

To evaluate a piece of equipment in use, an analysis of the expenditures for care and upkeep is made, and the condition of the equipment is checked to determine if the deterioration has been more rapid than it should have been under normal usage, exposure, cleaning operations, and contacts with food and heat. A factual basis for appraising upkeep costs and depreciation of kitchen equipment can be obtained by keeping careful records on each major piece. Fig. 9.11 is a suggested method for keeping such records.

Successful maintenance of equipment requires definite plans to prolong its life and maintain its usefulness. Such plans place emphasis on a few simple procedures: keep the equipment clean; follow the manufacturer's printed directions for care and operation, including lubrication; keep the instruction card for each piece of equipment posted near it; stress careful handling as essential to continued use; and make needed repairs promptly. Some pertinent suggestions for the care of machines and instructions for their use are: the assignment of the care of each machine to a responsible person; daily inspection for cleanliness and constant supervision by the manager when in use; immediate adjustment of even minor repairs; thorough knowledge of operating

Name of Institution:_____

A. LARGE EQUIPMENT RECORD

Equipment or
Appliance Item: Purchase Date:

Motor Serial Number	Motor Make Model	Equipment Number	Location
Original Cost	Estimated Period of use: Months □ Years □	Make of Equipment item:	Description: Type____ Size____ Capacity____ Design____
Appraisal — Date | Value	Motor Specification: W V Amp. H.P. __ __ __ __	Estimated Depreciation per Month____Year____	Date fully Depreciated _____

Repairs and Replacements

Date	Nature	By Whom	Cost	Remarks

Name of Institution _____

B. SMALL EQUIPMENT RECORD

Name of Item: Purchase Date: Purchased From: Location:

Style Size	Amount of Original Purchase	Quality or Grade	Uses:
— —	_____	_____	

Appraisal — Date | Value	Repairs or Replacement			
	Date	Nature	By Whom	Cost	Amount on hand

Figure 9.11. Suggested form for recording information on each piece of (*a*) large equipment, and (*b*) small equipment.

directions; regular oiling and inspections; and repairs by a competent person. Printed instructions should be easily available; directions for operation with a simple diagram should be posted by the machine; and any special warnings should be printed in large or colored letters. When explaining its operation, the function and relationship of each part should be described in detail so that it is understood by the operator. There should also be a demonstration of proper use of the machine and an explanation of its value and the cost of repairs. (See Figure 7.6, Chapter 7 for the procedure for cleaning a food slicer.) Similar directions should be formulated for each piece of equipment and made into a manual for use by employees responsible for the care and cleanliness of the various items.

The operating cost is an important feature often overlooked in purchasing equipment. In some localities, electricity may be available for cooking purposes at a lower operating cost than gas, or vice versa. When all factors are considered, an electric range may be more economical in this particular instance, even though the initial cost may be more. Due consideration and investigation of the relative efficiency of various models and types are also necessary in selecting any piece of equipment.

Method of Purchase

The method of purchase of equipment varies somewhat with the institution. However, regardless of whether the actual placing of the order is done by the director of the foodservice, the purchasing agent, or the superintendent of the hospital, the preliminary procedures are much the same. All available data as to the needs and requirements of the institution are collected by the director, who is responsible for the smooth operation of the service and the satisfaction of its guests. Usually representatives of different firms are willing to demonstrate equipment and to give the prospective buyer information concerning the particular piece of equipment needed. Visits may be made to various institutions to see similar models in operation. After such investigations are made and a definite idea of what is wanted is established, specifications are written and submitted to reliable firms. Written bids are then received and tabulated and a comparison is made, after which the order is placed.

The reliability of the firm from which the equipment is purchased means much to any institution. A reputable company with a record of successful operation usually strives to sell dependable merchandise of good quality. The company can be counted on to stand in back of the guarantee and to do all possible to keep the goodwill and confidence of the customer. In their planning and engineering departments, equipment dealers employ experts whose services are always available to the prospective customer. Years of experience and constant contact with both the manufacturing and operating units in the field enable them to be of valuable assistance. Most companies keep records of the sale, service calls, and repairs of the various pieces of equipment. In return, they deserve fair treatment and consideration from the director of the foodservice or the purchasing agent for the institution.

To be of value, a specification for equipment must be specific and definite. It covers every detail in relation to material, construction, size, color, finish, and cost, eliminating any question in the mind of either the buyer or the manufacturer as to what the finished product will be. When delivered, if the equipment does not measure up to the specified order, it need not be accepted. If the buyer is disappointed but has permitted loopholes in the specification, and the product meets the requirements of the specification, it must be accepted. However, most firms are so desirous of selling satisfaction that they check orders carefully with the buyer to see that everything is included before the equipment is made or delivered.

The vague and the definite specifications that follow for a particular piece of equipment illustrate the difference between the two types. Specifications may be indefinite, and yet to the casual observer all points may seem to be included. After reading the second example, one can readily see the weak spots in the first.

VAGUE SPECIFICATIONS

- Item number: xx
- Name of item: Cook's table with sink
- Dimensions: 8 ft long, 2 ft 6 in. wide, 3 ft high
- Material and construction: Top of this table to be made of heavy-gauge stainless steel with semirolled edge and to be furnished with one sink, 18 in. long, 24 in. wide, 12 in. deep, fitted with drain. Sink to be located 3 in. from left end of table. The under side of this table to be reinforced with channel braces. Table to be supported by 4 stainless steel tubular standards with adjustable feet. Stainless slatted shelf to rest on cross rails 10 in. above floor. Table to be equipped with one drawer, 24 in. long, 22 in. wide, and 5 in. deep. Drawer to be made of heavy stainless steel, reinforced on front facing. All joints of this drawer to be welded, and drawer equipped with ball-bearing drawer slides. This drawer to be fitted with a white metal handle.
- Price: $ . . . .

DEFINITE SPECIFICATIONS

- Item number: xx
- Name of item: Cook's table with sink
- Dimensions: 8 ft long, 2 ft 6 in. wide., 3 ft high
- Material and construction: Top of this table to be made of No. 14 gauge. No. 4 grind, No. 302 stainless steel with all edges turned down 1½ in., semi-

rolled edge. All corners to be fully rounded bull-nose construction and integral with top. Top of this table to be fitted with one sink, 18 in. long, 24 in. wide, and 12 in. deep, with all corners and intersections fully rounded to a 1-in. radius. All joints to be welded, ground smooth, and polished. Bottom sloped to drain in center. Sink to be located 3 in. from left end of table, 3 in. from each side. Sink to be equipped with 2-in. white metal drain with plug and chain complete.

The under side of this table top to be properly reinforced and braced with 4-in. No. 14-gauge stainless steel channel braces welded on. Four tubular leg standards to be welded to these channel cross braces. Standards to be made of seamless stainless steel tubing $1\frac{5}{8}$ in. outside diameter, cross rails and braces of the same material, fitted and welded together. Resting on these cross rails and braces will be a slatted bar shelf elevated 10 in. above floor. Slats to be made of No. 16 stainless steel, No. 4-grind, welded to 2-in. No. 16 stainless-steel supports. Slats 2 in. wide and bent down at ends and formed to fit over cross rails. Slatted shelf to be built in two removable parts of equal length. Leg standards to be fitted with adjustable inside threaded, stainless-steel, tubular, closed, smooth-finish feet.

Table to be equipped with one drawer, 24 in. long, 22 in. wide, and 5 in. deep. Drawer to be made of No. 16-gauge, No. 4-grind stainless steel throughout, reinforced on front facing with No. 14-gauge, No. 4-grind stainless steel. All joints of this drawer to be welded, ground, and polished. Each drawer to be equipped with nontilting, easy-glide roller-bearing drawer slides, and all metal tracks welded to under side of table top. This drawer to be fitted with a polished white metal pull handle.

- Price: F.O.B. . . . . . . $ . . . .
- Delivery date: not later than . . . .

When purchasing electrically operated equipment, it is essential that exact electrical specifications be given to the manufacturer at the time of placing the order. A motor is wound to operate on a certain voltage current, and when set up to operate on another, it may run more slowly or more rapidly than was intended, causing its output to be greater or less than its rated horsepower. There is danger of overheating and a breakdown of insulation, which will result in short circuits and the necessity for motor repairs or replacements. A three-phase motor is desirable because the absence of brushes lessens the maintenance problems. Motors of less than 1 horsepower may be used equally well on 110- or 220-volt currents but motors of larger horsepower should be operated on a 220-volt current. Manufacturers now use ball-bearing motors, fully enclosed and ventilated, which eliminate the necessity of frequent oiling. Most motors are built especially for the machines they operate. They must be adequate in power to easily carry the capacity loads of the machines.

Selection of Some Basic Items

An analysis of the basic considerations discussed thus far helps to determine whether the selection of certain items of kitchen equipment is justified and gives attention to the mechanics of buying. Standards for various types of equipment have been mentioned. The problem of selection is so important and errors are so costly that major characteristics to consider in the selection of certain types of items are given in Appendix C. No attempt is made to evaluate or identify equipment by trade name. The buyer may need to make a selection between the products of several competitive manufacturers or jobbers, each of whom may have quality products but with a wide variance in some details. All equipment should be a sound investment for the operator, be easily cleaned, safe to operate, and accomplish the work for which it was designed. Wise selection can be made only after an exhaustive study of all available data and observation of similarly installed equipment have been accomplished.

Manufacturers' specification sheets, brochures, and catalogs, trade shows, current professional and trade journals and magazines, and the representatives of the manufacturing companies are the best sources of up-to-date information on specific items. Special features may be changed fairly often so that detailed information on certain models is soon outdated in a publication like this one.

Some points for consideration when selecting foodservice equipment, other than price, cost of operation, and maintenance, are included in Appendix C to help acquaint the reader with possible features and variations of certain items. The availability of utilities and other factors might predetermine some decisions: for example, the choice between an electric or gas-heated range presents no problem if the advantages of one source of heat over the other are evident in the particular situation. Instead, the problem becomes one of a choice between various models manufactured by several different firms. Space permits only a limited amount of basic information on certain fundamental items. It is expected that supplementary material will be kept up-to-date and made available in library or office files for students and foodservice operators.

Cooking Equipment

This equipment must conform to requirements for material, construction, safety, and sanitation established by groups such as the American Standards Association, American Gas Association, National Board of Fire Underwriters, Underwriters Laboratories, Inc., American Society of Mechanical Engineers, and NSF International. One should be sure that parts are replaceable and service is available for all items selected, as well as give consideration to original and operating costs, the effectiveness in accomplishing the task to be done, and the time and skill required for ordinary maintenance. The life expectancy requirement depends somewhat on the situation, but the selection of durable, high-quality equipment is usually economical.

ELECTRIC AND GAS FIRED EQUIPMENT *Electrically heated* cooking equipment designed for alternating or direct current of specified voltage; rating required expressed in watts or kilowatts (1,000 watts = 1 kilowatt) per hour; wiring concealed and protected from moisture; switches plainly identified; thermostatic heat controls; flues not required for electric cooking equipment but the usual hood or built-in ventilating system necessary to remove cooking vapors and odors.

Gas fired cooking equipment designed for natural, manufactured, mixed, or liquefied petroleum fuel; adapted to given pressures; rating requirement expressed in British thermal units (Btus) per hour; individual shut-off valve for each piece of gas equipment; manifolds and cocks accessible but concealed; removable burners; automatic lighting with pilot light for each burner; thermostatic heat controls; gas equipment vented through hood or built-in ventilator instead of kitchen flue to exhaust combustible gases.

The most commonly used pieces of gas- and electric-heated cooking equipment are ranges, griddles, broilers, fryers, tilting frypans, and ovens. Steam-heated equipment includes steam-jacketed kettles and cabinet cookers. Specifics about each of these types of cooking equipment are included in Appendix C.

Noncooking Equipment

POWER OPERATED Modern foodservices depend on motor-driven machines for rapid and efficient performance of many tasks. Safety precautions are necessary. Capacity charts for all types of machines are available from manufacturers and distributors. Motors, built-in according to capacity of machine, must carry peak load easily; specify voltage, cycle, and phase; three-phase is usually used for three-quarters horsepower or larger; sealed-in motors and removable parts for ease of cleaning.

Power-operated noncooking equipment includes mixers, choppers, cutters, slicers, vertical cutter mixers, refrigerators, freezers, dish and utensil cleaning equipment, waste disposals, and transport equipment. Among the more common pieces of nonmechanical kitchen equipment are tables, sinks, storage cabinets, racks, carts, scales, cooking utensils, and cutlery. More detailed information about each of these types of noncooking equipment is included in Appendix C.

The most commonly used types of serving equipment are counters, utensils, dispensers, coffee makers, and mobile serving carts. These are also discussed in Appendix C.

Energy Conservation

According to the National Restaurant Association (NRA), energy management programs and the wise selection of equipment can result in savings of up to 20% on utility costs for the average foodservice establishment.

An energy management program requires the constant participation of every employee in the operation. Inservice training and incentive programs should be set up to ensure the cooperation of all involved. Some general guidelines for conserving energy in foodservice operations that should be included in any program are given in Chapter 5.

Using too large equipment at less than full capacity is one of the most common energy wasters. This includes but is not limited to dishwashers, ovens, griddles, fryers, ranges, and steam-jacketed kettles, when operated with partial loads and left on between loads.

Routine maintenance and cleaning of equipment are essential components of an energy reduction program. Weak or broken door springs on ovens and refrigerators may reduce efficiency by 35%. Carbonized grease and cooking residue on griddle plates can reduce cooking efficiency by 40%.

Utility companies often offer free equipment service adjustments, energy audits, and assistance in establishing effective energy management programs. Following is an example of information that may be obtained from a utility company.

HOW MUCH ENERGY DOES IT SAVE . . . To use OPEN BURNER RANGES instead of Hot Tops?
You are way ahead in conserving fuel and reducing operating costs when you use OPEN BURNER RANGES. Tests show dramatic savings in fuel consumption when OPEN BURNER RANGES are compared to Hot Top Ranges.

- Similar quantities of water boil in up to *one-third less time* on the OPEN BURNER RANGE.

- Boiling similar quantities of water requires up to *55% less fuel* on the OPEN BURNER RANGE.

- Hot Tops must be preheated. Preheat takes 30 to 60 minutes. The gas flame on the OPEN BURNER RANGE comes on instantly when you need it. *No preheat necessary!*

Tests show additional energy can be conserved no matter what kind of range top you have.

- Covering pans reduced energy consumption
  —on OPEN BURNER RANGES, covering pans reduced consumption up to 20%.
  —on Hot Tops, covering pans reduced energy consumption up to 35%.
- Heating larger quantities of food can be done more efficiently than heating smaller quantities of food.
  —on OPEN BURNER RANGES, BTU consumption per pound was reduced up to 19% when the quantity of water heated was doubled.
  —on Hot Top Ranges, BTU consumption per pound was reduced up to 20% when the quantity of water heated was doubled.

Other energy conservation suggestions for use of equipment in food service establishments follow:

- Ventilation systems, air conditioning, heating:
  Make-up air for hoods; use thermostatically controlled unheated and unrefrigerated air.
  Use heat recovery systems in hood; heat exchangers for hot water and/or comfort heating.
  Use evaporative coolers (swamp coolers) to comfort-condition kitchen air (do not use refrigerated air).
  Size air-conditioning units and comfort heaters accurately for climate area; limit size of heaters for kitchen area to take advantage of heat from cooking equipment.
  Use economizer cycle systems (use of outside air when cool enough to eliminate need for refrigerated air).
  Place air-conditioning and furnace filters in an easily accessible location to ensure frequent scheduled cleaning or replacement.
  Insulate heating and air-conditioning ducts adequately and completely, using 2 inches of insulation.
  Zone and wire air-conditioning and furnace units to permit zone control of unoccupied areas.
  Install covered and locked thermostats, 68° for heating, 78° for cooling.
  Use time clocks to decrease utility consumption by mechanical equipment in off-peak periods.
  Keep filters and extractors clean.
- Water heating:
  Locate water heater in close proximity to major use.
  Insulate all hot water lines.
  Size water heating equipment accurately; do not undersize or oversize; use quality equipment.

Install spring-loaded faucet valves or spring-loaded foot controls to limit hot water waste.

Use quality valves to minimize dripping faucets and repair all leaks promptly.

Consider solar-assisted and/or waste heat exchanger water heating systems to preheat water.

Use single system, high-temperature water heating equipment and automatic mixing valves.

Use water softening equipment to soften water in areas where water is hard.

Reduce water temperature where possible.

- Dishwashing:
  Size dishwasher to handle average maximum requirements.
  Install easily accessible switch to permit shut down of equipment in slack periods. Consider chemical dishwasher for small establishments.

- Cooking equipment:
  Be selective in specification of equipment offering greatest efficiency and flexibility of use.
  Careful planning can save on operating and initial equipment costs. Do not overestimate equipment requirements. Specify thermostatically controlled equipment whenever possible.
  Preheat just before use and turn off when not in use.
  Keep equipment clean for most efficient operation.
  Use the correct size equipment at all times.

- Ranges: Specify open top burners—they require no preheat and offer maximum fuel efficiency as compared to center fired and front fired hot tops, or even heat tops. Open burners reduce the air cooling load as there is minimal heat radiation when cooking operation is completed.

- Convection ovens: Versatile and perform most baking/roasting operations in shortest period of time.

- Steamers: Self-contained (boiler); high production at minimal operating cost.

- Grooved griddle: Replaces the underfired broiler; minimizes air pollution problems; operates much more efficiently than underfired broilers and places less of a load on air cooling systems; generally has greater cooking capacity.

- Broilers: Underfired—minimize specification—reasons stated in grooved griddles. Overfired—preferred over underfired. More efficient, faster, no pollution problems. Compartment over broiler provides use for waste heat as plate warmer, finishing foods, browning, cheese melting (may be used for these purposes in lieu of salamander).
  Salamanders/cheese melters: Specify those employing infrared ray radiation; they reach full operating temperature within seconds, are efficient, can be turned off when not in use.

- Braising pans/tilting skillets: A versatile volume production piece of equipment that can serve many cooking operations—fry, boil, braise, roast, steam, food warmer. Consider caster equipped pans and installation of additional gas outlets near serving lines, banquet facilities, and such to obtain maximum utilization of this equipment and reduce gas consumption.
- Fryers: Floor fryers provide maximum production capabilities, have self-contained power oil filter units for ease and speed of filtering, which prolongs oil life. Consider inclusion of multiproduct programmed computers; they are available built into the fryer and will provide consistently high-quality fried products with novice operators; lowers labor, food, and oil costs. Specify more than one size of fryers; full production capacity and standby or nonpeak period smaller capacity fryers; save on initial equipment cost; fuel costs and oil costs.

Dining Room Furnishings

A dining area that is attractive and appealing does much to make patrons feel comfortable and adds to the enjoyment of the food they are served. The foodservice director may be responsible for the selection of some of the furnishings, especially for the dinnerware, tableware, and glassware. The services of an interior designer or decorator may be employed, however, to help create the desired atmosphere through selection of the appropriate style and type of tables and chairs, window treatment, and a color scheme that will coordinate all furnishings into a harmonious effect.

Basic information needed for the wise selection of dinnerware (dishes), tableware (knives, forks, spoons), glassware, and table covers is presented in Appendix C. Specialized assistance likely will be sought for the purchase of furniture, drapes, curtains, and other furnishings. All furnishings should be pleasing, durable, serviceable, and easy to maintain.

Dinnerware

There are many choices of materials used in making dishes for today's foodservice market, including china, glass, and melamine or other plastic ware or combinations of other materials kept secret by their manufacturers. Dinnerware suitable for foodservices varies with the type of service given. A club or luxury restaurant may wish to use fine china such as that found in the homes of its patrons. In contrast, a school foodservice needs more durable ware to withstand the hazards attendant on its use. Fast-food establishments usually find disposable dinnerware best fills their needs.

Tableware

The most satisfactory type of eating utensils for institutions is that which has been designed and made especially for heavy duty. Such ware falls into two classes: *flatware* of the usual array of knives, forks, and spoons; and items such as teapots, sugar bowls, pitchers, and platters, known as *hollow ware* if made of silver. All must be durable and serviceable and, at the same time, attractive in line and design. Silver and stainless steel tableware are the two types used, and the decision to select one or the other will depend largely on the type of foodservice, the tastes of the clientele served, and the amount of money available for this expenditure and upkeep.

Glassware

Glassware is a major item of purchase for dining room furnishings for food services, since it is easily broken and replacement is frequent. It is usually more economical to purchase good quality glassware than inexpensive types.

Table Covers

One other furnishing to consider is the type of covering, if any, to be used on the dining tables, or trays if that type of service is used. Many tabletop surfaces are attractive, durable, and suitable for use without a cover. Simplicity and informality in dining have made this custom popular, and it does reduce laundry costs.

For many people, much of the charm of a foodservice is conditioned, if not determined, by the use of a clean tablecloth of good quality, freshly and carefully placed. Paper napkins and place mats and plastics have replaced cloth in many foodservices for convenience and economy. Whatever the choice, the cover should be of a type and color appropriate for the facility, contribute to the total atmosphere of the room, and be harmonious with the dishes to be used.

Summary

Prospective foodservice managers, as well as those already employed in the field, should have a "working" knowledge of equipment and furnishings— construction, materials suitable for various uses, something of the sizes or capacities available, and how to relate that information to meeting the needs of the individual foodservice. Wise selection and proper care of the many items that must be provided for efficient operation of the foodservice should result in economies for the organization and a satisfied working crew who have been supplied with the correct tools to accomplish their tasks.

Summary Questions

1. If labor cost is high in a particular area, what type of equipment should be given strong consideration?

2. In an assembly/serve foodservice system, what pieces of equipment are most warranted?

3. What are the most common materials used in the manufacture of foodservice equipment and for what are they usually used?

4. What are the disadvantages of a vague specification for a piece of foodservice equipment?

5. Describe some ways in which energy may be conserved in a foodservice operation.

6. List and briefly explain the various types of ovens now in use in foodservice operations.

7. What are the advantages and disadvantages of the various range tops available to a foodservice buyer?

Bibliography

Avery, A. C.: A Modern Guide to Foodservice Equipment. New York: Van Nostrand Reinhold, 1985.

Hirschfeld, J.: Baking ovens. FoodService Director 4(6):124, 1991.

Hirschfeld, J.: Rethinking ovens. FoodService Director 5(2)124, 1992.

Mitchell, T.: How-to's of energy efficiency. Western Foodservice 8:13, 1983.

National Sanitation Foundation International (NSFI): Standard 2 Food Service Equipment. Ann Arbor: NSF International, 1988.

Scriven, C. and Stevens, J.: Food Equipment Facts. New York: Van Nostrand Reinhold, 1989.

Spertzel, J. K.: Combi ovens: A revolution in cooking. School Food Service Journal 45(8):94, 1991.

Spertzel, J. K.: Mix it up! School Food Service Journal 46(3):77, 1992.

Spertzel, J. K.: More than just a pizza oven. School Food Service Journal 45(11):54, 1991.

Spertzel, J. K.: Steamed up about kettles! School Food Service Journal 45(10):58, 1991.

Ullmann, L.: Cooking on the double. Foodservice Equipment and Supplies Specialist 44(11):45, 1992.

For More Information

Birchfield, J. C.: Design and Layout of Foodservice Facilities. New York: Van Nostrand Reinhold, 1988.

Hirschfeld, J.: Rethermalization. FoodService Director 4(7):94, 1991.

Hopkins, R. E.: HACCP by the numbers. Food Mgmt. 26(9):74, 1991.

Humes, S. J.: 6 tips about walk-ins. FoodService Director 2(2):52, 1989.

Kazarian, E. A.: Foodservice Facilities Planning, 3rd ed. New York: Van Nostrand Reinhold, 1989.

Kotschevar, L. H. and Terrell, M. E.: Foodservice Planning: Layout and Equipment. New York: John Wiley & Sons, 1985.

Restaurants & Institutions: Equipment. Restaurants & Institutions 101(25):112, 1991.

Romano, S. N.: Future trends in institutional and commercial foodservice. The Consultant 24(3):40, 1991.

Spertzel, J. K.: Getting carried away with transport equipment. School Food Service Journal 45(9):70, 1991.

Spertzel, J. K.: Merchandising equipment sells school lunch. School Food Service Journal 46(1):54, 1992.

Spertzel, J. K.: Scaling up your kitchen. School Food Service Journal 45(3):30, 1991.

Townsend, R.: Equipment. Restaurants & Institutions 99(4):130, 1989.

Ward, B.: Cold facts on quick chillers. Foodservice Equipment and Supplies Specialist 44(9):65, 1991.

Wildow Jr., C. W.: Foodservice waste: Pulping systems help ease the crisis. The Consultant 24(4):65, 1991.

Organization and Administration of Foodservices

Designing and Managing the Organization

Society is composed of a variety of interdependent, overlapping organizations. In order to function effectively, organizations must be properly designed. This chapter examines the basic principles of organizational structure.

Organizations need competent managers to be able to meet their objectives both efficiently and effectively. The growing complexity of organizations today means a greater need to examine them as a whole. Using the systems approach, a manager can diagnose situations and choose the proper fit between subsystems of the organization. The contingency approach leads management to apply different basic guidelines depending on the particular situation. Low productivity in foodservice operations suggests that greater attention be paid to the quality of work life. The quality of work life approach promotes greater productivity through greater attention to the needs of both individual workers and groups. Most recently, the increasingly competitive foodservice environment has led to the need to reexamine quality in all aspects of an organization. Total quality management (TQM), a philosophy and system of management that has been touted as a fundamentally better way to conduct business and as necessary for the economic well-being of America, is discussed in this chapter.

To accomplish the common managerial functions of planning, organizing, staffing, directing, coordinating, reporting, and budgeting, a manager engages in a variety of activities that can be grouped into three basic categories: interpersonal relationships, information processing, and decision making. The three categories can be further divided into 10 observable working roles. In this chapter, the functions and roles of managerial work are explored. The skills required to perform these various functions and roles are also discussed.

The chapter concludes with a discussion of some important management tools. The organization chart is a map of the organization. The organization manual with its job descriptions, job specifications, and job schedules goes even further as a model of the organization.

Learning Objectives

After studying this chapter, the reader should be able to

1. describe the systems approach as it pertains to the management of a foodservice organization

2. discuss how concepts from the classical and human relations theories have been incorporated into the modern or systems theory in organizational management today

3. explain what is meant by quality of work life and total quality management (TQM) and describe how these two philosophies differ

4. compare and contrast the division of managerial work into functions versus roles

5. list and briefly explain some important management tools

6. explain the difference between line and line and staff organizations

7. list and briefly explain the relationship between Katz's three managerial skills and the manager's level in the organizational hierarchy

Organization

Theories of Organization

Organization for management is as old as human society and grew out of a common interest and combined effort to accomplish a common goal. Through the years many theories have been proposed, particularly since the early part of the twentieth century. Most of them fall into three categories: classical or traditional, human relations, and the modern or systems approach.

CLASSICAL   Classical organization theory rests on several premises—that division of work is essential for efficiency, that coordination is the primary responsibility of management in the organization of work, that the formal structure is the main vehicle for organizing and administering work activities, and that the span of control sets outside limits on the number of people responsible to a given manager. Other principles that emerged are: (1) *the scalar principle,* in which authority and responsibility flow in a direct line vertically from the highest level of the organization to the lowest; (2) *delegation,* in which decisions are delegated to the lowest competent level; (3) *unity of command,* which specifies that each person should be accountable to only one superior; (4) *the functional principle,* based on specialization of work; and (5) *the line and staff principle,* in which support and advisory activities are provided for the main functions of an organization. Classical organization theory continues to have great relevance to basic managerial problems, but it has been criticized as too mechanistic and not recognizing the interaction of groups and the decision-making processes in the formal structure.

HUMAN RELATIONS   The human relations theory evolved from the effort to compensate for some of the deficiencies of the classical theory. Where classical organization advocates focus on tasks, structure, and authority, human relations theorists have introduced the behavioral sciences as an integral part of organization theory. They view the organization as a social system and recognize the existence of the informal organization, in which workers align themselves into social groups within the framework of the formal organization. Many human relations theorists hold that employee participation in management planning and decision making yield positive effects in terms of morale and productivity.

SYSTEMS APPROACH   The systems approach, introduced in Chapter 2, is defined as a set of interdependent parts that work together to achieve a common goal. There are several important systems concepts that apply to organizations. Being predominantly open systems, human organizations interact with various elements of their environment. (For example, a hospital dietary department interacts with many external groups such as patients, customers, medical staff, hospital administration, and some regulatory agencies. The department, in turn, affects the external groups with which it interacts).

Organizations tend toward a dynamic or moving equilibrium. Members seek to maintain the organization and to have it survive. They react to changes and forces, both internal and external, in ways that often create a new state of equilibrium and balance. *Feedback* of information from a point of operation and from the environment to a control center or centers can provide the data necessary to initiate corrective measures to restore equilibrium.

Organizations and the world of which they are a part consist of a *hierarchy of systems.* Thus, a corporation is composed of divisions, departments, sections, and groups of individual employees. Also, the corporation is part of larger systems, such as all the firms in its industry, firms in its metropolitan area, and perhaps an association of many firms from many industries such as the National Restaurant Association (NRA) or the American Hospital Association.

Interdependency is a key concept in systems theory. The elements of a system interact with one another and are interdependent. Generally, a change in one part of an organization affects other parts of that organization. Sometimes the interdependencies are not fully appreciated when changes are made. A change in organization structure and work flow in one department may unexpectedly induce changes in departments that relate to the first department.

Systems theory contains the doctrine that the whole of a structure or entity is more than the sum of its parts. This is called *wholism*. The cooperative, synergistic working together of members of a department or team often yields a total product that exceeds the sum of their individual contributions.

Systems theory helps organize a large body of information that might otherwise make little sense. It has made major contributions to the study of organization and management in recent years. Systems theory aids in diagnosing the interactive relationships among task, technology, environment, and organization members.

In contrast to the classical models of organization, the systems approach has shown that managers operate in fluid, dynamic, and often ambiguous situations. The manager generally is not in full control of these situations. Managers must learn to shape actions and to make progress toward goals, but they know that results are affected by many factors and forces.

Systems theory has become popular because of its apparent ability to serve as a universal model of systems, including physical, biological, social, and behavioral phenomena.

Organization Structure

An organization is a system, having an established structure and conscious planning, in which people work and deal with one another in a coordinated and cooperative manner for the accomplishment of common goals. The formal organization is the planned structure that establishes a pattern of relationships among the various components of the organization. The informal organization refers to those aspects of the system that arise spontaneously from the activities and interactions of participants.

Whenever several people work together for a common goal, there must be some form of organization; that is, the tasks must be divided among them and the work of the group must be coordinated. Otherwise, there may be duplication of effort or even work at cross purposes. Dividing the work and arranging for coordination make up the process of organization, and once that is completed the group may be described as "an organization."

Certain steps are necessary in developing the framework of an organization's structure if goals of an enterprise are to be accomplished and the workers' talents developed to their fullest potential. These steps may be summarized as follows:

1. *Determine and define objectives.* The purpose of every organization dealing with personnel is to accomplish, with the efforts of people, some basic purpose or objective with the greatest efficiency, maximum economy, and minimum effort, and to provide for the personal development of the people working in the organization. Specifically, a foodservice has as its goal the production and service of the best food possible within its financial resources. It is important

that these objectives and the plans and policies for their achievement be presented in writing and understood by all responsible.

2. *Analyze and classify work to be done.* This is accomplished by dividing the total work necessary for the accomplishment of overall goals into its major parts and grouping each into like, or similar, activities. Examination of the work to be done will reveal tasks that are similar or are logically related. Such classification may be made by grouping activities that require similar skills, the same equipment, or duties performed in the same areas. There are no arbitrary rules for grouping. In a foodservice, the activities could be grouped as purchasing and storage preparation and processing, housekeeping and maintenance, and service and dishwashing. Each of these groupings might be broken into smaller classifications, depending on the type and size of the enterprise. With the increasing complexity of foodservice organizations and the trend toward centralization of certain functions, the organization structure takes on new dimensions and must consider the total management structure as well as the organization of its individual units.

3. *Describe in some detail the work or activity in terms of the employee.* This step is discussed in more detail later in this chapter under "Job Description."

4. *Determine and specify the relationship of the workers to each other and to management.* The work should be grouped into departments or other organizational units, with responsibility and authority defined for each level. It is generally understood that each person assigned to a job will be expected to assume the responsibility for performing the tasks given him or her and that each person will be held accountable for the results. However, persons can be accountable only to the degree that they have been given responsibility and authority. Responsibility without authority is meaningless. An assignment should be specific and in writing. For an organizational structure to become operational, of course, requires the selection of qualified personnel, provision of adequate financing and equipment, and a suitable physical environment. No successful organization structure remains static. It must be a continuing process that moves with changing concepts within the system and with changing conditions in its environment.

Application of the principles of organization and administration to a specific situation should precede any attempt at the operation of a foodservice unit. A detailed plan may be outlined for use as a guide in initiating a new foodservice of any type or for reorganizing one previously in operation.

Types of Organizations

Two types of authority relationships most often found in foodservice operating systems are line and line and staff. Large, complex operations may be organized on a functional basis.

LINE   In the line organization, lines of authority are clearly drawn, and each individual is responsible to the person ranking above him or her on the organization chart. Thus, authority and responsibility pass from the top-ranking member down to the lowest in rank. In such an organization structure, each person knows to whom he or she is responsible and, in turn, who is responsible to him or her.

Organization line structure can grow in two directions, vertically or horizontally. Vertical growth occurs through the delegation of authority, in which the individual at the top delegates work to her immediate subordinates, who redelegate part or all of their work to their subordinates, and so on down the line. For example, the director of a growing cafeteria operation may add an assistant manager, thus creating another level in the chain of command. When the distance from the top to bottom becomes too great for effective coordination, the responsibilities may be redistributed horizontally through departmentalization. In establishing departments, activities are grouped into natural units, with a manager given authority and accepting responsibility for that area of activities. There are several ways of dividing the work, but, in foodservices, the most usual are by function, product, or location. The work may be divided in a restaurant, into production, service, and sanitation, in dietetics, by administrative, clinical, and education; in a central commissary, by meat, vegetable, salad, and bakery departments; or by individual schools in a multiunit school foodservice system.

Advantages of the line organization include expediency in decision making, direct placement of responsibility, and clear understanding of authority relationships. A major disadvantage is that the person at the top tends to become overloaded with too much detail, thus limiting the time that he or she can devote to planning and research necessary for development and growth of the organization. There is no specialist to whom one can turn for help in the various areas of operation.

LINE AND STAFF   As an enterprise grows, the line organization may no longer be adequate to cope with the many diversified responsibilities demanded of the person at the top. Staff specialists, such as personnel director, research and development specialist, and data processing coordinator, are added to assist the lines in an advisory capacity. The line positions and personnel are involved directly in accomplishing the work for which the organization was created; the staff advises and supports the line. A staff position also may be an assistant who serves as an extension of a line officer. The potential for conflict exists between line and staff personnel if there is not a clear understanding of the lines of authority. For example, if a staff specialist recommends a change in procedure, the order for the change would come from the line personnel. Friction may arise if a strong staff person tries to overrule the manager or if the manager does not make full use of the abilities of the staff.

FUNCTIONAL   Some researchers consider functional authority as staff and others consider it—a distinct type in itself. Functional authority exists when an individual delegates limited authority over a specified segment of activities to another person. In a multiunit foodservice company, for example, the responsibility for purchasing or for menu planning and quality control may be vested in a vice president who then has authority over that function in all units.

Management

Organizations need competent managers to be able to meet their objectives both efficiently and effectively. The return that organizations realize from human resources will be determined, in large part, by the competence of their managers.

Theories of Management

In this era of constant societal change and "turbulent times," several management trends have emerged in response to perceived needs. *The systems approach,* described earlier in this chapter, gives managers a way of looking at the organization as a whole that is greater than the sum of its parts. The systems manager recognizes the contribution of each part to the whole system and that a change in one part will have an impact on other parts of the system. This approach allows a manager to diagnose and identify reasons for the occurrence of a situation.

The *contingency approach* holds that managerial activities should be adjusted to suit the situation. Factors within the situation, such as characteristics of the work force, size and type of organization, and its goals, should determine the managerial approach that is used.

In the late 1960s, *quality of work life* (QWL) was introduced. QWL represents an attempt to increase productivity by providing greater opportunity for satisfaction of human needs in the workplace. QWL is discussed in greater detail in Chapter 13.

Total quality management (TQM), as with many management philosophies, is a blend of the most effective facets of some previously tried approaches to quality improvement. Principles of quality assurance, participative management, and QWL are all found within the TQM framework. Each of these strategies was designed to improve the organization's products and services over time. TQM differs from the older approaches in its degree of pervasiveness. All aspects of the organization are involved in a TQM initiative. Changes are made throughout the organizational structure and culture. Employees at the lowest levels of the organization are empowered with decision-making and task-shaping authority.

Functions of Management

The basic purpose of management has been recognized as the leadership of individuals and groups in order to accomplish the goals of the organization. Fayol, a French mining engineer/manager, recognized that managerial undertakings require planning, organization, command, coordination, and control. Gulick developed the following seven major functions of management: planning, organizing, staffing, directing, coordinating, reporting, and budgeting. Various combinations of these functions with some modifications, deletions, and additions are found in modern management texts.

POSDCORB, the acronym created from the names of seven functions described by Gulick, is still widely accepted as describing the basic framework of the manager's job. Some disagreement does exist as to whether these functions are common to all levels of management. Others believe that even more functions should be included. Leading, actuating, activating, motivating, and communicating are concepts often fitted into the POSDCORB framework. That there is a degree of overlapping is evident in the functions themselves and in the efforts to classify them.

PLANNING   The planning function, described by Gulick and still relevant today, involves developing in broad outline the activities required to accomplish the objectives of the organization and the most effective ways of doing so. Planning is the basic function and all others are dependent upon it. The objective of planning is to think ahead, clearly determine objectives and policies, and select a course of action toward the accomplishment of the goals. Day-to-day planning of operational activities and short- and long-range planning toward department and institution goals are part of this function. Overall planning is the responsibility of top management, but participation at all levels in goal setting and development of new plans and procedures increases their effectiveness.

Forecasting is an important factor in effective planning for the future operating program of any company. Predictions of trends for the immediate and distant future based on an objective study of past and present situations usually are more reliable than mere guesses. Outside or external factors, such as social, economic, political, and other environmental conditions, are involved in forecasting, as are internal factors, such as size of plant and productivity of the personnel. A study of the interrelationships of such factors and their effects on the business, from data such as personal incomes, population growth, cost of living, and technological developments in food and equipment, should help the food manager to interpret possible future needs for personnel, physical facilities, and other budgetary items. A high degree of accuracy in forecasting is difficult to attain because of the uncertainties of the future. However, forecasting has merit in that it requires creative thinking, provides some helpful information, and may call attention to current problem areas within the organization. Examples of forecasting in foodservices are given in Chapter 5 on production planning and control and Chapter 14 on financial management.

ORGANIZING   Organizing includes the activities necessary to develop the formal structure of authority through which work is subdivided, defined, and coordinated to accomplish the organization's objectives. The organizing function identifies activities and tasks, divides tasks into positions, and puts like tasks together to take advantage of special abilities and skills of the workers and to use their talents effectively. Perhaps the chief function of the organizing process is the establishment of relationships among all other functions of management.

STAFFING   Staffing is the personnel function of employing and training people and maintaining favorable work conditions. The basic purpose of the staffing function is to obtain the best available people for the organization and to foster development of their skills and abilities. Chapter 11 discusses this important management function.

DIRECTING   Directing requires the continuous process of making decisions, conveying them to subordinates, and assuring appropriate action. Delegation of responsibility is essential to distribute workloads to qualified individuals at various levels. Whoever delegates a responsibility should not do so without detailed instructions as to what is expected of the subordinate and the necessary authority to carry out the responsibilities. If a subordinate is not given sufficient authority, the job is merely assigned, not delegated.

A very important part of the directing function is the concern with employees as human beings. Studies have shown that most people work at only 50% to 60% efficiency, and some investigators place this figure as low as 45%. The alert manager is aware that through careful, intelligent guidance and counseling and by effective supervision, the worker's productivity may be increased as much as 20%. This may mean the difference between financial success and failure of an enterprise.

COORDINATING   Coordinating is the functional activity of interrelating the various parts of work for smooth flow. In order to function effectively, organizations must be properly designed. Division of work is usually accomplished through departmentation, or specialization by function, product, client, geographical area, number of persons, or time. Different methods of coordination are required for different types of departmentation. As stated in Chapter 2, management's role in the systems approach is one of coordinating. This requires recognition of the need of all the parts and decisions made based on the overall effect of management on the organization as a whole and its objectives.

REPORTING   Reporting involves keeping supervisors, managers, and subordinates informed concerning responsibility through records, research, reports, inspection, and other methods. Records and evaluations of the results of work done are kept as the work progresses in order to compare performance with the yardstick of acceptability.

BUDGETING   Budgeting includes fiscal planning, accounting, and controlling. Control tends to ensure performance in accordance with plans and is a necessary function of all areas of foodservice. This necessitates measuring quantity of output, quality of the finished product, food and labor costs, and the efficient use of workers' time. Through control, standards of acceptability and accountability are set for performance. A good control system prevents present and future deviation from plans and does much to stimulate an employee to maintain the standards of the foodservice director. The budgeting function should be one of guidance, not command. It is concerned with employees as human beings with interests to be stimulated, aptitudes and abilities to be directed and developed, and comprehension and understanding of their responsibilities to be increased (see Chapter 14).

Skills of Managers

The most widely accepted method of classifying managerial skills is in terms of the three-skill approach initially proposed by Katz. He identified *technical, human,* and *conceptual* skills as those that every successful manager must have in varying degrees, according to the level of the hierarchy at which the manager is operating. Katz contended that managers need all three skills to fulfill their role requirements, but the relative importance and the specific types within each category depend on the leadership situation.

Based on the concept of skill as an ability to translate knowledge into action, the three interrelated skill categories may be briefly summarized as: (1) technical—performing specialized activities, (2) human—understanding and motivating individuals and groups, and (3) conceptual—understanding and integrating all the activities and interests of the organization toward a common objective. Technical skills are usually more important than conceptual ones for lower level managers. Human skills are needed at all levels of management, but are relatively less important for managers at the top level than the low level. Conceptual skill becomes more important with the need for policy decisions and broad-scale action at upper levels of management.

Managerial Activities and Roles

Whereas a number of studies have investigated the personal styles and characteristics of managers, relatively few have researched what managers actually do in fulfilling job requirements. After reviewing and synthesizing the available research on how various managers spend their time, Koontz reported that Mintzberg designed a study to produce a more supportable and useful description of managerial work. Mintzberg's resulting role theory of management has received attention as a useful way of describing the duties and responsibilities of managers. Mintzberg defined a role as an organized set of behaviors belonging to an identifiable position. He identified 10 roles common to the work of all managers and divided them into interpersonal (three roles), informational (three roles), and decisional (four roles). Although the roles are described here individually, in reality they constitute an integrated whole. In essence, the manager's formal authority and status educe interpersonal relationships leading to information roles and these, in turn, to decisional roles.

The three *interpersonal* roles of figurehead, leader, and liaison devolve from the manager's formal authority and status. As *figureheads,* managers perform duties of a symbolic, legal, or social nature because of their position in the organization. As *leaders,* managers establish the work atmosphere within the organization and activate subordinates to achieve organizational goals. As *liaisons,* managers establish and maintain contacts outside the organization to obtain information and cooperation.

The three *informational* roles of monitor, disseminator, and spokesperson characterize the manager as the central focus for receiving and sending of nonroutine information. In the *monitor* role, managers collect all information relevant to the organization. The *disseminator* role involves the manager in transmitting information gathered outside the organization to members inside. In the *spokesperson* role, managers transmit information from inside the organization to outsiders.

The four *decisional* roles are entrepreneur or initiator, disturbance handler, resource allocator, and negotiator. Managers adopt the *entrepreneurial* role when they initiate controlled change in the organization to adapt and keep pace with changing conditions in the environment. Unexpected changes require the manager to perform as a *disturbance handler.* As *resource allocators,* managers make decisions concerning priorities for utilization of organizational resources. Finally, managers *negotiate* with individual or other organizations. These interlocking and interrelated roles are shown in Figure 10.1.

Tools of Management

Directors of foodservices commonly use the organization chart as a means of explaining and clarifying the structure of an organization. They also use job descriptions, job specifications, and work schedules as devices for the clear presentation of personnel and their responsibilities to top management and to employees. These mechanical or visual means are indispensable in the able direction and supervision of a foodservice, and for convenience they may be called *tools of organization and management.* Performance appraisal as a tool of management is discussed in Chapter 11.

Figure 10.1. Interlocking and interrelated roles of managers.

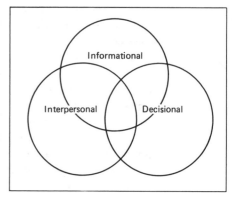

ORGANIZATION CHART   The chart of an organization may be considered the first tool of management. It graphically presents the basic groupings and relationships of positions and functions. The chart presents a picture of the formal organization structure and serves many useful purposes, but it does have some limitations. Whereas lines of authority are depicted on the chart, the degree of authority and responsibility at each level is not shown. Informal relationships between equals or between people in different parts of the organization are not evident. For this reason, job descriptions and organization manuals are valuable supplements to the organization chart.

The organization chart is usually constructed on the basis of the line of authority, but it may be based on functional activity or a combination of the two. Functions and positions are graphically presented by the use of blocks or circles. Solid lines connecting the various blocks indicate the channels of authority. Those persons with the greatest authority are shown at the top of the chart and those with the least at the bottom. Advisory responsibility and lines of communication often are shown by use of dotted lines. Organization charts for a small and a large hospital are shown in Figs. 10.2 and 10.3, for a college foodservice in Fig. 10.4, and for a campus restaurant in Fig. 10.5.

JOB DESCRIPTION   A job description is an organized list of duties that reflects required skills and responsibilities in a specific position. It may be thought of as an extension of the organization chart in that it shows activities and job relationships for the positions identified on the organization chart. Job descriptions are valuable for matching qualified applicants to the job, for orientation and training of employees, for performance appraisal, for establishing rates of pay, and for defining limits of authority and responsibility. They should be written for every position in the foodservice and should be reviewed and updated periodically. In many organizations, the job descriptions are incorporated into a procedure manual or kept in a looseleaf notebook for easy access.

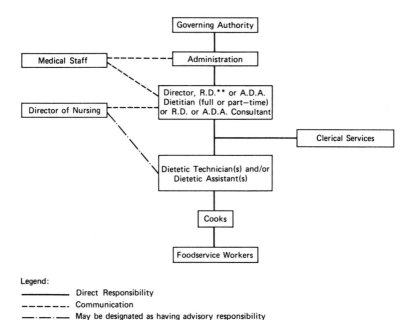

Figure 10.2. Organization chart for the department of dietetics in a hospital or other group care facility of less than 150 beds.* (Courtesy, The American Dietetic Association.)

Job descriptions may be written in either narrative or outline form or a combination of the two. The format probably will vary according to the job classification; for example, the work of the foodservice employee is described in terms of specific duties and skill requirements, but the job description for the professional position is more likely to be written in terms of broad areas of responsibilities. Most job descriptions include identifying information, a job summary, and specific duties and requirements. The initial job descriptions for a new facility would reflect the responsibilities delegated to each position on a trial basis and subject to early revision. In the case of an established unit, they are developed from information obtained from interviews with employees and supervisors and from observations by the person responsible for writing the job description. A *job analysis,* in which all aspects of a job are studied and analyzed, may be conducted first to collect information for the job description.

The job description in Fig. 10.6 may be useful as a guide. The exact content and format, however, varies according to the position being described and the needs and complexities of the institution.

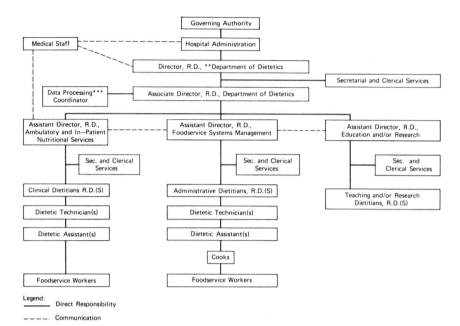

Figure 10.3. Organization chart for the department of dietetics in a large hospital (500 beds or more), health center, or other group care facility.* (Courtesy, The American Dietetic Association.)

In order to empower employees, as discussed earlier in this chapter, job descriptions have been replaced by a skills matrix system in some progressive companies. Each skills matrix describes steps in the career ladder along a vertical axis, as well as skills and competencies that are required for each step across the horizontal axis. The skills matrices specify roles and levels of performance for a "family of jobs," rather than a description of a specific job.

JOB SPECIFICATION   A job specification is a written statement of the minimum standards that must be met by an applicant for a particular job. It covers duties involved in a job, the working conditions peculiar to the job, and personal qualifications required of the worker to carry through the assigned responsibilities successfully. This tool is used primarily by the employing officer in the selection and placement of the right person for the specific position. Many small institutions use the job description as a job specification also (see Fig. 10.7).

WORK SCHEDULE   A work schedule is an outline of work to be performed by an individual with stated procedures and time requirements for his or her duties. It

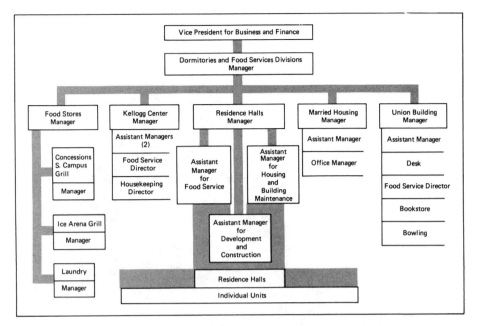

Figure 10.4. Organization chart for large housing and foodservice system. (Courtesy, Michigan State University.)

is important to break down the tasks into an organized plan with careful consideration given to timing and sequence of operations. Work schedules are especially helpful in training new employees and are given to the employee after the person has been hired and training has begun. This is one means of communication between the employer and employee. Work schedules should be reviewed periodically and adjustments made as needed to adapt to changes in procedures.

An example of a work schedule for a cafeteria worker is given in Fig. 10.8. For food production employees, the individual work schedule would outline in general terms the day's work routine, but would need to be supplemented by a daily production schedule giving specific assignments for preparation of the day's menu items and prepreparation for the next day. A more detailed discussion of production scheduling is included in Chapter 5.

Van Egmond-Pannell suggests three basic types of work schedules: individual, daily unit, and organization. Because the individual schedule on a daily basis would be too time-consuming for most managers, she recommends the daily unit schedule shown in Fig. 10.9.

The organization work schedule gives the standing assignments by half-hour periods for all employees in chart form. It does not relate specifically to the day's menu. This type of schedule shows graphically the total work load and its division among employees, but would not be effective unless accompanied by daily assignments or a production schedule.

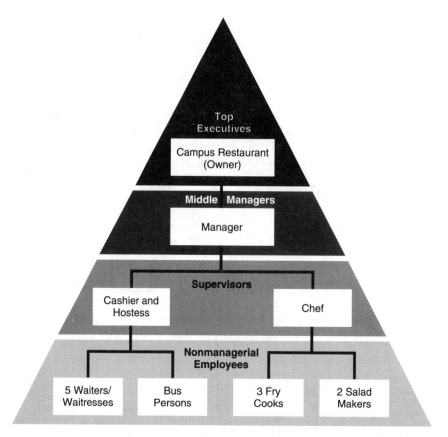

Figure 10.5.   The organizational pyramid for a campus restaurant. (Reprinted by permission from page 25 of *Management: Concepts and Effective Practice,* Third Edition, by Hitt, M. P., Middlemist, R. D., Mathis, R. L.; Copyright © 1989 by West Publishing Company. All rights reserved.)

SCHEDULING OF EMPLOYEES   Workers may be scheduled successfully only after thorough analysis and study of the jobs to be done, the working conditions, and the probable efficiency of the employees. The menu pattern, the form in which food is purchased, the method of preparation, and the total quantity needed are important factors in determining the amount of preparation time and labor required to produce and serve meals in a given situation. Good menu planning provides for variation in meal items and combinations from day-to-day, with a fairly uniform production schedule. Workers cannot be expected to maintain high interest and to work efficiently if they have little to do one day and are overworked the next.

Analysis of several sample menus in terms of total labor hours and the time of day required for the amounts and types of preparations is a basic consideration

JOB DESCRIPTION

Job title: First Cook   *Date:*   September 2, 19____
Job code: 2–26.32 Dept. 10   *Location:*   Kitchen of University Cafeteria
Job summary
   Prepares meats and main dishes, soups and gravies for noon meal.
   Cleans and washes small equipment used in cooking.
   Keeps own working area clean.
Performance requirements
   Responsibilities: responsible for the preparation of meat and main dishes,
   soups and gravies to be served at a stated time.
   Job knowledge: plan own work schedule, know basic principles of quantity
   food cookery and how to use certain equipment.
   Mental application: mentally alert.
   Dexterity and accuracy: accurate in weighing and measuring of food ingre-
   dients and portions.
   Equipment used: food chopper, mixer, ovens, ranges, steam cooker,
   steam-jacketed kettle, fryer, broiler, meat slicer.
   Standards of production: preparation of foods of high quality in specified
   quantities.
Supervision
   Under general supervision of dietitian.
   Gives some supervision to assistant cooks.
Relation to other jobs
   Promotion from: Salad maker or vegetable preparation worker.
   Promotion to: Foodservice supervisor (if education and ability warrants).
Qualifications
   Experience desirable but not required.
   Education and training.
     Technical or vocational training: none.
     Formal education: grammar school.
     Ability to read, write, and understand English.

Figure 10.6.   Job description; write up for a cook's position. Job description should be available for all positions in the department.

in determining the number of employees necessary in any foodservice. The total estimated work hours required to cover all activities in the organization divided by the number of working hours in the day would give an indication of the number of full-time employees needed. However, careful attention must be given to time schedules so that each employee will be occupied during his or her hours on duty. Certain preparations or service duties may require a reduction in the estimated number of full-time workers and the addition of some part-time workers during peak periods in order to maintain the desired standards at an even tempo. A graphic presentation of the estimated work hours needed for each job helps to clarify the problems of scheduling and the distribution of the work load (Fig. 10.10).

JOB SPECIFICATION

Payroll title: First Cook
Department: Preparation Department   *Occupational code:*   2–26.32
Supervised by: Dietitian
Job summary: Prepares meat, main dishes, soups, and gravies for noon meal.
Educational status: Speak, read, write English. Grammar school graduate or higher.
Experience required: Cooking in a cafeteria or restaurant 6 months desirable but not required.
Knowledge and skills: Knowledge of basic principles of quantity food preparation; ability to adjust recipes and follow directions; ability to plan work.
Physical requirements: Standard physical examination.
Personal requirements: Neat, clean; male or female.
References required: Two work and personal references.
Hours: 6:30 a.m. to 3:00 p.m., 5 days a week; days off to be arranged; 30-minute lunch period.
Wage code: Grade 3.
Promotional opportunities: To foodservice supervisor.
Advantages and disadvantages of the job: Location, environment, security.
Tests: None.

Figure 10.7.   Job specification. Example of a typical format used for each job in the department.

Working conditions such as the physical factors of temperature, humidity, lighting, and safety influence the scheduling of personnel and affect workers' performance. Of particular importance is the amount and arrangement of equipment. The distance each employee must travel within his or her work area should be kept at a minimum in order to conserve the individual's energy and time. Use of mechanical devices in the processing and service of food may decrease the total labor hours needed and increase the degree of skill and responsibility of employees. Arrangement of work areas for efficient operation cannot be overemphasized.

A work distribution analysis chart of the total activities within a department will show where tasks may be eliminated, combined, or modified in the overall picture. One must be sure that the activities are so organized and combined that efficient use is made of the labor hours of each individual worker. Studies may be made to determine a good standard for each procedure, such as the time required for the average worker to combine and shape 25 pounds of ham loaf mixture into loaves in pans for baking. The standards set for each procedure should be such that the workers in a particular organization will be able to maintain them. The standard time should be established at a level that the average employee could do 20% to 30% more work without undue fatigue.

WORK SCHEDULE FOR CAFETERIA COUNTER WORKER

Name: _____

Hours: 5:30 to 2:00 p.m.
30 min for breakfast
15 min for coffee break

Position—Cafeteria Counter Worker—No. 1
Days off: _____

Supervised by: _____
Relieved by: _____

5:30 to 7:15 A.M.:	1. Read breakfast menu
	2. Ready equipment for breakfast meal
	   a. Turn on heat in cafeteria counter units for hot foods, grill, dish warmers, etc.
	   b. Prepare counter units for cold food
	   c. Obtain required serving utensils and put in position for use
	   d. Place dishes where needed, those required for hot food in dish warmer
	3. Make coffee (consult supervisor for instructions and amount to be made)
	4. Fill milk dispenser
	5. Obtain food items to be served cold: fruit, fruit juice, dry cereals, butter, cream, etc. Place in proper location on cafeteria counter
	6. Obtain hot food and put in hot section of counter
	7. Check with supervisor for correct portion sizes if this has not been decided previously

6:30 to 8:00 A.M.:	1. Open cafeteria doors for breakfast service 2. Check meal tickets, volunteer lists, guest tickets, and collect cash as directed by supervisor 3. Replenish cold food items, dishes, and silver 4. Notify cook before hot items are depleted 5. Make additional coffee as needed 6. Keep counters clean; wipe up spilled food
8:00 to 8:30 A.M.:	Eat breakfast

8:30 to 10:30 A.M.:	1. Break down serving line and return leftover foods to refrigerators and cook's area as directed by supervisor
	2. Clean equipment, serving counters, and tables in dining area
	3. Prepare serving counters for coffee break period
	   a. Get a supply of cups, saucers, and tableware
	   b. Make coffee
	   c. Fill cream dispensers
	   d. Keep counter supplied during coffee break period (9:30–10:30)
	4. Fill salad dressing, relish, and condiment containers for noon meal

10:30 to 11:30 A.M.:	1. Confer with supervisor regarding menu items and portion sizes for noon meal
	2. Clean equipment, counters, and tables in dining area
	3. Prepare counters for lunch:
	   a. Turn on heat in hot counter and dish warmers
	   b. Set out tea bags, cream, ice cups, glasses
	   c. Place serving utensils and dishes in position for use
	4. Make coffee
	5. Fill milk and clean dispensers
	6. Set portioned cold foods on cold counter

11:30 A.M. to 1:30 P.M.:	1. Open cafeteria doors for noon meal service 2. Replenish cold food items, dishes, and silver as needed 3. Keep counters clean; wipe up spilled food 4. Make additional coffee as needed
1:30 to 2:00 P.M.:	1. Turn off heating and cooling elements in serving counters 2. Help break down serving line 3. Return leftover foods to proper places 4. Serve late lunches to doctors and nurses 5. Clean equipment and serving counter as directed by supervisor
2:00 P.M.	Off duty

Figure 10.8. Work schedule for a counter worker in any type of cafeteria.

WORK SCHEDULE

MENU:
LASAGNA CASSEROLE   BUTTERED FRENCH BREAD
TOSSED SALAD   MILK
CHILLED PEACH HALVES

Time	Manager 7 1/2 hr	6-Hr Assistant	5-Hr Assistant	4-Hr Assistant
7:30– 8:00	Make coffee or tea for teachers			
8:00– 8:30	Help with lasagna sauce	Prepare lasagna		
8:30– 9:00	Lunch count—Tickets		Dip up fruit and refrigerate	
9:00– 9:30				
9:30–10:00	Teachers' salads		Wash vegetables for salad	
10:00–10:30	Cut bread and butter	Prepare bread crumbs for fried chicken tomorrow		Cut up vegetables for salad
10:30–11:00			Put out desserts	Set up line—napkins, straws, dishes
11:00–11:30	Eat lunch—20 min	Eat lunch—20 min	Eat lunch—20 min	
	Put food on steam table	Put food on steam table	Wash pots and pans	Mix salad for first lunch
11:30–12:00	Cashier	Serving Set up for next line	Serving Help in dishroom	Back up line Dishroom
12:00–12:30	Serving	Serving Set up for next line	Cashier Help in dishroom	Back up line Dishroom
12:30– 1:00	Serving	Serving Put away food	Cashier 10 min break	Back up line Dishroom
1:00– 1:30	Count money—10 min break Help to clean tables	10 min break Clean tables	Clean steamtable	Eat lunch (eat on own time)
1:30– 2:00	Prepare reports	Clean up		Clean dishroom
2:00– 2:30	Place orders			Help with kitchen cleanup
2:30– 3:00	Take topping out of freezer and put in refrigerator for tomorrow			

Figure 10.9. Sample work schedule for school foodservice employees. (Courtesy, Dorothy VanEgmond-Pannell, *School Foodservice,* Westport, CT: AVI Publishing Co.)

Written schedules clarify the responsibilities of workers and give them a feeling of security. It is wise to include a statement indicating that additional duties may have to be assigned from time to time. However, work schedules must be kept flexible and adjustments made as needed to adapt to the daily menu. Also, the introduction of new food products may decrease the amount of time needed for prepreparation as well as the time of cookery; likewise, additional processes may become necessary.

Information pertaining to the broad subjects of organization and management is voluminous. Only basic concepts with limited application are included in this chapter. The following chapters discuss some special areas of concern to persons in the management of foodservices. Supplementary reading of current literature is advised to become acquainted with newer developments as they evolve.

Figure 10.10. Bar graph used to detail employee time schedules and task assignments for patients' foodservices. Total time spent on each separate task can be easily calculated.

Summary Questions

1. List and briefly describe five principles of the classical management theory.
2. Give several examples of the application of human relations theory.
3. Why is interdependency considered a key concept in systems theory?

4. List the steps required to establish an organizational structure.

5. What are the advantages and disadvantages of line and line and staff organizations?

6. What are the seven widely accepted functions of management?

7. How do job descriptions, job schedules, and job specifications differ, and for what purpose is each used?

Bibliography

Armstrong, L. and Symonds, W. C.: Beyond "may I help you?": Services finally are trying to put their house in order. Business Week Special issue # 3237, p. 100, 1991.

Axline, L. L.: TQM: A look in the mirror. Mgmt. Review 80(7):64, 1991.

Drucker, P. F.: Managing in Turbulent Times. New York: Harper & Row, 1980.

Fayol, H.: General and Industrial Management. London: Sir Isaac Pitman and Sons, 1949.

Gift, B.: On the road to TQM. Food Mgmt. 27(4):88, 1992.

Gulick, L.: Notes on the theory of organization. In L. Gulick and L. Urwick (Eds.), Papers on the Science of Administration. New York: Columbia University Press, 1937.

Hitt, M. A., Middlemist, R. D., and Mathis, R. L.: Management Concepts and Effective Practice. Saint Paul, MN: West Publishing Co., 1989.

Katz, R. L.: Skills of an effective administrator. Harvard Bus. Rev. 52:90, 1974.

King, P.: A total quality makeover. Food Mgmt. 27(4):96, 1992.

Koontz, H.: The management theory jungle revisited. Acad. of Mgmt. J. 5:175, 1980.

Mintzberg, H.: The Nature of Managerial Work. New York: Harper & Row, 1973.

Moravec, M. and Tucker, R.: Job descriptions for the 21st century. Pers. J. 71(6):37, 1992.

Schecter, M.: Restaura makes the CQE commitment. Food Mgmt. 27(4):112, 1992.

Schecter, M.: The quest for quality. Food Mgmt. 27(4):82, 1992.

VanEgmond-Pannell, D.: School Foodservice Management, 4th ed. New York: Van Nostrand Reinhold, 1990.

For More Information

Bolman, L. G. and Deal, T. E.: Reframing Organizations—Artistry, Choice, and Leadership. San Francisco: Jossey-Bass, 1991.

Coffey, R. J., Eisenberg, M., Gaucher, E. M., and Kratochwill, E. W.: Total quality progress at the University of Michigan Medical Center. J. of Quality and Participation Jan/Feb:22, 1991.

Cummings, A. R.: Quality control principles: Applications in dietetic practice. J. Am. Diet. A. 92:427, 1992.

Dessler, G.: Organization Theory—Integrating Structure and Behavior, 2nd ed. Englewood Cliffs, NJ: Prentice Hall, 1986.

Drucker, P. F.: The Frontiers of Management. New York: E. P. Dutton, 1986.

Imai, M.: Kaizen. New York: Random House Business Division, 1986.

Ivancevich, J. M. and Matteson, M. T.: Organizational Behavior and Management. Homewood, IL: Business Publications, Inc., 1987.

Koury, S. D.: Food Sanitation and Safety Study Course, 2nd ed. Ames: Iowa State University Press, 1989.

Mintzberg, H.: Mintzberg on Management. Inside our Strange World of Organizations. New York: The Free Press, 1989.

Mintzberg, H.: Structure in Fives: Designing Effective Organizations. Englewood Cliffs, NJ: Prentice Hall, 1983.

Mintzberg, H.: The Structuring of Organizations. Englewood Cliffs, NJ: Prentice Hall, 1979.

Naisbitt, J. and Aburdene, P.: Megatrends 2000. New York: William Morrow & Co., 1990.

Quinn, R. E., Faerman, S. R., Thompson, M. P., and McGrath, M. R.: Becoming a Master Manager. New York: John Wiley & Sons, 1990.

Roberts, W.: Leadership Secrets of Attila the Hun. New York: Warner Books, Inc., 1987.

Robey, D.: Designing Organizations, 2nd ed. Homewood, IL: Irwin, 1986.

Schermerhorn, Jr., J. R.: Management for Productivity. New York: John Wiley & Sons, 1989.

Senge, P. M.: The Fifth Discipline. New York: Doubleday Currency, 1990.

Szilagyi, Jr., A. D.: Management and Performance. Glenview, IL: Scott, Foresman, 1988.

Staffing and Managing Human Resources

Staffing and managing human resources involves all the methods of matching tasks to be performed with the people available to do the work. The *acquisition* of human resources (e.g., job analysis; human resource planning, recruitment, and selection); the *development* of human resources (e.g., placement, orientation, training, performance appraisal, and personnel development); the *rewards* of human resources (e.g., compensation and promotion); and the *maintenance* of human resources (e.g., health and safety, transfer, discipline, dismissal, supervision, decision making, grievance handling, and labor relations) are all intertwined in this process. Each of these subjects is discussed in this chapter.

An important aspect of the human resource management function is the establishment, acceptance, and enforcement of fair labor policies within an organization. Four areas in which policies are generally established are discussed: wages and income maintenance, hours and schedules of work, security in employment, and employee services and benefits. Major federal legislation that has an impact on these organizational policies is included in each section. The chapter concludes with a discussion of labor-management relations including relevant legislation and the impact of unionization on foodservices.

Learning Objectives

After studying this chapter, the reader should be able to

1. name the characteristics beyond good pay and benefits that are common to the companies considered the best to work for in the United States today

2. identify the tasks that are included in the staffing function of management

3. graph an integrated staffing system

4. list and briefly describe the sources of potential employees

5. discuss the purposes of the employment interview

6. describe what should be included in an employee orientation program

7. discuss when and how disciplinary action should be taken

8. identify legislation that has had an impact on foodservice management operations

Staffing

Foodservice has been called the ultimate people business. As the single most important resource in any enterprise, the human factor is the key to success. The ability of foodservice managers to understand people, recognize their potential and provide for their growth and development on the job is of inestimable worth in helping to create good human relations. Realization by workers that they are useful and important to efficient functioning of the business contributes to their sense of responsibility, ownership, and pride in the organization. Increase in pay alone does not buy good will, loyalty, or confidence in self and others. Often only simple changes or considerations such as beautification of the work area, elimination of safety hazards, rearrangement of equipment, modification of work schedules, or even cheerful words of appreciation and encouragement produce incentives with resultant increased and improved quality output. Mutually understood and accepted objectives and policies of the foodservice and well-defined channels of communication also contribute significantly to high-level employer–employee relationships.

Characteristics beyond good pay and benefits that are common to those companies considered best to work for in the United States include: encouraging open communication, flowing up and down; promoting from within; stressing quality to foster a sense of employee pride in output; allowing employees to share in profits; reducing distinctions between ranks; creating as pleasant a workplace environment as possible; encouraging employees to be active in community service; helping employees save by matching funds that they save; and making people feel part of a team. The presence of these characteristics results in a good workplace climate and low absenteeism and turnover of good employees.

Staffing is not simply a synonym for employment. Staffing includes all the methods of matching requirements of tasks to be performed with skills available. Hiring, placement, promotion, transfer, job design, and training are all intertwined in this process. People must be hired and promoted who can be trained to perform the necessary tasks. And training must be designed around the needs of the employees and the organization. Staffing may be thought of as an integrated system for moving people into, through, and eventually out of the organization. The components of an integrated staffing system are shown in Fig. 11.1.

A detailed plan of organization for a foodservice indicates the number and types of human resources needed, presents their distribution among the various work areas of the service, and shows their work schedules, the provision made for their training, and the responsibilities assigned to each. Far more difficult than the formulation of such a plan on paper is its actual inauguration. Then, all the neat little blocks on the chart designating individuals assigned certain responsibilities become persons with diverse energies and loyalties, egocentric ideas, and unclarified codes of values, some skillful, others not, some with acceptable food standards, and others apparently totally lacking in this regard. Left to chance, the introduction of the human element into an orderly plan is likely to plunge it into chaos. With wise selection, intelligent and adequate direction, and careful supervision, the human element vitalizes and enriches the plan.

Foodservices in many large companies have personnel departments responsible for the staffing function. In such organizations, the foodservice director works closely with the personnel department. However, in many small

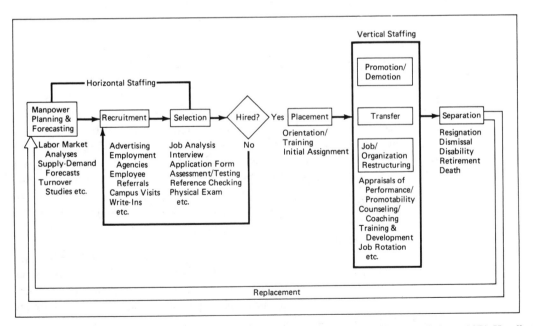

Figure 11.1. Components of an integrated staffing system. (Reprinted by permission. *ASPA Handbook of Personnel and Industrial Relations,* by Dale Yoder and H.G. Heneman Jr., p. 4-3, copyright © 1979, by Bureau of National Affairs, Inc., Washington, DC)

foodservices, personnel management responsibilities are assumed by the director of that department. Thus, the director may be responsible for the organization plans, the procurement, placement, induction, on-the-job training, and supervision of all employees in the department.

Management of human resources presents unique problems that can be solved only by persons with an understanding of human nature, a respect for the personalities of others, and an appreciation of the labor requirements and employment opportunities of the company. Insight into and respect for the rights of all individuals in an organization is the responsibility of the person in charge. These time-honored rights include: (1) the right to be treated as an individual and respected as a person, (2) the right to have a voice in one's own affairs, which includes the right to contribute to the best of one's own abilities in the solution of common problems, (3) the right to recognition for one's contribution to the common good, (4) the right to develop and make use of one's highest capabilities, and (5) the right to fairness and justice in all dealings with one's supervisors.

As soon as employed, a worker becomes a member of the group and begins to share in forming that intangible but all-important element termed group morale or group spirit. An understanding, cooperative, and helpful worker contributes to group morale; an irritable, carping, complaining, and obstructive worker destroys it. Many organizations have learned through sad experience how very great a destructive force one malcontent member can exert on group spirit. Since discipline of workers who are a disturbing force or their elimination from the work group is neither easy nor pleasant, the selection of those who will build morale rather than destroy it is of great importance in the choice of staff.

The skill, craftsmanship, dependability, and regularity of workers and their contribution to group morale in previous positions can determine whether they are chosen as new employees. Certain other things indicate probable contributions in the future. For example, capacity for growth, desire for self-improvement in order to render greater service, ambition for promotion, and identification with the firm are all important in the selection of a work force for tomorrow. However, not every person is equally desirous of assuming responsibility and carrying out a project to conclusion. This is also true of workers who are unwilling to face problem solving. Some people are overdependent and eager to avoid directing themselves or others.

After the foodservice director has considered personnel needs, what the foodservice has to offer in return should be considered. Everybody works smarter when there's something in it for them. Part of the reward is money. Adequate compensation and steady employment are basic to any satisfactory employer–employee relationship.

Another part of the compensation may be intangible; that is, just as employees contribute to the morale of the group spirit of the service, so the administration will contribute to their sense of personal satisfaction. The provision of meaningful work and the recognition of achievements are important motivational elements.

A third part of the compensation will be the opportunity to do a good job. Full instructions as to accepted procedures and standards and adequate on-the-job supervision are vital to satisfactory performance by workers. Only then will they experience pride in their accomplishments and attain and maintain a high level of performance on the job.

The job should provide opportunity for growth and a reasonable chance for promotion. Workers should have an opportunity to make their service a creative experience. They should be encouraged to regard improvement in techniques as possible and welcome and to feel that suggestions toward this end will be cordially received. They have a right to expect fairness in dealing with management, freedom from misrepresentation and misinformation about the employing organization, a reasonable opportunity for continued education, promotion when earned, and provision for satisfying recreation.

The foodservice director should synthesize the two points of view—the employer's and the employee's—into an adequate, functioning personnel program. Such a program should be characterized by wise selection, careful placement, adequate supervision, and education for the present job and for the future; fair employment policies; services desirable for the comfort and welfare of employees; and the keeping of records that will facilitate the evaluation and revision, if needed, of the management program.

The Employment Process

Organization charts indicate the number of workers needed in each department of a foodservice, and job descriptions and job specifications outline the specific conditions under which each employee will work, the job requirements, and the training and other personal qualifications deemed desirable. Such information affords the foodservice director charged with human resource management an inventory of employment needs.

Recruitment

The next step is to survey the sources of labor supply and determine which one or ones shall be used to bring the open positions to the attention of the best qualified prospective employees. There should be active recruitment of minority group members if the organization is to stay in line with public policy. Labor sources are many and varied, dependent somewhat on which sources are available locally and on the general labor market. Most sources may be classified as either internal or external.

INTERNAL SOURCES Promotion of employees to a position of higher level, transfer from a related department or unit, and the rehire of a person formerly on the payroll are examples of internal sources. Promotions or transfers within an organization help to stimulate interest and build morale of employees when they know that on the basis of measured merit they will be given preference over an outsider in the event of a good vacancy. Caution must be taken to ensure that the individual has the necessary personal attributes as well as training and experience for the position open and that equal opportunity employment regulations have not been violated.

An indirect internal source of labor is a present employee who notifies friends or relatives of vacancies and arranges for an interview with the employer. Recruiting labor in this way has advantages and disadvantages. Present employees generally prefer working with those who are congenial, and a pleasant spirit within the group may be built by utilizing this source of labor supply. In contrast, personal ties may be stronger than business loyalties, and inept, unskilled workers may be highly recommended by relatives and friends. Furthermore, a strongly clannish feeling among the workers may lead to an unfortunate generalized reaction against any disciplinary measure, no matter how well justified. The many phases of this situation should be considered before extensive use is made of this source of labor.

EXTERNAL SOURCES Some foodservice organizations may plan to fill vacancies by promoting from within; however, replacements will eventually be needed to fill the depleted ranks. The most common external sources are the press, employment agencies, schools, and labor unions.

Advertising: Newspaper advertising is a means of reaching a large group of potential applicants. Such advertisements cite the qualifications desired; otherwise, a mass of applicants may respond, none of whom are qualified. Definite statements as to desired training and experience in the foodservice field tend to limit the applicants to those who are truly qualified. Details concerning salary, sick leave, time schedule, and vacations are much better left until the personal interview. The advertisement should state whether application is to be made first in person or by letter.

Employment Agencies: Private employment agencies have long served as a means of locating labor. Usually, these agencies are supported by a registration fee charged to persons who are seeking employment. They generally provide a preliminary "weeding out" of would-be applicants, eliminating the unfit. Often these agencies tend to deal with specialized groups in the professional or technical areas and are of most value to those seeking employees on the managerial level.

Federal, state, and local employment agencies are a significantly important labor source. The value of these agencies has increased since they have studied the employer's needs and set up machinery to test aptitudes and skills of the workers. Such procedures benefit foodservice managers who are endeavoring to reduce turnover to a minimum and develop a stable work force.

School: In some localities, vocational and technical schools offer training for the food industry. These graduates are excellent candidates for available foodservice positions. The adequacy of their specific preparation for this work may greatly shorten the period of preliminary training necessary.

Another source, important in the foodservices of colleges and universities, is the student employment office of the college. Utilizing this type of labor offers financial assistance to worthy students and often provides experience to those majoring in food systems management. Perhaps the greatest advantage of student employees to the college foodservice manager is their availability for short work periods during the peak of the service load. However, the labor cost is high because the workers are inexperienced, and the labor turnover is great, thus much energy is expended in introducing new workers to the jobs. The short work periods necessitated by student classroom assignments make the planning of work far more complicated than when full-time employees are used. The immaturity and inexperience of the worker can also result in a waste of food supplies and labor hours unless constant and thorough supervision is provided. The maintenance of high food standards and acceptable service is often much more difficult with student employees than with carefully chosen, well-trained employees of long-time service.

Labor Unions: In organizations where employees are unionized, the labor union may be an important source for workers.

Selection

After the prospective workers have been recruited, the next step is for the employer to select the most capable person available for the particular opening. The cost of hiring, training, and discharging or transferring a worker is too great to allow many mistakes in the employee procurement process. Failure at this point is far more expensive than is commonly recognized.

Recognition of the heavy initial cost of employment means, when the labor market permits, a trend toward careful selection of each appointee.

APPLICATION FORM The application form plays an important role in the employment of any worker. The information requested should be phrased in direct simple statements pertinent to the particular job in which the applicant shows interest, and questions raised should be easily answered. Obviously, quite different information would be required of the person applying for a management position than for one who expects to be a counter worker. However, both application forms, when completed, must contain biographical data that will provide the employer with all the facts necessary not only to determine the fitness of the applicant for the job, but also to compare the qualifications of all applicants. The Fair Employment Practice laws adopted by many states make it illegal to ask questions that would be discriminatory because of race, religion, sex, age, marital status, or national origin. After the employee has been hired, such information can be obtained for the individual's personnel records. The manager should check with the personnel department or other authoritative source regarding restrictions in the application form and the interview. References of former employment are usually requested and should be checked.

INTERVIEW   The purposes of the selection interview are: (1) to get information—not only all the facts, but attitudes, feelings, and personality traits that determine "will-do" qualifications; (2) to give information—just as it is essential that the interviewer know all about the applicant, it is also essential that the applicant know all about the establishment and the job; and (3) to make a friend—treat an applicant with the same courtesy that you would give to a customer, for every applicant is a potential customer.

The direct personal interview is advantageous in that the interviewer has the opportunity to become acquainted with the applicant and to observe personal characteristics and reactions that would be impossible to learn from an application form or letter. Also, the great majority of employees of a foodservice are persons relatively untrained, whose qualifications cannot be ascertained in any other way than by a personal interview and possible communications with previous employers. Documents that could be termed credentials are rarely available; therefore, the personal interview becomes of great importance in making a wise choice. In filling administrative positions, the personal interview serves as a final check on the fitness of a person whose credentials have been considered carefully.

The applicant should be treated as a person whose concern with the decision is as real and vital as that of the employing agency. The job should be discussed in relation to other positions in the foodservice to which the job might lead. Reasonable hopes for promotion should be discussed and fringe benefits should be presented. Appraisal of the job specifications in terms of the applicant's own fitness should motivate the applicant toward either self-placement or self-elimination.

The development of a successful technique in interviewing requires thought, study, and experience. Some interviewing suggestions include these *do's:*

Do's 1–16

1. Have a purpose and a plan for the interview—a guided interview pattern.
2. Have and study carefully, an analysis of the job, a job description, and a job specification.

3. Provide a private place for the interview, free from interruptions and distractions.

4. Put the applicant at ease; establish confidence and a free and easy talking situation.

5. Use the pronoun *I* very, very sparingly; *we* is much better.

6. Listen with sincere and intensive interest.

7. Do ask questions beginning with *what, why,* and *how*. Useful phrases to keep in mind are:
   Would you give me an example?
   For instance . . .
   In what way . . .
   Suppose . . .

8. Do safeguard personal confidences.

9. Do strive to learn not only what the applicant thinks and feels, but *why the applicant thinks and feels that way*.

10. Do be pleasant and courteous.

11. Do strive to be a good sounding board or mirror for the applicant's expressions of attitudes, feelings, and ideas.

12. Do ask questions that encourage self-analysis.

13. Do prod, search, and dig courteously for all the facts.

14. Maintain an attitude of friendly interest in the applicant. Make a friend and a customer even though you do not hire the applicant.

15. Do make notes for record purposes either during or after the interview.

16. Do, immediately after the interview, write a summary on the interview form in the space provided.

Suggestions of things to avoid in interviewing include these:

Don'ts 1-15

1. Do not interrupt the applicant.

2. *Do not talk too much.* Talkative interviews usually are failures.

3. Do not rush the interview. This is not only discourteous, but it results in failure of the interview.

4. Do not ask leading questions. If the question is so worded that the answer you want is apparent to the applicant, you are actually interviewing yourself.

5. Do not ask questions that demand only a yes or no response.

6. Do not merely talk when the applicant has finished a statement. Use such responses as "I see," "I think I understand," or "What else can you add to that statement?"

7. Do not agree and do not disagree. Be interested but noncommittal.

8. Do not argue, or else the interview is finished.

9. Do not lose control of self or the interview.

10. Do not get in a rut. Do not leave any impression with the applicant that the interview is routine and perfunctory.

11. Do not "talk down."

12. Do not express or imply authority. The good employment interview is a free and easy exchange of attitudes and ideas between equals.

13. Do not jump to conclusions. The purpose of the interview is to get information. Appraisal and conclusions will come *after* the interview.

14. Do not preach or moralize. This is not the purpose of the interview.

15. Do not interview when either you or the applicant is upset.

TESTS   Impressions of the prospective employee gained in the interview and from the follow-up of references are admittedly incomplete. They may be checked or replaced by tests of various types, the most common being intelligence, trade, and aptitude. A number of companies, including foodservices, have improved the results of their selection decisions by the use of psychological tests. These companies have found the benefits derived from psychological testing far exceed the costs. An applicant's probable tenure, customer relations, work values, and safety record may be predicted with such tests. In order to be considered legal, all psychological test questions must be job-related and legal to ask. In addition, all applicants must be asked the same questions, and scoring methods must be the same for all applicants.

The physical fitness of an applicant for a foodservice appointment is highly important. A health examination should be required of all foodservice workers. Only physically fit persons can do their best work. Quite as important is the need for assurance that the individual presents no health hazard to the foodservice. Managers are well aware of the devastation that might result from the inadvertent employment of a person with a communicable disease.

The Worker on the Job

Personnel Records

After an agreement on employment terms has been reached, a record of appointment is made. This becomes the nucleus of the records of the activity and progress of the worker within the organization. Records may be kept on data-processing cards, in card files, or in looseleaf form. Included among the items listed on the forms are name, address, name of spouse, number of children, other dependents, educational background, former employment (including company and length of time), date of hiring, job assigned, wage rate, whether or not meals are included, absences with reasons, adjustments in work and wages, promotions, demotions, or transfers with reasons, and information concerning insurance and health benefits. Such complete records are useful in indicating the sense of responsibility and the serious intent of employees, and as a basis for merit ratings, salary adjustments, or other benefits.

Orientation

The induction of the newly employed worker to the job is a most important phase of staffing. Smith (1984) outlines 10 steps to be included in an orientation program that is designed to challenge the new employee's interest and elicit support for the goals and objectives of the company.

1. *Introduction to the company.* Introductions are simply a matter of identifying the company, where it has been, and where it is going. The key is to make the new employee feel good about the company and begin to instill the pride of belonging, being a part of the company.

2. *Review of important policy and practice.* Policy review will vary from company to company, but certainly must include standards of conduct and performance, and an introductory (probation) period of employment, a discipline policy, and a safety policy.

3. *Review of benefits and services.* A review of benefits is crucial. It is not as important to sell a benefits program and all its virtues as it is to communicate what is provided and at what expense. Employees need to appreciate the cost of benefits, and the interviewer should be able to relate the percentage of payroll spent on their behalf. In addition, discuss services that the employee might not construe as a benefit, such as a credit union, parking, food, medical care, discounts, and social-recreational services.

4. *Benefit plan enrollment.* Complete necessary benefit enrollment forms with assistance and with the assurance that the employee understands his or her options. Provisions should be made to allow the employee to discuss plan options with a spouse before making a commitment.

5. *Completion of employment documents.* Payroll withholding, emergency information, picture releases, employment agreements, equal employment opportunity data, and other relevant and appropriate documents must be completed.

6. *Review of employer expectations.* This deals with employer–employee relationships. Discuss teamwork, working relationships, attitude, and loyalty. A performance appraisal form makes a good topical outline for a discussion of employer expectations.

7. *Setting of employee expectations.* If employees meet company expectations, what can they expect from the company? Training and development, scheduled wage and salary reviews, security, recognition, working conditions, opportunity for advancement, educational assistance programs, counseling, grievance procedures, and other relevant and appropriate expectations should be detailed.

8. *Introduction to fellow workers.* Introduce people a few at a time to let the names be assimilated. Use of name tags is helpful and so is the buddy system. Assign someone to be mentor to the new employees, to introduce them around, take them to break periods, have lunch with them. A few days is usually enough introduction time.

9. *Introduction to facilities.* Take a standard tour of the facility. This is more effective if you break it into several tours. The first day tour the immediate work area and then expand the tour on subsequent days until the facility is covered.

10. *Introduction to the job.* Have your training program in place. Be prepared and ready to get the employee immediately involved in the work flow. (p. 48)

Training

After the individual worker has been properly introduced to the job, there still remains the need for training through qualified supervision, especially in the initial period of employment. Familiarity with established operational policies and procedures, presented by management in a well-organized manner, can do much to encourage the new worker and help in gaining self-confidence. Generally, advantages of a good training program include reduction in labor turnover, absenteeism, accidents, and production costs, and an increase in the maintenance of morale, job satisfaction, and efficient production at high levels.

The first step in establishing a training program is to decide when training is needed. Next, determine exactly what needs to be taught and who should receive that training. Goals should be established for the program and an outline developed containing the steps required to help meet those goals.

ADULT TRAINING   The unique characteristics of adults as learners must be considered when planning for on-the-job training. Children learn for the future and in order to advance to the next level of learning. Adults, however, learn for immediate application or to solve a present problem. For this reason, they require practical results from the learning experience. Other distinguishing characteristics of the adult learner are a reduced tolerance for disrespectful treatment, the preference for helping to plan and conduct one's own learning experiences, and a broader base of life experiences to bring to the learning activity.

GROUP TRAINING   Often training can be given efficiently and economically through group instruction. This type of teaching saves time for the instructor and the worker, and also has the advantage of affording the stimulus that comes as the result of group participation. In a foodservice, basic group instruction concerning the policies of management is practical and valuable. Among the areas that might be included are the history and objectives of the organization, relationships of departments and key persons within the particular department, the operational budget as it affects the workers, the preparation and service of food, the sanitation and safety program, and the principles and values of work improvement programs.

Perhaps the most important psychological principle of group training is the use of well-prepared teachers instead of a fellow worker who may have had successful experience in a limited area. Often the stimulation and the inspiration given to the employee by an able instructor are highly motivating and more important in the development of the individual worker than the immediate mastery of routine skills. Tools found to be of value in such an instructional program are audio and visual aids, including films and television, illustrative material, such as posters, charts, and cartoons, and demonstrations in which both the instructor and the employees participate. Spending time and money merely showing films in group training classes is wasteful unless the workers have been alerted to the points of emphasis, time allowed for discussion after the presentation, and follow-up through application on the job. Other psychological principles of group education cannot be considered here, although they should be understood by those in charge of such programs.

ON-THE-JOB TRAINING   Some large foodservice organizations have inaugurated rather extensive programs to provide on-the-job training of employees, with highly satisfactory results. Important objectives of such programs are: (1) to reduce time spent in perfecting skills for the production and service of attractive, wholesome food of high quality at reasonable cost; (2) to avoid accidents and damage to property and equipment; and (3) to promote good understanding and close working relationships among employees and supervisors. In these programs, emphasis is given to certain requirements common to all good job instruction, such as job knowledge, manipulative skills, human relations, adaptability, and ability to express oneself. These requirements are necessary for the instructor to be an effective teacher, able to do an effective job of instruction.

Teacher preparation for instruction to be given on the job and teaching steps include, first, to prepare to instruct:

1. Break down the job—list principal steps, pick out the key points.
2. Have a timetable—how much skill you expect your pupil to have and how soon.

3. Have everything ready—the right tools, equipment, and materials.

4. Have the workplace properly arranged—just as the worker will be expected to keep it.

And second, to instruct:

1. *Prepare the worker.* Put the worker at ease. A frightened or embarrassed person cannot learn. Find out what is already known about the job. Begin where knowledge ends. Interest the worker in learning the job. Place the worker in the correct position so that the job won't be viewed from the wrong direction.

2. *Present the operation.* Tell, show, illustrate, and question carefully and patiently. Stress key points. Make them clear. Instruct slowly, clearly, and completely, taking up one point at a time, but no more than the trainee can master. Work first for accuracy, then for speed.

3. *Try out the worker's performance.* Test by having the worker perform the job under observation. Have the worker tell and show you, and explain key points. Ask questions and correct errors patiently. Continue until you know the worker knows.

4. *Follow up the worker's performance.* Let the worker perform alone. Check frequently, but do not take over if you can give the help needed. Designate to whom the worker goes for help. Encourage questions. Get the worker to look for key points as progress is made. Taper off extra coaching and close follow-up until the worker is able to work under usual supervision. Give credit where credit is due.

A job breakdown is the analysis of a job to be taught and a listing of the elemental steps of what to do and the key points of how to do them. This serves as a guide in giving instruction so that none of the necessary points will be omitted. Fig. 11.2 is an example of a job breakdown for making change. There should be a job breakdown for every task and/or job to be performed in the organization.

Slide-tape programs for individual instruction in work methods and procedures have proven to be satisfactory, and although it is time-consuming to prepare such a program, the results appear to justify their use. Slides showing correct techniques are accomplished by oral examinations on tape. For techniques involving motion or rhythm, videotaping may be helpful.

Encouragement of the worker by the supervisor during the first days on the job and during the training period is important in stabilizing interest and sustaining a sense of adequacy. Informal interviews may serve as a means of determining areas in which help is needed, as well as those in which ability is most marked. Every expression of friendly, courteous interest is appreciated by the worker and aids in a successful adjustment to the new environment.

Job: Making Change
_____

Equipment and Supplies   Money and Cash Register
_____

Important Steps	*Key Points*
REGISTER FIRST—WRAP AFTERWARDS	
1. Accepts money from customer.	1. State amount of sale* "out of" amount received from customer.
2. Place customer's money on plate.	2. Stand in front of cash register. Do not put bill in drawer until after change has been counted.
3. Record the sale on cash register.	3. Check amount of change recorded on viewer.
4. Count change from till.	4. Begin with amount of sale picking up smallest change first up to amount received from customer.
5. Count change carefully to customer.	5. Start with amount of sale—stop counting when amount is the same as the customer gave.
6. Place customer's money in till.	6. Close the drawer immediately.
7. Deliver change, receipt or sales slip, and merchandise to customer.	7. Say *Thank You.* Let customer know you mean it.
*Including tax (state and federal).	

Figure 11.2.   Job breakdown for making change at the cash register. Important steps are "what to do"; key points are "how to do."

In addition to the satisfaction attained by establishing pleasant employer–employee relations, the right induction of the new worker has a dollar-and-cents value that cannot be overlooked. An employee who is unhappy, disinterested, and discontented will tend to look for placement elsewhere after a short experience with the company. Then all the money, time, and effort spent in obtaining and introducing the employee to the job will have been lost, and a similar expenditure must be made before another worker can be assigned the task.

Training budgets have been steadily increasing in restaurants, hotels, and fast-food operations because industry experts see employee training as a solution not only to increased turnover, but also as a way to solve other current problems. Among employees and in business, decreased productivity and intense competition have been the stimulants for training programs that are both intensive and progressive.

Performance Appraisal

For maximum effectiveness from the work force, every employee should know what is expected and how he or she is performing on the job. Workers are entitled to commendation for work well done and to the opportunity to earn greater responsibility, either with or without increased remuneration. One of the responsibilities of management and supervision is the performance appraisal. Management then has an obligation to communicate this information to each worker regarding individual progress. The personal development of and efficient production by each worker is of concern to management, but an individual worker cannot be expected to improve if evaluations are not made known or counsel is not made available for assistance. Performance appraisals are used to determine job competence, need for additional training or counseling, and to review the employee's progress within the organization. Ratings made objectively and without prejudice furnish valuable information that can be used in job placement, training, supervision, promotion, replacement, and future recommendations. Careful selection and placement and proper training of employees are prerequisites to a successful evaluation program. The performance appraisal may be accomplished by several methods, including rating scales, checklists, narrative evaluation, personal conferences, and management by objectives.

There are few, if any, objective standards that can be used for measuring subjective personal characteristics such as character, reliability, and initiative. Yet these traits, as they relate to the capabilities, efficiency, and development of each employee, are important to an organization. Such characteristics must be appraised in some way if management is to have an intelligent basis for classifying workers according to rank or grade and, thus, help to provide a standard for salary increases, promotions, transfers, or placement into a job for which the worker is well-suited.

Rating procedures have been developed that provide a measurement of the degree to which certain intangible personality traits are present in workers and in their performance on the job. Care should be taken to design the scale to meet the objective desired. Will this estimate of the relative worth of employees be used as a basis for rewards or recognitions or as a tool for explaining to workers why they may or may not be making progress on the job? In the hands of competent administrators, the rating form could be designed to obtain information to accomplish both purposes.

Distinguishable personal traits most likely to affect performance are honesty, initiative, judgment, and ability to get along with other workers. Examples of qualities on a rating chart are: quality of work, quantity of work, adaptability, job knowledge, and dependability.

These so-called rating scales, from which the variously known merit, progress, development, or service ratings are derived, are not new in industrial management, although few are directly applicable to foodservices. Some administrators prefer a system of gradation checking where each quality, factor, or characteristic may be marked on a scale ranging from poor to superior, or the reverse, with two or three possible levels within each grade. For example:

Another format might describe the grade for each factor listed.

Fig. 11.3 is an example of a rating scale with definitions of the various factors attached for use of the rater. Fig. 11.4 shows one of a different format.

The critical-incident appraisal method requires that supervisors identify behaviors that are indicators of excellent and poor performance. Throughout the rating period, records are kept of such critical incidents for each employee. These records are then compared to the previously identified indicators of performance appraisal.

Combining both the rating scale and critical-incident methods led to the behaviorally anchored rating scale (BARS) method of performance appraisal. BARS is generally considered the best and most effective means of appraisal. The disadvantage of this method is that the scales are difficult and time-consuming to develop. An example of a BARS rating scale is shown in Fig. 11.5. Specific behaviors are identified for each performance level for each job category. Employees are then rated according to the scale developed.

One of the original purposes of management by objectives (MBO) was to simplify and overcome the limitations of the more traditional performance appraisal. This approach emphasizes the setting of measurable performance goals that are mutually agreed on by the employee and the immediate supervisor. At stated intervals, the employee's progress toward the goals is assessed by the employee and the superior. Participation by employees in the performance appraisal process has resulted in favorable perceptions regarding the performance appraisal interview as well as positive performance outcomes.

Regardless of the rating systems selected, the person making the ratings should be well-qualified for the responsibility of evaluating people. Usually the immediate supervisor is in a position to do the best job, since this person can observe activities continuously. However, adequate instructions are needed as to the purpose and values of the program so that follow-through with assistance is provided when needed. Also, a thorough explanation and understanding of the factors to be rated is necessary to avoid misinterpretation of the forms or to

EMPLOYEE PERFORMANCE REVIEW RATING

NAME _____ DATE_____

PRESENT JOB _____ DEPARTMENT_____

PAY RANGE _____ TO _____

CURRENT RATE _____ NEW RATE _____

REVIEW PERIOD FROM _____ TO_____
                            Date   Date

REASON
FOR REVIEW: ☐ PROBATIONARY ☐ ANNUAL ☐ SPECIAL _____
                                                 Explain

Date to be returned to Personnel Department _____

PART I
The purpose of the Employee Performance Review is twofold.

    1. To identify the areas in which the employee is proficient, to encourage more effective utilization of known and demonstrated strengths, and to apply these proficiencies to the best advantage in accomplishing the objectives of the job and the department.

    2. To identify areas in which improvement is desirable and to assist the employee to plan and execute a program of study, practice and/or discipline to develop total competency in the job.

It is the responsibility of the employee's supervisor to do the utmost to see that these purposes are accomplished. With this in mind, make every effort to state your comments so that they are constructive and positive.

It is important to remember that a rating of "Successful Performance" represents the performance level of a fully competent employee who is successfully performing all job duties and responsibilities and is doing a good job. Performance levels either above or below "Successful Performance" should be fully documented in Part II with regard to what was done to merit the rating given.

Indicate your evaluation of the employee's performance on each of the factors below by placing a (✔) at the proper place on each scale.

For your convenience the midpoint on the rating scale has been indicated *but* it is important to remember that the evaluations criteria have been weighted. Therefore, the relationship between the score checked on the rating scale and the amount of the merit increase is minimal (a score of 5 on the rating scale does not mean a 5 percent increase).

KNOWLEDGE OF WORK. Consider the knowledge and understanding the employee has regarding the job. Does the employee know the methods or techniques to be used? Does the employee know the reasons for the procedure to be followed? Does the employee know the purpose of the job and what is required to be accomplished and how it contributes to the objectives of the department?

Figure 11.3. Scale for review of employee performance. (Courtesy, Lincoln General Hospital, Lincoln, Nebraska.)

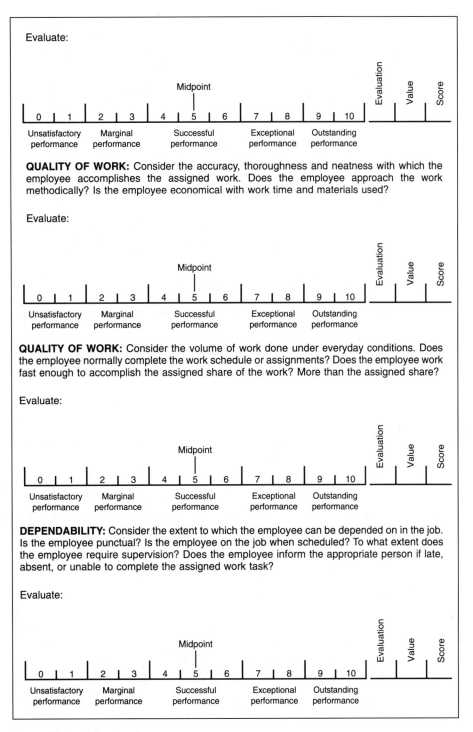

Evaluate:

QUALITY OF WORK: Consider the accuracy, thoroughness and neatness with which the employee accomplishes the assigned work. Does the employee approach the work methodically? Is the employee economical with work time and materials used?

Evaluate:

QUALITY OF WORK: Consider the volume of work done under everyday conditions. Does the employee normally complete the work schedule or assignments? Does the employee work fast enough to accomplish the assigned share of the work? More than the assigned share?

Evaluate:

DEPENDABILITY: Consider the extent to which the employee can be depended on in the job. Is the employee punctual? Is the employee on the job when scheduled? To what extent does the employee require supervision? Does the employee inform the appropriate person if late, absent, or unable to complete the assigned work task?

Evaluate:

Figure 11.3. (*Continued*)

COMPATIBILITY: Consider the extent to which the employee's attitude toward the work, the responsible supervisor, and the hospital are compatible with the objectives of the hospital. Is the employee cooperative, easy to work with? Is the employee's attitude toward patients and fellow employees friendly and cooperative? Where contacts outside the hospital are required in fulfilling job responsibilities, does the employee represent the hospital with confidence and discretion? Does the employee conform to the personal grooming standards?

Evaluate:

INITIATIVE: Consider how well the employee applies the knowledge of work. Is the employee a self-starter who makes frequent practical suggestions? Does the employee proceed on assigned work voluntarily and readily accept suggestions? How much does the employee rely on others in getting started on assigned work? How effectively does the employee share acquired skills with others?

Evaluate:

SAFETY: Consider the extent to which the employee is aware of unsafe practices and conditions in the work setting. Is the employee quick to sense possible hazards and then to take the appropriate steps to get them corrected? How careful is the employee insofar as safe work practices are concerned with regard to regular work assignments? Does the employee always follow the established work procedure for assigned tasks?

Evaluate:

Figure 11.3. (*Continued*)

Total Score (%)_____
(Maximum = 10.0 or 10%)

General Comments:_____

_____

_____

_____

_____

PART II
The purpose of this section is to present the employee a well-conceived and workable program for:
1. Optimum application of known and demonstrated strengths and;
2. Study, practice, and/or discipline to develop competency in the areas requiring improvement. Be specific. Formulate benchmarks, attainable objectives so that the employee can recognize accomplishment and be aware of growth.

Knowledge of Work:_____

_____

_____

_____

Quality of work:_____

_____

_____

_____

_____

Quantity of work:_____

_____

_____

_____

_____

Dependability:_____

_____

_____

_____

_____

Compatibility:_____

_____

_____

_____

_____

Figure 11.3.   (*Continued*)

Initiative:_____

_____

_____

_____

_____

Safety:_____

_____

_____

_____

_____

Prepared by _____ _____ _____
                Name   Title   Date

Department head_____ _____
                            Name   Date

FOR EMPLOYEE: My signature on this form indicates that I have reviewed my performance evaluation as presented on this form and a copy has been given to me.

For Probationary Rating ONLY
Recommended for:

☐ Permanent Status
☐ Extension of Probation

_____

Signature   Date   ☐ Termination

Figure 11.3. (*Continued*)

Associate Rating Form: Kitchen Worker

1. *Job Skill* (Max. points: 25)

   Consider job performance and skill. Does the worker keep up with the work and keep the station clean; make all products uniformly, waste conscious, and economical; work quietly and reasonably fast; refrain from visiting with fellow associates while on duty?

Excellent	25
Good	20
Average	15
Fair	10
Poor	5

2. *Cooperation* (Max. points: 25)

   Consider attitude. Does the worker respond quickly to a call for assistance from a fellow associate? Have a spirit of willingness? Receptive to change and new ideas? Accept new suggestions regarding his/her work?

Excellent	25
Good	20
Average	15
Fair	10
Poor	5

3. *Sanitation* (Max. points: 10)

   Consider health regulations: "No Smoking — Wash Hands When Leaving Rest Rooms." Does worker keep: paper, trash, liquids, vegetable leaves, and other foreign materials off floor, hot foods hot, and other food under refrigeration?

Excellent	10
Good	8
Average	6
Fair	4
Poor	2

4. *Care of equipment* (Max. points: 10)

   Does worker keep equipment clean and everything returned to proper place, know correct way to operate ovens, steamers, mixers, and other appliances?

Excellent	10
Good	8
Average	6
Fair	4
Poor	2

5. *Safety* (Max. points: 10)

   Does worker work safely and is worker safety conscious? Correct or report all hazards that may cause an accident? Know whereabouts of fire extinguisher and how to use it?

Excellent	10
Good	8
Average	6
Fair	4
Poor	2

6. *Appearance* (Max. points: 10)

   Consider personal cleanliness and neatness. Does worker seem to enjoy the work? Is he/she clean of body? Are clothes clean and appropriate?

Excellent	10
Good	8
Average	6
Fair	4
Poor	2

7. *Attendance* (Max. points: 10)

   Consider regular daily attendance and promptness. Does worker return from 10 minute breaks and meal periods on time?

Excellent	10
Good	8
Average	6
Fair	4
Poor	2

Figure 11.4. An example of a rating form designed for evaluating a kitchen worker. Comparable forms could be made applicable for each classification of worker.

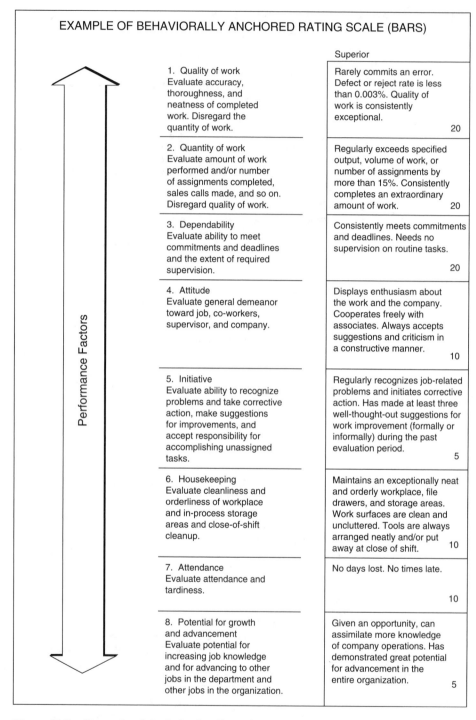

Figure 11.5. Example of the behaviorally anchored rating scale (BARS). (Source: Bittel, L. R. and Newstom, J. W.: *What Every Supervisor Should Know*, 6th ed. New York: McGraw-Hill, © 1990, pp. 189–190. Reproduced with permission of McGraw-Hill.)

Very good	At expected level	Below expected level	Unsatisfactory
Makes only an occasional error. Defect or reject rate is consistently less than 0.010%. Quality of work is high grade, but not exceptional. 16	Errors are only occasionally troublesome. Defects or reject rate rarely exceeds standard of 0.010%. Quality of work is average. 12	Errors are frequently troublesome. Defect or reject rate often exceeds standard of 0.010%. Quality of work is below average. 8	Errors are frequently troublesome. Defect or reject rate regularly exceeds standard of 0.010%. Quality of work is unsatisfactory. 4
Regularly exceeds specified output, volume of work, or number of assignments. Consistently turns out a good volume of work. 16	Usually meets the specified output, volume of work, or number of assignments. Amount of work completed is about average for this job. 12	Often fails to meet specified output, volume of work, or number of assignments. Amount of work completed is about 10% less than average for this job. 8	Regularly fails to meet specified output, volume of work, or number of assignments. Amount of work is almost always greater than 11% less than average for this job. 4
Meets commitments and deadlines 95% or more of the time. Needs minimum supervision on routine tasks. 16	Meets commitments and deadlines 90% or more of the time. Needs occasional supervision on routine tasks. 12	Meets commitments and deadlines less than 85 to 90% of the time. Needs constant checking, even on routine tasks. 8	Meets commitments and deadlines less than 95% of the time. Work and progress must be checked all the time. 4
Appears to be happy at his or her work. Cooperates freely with associates. Usually accepts suggestions or criticism in a constructive manner. 8	Accepts most assignments without complaint. Cooperates with associates when requested to do so. Follows instructions. 6	Frequently questions suitability of assignments. Complains regularly about the nature of the work. Cooperates with associates when requested to do so. Often rejects suggestions or criticism. 4	Constantly complains about the work and the company. Regularly voices objection to assignments. Does not cooperate with co-workers. Is always negative toward suggestions and criticism. 2
Usually recognizes job-related problems and initiates corrective action. Has made at least one well-thought-out suggestion for work improvement during the past evaluation period. 4	Occasionally recognizes and acts upon job-related problems. Occasionally makes well-thought-out suggestions for work improvement. 3	Fails to recognize job-related problems or to initiate action to correct them. Usually waits to be told what to do. 2	Fails to recognize job-related problems or to initiate action to correct them. Always needs to be told what to do. Never displays any kind of initiative. 1
Maintains a neat and orderly workplace, file drawers, and storage areas. Work surfaces are usually clean and uncluttered. Tools are put away at close of shift. 8	Maintains a reasonably neat and clean workplace. Work surfaces are acceptably free from soil or debris that would interfere with work. Only occasionally does not put tools away. 6	Often fails to maintain a reasonably neat and clean workplace. Work surfaces are often cluttered and not conducive to quality craft. Often fails to put tools away. 4	Consistently fails to maintain a neat and clean workplace. More often than not, fails to clean up or put tools away at close of shift. 2
1 to 2 days out sick, or 1 day absent of own accord, or 1 time late. 8	2 to 3 days out sick, or 2 days absent of own accord, or 2 times late. 6	3 to 5 days out sick, or 3 days absent of own accord, or 3 times late. 4	More than 5 days out sick, or more than 3 days absent of own accord, or more than 3 times late. 2
Given an opportunity, can assimilate more knowledge of company operations. Has demonstrated good potential for advancement in the department. 4	Has pretty much acquired as much knowledge here as he or she can assimilate. Has demonstrated some potential for advancement in the department. 3	Has difficulty in acquiring knowledge and skills here. Has demonstrated only limited potential for advancement. 2	Has great difficulty in acquiring knowledge and skills here. Has demonstrated no potential for advancement here. 1

Figure 11.5. (*Continued*)

avoid failure to meet the intended standards. The person who is charged with the responsibility of rating employees must be able to be objective and evaluate individuals in terms of the factors to be rated, to be guided by the pattern of performance instead of isolated happenings, to communicate fairly and accurately what is observed, and to be consistent from one time to the next. These are prime requisites of the rater.

An interview is a vitally important part of the performance appraisal process. The purpose of the interview is to provide information and set goals. It should be scheduled in advance and both employee and supervisor should be prepared. The proper atmosphere for two-way communication must be established. The supervisor should begin with a statement of purpose and then encourage the employee to participate in the dialogue. Total performance, both positive and negative, should be discussed. The evaluation stage of the interview should conclude with a summary and documentation of the interview for the employee's file. In the second stage of the interview, the emphasis should be on setting mutual goals, including personal growth and formulating follow-up procedures. The employee should never be left in doubt of the rating given, or of what must be done to change or improve if there is need to do so.

A relatively new trend that has been gathering momentum is the implementation of upward feedback performance appraisals, in which employees rate their bosses' people management skills. Upward feedback performance appraisals have proven to be valuable tools for the improvement of management performance and subordinates' morale. They provide employees with an opportunity to have a say in how they are supervised.

Promotions and Transfers

On the basis of sound ratings by members of staff, the foodservice manager is fairly able to predict the probable future development of various members of the organization. In the application of a rating scale, one group may rate high. This scale helps to identify the people deserving the stimulus and encouragement of promotion. The term *promotion* commonly implies an increase in responsibility and salary. Sometimes promotion carries only the opportunity for experience in a desired field. It may mean shorter hours and greater assurance of security. Regardless of the nature of the promotion, it is an expression of appreciation of an individual's worth. The skills matrix system described in Chapter 10 may be used as part of a personal development planning system that affords employees the opportunity to plan their own professional growth and self-marketing within the company.

Often a worker found unfit for one job may do well in another. The apparent lack of fitness may arise in the supervisory relationship or in contacts with coworkers. Personal prejudice against a particular type of work or physical inability to do the job may be the cause. In some cases, a minor shift may enable the worker to become a contented and valuable employee. Transfer of an employee who is not finding satisfaction in the current job to another opening within the organization offering a different challenge or opportunity has salvaged many workers. Different jobs may present wide variation in skill requirements, which makes possible the transfer of workers if necessary. Relative levels of difficulty should be considered in placement and in replacement. Continued training of the employee in this new position is critical to the success of a relocated worker.

Discipline

Discipline is required when other measures have failed to make sure that workers perform according to accepted standards. Leadership must first ensure that work rules are clear, reasonable, fair, reviewed regularly, and consistent with the collective bargaining agreement. Rules must be disseminated to employees orally and posted in a visible location. And they must be enforced promptly, consistently, and without discrimination. Leadership must set a good example by complying with all rules and requirements.

Any disciplinary action must be undertaken with sensitivity and sound judgment. The supervisor should first thoroughly investigate what happened and why. As a general rule, disciplinary action should be taken in private. Personnel policies usually fit the severity of the penalty to the severity of the infraction, with the steps in progressive discipline ranging anywhere from an informal talk, an oral warning or reprimand, a written or official warning, a disciplinary layoff, a demotion or transfer, to a discharge.

As an aid to supervisors, Metzger proposed the "hot stove" analogy to disciplinary action. Experiencing discipline should be like touching a hot stove. The burn gives advance warning, is immediate, consistent, and impersonal. Advance warning—everyone knows what will happen if you touch a hot stove. Employees should know what is expected of them. Immediate—the burn is immediate. Discipline should not be hasty, but should be taken as soon as possible after the infraction. Consistent—the hot stove burns every time. Disciplinary action should be taken every time an infraction occurs. Impersonal—whoever touches the stove is burned. The act not the person should be disciplined. After disciplinary action, the employee should be treated as before.

Dismissals

If employee is terminated without the consent of the employee, the act is termed dismissal. An individual may be discharged because of failure to perform assigned duties, but this should be the final step and should follow counseling, warning, or possibly disciplinary layoff. Each person discharged from a foodservice should be given a terminal or "exit" interview in which strong points are recognized and the reasons for dismissal are dispassionately reviewed. If the situation merits that the employee be recommended for another position, aid should be given in the placement problem. In any event, the discharged employee should not leave the service without having had a chance to speak regarding the dismissal and without being made aware, if possible, of the fair deal given by the supervisor.

Opinions differ regarding the discussion of a dismissal with other employees. If there is a possibility that the incident may foster a sense of insecurity among the group, a presentation of the facts, not necessarily full and complete, may be desirable from the standpoint of group morale. Often, employees understand far more of such situations than the director believes.

Supervision

Supervision encompasses coordinating and directing the work of employees to accomplish the organization's goals. In small foodservice systems, the total supervisory function may be the responsibility of the manager. In larger systems, the supervision of the day-to-day technical operations may be delegated to foodservice supervisors, dietetic technicians, or cook-managers. The manager is thus able to concentrate on planning, policy and goal setting, and interdepartment relationships, and on solving overall problems of the department. In a large department, the director, chief dietitian, or other administrator may delegate these management functions in part to other professionally trained staff.

When responsibility and authority are delegated, management must provide guidance so that the supervisor understands the limits of authority; that is, what decisions can be made without consultation and what actions can be taken on one's own. Management has a responsibility for training supervisors so that they can solve problems and meet emergencies.

The supervisor represents both management and employees. In a foodservice unit, as with industry in general, the supervisor is one of the key persons in the organization. The supervisor is the one to whom the employees look as a representative of management, whereas to management the supervisor represents the working force. Both groups, therefore, are interested in the quality of the supervision as represented by this staff member. The supervisor must be able to: (1) interpret the objectives and policies of the company to the employees in such a way as to encourage their cooperation and elicit their confidence, and (2) inspire and lead employees as evidenced through fair and intelligent dealings with them and through the personnel program.

Throughout an employee's term of service, supervision should play a large part in relating the employee to the task and to coworkers. When the probation period is past and the employee is regarded as a member of the permanent staff, familiar with the task and able in its performance, supervision is still necessary to maintain interest and provide for personal growth. To a large extent, recognition and approbation by superiors remain potent incentives to the average worker. The supervisor must accept the responsibility of finding and using incentives that lead to sound development. Adjustments in work assignments to meet changes in the individual's abilities and interests are wisely made only when supervision is adequate, both in kind and amount.

ROUTINE SUPERVISION   Routine supervision varies with the situation, but it is, for the most part, a matter of personal contact reinforced through checking by observations, records, and charts. Routine supervision may consist of greeting employees each day by name; checking for cleanliness, appearance, and state of health; checking menus and work schedules; making work assignments; explaining to employees any instruction they seem not to understand; checking continuously for quality and quantity of production and service; inspecting for sanitation of work areas and equipment; and, in general, maintaining good working conditions. The supervision of personnel is too often left to chance or to the "free time" that never seems a part of the foodservice manager's busy day. To avoid the hit-and-miss contact with employees, the wise supervisor sets aside a certain time each day for checking on the work in progress and for stimulating interest and cooperation in the individual and in the group. Schedules are needed for checking daily, weekly, and periodic jobs. Checking at the end of the day to see that the work as scheduled has been carried out completes the "routine" supervision.

Decision Making

Much of the supervisor's time is spent in making decisions and solving problems. Decision making can be thought of as the generic process, whereas problem solving is one type of decision making that applies to a specific situation.

The ability to make decisions in a timely and logical manner is an important skill for supervisors to possess. Better decisions are likely to be made when a number of steps are followed in the proper sequence. These are: (1) define the problem—nothing is as useless as the right answer to the wrong question, (2) analyze the problem, (3) develop many alternatives—brainstorm and then think them through considering the consequences of each, (4) choose the alternative with the most positive consequences and the least negative consequences, and (5) follow-up and appraise the decision.

Handling Grievances

The wise supervisor gives active supervision; that is, the wise supervisor does not sit at a desk waiting for employees to come with problems. The wise supervisor foresees and is prepared to meet possible difficulties instead of merely waiting for something unpleasant to happen. Grievances are not always expressed in verbal or written form. Supervisors should be alert for symptoms of unexpressed dissatisfaction such as excessive tardiness or absenteeism, decline in quantity or quality of work, change in attitude, or indifference.

Many grievances can be settled by the supervisor and employee on an informal basis. If the employees are unionized, the contract includes formal grievance procedures, which usually include presentation of the grievance in writing (see Fig. 11.6) and an attempt to settle the dispute at the first-line supervisory level. If this is not possible, the grievance moves through higher levels of authority until settled.

Staff Conferences

Regular staff conferences, department meetings, and the use of rating scales are all valuable in personnel direction. Continued effort to relate workers to their tasks and to the organization as a whole is often expressed in conferences scheduled at regular intervals by the supervisor. At these conferences, points of general interest are presented and suggestions for improvement of the foodservice are exchanged. Knotty problems, such as waste, breakage, and low productivity, that have not been mastered by direct supervisory approach can be resolved as the interest and awareness of the whole group is focused on them. Never should a staff conference be used for disciplinary action for certain members of the group. As previously stated, the adult worker, like the schoolchild, rarely benefits from public reprimand and unkind ridicule.

In addition to group contact, time should be taken by the supervisor for a talk with each individual worker at least once a week. All employees want to feel that someone is interested in them as an individual and recognizes their present and potential worth to the organization.

Labor Policies and Legislation

Policies are guides for future action. They should be broad enough to allow some variation in management decisions at all levels, yet offer guidelines for consistency in interpretation, and to commit personnel to certain predictable actions. Policies should not be confused with directives or rules. Policies are adopted to provide meaning or understanding related to a course of action; directives and rules are aimed at compliance.

LINCOLN GENERAL HOSPITAL
LINCOLN, NEBRASKA
GRIEVANCE CONTROL FORM

1. _____
   (Name)   (Position Title)   (Dept.)   (Employment Date)

   _____   _____
   (Supervisor)   (Department Head)

2. *Nature of Dissatisfaction:* (Be specific in writing up the dissatisfaction. Be sure to state who is involved, what happened, where did it occur, what were the circumstances, how did it happen, and what is the solution being sought.) _____

   _____

   _____

   _____

   _____

3. *The Final Settlement Was:* (Resolution at what step; what was the recommended solution and all other pertinent information significant to the solution.) _____

   _____

   _____

   _____

4. *Action Taken:*

*Work Days	Step	Date	Action Taken By:	Schedules Met (Yes/No)	**Work Days	Resolved (Yes/No)
2	I	_____	(Supervisor, Verbal)	_____	2	_____
2	II	_____	(Department Head, Verbal)	_____	2	_____
5	III	_____	(Grievance Committee, Written)	_____	2	_____
4	IV	_____	(Administrator, Written)	_____	2	_____

Comments: (Regarding any exceptions made at any step) _____

_____

_____

_____

*Any of the time limits specified in the procedure may be extended by mutual agreement of the parties involved.

**In the event that the employee fails to appeal the decision to the next step in the grievance procedure within two (2) working days, the employee will be deemed to have accepted the decision and waived the right to further appeal.

Figure 11.6.   Form for written record of a grievance and action taken. (Courtesy, Lincoln General Hospital, Lincoln, Nebraska.)

An important aspect of personnel management is the labor policies accepted and put in force. This is true regardless of the size of the organization. There is an old saying that when two men (or women) meet, there is a social problem; when one undertakes a task at the other's behest, there is a labor problem; and when wages are paid for this labor, there is an economic problem. The policies controlling the approach to these problems have slowly developed as civilization has grown and as the number of workers has increased. They have been formed, reformed, and revised, particularly in recent years, due to legislation enacted at federal, state, and local levels.

Policies relating to personnel are known as labor policies. Procurement policies may be related to preferred sources to be used for obtaining applicants, instruments such as tests to be used in selection, or a ratio of employees, such as women to men or minority to major racial groups to be hired. Policies for development of personnel may concern the type of training programs the company offers, whether or not fees or tuition for continuing education are paid, the amount of time to be allowed from work for personnel to attend classes or meetings, and the bases for promotions and transfers.

Those policies regarding compensation have to do with wage scales to be followed; vacation, sick leave, and holiday pay to be given; bonus or profit-sharing plans to be offered; and group insurance or other benefits that are available to the personnel.

Integration policies refer whether labor unions are recognized, the way that grievances and appeals are handled, or the degree of employee participation to be permitted in decision making.

Maintenance policies are about the services to be provided for employees' physical, mental, and emotional health. They may be related to safety measures, compensation for accidents, retirement systems, recreational programs, or other services, all of which are a part of the organizational plan.

Once policies have been developed and accepted, they should be written. The wise employer of today makes available to every worker a copy of the labor-management policies presented in a company handbook. This publication may be an impressive volume of many pages and elaborate illustrations or a few mimeographed sheets, but whatever its format, the contents should include information that the worker wants to know about the organization and that the employer wants him or her to know. Employees are not interested in cooperating as members of the team without understanding the policies, especially as these affect them. They want to know what is expected of them and to be kept informed of their accomplishments, the basis for promotion, for wage increases, fringe benefits, opportunities for steady work, and the possibilities of any seasonal layoffs.

From the standpoint of the employee, labor policies should be explicit in their provisions for a fair rate of pay, for promotions and transfers, for stabilization of employment, and for ways of keeping jobs interesting so that life does not become mere dull routine. They should offer provisions for fair disciplinary action among employees, recognition of industrial health hazards and provisions for their control, participation in the formulation of future plans and policies of the company, usually expressed by demands for collective bargaining, and certain fringe benefits.

Managers wish to have employees informed of policies about the goals and objectives for which the organization is in business, the products and services offered, the effect of high productivity as a benefit to both the employee and the company, cost-expenditure ratios and how they affect profits and resulting benefits, and the relationships desired with the public and with other departments of the organization.

There is general agreement on the list of topics that the employer has found must be covered in labor policies conducive to productive management and those desired by employees as vital to satisfactory working conditions. The ones cited by both—wages and income maintenance; hours of work; schedules and overtime provisions; security in employment, including transfers and promotions; safe and otherwise satisfactory working environment; insurance, retirement, or pension plans; equal employment opportunities; and fair employment practices and civil rights—may be regarded as the major issues in labor policies for most foodservice operations.

These topics can be grouped under four headings: wages and income maintenance, hours and schedules of work, security in employment, and employee services and benefits. Major federal legislation applicable to employment in the private sector is included as appropriate under each of the following discussions.

WAGES AND INCOME MAINTENANCE   From the point of view of the worker, the most important characteristic of the wage, the take-home pay received for labor performed, is its purchasing power. This represents the measure of the wants that the worker is able to satisfy and largely determines the adequacy of his or her standard of living, sense of financial security, and identification of self as a worthy and responsible member of the community. In the past, foodservices, like other service organizations, have tended to offer an annual wage rate below that necessary for a fair standard of living. This situation has improved as desirable policies on wages have been adopted and as state and federal laws have been enacted.

The formulation of satisfactory policies regarding wages and other income maintenance is contingent on many factors, among them: (1) the desire and intent of the company to pay fair wages to all employees and at the same time to maintain just control over labor costs; (2) recognition of the relationship between the duties and responsibilities of various jobs within the organization and the wages paid; and (3) acknowledgment of individual differences in experience, ability, and willingness to take responsibility. Management has the obligation to reflect such differences in the wage scale established for a particular job and to communicate freely with the workers on these points. Policies based on such considerations will lead to a systematic classification of jobs and wages that could be developed jointly by the employer and the employees. It would then be possible to express the value or worth of each job in terms of wages.

The application of the wage policy to kitchen and dining room personnel would lead to certain groupings, such as

1. busers, pot and pan washers, dishwashers
2. workers in preliminary or prepreparation
3. foodservice groups, including counter workers and waiters or waitresses
4. cook's assistants and second cooks; dining room host or hostess, cashiers
5. cooks, including meat, vegetable, salad, and pastry cooks
6. supervisors on the nonprofessional level

A wage differential will exist between groups. Civil service and labor unions, as well as many other organizations, have established steps within each wage level or grade so that employees who merit wage increases may be given such recognitions for superior service, although not qualified for advancement to a higher grade or job category.

The *Fair Labor Standards Act* of 1938, also known as the Federal Wage and Hour Law, was first enacted to help eliminate poverty, to create purchasing power, and to establish a wage floor that would help prevent another depression. The minimum wage set at that time was $.40 per hour! Gradually over the years, the base was increased. The act was amended in 1966, and, under new provisions, most foodservice employees were included for the first time. The minimum wage that year was $1.60, and the law included provisions for gradual increases that would continue as cost of living increased. The act applies equally to all covered workers regardless of sex, number of employees, and whether they are full- or part-time workers.

The *Equal Pay Act,* a 1963 amendment to the Fair Labor Standards Act, prohibits employers from discriminating on the basis of sex in the payment of wages for equal work for employees covered by the act. It requires employers to pay equal wages to men and women in their employ doing equal work on jobs requiring equal skill, effort, and responsibility that are performed under similar working conditions.

Another provision of the Fair Labor Standards Act of special interest to restaurant foodservice managers relates to wages for tipped employees. Tips received by an employee may be considered by the employer as part of the wages of the employee, but cannot exceed 50% of the applicable minimum rate. A "tipped" employee is a worker engaged in an occupation in which the worker customarily and regularly receives more than $30 a month in tips.

Many foodservice operations employ student workers; this is especially true in colleges and universities, schools, retirement homes, and other homes for congregate living. Minimum wage laws adopted by various states may make provision for compensation at an adjusted rate below the federal standard. Usually students who work less than 20 hours per week are not affected by provisions of such laws.

Unless specifically exempt by this law, all employees must be paid at least one and one half times the employee's regular rate of pay for all hours worked in excess of 40 hours in a work week of 7 days. Extra pay is not required for Saturday, Sunday, holiday, or vacation work.

All foodservice managers should become familiar with the state and federal laws regulating minimum wages for their various classifications of employees. Information may be obtained from the nearest office of the Wage and Hour Division of the U.S. Department of Labor.

Unemployment compensation is another piece of federal legislation that, in addition to regular pay for work on the job, partially assures income maintenance. This nationwide system of insurance to protect wage earners and their families against loss of income because of unemployment was first established under the Social Security Act of 1935. The purpose of this insurance is to provide workers with a weekly income to tide them over during periods of unemployment between jobs. Persons covered must have been employed for a specific period of time on a job covered by the law, who are able and willing to work, and who are unemployed through no fault of their own.

Unemployment insurance is a joint federal-state program, operated by the states with the assistance of the U.S. Department of Labor. Each state has its own specific requirements and benefits. Basically, employers pay a tax based on their payrolls. Benefits to unemployed workers are paid out of the fund built up from these taxes. In most states, firms employing three or four or more workers for 20 weeks throughout the year must participate. Each state law specifies conditions under which workers may receive benefits, the amount they receive, and the number of weeks they may draw benefits. In most states, the employer alone contributes to this fund; in only a few do employees make payment to it. Thus, unemployment compensation is an added payroll cost for many foodservice managers and an added benefit to the employees.

HOURS AND SCHEDULES OF WORK   The 40-hour work week established under the Minimum Wage and Hour Law is generally in use throughout the United States. Some organizations have adopted a 37½- or a 35-hour week. Time worked beyond 40 hours in a 7-day or 80 hours in a 14-day period (in hospitals or other facilities that care for the sick, elderly, or persons with mental illness) as specified under the law requires extra compensation, as previously noted.

The schedule of specific hours of the day when each employee is to be on duty should be carefully considered by all foodservice managers. As discussed, many different factors enter into the planning of satisfactory schedules. Employers have a responsibility for scheduling their employees so that their time at work is as needed and is used to their best advantage in order to help control labor costs. Split shifts are almost a thing of the past; straight shifts are usually preferred. An 8-hour day, 5 days a week is common practice also. However, some organizations have experimented with variations, notably a 10-hour day and 4-day week to allow a 3-day off-duty period for the employees and a 12-hour day, 3-day week. Most foodservice organizations have not found this scheduling practical because of the nature of the work to be done.

In addition to the needs of the employer and the organization, consideration is given to the employee and to stipulations in union contracts, if in effect, when planning scheduled time on and off duty for each member of the staff. Most state labor laws require break times for meals and between meal rest periods for employees, which is a further consideration when planning schedules to cover work that must be done. Familiarity with these regulations is a necessity for the manager.

SECURITY IN EMPLOYMENT   One of the major concerns of the working world in recent years is equal opportunity for employment for all persons who desire employment and who are qualified. Equal employment opportunity (EEO) is the umbrella term that encompasses all laws and regulations prohibiting discrimination or requiring affirmative action. The Equal Employment Opportunity Commission (EEOC) regulations and interpretive guidelines provide guidance to management for compliance with Title VII of the Civil Rights Act of 1964, the Age Discrimination in Employment Act, and the Americans with Disabilities Act (ADA) of 1990, all of which are federal EEO statutes.

Most states also have legislation that prohibits discrimination. In some cases, these statutes are broader than the federal laws. Marital status, sexual preference and orientation, race, color, religion, national origin, or ancestry are demographics protected from discrimination in various states. These are designated as fair employment practice laws. A public accommodation law, when in effect, requires that service be given in an equal manner to all persons.

The *Civil Rights Act of 1964* stipulates that "No person in the United States shall, on ground of race, color, or national origin be excluded from participating in, be denied the benefits of, or be subjected to any program or activity receiving Federal Financial assistance." Title VII under this act extended the provision to include prohibition of discrimination "by employers, employment agencies and labor unions."

Thus, employees who are in covered positions are entitled to be free of unlawful discrimination with regard to recruitment, classified advertising, job classification, hire, utilization of physical facilities, transfer, promotion, discharge wages and salaries, seniority lines, testing, insurance coverage, pension and retirement benefits, referral to jobs, union membership, and the like. All potential employees have equal opportunity, regardless of background.

The *Civil Rights Act of 1991* increases the likelihood that employees will sue because discrimination cases will be easier to win and the damages that are awarded would be more substantial. This act does not make anything illegal that wasn't already illegal, but it does relax the burden of proof and make possible recovery for pain, suffering, and punitive damages.

The *Age Discrimination in Employment Act of 1967* promotes the employment of the older worker, based on ability instead of age. It prohibits arbitrary age discrimination in employment and helps employers and employees find ways to meet problems arising from the impact of age on employment. The act protects most individuals who are at least 40 but less than 65 years of age from "discrimination in employment based on age in matters of hiring, discharge compensation or other terms, conditions, or privileges of employment."

Sexual harassment takes two forms and is a form of sexual discrimination that violates federal, state, and most local laws. The first form is *quid pro quo* and occurs when a supervisor either rewards or punishes a subordinate for providing and or not providing sexual favors. The second form is the *hostile work environment,* which occurs when an employee's ability to work is undermined by an atmosphere infused with unwelcome sexually oriented or otherwise hostile conduct created by supervisors or coworkers.

The *Americans with Disabilities Act* (ADA) of 1990 prohibits discrimination against qualified persons with disabilities in all aspects of employment from application to termination. No job may be denied an individual with a disability if the individual is qualified and able to perform the essential functions of the job, with or without reasonable accommodation. If needed, an employer must make the reasonable accommodation unless it would result in undue hardship for the employer. Existing performance standards do not have to be lowered, but such standards must be job-related and uniformly applied to all employees and applicants for that particular job. Equal opportunity must be provided to individuals with disabilities to apply and be considered for a job. The applicant cannot be asked preemployment questions regarding his or her disability, but the applicant can be asked about his or her ability to perform specific job functions. He or she may also be asked to describe or demonstrate how these job functions could be accomplished. Medical histories and preemployment physical exams are not allowed under the ADA legislation; however, the job offer may be conditional depending on the results of a post-offer physical exam. This exam must be required of all applicants in the same job category. Tests for the use of illegal drugs are not considered as physical exams under the ADA and are, therefore, still legal.

Quotas are fixed, inflexible percentages or numbers of positions that an employer decides can be filled only by members of a certain minority group. This is a form of reverse discrimination and is almost always illegal.

Affirmative action does not involve the setting of specific quotas but rather the desire to reach general goals to increase the numbers of women and minorities in specific positions. Required for certain federal contractors, affirmative action is legal if ordered by a court to remedy past discrimination or if limited in time and scope.

As can be seen, our economic society is characterized by many areas of friction in industry. Students of labor quite generally agree that in no area is there an economic problem more important to human beings than security of job tenure, which means assurance of the satisfaction of physical needs, a place in the esteem and affection of others, an opportunity for self-expression, and a chance to enjoy leisure. The three risks that more than any others tend to make the position of most wage earners in industry insecure are unemployment, physical impairment, and old age. The definition for unemployment used by the Bureau of Census in making its enumeration is: "Unemployment may be described as involuntary idleness on the part of those who have lost their latest jobs, are able to work, and are looking for work." This definition is obviously narrow, because it excludes all those persons who are unwilling to work, are unemployable because of physical or mental disabilities, or are temporarily idle for seasonal reasons. However, the definition covers the group whose unemployment usually arises from conditions inherent in the organization and management of industry.

Problems of tenure must concern all persons charged with the direction of the foodservice industry. Fortunately, foodservices on the whole lend themselves to steady employment, and many managers take pride in the long tenure of large numbers of their workers. Sometimes, however, the workers' acceptance of tenure as a matter of course brings definite problems such as laxity and inefficiency in the performance of assigned tasks and lack of interest in improved practices. Standards of performance in some instances have been lowered as security of employment has been assured. Personnel policies should cover such contingencies.

EMPLOYEE SERVICES AND BENEFITS   Benefits that employees receive often represent as much as 39% of wages earned. Some of these are so taken for granted that they are scarcely realized or appreciated by those who receive them. Yet, if such services were not provided, the lack would be acutely noticed. Managers recognize the humanistic desirability of making available certain programs and services in addition to a fair wage for their employees' comfort and well-being. A less altruistic point of view may cause managers to offer those same benefits in order to compete in the job market and attract desirable applicants.

Extra benefits, sometimes called "fringe" benefits, fall into three general groups: health and safety, economic, and convenience and comfort. The first, *health and safety*, is an important basic factor in all personnel problems. This matter affects social and economic life, being of interest not only to the employee but to the employer and the public as well. Time lost because of illness and accidents is expensive for both management and labor, results in lowered productivity and increased losses for the employer, and directly affects the income of the employee. Maintaining the good physical condition of employees is economically desirable as well as necessary for achievement of the many goals of the department. Also, managers of any foodservice recognize that the health of the worker may affect the health of the public through both direct and indirect contact. Additional discussions regarding the importance of good health for the foodservice employee are given in Chapters 5 and 7.

Safe working conditions are of first importance to employer and employee alike. A foodservice does not present the identical hazards found in any other industry, but duplicates some of those found in several industries. Falls, burns, shocks, and cuts are possible, as they are in any other place where mechanical equipment is used. It is the responsibility of the manager to see that safeguards are maintained, that the equipment is kept in safe condition, and that all working conditions are safe and clean.

The *Occupational Safety and Health Act* (OSHA) of 1970 has forced managers to look critically at working conditions and to bring any that are undesirable up to a standard demanded by law. Every employer covered by the law is required to furnish employment and places of employment that are free from recognized hazards that are causing or are likely to cause death or serious physical harm and must comply with all safety regulations promulgated by the Secretary of Labor in accordance with the provisions of the act.

Another benefit for employees is provided for in the *Workmen's Compensation Insurance* program. This legislation is administered by the states, and the liability insurance premiums are paid for by employers. Workmen's compensation laws are based on the theory that the cost of accidents should be a part of production costs, the same as wages, taxes, insurance, and raw materials.

This insurance covers employers' liability for the costs of any accident incurred by an employee on or in connection with the job. The workers must show that they were injured on the job and the extent of their injuries. Compensation laws state the specific amount of payment allowed for each type of injury in addition to hospital, surgical, and, in case of death, funeral expenses. All foodservice directors will need to determine, through their state department of labor, who can be covered by Workmen's Compensation, the methods of payment, and the amount of benefits to which the worker is entitled.

Health and accident insurance plans provide some assistance to employees who may become ill or who are injured off the job. Fear of injury or illness is the cause of much worry, even when an insurance plan is available to employees. Without it, many workers would be in financial straits, trying to pay medical and hospital bills on their own.

Many forms of health and accident insurance are available for groups. In some cases, the company alone pays for the employees; in others, it is jointly borne by the company and those who participate in it. Through labor union efforts and the efforts of concerned managers, more and more health services are being made available to employees, many at employer expense. Flexible benefit plans, which allow the employee to choose from a wide array of benefit options, are gaining in popularity. Whereas early benefit plans included only health and retirement, employees can now often choose profit sharing; stock ownership benefits; legal, educational, and childcare assistance; dental and vision insurance; and life insurance, depending on their own particular needs and wants.

The extent to which foodservices provide these benefits to employees usually depends on the size of the organization and the facilities it has available, for example, the emergency room of a hospital and the concern of those at the decision-making level.

The second group of employee services and benefits are those labeled *economic.* Most of the programs discussed so far provide some economic benefit to workers, even if indirectly. All insurance plans undoubtedly could be put under this classification instead of putting some under the classification of health and safety. However, benefits to be discussed in this economic group have a direct monetary value in returns to the employee; the employer carries the cost of some, and others are shared by the employee.

Social Security benefits are provided by the *Social Security Act,* a nationwide program of insurance designed to protect wage earners and their families against loss of income due to old age, disability, and death. A designated percentage of the salary of each employed person must be withheld from his or her wages and the same amount from the business added to the Social Security Fund, or to a comparable retirement-system fund if a nonprofit type of organization is involved. Provisions and benefits of Social Security change from time to time, so details soon become outdated. Managers must keep in touch with their local Social Security office to be informed of current changes.

Other economic benefits offered by some organizations to their employees may include group life insurance programs, profit-sharing plans, and pensions or retirement plans. All of these add to the economic security of those who continue in the service of a particular organization long enough to build a fund that is significant for them after regular employment ceases, either because of retirement or death. Vacations, holidays, and sick leave, all with pay, are other forms of fringe benefits for personnel. Properly administered, they are of advantage to the organization as well.

Employee convenience and comfort benefits make up the third group of fringe benefits. Services provided for the comfort or convenience of employees compile a long list and include, among others, adequate rest and locker rooms, meal service available to employees often at reduced or at-cost levels, free medical service on an emergency basis, credit unions, and recreational facilities. Educational tuition or fees for personnel to attend workshops or classes for self-development and skill development are also among these. Various foodservices participate in many of these or in different ones for their employees. In turn, these benefits help in building a loyal, contented working group with high morale.

Although many of the labor laws enacted are directed toward the protection of specific groups, the regulations applicable to all workers are well-established. Familiarity with federal, state, and local laws applying to foodservice employees is obligatory for every foodservice administrator and manager. Only then can labor policies be of benefit to both the worker and his or her organization and be put into action for implementation.

Labor-Management Relations

Foodservice managers are concerned with problems arising from directing employees' activities; that is, in handling the people who must translate the policies, procedures, and plans into action. When groups of people work together, there is always potential for conflict. Some people must manage and some must carry out the technical operations. Everyone wants more of whatever improves his or her position. The closer the relationship between the employee and manager, with open and free discussion on both sides, the less danger there is for grievances to arise.

Many foodservices are so small that the relationship between employer and employee is immediate and direct. Under such circumstances, discussion of mutual concerns is possible right in the work place. Direct face-to-face contact tends to develop a sense of real association and mutual interest. Employees with a somewhat complete picture of a relatively small business may see their job in relation to the whole. Many services, however, are so large that there is limited personal contact between employer and employee. Workers may feel there is little chance for the individual to be recognized as an important person in the organization. Also, they may not have an overall view of the business that would make possible self-evaluation of their own jobs in terms of the whole. Workers engaged in a limited phase of total large-scale production may find that they lack the direct contact that tends to humanize employer–employee relationships in a small foodservice.

Legislation

Managers who are not attuned to the concerns of employees, who do not recognize that a small complaint or conflict that arises is probably a symptom of a deeper problem, and who fail to investigate and correct the situation are opening the door for labor unions to come in to represent the employees better.

During the years, much legislation has been enacted to attempt to balance the power between labor and management. In 1935, the passage of the *Wagner Act* [or *National Labor Relations Act* (NLRA)] was the beginning of positive support of unionization and collective bargaining by the federal government. Prior to this legislation, workers had been exploited by management. This exploitation is documented in court cases as early as 1806. The terms of the Wagner Act regulate employees' rights to join a union and unfair management practices, prohibit management from interfering with their employees who wish to join a union and from discriminating against those who do join, and requires employers and union members to bargain collectively (an obligation to meet and discuss terms with an open mind, but without being required to come to an agreement). The majority of today's collective bargaining agreements provide for an impartial arbitrator to hear and decide grievances under the bargaining agreement. The NLRA also establishes the National Labor Relations Board (NLRB) to administer and interpret the provisions of the act.

The procedures followed in unfair labor practice cases are: (1) a private party files a charge that an unfair labor practice has been committed; (2) the regional office at which the charge is filed investigates the case and decides whether to proceed with the complaint; (3) if the regional director issues a complaint, an attorney from the regional office will prosecute the case; (4) if the case is not settled at this level, a hearing is necessary with a staff attorney representing the NLRB controlling the case; and (5) finally, an administrative law judge hands down a recommended decision and order.

One of the major responsibilities of the NLRB is to determine whether employees should be represented by a union. Employees usually initiate a union campaign if they desire union representation. At least 30% of the employees in the bargaining unit must support their petition to the NLRB; this support is shown by employees' signatures on authorization cards. These cards are investigated and authenticated by the NLRB before ordering that an election be held. The secret ballot election is conducted, and the results are tabulated by an NLRB representative. If the union wins the election, a contract is then drawn up, and the union designates a bargaining unit employee as its union "steward." This person handles the union business in the workplace.

Employees of hospitals operated entirely on a nonprofit basis were exempt from the original NLRA. However, an amendment to the NLRA brought nonprofit hospitals under the provisions of the act. In such situations, dietitians may be called on to defend their positions as "management" instead of as "labor."

The *Taft-Hartley Act* (or *Labor-Management Relations Act*), passed in 1947, was enacted to offset some of the power and unfair practices that labor unions seemed to acquire since 1935. Among other provisions, it prevents unions from coercing employees to join, outlaws the "union shop" (which requires an employee to become a member of the union in order to retain a job) and the "closed shop" (which obligates an employer to hire only union members and to discharge any employee who drops union membership), and makes it illegal for unions to refuse to join in collective bargaining. This statute marked a shift away from encouragement of unionization to a more neutral position on the part of the federal government.

Further legislation, passed in 1959, was the *Landrum-Griffin Act* (or *Labor-Management Reporting and Disclosure Act*), which is in the interests of both labor and management but is especially pro-individual labor union member. It contains a bill of rights for union members, requires certain financial disclosures by unions through a specified reporting system, prescribes procedures for the election of union officers, and provides civil and criminal remedies for financial abuses by union officers.

The labor legislation discussed and the area of human resource management on which it makes an impact is summarized in Table 11.1.

There are numerous reasons for employers to become the target of union organizing attempts or for employees to turn to a union. Chief among these reasons are poorly developed or administered personnel policies and practices, or a breakdown in some facet of employer–employee relations. A number of steps should be taken by managers long before organizational attempts begin. Most important among them is a review of personnel policies and employee relations, making every effort to maintain good personnel practices, put policies into writing, and communicate them to employees with frequent reviews and discussions.

TABLE 11.1.   Selected Labor Legislation Classified by the Relevant Area of Human Resource Management.

Acquisition of Human Resources	Development of Human Resources	Rewarding of Human Resources	Maintenance of Human Resources
Civil Rights Act—1964	Civil Rights Act—1964	Civil Rights Act—1964	Civil Rights Act—1964
Equal Pay Act—1963	Equal Pay Act—1963	Fair Labor Standards Act—1938	State Fair Labor Practices Act—1913
Age Discrimination in Employment Act—1967	Age Discrimination in Employment Act—1967	Equal Pay Act—1963	Wagner Act—1935
Americans with Disabilities Act—1990	Americans with Disabilities Act—1990	Age Discrimination in Employment Act—1967	Social Security Act—1935
Civil Rights Act—1991	Civil Rights Act—1991	Americans with Disabilities Act—1990	Taft–Hartley Act—1947
		Civil Rights Act—1991	Landrum–Griffin Act—1959
			Age Discrimination in Employment Act—1967
			Occupational Safety & Health Act—1970
			Americans with Disabilities Act—1990
			Civil Rights Act—1991

The impact of unionization on foodservices may be great for those who are naive in the ways of collective bargaining. Legal counsel to assist in negotiating a fair, workable contract for both labor and management is to be encouraged. If unionization is to become a reality, it is important to create a favorable climate for cooperation, to make sure that the negotiator understands the economic as well as the administrative problems of a foodservice operation, such as scheduling required to cover meal hours, the services necessary, especially to patients in health care facilities, the equipment to be used, and the prices charged in relation to the labor costs.

Certain rights of management may be lost when unionization takes place, since some of the authority but little of the responsibility will be shared with the union. Some of the freedoms lost are the right to hire, discharge, change work assignments and time schedules, set wages and fringe benefits, change policies without appeal, discipline workers without being subject to appeal to the union, and receive and act on grievances directly. The loss of the right to use volunteer workers in the department may also be realized.

It is imperative, therefore, that the collective bargaining agreement contain a management rights clause. There are two major categories of management rights clauses. One is a brief, general clause not dealing with specific rights, but with the principle of management rights in general. The other is a detailed clause, which clearly lists areas of authority that are specific to management.

Certain cost increases will be noted also: for time loss from the job by the person selected to be the union steward, and the cost of management support to the union based on a given sum per member per month in contributions.

The nature of labor organizations and the method they use differ according to the understanding and goals of the leaders and members, their convictions as to remedies needed, and by legal and other forms of social control. Ordinarily, management and organized labor have different approaches to solving their problems. This often leads to long hours of negotiations before a satisfactory mutual agreement can be reached. It is important that each group try to see the other's viewpoint with fairness and with an honest belief in the good faith of the other.

Summary Questions

1. What are the rights of individuals in an organization?

2. Discuss the advantages and disadvantages of using internal sources to select future employees.

3. List the five teaching steps that should be included in an on-the-job training program.

4. What are the purposes of the performance appraisal interview?

5. What is the sequence of steps recommended for good decision making?

6. Discuss the impact of unionization on a foodservice management operation.

7. Define the term "policy."

Bibliography

Barber, A. E., Dunham, R. B., and Formisano, R. A.: The impact of flexible benefits on employee satisfaction: A field study. Pers. Psych. 45(1):55, 1992.

Barlow, W. E. and Hane, E. Z.: A practical guide to the Americans with Disabilities Act. Pers. J. 71(6):53, 1992.

Bittel, L. R. and Newstrom, J. W.: What Every Supervisor Should Know, 6th ed. New York: McGraw-Hill, 1990.

Desatnick, R. L.: Managing to Keep the Customer. San Francisco: Jossey-Bass, 1987.

Leslie, D. L.: Labor Law in a Nutshell. St. Paul, MN: West Publishing Co., 1992.

Levering, R., Moskowitz, M., and Katz, M.: The 100 Best Companies to Work for in America. Reading, MA: Addison-Wesley, 1984.

Martin, S. L. and Lehnen, L. P.: Select the right employees through testing. Pers. J. 71(6):46, 1992.

Metzger, N.: The Health Care Supervisor's Handbook, 2nd ed. Rockville, MD: Aspen Systems Corp., 1982.

Moravec, M. and Tucker, R.: Job descriptions for the 21st century. Pers. J. 71(6):37, 1992.

Plavner, J. T.: Employment law lingo. HR Magazine on Human Resource Management 37(5):48, 1992.

Smith, R. E.: Employee orientation. Pers. J. 63(12):43, 1984.

United States Code, Volume 12: Title 29 (Labor). Washington, DC: U.S. Government Printing Office, 1989.

For More Information

Armstrong, M.: A Handbook of Human Resource Management. New York: Nichols Publishing Co., 1988.

Brymer, R. A.: Employee empowerment: A guest-driven strategy. Cornell HRA Quarterly 32(1): 1991.

Bureau of National Affairs: Employee Discipline and Discharge. Washington, DC: Bureau of National Affairs, 1985.

Bureau of National Affairs: BNA policy and practice series: Compensation. Washington, DC: Bureau of National Affairs, 1988.

Durocher, J. F.: Beat the training challenge with interactive videodiscs. Cornell HRA Quarterly 31:46, 1990.

Famularo, J. J.: Handbook of Human Resources Administration, 2nd ed. New York: McGraw-Hill, 1986.

Feldman, D. C.: Managing Careers in Organizations. Glenview, IL: Scott, Foresman and Company, 1988.

Flamholtz, E. G. and Das, T. K., eds.: Human Resource Management and Productivity. Los Angeles: Institute of Industrial Relations, 1986.

Greenlaw, P. S. and Kohl, J. P.: Personnel Management. New York: Harper & Row, 1986.

Hall, D. T. and Goodale, J. G.: Human Resource Management. Glenview, IL: Scott, Foresman and Co., 1986.

Hamilton, A. J. and Veglahn, P. A.: Sexual harassment: The hostile work environment. Cornell HRA Quarterly 33:88, 1992.

Kelly, M. A.: Labor and Industrial Relations. Baltimore: Johns Hopkins University Press, 1987.

Kinlaw, D. C.: Coaching for Commitment: Managerial Strategies for Obtaining Superior Performance. San Diego, CA: University Associates, Inc., 1989.

Lehr, R. I., Middlebrooks, D. J., and Rutledge, D. J.: How to Avoid Charges of Age Discrimination in the Workplace. New York: Executive Enterprises Publications Co., Inc., 1989.

Makin, P. J., Cooper, C. L., and Cox, C. J.: Managing People at Work. New York: Quorum Books, 1989.

Nadler, L. and Wiggs, G. D.: Managing Human Resource Development. San Francisco: Jossey-Bass, 1986.

Pfeiffer, J. A. and Ballew, A. C.: Using Instruments in Human Resource Development. San Diego, CA: University Associates, Inc. 1987.

Rhodes, S. R. and Steers, R. M.: Managing Employee Absenteeism. Reading, MA: Addison-Wesley Publishing Co., 1990.

Spencer, L. M., Jr.: Calculating Human Resource Costs and Benefits. New York: John Wiley & Sons, 1986.

Stone, F. M., ed.: The AMA Handbook of Supervisory Management. New York: AMACOM, 1989.

Taylor, B. J.: Labor Relations Law. Englewood Cliffs, NJ: Prentice Hall, 1992.

Administrative Leadership

As administrative leaders, those individuals who assume the management of foodservice organizations will be successful to the degree that they are willing to assume responsibility and are able to maintain good human relations. Goals and objectives of the department cannot be attained by the administrator alone; working satisfactorily through other people constitutes the major part of the job.

Most people would assume that without administrative leadership no organization could achieve its goals and plans. This assumption is generally valid, but what is meant by administrative leadership? In this chapter, the difference between leadership and management is discussed, and the characteristics displayed by managers and leaders in administrative positions are compared.

The topic of leadership effectiveness is of special interest. An historical view of leadership is presented tracing the evolution of effective leadership theories from the era of scientific management to the present-day systems concept and contingency approach. The major contributions of each period are summarized.

Communication is a key part of effective leadership. Some of the barriers to successful communication are described as well as some techniques to improve in this area.

Although profit and productivity are still major goals of administrative leadership, managerial ethics, and social responsibility have assumed equal importance. This chapter concludes with a discussion of the ethical and social responsibilities required by administrative leaders in today's foodservice industry.

Learning Objectives

After studying this chapter, the reader should be able to

1. compare and contrast the concepts of management and leadership
2. describe the difference between McGregor's Theory X and Theory Y approaches to leadership

3. trace the history of leadership theories, and describe the contributions that each theory has made to the current approaches

4. list and briefly describe some of the barriers to good communication

5. identify some techniques that may be used to improve communication

6. discuss social responsibilities a manager has in today's organizations

7. discuss a foodservice manager's professional responsibilities

Leadership

Leadership is one of the most observed and least understood phenomena on earth according to Burns; in fact, he cites more than 130 definitions of the term. After reviewing more than 5,000 research studies and monographs on leadership in *Stogdill's Handbook of Leadership,* the editor of the book concluded that there is no common set of factors, traits, or processes that identifies the qualities of effective leadership.

Leadership, like the concept of management, means different things to different people—ranging from being the first to initiate a change to inspiring bravery on the battlefield. This fact has caused many to use other, more definitive terms, such as activating or influencing. At times, leadership and management have been used synonymously. However, *leadership* is essentially the business or activity of trying to *influence* people to strive willingly to attain the goals and plans of the organization. *Management* is the function of running an organization from a conceptual or policy standpoint. Leadership may then be defined as working with people to get them to willingly produce the results the leader wants or needs to accomplish.

Hickman suggests that although managers and leaders both have minds and souls, they tend to emphasize the use of one over the other as they function in the organization. That is, the mind represents the analytical, calculating, structuring, and ordering side of tasks, while the soul represents the visionary, passionate, creative, and flexible side.

Abraham Zaleznik, a professor of social psychology of management, writes that managers and leaders are very different kinds of people who differ in motivation, personal history, and how they think and act. Management and leadership require different responses to different demands, and there are situations when each is required. In order to see how the roles of leaders and managers differ, some of the characteristics of each are tabulated in Table 12.1.

Koontz and O'Donnell (1968) suggest that subordinates will respond to authority alone to do the bare minimum to maintain their jobs. But "to raise effort toward total capability, the manager must induce devoted response on the part of subordinates by exercising leadership."

TABLE 12.1.   Some Characteristics of Managers and Leaders.

Manager	*Leader*
How They View Themselves:	
Managers have a strong sense of belonging to their organizations.	Leaders see themselves as separate from their organizations and the people of their organizations.
Managers see themselves as protectors of existing order with which they identify.	Leaders have strong personal mastery that impels them to struggle for change in existing order.
How They View Their Function:	
Managers work through other people within established organizational policies and practice to reach an organizational goal. They limit their choices to pre-established organizational goals, policies, and practices. Managers are concerned with process.	Leaders question established procedures and create new concepts. They inspire people to look at options. They are concerned with results.
Personality:	
Managers have a strong instinct for survival.	Leaders seek out risks, especially if rewards seem high.
Managers can tolerate mundane, practical work.	Leaders dislike mundane tasks.
Relationships:	
Managers relate to people according to their role—boss, employee, peer, and so forth.	Leaders relate to people in an intuitive and empathetic way.
Primary Concern:	
Managers are concerned with achievement of organizational goals.	Leaders are concerned with achievement of personal goals.
Place in Organization:	
Managers are supervisors, department heads, and administrators. They are usually considered higher echelon.	Leaders may be found at any level in the plan of organization from technician to highest echelon.
Power:	
Managers derive power from their positions.	Leaders derive power through personal relationships.
Goals:	
Managers are concerned with pre-established, organizational goals. Their personal and subgoals arise out of necessity to conform to organizational structure, rather than a desire to change.	Leaders are concerned with personal goals. They are not comfortable with the status quo of established organizational goals and policies. They enjoy innovating.

SOURCE: Tramel, Mary E. and Reynolds, Helen: *Executive Leadership*. Englewood Cliffs, NJ: Prentice-Hall, Inc., 1981, p. 59. Used with permission.

Leadership has been viewed as a special form of power involving relationships with people. These relationships are developed when leaders successfully fuse organizational and personal needs in a way that allows people and organizations to reach levels of mutual achievement and satisfaction. This can be an exceedingly difficult task. Each employee is different with different motivations, ambitions, interests, and personalities. As a result, each must be treated differently. Work situations differ. How managers can handle these divergent factors effectively has been the subject of study for many years, and such research, both past and present, can be used to improve managerial leadership effectiveness.

Drucker contends that the essence of leadership is performance—not charisma or a set of personality traits. He states that there are three basic requirements for effective leadership: (1) The leader must think through the organization's mission, defining it and establishing it, clearly and visibly. Any necessary compromises made are compatible with the leader's mission and goals, and standards are maintained; (2) The leader sees leadership as a responsibility, not rank and privilege. The effective leader accepts responsibility for subordinates' mistakes but sees their triumphs as well as his triumphs. For this reason, the effective leader does everything possible to surround herself with able, independent, and self-assured people; and (3) The leader must earn trust. This means that a leader's actions and professed beliefs must be congruent. Drucker states that being a good leader is not based on being clever but on being consistent, and that these are the same characteristics required of a good manager.

Bennis agrees with Drucker's idea and, based on his research, finds that managers must grow to become leader-managers. He puts forth four essential traits of effective leadership: (1) the capacity to engage people and draw them to a compelling vision of what is possible; (2) the ability to communicate their vision in a way that allows people to make it their own and give it personal meaning; (3) trust, total reliability, and integrity, as well as the performance of actions that are congruent with their vision; and (4) the possession of high regard for self and others. The combined effect of these personal characteristics empowers people by: (1) making them feel significant; (2) focusing on their developing competence rather than their failures; (3) creating a shared sense of community; and (4) making work exciting and worthy of dedicated commitment.

As a leader of people, the foodservice manager has the task then to empower employees by clearly establishing and communicating the organization's mission, accepting the responsibility of leading the group, and earning employee's trust by showing a high regard for self and others. An empowered team is necessary to create an effective, smoothly operating work unit.

The Traditional Leadership Role

SCIENTIFIC MANAGEMENT   The era of "scientific management" was founded on the belief that the main common interest of both the organization and the employee was money, and only money. The leader/manager's role consisted of issuing orders and handing out rewards and punishment. The founders of the scientific management theory, such as Frederick W. Taylor and Frank and Lillian Gilbreth, were primarily concerned with the best method and "right wage" for doing the job. The employee was viewed as a machine or tool. This type of thinking met the needs of the day. But times change. The practices of the scientific management movement began to be questioned in the late 1920s.

HUMAN RELATIONS APPROACH   The turning point came as a result of the Hawthorne studies. Western Electric Company conducted some experiments at their Hawthorne plant outside Chicago to determine the relationship between the physical working environment and productivity. Lighting was one variable that was tested. Researchers were surprised to find that no matter how they varied the intensity of the lighting, productivity increased. They concluded that the level of performance had nothing to do with the lighting intensity but rather was a result of the interest shown in the worker as a person rather than as a machine. Thus, the human relations era was born. Human relationists such as Mayo, Maslow, Roethlisberger, and Dickson brought a more tolerant approach to the leadership of people—consideration of the individual and an understanding of why people work. The theory was good. The implementation, in many cases, was poor.

Newer Approaches to Leadership

THEORY X AND Y   The human relations movement began to lose favor in the early 1950s. McGregor introduced his Theory X and Theory Y analysis of leadership strategies, suggesting that the basic attitude of a manager toward employees has an impact on job performance. He divided these supervisory attitudes into two categories—Theory X and Theory Y. *Theory X* attitude was held by the traditional and "old-line" managers. *Theory Y* was the attitude held by the emerging manager of the 1960s and 1970s. However, again implementation was the problem. Managers trained in Theory Y management found that, in many cases, the resulting job performance was not the desired level or quality.

SITUATIONAL MANAGEMENT   The work done at Ohio State and by Blake and Mouton, as well as others, culminated in the theory that effectiveness as a leader depends on a multiplicity of factors, not only human behavior and motivation. The situational approach to management concentrates on the theory that leadership effectiveness is a function of the individual leader (including traits and personalities), of that leader's subordinate (including attitude toward working, socioeconomic interests, and personality), and of the situational variables involved.

Since followers are the ones who determine whether a person possesses leadership qualities, the expectations of followers have been studied. Table 12.2 shows the characteristics that followers admire in superiors. From this study, it may be concluded that honesty, competence, forward-looking, and inspiration are important leader attributes.

Early studies by Stogdill at the Ohio State University attempted to define more global leader behaviors. Two separate and distinct dimensions of leader behavior were identified—initiating structure and consideration. *Initiating structure* refers to the relationship between the leader and the members of the work group in seeking to establish well-defined patterns of organization, channels of communication, and procedures. *Consideration* refers to behavior that indicates friendship, mutual trust, respect, and warmth in the relationship between the leader and the work group. This was the first study to plot leader behavior on two axes. Leadership quadrants drawn from the Ohio State studies are illustrated in Figs. 12.1, 12.2, and 12.3. The effects of initiating

TABLE 12.2.   Characteristics of Superior Leaders.

Characteristic	U.S. Managers (N = 2,615)	
	Ranking	Percentage of Managers Selecting
Honest	1	83
Competent	2	67
Forward-looking	3	62
Inspiring	4	58
Intelligent	5	43
Fair-minded	6	40
Broad-minded	7	37
Straightforward	8	34
Imaginative	9	34
Dependable	10	33
Supportive	11	32
Courageous	12	27
Caring	13	26
Cooperative	14	25
Mature	15	23
Ambitious	16	21
Determined	17	20
Self-controlled	18	13
Loyal	19	11
Independent	20	10

SOURCE: Kouzes, James M. and Posner, Barry Z.: The Leadership Challenge: How to Get Extraordinary Things Done in Organizations, Table 1, p. 17. Copyright © 1987 by Jossey-Bass Inc., Publishers. Used with permission.

STYLE OF LEADER

Figure 12.1. Style of leader versus maturity of follower(s). (From Paul Hersey and Kenneth Blanchard, *Management of Organizational Behavior: Utilizing Human Resources,* 4th ed., © 1982, p. 152. Reprinted by permission of Prentice Hall, Englewood Cliffs, New Jersey.)

MATURITY OF FOLLOWER(S)

structure on employee satisfaction and performance have been found to depend entirely on the situation. Research has shown that consideration behavior is positively related to employee satisfaction, but its effect on performance is unclear.

Building on the work done at Ohio State, Blake and Mouton developed the Managerial Grid, shown in Fig. 12.4. Originally, the team leadership style (9,9) was believed ideal—high concern for people and production. However, it was soon found that some of the other leadership styles were equally effective and that some managers using a team leadership style were not effective. The Managerial Grid labels were modified as shown in Figs. 12.5 and 12.6.

One researcher, House, proposed a theory that helps to explain the situational nature of the initiating structure dimension of leader behaviors. Called the path-goal theory of leadership, it states that the functions of a leader should consist of increasing personal rewards for subordinates for goal attainment and making the path to these rewards easier to follow by clarifying it, removing and reducing roadblocks, and increasing opportunities for satisfaction along the way. House based his theory on the expectancy theory of motivation proposed by Vroom, which states that motivation is a function of both the person's ability to accomplish the task and his or her desire to do so. In the late 1960s, the theory that leadership effectiveness is contingent upon not only leadership style but the attitude and outlook of the follower and the situational constraints came to be accepted.

High Relationship—Low Task: **Leadership through Participation** Use when followers are "able" but "unwilling" or "insecure."	*High Relationship—High Task:* **Leadership through Selling** Use when followers are "unable" but "willing" or "motivated."
Low Relationship—Low Task: **Leadership through Delegation** Use when followers are "able" and "willing" or "motivated."	*Low Relationship—High Task:* **Leadership through Telling** Use when followers are "unable" and "unwilling" or "insecure."

Figure 12.2.   Interpretation of the Situational Leadership Model. (From Bolman, Lee G. and Deal, Terrance E.: *Reframing Organizations: Artistry, Choice, and Leadership,* p. 418. Copyright © 1991 by Jossey-Bass, Inc., Publishers. Used with permission.)

CONTINGENCY THEORIES OF LEADERSHIP   Basically, contingency theory holds that there is no one "best" style of leadership but that style must be adjusted to fit the situation. Effective leadership in any given situation is dependent on a number of circumstances: The situation—how structured is the task involved, whether or not the leader has any power as perceived by subordinates, and how well the leader gets along with subordinates. Fiedler developed a continuum identifying possible states of each of the three factors. He concluded that in very "favorable" or in very "unfavorable" situations for getting a task accomplished by group effort, the task-oriented management style works best. In intermediate situations, the human relations style is more successful.

In 1958, Tannenbaum and Schmidt wrote a now classic article, "How to Choose a Leadership Pattern," in which they described how a manager should successfully lead his organization. Fifteen years later, they reconsidered and updated their original statements to reflect new management concepts and societal changes. The revised continuum of manager-nonmanager behavior is shown in Fig. 12.7.

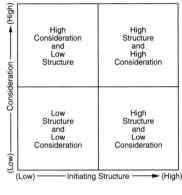

Figure 12.3. The Ohio State leadership quadrants. (From Paul Hersey and Kenneth Blanchard, *Management of Organizational Behavior: Utilizing Human Resources,* 4th ed., © 1982, p. 96. Reprinted by permission of Prentice Hall, Englewood Cliffs, New Jersey.)

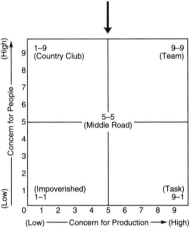

Figure 12.4. The Managerial Grid leadership styles. (From Blake, R. and Mouton, J. S.: *Executive Achievement,* p. 16. Copyright © 1986. New York: McGraw-Hill, Inc. Reproduced with permission of McGraw-Hill.)

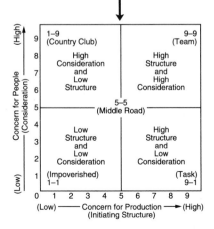

Figure 12.5. Merging of the Ohio State and the Managerial Grid theories of leadership. (From Blake, R. and Mouton, J. S.: *Executive Achievement,* p. 16. Copyright © 1986. New York: McGraw-Hill, Inc. Reproduced with permission of McGraw-Hill.)

Figure 12.6. The Updated Managerial Grid.

1,9
Seeking Acceptance and Approval

Thoughtful attention to needs of people for satisfying relationships leads to a comfortable, friendly organization atmosphere and work tempo.

9,9
Making Contributions That Make a Difference

Work accomplishment is from committed people; interdependence through a "common stake" in organization purpose leads to relationships of trust and respect.

5,5
Being Popular and "In"

Adequate organization performance is possible through balancing the necessity to get out work with maintaining morale at a satisfactory level.

1,1
Desire to Hang On

Exertion of minimum effort to get required work done is appropriate to sustain organization membership.

9,1
Domination, Mastery, and Control

Efficiency in operations results from arranging conditions of work in such a way that human elements interfere to a minimum degree.

Figure 12.6. The Updated Managerial Grid. (From Blake, R. and Mouton, J. S.: *Executive Achievement,* p. 16. Copyright © 1986. New York: McGraw-Hill, Inc. Reproduced with permission of McGraw-Hill.)

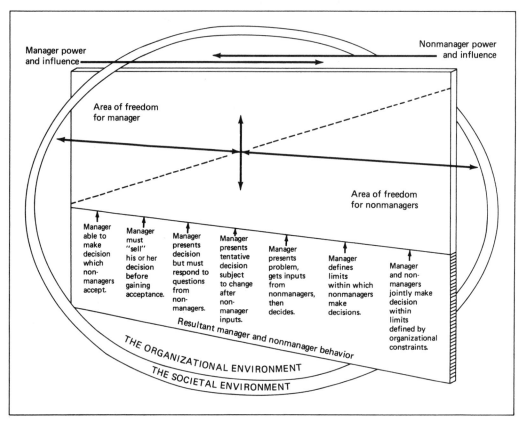

Figure 12.7. Tannenbaum-Schmidt's continuum of manager-nonmanager behavior. [Reprinted by permission of *Harvard Business Review*. An exhibit from "How to choose a leadership pattern" by Robert Tannenbaum and Warren H. Schmidt (May/June 1973). Copyright © 1973 by the President and Fellows of Harvard College; all rights reserved.]

The total area of freedom shared by managers and nonmanagers is constantly redefined by interactions between them and the forces in the environment. The points on the continuum designate types of managers and nonmanager behavior that are possible with the amount of freedom available to each. This continuum allows managers to review and analyze their own behavior within the context of alternatives available. It is important to recognize that there is no implication that either end of the continuum is inherently more effective than the other. The appropriate balance is determined by forces in the manager, in the nonmanager, and in the particular situation. The model also suggests that neither manager nor nonmanager has complete control. The nonmanager always has the option of noncompliance, and managers can never relieve themselves of all responsibility for the actions and decisions of the organization.

Also based on the premise that there is no one best way to influence people, Hersey and Blanchard's Situational Leadership Model, shown in Fig. 12.1, bases the recommended style of leadership on: (1) the amount of guidance and direction (task behavior) a leader gives; (2) the amount of socioemotional support (relationship behavior) a leader provides; and (3) the readiness (maturity) level that followers exhibit in performing a specific task, function, or objective. Each of the leadership styles shown (delegating, participating, selling, and telling) is a combination of task and relationship behavior (the two dimensions identified in the Ohio State studies).

It is probable that most people are able to operate within a narrow band of preferred ways of leading and tend to use these styles over and over. Self-development and training should be directed to a wider range of styles for use in the appropriate situations. Ideally, persons in foodservice management positions should accept as a personal philosophy that their human resources are their greatest assets and that to improve their value is not only a material advantage but a moral obligation as well.

The historical view of leadership and the contributions of each of the periods is summarized in Fig. 12.8.

Effective Communication

One leadership model shows the central role of communication for leadership effectiveness. In this model, communication is the glue that binds the behavior between leader and follower. The messages transmitted between them present the styles, attitudes, values, motives, skills, and personality variables that are possessed by the leader. The amount of control exerted will vary depending on the situation, task, personnel, and the interrelationships of these components. Good communication is a critical component of effective leadership. It is the process that links all of the management functions. In fact, estimates indicate that between 70% and 90% of a manager's time is spent communicating.

DEFINITIONS   *Communication* can be defined as the constant development of understanding among people. *Effective communication* means that there is successful transfer of information, meaning, and understanding from a sender to a receiver. It is not necessary to have agreement, but there must be mutual understanding for the exchange to be considered successful. For a leader to lead, directions must be followed. For directions to be followed, they must be understood. The best plans will fail if communication is not comprehended. It is almost certain that no message will be transmitted or received with 100% accuracy. The average employee remembers

10% to 15%   of what (s)he hears

15% to 30%   of what (s)he hears and sees

	Scientific Management–1910 to 1926
Taylor and Gantt	The one best way
F. and L. Gilbreth	"Efficiency" and work simplification
	Human Relations–1926 to 1947
Mayo	Employees must be treated like people, not machines
Roethlisberger and Dickson	Satisfaction in work
Maslow	
	The Behavioral Scientists–1947 to 1967
McGregor	Under the right conditions, people will manage themselves
Argyris	People work best when their social and psychological needs
Likert	are met
Drucker	
Herzberg	
	The New Thinkers–1967 to 2000
Reddin	The situation, the type of work, and the type of manager all
Tannenbaum and Schmidt	determine the most appropriate leadership style
Hersey and Blanchard	There is no "one best way"
Blake and Mouton	
House	

Figure 12.8.   A summary of the historical view of leadership.

30% to 50%   of what (s)he says

50% to 75%   of what (s)he does
  but (s)he remembers

75%   of what (s)he does with proper
  instruction

Proper instruction includes hearing, seeing, saying and doing, and then repeating it all again.

CHANNELS OF COMMUNICATION   An organization's channels of communication can be divided into the formal channel (that established by the organizational structure) and the informal channel. In the formal channel, communication can be downward, upward, or horizontal. Communication from the top down is the most frequently used channel. Equally important is the upward flow of information. Management should encourage the free flow of suggestions, complaints, and facts.

The informal channel of communication includes the "grapevine." News acquired through the grapevine contains some factual information but, most of the time, it carries inaccurate information, half truths, rumors, private interpretations, suspicions, and other kinds of distorted information. The grapevine is constantly active and spreads information with amazing speed, often faster than formal channels.

An alert manager acknowledges the grapevine's presence and tries to take advantage of it, if possible. The grapevine can carry a certain amount of useful information. It can help to clarify and disseminate formal channel information. Rumors and inaccuracies should be dispelled by stating the facts to as many people as possible.

TYPES OF COMMUNICATION   Oral, or spoken, communication is the most common form of communication and is generally superior. Oral communication takes less time and is more effective in achieving understanding. Face-to-face communication has the advantage of also providing information through body language, personal mannerisms, and facial expressions. Oral communication should be used when: (1) instruction is simple; (2) quick action is required; (3) a method to be followed needs to be demonstrated; (4) privacy is required; and (5) employees have proven they are capable and meet their commitments.

Written communication should be used in some circumstances, particularly when: (1) a policy or some other authority is being quoted; (2) employees are to be held strictly accountable; (3) a record is needed; (4) employees are inexperienced; and (5) distance makes oral communication impossible. A well-balanced use of both oral and written communication is often very effective.

Other types of communication include visual aids, gestures, and actions. Visual aids, such as pictures, charts, cartoons, symbols, and videos, can be effective particularly when used with good oral communication. "Actions speak louder than words" is sage advice to any manager. Gestures, handshakes, a shrug of the shoulders, a smile, and silence all have meaning and are powerful forms of communication to subordinates.

BARRIERS TO GOOD COMMUNICATION   Some of the barriers to communication have to do with the language used, differing backgrounds of the sender and receiver, and the circumstances in which communication takes place. The receiver hears what he or she expects to hear and may shut out or ignore what is not expected. There is a tendency to infer what is expected even when it has not been communicated. Senders and receivers have different perceptions based on their different backgrounds. It is important to consider where the other person "is coming from." Receivers evaluate the source and interpret or accept communication in light of that evaluation. A trusted and respected leader will have more open channels of communication than a leader who does not command trust and respect. Conflicting information is often ignored. Different people most often attach various meanings to certain words. The sender or communicator must carefully choose words that convey the meaning in such a way that the receiver understands. Nonverbal cues are often ignored. Body language and facial expression often say more than the words they accompany. A receiver who is emotionally upset often stops listening in order to

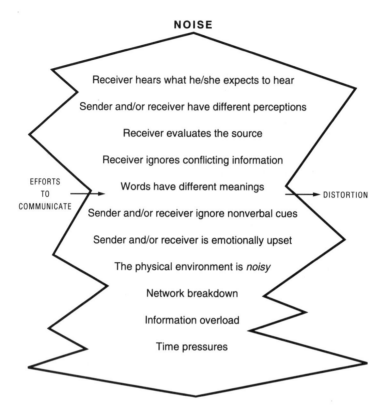

NOISE

Receiver hears what he/she expects to hear

Sender and/or receiver have different perceptions

Receiver evaluates the source

Receiver ignores conflicting information

EFFORTS TO COMMUNICATE → Words have different meanings → DISTORTION

Sender and/or receiver ignore nonverbal cues

Sender and/or receiver is emotionally upset

The physical environment is *noisy*

Network breakdown

Information overload

Time pressures

Figure 12.9.   Barriers to successful communication.

think about what he or she will say next. Noise and the environment often form a physical barrier to communication. There is a right place and a wrong place to conduct good communication. There is a right time and a wrong time.

A network breakdown occurs when there is a disruption or closure of a communication channel. This can be caused by a number of factors, both intentional and unintentional. Some reasons for the network to break down are forgetfulness, jealousy, fear of negative feedback, and to gain an edge over the competition. Information overload occurs when someone receives more information than they are able to process. Time pressures on the sender form a barrier to effective communication because of hastily developed messages, use of the most expedient (often, not most effective) channel, and allowing insufficient time for feedback. These barriers to successful communication are summarized in Fig. 12.9.

IMPROVING COMMUNICATIONS   Communication is not a one-way process. One of the most important parts of effective communication is to listen to the reply, which may be either words, facial expression, body language, or even silence.

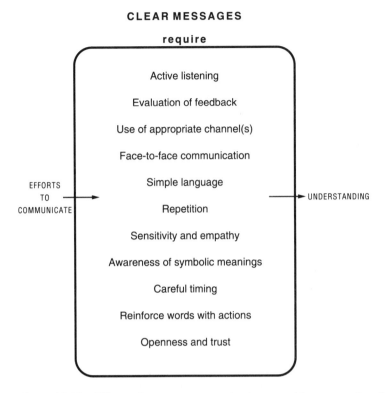

CLEAR MESSAGES

require

Active listening

Evaluation of feedback

Use of appropriate channel(s)

Face-to-face communication

Simple language

EFFORTS TO COMMUNICATE → Repetition → UNDERSTANDING

Sensitivity and empathy

Awareness of symbolic meanings

Careful timing

Reinforce words with actions

Openness and trust

Figure 12.10.   Ways to improve communication to achieve mutual understanding.

The evaluation of feedback can tell much about how the message has been received. Empathy or the ability to put yourself in the receiver's shoes in a conversation can also be crucial to mutual understanding.

Face-to-face communication is advantageous to use, when possible, because of the ability to gain immediate feedback from multiple channels, such as oral, facial expression, and body language. Long, technical, and complicated words should be avoided as much as possible. To secure understanding, repeating information using slightly different words, phrases, or approaches is often effective. Being sensitive to the receiver or being able to put yourself in the receiver's place can improve communication. One should be aware that some words or phrases can have symbolic meaning to others and avoid using them. Proper timing is also important. The old maxim, "criticize in private, praise in public" is an example of timing. Reinforcing words with congruent actions has already been discussed as essential to effective communication. Finally, an atmosphere of openness and trust, fostered by self-disclosure, builds healthy relationships that contribute to effective communication. These methods to improve communication are summarized in Fig. 12.10.

Managerial Ethics and Social Responsibility

The major goals of administrative leadership in the scientific management era were profit and productivity. Today, leadership in organizations involves managerial ethics and social responsibility as well. Among the ethical challenges facing foodservice managers today are identifying and understanding different cultural values, dealing with unethical behavior in the organization, balancing the organization's need to know with the employees' rights to privacy, balancing management and employees' rights, and identifying and implementing programs to ensure that the organization is operating in a socially responsible manner. Some areas of each of these are controlled by government regulatory agencies and legal mandates, but many other areas are not.

Ethics can be defined as the rightness or wrongness of actions and as the goodness or badness of these actions' objectives. Many professional organizations have a code of ethics that provide guidelines for their members to use in their work with others. A bill of rights for employees also provides a valuable set of guidelines for managers to use in dealing with subordinates and, at the same time, assures certain rights to employees, such as the right to follow a grievance procedure or the right to a safe workplace.

Social responsibility is an ethical issue because it deals with the goodness or badness of organizational actions as they have an impact on society as a whole. The classical view of social responsibility is that organizations have no obligations to society other than to achieve organizational objectives. The modern view holds that organizations must operate to achieve the greatest good for the greatest number of people. In other words, social responsibility is demonstrated when a company goes beyond profit maximization in order to benefit society in other ways. This may be demonstrated in a number of ways. On the lowest level, organizational "image-building" occurs when managers support good causes in an effort to promote the company and its products. The middle-of-the-road approach includes "good citizenship," which is demonstrated by company support of charities or public interest issues, employee time off to work in problem areas, and employee wellness programs. At the highest level is "full corporate social responsibility," demonstrated by enthusiastic support for social problems.

The areas in which managers are expected to take a proactive, socially responsible stance include the environment, minority group relations, consumer responsibility, and employee rights. Foodservice has a major impact on the environment. Conservation, including the wise use of water and energy, and pollution prevention are real concerns for the industry, as well as being economically and socially mandated practices. The major pollution concern for foodservice is solid waste management. The National Restaurant Association (NRA) (the representative of 636,000 foodservice units) lends its full support to socially responsible, multi-tiered solutions to the solid waste crisis. In order to be successful, such a solution would require the integration of recycling, source reduction, incineration and landfilling, and the support of local and state government. Policies for solid waste management depend on: (1) cooperation of customers to sort and separate solid waste; (2) interest and support of employees and management; (3) the ability to store waste; (4) the cost of transporting waste to recycling centers; (5) the availability of buy-back centers or reclaimers; and (6) a market demand for recycled products.

Social responsibility and minority group relations means going beyond the minimum EEOC (Equal Employment Opportunity Commission) requirements and actively recruiting and promoting members of minority groups, as well as training them if they lack necessary entry-level skills.

Responsibility to consumers in the foodservice field means ethical pricing and advertising practices. It also means serving good quality food that has been prepared under the most sanitary conditions humanly possible.

In the area of management and employee rights, several areas of social responsibility are important. Freedom of speech, assembly, due process of law, privacy, fair compensation, and safe working conditions are all mandated by law. As with EEOC regulations, OSHA (Occupational Safety and Health Act) sets minimum safety requirements. An employer must use his or her own sense of responsibility to determine how much additional cost to incur to ensure the safest of working conditions. More controversial areas of employee rights are substance abuse and drug testing, smoking in the workplace, and surveillance of employees. Random drug testing is illegal unless certain criteria are met. For example, the employer must have employee written consent, the job consequences of abuse must be severe, and the results must be held strictly confidential. No smoking facilities are becoming more widespread. This threatens the rights of the smoker; however, thus far, opposition has not been strong. Modern technology has made sophisticated employee surveillance techniques more effective, readily available, and affordable. If this practice occurs without employees' knowledge, a question of ethics could be raised.

Functional Responsibilities and Skills Required

Certain basic responsibilities are common to all foodservice administrators in whatever type of organization they are employed. Most of the responsibilities that are specific to foodservice are discussed in detail in other chapters of this book. They include

- establishment of goals, objectives, and standards
- personnel selection, education, and welding an effective staff
- overall planning and delegation of work to be done; scheduling of workers
- purchase of food, equipment, and supplies according to specification
- planning for physical facilities and equipment needs

- supervision of all technical operations: production, delivery and service of food, sanitation, safety, security
- financial planning and control

These responsibilities may be classified under the functions of management given in Chapter 10.

Effective administrative leadership is a professional responsibility. Some of the key characteristics of successful—and, thus, professionally responsible—leaders are given by Lester (1981):

> (1) Sense of responsibility—This may mean sometimes subordinating personal desires to the needs of the organization or the profession; (2) Technical and professional competence—The input of others to make decisions may provide guidance, but the final decision will require personal technical and professional knowledge and skills; (3) Enthusiasm—Honest, genuine enthusiasm for the goals and plans of the leader are vital to the generation of commitment and enthusiasm on the part of employees. New directions and unfamiliar areas should be sought without reluctance; (4) Communication skills—Communication is one of the vital linking processes that holds the organization together. It is a key variable in leadership effectiveness. Verbal, written, and nonverbal communications should be understood and utilized effectively. Active listening, avoiding distortion, is a key to good communication; (5) High ethical standards—Ethics are the basis of all group interaction and decision-making processes. Therefore, they play a key role in the leadership function. Professional ethics require leaders to maintain high standards of personal conduct in all situations so that employees may rely on their actions. Integrity is demonstrated when concern for company interests is greater than personal pride; (6) Flexibility—Leaders must have the ability to take whatever comes along and thrive on it. This requires an understanding and acceptance of the fact that no two people or two situations are ever exactly alike. Approaches must be adapted. Change and stress must be understood and managed; (7) Vision—An ability to see the organization as a whole made up of interdependent and interrelated parts; to see where it is going and how it can get there is necessary for effective leadership. Leaders with ideas and images that can excite people and develop timely and appropriate choices will inspire those they lead.

Leadership is widely touted as a cure-all for organizational problems. It is also widely misunderstood—a fact that can result in oversimplified advice to managers. Leadership in foodservice organizations can be defined as the privilege of having the responsibility to direct the actions of others in carrying out the purposes of their organization. This can be accomplished at various levels of authority, but at all levels the leader is accountable for both successes and failures. Many researchers believe that they can systematize or develop models to capture the elusive nature of the leadership phenomenon; however, there are just as many researchers who believe that it cannot be systematized or modeled. This latter group contends that there are too many variables inherent in the environments in which the leader must function, and that the currently popular models of leadership, such as the Managerial Grid, the Tannenbaum-Schmidt continuum, and the Hersey-Blanchard situational model, neglect many of the most critical challenges that leaders must face.

Managers and leaders—are they different? Bennis makes this insightful distinction between managers and leaders: "Managers do things right" while "leaders do the right things." He contends that both functions are necessary in any organization, but that American businesses today are dangerously overmanaged and underled. Drucker agrees and suggests that leadership is made up of a few essential principles, the very same ones that constitute effective management. What needs to be done now is the integration of all the principles of management and leadership—a blending of innovation, stability, order, and flexibility.

Clearly, leadership has been the subject of exhaustive study for many years and will continue to be studied. Many researchers would agree that the knowledge that we already have is enough to improve the situation in American business. Managers now need to do a better job of applying what is known about leadership in order to become leader-managers. To be competitive in today's world, one must not only make a profit but also develop competent and motivated people who can adapt rapidly to changing technology and markets, work together and create synergies, and interact with customers as though they were speaking for the company.

For foodservice managers, this could mean a careful, critical selection of new employees and a training program for all workers to keep them abreast of any changes in the organization, new equipment to be used, and other developments that would affect their work.

Summary Questions

1. What is situational management?
2. Describe how the Tannenbaum-Schmidt continuum of manager behavior fits into a contingency theory of leadership.
3. Define communication.
4. List the various modes of communication that are used in an organization.
5. Describe some ways in which communication can be made a two-way process.
6. List some of the characteristics of a professionally responsible leader.
7. Describe how social responsibility has been legally mandated.

Bibliography

Barnes, L. B. and Kriger, M. P.: The hidden side of organizational leadership. Sloan Mgmt. Rev. 27:15, 1986.

Bass, B. M.: Stogdill's Handbook of Leadership. A Survey of Theory and Research, rev. ed. New York: The Free Press, 1981.

Bennis, W. and Nanus, B.: Leaders: The Strategies for Taking Charge. New York: Harper & Row, 1985.

Blake, R. R. and Mouton, J. S.: Executive Achievement: Making It at the Top. New York: McGraw-Hill, 1986.

Bolman, L. G. and Deal, T. E.: Reframing Organizations. San Francisco: Jossey-Bass, 1991.

Burns, J. M.: Leadership. New York: Harper & Row, 1978.

Dessler, G.: Organization Theory. Englewood Cliffs, NJ: Prentice Hall, 1986.

Drucker, P. F.: Managing for the Future. New York: Truman Talley Books/Dutton, 1992.

Ewing, D. W.: Freedom Inside the Organization. New York: E. P. Dutton, 1977.

French, J. R. P. and Raven, B. H.: The bases of social power. *In* D. Cartwright (Ed.), Studies in Social Power. Ann Arbor, MI: University of Michigan Press, 1959.

Hersey, P. and Blanchard, K. H.: Management of Organizational Behavior: Utilizing Human Resources. Englewood Cliffs, NJ: Prentice Hall, 1982.

Hickman, C. R.: Mind of a Manager Soul of a Leader. New York: John Wiley & Sons, 1990.

House, R. J.: A path-goal theory of leader effectiveness. Administrative Science Quarterly 16:321, 1971.

Koehler, J. W., Anatol, K. W. E., and Applbaum, R. L.: Organizational Communication, 2nd ed. New York: Holt, Rinehart and Winston, 1981.

Kouzes, J. M. and Posner, B. Z.: The Leadership Challenge. San Francisco: Jossey-Bass, 1987.

Lester, R. I.: Leadership: Some principles and concepts. Personnel J. 50:868, 1981.

Maccoby, M.: Why Work? New York: Simon & Schuster, 1989.

McGregor, D.: The Human Side of Enterprise. New York: McGraw-Hill, 1985.

Roberts, W.: Leadership Secrets of Attila the Hun. New York: Warner Books, Inc., 1987.

Spence, H. and Duncan, P., eds.: Food Service and the Environment. Proceedings of the Food Service and the Environment Conference, Victoria University of Wellington, New Zealand, April 6–7, 1992.

Stogdill, R. M. and Coons, A. E., eds.: Leader Behavior: Its Description and Measurement, Research Monograph No. 88. Columbus: Bureau of Business Research, The Ohio State University, 1957.

Stone, F. M., ed.: The AMA Handbook of Supervisory Management. New York: AMACOM, 1989.

Tamel, M. E. and Reynolds, H.: Executive Leadership. Englewood Cliffs, NJ: Prentice Hall, 1981.

Tannenbaum, R. and Schmidt, W. H.: How to choose a leadership pattern. Harvard Business Review, 51(3):162, 1973.

Williamson, J. N., ed.: The Leader-Manager. New York: John Wiley & Sons, 1986.

For More Information

Adams, J. D., ed.: Transforming Leadership. Alexandria, VA: Miles River Press, 1986.

Agor, W. H., ed.: Intuition in Organizations. Newbury Park, CA: Sage Publications, 1989.

Armstrong, M.: The Handbook of Human Resource Management. New York: Nichols Publishing Company, 1988.

Axline, L. L.: TQM: A look in the mirror. Mgmt. Review 80(7):64, 1991.

Bailey, F. G.: Humbuggery and Manipulation. Ithaca, NY: Cornell University Press, 1988.

Batten, J. D.: Tough-Minded Leadership. New York: AMACOM, 1989.

Bednar, D. A.: Relationships between communicator style and managerial performance in complex organizations: A field study. J. of Bus. Comm. 19:51, 1982.

Berenbeim, R. E.: Corporate ethics. The Conference Board Research Report No. 900, p. 4, 1987.

Bittel, L. R. and Newstrom, J. W.: What Every Supervisor Should Know, 6th ed. New York: McGraw-Hill, 1990.

Cadbury, Sir A.: Ethical managers make their own rules. Harvard Bus. Rev. 87(5):69, 1987.

Cichy, R., Sciarini, M. P., and Patton, M. E.: Foodservice leadership. Cornell HRA Quarterly 33:46, 1992.

Clemens, J. K. and Mayer, D. F.: The classic touch: Lessons in leadership from Homer to Hemingway. Homewood, IL: Dow Jones-Irwin, 1987.

Cohen, W. A.: The Art of the Leader. Englewood Cliffs, NJ: Prentice Hall, 1990.

Conger, J. A., Kanungo, R. N., and Associates: Charismatic Leadership. San Francisco: Jossey-Bass, 1988.

Daft, R. and Lengel, R.: Information richness: A new approach to managerial behavior and organization design. Research in Organizational Behavior 6:191, 1984.

Fiedler, F. E. and Garcia, J. E.: New Approaches to Effective Leadership. New York: John Wiley & Sons, 1987.

Geldt, T. E.: Drug and alcohol abuse in the workplace: Balancing employer and employee rights. Employee Relations Law Journal 11:183, 1986.

Hamilton, J. O., Smith, E. T., Angiolillo, P., and Rhein, R.: No smoking sweeps America. Business Week July 27, 1987, p. 40.

Kanter, R. M.: Men and Women of the Corporation. New York: Simon & Schuster, 1983.

Kanter, R. M.: When Giants Learn to Dance. New York: Simon & Schuster, 1989.

Kaplan, R. D.: The Expansive Executive. Greensboro, NC: Center for Creative Leadership, 1989.

Kets de Vries, M. F. R.: Prisoners of leadership. Human Relations 41(3):261, 1988.

Kinlaw, D. C.: Coaching for Commitment: Managerial Strategies for Obtaining Superior Performance. San Diego: University Associates, Inc., 1989.

Kirmeyer, S. L. and Thung-Rung, L.: Social support: Its relationship to observed communication with peers and superiors. Acad. of Mgmt. J. 30:138, 1987.

Koten, J. A.: Corporate communications: All together now. Business Horizons 27:18, 1984.

Kotter, J. P.: The Leadership Factor. New York: The Free Press, 1988.

Lehr, R. I. and Middlebrooks, D. J.: Workplace privacy issues and employer screening policies. Employee Relations Law Journal 11:407, 1986.

Leipzig, J. S. and More, E.: Organizational communication: A review and analysis of three current approaches to the field. J. of Bus. Comm. 19:77, 1982.

Peters, T. and Austin, N.: A Passion for Excellence. New York: Random House, 1985.

Rothstein, M. A.: Screening workers for drugs: A legal and ethical framework. Employee Relations Law Journal 11:424, 1986.

Rowe, M. P. and Baker, M: Are you hearing enough employee concerns? Harvard Bus. Rev. 62:127, 1984.

Ruben, B. D.: Communication and Human Behavior, 2nd ed. New York: Macmillan, 1988.

Sayles, L. R.: Leadership: Managing in Real Organizations, 2nd ed. New York: McGraw-Hill, 1989.

Smeltzer, L. R.: The relationship of communication to work stress. J. of Bus. Comm. 24:47, 1987.

Smith, P. B. and Peterson, M. F.: Leadership, Organizations and Culture. Newbury Park, CA: Sage Publications, 1988.

Weiner, S.: Profit without pollution. Forbes 139(11):46, 1987.

Whitely, W.: An exploratory study of managers' reactions to properties of verbal communication. Personnel Psychology 37:41, 1984.

Zaleznik, A.: The Managerial Mystique. New York: Harper & Row, 1989.

Work Improvement and Productivity

Raising productivity has been called the first responsibility of management in a knowledge society. Predictions are that it will be the biggest and toughest challenge facing managers during the next few decades. Past experience has shown that an increase in productivity as a result of investment of capital and new technology depends entirely on how people use them. However, people "working smarter" is believed to be the real key to productivity increases in foodservice operations.

Productivity, the ratio of input to output, can be used as a measure of work improvement. However, using the input/output ratio as a definition of productivity in the practical world of foodservice today is inadequate and somewhat irrelevant. A wider conception of productivity, which encompasses factors such as product quality and customer satisfaction, is necessary. In addition, any attempt at work improvement must take into consideration the people involved. An understanding of human nature on the part of management and improvement in the overall quality of work life are critical components of any productivity improvement program.

Increased production with less human effort has been another objective in the foodservice industry for years. Some methods for designing effective and efficient ways of accomplishing work are included in this chapter. This work design must consider improved job content, a safe and healthy work environment, and efficient and effective work methods.

Each of these requires a careful study of existing conditions before any change is implemented. The study of work methods begins with the establishment of standards. The method employed can then be analyzed using one of several techniques. Work simplification is one such technique for identifying and eliminating the uneconomical use of time, equipment, materials, space, or human effort.

In foodservice operations, the focus on increased productivity has to center around performance. Work performance in some jobs means that quality, quantity, and/or both quality and quantity must be considered. Quality management philosophies, such as total quality management (TQM), are receiving increased attention in all segments of foodservice.

Learning Objectives

After studying this chapter, the reader should be able to

1. define productivity as it relates specifically to foodservice management
2. describe the quality of work life (QWL) concept
3. list and briefly discuss the environmental factors that can minimize worker fatigue
4. describe what is meant by work simplification
5. list and briefly explain the principles of motion economy
6. list the steps required for the analysis and revision of a job method
7. explain the use of work sampling, pathway or flow diagram, operation and flow charts, and micromotion studies as tools for a work improvement study
8. describe the concept of total quality management (TQM)

A step-by-step procedure for implementing a work improvement program is outlined in this chapter. One very important step requires that the job be broken down into its component parts in detail. This may be accomplished by work sampling, a pathway or flow diagram, operation and process charting, or micromotion studies. Each is discussed briefly.

What Is Productivity?

The successful and efficient day-to-day operation of a foodservice is a constant challenge to its management group. No foodservice system can afford to remain static for long, but must keep pace with the socioeconomic changes and technological developments in food and equipment and their effects on the overall pattern of operation. Changes in consumer attitudes and behavior, labor and energy costs, regulatory considerations and the general business environment have created new and challenging problems. The present-day foodservice consumer shows a much greater awareness of economic value and sanitary requirements and demands quality food and efficient service at a reasonable price.

Increased production with less human effort has long been an objective in industry. Interest in the designing of work systems to convert human work practices to machines was a contributing factor to the Industrial Revolution. Since then the development has not been steady, but we do rely heavily on mechanization and automation to increase productivity and develop manpower effectiveness. Current high material and labor costs make it imperative that every effort be made to study the work design and perfect efficient operation if high standards of production and quality of products are to be maintained at a reasonable cost.

Simplification of tasks and techniques designed to decrease fatigue of workers are effective aids to good management that are accorded wide recognition and attention by both managers and workers in the foodservice field.

Increased productivity and employee satisfaction are frequently considered to be the overall objective of work design. Many definitions have been given for productivity but essentially, in foodservice management, it is a measure or level of *output* of goods produced or services rendered in relation to *input* in terms of time (labor hours, minutes, or days), money spent, or other resources used.

In order to relate such diverse quantitative units of measurement as number of meals and amounts of service, pounds of materials, labor hours, BTUs, and capital equipment, they can be expressed in dollar values. The resulting formula is a profitability ratio that must be greater than one to produce a profit.

A crucial problem facing some companies is their inability, due to competition (and cost containment), to recover increases in the cost of materials, labor, or other resources by raising prices. They are also unable to decrease the cost of the resources or substitute others. Therefore, if the profit margin is to be maintained or increased, productivity must be improved.

In foodservice organizations, productivity is measured using indicators such as: meals per worked hour, meals per paid hour, meal equivalents per worked hour, meal equivalents per paid hour, transactions per worked hour, and transactions per paid hour. When measured for successive periods, these productivity indicators show a trend. Comparisons can also be made between similar institutions.

The QWL Approach

Quality of work life (QWL) is a term that has been used to describe values that relate to the quality of human experiences in the workplace. QWL is affected by a composite of factors on the job, including factors that relate to work itself, to the work environment, and to the employee personally. People are the key factor in improving productivity. If productivity is to be improved, both the nature of people and the organizations in which they work must be understood. People are the highest order of resources and, as such, are responsible for controlling and utilizing all other resources.

If the source of improving the productivity position of an organization is directly traceable to people, then it follows that the achievement of a better bottom line of productivity must be *everybody's* business. Managers must be capable of utilizing the human resources of the organization and use a systems approach to productivity improvement in which all members of the organization are involved.

Increased productivity means motivation, dignity, and greater personal participation in the design and performance of work in the foodservice organization. It means developing individuals whose lives can be productive in the fullest sense.

Judson reported a study of 195 U.S. companies found that management ineffectiveness was by far the single greatest cause of declining productivity and that the only successful effort to raise productivity was an integrated QWL approach.

QWL is a multifaceted concept. Incentive plans such as a contingent time-off plan under which the company agrees to award specific time off if the workers perform at an agreed-upon level have been successful in improving productivity. Such factors as reducing worker fears, providing opportunity for advancement, implementing job enrichment by adding responsibility, budget, or staff to the job, allowing the exercise of professional skills, and improving communication skills also aid in increasing productivity.

A classic study conducted a number of years ago by Katz and Kahn, two behavioral science researchers, found that a particular leadership style was more effective in increasing productivity and employee satisfaction. The characteristics of this style of leadership are: (1) general supervision rather than close, detailed supervision of employees; (2) more time devoted to supervisory activities than in doing production work; (3) much attention to planning of work and special tasks; (4) a willingness to permit employees to participate in the decision-making process; and (5) an approach to the job situation described as being employee-centered, that is, showing a sincere interest in the needs and problems of employees as individuals, as well as being interested in high production.

Increased involvement of workers in their organizations has received much attention in the last few years. Today's workers no longer want to be separated from responsibility. Productivity appears to be maximized when a unity of purpose and a feeling of ownership exists among employees. This unity is created when the greatest possible responsibility is given to the lowest possible levels of the organization; compensation systems are designed so that employees are salaried with incentive earnings tied to competence and performance; the greatest degree of involvement and consensus is sought from all levels; and management exhibits the unity with the employee.

In addition to these characteristics, improvements in resources (supervision, methods, and technology) to facilitate greater effectiveness and reduce frustrations seem effective in improving productivity and employee satisfaction.

The QWL approach, in essence, attempts to replace the typical adversary relationship between management and employees with a cooperative one. Key words of QWL are cooperation, trust, involvement, respect, rapport, and openness.

Work Design

The overall objectives of work design are to increase productivity and employee satisfaction. The specific objectives are to improve the content of the job, provide a safe and healthy work environment, and to design a staff of fit people, optimum work environment, and effective and efficient work methods.

JOB CONTENT   Job content in foodservice systems is being improved through automation of the production and distribution systems. Food factories and commissary-type operations employ large-volume machinery in long, integrated production runs to prepare one specific product at a time. This system makes possible a more orderly pace and, usually, more desirable working hours.

Another approach to changing job content is to redelegate some parts of the job. A growing number of jobs are becoming encumbered with routine "busy work" that has little or no value and that could be delegated to less skilled employees. High levels of productivity, profitability, motivation, and morale are dependent on allowing employees to do what they have been trained and paid to do. The ingredient room where foodservice employees weigh, measure, and assemble all the ingredients for each production formula is an example of this downward shift of responsibility. Such work would normally be performed by a cook, chef, or cold prep person. The use of support personnel such as dietetic technicians and assistants is another example. Delegation of this type must be done carefully. It is a complex process requiring skill in planning, organizing, and controlling. The different needs and abilities of employees must be effectively managed.

SAFETY AND HEALTH   To provide a safe and healthy work environment is both economically and sociologically important. From an economic standpoint, accidents and job-related illnesses are extremely costly in terms of productivity. The safety and health of the work force is the responsibility of its management and is discussed further in the sections that follow.

EQUIPMENT DESIGN   Kazarian (1983) stated that, "Probably the greatest change that will be evident in the future planning of foodservice facilities is the physical arrangement of spaces and equipment to increase the productivity of workers." Avery (1985) said:

> In order for the equipment and workers to combine productively, one must call on the science variously known as ergonomics, human factors, or human engineering.

This may be defined as adapting tasks, equipment and working environment to the sensory, perceptual, mental, and physical attributes of the human worker. The employee works best if his equipment is designed for the job to be done, his capabilities, and if it is well placed in pleasing surroundings. (p. 15)

To maximize productivity in foodservice, Avery (1985) sets forth these principles of human engineering:

1. Design and arrangement of equipment should be such that the equipment's use requires a minimum application of human physical effort.

2. Only essential information should be provided for the equipment, and this should be presented when and where it is required with maximum clarity. It should be arranged in a step-by-step order.

3. Control devices on equipment should be easily identified, minimum in number, logical in placement, and in consonance with displays in operation. They should relate precisely to the functions they control.

4. Equipment should be designed to provide maximum productivity while utilizing the worker's physical and mental attributes most effectively. It should take into account the dimensions of the worker and his or her strengths.

5. Equipment should be selected on the basis of need in utilizing specific ingredients to prepare a selected menu, grouped in most used combinations, and arranged in order of most frequent interuse proceeding from left to right. Those tasks demanding the greatest skill should be grouped around the worker having these skills, and his or her movements to provide for his or her needs should be minimal.

6. The environment in which the foodservice worker operates should be designed and controlled to allow him or her to be most productive, comfortable, and happy with his or her job. This control involves consideration of lighting, facility and equipment coloration, temperature, humidity, noise, smells, facility design, floor conditions, and safety, among others. (p. 16)

WORK ENVIRONMENT   One of the goals of human engineering is the prevention of fatigue. The manager of a foodservice may find that fatigue or tiredness of some workers, with a resultant drop in their energy, enthusiasm, and production output, is due to external factors beyond his or her control, such as irregularities in the home situation, extraordinary physical exertion away from the job, or a nutritionally inadequate food intake. However, in the organization, while the workers are on the job, there are unlimited opportunities to study causes of fatigue and to possibly correct them.

Certain psychological factors such as attitude because of disinterest in and boredom with the job, dislike of the supervisor, or a low rate of pay may contribute to the fatigue and low output of some workers, but such situations often can be improved through changes in personnel policies and administration. Emphasis in this section is relative to the environmental and physical factors on the job affecting fatigue and work improvement methods.

With a given set of working conditions and equipment, the amount of work done in a day depends on the ability of the worker and the speed at which he or she works. The fatigue resulting from a given level of activity depends on such factors as: (1) hours of work, that is, the length of the working day and the weekly working hours; (2) number, location, and length of rest periods; (3) working conditions such as lighting, heating, ventilation, and noise; (4) the work itself.

The amount of reserve energy brought to the job varies with individuals. Some workers can maintain a fairly even tempo throughout the day, whereas others tire rather quickly and need to rest periodically to recoup nervous and physical energy. Short rest periods appropriately scheduled tend to reduce fatigue and lessen time taken by employees for personal needs.

Lighting, heating, ventilation, and noise are environmental factors that often contribute to worker fatigue. Satisfactory standards for the lighting of kitchen areas is 35 to 50 foot-candles on work surfaces with reflectance ratios of 80 for ceiling, 30 to 35 on equipment, to a minimum of 15 for floors. Temperature and humidity also influence worker productivity. A desirable climate for food preparation and service areas is around 68° to 72° F in the winter and 74° to 78° F in summer with relative humidity 40% to 45%. Higher temperatures tend to increase the heart rate and fatigue of most workers. Air conditioning in hot and humid locales is considered a necessity, whereas in some parts of the country a good fan and duct system is satisfactory to give an air change every 2 to 5 minutes. Hoods over cooking equipment provide for the disposal of much heat and odor originating from these units. Noise has a disturbing and tiring effect on most people. Effective control of the intensity of noise in a foodservice area is possible through precautionary measures such as installation of sound-absorbing ceiling materials, the use of rubber-tired mobile equipment and smooth-running motors, and training the employees to work quietly.

Much has been written about the value of the study of physical facilities and the procedures followed in specific jobs, aimed at increasing efficiency in the operation of a foodservice. A thorough analysis of a floor plan, on paper or in actuality, would provide facts on which to base decisions regarding changes needed in order to make the most compact arrangement possible, yet provide adequate equipment in an efficient arrangement.

WORK METHODS   In order to design the most effective and efficient work methods, existing methods must first be studied. A very important part of the manager's job is the establishment and maintenance of standards by which performance can be judged. Standards are criteria against which results are judged.

Foodservice managers and administrative dietitians have responsibility for determining the standards of time, quantity, quality, and cost for their own department. How much work of what quality is to be accomplished in what length of time and at what cost? Managers must be able to answer these questions realistically and provide the information for the workers if any degree of competence and *high productivity* are to be achieved. Otherwise, employees develop their own standards and may never reach their potential or produce at an acceptable level. Managers who allow this to happen have lost control of operations; events then control the manager.

Standards are derived from objectives, the statements of what is to be achieved. Behavioral objectives relate specifically to what an individual should be able to do as a result of the learning process. Such objectives usually form the basis of a training program and give specific measures for trainee attainment. Although workers learn proper techniques and procedures throughout training program, actual work experience is usually necessary for them to develop speed and accuracy in completing a given task. This is a situation in which preestablished standards are necessary so the employees will know exactly what is expected of them and so a goal is provided for them to attain. An example of a behavioral objective for a kitchen worker is "the employee will be able to make and wrap 90 sandwiches in 30 minutes."

Time and quantity studies must be made within a given foodservice department in order to establish desirable standards for that department with its own equipment, space arrangement, facilities, and procedures. These variables make it difficult if not impossible to have universal standards among foodservice organizations. The employee who knows she is expected to make 45 sandwiches in 15 minutes, or 3 sandwiches per minute, is much more apt to respond to meet the challenge of a goal to be reached than the employee who is told to "just work as fast as you can."

Each operation or task to be performed requires similar questions to be asked and answered. Actual time studies may be made in order to arrive at realistic time-quantity standards. Quality and cost standards come from the knowledge of the dietitian or foodservice manager, who must have acquired this from his or her basic education and preparation for the position. Standards for personnel to which applicants can be compared include minimum acceptable qualities necessary for adequate performance of the job duties. These standards or qualifications are stated in job specifications for use by those who select personnel. (See Chapter 10 for more on job specifications.)

Although no one can set standards for someone else's department, results of some research studies can prove helpful as a guide to foodservice managers undertaking a standards-setting project. A formula for determining how long it takes to accomplish a given task is

$$\frac{a + 4m + b}{6} = \text{Probable time required}$$

$a = $ the "least" amount of time to do a given task

$b = $ the "most" amount of time to do a given task

$m = $ the most "likely" time to do a given task

Let us say, for instance, that we want to know how much time should be allowed to mop a heavily obstructed 1600-square foot institutional kitchen.
A sloppy, cursory job will take 20 minutes.

$$a = 20 \text{ (minutes)}*$$

An extremely thorough job will take 120 minutes.

$$b = 120 \text{ (minutes)}*$$

The job, done adequately, will most likely take 45 minutes.

$$m = 45 \text{ (minutes)}*$$

Using the formula.

$$\frac{a + 4m + b}{6} = \frac{20 + (4 \times 45) + 120}{6} = \frac{20 + 180 + 120}{6} = \frac{320}{6} = 53\tfrac{1}{3} \text{ minutes}$$

Knowing that the most probable time to mop the floor is $53\tfrac{1}{3}$ minutes, we will allot that amount of time daily to that task.
*Derived from actual time study of cursory, thorough, and adequate sampling.

Studies throughout the years have given suggested standards in terms of number of labor minutes required for one meal served. These ranged from a low of 4 or 5 minutes for some school foodservices, to 9 or 10 minutes for college and industrial cafeterias, up to 18 to 20 labor minutes per meal including supervisory time in hospitals. Greater efficiency (lower number of minutes required) is usually achieved when a larger number of meals are served as compared with a small organization serving few meals. Foodservice managers may wish to make a study of their own operations and develop a standard for themselves based on number of labor minutes needed for each meal served.

School foodservice standards for personnel staffing are stated in terms of number of labor hours needed for number of lunches served, as in the table that follows.

Number of Lunches Served	Meals Per Labor Hour	Total Hours
Up to 100	$9\frac{1}{2}$	9–11
101–150	10	10–15
151–200	11	15–17
201–250	12	17–20
251–300	13	20–22
301–350	14	22–25
351–400	14	25–29
401–450	14	29–32
451–500	14	32–35
501–550	15	35–36
551–600	15	36–40
601–700	16	40–43
701–800	16	43–50
801+	18	50+

Worker efficiency in foodservices is estimated to be from 40% to 55%. Although the nature of the work involved in preparing meals for specified periods of the day, causing uneven workloads, can be part of the reason for such low productivity as compared with that in other industries, foodservices can no longer afford the luxury of inefficiency. Labor costs are too high, and every means possible should be used to improve productivity.

Productivity is sometimes equated with efficiency. Kaud proposed this formula for expressing work efficiency.

$$\text{Efficiency \%} = \frac{\text{earned (standard) hours}}{\text{actual (worked) hours}} \times 100$$

The time that the worker actually performs necessary work can be determined through the use of the work sampling (see later in this chapter under "Methods for Work Improvement Study").

WORK SIMPLIFICATION   Detailed studies of activities within an organization often reveal that cost and time requirements are high because of unnecessary operations and excess motions used by the workers in performance of their jobs. When proper adjustments are made in both the physical setup and the work procedures, the conservation of energy of the workers, increased production, and a reduction in total man-hours should result. Such studies have proved highly effective in the simplification of effort in both repetitive and nonrepetitive activities and apply either in a new situation or where long-established procedures have become accepted practices.

What has become known as *work simplification* began in the late 1920s. An industrial engineer, Allan H. Mogensen, developed the philosophy as a result of his work at Eastman Kodak. He found that workers were creative at thwarting his attempts to prescribe more efficient methods and, when not under surveillance, would develop more productive methods that would enhance their rewards. He reasoned that this creativity could be harnessed in a way that would enable every employee to be his or her own industrial engineer. Thus, the slogan, "Work smarter, not harder," emerged.

Work simplification is more than a technique or set of how-to-do-its. It is a way of thinking or a philosophy that there is always a better way. The emphasis is on the elimination of any uneconomical use of time, equipment, materials, space, or human effort. Conservative estimates show that through an effective work simplification program, foodservice worker productivity can be increased by 20% to 50%.

Employee interest, understanding, and cooperation are essential to the successful operation of a work simplification program. Thinking through and planning before starting any task is necessary if it is to be accomplished efficiently and in the simplest manner possible. The elimination of wasted effort is easy once the worker becomes "motion conscious," learns to apply the principles that may be involved, and sees objectively the benefits of changed procedures. Such benefits can be evidenced by lessened fatigue of workers, safer and better working conditions, better and more uniform quality production, and possibly higher wages through increased production. Agreement and understanding of the objectives and realization that benefits will be shared mutually by workers and management are factors for success. The solicitation and incorporation of suggestions for job improvement methods from the workers are conducive to enthusiastic interest and participation. Usually, any employee resistance to change in established work routines can be overcome by the proper approach of management before and after the inauguration of a work simplification program. The selection of personnel qualified by personality and training for leadership in this work is of prime importance to its implementation.

MOTION ECONOMY The same principles of motion economy adopted by engineers many years ago are applicable in a foodservice operation. Analysts and supervisors need to have an understanding of these principles and the ability to interpret them to workers effectively before job breakdown studies and revision in procedures, arrangement of work area, and equipment are inaugurated. A listing of these fundamental principles of motion economy is given in Table 13.1.

TABLE 13.1.   Principles of Motion Economy.

A check sheet for motion economy and fatigue reduction

Use of the Human Body	Arrangement of the Workplace	Design of Tools and Equipment
1. The two hands should begin, as well as complete, their motions at the same time.	10. There should be a definite and fixed place for all tools and materials.	18. The hands should be relieved of all work that can be done more advantageously by a jig, fixture, or a foot-operated device.
2. The two hands should not be idle at the same time, except during rest periods.	11. Tools, materials, and controls should be located close to the point of use.	19. Two or more tools should be combined wherever possible.
3. Motions of the arms should be made in opposite and symmetrical directions, and should be made simultaneously.	12. Gravity feed bins and containers should be used to deliver material close to the point of use.	20. Tools and materials should be prepositioned whenever possible.
4. Hand motions should be confined to the lowest classification with which it is possible to perform the work satisfactorily.	13. "Drop deliveries" should be used wherever possible.	21. Where each finger performs some specific movement, such as in typewriting, the load should be distributed in accordance with the inherent capacities of the fingers.
5. Momentum should be employed to assist the worker wherever possible, and it should be reduced to a minimum if it must be overcome by muscular effort.	14. Materials and tools should be located to permit the best sequence of motions.	22. Levers, crossbars, and hand wheels should be located in such positions that the operator can manipulate them with the least change in body position and with the greatest mechanical advantage.
6. Smooth continuous motions of the hands are preferable to zigzag motions or straight-line motions involving sudden and sharp changes in direction.	15. Provisions should be made for adequate conditions for seeing. Good illumination is the first requirement for satisfactory visual perception.	
7. Ballistic movements are faster, easier, and more accurate than restricted (fixation) or "controlled" movements.	16. The height of the workplace and the chair should preferably be arranged so that alternate sitting and standing at work are easily possible.	
8. Work should be arranged to permit easy and natural rhythm whenever possible.	17. A chair of the type and height to permit good posture should be provided for every worker.	
9. Eye fixations should be as few and as close together as possible.		

(SOURCE: Ralph M. Barnes: *Motion and Time Study*, Fifth Edition, p. 220. Copyright © 1963 by John Wiley & Sons, Inc. Reprinted by permission of John Wiley & Sons, Inc., New York.)

Practical application of most of these principles can be made easily in the foodservice field and lead to increased efficiency; that is, reduction in the motion and time required for the job. Also, the steady output of production with less fatigue on the part of the worker can be a result. A few specific examples of application follow.

- *Principles 1, 2, and 3.* To serve food onto a plate at the counter, pick up plate with left hand and bring to a center position while right hand grasps serving utensil, dips food, and carries it to the plate, both operations ending simultaneously; when panning rolls, pick up a roll in each hand and place on pan.
- *Principle 6.* Stir a mass of food easily and with minimum fatigue by grasping the handle of a wire whip (thumb up) and stirring in a circular motion instead of pushing the whip directly back and forth across the kettle. Principles 5 and 7 are also applied in this same example, since greater force may be gained easily at the beginning of the downward and upward parts of the cycle.
- *Principle 8.* Gain and maintain speed in dipping muffin or cupcake batter through the use of rhythmic motions; use regular and rhythmic motions in slicing or chopping certain vegetables and fruits with a French knife on a board.
- *Principles 8 and 10.* Equip and arrange each individual's work area so that body movements are confined to a minimum in his or her job performance.
- *Principle 11.* Store mixing-machine attachments and cooking utensils as close as possible to place of use; remove clean dishes from washing machine directly to carts and lowerator units that fit into serving counter; store glasses and cups in racks in which they were washed; cook certain foods in containers from which they will be served.
- *Principle 12.* Install vegetable peeler at end of preparation sink so that peeled potatoes can be dumped directly into the sink; install water outlets above range and jacketed kettles so utensils can be filled at point of use.
- *Principle 14.* For breading foods, arrange container of food to be breaded, flour, egg mixture, crumbs, and cooking pan in correct sequence so that no wasted motions are made.
- *Principle 16.* Provide some means of adjusting height of work surface to the tall and short worker; include one or two adjustable-height stools in list of kitchen equipment.
- *Principle 18.* Provide knee lever-controlled drain outlets on kitchen sinks; install electronic-eye controls on doors between dining room and kitchen.

WORK IMPROVEMENT PROGRAM   Improvement in any work program is contingent on a study of the environmental factors and the activities of the workers in meeting the objectives of the organization. Such a study can involve one or more jobs in an organization. The usual approach for analysis and revision of a job method is:

1. *Select the job to be improved.* What needs improvement most? A bottle-neck job is the best one to start thinking about. Jobs that require much time or that require much worker movement for materials, tools, and such are also good choices.

2. *Break down the job in detail.* Get in the habit of seeing every job as: make ready—the effort and time put into getting the equipment, tools, and materials with which to work; do—the actual productive work; and put away—the clean up or disposal following the "do." Analyze each operation, noting procedure, equipment used, distance moved, and time required. Some methods for performing this step are discussed in the next section.

3. *Challenge every detail.* Ask these questions of the entire job and of every part of the job. *What* is done? *Why* is it done at all? Is it necessary? *Where* is it done? Why is it done there? Is this the right place for it? Where is the best place? *When* is it done? Why is it done then? Is there a better time? *Who* does it? Why does this person do it? Is he or she the right person? *How* is it done? Why is it done this way? Is there a better way? Is there an easier way? Also question the materials, tools, and equipment that are being used. A form such as that shown in Fig. 13.1 is useful for this step.

4. *Develop a better method.* The process- or activity-activity analysis chart affords opportunity to study any job objectively and to evaluate the efficiency of performance. Checks can be made easily to determine the necessary and the excess operations, where and how delays occur, the distances either product or worker must travel, and where changes can be made.

5. *Put the new method into effect.* Teach the new method and follow up with proper supervision. Continue to seek new and better ways to do the job.

Much of the analysis or breakdown of jobs is accomplished through motion and time studies. Barnes (1980) defines motion and time study as

the systematic study of work systems with the purposes of (1) developing the preferred system and method—usually the one with the lowest costs; (2) standardizing this system and method; (3) determining the time required by a qualified and properly trained person working at a normal pace to do a specific task or operation; and (4) assisting in training the worker in the preferred method.

METHODS FOR WORK IMPROVEMENT STUDY   The breakdown of job activities can be made in various ways and recorded appropriately for analysis, study, and evaluation. Among the possibilities are work sampling, pathway or flow diagram, operation and process charting, and micromotion studies. The objective is to be able to gain a complete and detailed picture of the process, regardless of the method of recording.

Situation Studied _Lettuce Chopping_		**Date** _9-17-81_	
Why Studied _To improve efficiency of the process_		**Study by** _Gregoire/Palacio_	
Where _Kramer Food Center Salad Area_		_31.03_ minutes/occurrence	
How Often Repeated per Year _690_		_21410.7_ minutes/year	

Purpose	**What is achieved?** _Lettuce is chopped for salads_	**What would happen if it weren't done?** _There would be no tossed salads_	**What could be done and still meet requirements?** _Lettuce could be bought chopped_	**What should be done?** _Lettuce should be chopped at the facility_
Place	**Where is it done?** _Salad area_	**Disadvantages of doing it there:** _Don't always have enough heads of lettuce to fill barrels of chopped lettuce_	**Where else could it be done?** _Veg. Prep (downstairs)_ **Advantages of doing it elsewhere:** _Barrels could be filled to capacity._	**Where should it be done?** _Salad area for control and better use of existing space._
Sequence	**When is it done?** **Before:** _Each meal_ **After:** _Lettuce is cleaned_	**Disadvantages of doing it then:** _Requires set-up and clean-up three times a day_	**Advantages of doing it sooner:** _Clean-up and set-up only once_ **Advantages of doing it later:** _Lettuce would be fresher_	**When should it be done?** _Once a day_
Person	**Who does it?** _Student salad employee_	**Why that person?** _Assigned to students because this job is routine and disliked by full-time employees_	**List two others who could do it.** _Veg. Prep employee Salad foodservice worker_	**Who should do it?** _Salad foodservice worker_
Means	**What equipment and methods are used?** **Equipment:** _Cutting board French knife_ **Method:** _Manual chopping_	**Disadvantages of equipment:** _Somewhat dangerous_ **Method:** _Slow, tedious_	**How else could it be done?** _Purchase chopped Manual lettuce chopper VCM–Meat slicer_ **Advantages:** _Faster, safer_	**How should it be done?** _VCM_

Figure 13.1. Critical examination of the process of lettuce chopping. Example of how such a study is recorded on a suitable form.

Work sampling is a tool for fact-finding and is often less costly in time and money than a continuous study. It is based on the laws of probability that random samples reflect the same pattern of distribution as a large group. The primary use of work sampling is to measure the activities and delays of people or machines and determine the percentage of the time they are working or idle instead of observing the detailed activities of a repetitive task. The shorter and intermittent observations are less tiring to both the worker and the observer than continuous time studies; several workers can be observed simultaneously; interruptions do not affect the results; and tabulations can be made quickly on data-processing equipment, although neither management nor workers may have the knowledge of statistics involved. This process is sometimes known as random ratio-delay sampling.

A *pathway chart* or *flow diagram* is a scale drawing of an area on which the path of the worker or movement of material during a given process can be indicated and measured, but with no breakdown of time or details of the operation. Measurement of the distance traveled as the worker moves about in the performance of a task is made by computing the total length of lines drawn from one key point to another simultaneously with the worker's movements and multiplying by the scale of the drawing. A more convenient method is to set up pins or string supports at key points on a scale drawing of the worker's area and wind a measured length of string around the supports as the worker progresses from one position to another.

Operation charts can be used as simple devices to record, in sequence, the elemental movements of the hands of a worker at a given station, without consideration of time. A diagram of the work area might head the chart with the observed activities of both hands listed in two columns—left side for left hand, and right side for right hand. In such a chart, small circles are usually used to indicate transportation and large circles to denote action. Analysis of the chart gives a basis for reducing transportation to the lowest degree possible and for replanning the work area and procedures. It is important that both hands be used simultaneously and effectively. A chart showing the procedures used in making a pineapple and cottage cheese salad is given in Fig. 13.2. The lettuce cup had been prearranged on the plate.

The *process chart* is a fairly simple technique for recording and analyzing the breakdown of a job. It graphically presents the separate steps or events by the use of symbols for a given process so that the entire picture of the job can be condensed into a compact yet easily interpreted form. A process chart can present either *product analysis,* which shows in sequence the steps that a product goes through, or *person analysis,* which is a study of what the person does. Many different symbols were used by the Gilbreths when they devised this method of recording job activity years ago. Today, for most practical purposes, only four or five symbols are used that simplify and list quickly the steps or activities in a process. The symbols often used are

○ = operation or main steps in the process
⇨ = transportation or movement
D = delay
▽ = storage or hold
□ = inspection such as examination for quality or quantity

Symbols can be arranged in a vertical line in sequence or, as in the activity-analysis charts (Figs. 13.3 and 13.4), with lines drawn from one symbol to another in each succeeding step. This method of charting makes for ease in checking time and in determining the number of repeats in any process as a basis for their reduction through revision of the method.

Without benefit of an elaborate process chart form, a simple listing of the procedures and times used in the preparation of a menu item can be made and used to improve either the physical setup or the method; for example, the observance of the cook mixing and portioning meat balls, beginning at the worktable.

A *micromotion study* is a technique whereby movements of the worker may be photographed and recorded permanently on film. This method affords a more accurate presentation of detail than others, and projection for analysis can be made at different rates of speed. In addition, the time of each movement can be recorded.

Procedure Chart

Approximate Distance (ft.)	Time (min)	Description of Operation
6	9:00	Fasten bowl and beater in position on mixer
15	9:01	Go to refrigerator for milk, ground meat, and other weighed recipe ingredients (use cart)
15	9:035	Return to mixer
3	9:04	Place seasonings, eggs, milk, and cut-up bread in mixer bowl
	9:05	Mix slightly (observe)
	9:06	Add meat and mix to blend (observe)
3	9:075	Remove beater and take to wash sink
5	9:085	Lift bowl of meat mixture to low bench near worktable
50	9:09	Assemble portion tools and pans
	9:10	Portion onto pans with number 12 dipper
	9:25	Complete portioning

A detailed motion breakdown of the activities portrayed on micromotion film is easily made and recorded in graphic form by use of *therbligs*, expressed through letter, line, or color symbols. The word *therblig*, formed by spelling

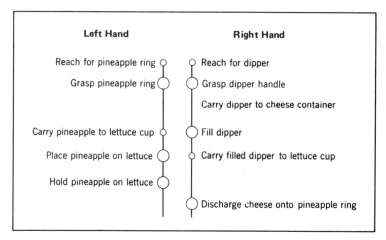

Figure 13.2.   Operation Chart showing movement of the two hands in making pineapple and cottage cheese salad.

Gilbreth backward but retaining the original order of the last two letters, was coined by Frank Gilbreth at the time he introduced the system of breaking down, into 17 subdivisions or elements, basic hand movements employed in job performance. The therbligs are: search (Sh), select (St), inspect (I), transport empty (TE), grasp (G), hold (H), transport loaded (TL), release load (RL), position (P), preposition (PP), assemble (A), disassemble (DA), use (U), avoidable delay (AD), unavoidable delay (UD), plan (Pn), and rest (R).

Most often letter symbols are used in recording the breakdown of a procedure, for example, cutting a cake.

P   Place cake on table in position to cut
TE   Move right hand toward knife rack
Sh   Look over supply of knives
St   Decide knife to use
G   Take knife in right hand
TL   Move knife to cutting position above cake
U   Cut cake

Any human activities can be analyzed by this system as a basis for eliminating the unnecessary and excess motions in the formulation of an improved method of procedure.

The chronocyclegraph is a photographic technique designed to show motion patterns of hands performing rapid repetitive operations. It is made by attaching lights to the hands, which show as dotted lines on the finished photograph. The entire workplace must be included in order to study the relationship of the worker and direction of his or her hand movements to the work setup.

PROCESS CHART

Present ☒ Proposed ☐

1951 – H.Q. Davidson

FILE NUMBER   page

SUMMARY		No.	TIME ( )	TASK or JOB	: Dishwashing Procedure, Operations I Scrapping Trays
OPERATIONS	○	1,546			
INSPECTIONS	☐	0		DEPT.	10th Floor Pantry
MOVES	⇨	99		EQUIPMENT, TOOLS' etc.	Scrapping counter, prerinse counter with disposal unit, trash can, carts, cloth
DELAYS	D	70			
UNITS PRODUCED: 70 trays			1½ hr.	OPERATOR	Pantry Maid A
TOTAL DISTANCE MOVED				ANALYST	DATE March 20, 1963

Descriptive Notes	Activity	Dist.	Time	Analysis Notes
Rinses cloth at sink.	⊗☐⇨D			Damp cloth is used to wipe trays
Carries cloth to scrapping table.	○☐⇨D	8' 6"		
Brings loaded cart into pantry from hall.	○☐⇨D	5' 6"		Positions cart at left of operator. Each cart holds 6-9 trays.
Moves to side of table.	○☐⇨D			
Takes tray from cart and places on scrapping table.	⊗☐⇨D			
Moves around in front of table.	○☐⇨D	1' 0"		Convenient position for working.
Changes position of tray.	○☐⇨⊗			
Places tray on stack of empty trays.	⊗☐⇨D			
Pulls menu from tray.	⊗☐⇨D			
Places name card on tray at extreme right of scrapping table.	⊗☐⇨D			Name cards in stacks by sections.
Picks up salt and pepper with left hand.	⊗☐⇨D			
Places salt and pepper on tray with name cards.	⊗☐⇨D			
Empties coffee pots into disposal.	⊗☐⇨D			
Places empty coffee pots on prerinse counter.	⊗☐⇨D			
Picks up plate and scrapes waste into disposal.	⊗☐⇨D			
Adds plate to stack on prerinse counter.	⊗☐⇨D			
Picks up creamer and empties contents into disposal.	⊗☐⇨D			
Places creamer on prerinse counter.	⊗☐⇨D			
Places cup and saucer on prerinse counter.	⊗☐⇨D			Saucers stacked.
Removes glasses from tray and empties contents into disposal.	⊗☐⇨D			
Places empty glasses upside down in wash rack on prerinse counter.	⊗☐⇨D			
Picks up bowl with right hand.	⊗☐⇨D			
Transfers bowl to left hand.	○☐⇨⊗			Unnecessary handling.
Scrapes waste food from bowl with spoon into disposal.	⊗☐⇨D			Rubber scraper better tool.
Stacks bowls on prerinse counter.	○☐⇨D			

DEPARTMENT OF INDUSTRIAL ENGINEERING—THE OHIO STATE UNIVERSITY

Figure 13.3. Process Chart of tray scrapping as observed in a hospital floor-service pantry.

PROCESS CHART

Present ☐ Proposed ☒

1951 – H.Q. Davidson

FILE NUMBER   page

SUMMARY		No.	TIME ( )	TASK or JOB :	Dishwashing Procedure, Operation I Scrapping Trays
OPERATIONS	◯	1,024			
INSPECTIONS	☐	2		DEPT. :	10th Floor Pantry
MOVES	▷	13		EQUIPMENT, TOOLS' etc.:	Scrapping counter, prerinse counter with disposal unit, trash can, carts, pan, rubber scraper
DELAYS	D	0			
UNITS PRODUCED: 70 trays			1 hr. TOTAL	OPERATOR :	Pantry Maid A
TOTAL DISTANCE MOVED 117 feet				ANALYST :	DATE: April 3, 1963

Descriptive Notes	Activity	Dist.	Time	Analysis Notes
Rinses cloth at sink and fills pan with water.	⊗☐▷D			Cloth is rinsed several times during operation.
Carries cloth and pan to scrapping table.	◯☐▷D	7' 0"		Pan of water at counter reduces trips to sink.
Goes to silver storage unit.	◯☐▷D	4' 9"		
Gets rubber spatula from drawer.	⊗☐▷D			
Returns and places spatula on scrapping table.	◯☐▷D	5' 0"		
Brings loaded cart into pantry from hall.	◯☐▷D	5' 6"		Pre-positioned tray on scrapping counter facilitates placement of name cards, and salts and peppers.
Takes tray from cart and places on scrapping table.	⊗☐▷D			
Picks up salt and pepper and places on tray at extreme right of worker.	⊗☐▷D			
Places name-card holder with menu on same tray.	⊗☐▷D			Menu pulled after name-card holder is on tray while hand is in position. Drops menu on table; all menus later put into trash can at one time.
Scrapes waste food from bowl with rubber scraper.	⊗☐▷D			All refuse from one tray scraped into one dish; then, into disposal.
Stacks bowls on prerinse counter.	⊗☐▷D			
Places silver in rack on prerinse counter.	⊗☐▷D			
Removes glasses from tray, empties contents into disposal.	⊗☐▷D			
Places glasses upside down in wash rack on prerinse counter.	⊗☐▷D			
Empties coffee pot and creamer into disposal, transfers directly to dish rack.	⊗☐▷D			Both hands used simultaneously. Movements combined or continuous wherever possible.
Removes paper tray-cover, folds once and places in trash can.	⊗☐▷D			
Wipes off bottom of tray, places on stack than wipes off top of tray.	⊗☐▷D			Handling of each tray reduced to a minimum.
Reaches to cart for next tray.	⊗☐▷D			
Operations repeated until all trays are scrapped.	◯☐▷D			
	◯☐▷D			

(vertical text, left margin: DEPARTMENT OF INDUSTRIAL ENGINEERING—THE OHIO STATE UNIVERSITY)

Figure 13.4.   Process Chart of same operation as shown in Fig. 13.3 after a study and revision of the original procedures had been made. By changing the sequence of operations and moving the tray cart near the working area, the operations, moves, and delays were reduced materially.

Complete calculation of velocity and acceleration of hand motions is limited by the two-dimensional factor of this technique.

Applications of Work Improvement

Analysis of the data accumulated in the study of the work situation and the methods used in a foodservice may show that certain changes could be made immediately, whereas others involve time, money, and an educational program for the workers. No one set of rules can be used to bring about the desired improvements, but through the cooperative effort of management and worker groups, many things can be made possible. A few suggestions for making improvements follow.

One of the first steps in a job improvement plan is to try to *eliminate unnecessary operations, delays, and moves* without producing deleterious effects on the product or worker. Habit plays an important part in the work routines of people, and it is easy for them to continue in the old pattern; for example, even though the improved methods of processing dehydrated fruits eliminates the necessity of soaking before cooking, some cooks might continue to soak them. A common example of good practice is to have one person fill and deliver storeroom requisitions once a day instead of each cook going to the storeroom for single items as needed.

Operations can be combined as in the making of certain types of sandwiches when the butter could be combined with the spread mixture and applied in one operation instead of two. Other examples of simplified practice are the one-bowl method for combining ingredients for cakes, and cutting a handful of celery stalks at one time on a board instead of singly in the hand.

A *change in sequence of operations* to make the most efficient use of time and equipment and to reduce distance is important. Instead of trying to pare and cut dry, hard squash, put it into the steamer for a short time until the hard cover softens; then it can be pared and cut quickly and easily.

The *selection of multiple-use equipment* reduces to a minimum the items needed. A mixing machine with all of the chopper, slicer, and grinder attachments might be more desirable for a given situation than the purchase of a chopping machine in addition to the mixer without attachments. Where and when the item will be used determines its best location. A mixing machine to be used in one department only should be located convenient to that center of activity, whereas a machine shared by two departments would be located between the two but nearest and most accessible to the department requiring the heaviest and most frequent usage. Duplication of some equipment can be compensated in reduced labor hours required for certain jobs.

Equipment can be relocated or removed entirely to facilitate a more direct flow of work in any area. To reduce "searches" a definite place should be provided for every item and, in a well-regulated foodservice, everything is kept in the designated location except when in use. This storage location or prepositioning of the items should be convenient to the center of their first use; for example, the bowls, beaters, and attachments for the mixing machine should be stored next to or underneath the machine, the cook's cutlery stored in a drawer or on a rack at the cook's table, and clean water glasses returned to the water cooler in the wash racks for storage. Some kitchens may have retained a meat block, even though pan-ready meats are now used. Others may have more range space than is needed for modern cookery. In either case, the removal of certain equipment would provide space for more efficient utilization. Some kitchens may need additional equipment to provide adequate physical facilities for satisfactory operation. Most kitchen machines are designed as labor-saving devices and can do many times the amount of work that could be accomplished by hand in a comparable time and should be used whenever feasible. Improvements in design and operation of kitchen machines influence the method of operation. Automatic timing and temperature-control devices release the worker for other duties more than was possible when frequent checking and manual control were necessary.

The *reduction of transportation or movement of materials and equipment* often can be made through rearrangement of equipment, mobile equipment, and the use of carts to transport many items at one time. The relation of the receiving, storage, and preparation areas requires careful planning to be sure that the flow of the raw product through preparation and service is kept direct and in as condensed an area as practicable. Some delays in operation can be avoided by the installation of additional equipment, by a change in the sequence of operation, such as the assembly-line technique in pie making, by the training of the workers to use both hands at one time and to practice certain shortcuts in preparation, or by a better understanding of the timing standard for various processes.

The *use of a different product* could become a deciding factor in changing the method of procedure. The present tendency is toward the increased use of preprepared foods. Peeled carrots; processed potatoes; peeled and sectioned citrus fruit, frozen fruits, and vegetables; basic mixes for baked products, freeze-dried shrimp; and pan-ready poultry are only a few such items that definitely change the preliminary procedures necessary in many food production jobs.

Consideration of these suggestions and other factors peculiar to the situation provides a basis for outlining an improved method that can be tried and reevaluated for further streamlining. An example of the advantages to be gained from such a revision are indicated in the summaries at the tops of Figs. 13.3 and 13.4.

Quality Management Approaches to Productivity

The discussions thus far on improving productivity have concentrated more on the quantitative aspects of work performance than the qualitative aspects. However, any attempt at productivity improvement must not leave out a consideration of such qualitative aspects. It is important for quality standards to be defined and built into the process. The difficulty has been in measuring quality. A number of attempts have been made in the past, but most, such as the quality assurance programs, were limited-time approaches. Currently, three quality management approaches are being implemented in foodservice operations—quality improvement process (QIP), continuous quality improvement (CQI), and total quality management (TQM). Even though these approaches differ in title and purpose, they all have certain features in common. First, each encompasses a management strategy designed to improve the organization's quality of products and services continuously over time. Second, each promotes positive changes in the structure and culture of the organization to allow for employee participation in decision making and task shaping. This is often referred to as empowerment of employees. Finally, each provides means for assessment of the level of quality improvement and whether quality standards are being met.

Continuous improvement of quality and quantity of products and services is essential for the requisite productivity increases of the future. It will not be enough to make a one-time attack. Continuous learning is also required for increased productivity. The greatest benefit from training employees is not in learning new information, but in doing what is already done well even better. Continuous learning can also be promoted by utilizing the insight that people learn when they teach.

In seeking to empower employees, the goal should be to build responsibility for productivity and performance into every job regardless of level, difficulty, or skill. Drucker contends that partnership with the responsible worker is the only way that will work; nothing else will work at all.

Quality standards can be made more quantifiable by establishing key result areas (KRAs) such as food and service quality, financial management, human resource management, productivity, planning and marketing, and facilities management. Within each KRA, measurable and quantifiable critical factors are listed.

Summary

The need for raising productivity is urgent; so urgent, in fact, that it has been called the first social responsibility of management in a knowledge society. Research conducted during the past 100 years confirms that productivity can be raised and provides the information on how this can be accomplished. Simply stated, it is a matter of defining the task; concentrating work on it; defining the performance; continuously working on improvement and learning; and making the employee a complete partner in the productivity improvement program.

Summary Questions

1. Give some examples of useful profitability ratios that would be useful in the management of a foodservice.
2. List some key words that embody the QWL approach.

3. What are the overall objectives of work design?

4. What factors can cause worker fatigue?

5. Give the formula for determining a worker's efficiency.

6. List some suggestions that may be implemented for work improvement.

7. Why is work improvement and productivity so important in today's work environment?

Bibliography

Armstrong, L. and Symonds, W. C.: Beyond 'may I help you?' Bus. Week 25:100, 1991.

Avery, A. C.: A Modern Guide to Foodservice Equipment, rev. ed. Boston: CBI Publishing Co., 1985.

Axline, L. L.: TQM: A look in the mirror. Mgmt. Rev. 80(7):64, 1991.

Baille, A. S.: The Deming approach: Being better than the best. SAM Advanced Mgmt. J. 51:15, 1986.

Bain, D.: The Productivity Prescription. New York: McGraw-Hill, 1982.

Barnes, R. M.: Motion and Time Study—Design and Measurement of Work, 7th ed. New York: John Wiley & Sons, 1980.

Bennett, A. C.: Productivity and the Quality of Work Life in Hospitals. Los Angeles: American Hospital Publishing, Inc., 1983.

Bowman, J. and Gift, B.: Continuing to do well. Food Mgmt. 24:138, 1989.

Brayton, G. N.: Simplified method of measuring productivity identifies opportunities for increasing it. Industrial Engineering 15:49, 1983.

Deming, W. E.: Quality, Productivity, and Competitive Position. Cambridge, MA: MIT Press, 1982.

Drucker, P. F.: Managing for the Future. New York: Truman Talley Books/Dutton, 1992.

Flamholtz, E. G., Das, T. A. K., eds.: Human Resource Management and Productivity. Los Angeles: Institute of Industrial Relations, University of California, Monograph and Research Series, 39, 1984.

Gift, B.: On the road to TQM. Food Mgmt. 27:88, 1992.

Imai, M.: Kaizen. New York: Random House Business Division, 1986.

Judson, A. S.: The awkward truth about productivity. Harvard Bus. Rev. 60:93, 1982.

Kahn, R. L. and Katz, D.: Leadership practices in relation to productivity and morale. In D. Cartwright and A. Zander (Eds.), Group Dynamics Research and Theory, 2nd ed. New York: Harper & Row, 1960.

Katzell, R. A. and Yankelovich, D.: Work, Productivity, and Job Satisfaction. New York: The Psychological Corp., 1975.

Kaud, F. A.: Productivity: Measures and improvement approaches. In J. C. Rose (Ed.), Handbook for Health Care Food Service Management. Rockville, MD: Aspen Systems Corp., 1984.

Kazarian, E. A.: Foodservice Facilities Planning, 2nd ed. Westport, CN: AVI Publishing Co, 1983.

King, P.: A total quality makeover. Food Mgmt. 27:96, 1992.

Konz, S.: Work Design: Industrial Ergonomics, 2nd ed. Columbus, OH: Grid Publishing, Inc., 1983.

Lockwood, D. L. and Luthans, F.: Contingent time off: A nonfinancial incentive for improving productivity. Mgmt. Rev. 73:48, 1984.

Matthews, M. E.: Productivity studies reviewed, trends analyzed. Hospitals 49:81, 1975.

Miller, L.: Tearing down the barriers between management and labor leads to increased productivity and greater profits. Mgmt. Rev. 73:8, 1984.

Myers, M. S.: Every Employee a Manager. New York: McGraw-Hill, 1981.

Pedderson, R.: Motivation and worker productivity. *In* J. Wilkinson (Ed.), Increasing Productivity in Foodservice. Boston: Cahners Books, 1973.

Schecter, M.: Restaura makes the CQE commitment. Food Mgmt. 27(4):112, 1992.

Schecter, M.: The quest for quality. Food Mgmt. 27:82, 1992.

The roots of quality control in Japan: An interview with W. Edwards Deming. Pacific Basin Quarterly Spring/Summer:1, 1985.

VonEgmond-Pannell, D.: School Foodservice, 4th ed. New York: Van Nostrand Reinhold, 1990.

For More Information

Andrews, C. G. and Johnson, G. A.: The crucial importance of production and operations management. Acad. Mgmt. Rev. 7:145, 1982.

Barrier, M.: Small firms put quality first. Nation's Business 80:22, 1992.

Bartscht, K. G., Bayha, F. H., Molhoek, D. G., and Kausler, G. J.: Hospital Staffing Methodology Manual, MM-3 Dietary. Ann Arbor, MI: Community Systems Foundation.

Batten, J. D.: Tough-Minded Leadership. New York: AMACOM, 1989.

Berger, J.: Productivity: Why it's the no. 1 underachiever. Business Week 2995:54, 1987.

Crosby, P. B.: The Eternally Successful Organization. New York: McGraw-Hill, 1988.

Dreyfack, K. and Port, O.: Even American know-how is headed abroad. Business Week 2935:60, 1986.

Main, J.: Under the spell of the quality gurus. Fortune 114:30, 1986.

Scholtes, P. R.: The Team Handbook. Madison, WI: Joiner Associates, Inc., 1988.

Spencer, L. M., Jr.: Calculating Human Resource Costs and Benefits. New York: John Wiley & Sons, 1986.

Financial Management

Financial planning and accountability for the foodservice organization is a major responsibility for the manager. Cost effectiveness is essential for a successful operation, especially with today's economy and competitive market.

Every person responsible for the financial management must know, day by day, what transactions have taken place and how they compare with established goals. Otherwise, downward trends may not be detected in time to take corrective action before financial disaster occurs. The primary purpose of this chapter is to provide information necessary for managers to be able to: (1) plan a budget, (2) set up a system of records that provide financial operating data, (3) use records to prepare financial reports, (4) review and evaluate data from the records and reports by comparing them with budgeted figures, and (5) know what kinds of corrective action can and should be taken to keep financial operations in line with anticipated and desired goals. Basic information required for this kind of cost control and good financial management is the same whether a computerized or manual system is used. Decision making regarding objectives and goals, cost justification, control measures, and the kind of corrective action to take when needed remains a personal activity and responsibility of the foodservice manager.

Learning Objectives

After studying this chapter, the reader should be able to

1. list and briefly describe the four actions basic to achieving financial maturity
2. define the term budget and discuss its purpose
3. describe the advantages and disadvantages of budgetary planning

4. compare and contrast a fixed budget, a flexible budget, and a zero-based budget

5. list the recommended steps in planning the foodservice financial budget

6. describe why the budget process is one of the most effective management tools

7. name the areas in which records for control purposes should be kept

8. describe what is included in a profit and loss statement

9. discuss the conventional and prime-cost methods used to determine selling price

10. calculate productivity and cost ratios for financial analysis

11. suggest appropriate action plans to bring actual spending in line with the budget

Financial Planning

Good financial planning and management are essential for the success of every foodservice operation. It is essential that management has knowledge of the techniques used to control costs and to provide data for sound financial decision making. The following four actions are basic to achieving financial maturity on the part of the manager and, when followed, should provide the guide to achieving the success desired:

1. setting financial goals or standards to be attained, usually through a planned budget

2. knowing what is being accomplished through a system of records to provide pertinent data on current operations

3. using the data from the records to evaluate progress that has been made toward reaching the set goals, best done through daily, monthly, and yearly reports that compare actual achievement with the standard

4. taking any corrective measures necessary to bring operations in line with those desired

The financial goals of various foodservices differ. Some are in business to make as large a profit as possible; others are nonprofit but seek to provide the best possible food and service that their available resources allow. In all situations, however, some type of financial plan is a key to achieving desired departmental goals. Without such a guide, problems may arise before management is aware of them and could lead to financial downfall.

The financial plan most commonly used is a budget. All foodservice managers should prepare and use a budget as a guide for maintaining a sound, healthy organization. Such planning is, of course, done within the policies of the organization.

Budgets

A budget is a forecast of future needs. It covers the planned activities of the department for a given period of time, usually the fiscal or calendar year, and should be arranged in some orderly manner. Budgets are usually thought of as a *financial* plan, but foodservice budgets also include operating data, such as the number of meals to be served and labor time requirements. Kaud stated, "It is generally agreed that the proper design and use of the budget process is one of the most effective management tools because it does the following":[1]

- States goals and objectives in a quantifiable manner.
- Serves as a communication and commitment device for management.
- Acts as a measurement tool and feedback for corrective action.
- Points out deficiencies.
- Forecasts when shortages might occur.

Budgets are based on factual data from past records of income, expenditures, census and labor hours used, and a consideration of any anticipated changes that can affect future operations. This method alone, however, can focus too much on desired additions to the budget unless there is a cost evaluation made to justify both past and newly planned expenditures.

For any foodservice that is just beginning operation, a detailed budget will not be possible. Since the service has not operated previously, there will be no records of past operations available on which to base a plan. An established goal of percentage of income to be spent for food can serve as a general guide for the first few months of business and be compared daily with actual operations.

With the current emphasis on cost containment and better management of all resources, it is important that foodservice managers understand the budget planning process and techniques used to prepare a realistic budget. Too many managers operate without a budget as a guide because it is time-consuming to prepare, predictions are difficult, and incomplete records fail to provide the necessary data. The value of a budget and the budgeting process must be clearly understood and accepted by management; otherwise, if one is planned, it may be an empty gesture, not used for its intended purpose.

---

[1] Reprinted, with permission, from *Financial Management of the Hospital Food Service Department,* published by American Hospital Publishing, Inc., copyright 1983, out of print.

VALUE OF A BUDGET   To some, the word *budget* has the connotation of curtailed spending and inflexibility, and is, therefore, undesirable. This is not true. Instead, a budget is a valuable management tool used as a guide for allocation of resources and for comparison with actual operations, the basis for financial control.

The advantages of budget planning and budgets are many, far outweighing any possible disadvantages. For example,

1. Budget planning forces those in management positions to seriously consider the future directions and development of their department, and to reaffirm old or establish new financial goals. All those with decision-making authority in the department should be involved in budget planning and contribute to final decisions.

2. The budget planning committee's review of previous expenditures provides an evaluation process and a base for justifying future requests for funds.

3. A budget is an important control device. It gives a standard for comparison against actual transactions. Deviations from the anticipated (budgeted) are evident and can be corrected or justified as they occur.

4. Since persons involved in planning establish priorities of need, they should be committed to staying within the limits they were responsible for setting.

5. A budget provides a goal for achievement. Employees made aware of those goals are apt to feel responsibility toward meeting them.

6. A budget provides for continuity in the event of a changeover in management.

Disadvantages of the budget process are minor compared with the positive results of having a budget for a guide. Such disadvantages include the following:

1. A budget that is rigid is often ignored as unworkable. Budgets should be flexible and adjustable according to changing situations.

2. Budget preparation is tedious, requires time, and takes personnel away from other management activities.

3. Unless the entire managerial staff is in support of budgeting and cooperates in preparation and use of the budget, the process may be only a gesture and have limited value.

4. Departments within the organization may vie with each other for funds, which could cause undesirable competition and problems.

TYPES OF BUDGETS   Although there are many types of budgets, all have the same focus: to determine how much money (or other resources) are available to be used, and then to allocate that amount fairly to cover various expenses plus a margin for profit.

Following are descriptions of some types of budgets used by foodservice managers and some terms used in the budgeting process.

- **Operating budget,** as the name implies, is a plan for operating the foodservice, including both financial forecasts for income and expense items and the numbers of customers (guests, patients, students, and so on) and the projected labor hour requirements. Accurate historical data from records and reports must be available in order to project reliable forecasts. If new equipment is needed, an **equipment budget** with costs and priorities may be included. Likewise, a **facilities remodeling or repair budget** section may be a part of the total budget plan. A separate **labor budget** that details the number of labor hours or days and total personnel needs with labor cost totals is also a budget component. A **sales budget** or forecast of number of meals the operation expects to serve and the dollar volume of income is especially valuable to the profit-type organizations.

- **Fixed budget** is one based on a fixed annual level or volume of transactions such as the number of meals served, number of hospital patient days, or similar classification, and computed with the projected average rate figure, as cost per meal.

- **Flexible budget** considers the ranges from high to low activity figures rather than averages as with the fixed budget. This type of budget gives "flexibility" in operating, but may be more difficult to use as a control than the fixed budget.

- **Zero-based budget** requires managers to justify in detail each request for funds and to reevaluate all activities each year. There is no carryover from previous years, so each new budget begins with a "zero" balance.

Steps in Budget Planning

As mentioned, budgets are time-consuming to prepare and require thought-provoking effort on the part of all who are involved. A timetable should be set up for various phases of data collection and planning. The schedule must allow ample time for careful completion of the project so it can be evaluated and approved well in advance of the beginning of the next fiscal period. Budget planning as a joint endeavor represents many points of view. Final agreement by participants should ensure a fair allocation of funds for the goals to be met.

The steps involved in arriving at a good, carefully planned budget are outlined according to Minno and Bhayana. There are three distinct phases, each one deriving information from the one before. For example,

- *the evaluation phase,* which makes sense of an operation's past performance and identifies those factors that can influence the future

- *the planning phase,* which uses the information compiled during the evaluation to forecast the budget

- *the control phase,* which uses the budget cost during planning to keep track of monthly performance

More specifically, the following steps are usually used in planning the foodservice budget:

1. Collect operating data from records and reports. (See later in this chapter under "Financial Operations: A System of Records and Reports.")

2. Study these data and evaluate them against departmental goals. Information reviewed should cover actual operating and budget variance figures from the previous 3 or 4 years with justification or explanation of variances; income and expense trends; sales reports and statistics; menu, prices, customer selection, portion sizes, and food cost per portion; such labor statistics as the number of employees, their duties, schedules, and wage rates.

3. Analyze and discuss any factors that can affect future operations. These include both external (outside your control) and internal (within your control) influences that can be identified as having a possible effect on foodservice costs or activities in the future. Examples of *external* factors: the local economy, actions by government (change in taxes or laws), changes in utility costs, new construction that might bring in new business or divert traffic and so reduce patronage, or increases in competition. Examples of *internal* factors: a planned addition to the facility that will change the number of persons to be served; a change in type of foodservice system as from conventional to assembly/serve; converting to computerized record keeping; change in hours of service to better accommodate patrons.

4. Discuss and plan for new goals or activities desired, such as a remodeling project, purchasing new equipment, or a new service (e.g., catering) to be offered. These are all considered in light of anticipated changes and current prices.

5. Set priorities and make decisions as to what can be included in the budget for next year. In establishing budgetary priorities, the director must weigh the relative desires and needs of each unit, search out nonessentials, decide if any items could be provided at a lower cost, plan for upkeep and expansion of the plant, and provide for the development of personnel. Even though the income remains approximately the same year after year, careful appraisal of past expenses should be made whenever a new budget is prepared in order to prevent overspending for some items to the neglect of others.

The *budget* must reflect the objectives and policies of the organization for which it is planned. For example, the school foodservice has as its objective the serving of good food at a minimum cost. The foodservice may pay for food, labor, and laundry only, while the school subsidizes the overhead and operating costs. In such a case, the percentage of income spent for food is high. The foodservice budget of a college residence hall that is helping to pay for retirement of bonds is quite different from one whose physical plant and equipment are not encumbered. In each situation, the proportion of the income spent for various expense items varies with the size and type, objectives, and policies of the individual foodservice.

The budget planning committee has responsibility for making decisions as to what expense items can be included in the budget with a fixed income, or how the income can be expanded to cover the cost of the items of expense deemed essential. Forward-looking managers establish priorities and plan an orderly way of achieving these goals, even if it means looking beyond next year's budget.

6. Write the budget for presentation. Although there is no established format for the formal write-up of the budget, it contains an organized listing of expected income, classified as to sources, and the classified list of all expense items. Usually a form similar to the one shown in Fig. 14.1 is used as a work sheet to organize data in the budget. Writing the budget follows these steps:

   a. List all sources of expected income. Fig. 14.2 illustrates those for a college residence hall where income comes from student board fees. Commercial operations derive income from cash sales. Record this year's dollar figures for each of the sources of income and then the anticipated changes for the next budget period. Calculate and record the total expected income.

   b. Classify and list the items of expense with the cost calculated for each. Basically, these are food, labor, overhead (e.g., fixed costs as amortization or rent, taxes, and insurance), and operating costs (e.g., utilities, telephone, supplies). Fig. 14.1 shows one such chart of accounts, as the listing is called. The National Restaurant Association (NRA) has provided comparable information for commercial operations in its Uniform System of Accounts for Restaurants.

   c. Add other pertinent data, such as number of meals served, labor hours for both total and per meal served, last period, expected changes, and new totals.

   d. Prepare a justification for requests of new funds.

Budget Work Sheet—Income and Expense

	Estimated Last Year		Actual Last Year		Anticipated Changes		Estimated Next Year	
	Total	%	Total	%	+	−	Total	%
Income								
Regular Sales								
Special Meals								
Other (Itemize for specific Foodservice)								
Total								
Expenses								
1. Food								

Figure 14.1.   Budget planning work sheet, adaptable for use in any foodservice.

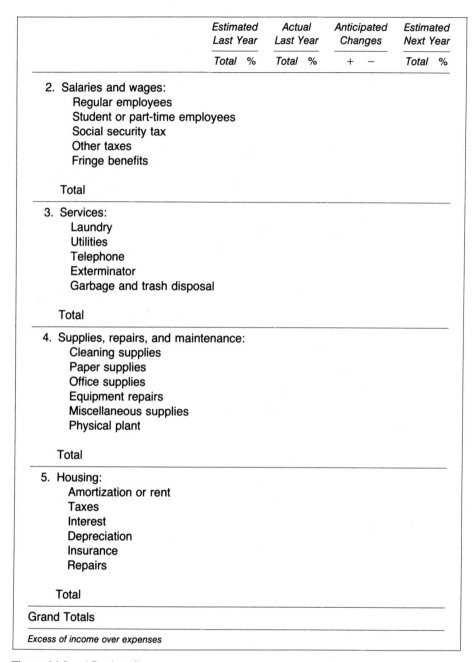

	Estimated Last Year		Actual Last Year		Anticipated Changes		Estimated Next Year	
	Total	%	Total	%	+	−	Total	%
2. Salaries and wages:								
Regular employees								
Student or part-time employees								
Social security tax								
Other taxes								
Fringe benefits								
Total								
3. Services:								
Laundry								
Utilities								
Telephone								
Exterminator								
Garbage and trash disposal								
Total								
4. Supplies, repairs, and maintenance:								
Cleaning supplies								
Paper supplies								
Office supplies								
Equipment repairs								
Miscellaneous supplies								
Physical plant								
Total								
5. Housing:								
Amortization or rent								
Taxes								
Interest								
Depreciation								
Insurance								
Repairs								
Total								
Grand Totals								
Excess of income over expenses								

Figure 14.1. (*Continued*)

Sources of Income	Income Past Period	Anticipated Increase	Anticipated Decrease	Anticipated Income
Board fees				
Cafeteria receipts				
Guest meals				
Special meals				
Catering				
Special food orders				
Miscellaneous				
Total				

Figure 14.2.   Income sources and detailed information for use in budget planning.

e. Review and make any changes necessary.

f. Write the budget in final form with any cost-benefit statements attached. If the budget is to be forwarded to a higher administrator for approval, an explanation of certain items can prove helpful for better understanding of requests.

g. Once it has been approved, use the budget. The yearly budget figures are divided into appropriate time periods for comparative purposes. For example, a calendar month may be used for those with year-round operations. Schools may wish to use a 20-school-day period, since holidays and vacations result in more or fewer operating days some months, making comparisons unrealistic.

A form similar to the one illustrated in Fig. 14.3 should be used for recording the budgeted figures. At the close of the month or other specified time period, the actual operating figures are recorded from the income, expense, and census records for easy comparison. A quick glance at this comparative report will show any discrepancies or variances between anticipated and actual business. Any deviation, positive or negative, should be analyzed to determine the reasons for the deviation and plan correct action. The data on the comparative form should be used in connection with information from the daily food cost report and profit and loss statements to evaluate activities and decide what actions to take. This is discussed in more detail later in the chapter.

Financial Operations: A System of Records and Reports

Knowledge of the day-to-day financial transactions and an awareness of "where the money is going before it is gone" is an ongoing responsibility of the foodservice manager. The use of records is essential for providing readily available operating data.

Name of Food Service

Month_____ , 19_____

	Number of Meals	Food Cost		Payroll Expense		Other Costs and Expenses	
	Total for month	Total for month	Per meal served	Total for month	Per meal served	Total for month	Per meal served
Budgeted							
Actual							
Over + – Under							

Cumulative for Year to Date

	Jan.	Feb.	Mar.	April	May	June	etc.
Budgeted							
Actual							
Over + – Under							

Figure 14.3.   Budgeted figures are compared with actual operating figures for management control of finances.

Records, like all forms of control, vary with the type, size, and policies of the institution, so that the management must ascertain what information is needed and how it may be obtained with the least expenditure of effort, time, and money.

Most foodservice organizations today utilize the computer for much of their record keeping and reporting. Data required for computer input is essentially the same as that for noncomputerized record keeping: forms and procedures vary. Good manual control and decisions on what information should be provided by computer are prerequisites to a good computerized control system. Designing appropriate forms for data organization is the first step in setting up either a manual or computerized system.

Records for Control

Records deemed essential for a noncomplex foodservice operation include those that control the major phases of the operations. These essential records may be classified as those for purchasing and receiving, storage and storeroom control, production and service of food, number of people served, cash transactions, operating and maintenance, and personnel. More specifically, these include the following:

Purchasing and receiving records
  Purchase order
  Invoice
  Receiving record
  Purchase record
  Summary of purchases record
Storage and storeroom records
  Storeroom control
  Requisition or storeroom issue records
  Perpetual inventory
  Physical inventory
Food production
  Menu
  Standardized recipes
  Portion control standards
  Production schedule and leftovers report
  Menu tally
Service records
  Census reports: number of meals served
  Regular and special meals' count
  Catering and vending
Cash transactions records
  Cash sales register reports
  Guest checks
  Cash disbursement records for all expense items
Operating and maintenance
  Maintenance records
  Repair invoices
Personnel records (related to cost control)
  Time card/payroll records
  Work schedules
  Fringe benefits record

Illustrations of record forms are given in the chapters appropriate for each topic. Therefore, only census and income/expense records are presented in this chapter. Since these are given as examples only, each foodservice director should design forms for his or her own department according to the specific situation.

SERVICE RECORDS   A record of the number of people served is vital for forecasting, purchasing, and production needs. The data from a census report are necessary for determining per meal costs, average sales per person, and the distribution of meals served to various categories of consumers for each meal of the day.

A form designed for recording the census should be large enough to include figures for the entire month (or other accounting period) and for each category of consumers. Figs. 14.4a and b give examples of typical census report forms for two types of foodservices. If more detailed information is desired, patient meals could be divided into "regular" and "therapeutic" or "modified" diets, and personnel meals into "staff" and "employees."

Information to be recorded on this form comes from cash register reports for personnel and guest meals; dietary count of patient meals and of meals served at any special functions.

Catering Records: A record of catering functions is necessary for foodservices that provide this service in addition to their own regular meal service. Each event has a different menu and demands specialized service, for which customers pay accordingly. In all cases, it is necessary to have definite policies and procedures outlined that can be followed through from the planning to the billing of the charges in order to ensure successful and satisfactory operation. Fig. 14.5 is a typical agreement form for special group meetings and meals with a record of price and total charges and number of people served.

INCOME AND EXPENSE RECORDS   A record of daily transactions is essential for preparation of monthly financial statements. Managers must know the sources and amounts of income, and where that income goes. Several records are needed to provide that information in a simplified way.

Sales and Cash Receipts: Even small operations such as school lunchrooms handle some cash, and business-like procedures are needed for accounting of the money. Cash registers provide a relatively safe place for money during serving hours and also provide accurate data on number of sales made and total cash received. Larger organizations may use cash registers of varying degrees of sophistication including electronic point-of-sales (POS) computer terminals. These produce summary printouts and proofs of cash collected, which can replace the use of the cash register record shown in Fig. 14.6. The POS terminal

Monthly Census Report

Name of Organization _____

Date _____ Month _____ 19 _____ Year

Day/Date	Regular Guest Count			Totals		Employee Meals			Totals		Special (Catering) Functions			Totals		Grand Totals	
	Break-fast	Lunch	Dinner	Today	To Date	Break-fast	Lunch	Dinner	Today	To Date	Break-fast	Lunch	Dinner	Today	To Date	Today	To Date
Su 1																	
Mo 2																	
Tu 3																	
—																	
Tu 31																	

Figure 14.4a. Census record-keeping form, which is adaptable to commercial foodservice. The "To Date" figures are cumulative for the month.

MONTHLY MEAL CENSUS

Hospital _____

Date _____ 19 ___

mo.

Date	Patient Meals					Personnel Meals					Patient and Personnel	
				Total Meals					Total Meals		Total Meals	
	Break-fast	Lunch	Dinner	Today	To Date	Break-fast	Lunch	Dinner	Today	To Date	Today	To Date
1												
2												
3												
—												
30												
31												

Figure 14.4b.   Meal census summary sheet suitable for health care facilities.

can be programmed to provide as much information and detail as management desires. This may include

- number of sales
- total sales dollars by cash, check, credit card
- tax collected
- a total customer count of those who paid by cash and a count by number of those customers who received meals other than by the cash system
- the total number of servings for each type of food, such as entrées, vegetables, desserts, salads, and beverages (menu tally)
- the dollar volume for each type of food sold

Also the computer can perform the following tasks:

- Print out an itemized receipt for each customer.
- Calculate automatically the change to be returned to the customer and print the transaction on the receipt.
- Report totals and productivity by hour or shift.

A record of income from sales other than cash sales and of payments made for all expense items is also essential. A *cash receipts and disbursements* book is used by bookkeepers to record these transactions. Also, they can be kept by computer. Sample forms of the two parts of the cash record are given in Figs. 14.7a and b. These should be filled in daily, posting the disbursements amounts from bills received and paid by check; the cash received from the cash register reports and report of any other cash payment received. Much of this bookkeeping and

Name of Foodservice

Organization _____   Function _____

Date _____ Time _____   Arranged by _____

Room_____   Address _____

Number Guaranteed_____ Served _____   Phone No._____

Price _____   Booked by _____ Date _____

Total Charge _____   Approved by _____

Menu	Details
	Setup
	Speaker's Table
	Flowers
	Music
	Public Address
	Tickets
	Misc.

Guarantees are not subject to change less
than 24 hours in advance of party. We
are prepared to serve 10% in excess of the
number guaranteed.

Accepted _____

Union Office_____

Copies: Manager
        Food Director
        Catering
        Maintenance
        Kitchen
        Accounting

Figure 14.5.   Catering agreement form also serves as record of number served.

Form 7158							FOOD SERVICE	Report No........................		
								Dep't. No........................		
						REPORT OF CASH RECEIVED		Page.........of.........		
............(Unit)............							Period from................to................Incl.			

Present Reading	Less: Previous Reading	Difference	Void	Register Sales	Tax on Register	Over Short	Description	Validated Receipt	Code
							REGISTER 1		
							TOTAL 1		
							REGISTER 1		
							TOTAL 2		
							REGISTER		
							TOTAL 1		
							REGISTER		
							TOTAL 2		
							REGISTER		
							TOTAL 1		
							REGISTER		
							TOTAL 2		
							TOTALS		

Receipt No.	Received from (Name and Description)	Date of Charge or Period Covered	Received on Account (Tax Incl.)	Other Receipts		
TOTAL CASH RECEIVED						

Signed........................   Total Deposit........................
        Supt. or Manager

Figure 14.6. Cash report form to be filled in by cashiers using cash registers.

record keeping is computerized in today's foodservices (described in more detail in Chapter 15). However, the data and information presented here are basic for either manual or computer record keeping.

No records, however carefully designed, are of value unless they are kept *daily,* are *accurate,* and are *used by management.*

Cash Receipts Record (a)

Name of Organization _____   Month _____ 19 _____

Date	Total Amount Received	Food Sales	Beverage Sales	Accounts Paid	Misc. Sales	Other Source	Amount
1							
2							
3							
4							
—							
31							
Totals							

Source of Income

Cash Disbursements Record (b)

Name of Organization _____   Month _____ 19 _____

Date	Name of Account	Check No.	Amount Paid	Food	Beverages	Supplies	Utilities	Payroll	Rent
1									
2									
3									
4									
—									
31									
Totals									

Classification of Expense Accounts

Figure 14.7.   (*a*) Sample cash receipts, and (*b*) cash disbursements forms for financial control. Income sources and expense accounts vary with type of operation. Totals on each form are posted to the appropriate classification column.

Financial Accountability

Accountability for expenditures made with the company's or institution's money is not assured by merely keeping records. The data and information provided by the records just described must be used to analyze and improve the financial situation. To do that, certain reports are prepared using data from the records. Essential ones are: a Daily Food Cost Report; a Monthly Report, or Profit and Loss Statement; a Yearly Summary Report; and Comparative Reports of Operations.

Reports

DAILY FOOD-COST REPORT   A simple daily food-cost report as illustrated in Fig. 14.8 is prepared from four records: the cash receipts record of *total income from sales* for the day, the *census record* of number of people served, the *storeroom issues* record, and the *invoices for perishable foods,* issued directly to the kitchen and not kept on inventory (known as direct purchases). A total of storeroom issues and direct purchases gives the cost of food for the day.

This is the most valuable of the three reports as a management tool because it provides up-to-the-minute information about sales, food costs, and number of people served. Expenses other than food usually are not included in the daily report, since they do not fluctuate as greatly as food costs.

The relationship between food cost and income expressed in terms of percent is the most significant single figure to be observed. This percentage figure is found by dividing the cost of food used today by the income for today. For example, if the income from sales (or budgeted allocation) is $1,280 and the food cost is $530,

$$\frac{\text{Food Cost} - \$530}{\text{Income} - \$1,280} = .414 \times 100 = 41.4\%$$

41.4% is the food-cost percentage, or
percent of income spent for food

By looking at this figure, the manager can quickly tell whether or not it meets the standard set for his or her operation. Each foodservice sets its own food-cost percentage standard based on the type of organization, its goals, characteristics, and expenses. A luxury restaurant with elaborate service and high overhead may set 20% to 25% of the sales for food as its standard. Other expenses and profit take up the other 75% to 80% of the income.

In contrast, a school foodservice in which some of the foodservice overhead is paid by the school and in which labor costs are not excessive, 50% to 60% may be the standard for food. Although the percentage is much higher, the actual amount spent for food is considerably lower, since the income per meal is so much greater in the restaurant than in the school.

In addition to the daily food-cost calculation, *cumulative* figures for the month are important (see Fig. 14.3). The sales and food-cost figures for the first day of the month are added to those of the second; the total of the first 2 days is added to the third day's figures, and so on throughout the month.

UNIVERSITY COMMONS
DAILY FOOD-COST REPORT

Year _____

Day and Date	Tuesday May 1		Wednesday May 2		Thursday May 3		Friday May 4		Saturday May 5		Sunday May 6	
Income and Census:	Census	Sales	Census	Sales	Census	Sales	Census	Sales	Census	Sales	Census	Sales
A. From cafeteria sales (Cash register report)												
B. From parties (Charges)												
C. Total today												
D. Total to date												
E. Cumulative total for month												
Food Cost:												
F. Food cost today												
G. Total food cost to date												
H. Cumulative total for month												
Food-cost percentage												

Figure 14.8. Daily food-cost report form; used continuously for each accounting period, usually a calendar month. Food-cost percentages are calculated on the cumulative totals; the one for the last day is the average for the month.

The cumulative (rather than daily) figures should be used to determine the food-cost percentage because they tend to average out the "ups and downs" of a single day's operation and give the picture of operations to date. If the food-cost percent figure varies from day-to-day within reasonable limits, there is little cause for concern. It is the cumulative or average figure, calculated each day, that should be in line with the desired food-cost percentage. Variations in the figure indicate the need for investigation to determine the reasons and take corrective action.

The *daily* cumulative food-cost report is valuable because it shows deviations from the budget at the time they occur and corrective action can be taken *at once.* An end-of-the-month report (profit and loss statement) shows deviations that occurred sometime during the month, and any action taken does not bring expenditures in line for that month.

Another daily report that can help managers pinpoint and evaluate expenditures is the record of charges for *raw* food sent to various production and/or service units. For example, large foodservice operations distribute food to a pantry, salad unit, and cafeteria among others. On a form as in Fig. 14.9, the direct and storeroom issue costs are recorded. This information shows trends in unit spending and can also be used for comparison with income generated from production in each unit. These figures also provide a helpful productivity analysis.

A record of cost of *prepared* food sent from a main production center to various service units as in a hotel to its coffee shop, main dining room, catering

SUMMARY OF DAILY FOOD COST EXPENSE BY PRODUCTION AND SERVICE UNITS								
Month _____ , 19_____								
Day and Date		Main Production Unit	Vegetable Preparation	Salad Unit	Bakery	Serving Counter	Totals Today	To Date
Mon. 1	Direct purchases							
	Storeroom issues							
Tues. 2	Direct purchases							
	Storeroom issues							

Figure 14.9.   Charges for raw food issued to production and service units can be accounted for by use of this form.

and room service, or in a large medical center to its patient areas, visitor/staff cafeteria, and perhaps separate children's, psychiatric, rehabilitation, and other hospital units is another necessary cost control record.

The charge for food prepared and sent to these units can be based on the number of portions issued, or on total weight or volume of the food. In either case, precosting with current prices of the various menu items is the preliminary step. A form for recording these daily issues and charges may be developed by the dietitian or foodservice manager so that the appropriate transfer of charges can be made.

The daily food-cost report, although more or less approximate, is usually sufficiently accurate to pinpoint trouble spots before serious financial reverses can occur. If a detailed breakdown of costs each day is important to the manager, a computer program can be planned to make such information quickly available. A computer printout of essential data from the previous day's transaction can be on the manager's desk each morning for study and evaluation. As with all reports, the daily food-cost report, of whatever form, provides a working tool for foodservice managers, who are expected to know how to use it.

PROFIT AND LOSS STATEMENT   The profit and loss report is a summary comparison in dollars and cents of the income, including *all* expenses of the department, to determine the amount of profit or loss for a given period. Usually, it is prepared at the end of each calendar month. In schools, however, the accounting period may be the number of operating days per year divided into equal periods of about 20 or 25 days each. This gives a basis for better comparison of operations from period to period. The profit and loss statement shows the true cost of food used based on purchases, adjusted with inventories, and all other actual expenditures.

The figures for preparing this statement are taken from the cash ledger, income and disbursements, and from the beginning and ending physical inventory figures. A simple summary of the profit and loss statement is

	Income (sales)
Less:	Cost of food sold
Equals:	Gross profit
Less:	Labor, overhead, and operating costs
Equals:	Net profit or loss

The "cost of food sold" in the profit and loss statement is determined by adjusting the cost of food purchased during the month with the beginning and ending inventories for that month:

Purchases

(Figure obtained from vendors' end-of-month statements verified by manager's check on daily invoices)

+ Beginning inventory

(Value of goods on hand in the storeroom available for use. Figure obtained from costed inventory taken on *last* day of preceding month, which becomes the beginning inventory the *first* day of the month)

= Cost of goods available to be used
− Ending inventory

(Value of goods on hand on the last day of the month; goods not used during the month but available for use in the next month)

= Cost of goods used

An example of a typical profit and loss statement is given in Fig. 14.10. Percentage ratios of the major items of expense and of the profit to the sales are included for better interpretation of operations, as dollar and cents figures in themselves have little meaning here. The percentage figures are determined by dividing each expense item *by* total income; that is, the percentage of income that is spent for food, labor, other expenses, and a profit, or if expenses exceed income, a loss.

As with the daily food-cost report, a cumulative statement of profit and loss, recorded month by month, together with the budgeted figures gives comparative data for the manager's use.

If this report is to be effective, it must be completed and available as early in the month as possible, and certainly no later than the tenth of the month. Reports coming to the food manager's desk a month or 6 weeks after the end of the operating period have little or no control value at that late date. The amount of profit or loss should be no surprise, however, to the manager who has used the daily reports to "keep a finger on the pulse of operations."

Large organizations where foodservice is but one of several departments, such as hospitals, colleges and universities, and hotels or motels, have their own bookkeeping departments. However, in most situations the foodservice manager generates his or her operating data for closer control and speedier, more complete reports than may come from a central business office. They do provide good checks on each other, however, and managers of both departments are well-informed about needs and requests presented in the budgeting process.

**COLLEGE COMMONS
PROFIT AND LOSS STATEMENT**

April, 19___
(Operating days, 22)

				Per cent of Sales
Sales	$26,476.72			
Less: sales tax	1,040.00			
Net sales		$25,436.72		100.00
Cost of food sold				
Inventory—April 1	1,976.05			
Freight	35.16			
Purchases	10,632.07			
	12,643.28			
Less: inventory April 30	2,258.99			
Net cost of food sold		10,384.29		40.82
Gross profit on food			$15,052.43	59.18
Labor:				
Regular employees	4,651.48			
Student employees	3,081.51			
Supervision	2,479.53			
		10,212.52		40.15
Operating expenses:				
Social security tax	386.96			
Other taxes	291.16			
Maintenance and repair	590.06			
Utilities	757.56			
Supplies (cleaning, paper, office)	766.73			
Laundry	527.39			
Depreciation on equipment	600.00			
		3,919.86		15.41
Total labor and operating expense			14,132.38	
Excess of income over expenses			$ 920.05	3.62

Figure 14.10. Monthly profit and loss statement for a college foodservice unit.

ANNUAL REPORTS   An annual report is usually prepared for higher administrative officials and provides a resumé of the activities and accomplishments of the year just completed, as well as plans for future developments. Although an annual report contains statistical data, it should be much more than a mere listing of facts and figures. It is the interpretation of these data that makes the report significant to those who read it.

The preparation of such a report usually requires staff participation and planning together as a group. It calls for creative thinking and provides opportunity to dream while forecasting ways in which the department can be improved, not just next year but 2, 5, or 10 years hence. If there is a specific message that the managers wish to convey, such as the need for enlarging or remodeling the facility, the report should emphasize that theme for maximum impact.

The cumulative profit and loss statements, census reports, and other records of income and expense are the bases for the financial part of an annual report. Comparisons should be made of the actual and budgeted figures for the year and explanations given for increases or decreases. Often, the presentation of these data in graphic form, such as a pie chart illustration of the expenditure of the income dollar, are more quickly understood than the mere statement of words. The use of bar graphs to show comparisons and the plotting of income or census figures month by month on a graph are other examples of effective reporting.

Information on the personnel situation should be included as well, since the cost of labor is high. Administrators are interested in percentage of turnover, promotions, length of service, and outstanding achievements of the staff and employees. Reasons for terminations of employment are important, too; they may help to point out some weakness in the organization. Interpretations of labor hours worked in terms of ratios to meals served, income received, or other comparisons of special significance are also included.

The physical plant and the equipment changes or repairs that have been made, as well as anticipated needs in all areas of operation, should be reported. Any situation that calls for a major expenditure of money requires explanation and justification.

The annual report also includes a summary of accomplishments or goals reached during the period. Special problems encountered and solved, unusual occurrences or services rendered, and the projected plans for the future complete an annual report.

Factors Affecting Cost Control: Evaluation of Operations

A critical step in achieving a good financial position involves the manager making follow-up decisions and taking actions after review of the records and reports. If operations are in line with the budget plan, no action is indicated. If, however, costs are excessively high and profits not what were predicted, or volume indicators are lower than anticipated, a review of the many factors involved in cost control is necessary. There are many alternatives to consider before raising prices or reducing portion size. These may be required actions at some time, but not as the first approach.

Managers with professional preparation and experience search for causes of deviation from the expected by reviewing the many factors that have a bearing on overall expense. These include every activity in the department from the physical arrangement and layout of equipment to customer satisfaction. A brief review of some of these factors is given here. Table 14.1 summarizes some of the key questions that the manager should consider when analyzing budget deviations.

FOOD COSTS   Food is the most readily controlled item of expenditure and the one subject to greatest fluctuation in the foodservice budget. If control of food costs is to be effective, efficient methods must be employed in planning the menu, purchasing, storing, preparing, and serving. The expenditures for food vary greatly from one type of institution to another and often for institutions of the same type because of the form of food purchased, the amount of on-premise preparation, geographic location, and delivery costs.

In spite of the variation in the amounts spent for food, the underlying bases of food cost control are the same for all types of foodservices. The effectiveness of control is determined by: the menu, menu costing and establishing selling price, the purchasing, receiving, storage, and storeroom control procedures, methods used in the production of food, including prepreparation, cooking, and use of leftovers; portion size and serving waste; and the cost of employees' meals.

Menus: Menu planning is the first and, perhaps, the most important step in the control of food costs. The menu determines what and how many foods must be purchased and prepared. Knowledge of these food costs, as well as labor cost and intensity, and the *precosting* of the menu to determine whether or not it is within budgetary limitations are essential for control procedure. Menu planning is discussed in detail in Chapter 3.

Menus that provide extensive choices require preparation of many kinds of foods, several of which are not sold in quantities sufficient to pay for their preparation. If a widely diversified selection is offered, the investment of too large a sum in food or labor for its preparation can result. Also, it may result in carrying an extensive inventory of small quantities of food items, or of foods infrequently used.

Foodservice managers should remember also that although menus are made some days or even weeks in advance, they can be adjusted daily to the inventory of food on hand and to local market conditions. Waste can be prevented only by wise utilization of available supplies, which helps to keep food costs under control and adds to variety of the menus.

TABLE 14.1.   Some Factors to Consider When Analyzing Budget Deviations.

Factor	Key Analytical Questions
Food Costs	
Menus, menu costing, selling price	1. How many choices are offered? 2. What are the food and labor costs of each menu item? 3. Which items are most profitable? 4. How many of each item are sold? 5. Could menu items be better merchandised?
Purchasing	1. Are appropriate specifications used? 2. Has prime vending or group purchasing been considered? 3. Has buyer kept current with market trends and conditions?
Receiving	1. Are deliveries checked against the purchase order? 2. Are qualities and quantities verified with specifications?
Storage	1. How does current turnover rate compare with previous calculations? 2. Is there opportunity for theft? 3. Are storeroom requisitions controlled? 4. Are store areas properly arranged to minimize spoilage? 5. Are proper temperatures maintained in all storage units?
Food production	1. Are standardized recipes available and used? 2. Has establishing central ingredient assembly been considered? 3. Is production equipment adequate and well-maintained? 4. Are forecasts accurate and followed by production staff?
Portion size	1. Have portion sizes been established for each menu item? 2. Are employees aware of the portion sizes, and have they been trained in portion control? 3. Are appropriate and adequate portioning utensils available for employee use?
Employee meals	1. Have the costs of employee meals been calculated? 2. Are proper accounting methods used to justify these costs?
Labor Costs	
Type and extent of service offered	1. Can more self-service opportunities be offered without sacrificing customer satisfaction?

TABLE 14.1.   (*Continued*)

Factor	Key Analytical Questions
Hours of service	1. Is there enough customer volume to justify current hours of service? 2. What merchandising techniques can be implemented to stimulate sales during slack times? 3. Are there tasks done at peak times that could be transferred to slack times?
Physical plant	1. Is equipment arranged logically to minimize human energy expenditure? 2. Are carts available and are size and number adequate to minimize trips to storage areas? 3. Does sharing equipment delay production?
Personnel policies and productivity	1. Have production standards been determined and communicated to the employee? 2. Are employees properly trained and supervised to assure productivity standards are met? 3. Can overtime expenditures be justified?
Supervision	1. Are supervisors monitoring departmental activities? 2. Do supervisors recognize key productivity times and take action to assure that standards are met? 3. Does supervisor know how to allocate resources on a day-by-day basis to keep within budgetary guidelines?
Operating and Other Expenses	
Maintenance and repair	1. Is a preventative maintenance system defined and used? 2. Can repair costs be justified compared to equipment replacement? 3. Are employees trained to report broken equipment?
Breakage	1. Are records of china and glass breakage kept and summarized periodically to monitor changes in amounts broken? 2. Are employees aware of costs? 3. Are proper handling techniques used to minimize breakage?
Supplies	1. Do employees have access to supplies? 2. Are procedures for use of chemicals established to minimize waste?
Energy and utility costs	1. Does preventative maintenance include energy efficiency check? 2. Is equipment used properly to minimize energy utilization?

Menu Costing and Establishing Selling Price: One important responsibility of foodservice managers is to determine a sound basis for establishing the selling price for food. Haphazard methods may lead to financial disaster or dissatisfaction of the patron.

Foodservices use a variety of methods for determining a selling price. The most common method is based on the raw-food cost of menu items plus a "markup" to give a selling price appropriate for the type of organization and the desired food cost percentage level that the foodservice wishes to maintain.

The *raw-food cost* is found by costing the standardized recipe for each menu item. An example of a costed recipe is shown in Fig. 14.11. Storeroom purchase records provide the price of ingredients to use in costing the recipes. Many foodservices have the costed recipes and storeroom records on computer with programs to update recipe costs as ingredient prices fluctuate.

The *markup* is determined by dividing the desired food cost percentage that the foodservice wishes to maintain, into 100 (representing total sales or 100%). The resulting figure is called the "markup factor." This is the figure by which the raw-food cost is multiplied to obtain a selling price. To illustrate: assume the foodservice wishes to maintain a 40% (of income) food cost:

$\dfrac{100}{40}$ (represents total sales) (percent of income for food) = 2.5
2.5 is the markup factor.

Cost of the recipe in Fig. 14.11 is .2687 × 2.5 = $.672, or .70, the suggested selling price.

The markup factor cannot be used alone, however, to calculate selling price. There are many "free" items given with a meal that must be added in—salt and pepper, condiments, sugar and cream, and jams, jellies and sauces. These do not show up in recipe costing, but they must be accounted for.

Also, it is imperative that the food manager know not only the raw-food cost of menu items but also the cost of the many hidden losses in preparation, cooking, and serving, which if not controlled add appreciably to the total food cost. Overproduction and unavoidable waste likewise add to the costs, and the wise manager analyzes these, controls what is possible, and considers the other in the establishment of selling prices. To compensate for these "unproductive and hidden costs," many foodservice managers add 10% (or some such standardized amount) to the recipe cost before markup. Thus, in the illustration given, the suggested selling price of $.70 would be changed:

Raw-food cost of $.2687 × .10 = .0269
+ .2687 = $.2956
× 2.5 = .739, or .75, a more realistic selling price.

Name of product _Quiche Lorraine_   Size of Pan _12 x 20 x 2_

Yield (Total Quality) _2 Pans_   How Portioned _4 x 6; 24/pan_

Size Portion _7 oz_   Date Prepared _8/31/92_

No. of Portions _48_   Prepared by _L.L._

NUMBER OF SERVINGS: _48_

INGREDIENTS	EP Weight	Measure	AP Weight	Measure	Unit Price		Cost
Flour, Pastry			3 lbs. 2 oz		.523/lb	1	6343
Salt, Cooking			2 oz		.058/lb		0072
Shortening			1 lb 12 oz		.73/lb	1	277
Water		2½ c					—
Onion, Chopped	4.2 qt		4.5 oz		.238/lb		074
Milk		1 gal			2.44/gal	2	44
Swiss Cheese, Grated			2 lb		2.95/lb	5	90
Eggs, fresh, whole		3 doz			.68/doz	2	04
Mustard, dry			½ oz		.92/lb		0287
Ham, ground (optional)	1 lb 4 oz				2.72/lb	3	40

Procedure:

Total Cost _$16.8012_

Portion Cost _.3500_

Figure 14.11. Costed recipe is the basis for establishing selling price.

Pricing of table d'hote, selective, elective, or other combination menus usually found on printed menus in commercial foodservices follows the same procedure as illustrated. However, all items that are served together at one price (as meat, potato, vegetable, salad, and beverage) are costed, and total raw-food cost is obtained before the markup factor is used to calculate the selling price.

Obviously, the exact markup price cannot be used when a fraction or an "awkward" number results. Such numbers are rounded up to the nearest reasonable figure; $1.87 might become $1.90 or even $2, for example.

Another method, called "demand-oriented pricing," is based on what the customers perceive the value/cost should be and what they are willing to pay for what they receive. This is also known as "what the traffic will bear." Prices are set as high above raw-food cost as the customers will pay, without lowering the number of sales on the item. Close control and watch on sales with good records to support pricing decisions are necessary.

Sometimes managers set their selling prices to be comparable with their competitors. This is unrealistic if used as the only basis, for there are too many variables in each operation. This method may be used for a single food item, perhaps for a cup of coffee, but it is not a "scientific" way of pricing.

These two methods, demand-oriented and competitive pricing for establishing a selling price, have been questioned by some foodservice managers, especially in these times of soaring labor and operating costs. Overhead costs remain about the same regardless of the menu and do not vary from day-to-day. Labor costs are affected by the menu, however, as preparation time is different for each item of food. Roasts and steaks, for example, usually are high-cost foods but require relatively little labor time to prepare. Stew and quiche, traditionally lower cost items, require much more time to prepare. It seems logical to some operators, therefore, to base selling prices on labor cost plus raw-food cost. In this way, all customers share more equally in the expenses of the foodservice. This method is called "prime-cost" pricing because food and labor are the primary expense items in the budget. Together, these two items of expense usually make up 70% to 85% of the total of all expenses, on the type of organization. The markup in this case is figured on the prime costs,

$$\text{Food} + \frac{\text{Sales: 100}}{\text{Labor: 70}} = 1.43 \text{ or } \frac{100}{85} = 1.18$$

instead of the 2.5 used in the traditional method example given previously.

To utilize the prime cost system requires accurate records of labor time spent in preparing the various foods. The amount of labor time used multiplied by the employee's wage rate gives this cost of labor.

An example of pricing by this method and by the conventional for steak and for quiche shows

<table>
<tr><td>

Conventional Method

at 33⅓% food-cost
markup = 3x
plus 10% of raw-food
cost

</td><td>

Prime-Cost Method

at 33⅓% food cost
+ 46⅔% labor cost
80% prime cost
Markup = 1.25x

</td></tr>
</table>

STEAK

Raw-Food Cost	1.80	Raw-Food Cost	1.80
+ 10% Hidden Cost	+ .18	+ Labor Cost	
	1.98	of 5 min.	
× Markup	× 3	@ 12.00/hr.	+ 1.00
	5.94		2.80
		or × Markup	× 1.25
Selling Price =	6.00	Selling Price =	3.50

QUICHE

Raw-Food Cost	.850	Raw-Food Cost	.85
+ 10% Hidden Cost	+ .085	+ Labor Cost	
	.935	of 20 min.	
× Markup	×3	@ 12.00/hr.	+ 4.00
	2.805		4.85
		× Markup	× 1.25
Selling Price =	2.80		6.06
			or
		Selling Price =	6.00

Due to customer perception of value/cost, it is doubtful that many portions of quiche would be sold for $6 in the same foodservice in which steak is sold for $3.50. At the same time, management could likely apply the "demand-oriented pricing" to the steak item in the prime-cost method, because customers would be willing, and expect, to pay more for a steak than for quiche.

The conventional method, with management decision making to adjust certain costs from time to time, is used by a majority of foodservice directors.

Purchasing: Food purchasing is fully described in Chapter 5. However, when managers are reviewing and evaluating overall expenses, purchasing methods should be included.

The market is ever-changing and the buyer must keep abreast of new developments and learn what best suits the needs of the foodservice and at the most advantageous price. Specifications may need to be changed from time to time according to market trends. Certain costs are controlled through wise purchasing by an informed, capable buyer who is alert to ever-changing market conditions and has a knowledge of new products as they become available.

Receiving: Losses may easily occur at the point of receiving goods if management is negligent about checking in orders as they are received. This task may be entrusted to an assistant, but should be someone with managerial authority.

Storage and Storeroom Control: Protection of the company's large investment of money in the food after it is purchased and received contributes greatly to overall cost control. It has been said that one should buy only the amount that can be used at once or stored adequately. Furthermore, one should store only what is essential for limited periods of time because unnecessarily large inventories tend to increase the possibility of loss through spoilage, waste, or theft.

The value of the inventory can be monitored by calculating the turnover rate, which is a measure of how many times storeroom goods are used and replenished during a specified time period. The rate is determined by dividing the cost of goods sold by the value of the ending inventory (from the profit and loss statement). A turnover of three to five times a month is fairly average for many foodservices, although this varies considerably. A small fast-food restaurant in a large city may have a high turnover of inventory, for foods are used quickly and deliveries can be made frequently. In contrast, a large university that is located in a somewhat geographically isolated area may keep a large inventory of staple items to carry through a school year, and so the inventory turnover would be very low.

If the turnover rate is excessively high, it may indicate a shortage of funds to purchase in sufficient quantities, and small amounts that are used almost at once are purchased. This is an expensive method. It may also limit the foodservice's credit rating and ability to buy competitively.

If the turnover rate is low, probably too much stock is remaining on the storeroom shelves too long, or many items are not being used. Managers should check the inventory from time to time and include on the menu those items that need to be "moved" before they deteriorate and cause "waste" cost.

Food Production: Preparation, Cooking, and Leftovers Control: Foodservice managers are well aware of the many costs and potential losses that can occur in the production of food for service. Foodservice workers, although well-trained, need continuous supervision to assure that standardized recipes are used properly, and equipment is operated appropriately to minimize preparation losses. See Chapter 5 for details.

Reducing the amount of leftover prepared foods is another step that can be taken toward cost containment. The manager's ability to forecast accurately the number of portions that are used or sold is critical and should not be based on guesswork or left to the cooks to decide how much to prepare. Rather, the use of records to show *amounts prepared, amounts sold or used,* and *amounts left* gives a realistic basis for estimating quantities required the next time an item is served.

Portion Size and Serving Wastes: An established portion size is a part of the standardized recipe, the basis for costing and setting the selling price. The size of a portion or serving to be offered to the consumer is a management decision and must be communicated in writing to the employees.

One means of assuring standardized portions is to know size and yield of all pans, measures, ladles, and other small equipment used in the serving. For example, if 1 gallon of soup is to yield 16 1-cup servings, there must be accurate measurements both of the original quantity and the amount taken up in the ladle. A 1-cup ladle should be provided for the server's use, not a three-quarter cup or some other size, to obtain the standard portion. Other appropriate-size serving equipment should be used for other food items.

Employees' Meals: Sometimes employees are given a discount on their meals or are charged "at-cost" prices rather than the usual marked up selling price. The value of food consumed by employees should be of real concern to management in attempting to better control both food and labor costs. The philosophy of management regarding employees' meals, to charge or not for them, varies with the individual institution. Managers should question the present policy in view of overall cost control. If meals are provided, the value of them must be determined for use in the financial statement.

Meals provided as part of employees' compensation should be handled as a labor cost, not food cost, in the profit and loss statement. A cost determination of the value of the meals is made by management, and the total of all employees' meals is deducted from the "cost of food sold" and added to "labor" as an employee benefit to reflect their true place in financial accounting.

LABOR COST CONTROL   Labor costs represent a major component of the total foodservice expense in most organizations today. Until recent years, food was first in importance and labor was second. Together, food and labor made up around 75% of the total expense. With ever-increasing wage rates and employee benefits, it now is estimated that labor constitutes 50% to 70% of the total, as an overall average.

However, there are so many variables in each situation that even "averages" have little meaning. Restaurants with full table service in luxurious surroundings and French-style service have quite a different labor cost than a serve-yourself buffet operation. In the first case, the income per meal may be $20; in the second, $2.95. The labor cost may be 50% in each case—$10 for labor in the luxury restaurant and $1.48 in the self-service establishment—but each shows the same *percentage* of income spent for labor. Dollar figures need to be closely monitored in any evaluation, and managers should not rely on percentages only.

Production employees can prepare more servings of most menu items with little extra time expenditure; supervisors can handle a somewhat larger volume of trade during their time on duty; and probably no additional office help would be required as the volume of business increases. Good managers should be able to determine when additional labor is required to handle increased volume. Generally speaking, the greater the volume of business, the greater the returns on labor dollars spent. Labor costs are less controllable than food costs, and their percentage of payroll costs to sales fluctuates with sales. It is impractical if not impossible to change the number of employees day by day in proportion to the number of customers, patients, or students, as one might change the menu to meet fluctuating needs. Therefore, it is necessary to consider ways to get full returns from the payroll dollar.

The following ratios are commonly used in the foodservice industry to analyze labor productivity and costs:

$$\text{Meals per labor hours} = \frac{\text{Total number of meals served}}{\text{Total hours of labor to produce the meals}}$$

$$\text{Meals per full-time equivalent (FTE)} = \frac{\text{Total number of meals served}}{\text{Total FTEs to produce the meals}}$$

$$\text{Labor minutes per meal} = \frac{\text{Total minutes of labor time to produce the meals}}{\text{Total number of meals served}}$$

Type of Foodservice System: The various types of systems and the labor required in each are described in Chapter 2. Foodservice organizations faced with excessively high labor costs might investigate the feasibility of converting to another, lower labor requiring system. Or if a complete conversion is not possible, consideration could be given to the use of more preprepared frozen food items, thus reducing labor time/cost for food production.

Type and Extent of Services Offered: The extent of service offered within the organization affects total labor costs. In cafeterias, for example, the patrons may carry their own trays and bus their own soiled dishes, or if table service is used, the ratio of servers to guests varies as does the cost of labor. If the menu and service are simple, one waiter is able to serve many guests. When the formality of dining calls for personalized service and several echelons of dining room employees from the maitre d' to the head waiter or waitress, server, wine steward, coffee server, and bus person, it is easy to understand the high cost of labor in such establishments.

Hours of Service: The hours of service determine the number of "shifts" of personnel as well as the total number of labor hours required to accomplish the work. The hospital cafeteria that is open 7 days a week and serves 4 or 5 meals daily—breakfast, lunch, dinner, night supper, and 3 A.M. lunch for the night workers—demands a larger complement of employees than does the school lunchroom that serves only one meal per day for 5 days. The restaurant that is open 24 hours a day, 7 days a week has a different labor scheduling than the one that is open for business 10 to 12 hours a day, 6 days a week. Each situation has a different labor-cost expense.

Records of patronage and sales by 15-minute time segments throughout the serving period provide valuable data for management when evaluating labor needs and scheduling. Electronic or computer point-of-sales (POS) cash registers provide such data; small foodservices use a simple form such as shown in Fig. 14.12 for posting such data. Use of a graph as in Fig. 14.13 helps managers evaluate labor distribution.

Physical Plant: Size and Equipment Arrangement: An efficient kitchen arrangement and a convenient location are positive factors in labor cost control. Facility planning and layout are discussed in detail in Chapter 8. The foodservice manager may not be the one responsible for the kitchen plan, but if he or she "inherited" one that is poorly arranged, some changes may be necessary. Work flow and productivity analysis provide information to determine if changes are needed (see Chapter 13).

Menu and Form of Food Purchased: Many questions can be asked about the menu and form of food purchased as they affect overall labor costs. (Various types of menus are presented in Chapter 3.) The number of menu choices

Name of Foodservice

Date _____ AM	Number of Customers	Amount of Sales	Average Sales	Labor Hours	Labor Cost
7:00–7:15					
7:16–7:30					
7:31–7:45					
(etc.)					

(Breakfast)

Figure 14.12.   Records of census and sales by time segments give managers data helpful for evaluating and scheduling personnel.

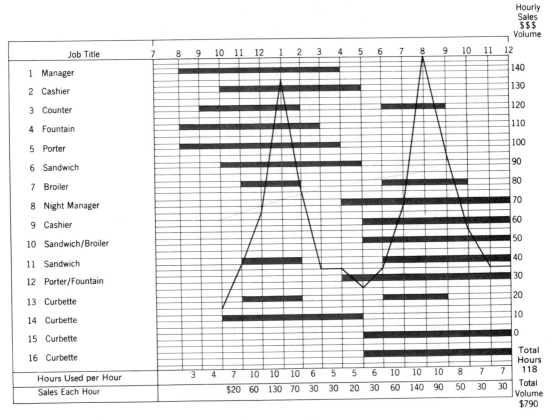

Figure 14.13. Graphic presentation of employee's time schedule in relation to volume of sales in one restaurant. (Courtesy, Ohio State Restaurant Association.)

offered, the complexity of preparation involved, the labor time/cost required, and the number of dishes to be washed, resulting from the menu items served, are only a few costs. Studies to determine the exact labor time/cost involved in preparing foods from the raw state versus the food and labor costs of using convenience foods give a preliminary basis for decisions on which form of food to buy.

Personnel Policies and Productivity: Labor is a commodity that cannot be purchased on short notice. The careful selection and placement of workers is basic to reducing turnover and its inherent costs. A study of overall personnel policies, including wage scales and employee benefits, can give managers possible clues to remedy excessive labor costs. However, the most important aspect of labor cost is probably employee productivity. As noted in Chapter 13, ineffective management is the single greatest cause of declining, or poor, productivity. Good supervision is vital to holding labor costs in line.

Supervision: Supervision is a major factor in the labor-cost picture. The effects of good or bad supervision cannot be underestimated when evaluating total labor cost. *Good* supervision assures adherence to established policies and rigid control of work schedules and standards, and influences employee morale; productivity is high and management receives fair returns on the labor dollar invested.

Too often, however, administration views supervision costs as excessive and attempts to cut labor costs by replacing competent, well-trained supervisors with inexperienced, immature ones. Sometimes, an experienced but unqualified person is promoted from the ranks to assume supervisory duties at a relatively low cost. Rarely does such replacement prove satisfactory. Neither the inexperienced nor the experienced untrained worker is able to see the full view of the foodservice operation. Usually the costs begin to rise until any slight saving entailed in the employment of an untrained director is absorbed many times over. Money spent for efficient supervision brings high returns in economic value to the organization. There is no substitute for good supervision.

OPERATING AND OTHER EXPENSES Control should not end with consideration of food and labor costs only; 12% to 18% of the departmental budget will probably be used for other items classified as overhead and operating expenses. These include utilities, laundry and linen supplies, repairs, replacement and maintenance, telephone, printing, paper goods, office supplies and cleaning materials, depreciation, rent or amortization, and insurance and taxes.

In addition, there is a real concern for conservation of energy resources within all foodservice establishments. Not only does conservation meet a national need, but it also helps to reduce departmental operating costs.

Maintenance and Repair: A planned maintenance program with the services of a maintenance engineer helps prevent breakdowns, extends the life of the equipment, and is usually a cost-effective procedure.

Breakage: Excessive breakage quickly adds to operating costs. Procedures should be in place to document breakage and employees should be well-trained on materials handling to prevent excess breakage.

Supplies: Supplies include linens, paper goods, cleaning compounds, dishwasher detergents, office supplies, and similar items. Although these items may be considered small in relation to other costs, any waste is costly. Accurate accounting of these items helps control costs.

Energy and Utility Costs: The energy "squeeze" of the 1970s made most foodservice managers and equipment manufacturers well aware of the need for conservation. New equipment designs are energy efficient, and managers continue to seek ways to conserve and to reduce utility bills. Energy-efficient equipment is discussed in Chapter 9; built-in energy efficient layout and design in Chapter 8; and ways of saving energy in storage and production of food in Chapter 4.

Summary

Financial planning and accountability is the responsibility of the foodservice manager. A basic understanding of accounting and financial management concepts is necessary to analyze the financial performance of the foodservice department and to make appropriate decisions for allocation of available resources.

The foodservice manager must recognize that the budget is the key management tool for financial planning and that he or she must take an active role in the budget development and implementation. Understanding and getting involved in the budget planning process assures a managerial commitment to the financial goals of the department.

The foodservice manager must know the day-to-day transactions and operational activities that take place in order to compare them with established goals. A sound system of records and reports provides the data base for making these comparisons. Without this close monitoring, downward trends are not detected and financial disaster can occur.

Summary Questions

1. What is the purpose of the budget?
2. Describe the three phases of budget planning.
3. What is the purpose of POS terminals?
4. In order to be effective, what are the three requirements for any record-keeping system?
5. What is the formula for determining food-cost percentage?
6. How are standards for food-cost percentages set?
7. Define markup. How is it calculated?
8. What three ratios are commonly used to analyze labor productivity and costs?

Bibliography

Horwath and Leventhol: Uniform System of Accounts for Restaurants, 6th ed. Washington, DC: National Restaurant Association, 1990.

Kaud, F. A.: Financial Management of the Hospital Food Service Department. Chicago: American Hospital Publishing, Inc., 1983, p. 13.

Minno, M. P. and Bhayana, R.: Restaurant budgeting: Step by step. NRA NEWS 40:21, 1984.

For More Information

Coltman, M. M.: Hospitality Management Accounting, 4th ed. New York: Van Nostrand Reinhold, 1991.

Keiser, J.: Controlling and Analyzing Costs in Foodservice Operations, 2nd ed. New York: Macmillan Publishing Co., 1989.

Sneed, J. and Kresse, K. H.: Understanding Foodservice Financial Management. Rockville, MD: Aspen Publishing, Inc., 1989.

Spears, M. C.: Foodservice Organizations. A Managerial and Systems Approach, 2nd ed. New York: Macmillan Publishing Co., 1991.

Stokes, J. F.: Cost Effective Quality Food Service. An Institutional Guide, 2nd ed. Rockville, MD: Aspen Systems Corporation, 1985.

Marketing in Foodservice Organizations

Marketing has been an essential function of commercial foodservice operations for a long time. In recent years, managers of noncommercial operations (i.e., hospitals, long-term care facilities, schools, and universities) have recognized the value of marketing principles as a means to survive in a highly competitive industry in which resources are increasingly scarce and costly. Serving good food is not enough. Today's customer is more sophisticated and has higher expectations of food and service than ever before. Good food must be accompanied by good service, a clean and pleasant atmosphere, an appropriate price, and convenience. These attributes can create a competitive edge or "point-of-difference"—the point at which a customer chooses one foodservice over another.

An individual does not need a business degree in marketing to develop a successful marketing program for a foodservice operation. In fact, this chapter introduces the reader to the basic principles of marketing and offers suggestions on how to develop and implement a successful program. It begins by defining some key marketing terms and concepts. Subsequent sections describe the unique aspects of the marketing process in foodservice, while the final section describes merchandising and promotion techniques appropriate for a foodservice operation and offers guidelines on how to plan and implement a specific promotion.

Learning Objectives

After studying this chapter, the reader should be able to

1. define the terms "marketing" and "marketing mix"
2. describe the premise of the marketing concept

3. apply the marketing concept and marketing strategies to a foodservice operation

4. recognize the responsibilities of a manager in planning, executing, and evaluating a marketing program

5. identify techniques and strategies useful in promoting products and services in a foodservice operation

The Definition of Marketing

Today, the word "marketing" is heard in many contexts. Earlier in the book, the marketing system is discussed in terms of agricultural products. In this chapter, however, marketing is examined as a specific managerial function. One definition of marketing is given by the American Marketing Association, which defines marketing as the performance of business activities that direct the flow of goods and services from the producer to the consumer. Others have defined marketing in more human terms. For example, Kotler defines marketing as a human activity directed at satisfying the needs and wants of customers through an exchange process; another author, Drucker, defines marketing simply as "creating customers."

In today's environment of limited resources and increased competition, it is easy to lose sight of the marketing concept in favor of financial stability. However, it is important for the manager to adopt the marketing concept and empower the employees to put customer needs first; without the customer, there would not be a foodservice organization. The marketing concept implies flexibility in changing with customers' evolving needs, wants, and demands.

Many marketing terms are used interchangeably. For the purposes of this chapter, the following terminology, as defined by Underwood, is used:

Marketing is the act or process of selling or buying in a marketplace.

Merchandising is a global term that describes sales promotion as a comprehension function, including market research, development of new products, manufacturing, marketing, advertising, and selling.

Promotion is a process or action meant to influence, increase, or improve the acceptance and sale of merchandise or services through advertising and publicity.

Advertising results when a promotion has been planned and presented to the public. It is the action of calling something to the attention of the public, making something public or generally known, and emphasizing desirable qualities to arouse a desire to buy a product or patronize a facility.

Publicity consists of acts or devices designed to attract public interest. It is the dissemination of information or promotional material, such as advertising.

Marketing activities identify and attract customers to an organization and its products and services, as well as serve an important function in the commercial foodservice industry. Marketing in the noncommercial foodservice setting, however, is a relatively new managerial concern. During the past decade, the health care and education industries have faced numerous challenges, including increased costs, inflation, increased government regulation, and competition for customers. As a result, many hospitals and long-term care facilities are struggling to maintain or increase their patient numbers. Schools, colleges, and universities are challenged with declining enrollment and competition from nearby restaurants.

The foodservices of these organizations can play an important role in attracting and keeping customers by creating good quality food and service and by increasing customer awareness of their availability. For example, good food and service can be a key factor in whether a family is willing to admit a loved-one to a long-term care facility. Variety and excitement in the school cafeteria can prompt a student to choose the cafeteria over a nearby fast-food restaurant for lunch. Furthermore, patients satisfied with their food will most likely comment favorably on their entire hospital stay.

Marketing is indeed a customer-driven process that includes specific activities. Fig. 15.1 illustrates a successful marketing cycle. Steps include: (1) identification of customers; (2) development of products, pricing, and distribution; (3) customer purchases; (4) generation of profits; and (5) appropriate action based on profits and customer feedback.

Marketing operates in a dynamic environment influenced by outside and inside forces. Outside forces include politics, the economy, government regulation, laws, social pressures, technology, local competition, industry trends, and, of course, customer attitudes and behavior. Inside influences can include organizational goals, budgetary constraints, and departmental policy.

The Marketing Cycle

The marketing cycle begins by identifying the customers who make up the potential market. The market, or target market, is defined as a group of people who, as individuals or organizations, have needs for products and possess the ability, willingness, and authority to make a purchase. The manager should ask the following questions:

• Who are the current customers?
• How many customers are in the potential market?
• Can we attract additional customers?
• What are the unique needs of these customers?

Figure 15.1. The marketing cycle. (Adapted from Robert D. Reid, Foodservice and Restaurant Marketing. New York: Van Nostrand Reinhold Co., Inc., 1983.)

For example, the director of a school lunch program may find that potential customers include students that currently bring their lunch or go home, as well as teachers, staff, and visitors that have not previously participated in the lunch program. Numbers can be estimated by calculating total student enrollment, total teaching and support staff, and the estimated number of visitors to the shool each day. Additional customers often include the elderly population of the community, who may participate in a congregate meal program at the school. Finally, the unique needs of each group must be identified. These unique needs may include fast-food type preferences for the student, foods of appropriate texture for the elderly, and speed and convenience for the teachers and staff.

Answering these questions helps the manager begin to define the market segments. Market segmentation divides the total market into smaller groups of people with similar product needs. Categories of customers emerge based on demographics, geographics, psychographics, and product preferences.

Demographic segmentation refers to the statistical data on customer profile characteristics such as age, sex, income, and educational background. *Geographic* segmentations categorize customers according to where they live. Segmentation by *psychographics refers to customers of similar life-styles, attitudes, and personalaties. Finally, product preference* is segmentation by customer behavior exhibited in a foodservice operation.

Once the needs and wants of potential customers have been identified, the manager can proceed with the marketing process by developing the products and services necessary to satisfy if not exceed these needs and wants. A product may be an object, service, or idea. It must also be available at the right place at the right time and be priced appropriately so that the customer identifies it as meeting a need, is willing to pay for the product, and prefers the product over that offered by the competition. To this end, the marketing process must be customer-oriented and customer-driven.

The Marketing Mix

A well-defined marketing program includes four elements: Product, Place, Price, and Promotion. These elements, often called the four Ps of marketing, and their unique combinations in any marketing program are called the marketing mix.

Product is the unique combination of products and service that satisfies a want or need. The product can be objects, services, ideas, places, or an organization. It is what is produced based on knowledge of the market and what is ultimately sold. Foodservice products include all items on the menu, as well as the many types of service options, such as cafeterias, vending machines, and catering, and other desirable attributes, such as pleasant atmosphere.

Place includes distribution and how products are sold. Products must be available at the right time and place, convenient for customers. Many foodservices today are accommodating customer desire for speed and convenience. For example, large-scale hospitals often set up mobile cafeterias or kiosks on nursing units during busy lunch periods as a convenience for medical staff with limited break time.

Price is the amount of money charged for a product or the sum of the values customers exchange for the benefit of the product. Strategic pricing encourages the customer to make a purchase, contributes to product image, and allows products to compete in the market. For example, a cafeteria manager may offer coffee at a reduced price during slow periods knowing that a customer is likely to make additional purchases such as sweet rolls, pie, or popcorn. See Fig. 15.2.

Promotion involves all communication with the customer. It introduces the customer to, or increases customer awareness of, the available product. (This is discussed in more detail later in the chapter.)

Training Staff on Their Role in Marketing

Employees are a very important part of a successful marketing program. They must be recruited and hired with great care and trained immediately on proper customer relations and professional behavior.

Figure 15.2. An example of a "preferred customer" coupon to increase cafeteria sales. (Copyright 1992 Board of Regents, University of Wisconsin Systems, University Hospital and Clinics, all rights reserved.)

Training time and costs should be valued as an investment in a successful marketing program. Reid suggests the following steps for employee training:

1. The training should be carefully planned and kept simple. An outline should be prepared to detail the subject matter covered in the training session.

2. The trainer should plan to cover only what the trainee can learn in a training session. Specific times should be set aside for training rather than trying to "squeeze it in." The marketing concept and all of its implications can be covered during several short sessions rather than during one long one.

3. The trainer should explain for the trainees specifically what it is they should be able to do; they should then be allowed to practice. For example, a cafeteria manager may wish to teach *suggestive selling* by training each cafeteria line employee to ask, "Would you like fries with your hamburger?", or to offer another appropriate suggestion.

4. All employees should be provided with feedback. Employees want to know how they are doing and follow-up is essential to evaluate the effectiveness of the training.

Managers, too, must take responsibility for self-development in marketing concepts, functions, and activities. Participation in professional associations, such as the National Restaurant Association (NRA), is a good way to stay current on a number of industry topics including marketing, planning, promotional ideas, and pricing strategies. Other self-development options include attending professional seminars and reading some of the numerous professional publications specific to the foodservice industry.

Marketing for Foodservice Operations

Unique Aspects of Foodservice Marketing

Marketing in foodservice requires a unique approach, because unlike many industries, foodservice includes a service component. Service is the application of human or mechanical efforts to people or objects. Service industries such as foodservice differ from most manufacturing industries in product, customer contact, perishability of inventory, and distribution.

Product

Foodservice is part of the multimillion dollar service industry in the United States. A service is an intangible product that is sold or purchased in a marketplace—one that does not result in ownership. *Intangibility* refers to the incapability of a product to be perceived, especially by touch. In this sense, food purchased for immediate consumption is referred to as a service because the customer leaves the operation without a tangible product. *Tangible* simply means that the product is capable of being perceived by the buyer. Televisions, dishwashers, and automobiles are examples of tangible products.

Customer Contact

The customer takes a more active role in the marketing function in a service industry. For example, in many cafeterias, patrons help themselves to displayed foods or, in the case of table service, there is direct and frequent customer-employee contact. Each contact represents an opportunity for the foodservice to market not only the food product but the organizational image as well.

In the cafeteria self-serve situation, the foodservice operation has the opportunity to entice the customer with attractive well-designed display (see Fig. 15.3). Table service offers more direct and personal contact. For example, wait staff can be trained to anticipate customer wants and needs such as a beverage refill or readiness for the check. One negative customer-employee interaction can generate lasting dissatisfaction that may result in the loss of business not only from the unhappy customer, but from all potential customers that the dissatisfied customer influences through word-of-mouth.

Perishability

Food is unique in that it is highly perishable and difficult to store in inventory. Unlike a tangible product, such as a television set, that can be stored in a

Figure 15.3.   Example of an attractively designed cafeteria line. (Courtesy, University of Wisconsin Hospital and Clinics, Department of Food and Nutrition.)

warehouse during low-demand periods, food is highly perishable and, if unsold or simply not used, it is lost income, or waste. For example, if customer count is lower than expected in a cafeteria or school these potential sales are lost forever and food prepared ahead of time is wasted.

Distribution

In many types of foodservice operations, food must be prepared in advance, held either hot or cold, and transported for distribution. For example, many elementary and high schools receive their food from commissary foodservice operations. Without careful consideration of the conditions during holding and transport, food quality can deteriorate significantly and, thus, it can be rejected by the paying customer.

Marketing as a Managerial Function

Management must recognize marketing as an essential function, similar to traditional management functions of organizing, leading, and controlling. The marketing function isn't a management fad that, if ignored, will go away. It is the customer who will not return if the marketing function is not understood or properly implemented.

Common marketing mistakes include

* lack of planning
* improper budgeting
* poorly defined goals and objectives
* lack of product development
* inadequate program evaluation

With a clear vision of and a commitment to the organization's mission, the wise manager can develop a marketing program that includes planning, implementation, and evaluation.

Planning

Planning begins with a clear understanding of and a commitment to the goals and objectives of the marketing plan. In other words, the manager should ask: "What are we as an organization or a department trying to do?" "What do we hope to accomplish?" For example, is the purpose of the marketing program to attract new customers, retain current customers, or influence specific purchasing behaviors?

General goals need to be defined as part of the organization's long-term or strategic planning. For a goal to become reality, specific objectives must be established. Objectives must be clear and, for purposes of program evaluation, they must be measurable. Responsibility for achieving the objective through specific activities should be assigned and a timetable established for meeting the objective.

For example, a high school may have a goal of maintaining student participation in the school lunch program. An appropriate objective in making strides to achieve this may be to have the foodservice department distribute surveys to at least 50% of the students enrolled in the school district during a 3-month period in order to determine student opinion concerning participation in the school lunch program. Fig. 15.4 is an example of a survey used in a high school to determine the food preferences of freshmen in an effort to retain their participation in the school lunch program. Using such survey results, the foodservice manager can create specific action plans to implement the objective. Without specific action plans, good objectives might be deserted and desired goals will not be met.

Implementation

Implementation is critical in keeping objectives from becoming good intentions that are left unchallenged. It involves empowering staff to embrace the

SURVEY - 9TH GRADE

Hello! We are interested in finding out how you feel about your school lunch program and how your opinions have or have not changed since Middle School. Please answer the following questions and hand it in TODAY. Your participation is appreciated!

Check how often you purchase cafeteria items:

_____ Always (5 times per week)
_____ Frequently (3 - 4 times per week)
_____ Sometimes (2 times per week)
_____ Rarely or never (0 - 1 times per week)

Check items you usually buy: _ hot items ____ salads ____ snacks ____ desserts

1. How do the following foods rank in comparison to those in Middle School? Please circle your response.

HOT ITEMS (Hamburgers, Fries, Tacos, etc)
   a) variety of choices   BETTER   WORSE   SAME
   b) taste   BETTER   WORSE   SAME
   c) appearance   BETTER   WORSE   SAME
   d) overall   BETTER   WORSE   SAME

SALADS
   a) variety of choices   BETTER   WORSE   SAME
   b) taste   BETTER   WORSE   SAME
   c) appearance   BETTER   WORSE   SAME
   d) overall   BETTER   WORSE   SAME

SNACKS
   a) variety of choices   BETTER   WORSE   SAME
   b) taste   BETTER   WORSE   SAME
   c) appearance   BETTER   WORSE   SAME
   d) overall   BETTER   WORSE   SAME

DESSERTS
   a) variety of choices   BETTER   WORSE   SAME
   b) taste   BETTER   WORSE   SAME
   c) appearance   BETTER   WORSE   SAME
   d) overall   BETTER   WORSE   SAME

What foods do you really like, that are offered in High School, but weren't offered in Middle School? Please list items here:

_____
_____
_____

Are there any foods offered in High School that you would like to see taken off of the menu? Please list items here:

_____
_____
_____

Are there any foods you would like to see added to the High School menu? Please list items here:

_____
_____
_____

Figure 15.4.   Survey tool designed to determine food preferences of high school freshmen. (Courtesy, Madison Metropolitan School District, Food Production Center.)

marketing plan, training employees to successfully execute the plan, defining and developing the promotion plans, effectively communicating marketing messages, and providing support to enable the plan to succeed. Part of this support includes implementing procedures to evaluate the marketing plan's effectiveness.

Evaluation

Evaluation is the process of determining the success of the plan as implemented. The manager must measure the degree to which the previously established objectives were achieved. For example, if the foodservice manager sets an objective of increasing school lunch participation by 5%, then the manager must review daily meal counts to determine if that objective was actually achieved. The knowledge gained from this evaluation can be used to refine objectives and action plans.

Marketing programs, in particular, are costly in time and resources; therefore, management must take steps to ensure that there is an actual, measurable return on this investment. Logically, the evaluation strategies come after implementation of the program and after a specific amount of time has passed. This allows the program ample opportunity to achieve anticipated objectives. Results of the marketing program can then be compared against the projected results. For example, a manager for a long-term care facility may wish to increase customer meal participation on holidays. Fig. 15.5 is an example of an invitation used in one long-term care facility to promote such an objective. After the holidays, the manager can simply compare participation following this promotion against guest participation for previous holiday seasons. The change in participation is an indicator of the program's success with this one objective. Obviously, clear and concise record keeping is also critical to assure that these comparisons are made effectively.

Merchandising and Sales Promotion in Foodservice Operations

As described, marketing is a process of identifying customers and their needs, and developing products to satisfy those needs. Merchandising and promotions are distinct functions used to continually pique the interest of customers in an effort to stimulate repeat business, as well as new business.

Merchandising

Merchandising is defined as a comprehensive function that includes market research, product development, manufacturing, marketing, sales promotions,

maplewood
sauk prairie

Skilled Nursing Facility

245 Sycamore Street, Sauk City, Wisconsin 53583
Phone (608) 643-3383

SEASONS GREETINGS!

In celebration of the Holiday Season, you are cordially invited to a complimentary dinner with your spouse at Maplewood on Christmas Day, December 25, 1992.

Dinner will be served to you and your spouse in the main dining room at 12:00 noon.

Please complete and return the attached RSVP by December 18, 1992. An envelope is enclosed for your convenience.

Happy Holidays!

Mary Leonard

Mary Leonard
Director of Dietary

_____   YES, I will attend Christmas dinner with my spouse.

_____   NO, I will not attend Christmas dinner with my spouse.

Signed: _____

Spouse's Name: _____

Figure 15.5.   An example of a personalized invitation used to promote increased guest participation of a holiday meal at a long-term care facility. (Courtesy, Maplewood of Sauk-Prairie, Sauk City, Wisconsin.)

advertising, and selling. Terms such as marketing, promotions, merchandising, and selling are used interchangeably, and clear, concise definitions are difficult to find.

No amount of merchandising, however, will be effective if the foodservice establishment is not clean, organized, pleasant, and comfortable. With these basic requirements achieved, the manager should consider the numerous opportunities available to tantalize the customer.

- Present all food attractively, regardless of whether it is being served in a dining room, on a patient tray, from a steam table, or from a vending machine. Use garnishes and appropriate plate-fill to visually attract customers to the food. Figs. 15.6, 15.7, and 15.8 are examples of catering platters designed with color and eye appeal.
- Arrange displayed foods in cafeterias or on buffet lines in an eye-appealing manner. Mix colors for preplated salads and arrange in mixed combinations. For example, alternate crisp, colorful vegetable plates with softer, less colorful salads (i.e., potato salad). Figs. 15.9 and 15.10 are examples of attractive buffet and cafeteria lines.
- Use bulk display techniques. Offer fresh fruit from baskets or bowls brimming with polished, clean apples, oranges, plums, and so forth. Fig. 15.11 is an example of an eye appealing fruit display.

Sales Promotion

As discussed earlier in this chapter, promotion is one of the four Ps of a marketing program. Promotion is a distinct function, different from merchandising

Figure 15.6.   Catering platter attractively arranged and garnished. (Courtesy, St. Joseph's Hospital, Marshfield, Wisconsin.)

Figure 15.7. Catering platter attractively arranged and garnished. (Courtesy, St. Joseph's Hospital, Marshfield, Wisconsin.)

Figure 15.8. Catering platter attractively arranged and garnished. (Courtesy, St. Joseph's Hospital, Marshfield, Wisconsin.)

Figure 15.9. An example of a buffet line. (Courtesy, St. Joseph's Hospital, Marshfield, Wisconsin.)

Figure 15.10.   An example of a cafeteria line with emphasis on color and design. (Courtesy, University of Wisconsin Hospital and Clinics.)

Figure 15.11.   Example of bulk fruit display for cafeteria. (Courtesy, University of Wisconsin Hospital and Clinics.)

and advertising. It is the function of influencing the customer's purchase and repurchase behavior, with a primary goal of increasing patronage and, in turn, improving sales and profit. Promotion can also be used for a number of nonprofit goals, such as increasing public awareness of a facility's services.

By planning, implementing, and evaluating promotional strategies, the manager can accomplish several goals. These goals are to: (1) present information to the customers, (2) reinforce desired purchasing behavior to stimulate repeat business, (3) stimulate first-time business by arousing curiosity, and (4) enhance the image of an organization. Such strategies are appropriate for all types of institution foodservices. Obviously, promotions are necessary for cafeterias, vending, and catering, which rely on a profit. There are, however, many other reasons for understanding the basics of promotional marketing.

There are two categories of promotions. First, there are the "share of market" promotions. These are volume-based; that is, designed to increase patronage, sales, or a combination of the two. Second, there are "share of mind" promotions, which seek to influence the customer's preference or feelings about a particular facility or product. Both of these can be used in institutional foodservices.

Promotion Planning

Promotion planning begins just like any other managerial function, by establishing clear, measurable objectives. The primary objectives of promotions are to increase the frequency of customer visits and the level of customer satisfaction. Table 15.1 suggests specific objectives for various types of foodservice operations.

The manager can generate ideas for specific objective(s) by asking the following questions:

1. What is it that we are trying to accomplish with this promotion?
2. Is it consistent with our mission statement?
3. Is it designed to meet customer needs?
4. How can we evaluate or measure the success of this promotion?

In contrast to marketing and merchandising, promotions are generally designed to run for a short period of time but may be extended or repeated if the objectives remain desirable. For example, a school may try a special promotion during National School Lunch Week to increase participation, offering a free dessert with each meal. If highly successful, the foodservice manager may wish to repeat the promotion at another time during the school year.

TABLE 15.1.   Examples of Promotions Objectives.

Schools
  • increase participation in the school lunch program
  • increase total à la carte sales
  • create an awareness of a new product

Hospital Cafeteria, Vending
  • increase average total profit
  • increase beverage to food ratio
  • increase salad and dessert sales

Long-Term Care Facilities
  • increase awareness of nutritional value of food
  • increase awareness of special services
  • increase family participation in holiday meals

Some guidelines for the development, implementation, and evaluation of a successful promotion are as follows:

1. Plan well in advance—at least 1 to 3 months before the event is to take place.

2. Establish goals and objectives.

3. Know the current and potential customers.

4. Select a promotional idea consistent with customer need and the organization's mission.

5. Seek advice and ideas from internal and external sources.

6. Verify availability of financial resources and compare costs of promotion to expected benefits.

7. Design a written plan for implementation and review the plan with employers.

8. Execute the plan, paying careful attention to all details.

9. Evaluate the results against the planned objectives and make changes as necessary for future promotions.

There are numerous means by which promotion objectives can be met including coupons, contests, discounts, combination pricing, signs, special events, menu boards, and theme days. The following illustrations (Figs. 15.12 through 15.20) are examples of promotions used in various types of foodservice organizations.

SAINT JOSEPH'S HOSPITAL-MARSHFIELD

A MEMBER OF MINISTRY CORPORATION
SISTERS OF THE SORROWFUL MOTHER

GIFT CERTIFICATE

TO: _____ $ _____

FROM: _____

Redeemable at: Four Seasons Dining
                  Take Me Home
                  Westwood Dining

Issue Date: _____ Initials: _____

Certificate can be redeemed up to six months after date of issue.

P546-244

TAKING
HEALTHY HABITS
TO HEART

Buy 12 of the featured Heart Healthy
entrees and your 13th is free.

P546-279

This coupon entitles any
patient or visitor to

*One Free
Cup of Coffee*

in

Westwood Dining

Figure 15.12. Examples of promotions to increase customer awareness of and participation in cafeteria options. (Courtesy, St. Joseph's Hospital, Marshfield, Wisconsin.)

(*a*)

(*b*)

Figure 15.13.   Examples of how specialized bakery products (*a*) and displays (*b*) can be used to stimulate cafeteria sales. (Courtesy, St. Joseph's Hospital, Marshfield, Wisconsin.)

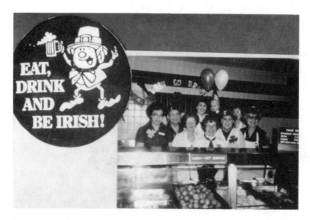

Figure 15.14.   Example of a theme day promotion for a cafeteria on St. Patrick's Day. (Courtesy, St. Joseph's Hospital, Marshfield, Wisconsin.)

Figure 15.15.   Example of build-your-own yogurt sundae to increase mid-afternoon cafeteria sales. (Courtesy, University of Wisconsin Hospitals and Clinics.)

Catering Services Newsletter
U.W.H.C. Food and Nutrition Services Department

Welcome to our catering services newsletter "Celebrations and Salutations!" This issue offers ready to serve party trays and desserts for creating special events with style, taste, and a personal touch with little effort by you the host or hostess. Just in time to help you through the holidays.

DELI PARTY TRAYS

Featuring outstanding deli combinations for any occasion or taste. From family birthday parties to receptions or a tailgate party, U.W.H.C. Catering Services will fill your order expertly and efficiently. From our deli area the following items are available:

* **Meat Trays** - Featuring Ham, Turkey, Roast Beef, Turkey Ham, Turkey Pastrami, and Hard Pastrami
* **Cheese Trays** - Featuring American, Swiss, and Lo-Fat/Lo-Sodium Monterey Jack, Cheddar, Farmer's Cheese
* **Combination Trays** - Featuring both Meats and Cheeses
* **Relish Trays** - With an assortment of fresh vegetables and homemade dips
* **Finger Sandwiches** - With Ham, Turkey, Ham Salad, Egg Salad, Avocado Spread
* **Shrimp & Seafood Platters** with Cocktail Sauce
* **Freshly Prepared Salads** - Potato Salad, Pasta Salad, Coleslaw, Marinated Vegetable Salad, Rotini and Vegetable Salad, Fruit Salad
* **Fruit Platters** - With an assortment of seasonal fresh fruit

Let us help you . . .
Call **3-1524** and we will gladly assist you in planning your function for your convenience . . .
Minimum three day advance notice preferred . . .

BAKERY FOR - U

Sweeten Your Family's Smile
Create a special event at home with one of our specialty pies, cakes, Baker's Dozen Cookies, or Ice Cream for dinner, social get togethers, or anytime.

BAKERY FOR - U Offerings:
Pies: Peach, Apple, Cherry, Blackberry, Blueberry, Pecan, Pumpkin and Lemon Meringue

Cream Pies: Heath Crunch, Peanut Butter Silk, French Silk, and Banana Cream

Cakes: Walnut Layer, Chocolate Layer, Carrot, Black Forest, German Chocolate Layer, French Cream Cheese

Cookies: Your choice of fresh baked Chocolate Chip, Oatmeal Raisin, Roasted Peanut or Chocolate Chip Pecan. Baker's Dozen (13) per package.

Ice Cream: UW's own Babcock specialty in 1/2 gallons. Vanilla and assorted flavors with or without nuts.

All baked goods are available for easy self service from the refrigerated display case in the cafeteria from **2:00 pm - 6:30 pm daily**. Phone orders are also available through **3-1526** with pick up in 20 minutes.

Figure 15.16.   An example of a catering services newsletter to increase awareness of catering services available through a hospital cafeteria. (Copyright 1992 Board of Regents, University of Wisconsin Systems, University Hospital and Clinics, all rights reserved.)

Figure 15.17.   Example of pizza promotions for a hospital cafeteria, designed to be hung on the doorknobs of offices. (Copyright 1992 Board of Regents, University of Wisconsin Systems, University Hospital and Clinics, all rights reserved.

PIZZARIFFIC
PIZZA

to go

"Buy" The Slice

"Buy" The Box

Call 263-1526

To order whole pizza
Ready in 20 minutes
Selections vary daily

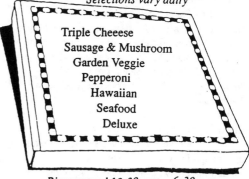

Triple Cheeese
Sausage & Mushroom
Garden Veggie
Pepperoni
Hawaiian
Seafood
Deluxe

Pizza served 10:30 a.m. - 6:30 p.m.
University Hospital Cafeteria

UWHC CAFETERIA

PIZZARIFFIC DEALS

HOT SUMMER SAVINGS

Figure 15.18. Example of pizza promotions for a hospital cafeteria. (Copyright 1992 Board of Regents, University of Wisconsin Systems, University Hospital and Clinics, all rights reserved.)

UNIVERSITY OF WISCONSIN HOSPITAL AND CLINICS

 Welcome **TO OUR CAFETERIA**

Family, friends and guests of our patients
Students, Faculty and Staff

BREAKFAST	*LUNCH*	*DINNER*	*SNACKS*
6:00 - 9:45 A.M.	11:00 - 2:00	4:30 - 7:00	ANYTIME

MONDAY
08/03/92
- LUNCH: Grilled Chicken Breast, Orange Roughy, Chicken Fajita, Vegetarian Lasagna with Garlic Bread, Kafta with Tahini Sauce
- DINNER: Vegetarian Lasagna with Garlic Bread, Sweet & Sour Pork, Roast Whole Turkey, Baked Pollock, Egg Roll

TUESDAY
08/04/92
- LUNCH: Pork Cutlets, Chicken Cordon Bleu', Carved Steamship Round on a Kaiser Roll, Cheese Strata, Lemon Peppered Pollock
- DINNER: Baked Lasagna, Carved Steamship Round on a Kaiser Roll, Chicken Breast Cordon Bleu', Walleyed Pike, Cheese Strata

WEDNESDAY
08/05/92
- LUNCH: Swiss Steak, Baked Sole, Chicken Breast Hoagie, Baked Sole, Italian Spaghetti, Vegetarian Spaghetti, Baked Potato with BBQ Roast Beef and Cheese
- DINNER: Vegetarian Spaghetti, Carved Whole Baked Ham, Bacon Burger, Italian Spaghetti & Meat Sauce, Poorman's Lobster

THURSDAY
08/06/92
- LUNCH: Baked Meatloaf, Baked Fish with Rice, Falafel, Broccoli Quiche, Beef Liver & Onions
- DINNER: Carved Roast Pork, Baked Chicken, Ranch Steak on Kaiser Roll, Broccoli Quiche

FRIDAY
08/07/92
- LUNCH: Carved Turkey, Pepper Steak Over Rice, Hot Turkey Ham and Cheese Sandwich, Eggroll with Sweet and Sour Sauce, Baked Potato with Broccoli, Cheese and Bacon, Vegetarian Chili, Fish Marinara
- DINNER: Stir Fried Beef with Vegetables over Rice, Chicken Kiev, Hot Turkey Ham and Cheese Sandwich, Baked Sole, Carrot Mushroom Loaf

SATURDAY
08/08/92
- LUNCH: French Fried Perch, Carved Roast Turkey, Sliced Roast Pork, Manicotti with Garlic Bread, Super Dog
- DINNER: Carved Roast Turkey, Manicotti, Sliced Roast Pork, Chimichanga

SUNDAY
08/09/92
- LUNCH: Carved Prime Rib of Beef, Baked Filet of Sole, Sliced Baked Ham Baked Potato with Broccoli & Cheese
- DINNER: Carved Prime Rib of Beef, Baked Filet of Sole, Sliced Baked Ham Baked Potato with Broccoli & Cheese

TRY OUR NEW PIZZARIFFIC PIZZA BY THE SLICE OR WHOLE!!

(2792o)

WE FEATURE LIGHT CHOICES AT EVERY MEAL
GO FOR THE GOLD!
WIN WITH OUR UPCOMING
OLYMPIC SPECIALS

Figure 15.19. Example of a cafeteria menu flyer to increase customer awareness of cafeteria specials. (Copyright 1992 Board of Regents, University of Wisconsin Systems Hospital and Clinics, all rights reserved.)

OCT '92 LUNCH MENU

MONDAY	TUESDAY	WEDNESDAY	THURSDAY	FRIDAY
			1 Oven Baked Chicken; Fluffy White Rice/Gravy; Whole Kernel Corn; Choice of Bread/Butter; Chilled Peach Slices	**2** Cardinal Burger/Bun w/Red & White Toppings; Football Fries; Victory Green Beans; Favorite Fruit Medley; Winning Rice Krispie Bar; HOMECOMING
5 Chicken Nuggets w/Sauces; Macaroni w/ Cheese Sauce; Broccoli Cuts; Choice of Fresh Fruit	**6** Italian Dunkers* (Cheese Bread w/ Meat Sauce); Tossed Salad w/ Choice of Dressing; Diced Pears; Sugar Cookie	**7** French Toast w/ Warm Syrup; Little Smokies; Choice of Juice; Fruit Cup w/Melon; Iced Cinnamon Roll; YOM KIPPUR	**8** Roast Turkey/Gravy; Snowy Mashed Potatoes; Wisconsin Blend Veggies; Dinner Roll/Butter; Fruited Jello Square	**9** Pepperoni Pizza or Cheese Pizza; Fresh Vegetable Sticks w/ Reduced Calorie Dip; Pineapple Tidbits
12 DISCOVER ETHNIC FOODS; Burrito* Ole w/Queso; Lechuga, Tomate; Frijoles (Refried Beans); Centennial Bread; Applesauce for 500; Italian Ice Discovery; COLUMBUS DAY (observed)	**13** Build-Your-Own Burger; Cheese Slice, Lett., Tom.; Straight Cut Fries; Fruit Cocktail Shapes; Future Fortune Cookie	**14** NATIONAL SCHOOL LUNCH WEEK (October 12-16); Grilled Unbreaded Chicken Breast Patty/Bun; Lettuce Leaf & Tomato Sl.; Seasoned Green Beans; Baked Fruit Bar	**15** Curley Noodles w/ Italian Meat* Sauce; Bread Stick; Confetti Salad/Dressings; Peach Smiles; PENCIL DAY – Elem. Schools	**16** WORLD SERIES TAILGATE; Home Run Turkey or Beef Stacker/Bun; Cheese Slice/Lettuce Leaf; Curve Ball Fries; Catch of Fresh Fruit; BASEBALL CARD DAY
19 Cheese & Sausage Pizza; Fresh Veggies w/ Ranch or Yogurt Dip; Mixed Fruit	**20** Chicken Nuggets/Sauces; Toasty Tritator; Green Beans; Bread/Butter; Strawberry Shortcake	**21** Meat & Cheese Lasagna*; Garlic Bread; Tossed Salad w/ Choice of Dressings; Pineapple Bites	**22** Sloppy Joe* /Bun; Tator Tots; Tiny Green Peas; Pear Halves; TELL THE COOKS YOUR NAME TREAT: Ice Cream	**23** Ham & Cheese Melt; Waffle Cut Fries; Golden Cut Corn; Choice of Fresh Fruit
26 Hotdog or Brat/Bun; Crinkle Cut Fries; Bubbly Baked Beans; Cinnamon Apple Crisp	**27** Breaded Chicken Patty on Bun w/Lettuce Leaf; Tator Tots; Broccoli & Cauliflower; Choice of Fruit	**28** NO SCHOOL; PROFESSIONAL DEV./ WORK DAY	**29** NO SCHOOL; TEACHER'S CONVENTION	**30** NO SCHOOL; TEACHER'S CONVENTION; HALLOWEEN (Saturday, 31st)

All menus subject to change

* Items may contain ground turkey or pork as well as ground beef

Figure 15.20. Example of a school lunch menu designed to promote National School Lunch Week. Copies of the menu are sent to student homes. (Courtesy, Sun Prairie Area School District, Sun Prairie, Wisconsin.)

Summary

Marketing has been an essential function of commercial foodservice operations for a long time. In recent years, managers of noncommercial operations, (e.g., hospitals, long-term care facilities, schools, and universities) have recognized the value of marketing principles as a means to survive in a highly competitive industry with limited resources and ever-increasing costs.

Foodservice managers today must have a sound knowledge base of marketing terminology, the marketing cycle, the marketing concept, and the unique aspects of marketing in foodservice in order to successfully implement a program. Implementation includes carefully planned training for foodservice employees and an evaluation strategy to assess the degree to which the program objectives were achieved.

Merchandising and promotions are very important activities related to a marketing program. The foodservice manager must become familiar with promotion design, planning procedure, implementation, and evaluation strategies as means to gain the competitive edge and retain or attract new customers to the foodservice operation.

Bibliography

Kotler, P. and Armstrong, G.: Marketing: An Introduction. Englewood Cliffs, NJ: Prentice Hall, 1987.

Reid, R. D.: Foodservice and Restaurant Marketing. New York: Van Nostrand Co., 1983.

Smith, D. I.: Merchandising: Influencing the customer purchase decision. In R. A. Brymer (Ed.), Hospitality Management (pp. 255–268). Dubuque, IA: Kendall/Hunt Publishing Co., 1991.

Spears, M. C.: Foodservice Organizations: A Managerial and Systems Approach, 2nd ed. New York: MacMillan Publishing Co., 1991.

Underwood, R. F.: Marketing and revenue-producing projects. In K. E. Lawrence and S. N. DiLima, (Eds.), Hospital Nutrition and Food Service: Forms Checklists and Guidelines (pp. 4:1–4:2). Gaithersburg, MD: Aspen Publishers, Inc., 1992.

For More Information

Albrecht, K. and Bradford, L. J.: The Service Advantage: How to Identify and Fulfill Customer Needs. Homewood, IL: Dow Jones & Company, Inc., 1990.

The Competitive Edge: Marketing Strategies for the Registered Dietitian. Chicago: American Dietetic Association, 1986.

DiDomenico, P.: Promoting Columbus Day. Restaurants USA 12:10–13, 1992.

Dollar, F. W.: Marketing: A constant commitment. Food Mgmt. 20:51–52, 1985.

Erffmeyer, R. C.: Incorporation of the marketing concept. Applications in university contract food service. J. Am. Diet. Assoc. 87:1215–1216, 1987.

Foodservice Manager 2000: National Restaurant Association. Current Issues Report: Washington, DC, 1992.

Isaken, R.: Nutrition and ambience: Consumer demands and restaurateur response. The Consultant 19:24–25, 1986.

Kaud, F. A., Miller, R. P., and Underwood, R. F.: Cafeteria Management for Hospitals. Chicago: American Hospital Association, 1982.

McCabe, G.: Anatomy of a promotion. Food Manager 26:74, 1991.

Parks, S. C.: Research techniques used to support marketing management decisions. In E. R. Monsen (Ed.), Research (pp. 295–314). Chicago, IL: The American Dietetic Association, 1992.

Parks, S. C. and Moody, D. L.: A marketing model: Applications for dietetic professionals. J. Am. Diet. Assoc. 86:37–43, 1986.

Pickens, C. W. and Shanklin, C. W.: State of the art in marketing hospital foodservice departments. J. Am. Diet. Assoc. 85:1474–1478, 1985.

Pond-Smith, D., Jennings, G., Funk, K., and Latif, L. A.: Alternative revenue sources school foodservice: A survey of school food and nutrition services. J. Am. Diet. Assoc. 90:1103–1104, 1990.

Puckett, B. B.: Food Service Manual for Health Care, 1988 Edition. Chicago: American Hospital Association, 1988.

Reid, R. D.: Hospitality marketing management in the 90's. In R. A. Brymer (Ed.), Hospitality Management (pp. 233–243). Dubuque, IA: Kendall/Hunt Publishing Co., 1991.

Sagowitz, S.: Anticipating customer demands. Food Mgmt. 21:67–68, 1986.

Sagowitz, S.: Reach out and get to know your customers. Food Mgmt. 20:33–34, 1985.

Sneed, J. and Burkhalter, J. P.: Marketing nutrition in restaurants: A survey of current practices and attitudes. J. Am. Diet. Assoc. 91:459–462, 1991.

Underwood, R. F.: 52 Cafeteria Promotions That Really Work. Gaithersburg, MD: Aspen Publishers, Inc., 1988.

Computer-Assisted Management

Managerial success in foodservice depends on the ability of a person to manage and use information to make decisions that are timely and effective. Every organization has an *information system*—a subsystem in the overall structure that affects all levels of the organization. This information system may range from the very informal (noncomputerized) to the very sophisticated (computer-based). For a small operation, a manual system can often perform the necessary tasks efficiently and accurately. Often, however, as the volume of work grows, procedures increase in complexity, activities become more interrelated, improvements in productivity are made, and computer support is implemented. The proliferation of computer-assisted information systems in foodservice operations can also be attributed to the information explosion, the rapid pace of change, the increasing complexity of management, the recognition of information as an essential resource, and the improvements in computer technology (e.g., expanded capabilities; decreased cost and size; faster, simplified programs; and a clearer understanding of potential benefits). The computers used in businesses today are 30 times faster and 200 times cheaper than the largest computers available in 1960.

A computer-assisted management information system does the following: it accepts data (input) from sources within and external to the organization; it acts on the data (transformation) to produce information; and, finally, it produces the information for the intended user (output).

This chapter presents information on the use of computerized data processing as a foodservice information system. Certain computer terminology, considerations to be made in selecting a suitable computer system, including programs, and some applications to foodservice administration are given. This information should aid managers who wish to change from a manual to a simple computerized information-producing system. Success of any such system depends on its design in relation to departmental needs and goals and the extent to which management uses the information provided.

Learning Objectives

After studying this chapter, the reader should be able to

1. describe how computer-assisted management information systems (MIS) facilitate the management functions of planning, organizing, delegating, leading, and controlling

2. list the purposes of MIS

3. identify the steps by which data can be converted into information

4. define the terms hardware, software, central processing unit (CPU), memory, input, output, peripherals, data base, and spread sheet

5. describe how a foodservice manager should prepare for computerization

6. list the six basic program categories of foodservice computer-based information systems

7. distinguish between artificial intelligence expert systems and robotics

8. list the three goals of computer-assisted MIS

Description of MIS

Management information systems (MIS) are networks of communication that provide management with information about the organization activities and serve as a basis for decision making.

The interrelated nature of the subsystems of the organization and the central role of the information subsystem is shown in Fig. 16.1. Each of the functional areas contributes to the information system and, in turn, the information system provides the managers with the needed information for the successful management of each of their areas.

Most often MIS are thought of as computerized data processing. That is increasingly true and, ultimately, the foodservice organization that does not utilize a computer system will be at a distinct disadvantage. However, MIS includes other modes for providing information that are used alone or in conjunction with computers. The computer is only a tool for running the MIS more effectively and efficiently.

All organizations have information systems. Some are informal, such as the grapevine, opinions, gossip, and hearsay; others are formal, such as written

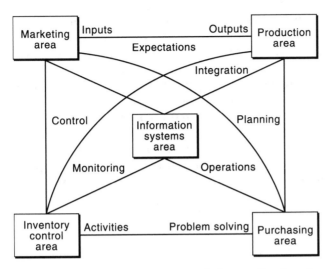

Figure 16.1.   Information systems role in coordinating. (From Senn, J. A.: *Information Systems in Management,* 3rd ed., 1987, p. 492. Reprinted by permission of Wadsworth, Inc.)

policies and procedures, and records and reports. Although both types may be necessary, only the formal information system is a valid basis for decision making. As noted in the discussion on records and reports in Chapter 14, information must be current, accurate, complete, clear, timely, and accessible when needed in order to be the greatest value to the manager. The department's MIS must be designed to meet those requirements.

Any successful information system must be well-organized and developed on the basis of wants and needs of the individual foodservice operation. MIS is a total process in which data are provided and refined to give desired information to management at all levels. To attain this goal, specific objectives as to what the formal information system is to accomplish must be stated and the information to be provided identified.

Usually, information systems are designed to: (1) monitor progress, (2) track trends, (3) assess performance, (4) consider alternatives, (5) make decisions, and (6) take corrective action needed. In other words, an MIS facilitates the management functions of planning, organizing, delegating, leading, and controlling.

It should be pointed out that *data* are raw facts that in themselves have little or no meaning. They must be translated into a meaningful form for whoever is to use them. Thus, data are transformed into information. For example, the data on a census report tells the number of people served on a given day or a monthly total. Those figures alone have little meaning, but become important information to the food buyer or production manager who uses that data to decide how much food to buy or to be prepared, or to the manager who compares the census data to the income to determine the degree of financial success achieved for a certain time period, and provides a basis for deciding whether or not any remedial action is required.

Since so much data are generated in any business, too much for most managers to cope with in the raw form, it is necessary that the data be screened, synthesized, compared, and analyzed according to the needs of a particular foodservice operation.

Although there are endless methods for producing information from data, Burch, Strater, and Grudniski tell us there are 10 steps or operations taken to convert data into information, whatever mechanism is used:

- capturing—recording
- verifying—checking data
- classifying—into specific categories meaningful to the user
- arranging or sorting—predetermined sequence (an inventory file, for example)
- summarizing—combining data
- calculating—mathematics/logical manipulation of data (as figuring employees' pay or customers' bills)
- storing for later retrieval
- retrieving—searching and gaining access to
- reproducing
- disseminating/communicating to final user—report, disc, screen, and so on

These steps may be accomplished by computer or manually. Selection of a system to perform the functions is of major concern to today's foodservice manager. For a discussion of the manual procedures for designing and keeping records and preparing reports, see Chapter 14. Informal information systems such as oral communication through group meetings, individual counseling, and training programs are discussed in Chapter 11. Written information provided through policy and procedure books, quality assurance evaluations, operating standards, and employee appraisals, also presented in this text, are a part of the total information system. In this section, data on the basics for selection and use of a computerized management information system and some of the applications to the foodservice are given.

MIS by Computer Systems

Computers are being used to some degree almost universally today, although foodservice organizations have been slower than other industries to convert to their use, especially for decision-making support. The primary function of computers is to record data that are created with every transaction and convert them into usable information in a matter of seconds or minutes instead of the days or weeks it takes to do so manually. It is important to recognize that the computer MIS is only as good as the manual system employed. Also, computers do not constitute the entire MIS, but are supplemented with other modes of communication.

Technological developments in computer design bring new types and models to the market almost daily. With the advent of microcomputers, the desktop personal computers, the price range is now within the budget of most foodservice departments. These machines can perform functions that formerly were almost prohibitively expensive when done by mainframe computer for many foodservices. Due to their wide availability and the competitive computer market, the price of automation has been greatly reduced. Foodservice computer systems have been, and can be, designed to handle a wide variety of programs. Whereas the foodservice manager does not need to be a computer scientist or have programming skills, a degree of computer literacy is necessary to recognize and utilize what a computer can do. Basic information, terminology, and foodservice applications presented here may serve as an aid in the selection of an appropriate computer system and programs to meet specific needs or in talking with computer analysts who may be employed to assist with computerization. However, a study of the market for available computer models and programs at any given time is essential to make sure selections will be current and the best available for the price.

Types of Computers

Computers have commonly been classified into three categories—mainframe, minicomputer, and microcomputer—based primarily on size and memory capacity. The classical descriptions of these are

- *Mainframe:* the very large, full-scale computers that require specially designed rooms to house them and specialists to operate and keep them in repair. These are appropriate for very large organizations and are usually shared by many departments, or time-leased to outsiders, which may result in time lags in obtaining the desired output. Cost is upward of a million dollars, but capabilities are extensive, and computer time is available to many users at once. Terminals at remote locations connected with the computer may be used to enter data or call for programs stored, and to receive printouts.

- *Minicomputer:* somewhat smaller and less costly than the mainframe, but with many of the same characteristics. Developed later than the mainframe, it has features that make it more flexible in programming. This type is often used for research projects with large quantities of data to process, or used by large business organizations. The cost range is wide, $25,000 and upward.

- *Microcomputer:* small, desk-top, single-user type (including personal computers). Price range approximately $2,000 to $5,000 (or more). Great variety of makes and models; capable of providing most information required by a foodservice department. Units may be interconnected or linked to provide a more complex, automated foodservice information system (see Fig. 16.2). The newest of the microcomputers is not desk-top or even lap-top, but palm-top! It weighs 16 oz., measures 6.3″ × 3.3″ × 9″, and runs for 50 hours on two AA batteries. The input disk for this computer is the size of a credit card, and it can interface with a desk-top microcomputer and printer.

Although these computer classifications are still used, they are no longer as useful and definitive to explain the capabilities of the computer. There are now numerous makes and models within each category from which to choose. All computers have been reduced in size during the years since World War II.

Figure 16.2. Typical microcomputer suitable for foodservice establishments. (Copyright 1986. Courtesy, Dytran Computer Systems, Inc., Beaverton, Oregon.)

Memory size has brought about the development of a class of computers, the supercomputer, which has greater memory than has generally been available.

Probably the biggest change has been in the availability of new peripherals (see later under "Computer System Requirements" for definitions) for all classes and/or categories of computers. A microcomputer, for example, may now be hooked up to a whole series of other microcomputers to form a local area network (LAN), to an expanded memory hard disk, or even to mainframe computers. Other new peripherals are being developed continuously for computers of all sizes. There are voice-activated, touch-sensitive devices, optical scan devices, and a variety of new printers.

Although all of these may make information gathering, storage, retrieval, and dissemination easier, one of the outstanding developments combines the technologies of a personal microcomputer with the telephone, and is known as the *telecomputer.* This instrument is capable of transmitting and receiving voice and electronic data and information. Data are transmitted through a digital display telephone equipped with a hands-free speakerphone. Although this is not an information-*producing* system, it does provide for rapid interdepartmental or outside transmission of data or information. Fig. 16.3 shows the components of a sophisticated voice and data display system that can be interconnected throughout the building.

Figure 16.3.   Digital voice/data communication system provides a range of flexible configurations from 20 to 240 stations, internally as a local area network (LAN), or externally to remote areas. Provides simultaneous voice and data display capabilities. GTE Starlog℠ Communication System. (Courtesy, GTE Communications System Corp., Phoenix, Arizona.)

Computer System Requirements

Most students today are conversant with computers and their use, therefore, needing little introduction to them. Some foodservice managers, however, may wish to become more familiar with terms used in discussing and selecting computers. A brief review of this terminology and requirements of a computer system follows:

COMPONENTS   The parts or elements of a computer system that make it functional include the following:

- **Hardware** is the computer equipment itself.
- **Software** is a series of instructions fed into the computer that tells it to perform certain functions (the program); also is output from a printer.
- **Central Processing Unit** (CPU) is the calculation or "brains" of the computer. It directs the flow of data (information) within the computer and controls the processing of it according to instructions given by the program used.
- **Memory** or the temporary storage unit; capacity of the computer is measured in binary digits or *bits*. Eight bits grouped together form a *byte*, which represents one character, letter or number, used in coding data. The greater the number of bytes specified for a computer, the larger it is and the greater the amount of data it can store and process at one time. *Kilobite* (K) equals 1,000 bytes of memory, so a 64K computer can store about 65,000 characters, or 35 typed pages.

    RAM (random-access memory) is data stored on chips and is erasable and changeable. It is entered by "loading" the computer from a tape or diskette, or from a keyboard.

    ROM (read-only memory) is permanently fixed data or programs supplied by the manufacturer and cannot be changed.
- **Input** is the data fed into the computer (software) and the device, or equipment, used to feed the data into the computer (hardware). Devices for mainframes and minicomputers are: terminal key board or keypunched (coded) cards, or data stored on magnetic or paper tapes; and devices for microcomputers are: discs, cassettes, solid-state cartridges, or terminal keyboard. Newer inputs include voice input, touch devices, and optical scanners.
- **Output** is the information given out after the data have been processed (software), and it is the device used for presenting the results (hardware). Mainframe and microcomputers have the same equipment for output:

    Printer—prints out a permanent copy

    Display screen—temporary display

CRT (cathode ray tube)
VDT (video display terminal)
Voice output

- **Peripherals** are the parts of a computer system other than the basics just described; also used to refer to accessory parts of the system not essential to its operation. Some of the more common peripherals are
  Graphics tablet and *plotter* for generating graphs, charts, and designs.
  Color graphics capacity device for obtaining colored designs.
  Joysticks or "game" paddles for manually directing or controlling a "pointer" or beam of light to a particular area on a display screen.
  Modem, a device that connects a computer to telephone lines to transfer messages to other computers; electronic signals from the computer are transformed to audible tones that can be transferred over the telephone lines to another computer at remote or nearby locations; especially valuable for accessing data bases and obtaining information not stored locally.

OTHER COMPUTER-RELATED TERMINOLOGY:

- **Data base**—a file of related data, stored item-by-item, that can be added to, changed, or deleted, and can be used by any user who has access to the file. Some data base files are prepared and stored by the user; others are available for purchase.

- **Computer program**—a set of instructions to be used directly or indirectly in a computer and designed to bring about a certain result. Must be expressed in a form "understood" by the computer.

- Types of **processing** include:
  Batch processing—data held and verified for accuracy by the computer before being used to change or update permanent files.
  Real-time processing—immediate processing of data to update files as soon as data are entered in a terminal.

- Types of **printers** for output onto paper, producing **hard copy** include:
  Dot-matrix printers that produce characters by means of dots that form patterns.
  Letter-quality printers that produce characters by means of a single impact similar to a typewriter.
  Laser printers that produce typewriter-quality printout.

- **Diskette** or **floppy disk**—a flexible magnetic-coated device resembling a phonograph record that is used to store information; the most commonly used means of permanent storage for microcomputers. Available in 8-inch, 5-¼ inch, and, most recently, 3-¼ inch sizes.

- **Micro chip** or **microprocessor**—a tiny silicon flake containing microscopic electronic switches connected by wires of metal film; designed as the "heart" of microcomputers, combines memory with logic. The ¼-inch square chip can hold a million electronic components and is virtually weightless.

- **Spreadsheet**—an electronic version of a multicolumnar bookkeeping sheet used for processing large volumes of numeric data to be analyzed according to predefined relationships; used, among other things, as an aid in decision making by showing likely results of "what if" certain changes were to be made.

Converting to a Computer and/or Computer System

Many questions need to be answered by any foodservice manager who wishes to "computerize" his or her department's activities. Much time, thought, and study are required before the decision is made to install a computer system. Expectations of benefits to be derived often exceed the commitment a manager is willing to make to prepare for computerization. However, for the manager who understands specifically which is desired, what may be expected, and what must be done to achieve desired results, success is usually assured. Many organizations find it money well spent to employ a reputable computer analyst to carry out the search for hardware and software and to set up a suitable system to meet their specific needs.

A foodservice manager who has a well-organized and functioning system of records and financial reporting will be able to understand computer processing and convert to it much easier than one who does not have such data readily available. A computer analyst must have such detailed information in order to design a computer system.

The first question to be addressed is what type of computer will be used? For those foodservices that are a part of a large organization with its own mainframe computer, time may be allocated for foodservice use. Then programs can be developed for use with that computer, usually with the help of a computer programmer. For other foodservices, the purchase and use of a microcomputer and perhaps programs that have been developed by others present a different situation. Since mainframe computers preceded the advent of microcomputers, much has been written and published about programming foodservice activities for mainframe processing.

Microcomputers are crowding the workplace today, so instead of using the huge, sometimes intimidating mainframe computer with its programmers and processors, foodservice managers can now control and disseminate information for themselves on their own "friendly" personal computers. Or work can be done on the microcomputer and transferred to a mainframe for storage. Selecting appropriate hardware and software is the challenge.

Fig. 16.4 outlines the suggested eight steps to be taken when considering a small computer system. The first and most critical step is to analyze the operation's needs. Questions should be asked such as: Do we really need a

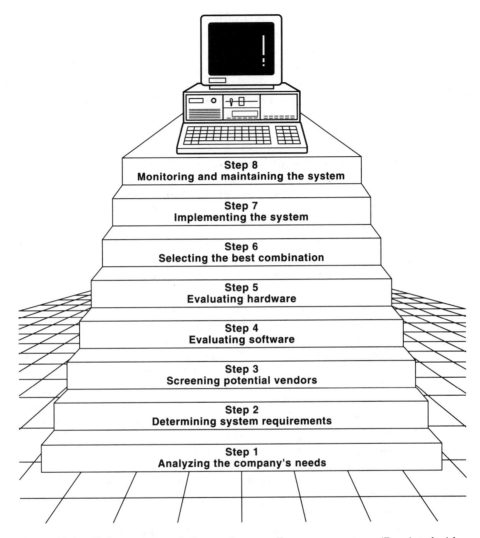

Figure 16.4. Eight recommended steps for a small computer system. (Reprinted with permission from the *Journal of Accountancy,* Copyright © 1985 by American Institute of Certified Public Accountants, Inc.)

computer system? Can we afford a computer now? What current information systems do we use, and what are the weaknesses of these systems? What are the benefits of computerization? What specific applications are we interested in computerizing? Answers to this last question might be to maintain a perpetual inventory or to calculate the payroll. More general goals might be to improve the cost-effectiveness of the department or to be able to redirect staff time now used for routine bookkeeping tasks.

The second step is to determine the organization's specific computer requirements: for example, what will the system need to do and in what areas? Research for this step can be divided into three main areas: (1) *administrative systems,* which include accounting, bookkeeping, financial analyses, budgeting, reporting, word processing, and other office automation; (2) *foodservice management systems,* which include recipe and menu cost analyses, ordering, food production, distribution, and inventory control; and (3) "*front of the house*" *systems,* which are point-of-sale based for controlling cash and capturing sales statistics.

Screening potential vendors is next. Vendors can provide invaluable assistance in selecting the appropriate computer system, training and implementing the system, and providing ongoing maintenance and software support.

The software programs that operate the computer must be chosen carefully in order to receive the desired output and to provide the operating functions desired. Note that software should be chosen before hardware; that is, software should serve as the basis for hardware decisions, not vice versa. This may be a good time to form a team of those who will use the programs and the data generated. Allowing input for buying decisions helps to create a commitment from those who will have to make the system function.

Begin a search to investigate the availability of software programs that are designed to meet the identified needs of your organization. It is estimated that there are some 150 to 200 companies producing programs designed for foodservice and dietary use. One good way to locate this information is to attend trade shows and/or professional meetings where hardware and software vendors exhibit their products. Another is to subscribe to computer-related periodicals (i.e., *Journal of Dietetic Software,* which usually carries some foodservice programs). Write to the companies featured, requesting information. Also, many courses in basic computer use are offered at community colleges, by computer companies, and others. Enrollment in such a course will prove most worthwhile for the uninitiated. Another important source is one's colleagues who are using computers at their workplace and can give good assistance.

Fetter discusses guidelines for evaluation of computer software and has developed an evaluation form (Fig. 16.5) that is helpful for recording the details of each program reviewed in the search process. Although designed specifically for education programs, it is readily adaptable to other types. Two other comprehensive sets of forms were developed by Byrd-Bredbenner and Pelican for nutrient analysis programs and educational programs. These may be of interest to some readers. Of special concern in the evaluation of programs are its

1. appropriateness

2. cost

3. flexibility

Evaluation of Computer Programs*

I. Product Title:_____   Computer
   Author/Publisher:_____   Developed for:_____
   Publishing/Copyright Date:_____   Unit Cost:_____

II. Type of Program Format (check appropriate description):
   Diskette:___   Text:____
   Cassette:___   Other:___
   Module:____

III. Target Population (check appropriate description):
   A. Students   ____   Grade Level:___   Ability Level: ___
   B. Teachers   ____
   C. Administrators___
   D. Other _____   (Describe: _____)

IV. Resources Needed:
   A. Cassette Recorder___
   B. Disk Drive_____
   C. Printer_____
   D. Other_____   (Describe: _____)

V. Type of Program: (check all that apply)
   A. Administrative Aid____   F. Simulation _____
   B. Drill and Practice_____   G. Testing_____
   C. Educational Game_____   H. Tutorial _____
   D. Entertainment_____   I. Word Processing___
   E. Problem-Solving_____   J. Other_____(Describe: _____
                                            _____)

VI. Appropriateness:
   A. Are the stated objectives of the course being met by this product?   Yes_____ No___
   B. Can materials be used with other than the stated population?   Yes_____ No___
   C. Can materials be used to accomplish other than the stated goals?   Yes_____ No___
   D. Is the product adaptable to various teachers or situations?   Yes_____ No___
   E. Are alternative learning opportunities suggested/provided for?   Yes_____ No___
   F. Is there a definite need for this particular product in teaching the course? Yes_____ No___

VII. Content:
   A. Is the content of this instructional material sufficient in quantity to adequately cover the
      topic as provided in the syllabus?   Yes_____ No___
   B. Is the content of this instructional material sufficient in quality to adequately cover the
      topic as provided in the syllabus?   Yes_____ No___
   C. Does the instructional material provide adequate quantity and quality of additional
      content to provide for remedial instruction?   Yes_____ No___
   D. Does the instructional material provide adequate quantity and quality of additional
      content to provide for enrichment exercises for individuals?   Yes_____ No___

*Readers of *Educational Technology* Magazine are hereby given permission to reproduce this Evaluation Form at will.

(Continued on Next Page)

Figure 16.5.   Form for evaluating computer software programs. (Courtesy, W. R. Fetter and
Educational Technology, March 1984.)

VIII. Organizational and Technical Components: (rate each of the following items)

	Exc.	Good	Fair	Poor
A. Instructions are clear, concise, and understandable	____	____	____	____
B. Content is accurate	____	____	____	____
C. Presentation of material is consistent with accepted practices	____	____	____	____
D. Reading level is appropriate for intended users	____	____	____	____
E. Program motivates learner	____	____	____	____
F. Program employs positive feedback and reinforcement	____	____	____	____
G. Program handles learner input errors effectively	____	____	____	____
H. Program helps student develop correct response	____	____	____	____
I. Program employs the following techniques: (rate each that applies; leave other items blank)	____	____	____	____
1. Graphics	____	____	____	____
2. Color	____	____	____	____
3. Sound/Music	____	____	____	____
4. Voice	____	____	____	____
5. Time Display	____	____	____	____
6. Score Display	____	____	____	____
7. Personalized Responses	____	____	____	____
8. Other (Describe)	____	____	____	____

IX. Technical or Teacher's Manual:

A. Is a manual included with the product?   Yes ____ No ____

B. Does the manual indicate the necessary qualifications of teachers for using the product effectively?   Yes ____ No ____

C. Does the manual describe the necessary support system needed for effective use of the product?   Yes ____ No ____

D. Does the manual list field data on the product's effectiveness as an instructional aid?   Yes ____ No ____

E. Does the manual list field data on typical users of the product?   Yes ____ No ____

F. Does the manual suggest a typical setting or time frame for product usage?   Yes ____ No ____

X. Evaluation: (of learners)

A. Are instruments for the evaluation of learners included with the product?   Yes ____ No ____

B. If YES, do the instruments meet the course objectives and the stated objectives of the materials?   Yes ____ No ____

C. If NO, can evaluation instruments be easily developed which will accomplish the evaluation of the learner meeting the course objectives through use of the product?   Yes ____ No ____

XI. Product Revision: Is there evidence that the product has been regularly revised and updated? Yes ____ No ____

XII. Narrative Comments: Use this space to make any comments concerning any question on the evaluation form. Please refer to *both* the section number *and* question letter when making comments.

Figure 16.5. (*Continued*)

4. availability/delivery schedule

5. revision policy and service support

Berst (1983) advises to "evaluate software in three distinct stages: first the documentation, then the support, and finally the program itself." *Documentation* is the user's manual. Without complete directions it is difficult to get full value from the program. Manuals should be well-organized, easily understood, and provide a sample printout, and a picture of the video display as it would look. Many programs can be eliminated from consideration if those features do not appear in the manual. Berst says that most good documentations contain six elements: *overview* or description of the program; *tutorial* section giving step-by-step instructions; a *command* summary, or brief review, of the instructions for follow-up reference; *technical section* that outlines the program logic for benefit of a programmer's use in case the program needs to be changed; *trouble-shooting* section that tells how to "get back on track" after making mistakes; and an *index* that is comprehensive and complete.

The *support* aspect of software evaluation refers to the service and assistance that the company selling the program will give. Look for one that will correct bugs. A *hotline* to the company provides a means of talking to an expert; a *warranty* replaces defective disks and refunds money paid if the program does not run on your machine, even though it was stated as being compatible. Other types of support may be offered in addition, such as a trade-in allowance on old software when a new one comes out, and a company-trained local dealer who may give assistance if needed.

Finally, evaluate the *program* itself in terms of matching or providing information and/or the needs outlined by the foodservice manager. Good programs are easy to use; they "talk" to the user in English, not in code numbers; they are set up to warn the user to follow certain steps so obvious mistakes are avoided; and they are standardized, that is, consistent throughout in commands, keys for same use, and location of data on the screen.

Some companies do not allow a program to be previewed before purchase for fear of "pirating." In this situation, the foodservice manager may wish to locate and talk with persons who are using the program to help determine its appropriateness. It is too costly to buy a program only to find it does not provide the information needed.

Critical evaluation of software programs, both of the general program characteristics and the subject matter content, is extremely important. Remember that no program is perfect. The manager should decide how much he or she is willing to compromise, or how a program can be adapted for a particular operation.

Develop your own program if suitable prepreparred programs are not available on the market. Some foodservice managers have the knowledge and ability to do their own computer programming. Others will work with a systems analyst to design the program desired. If this is the case, a clear presentation of the foodservice operations and transactions involved is essential for providing needed background information. Copies of written records and reports used and a step-by-step description of the procedures for obtaining data on the records, and how they are used are also important. Having a well-organized system of records as outlined in Chapter 14 is the basis for developing a good computerized program.

Step 5 in the process is the selection of the hardware. Hardware includes the central processing unit (CPU), input devices, output devices, and the peripherals. Select a microcomputer or system that is compatible with the program you designed or purchased. By having the software available first, the manager knows what makes of computers can be used, and so narrows the choices, which makes selection easier. If the organization is large and has other computers with which this new one may interface, be certain it is compatible with the others.

Features to evaluate and conditions to consider in making the selection and before purchasing a microcomputer include the following:

- Explore all local outlets to find dealers who carry the make and model you need. A local dealer is available to help set up or install the equipment and give follow-up support, which is not possible through a mail-order company.

- Compare makes and models available in relation to their capability and cost. As costs increase, capabilities or memory should increase and provide faster processing. Remember that the basic cost of the computer may be only the beginning of costs involved in making the system functional. A significant investment must be made in the computing process after the initial purchase. There is much overhead involved in installing and operating the system. The purchase price of a personal computer is just the beginning of the user's expenses—not the end. Therefore, in comparing prices, include the prices of all of the extras: paper, cables and wiring for installation, peripherals desired, printer ribbons, and, of course, service charges. Some companies may help set up a small computer at no extra charge, but complex systems with interacting units may cost thousands of dollars to install and make operable.

- Investigate the reputation of the companies that can provide equipment you need. How long have they been in business?

- How extensive are their sales? Do they give good support to users of their equipment? Have other users been satisfied with the service received? Is the company dependable?

- Ask about a warranty. What does it cover and for how long?

- Is a trade-in possible if a change in computer or system is desired?

- After making a selection, ask the vendor for a written statement of purchase/sales conditions agreed upon.

The next step involves putting together the best combination of vendor, software, and hardware. The relative merits of each must be weighed against system requirements, support needed and available, system's capacity and flexibility, costs, and financing arrangements. Although the initial cost of the system is apparent, the annual cost of maintaining the computer system should not be overlooked. This includes the annual cost for vendor support services, software and hardware program enhancements, labor cost for maintaining the system, ongoing training costs, printer cartridges, and other supply expenditures.

Installing and implementing the system purchased follows. Prepare the site for the computer and schedule installation. Preparation for placing a personal computer or single-unit microcomputer may require providing only a table or desk and space for storing discs, paper, and such. Or considerations may include designating an entire room for the system with its peripherals and accessories. Some installation of electrical wiring and placement of cables may be necessary before hardware and software can be put into place.

Employees who will spend much of their working day in front of a microcomputer deserve a comfortable setup, one that will prevent stiff necks, back pain, eye strain, and related problems. Guidelines have been developed related to ergonomics, that is, the design of computer space for efficiency and comfort. Fig. 16.6 illustrates the positioning of equipment to meet those guidelines for correct relationships between user and components of a personal computer.

In implementing the system, a plan should be written that includes the tasks to be performed in the proper sequence, the time frame for completing each, the person responsible for each task, and the end products desired from implementation. One specific person in the department should be given the time and responsibility for overseeing the installation of the equipment and implementing the program. This may be the foodservice manager or some other person who is knowledgeable and who can be given time to stay with the project until it is fully operable. This person should be charged with training all who will use the computer system. *Training* is the key to success in converting to a computer system. Permit ample time for this training, for even knowledgeable people need time to really learn the system.

It is not necessary to implement all of the programs at once. In fact, putting the system into operation one step at a time and maintaining audit checks against existing records to prove the accuracy of the computer program is more satisfying for building user confidence. Problems do occur in initiating new computer systems. It takes time and patience to iron them out. Close scrutiny of the implementation process and good training of the workers should help minimize any difficulties encountered.

The eighth and final step is the ongoing monitoring and maintenance of the new system. Included in this step should be the establishment of a procedure for addressing system problems; a backup schedule; plans to regularly update documentation, compare actual system performance to planned performance, and conduct an annual information system review; and the development of a preventive maintenance program.

Figure 16.6. Basic guidelines for correct relationship between user and computer components, designed to ease physiological strain of person using computer—ergonomics.

Foodservice Computer Application

The computer's primary function during the years has been to process operating data into usable information. Early computer programs in foodservice organizations, utilized for many years, have been expanded and interfaced until there are many new applications for them today.

Foodservice computer information systems may be classified into six basic program categories:

1. menu planning and analysis

2. inventory and purchasing control

3 production control (including ingredients and recipes, forecasting, and scheduling)

4. food-cost accounting

5. sales control

6. labor productivity and payroll

In addition, computer capabilities are used for decision-making support through simulation and various data manipulation programs, and for graphics designing of floor plans, equipment layouts, and similar projects. Although robots are often thought of as "equipment," they are computer controlled and programmable, and so, are included here. Some specific applications of computer uses in certain types of foodservices are mentioned.

The components of each of the six basic program categories with inputs, outputs, and capabilities are outlined below, adapted from unpublished work by Adams. The foodservice manager must be prepared to provide all of the input data listed in order for a computer program to be developed or a suitable one purchased for implementation. A good, manually operated system of records and reports is the basis for obtaining the required data. Additional references at the end of this chapter will lead readers to more information and detail.

Menu Planning and Analysis

INPUT

1. Recipe file—listing of all recipes (menu items) in use, stored in computer memory or data file (see Table 16.1)

2. Food inventory item file with costs—a listing of the food inventory, item by item with current price of each

3. Nutrient data base

4. Constraints—frequency of menu item use; cost limitations; color, texture, flavor, and shape of foods

OUTPUT

1. Menu planned and printed by computer for specified time period that meets objectives prescribed (see Fig. 16.7)

OTHER CAPABILITIES

1. Computer selects menu items that are within the desired constraints; substitutions are possible

2. Recipes/menus are costed to provide base for establishing a selling price

TABLE 16.1.   Portion of a Recipe File with Costs per Serving, Used by Computer for Menu Planning.

		* * * * Starch Items * * * *		
Code Number	Recipe Name	Portion Size		Cost/Serving
400041	Mashed potatoes	3	oz	$0.029
400050	Duchess potatoes	3.5	oz	$0.124
400100	Potato/carrots in broth	7	oz	$0.282
400131	Baked potato wedges	3	oz	$0.086
400173	Tator tots or fr fries	3	oz	$0.086
400175	Buttered whole potatoes	3	oz	$0.107
400181	Parsleyed potatoes	3	oz	$0.108
400185	Hash browns-oven fried	3	oz	$0.116
400190	Pan fried potatoes	3	oz	$0.093
400220	Creamed potatoes	4.5	oz	$0.119
400225	Creamed peas & potatoes	6	oz	$0.160
400262	Hot German potato salad	3.5	oz	$0.217
400301	Scalloped potatoes	3.5	oz	$0.072
400305	Buttered rice	3	oz	$0.039
400424	Macaroni salad	3	oz	$0.203
400467	Potato salad	3	oz	$0.101
400581	Buttered noodles	3	oz	$0.061
410306	Bread dressing	3	oz	$0.086
410705	Glazed sweet potato	4	oz	$0.166
410710	Sweet potatoes & apples	4	oz	$0.165
420107	Baked beans	3	oz	$0.063
421804	Black-eyed peas	3	oz	$0.027

SOURCE: Courtesy, Cook-Ware™, Dytran Computer Systems, Inc. Copyright 1986.

3. Computer can interact with POS (Point of Sales) registers for menu tally data and analysis for eliminating unpopular items (see Figs. 16.8 and 16.9)

4. Computer can plan patient special diets (health care facilities)

5. Total nutritional values calculated for a meal and/or for the day

6. Menu index—to reference menus however desired: by date, meal, cycle, (see Fig. 16.10) month or week, or by index number

INVENTORY AND PURCHASING CONTROL

INPUT

1. Master item file—a list of all items carried in stock (food and supplies) in computer memory

2. Maximum and minimum stock levels established for each item in master item file

Figure 16.7. A computer-generated menu for St. Clares-Riverside Medical Center, Denville, New Jersey. (Courtesy, Computrition, Inc.)

Figure 16.8.   A POS terminal, the basic input device that would be used by a server, cashier, or bartender in a typical full service or quick service restaurant. (Courtesy, TEC America, Garden Grove, CA)

3. Inventory transactions
    a. Orders—total amount for each item by vendor
    b. Goods received—by item, vendor, and cost
    c. Storeroom issues

OUTPUT

1. Master food and supplies item file—printout of all items in each file; example in Table 16.2
2. Daily report of purchases
    a. Printout of all items ordered
    b. Printout of goods received—item, amount, cost
3. Daily storeroom issues report—printout of items and amounts issued (from inventory) with cost for each item
4. Perpetual inventory update—items received, added to inventory; items issued subtracted and printout new master item file
5. Purchase order or recommended buy list—computer identifies items below minimum-quantity standard and generates a purchase order printout to bring stock up to maximum (Table 16.3)

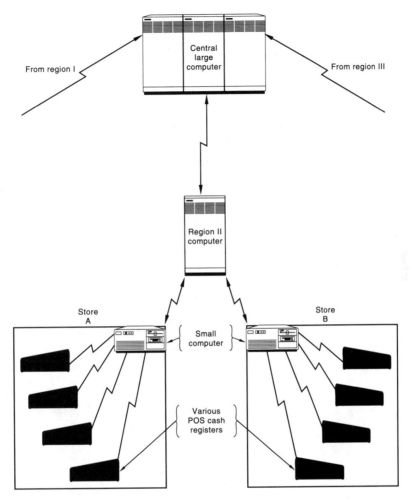

Figure 16.9. An integrated POS system. (From Scott, G. M.: *Principles of Management Information Systems.* Copyright © 1986 by McGraw-Hill, Inc. Reproduced with permission of McGraw-Hill, Inc.)

OTHER CAPABILITIES

1. Purchase summaries—by item with total cost by week, month, or year, or by vendor with total purchases from each (to be used for forecasting futures purchasing)

2. Issue summaries—total cost of issues, by category, to various service units (for charging costs to specific units; to track spending trends; to use to compare with income generated from each unit)

3. Physical inventory form—printout of items in inventory to use for recording actual count of goods on hand; example in Fig. 16.11

MENU CYCLE WEEK : 1
DAY OF WEEK :Sunday
MEAL :Breakfast

MASTER CYCLE MENU PLANNER

Cook-Ware™

DATE: _____

COST PER MEAL: $ .40

```
* * * * * REGULAR DIET * * * *
* HAM & CHEESE SCRAMBLE (3.25 OZ)
* MALT O MEAL^COLD CEREAL (1/2C)
*
* CRANBERRY JUICE (4 OZ)
*
*
* COFFEE, HOT TEA, 2% MILK
* BUTTERED TOAST (1 SL) JELLY PKG
* * * * * * * * * * * *
```

1-Entree   →
2-Starch   →
3-Vegetable →
4-Salad   →
5-Dessert   →
6-Soup/Other →
7-Beverage →
8-Bread   →

```
* * * * 2 GM SODIUM DIET * * *
* S.F. SCRAMBLED EGG (3 OZ)
* MALT O MEAL^COLD CEREAL (1/2C)
*
* CRANBERRY JUICE (4 OZ)
*
*
* COFFEE, HOT TEA, 2% MILK
* BUTTERED TOAST (1 SL) JELLY PKG
* * * * * * * * * * *
```

1-Entree   →
2-Starch   →
3-Vegetable →
4-Salad   →
5-Dessert   →
6-Soup/Other →
7-Beverage →
8-Bread   →

```
* * * PUREED DIET * * *
* PUREED HAM & CHEESE SCRAMBLE
* MALT O MEAL^COLD CEREAL (1/2C)
*
* CRANBERRY JUICE (4 OZ)
*
*
* COFFEE, HOT TEA, 2% MILK
* BUTTERED TOAST (1 SL) JELLY PKG
* * * * * * * *
```

1-Entree   →
2-Starch   →
3-Vegetable →
4-Salad   →
5-Dessert   →
6-Soup/Other →
7-Beverage →
8-Bread   →

```
* * * CALORIE CONTROLLED DIET * *
* SCRAMBLED EGG (2 OZ=1) HAM
*   (1OZ=1)
* MALT O MEAL (1/2C^4 OZ=1 EX)
*
* LC CRANBERRY JC (1/2C^4 OZ=1EX)
* TOAST (1 SL=1EX) LC JELLY PKG
* MARG PAT (1=1 EX)
* 2% MILK (1C^8 OZ=1 EX)
* COFFEE, HOT TEA
* * * * * * * * * *
```

```
* * * LIBERAL BLAND DIET * *
* HAM & CHEESE SCRAMBLE (3.25 OZ)
* MALT O MEAL^COLD CEREAL (1/2C)
*
* CRANBERRY JUICE (4 OZ)
*
*
* COFFEE, HOT TEA, 2% MILK
* BUTTERED TOAST (1SL) JELLY PKG
* * * * * * * *
```

```
* * 30-40 GM FAT DIET * *
* F.F. SCRAMBLED EGG (2 OZ)
* MALT O MEAL^COLD CEREAL (1/2C)
*
* CRANBERRY JUICE (4 OZ)
*
*
* COFFEE, HOT TEA, SKIM MILK
* UNBUTTERED TOAST (1SL) JELLY PK
* * * * * * *
```

```
* * * 2.4-4.5 GM SODIUM DIET *
* SCRAMBLED EGG (3 OZ)
* MALT O MEAL^COLD CEREAL (1/2C)
*
* CRANBERRY JUICE (4 OZ)
*
* MARG PAT (1)
* COFFEE, HOT TEA, 2% MILK
* BUTTERED TOAST (1 SL) JELLY PKG
* * * * * * * * * * *
```

```
* * * MECHANICAL SOFT DIET * * * *
* HAM & CHEESE SCRAMBLE (3.25 OZ)
* MALT O MEAL^COLD CEREAL (1/2C)
*
* CRANBERRY JUICE (4 OZ)
*
*
* COFFEE, HOT TEA, 2% MILK
* BUTTERED TOAST (1SL) JELLY PKG
* * * * * * * * * * *
```

Figure 16.10. Example of a menu, filed by cycle index in computer. (Courtesy, Cook-Ware®, Dytran Computer Systems, Inc. Copyright 1986.)

Inventory Control System
Cook-Ware®
Food Item File

Stock Number	Description	Qty-On Hand	Cost/Buy Unit	Buy-Unt Unit	Issue Unit	C.F.	Use-Wgt Grams	Min/Max Levels	On Order	Date	Vendor	Loc
01104	Corn beef, cooked 4/5#	11	$ 1.76	lbs	lbs	1	453	20/40	190	01/01/1980	Lady1	1
01147	Beef, stew cut 10#	30	$ 1.75	lbs	lbs	1	453	40/60	0	06/15/1982	Koncen	2
01180	Beef patty, ground 5/1#	1	$ 1.80	lbs	lbs	1	454	40/120	0	06/15/1982	Koncen	2
01201	Hamburger, bulk 5#	10	$ 1.35	lbs	lbs	1	453	40/200	0	06/15/1982	Burton	2
01228	Beef bones	10	$ 0.20	lbs	lbs	1	456	15/40	0	06/15/1982	Koncen	3
01252	Dried beef	0	$ 0.00	lbs	lbs	1	453	0/0	0	/ /		
01279	Cube steak 3 oz	0	$ 0.00	lbs	ind	6	85	0/0	0	/ /		
01325	Beef roast (inside)	0	$ 1.79	lbs	lbs	1	453	45/135	0	06/15/1982	Test vendr	3
01341	Corned beef	0	$ 0.00	lbs	lbs	1	453	0/0	0	/ /		
01342	Beef short ribs	0	$ 0.00	lbs	lbs	1	453	0/0	0	/ /		
01343	Beef brisket	0	$ 0.00	lbs	lbs	1	453	0/0	0	/ /		
02071	Fish square 3 oz	0	$ 0.00	box	ind	6	453	0/0	0	/ /		
02089	Cod fish 3 oz 6#	0	$10.54	box	lbs	6	453	35/70	0	06/15/1982	Koncen	4
02313	Fish cakes 2 oz	0	$ 0.83	lbs	ind	8	57	180/720	0	06/15/1982	Koncen	3
04073	Pork chop 4 oz	0	$ 0.00	lbs	lbs	1	453	0/0	0	/ /		
04146	Pork steaks 5 oz	0	$ 1.49	lbs	lbs	1	453	55/145	0	06/15/1982	Koncen	4
04341	Ham patty 20#box	161	$37.40	box	ind	160	86	180/360	0	02/16/1984	Pisc	1
04405	Ham roll, fresh 3/10#	0	$ 1.62	lbs	lbs	1	453	45/135	0	06/15/1982	Graves	1
04499	Chopped ham, canned	1	$ 1.45	lbs	lbs	1	453	24/100	0	06/15/1982	Pisc	1
04529	Ham roast, fresh	0	$ 1.35	lbs	lbs	1	453	50/150	0	06/15/1982	Koncen	1
04588	Sausage bulk 6#	0	$ 1.65	lbs	lbs	1	453	12/18	0	06/15/1982	Grav	1
04642	Sausage pty 1.5 oz 8/6#	0	$63.84	case	ind	512	43	360/100	0	06/15/1982	Graves	1
04677	Sausage link 1 oz 6#	0	$10.31	box	ind	96	28	150/100	0	06/15/1982	Grav	1
04707	Polish sausage 10#	0	$ 1.53	lbs	lbs	1	453	20/30	0	06/15/1982	Graves	1

TABLE 16.2. Sample Section of a Master Food Item File.

SOURCE: Courtesy, Cook-ware®, Dytran Computer Systems, Inc. Copyright 1986.

TABLE 16.3   Computer-Generated Listing of Food Items Below the Minimum Standard Stock Level.

Inventory Control System
Cook-Ware®
Listing of Items below Min.

Stock Number	Description	Qty-On Hand	Cost/Buy Unit	Buy-Unt Unit	Issue Unit	C.F.	Use-Wgt Grams	Min/Max Levels	On Order	Date	Vendor	Loc
01104	Corn beef, cooked 4/5#	11	$ 1.76	lbs	lbs	1	453	20/40	190	01/01/1980	Lady1	1
01147	Beef, stew cut 10#	30	$ 1.75	lbs	lbs	1	453	40/60	0	06/15/1982	Koncen	2
01180	Beef patty, ground 5/1#	1	$ 1.80	lbs	lbs	1	454	40/120	0	06/15/1982	Koncen	2
01201	Hamburger, bulk 5#	10	$ 1.35	lbs	lbs	1	453	40/200	0	06/15/1982	Burton	2
01228	Beef bones	10	$ 0.20	lbs	lbs	1	456	15/40	0	06/15/1982	Koncen	3
01325	Beef roast (inside)	0	$ 1.79	lbs	lbs	1	453	45/135	0	06/15/1982	Test vendr	3
02089	Cod fish 3 oz	0	$10.54	box	lbs	6	453	35/70	0	06/15/1982	Koncen	4
02313	Fish cakes 2 oz	0	$ 0.83	lbs	ind	8	57	180/720	0	06/15/1982	Koncen	3
04146	Pork steaks 5 oz	0	$ 1.49	lbs	lbs	1	453	55/145	0	06/15/1982	Koncen	4
04341	Ham patty 20#box	161	$37.40	box	ind	160	86	180/360	0	02/16/1984	Pisc	1
04405	Ham roll, fresh 3/10#	0	$ 1.62	lbs	lbs	1	453	45/135	0	06/15/1982	Graves	1
04499	Chopped ham, canned	1	$ 1.45	lbs	lbs	1	453	24/100	0	06/15/1982	Pisc	1
04529	Ham roast, fresh	0	$ 1.35	lbs	lbs	1	453	50/150	0	06/15/1982	Koncen	1
04588	Sausage bulk 6#	0	$ 1.65	lbs	lbs	1	453	12/18	0	06/15/1982	Grav	1
04642	Sausage pty 1.5 oz 8/6#	0	$63.84	case	ind	512	43	360/100	0	06/15/1982	Graves	1
04677	Sausage link 1 oz 6#	0	$10.31	box	ind	96	28	150/100	0	06/15/1982	Grav	1
04707	Polish sausage 10#	0	$ 1.53	lbs	lbs	1	453	20/30	0	06/15/1982	Graves	1
05185	Chicken, fine cooked	1	$ 1.60	lbs	lbs	1	453	40/120	0	06/15/1982	Koncen	1
05312	Chicken, diced 6/5#	1	$ 2.40	lbs	lbs	1	453	30/120	0	06/15/1982	Koncen	1
05576	Chicken fryer 8 cut/lb	1	$ 0.89	lbs	lbs	1	453	65/260	0	06/15/1982	Grav	1
05771	Turkey 60/40 2/10#	1	$ 1.10	lbs	lbs	1	453	25/100	0	06/15/1982	Graves	1
05894	Turkey breast, cooked	10	$14.60	lbs	lbs	20	453	25/75	0	06/15/1982	Lady	1
06203	Hot dogs 2 oz	20	$ 1.26	lbs	ind	8	57	180/360	0	06/15/1982	Pisc	1
06408	Beef liver 10#box	1	$11.70	box	ind	50	75	180/200	0	06/15/1982	Lady	1

SOURCE: Courtesy, Cook-Ware®, Dytran Computer Systems, Inc. Copyright 1986.

Physical Inventory Form

Location Code: _____   _____ , 19 ____
                                                                    month

Classification Code	Code No.	Item	Issue Unit	Quantity on Hand	Unit Price	Total Cost
Beverages						
0000	0001	Coffee	lbs			
	0002	Hot chocolate powder	2 oz packet			
	0003	Iced tea bags	each 1 gal			
	0004	Tea bags	100/box			
Cereals, prepared						
0100	0101	All-Bran	1# box			
	0102	Ass'td indiv.	50/cs			
	0103	Barley	1# pkg			
(etc.)						

Figure 16.11. Sample page of a computer-generated form for use in taking physical inventory. Food items in stock are preprinted on form.

4. Perpetual-physical inventories comparative report—printout of differences found between computer-stored perpetual inventory and physical inventory, item by item; used by management to reconcile reports

5. Recipe-ingredient cross reference—printout of all ingredients on inventory (food item file) and an accompanying list of all recipes that contain each food item (major ones); aid in identifying recipes in which a particular ingredient is no longer available or has changed form; may call for recipe adjustment or restandardization

6. Inventory location file (for foodservices with multistorage units: warehouse, daily stores, refrigerator, freezer)—can be used to identify location of all items and by order in which they were received; aid in inventory taking and proper costing of items

PRODUCTION CONTROL (RECIPES, INGREDIENTS, FORECASTING, SCHEDULING)

INPUT

1. Master food item (ingredient) file (with prices and yields)—stored in computer memory

2. Standardized recipe file, by name, classification (breads, desserts, meats, etc.), listing ingredients; procedures including preparation time, weight and/or volume of ingredients; and number and size of servings—stored in computer memory

3. Daily production forecast—number of servings to be prepared of each menu item (recipe)

4. Conversion file—to automatically convert food items from units in which purchased into units as used in recipes (e.g., baking powder purchased in 10-pound cans but used in ounces or tablespoons in recipe)

OUTPUT

1. Production schedule—printout of adjusted recipes to be used in the amount (number of servings) required; one recipe per page if desired (Fig. 16.10)

2. Storeroom issue request—printout of items to be issued from storeroom as required to produce recipes on the day needed

3. Advance freezer withdrawals—printout of any frozen foods called for in recipes to be used in days ahead. Alerts storeroom workers to remove frozen foods from freezer to refrigerator to defrost in time for use

4. Advance preparation lists—printout of recipes that require advance preparation, to alert cooks to schedule these items (as gelatin) far enough in advance to have them ready when needed

5. Recipe cost update—as new purchases are made, current costs in food item inventory file used to cost recipes whenever desired (Fig. 16.12)

OTHER CAPABILITIES

1. Daily production—time schedules for kitchen employees based on input detail of preparation procedures, time of service, equipment availability, and employees' time schedules

2. Interfaces with POS registers to report flow of sales of various menu items and triggers need for additional foods to be prepared (with batch cookery)

3. Production forecasts—based on historical census data for specific days of the week, seasons, holidays, or other

Food Cost Accounting (Records and Reports)

INPUT

1. Daily transactions of sales, census, storeroom issues, and purchases received, total income, and expenditures

2. Desired markup percentage

OUTPUT (SPREADSHEET SOFTWARE BEST USED FOR THESE REPORTS)

1. Daily food-cost report and analysis (spreadsheet program utilized)

2. Cumulative food-cost report with percentage of income spent for food

SNELL HALL 09/30/86	OREGON STATE UNIVERSITY	

Recipe Costing

170100
CLAM CHOWDER
DINNER/SUPPER   SOUP   NUMBER OF SERVINGS 100

ATTRIBUTES—   WHITE   MILD   LIQUID   hot
                        4 DAYS SEPARATION

ESTIMATED—   WEIGHT OF A SERVING   7.69 OZ
                        VOLUME   6.00 FL OZ
                        RECIPE YIELD   75.00 LB

Food Code No.	Ingredients	Quantity	Unit	Weight Cooked	Cost/ Ingredient
2500	Milk, whole	3.00	gallon	12.00	2.125
2400	Margarine	3.75	pound	3.75	1.560
5290	Flour	1.75	pound	1.75	.319
4354	Potatoes frozen	3.00	pound	3.00	.630
4426	Onions chopped	2.50	pound	2.50	.533
1200	Clams canned	28.75	pound	28.75	32.123
0	Water	3.00	gallon	10.80	0
5482	Salt	1.00	ounce	.06	.002
5470	Pepper	7.50	gram	.02	.016

Calculated recipe yield   62–63 lb   Total food cost $37.31
Calculated weight of a serving 10.02 oz   Food cost per serving $ .373
               (raw)

Figure 16.12.   Example of computer-costed recipe; one taken from complete recipe file.

3. Sales per hour (or other time period) and by salesperson

4. Monthly profit and loss statement

5. Summaries of transactions for various time periods

OTHER CAPABILITIES

1. Transaction entries programmed to automatically update general ledger accounts (accounts receivable and payable)

2. Comparative reports of food-cost data with other time periods

3. Precosting (cost of recipes used for menu of day plus other meal costs)—paper goods, condiments and accompaniments/garnishes—compared with postcosting (waste in preparation and cooking considered); postcost based on beginning inventory plus purchases, minus ending inventory, and should equal real cost

SALES AND CASH CONTROL

INPUT

1. Guest check information: table number, number of guests at table, check number, and server's code number, entered on a POS register or ECR (electronic cash register)
2. Guests' food orders
3. Individual charges for menu item
4. Cash sales report

OUTPUT

1. Guests' checks automatically calculated and totaled
2. Guests' orders displayed on screen on back-of-house computer or printout of the order may be given for cooks to fill orders (interfaced with POS register) No order should be prepared before this
3. Menu item tally of sales—for evaluation of menu mix and popularity
4. Total cash intake from sales, and total income per server
5. Automatic calculation and dispensing of customers' change
6. Reconciliation of actual cash on hand with records of cash transactions

OTHER CAPABILITIES

1. Develop sales and other expense budgets or analyses as in Fig. 16.13
2. Sales by time segments throughout serving period, by server or service unit
3. Special transactions as tax, employees' meal discounts, catering sales, payment by credit card, tip credits calculations
4. Revenue from sales data automatically posted to a general ledger; used for income statement and financial reports

LABOR PRODUCTIVITY AND PAYROLL

INPUT

1. Employee time-on-duty—"in/out" record data
2. Employee identification codes
3. Job codes with wage information
4. Work schedules for each employee
5. Employees' personal data stored
6. Income data

OUTPUT

1. Individual and total payroll reports automatically entered in accounts payable ledger

---

Inventory Control System

Cook-ware™
Expense Analysis Sheet

Facility: _____   Reporting Period: _____
Date: ___/_____/_____   Filed by: _____

# LINE	GENERAL DESCRIPTION	$ DOLLAR AMOUNT $
	** MATERIAL EXPENSE **	
1	Inventory value at beginning of reporting cycle: (note posting report for values)	_____
2	Total purchase for period (note posting report):	_____
3	Sub total (add #1 + #2)	_____
4	Value of inventory at end of reporting period: (note posting report for values)	_____
5	Total inventory expense (subtract #3 − #4):	_____
	** SALARY EXPENSE **	
6	Total dietary salary expense for period:	_____
7	Dietary supervisory salary expense for period:	_____
8	Dietary consultant expense:	_____
9	Total dietary labor expense (add #6 + #7 + #8):	_____
	** MISCELLANEOUS EXPENSE **	
10	Miscellaneous dietary expense during period:	_____
11	Cafeteria sales during period:	_____
12	Number of cafeteria meals served to non-residents:	_____
13	Total resident census (daily census × #days/period):	_____
14	Total resident meals served (#13 − #12):	_____
15	Total dietary expense (#5 + #9 + #10 − #11):	_____
16	Total dietary cost per resident per day (#15 / # 14)	_____

Figure 16.13. Data from analyzing expenses and census to be filled in as indicated. (Courtesy, Cook-Ware™, Dytran Computer Systems, Inc. Copyright 1986.)

2. Paychecks generated

3. Amount of time employee(s) spends on various tasks; total time calculated

4. Productivity indicators calculated
   a. Income/employee
   b. Labor hours/task (establish standards)
   c. Sales/labor dollar

OTHER CAPABILITIES

1. Productivity history for each employee

2. Labor budget variances from actual

3. Prepare labor budget; predict future demands

4. Labor cost for each menu item and per serving of prepared foods (aid in establishing selling prices)

OTHER COMPUTER USES

Artificial Intelligence: One of the newest and most exciting developments in the information technology arena is artificial intelligence (AI). AI includes expert systems, robotics, and neural networks. Expert systems and robotics have application in foodservice, while neural networks are used predominately in computer-based medical research.

Expert systems are software products designed to replace specific tasks performed by a specific person. These products are applicable when years of expertise, experience, and great amounts of knowledge are required to perform certain tasks. The computer is equipped with vast amounts of knowledge, which are intertwined with objective reasoning capabilities. Complex scenarios of decision strategies are developed to solve problems and to set plans in motion. Because expert systems have almost limitless storage capacities and are able to process information so quickly, the computer is able to solve problems and make decisions in only minutes or hours that would normally have taken days, weeks, or months.

Robotics involves computer-driven devices developed to perform specific tasks. Unlike automated machinery, robots can be reprogrammed and are multifunctional. The use of robotics is just beginning to see increased use in foodservice operations.

Some possibilities identified for foodservice use of robots include: loading/unloading, lifting product, and stocking shelves; steam cleaning carts; loading/unloading racks from dish machines; chopping, dicing, and slicing with equipment; stirring, filling, and sorting/picking operations; feeding materials into equipment; metering of ingredients; loading delivery carts (tray line); delivering supplies from storage to production areas and from production to service areas.

Although robots are not being utilized to a great extent in foodservice operations at present, the potential is there. If labor shortages and high costs intensify, the use of computerized robots may provide a solution for the future. Any possible negative effects on human productivity should not be overlooked.

Graphic Design: Computer use for floor planning and equipment arrangement is a growing application in the foodservice industry. As described in Chapter 8, computer-aided design (CAD) software programs are on the market to assist managers with designing projects. These programs allow for the use of specific variables, identified by the foodservice director, that are appropriate for one particular project/facility (see "Bibliography" at end of Chapter 8).

Data bases unique for facility designing are available also for any who may wish to utilize one for their own project planning. Some foodservice directors may utilize their own computer graphic tablet and plotter to develop their own schematic drawings. *Simulation* of proposed features of the facility, such as planning cafeteria configurations, are often used as a basis for considering alternatives and for decision making.

Decision-Making Support: The majority of foodservice computer applications in use at present tend to be for routine accounting functions. However, the potential of the computer for more management decision-making and problem-solving support should be emphasized. The current challenge is to focus on *management* of information and not merely on its manipulation.

Decision-support systems have to be individualized for each user since each need is unique. The information compiled is processed in whatever form the manager requires. Several possible alternatives resulting from a particular decision may be generated to aid the manager in making a wise choice. These are known as "what if" situations and show the overall effect a change may have on the system's operation before it is put into effect. Several processes may be used to achieve this result.

"*Electronic spreadsheets* are used primarily in financial planning and budgeting decisions. . . . The operator alters the sales data in a budget or financial plan and the computer shows the likely results of decisions based on the new assumptions (Patterson and Alvarez, 1985)." Spreadsheets may also be used to support purchasing choices, employee scheduling, inventory control, and menu analysis. Fig. 16.14 shows an example of a simple spreadsheet output.

Kasavana (1984) describes *menu engineering* as "a series of processes through which management can evaluate current and future menu pricing, design, and content decisions." The 12-step procedure in menu engineering focuses on *menu mix* or customer demand for each item, and *item pricing* analysis to determine the profit contribution of all menu items. "It provides a quantitative measurement scheme for evaluating success in menu and related decision areas" (Kasavana, 1984). These include answers to questions such as: What is the potential food cost for a given menu? At what price level and mix of sales does a (restaurant) foodservice maximize its profits? Which current menu items require replacing, repricing, or repositioning on the menu? How can the success of a menu change be evaluated?

Analyses can be achieved through use of the electronic spreadsheets or by matrix mathematical computations. The computer can be programmed for such computations. It integrates various pieces of data about each resource used (inputs) that has a bearing on the problem to be solved (output). The output provides management with the information on which to base a decision as the "best" action to take. "Best" is based on the organization's goals and

Name of Foodservice

Date _____   Day of Week _____

Meal	Time Segments	Sales for Period	Number of Customers	Average Check
Breakfast	7:00–7:29	32.20	35	.92
	7:30–7:59	65.10	62	1.05
	8:00–8:29	68.85	81	.85
	8:30–8:59	33.12	46	.72
	9:00–9:29	34.85	41	.85
	9:30–9:59	19.32	28	.69
Total/Averages:		253.44	293	.865
Continental Breakfast/ AM Break	10:00–10:15	40.50	54	.75
	10:16–10:30	32.30	38	.85
	10:31–10:45	45.08	49	.92
	10:46–11:00	13.49	21	.69
Total/Averages:		135.95	162	.839
Lunch	11:00–11:29	178.25	65	2.75
	etc.			

Figure 16.14. Simple spreadsheet used for analyzing sales by time periods.

limitations. It is up to management to initiate the action called for and to ascertain that it is integrated into the activities of the operation. This follow-up function cannot be performed by computer!

One type of computer program helpful to managers who wish easy retrieval of specific bits of information, or seek answers to questions by direct searching of data bases, is known as the "conversational" method. The user converses with the computer in foodservice terms that the computer can understand. Some examples of the kind of information that can be retrieved in this conversational manner are as follows:

1. the impact on cost and other resource use of exchanging one menu item for another in the menu plan

2. the impact on cost of changing ingredients in a recipe

3. the pattern of use for a specific ingredient over a range of meals

4. ingredient amounts in stock and anticipated orders for replenishing supplies

5. labor productivity information for individuals and the work force

6. budgetary comparisons—planned to actual

7. conversational menu planning—building a menu cycle plan and simultaneously testing it against budgetary and other constraints

8. anticipating the consequences to the foodservice of price changes of ingredients or changes in a labor contract

Managers of specific types of foodservice operations will find other needs that can be met with these decision-support computer systems. Applications seem to be limited only by the creativity of management.

Summary

Computer-assisted MIS have become sophisticated, accurate, and more timely since the development of microcomputer technology. Manual computations and record keeping that require hours of clerical time can now be accomplished in minutes, after a computer program has been designed or purchased and a computer system installed.

New types of computers and programs are marketed almost daily and open new possibilities for management support. Predictions for the future include more decision-support systems that integrate several types of computing (word processing, data processing, query languages, and more), which are presently used separately, into one unit. Dietitians and managers will be able to utilize this tool in their workplaces to maintain a cost-effective operation. The organizational structure of foodservice may change, with a flattening of the management pyramid and fewer levels between top and first-line management. With access to data formerly denied, supervisors may participate in greater decision making and so be better informed.

Computer-based voice-store-forward telephone systems that avoid time-wasting repeat calls; electronic mail exchange that simultaneously transmits memos, reports, and drafts; and teleconferencing to link remote managers to one another help to save time and reduce costs. Computers can be used to monitor production flow and quality and so free supervisors for more training, coaching, negotiating, and worker counseling and planning.

Other trends seem to be toward more voice-operated machines that allow customers to place their own orders and receive change and receipt automatically; computer hookups between service units in one foodservice system as in large school foodservice operations, medical centers, or restaurant chains; computerization of the human resources system—recruitment, training, placement (matching characteristics for success with those of applicants), and retention; and improved decision making at all levels by combining the organization's data with external economic sociological and technological factors for forecasting. These applications, as well as others not mentioned here, are in use, to some degree, in foodservices today; many more applications are sure to come.

Any information system is only as good as its design and use. In planning computer-assisted MIS, remember the desired result—placing data into a *meaningful context* for those who are to use it, *disseminating* the information to the right people *when needed,* and making certain that the data are *complete, accurate,* and *free of bias.* Only when this is accomplished will computer-assisted management have achieved its greatest potential value in the foodservice operation.

Summary Questions

1. Why are data by themselves considered useless?
2. What are the three categories of computers, and for what is each type most suitably used?
3. What criteria should be used to evaluate a computer program?
4. How is a robot different from automated machinery?
5. Describe CAD. What is its purpose and value?
6. What guidelines should be implemented to minimalize physiological strain on the computer user?
7. What is the desired result of computer-based MIS?

Bibliography

Adams, E.: Computer Usage in Food Systems. Unpublished graduate work, Food Systems Management Department, College of Home Economics, Oregon State University, Corvallis, Oregon, 1984.

Beasley, M. A.: The hidden costs of computerization. Food Mgmt. 27:36, 1992.

Berst, J.: The ABC's of evaluating packaged software. Interface Age 8(2):35, 1983.

Burch, J. G., Strater, F. B., and Grudniski, G.: Information Systems: Theory and Practice, 3rd ed. New York: John Wiley & Sons, 1983.

Fetter, W. R.: Guidelines for evaluation of computer software (with an evaluation form). Educational Technology 24:19, 1984.

Grossbauer, S.: Selecting software. FoodService Director 4:84, 1991.

Harris, P. R.: Management in Transition. San Francisco: Jossey-Bass, 1985.

Kasavana, M. L.: Computer Systems for Foodservice Operations. New York: Van Nostrand Reinhold, 1984.

Luros, E.: Automation for the Year 2000. (Script from slide presentation). Chatsworth, CA: Compurition, Inc., 1992.

Patterson, J. and Alvarez, R.: Computer systems for food-service operations. Cornell HRA Quarterly 26:132, 1985.

Scott, G. M.: Principles of Management Information Systems. New York: McGraw-Hill, 1986.

Senn, J. A.: Information Systems in Management, 3rd ed. Belmont, CA: Wadsworth
Publishing Co., 1987.

Watts, T.: Computer trends for the future. School Food Service J. 46:24, 1992.

Wilkinson, J. W. and Kneer, D. C.: Information Systems for Accounting and Management.
Englewood Cliffs, NJ: Prentice Hall, 1987.

For More Information

Adams, E. A. and Messersmith, A.: Robots in food systems: A review and assessment of
potential uses. J. Am. Diet. Assoc. 86:476, 1986.

Bedell, E. F.: The Computer Solution. Homewood, IL: Down Jones-Irwin, 1985.

Christensen, K. S.: Computerizing? Start with menu planning. School Food Service J.
45:46, 1991.

Encarnacao, J. and Schlechtendahl, E. G.: Computer Aided Design. Berlin: Springer-
Verlag, 1983.

French, J. A.: The Business Knowledge Investment. Englewood Cliffs, NJ: Yourdon Press,
1990.

Basic Cooking Methods

Basic Cooking Methods

Baking. Cooking by dry heat, usually in an oven.

Time and temperature: Baking temperature is determined by type of food and equipment. Oven load and size of containers must be considered when figuring required cooking time.

Equipment: Oven (deck, revolving, conveyor, range, or convection). A convection oven reduces cooking time by 30% or 40% and cooks at a temperature 25% to 50% lower than a traditional oven.

Barbecuing. Cooking on a grill or spit over hot coals, or in an oven, basting intermittently with a highly seasoned sauce.

Typical products: Meat, poultry.

Blanching. Cooking a food item partially and briefly.

Food usually is blanched in water, although some foods, such as french fries, are blanched in hot fat. To blanch in water, the food is placed in rapidly boiling water and held until the water returns to a boil, then quickly cooled in cold water.

Equipment: Steam-jacketed or other type of kettle.

Typical products: Vegetables or fruits; to set the color and destroy enzymes, or to loosen skins for easier peeling.

Boiling. Cooking food in a liquid that is bubbling rapidly.

Time and Temperature: The temperature of boiling water is 212°F at sea level. This point is raised by the presence of solids in the water and lowered by higher altitudes. At 5,000 feet, water boils at about 203°F; therefore, it takes *longer* to boil foods at high altitudes because of the lower boiling temperature.

Equipment: Steam-jacketed kettle, stock pot, or other kettle on top of the range.

Typical products: Vegetables, pasta, cereals, rice. Not generally used for high protein foods (meat, fish, or eggs) because heat toughens the protein, and the rapid movement of boiling breaks delicate foods. This type of food is usually brought to a boil, then the heat is reduced to simmering temperature for the rest of the cooking period.

Braising. A method of cooking that combines cooking in fat with the addition of moisture.

Food is browned in a small quantity of fat, then cooked slowly in liquid in a covered utensil.

Equipment: Tilting frypan or steam-jacketed kettle. For smaller amounts, a skillet or wok may be used. After the moisture is added to the browned food, the product may also be finished in the oven at a low temperature.

Typical products: Meats, poultry.

Broiling.   Cooking by radiant heat.

Food is placed on a rack either below or between the gas or electric heat source. The rack is positioned 3 to 6 inches from the heat source, depending on the type and intensity of the heat. The temperature required depends on the thickness of the food. Traditional broilers lack precise temperature controls and food must be closely monitored during cooking. In *panbroiling,* food is cooked without fat in a frypan. If fat is not poured off as it accumulates, the process becomes panfrying.

Equipment: Specially designed broilers for institutional use.

Typical products: Tender cuts of meat (steaks, chops), fish, poultry.

Deep-Fat Frying.   Cooking by submerging food in hot fat.

In this type of cooking, some of the medium becomes part of the food during the cooking process, and it is not unusual for foods to absorb 10% to 20% fat during frying. Foods may be dipped in a breading or batter before frying to form a protective coating between food and fat and to give the product crispness, color, and flavor. A well-prepared deep-fat fried food should have minimum fat absorption, attractive golden color, crisp surface or coating, and no off-flavors imparted by the frying fat. For the production of a high-quality product, use a good quality fat with a high smoke point, avoid overloading the baskets, fry at proper temperatures, and avoid frying strongly and mildly flavored foods in the same fat. About 10% to 30% of the fat should be replaced with fresh fat before each daily use. Modern fryers are equipped with automatic basket lifts, fat temperature sensors, and computerized timers to aid in the consistent production of good fried foods. Thermostatic control and fast recovery of fat temperature permits the rapid production of consistent quality fried foods.

Equipment: Deep-fat fryer. Pressure fryers and convection fryers are recent developments that reduce the frying time, thus enabling large volume food-services to produce fried foods more rapidly. Pressurized fryers are used most frequently in foodservice operations specializing in fried chicken.

Typical products: Fish, shellfish, chicken, vegetables, meat.

Fricasseeing.   Browning in fat, then simmering in gravy.

Similar to braising, but moisture is in the form of gravy rather than water or other liquid.

Equipment: Tilting frypan, steam-jacketed kettle.

Typical products: Chicken, some meat cuts.

Frying.   Cooking in fat or oil.

See Deep-Fat Frying, Ovenfrying, Panfrying, and Sautéing for frying methods.

Griddling.   Cooking on a solid cooking surface.

Food is placed on a flat surface and cooked with or without a small amount of fat.

Equipment: Griddle.

Temperature: The temperature on a griddle is adjustable and is lower than on a grill (usually around 350°F).

Typical products: Meat, eggs, pancakes, sandwiches.

Grilling.   Cooking on an open grid over a heat source.

Equipment: Grill, with heat source of charcoal, an electric element, or gas-heated element.

Typical products: Meat, fish.

Ovenfrying.   High temperature cooking in an oven.

Food is placed on greased baking sheets, melted fat brushed or drizzled over it, and baked in a hot oven (usually 400° to 450°F.) The resulting product resembles fried or sautéed food. This method is used when deep-fat fryers are not available or are inadequate to handle the production demand, usually in large health care facilities or other noncommercial foodservice operations.

Typical products: Chicken pieces, fish fillets.

Panfrying.   Cooking in a moderate amount of fat in a pan over moderate heat.

The amount of fat depends on the food being cooked. Only a small amount is used for eggs, while more may be needed for panfried chicken. Most foods must be turned at least once for even cooking. Some larger foods may be removed from the pan and finished in the oven, to prevent excessive surface browning.

Equipment: Skillet, tilting frypan.

Typical products: Meat, chicken, eggs, potatoes, onions.

Poaching.   Cooking by immersing food in hot liquid maintained at simmering temperature.

Food is added to hot liquid and simmered, keeping the temperature below boiling.

Equipment: Tilting frypan, steamer, oven, or a shallow pan on the range top.

Typical products: Fish, eggs out of the shell, fruit.

Roasting.   Baking of meat or poultry (uncovered) in an oven.

Cooking uncovered is essential to roasting because if the meat or poultry is covered with a lid or aluminum foil the steam is held in, changing the process from dry-heat to moist-heat cooking.

Equipment: Oven (range, deck, revolving, range, or convection).

Typical products: Poultry, tender cuts of beef, pork, lamb, or veal.

Sautéing.   Cooking quickly in a small amount of fat.

Food is placed in a preheated skillet with a small amount of fat and cooked quickly. Food should be cut or pounded to an even thickness and not overcrowded in the pan. After a food is sautéed, wine or stock is frequently added to dissolve brown bits of food sticking to the sides or bottom of the pan, a process called deglazing. Generally, this liquid is served with the sautéed item.

Equipment: Skillet, tilting frypan.

Typical products: Poultry, fish fillets, tender cuts of meat.

Searing.   Browning of food in fat over high heat before finishing by another method.

Equipment: Tilting frypan, steam-jacketed kettle, skillet on top of range.

Typical product: Meat.

Simmering.   Cooking of food in liquid below the boiling point.

Liquid should be kept at a temperature ranging from 185°F to just below the boiling point. Most foods cooked in a liquid are simmered because the higher temperatures and intense bubbling of boiling may be detrimental to the texture and appearance of the food. Food may be brought to the boiling point first, then the heat reduced for the rest of the cooking period.

Equipment: Steam-jacketed kettle, stock pot, or other kettle on top of the range.

Typical products: Soups, sauces, meat, poultry.

Steaming.   Cooking by exposing foods directly to steam.

Steam cookers provide for controlled cooking in constant temperatures. Food properly cooked in a pressure steamer is evenly cooked, retains a high vitamin content as well as its natural color and flavor, and suffers less of the usual cooking losses, such as shrinkage caused by prolonged cooking, boiling over, or burning. Pressure steaming is an extremely rapid method of cooking and must be carefully controlled and timed.

Equipment: Steamers may be low pressure, high pressure, or zero pressure. High-pressure steam cookers are used primarily for fast cooking and small batch cookery of vegetables. In a zero convection, a fan circulates the steam throughout the steamer cavity. Most steamers are designed to accommodate standard-size pans that can be used directly on the serving counter. Steam is the source of heat in jacketed kettles, but is not the cooking medium. The heat is transferred through the walls of the inner lining of the kettle by conduction, but no contact between food and steam is possible. The temperature is higher than in a double boiler because the steam is under pressure. The temperature increases with increase in pressure.

Typical products: Vegetables, fruits, poultry, dumplings, pasta, rice, cereals.

Stewing. Cooking in a small amount of water, which may be either boiling or simmering.

Whether a food is to be simmered, stewed, or boiled the liquid usually is brought to a full boil first. This compensates for the lowering of the temperature when the food is added. The heat is then adjusted to maintain a steady temperature.

Equipment: Steam-jacketed kettle, tilting frypan, kettle on top of the range.

Typical products: Meat, poultry, fruit.

Stir-Frying. Cooking quickly in a small amount of oil over high heat.

Food is cut into uniform strips or small pieces and cooked quickly in a small amount of oil. Light tossing and stirring motion is used to preserve the shape of the food.

Equipment: Tilting frypan, skillet, wok.

Typical products: Vegetables, chicken, pork, tender beef, or shrimp.

Cooking Methods for Specific Foods

Most foods are cooked by one of the basic methods described in the previous section. Broiling, frying, baking, and simmering are standard processes in food preparation, but there may be variations in exact procedures because of the type of product, available equipment and personnel, and the size and character of the operation. The following information is given to augment the basic definitions previously provided.

Meat

Cooking Methods Depends on the quality and cut of meat and the quantity that must be prepared at one time. For *beef,* dry heat (broiling, roasting) is generally used for tender cuts, and moist heat cookery (braising, stewing, simmering) for the less tender cuts. Table A.1 suggests methods of cooking appropriate for various cuts and grades of beef. Lower grades of meat and the less tender cuts of higher quality beef may be tenderized by scoring, cubing, grinding, or by the addition of enzymes. Adding tomatoes or vinegar to a meat mixture also has a tenderizing effect. For *veal, pork,* and *lamb,* practically any cut but the shank may be cooked by dry heat, although broiling is not as desirable for pork or veal as it is for lamb or beef. Veal, because of its delicate flavor and lack of fat in the tissues, combines well with sauces and other foods.

Time/Temperature Yield is an important factor in the cooking of meat. Reduction in the yield of cooked meat may occur as cooking losses or as carving or serving losses. Shrinkage during cooking usually is the major loss involved

TABLE A.1.   Suggested Cooking Guide for Beef.

The use of an appropriate method of cooking is essential to bring out
the desirable eating qualities of the specific cut and grade selected.
Below is a guide suggesting the most generally accepted method of
cooking retail beef cuts of each grade.

Flank, plate, brisket, foreshank, and the heel of the round should be
prepared in the same manner for all grades of beef. These less tender
cuts are used for stewing, braising, pot roasting, or boiling, or are
ground for use in meat loaves and similar dishes.

Cut	Prime	Choice	Select
Top round and sirloin tip (steaks and roasts)	Braise, broil, panfry, pot roast, or roast	Braise, broil, panfry, pot roast, or roast	Braise, panfry, pot roast, or roast
Bottom round (steaks and roasts)	Braise, panfry, pot roast, or roast	Braise, panfry, pot roast, or roast	Braise, pot roast, or roast
Rump roast	Roast or pot roast	Roast or pot roast	Roast or pot roast
Sirloin (steaks and roasts)	Broil, panfry, or roast	Broil, panfry, or roast	Broil, panfry, or roast
Porterhouse, T-bone, club, and rib steaks	Broil	Broil	Broil
Rib roast	Roast	Roast	Roast
Chuck, round bone, and blade (roasts and steaks)	Roast, pot roast, or braise	Roast, pot roast, or braise	Roast, pot roast, or braise

SOURCE: "U.S. Grades of Beef," *Marketing Bulletin No. 15,* U.S. Department of
Agriculture, Washington, DC.

and it may range from 15% to 30%. Some shrinkage occurs regardless of the
cooking method, but the cooking temperature and the cooking time have a
direct bearing on the amount of shrinkage. Low temperatures generally result
in fewer cooking losses and the most palatable product. If cooked too long,
meat dries out and tends to be less tender. Even meat that requires moist heat
and a comparatively long cooking time to become tender will be less tender
when overcooked.

Roasting: Time/weight relationship expressed in minutes per pound can
be used as a guide, but the most accurate way to determine the doneness of a
roast is with a meat thermometer that registers the internal temperature. For
ease in roasting and handling, the roasts to be cooked together should be

uniform in size. Frozen meat generally is thawed in the refrigerator before cooking to reduce both time and heavy drip losses during preparation. Roasts will continue cooking for a period of time after removal from the oven, and the internal temperature of the roast may rise as much as 5°. The roast should be allowed to sit or rest in a warm place for 15 to 20 minutes before it is carved. The roast becomes more firm, retains more of its juices, and is easier to carve. When cooking a number of roasts, it is possible to offer meat at different stages of doneness by staggering the times that roasts are placed in the oven. The well-done roasts are started first and, when done, are removed from the oven, allowed to stand 20 minutes, sliced, and placed in pans in the warmer or in the oven at low heat. The rare meat is put in the oven last and, when the thermometer reaches 125°F, is removed from the oven, sliced, and sent directly to the serving area. For optimum quality, roasts are cooked and sliced just prior to serving. However, this may not be possible in some foodservice operations. If the meat must be cooked the day before or several hours prior to serving, the quality is better if the cooked roasts are stored in the refrigerator, then sliced and reheated before serving rather than refrigerating and reheating the sliced meat.

Poultry

COOKING METHODS   Broiling (if not too large), panfrying, deep-fat frying, ovenfrying, roasting, barbecuing, fricasseeing, stewing, broasting.

TIME/TEMPERATURE   Moderate heat for tender, juicy, and evenly done meat. High temperatures result in stringy, tough, and unappetizing meat. When roasting, use a thermometer placed in the thickest part of the breast or inner part of the thigh muscle, being careful that the bulb does not rest against a bone. Temperature should reach 170° to 180°F. Poultry usually is cooked well-done, but overcooking results in loss of juiciness. Many foodservices prefer to purchase boneless turkey roasts or rolls for convenience in roasting, slicing, and portion control. Cooking time for ready-to-cook rolls is longer in minutes per pound than for whole turkeys, but the total cooking time is less. (See Table A.2 for a timetable for roasting turkey.) Stuffing or dressing should be baked separately and served with the roasted sliced meat.

Fish

THAWING   Frozen fish steaks or fillets need not be thawed prior to cooking unless they are to be breaded, but any defrosting should be at refrigerator temperature and only long enough to permit ease in preparation. Thawing at room temperature is not recommended. Once thawed, fish should be cooked immediately and never refrozen. Frozen breaded fish portions should not be thawed before cooking.

TABLE A.2.   Timetable for Roasting Turkey.

Form of Turkey	Weight of Turkey, Whole or Piece (lb)	Oven Temperature (°F)	Cooking[a] Time (hr)
Turkey, whole, ready-to-cook	12 to 16	325	3½ to 4½
	16 to 21	325	4½ to 6
	21 to 26	325	6 to 7½
Turkey parts			
Breast	8 to 12	325	3 to 4
Leg (drumstick and thigh)	3 to 8	325	1¾ to 3
Halves	8 to 12	325	2¼ to 4
Quarters	3 to 8	325	1½ to 3½
Turkey roasts, boneless			
Frozen	9½ to 11½	350	4 to 4½
Thawed	9½ to 11½	350	2¾ to 3½

[a]Turkey is done when thermometer registers 180° to 185°F in inner thigh or 170° to 180°F in breast of whole turkeys; or 170°F in turkey roasts.

SOURCE: Adapted from "Quantity Recipes for Type A School Lunches," PA-631, U.S. Department of Agriculture, revised 1971.

COOKING METHODS   Deep-fat frying, panfrying, ovenfrying, broiling, baking, poaching. The best cooking method is determined by size, fat content, and flavor. Baking and broiling are suitable for fat fish, such as salmon, trout, and whitefish. If lean fish is baked or broiled, fat is added to prevent dryness, and it often is baked in a sauce. Lean fish, such as haddock, halibut, and sea bass, are often poached, simmered, or steamed, although they may be broiled or baked if basted frequently. Fish cooked in moist heat (poaching) requires very little cooking time and usually is served with a sauce. Frying is suitable for all types, but those with firm flesh that will not break apart easily are best for deep-fat frying. Whatever the method, fish should be served as quickly as possible after cooking for optimum quality. See Table A.3 for suggested cooking methods.

EQUIPMENT   Deep-fat fryer, skillet, tilting frypan, oven, steamer.

TIME/TEMPERATURE   Low to moderate heat. Allow extra time for frozen fish that is not defrosted. Fish should be cooked only until the flesh may be easily separated from the bones.

Eggs

COOKING METHODS   Poaching, frying, scrambling, and cooking in the shell.

Poaching: Cooked to order in a shallow pan of hot water on top of the range, or in quantity, a counter pan deep enough to permit 2 to 2 1/2 inches of

TABLE A.3. Suggested Methods of Cooking Fish and Shellfish.

Species	Approximate Weight or Thickness	Baking Temperature (°F)	Baking Minutes	Broiling Distance From Heat (in.)	Broiling Minutes	Boiling, Poaching, or Steaming Method	Boiling, Poaching, or Steaming Minutes (per lb)	Deep-Fat Frying Temperature (°F)	Deep-Fat Frying Minutes	Panfrying Temperature	Panfrying Minutes
Fish											
Dressed	3 to 4 lb	350	40 to 60			Poach	10	325 to 350	4 to 6		
Pan dressed	½ to 1 lb	350	25 to 30	3	10 to 15	Poach	10	350 to 375	2 to 4	Moderate	10 to 15
Steaks	½ to 1¼ in	350	25 to 35	3	10 to 15	Poach	10	350 to 375	2 to 4	Moderate	10 to 15
Fillets		350	25 to 35	3	8 to 15	Poach	10	350 to 375	2 to 4	Moderate	8 to 10
Portions	1 to 6 oz	350	30 to 40					350	4	Moderate	8 to 10
Sticks	¾ to 1¼ oz	400	15 to 20					350	3	Moderate	8 to 10
Shellfish											
Clams—live, shucked		450	12 to 15	4	5 to 8	Steam	5 to 10	350	2 to 3	Moderate	4 to 5
Crabs—live, soft-shell				4	8 to 10	Boil	10 to 15	375	2 to 4	Moderate	8 to 10
Lobsters—live	¾ to 1 lb	400	15 to 20	4	12 to 15	Boil	15 to 20	350	2 to 4	Moderate	8 to 10
Spiny lobster tails—frozen	¼ to ½ lb	450	20 to 30	4	8 to 12	Boil	10 to 15	350	3 to 5	Moderate	8 to 10
Oysters—live, shucked		450	12 to 15	4	5 to 8	Steam	5 to 10	350	2 to 3	Moderate	4 to 5
Scallops—shucked		350	25 to 30	3	6 to 8	Boil	3 to 4	350	2 to 3	Moderate	4 to 6
Shrimp											
Headless, raw						Boil	3 to 5				
Headless, raw, peeled		350	20 to 25	3	8 to 10	Boil	3 to 5	350	2 to 3	Moderate	8 to 10

SOURCE: "How to Eye and Buy Seafood," National Marine Fisheries Service, U.S. Department of Commerce, 1970.

water to cover the eggs is used. Eggs should be broken onto saucers and slid into the water toward the side of the pan. The water should be simmering when the eggs are dropped in. The addition of 2 tablespoons of vinegar and 1 tablespoon of salt to 1 gallon of water prevents whites from spreading. Poaching may be done in a shallow pan on the range top or in the oven, tilting frypan, or steamer.

Frying: Usually cooked to order in frypan or on a griddle. Eggs cooked on a griddle are more apt to spread than those cooked in a small frypan, and so are less attractive. To prevent toughening, eggs should not be fried at a high temperature.

Scrambling: Cooked to order in a frypan or griddle, or in quantity in the steamer or oven. The addition of milk to the eggs keeps them from drying, and medium white sauce added in place of milk prevents the eggs from separating and becoming watery when held on the serving counter.

Cooking in the Shell: In a pan on top of the range, an automatic egg cooker, a wire basket in the steam-jacketed kettle, or in a steamer. If eggs are brought to room temperature before cooking, the shells will not crack when heat is applied.

TIME/TEMPERATURE Avoid high temperatures and long cooking times. Eggs should be cooked as close to service as possible or cooked to order.

Pasta and Cereals

COOKING METHODS

Pasta: Pasta is cooked uncovered in a large amount of boiling water in a stock pot or steam-jacketed kettle until tender but firm (al dente), then rinsed with cold or hot water and drained. If pasta is to be combined with other ingredients in a casserole, it should be undercooked slightly. If the pasta is not to be served immediately, it may be drained and covered with cold water. When pasta is cold, drain off water and toss lightly with a little salad oil. This will keep pasta from sticking or drying out. Cover tightly and store in the refrigerator. To reheat, place pasta in a colander and immerse in rapidly boiling water just long enough to heat through; or reheat in a microwave oven.

Rice: Rice is cooked in a steamer, the oven, or by boiling. It is cooked until all of the water is absorbed, so the right proportion of rice to water and the correct cooking time are important. Converted or parboiled long-grain white rice requires slightly more water and a longer cooking time than does regular long-grain or medium-grain rice. The cooking time for brown rice is almost double that of white rice.

Cereals: Cereals in quantity are generally cooked in a steam-jacketed kettle or steamer, but they may be prepared in a heavy kettle on top of the range. Add cereal and salt to boiling water, using a wire whip. Stir until some thickening is apparent, then reduce the heat and cook until cereal reaches desired consistency and the raw starch taste has disappeared. Cereal should be thick and creamy but not sticky. Overstirring or overcooking produces a sticky, gummy product.

Fruits and Vegetables

PREPREPARATION   Fresh fruits should be washed to remove surface soil, sprays, and preservatives before they are served raw or cooked. Apples, bananas, and peaches discolor rapidly after peeling so they should be immersed in pineapple, orange, or diluted lemon juice. Fruits also may be treated with ascorbic acid or other preparations that prevent oxidation. Berries deteriorate rapidly, so washing should be scheduled as near service as possible. A small amount of sugar sprinkled over the berries after cleaning keeps them fresh-looking.

Fresh vegetables should be washed, trimmed, peeled if necessary, and cut into even-sized pieces for cooking. Preparing fresh vegetables too far in advance causes them to discolor. Covering prepared vegetables with cold water helps retain color but reduces their nutritive value if they are held too long. Many foodservice operations have taken the preliminary preparation of fruits and vegetables out of the individual kitchens; they either centralize this function or buy convenience products that have some or all of the preparation completed. Peeled potatoes and carrots, washed spinach and other leafy vegetables, cut vegetables ready for cooking, and peeled and sectioned citrus fruits and fresh pineapple are examples.

METHODS OF COOKING VEGETABLES   Steaming, boiling, baking, frying.

EQUIPMENT   Steamer, steam-jacketed kettle, tilting frypan, kettle on top of the range.

Whatever method is used, vegetables should be cooked in as small a quantity at one time as is feasible for the type of service. The needs of most foodservices can be met by the continuous cooking of vegetables in small quantities. Vegetables should be cooked only until tender or, when stir-frying, until tender crisp. Vegetables should be served as soon as possible after cooking for optimum quality and should be handled carefully to prevent breaking or mashing. Appearance is important to customer acceptance of vegetables, as is the seasoning. Frozen vegetables are cooked by the same methods used for fresh vegetables, but because frozen vegetables have been partially cooked, the final cooking time is shorter than for fresh products. Most frozen vegetables do not need to be thawed, but they can be cooked from the frozen state and placed directly into steamer pans or boiling salted water. Exceptions are vegetables that are frozen into a solid block, such as spinach and winter squash. Results are more satisfactory if they are thawed in the refrigerator first for more even cooking.

To *steam,* place prepared vegetables not more than 3 to 4 inches deep in stainless steel inset pans. Perforated pans provide the best circulation, but if cooking liquid needs to be retained, use solid pans. To *boil,* add vegetables to boiling salted water in steam-jacketed kettle or stockpot, in lots no larger than 10 pounds. The amount of water used in cooking all vegetables is important for retention of nutrients. The less water used, the more nutrients retained. Addition of baking soda to the water also causes loss of vitamins. Mature root vegetables that need longer cooking require more water than young, tender vegetables. Spinach and other greens need only the water clinging to their leaves from washing. Cover and bring water quickly back to the boiling point. Green vegetables retain their color better if the lid is removed just before boiling begins; strong-flavored vegetables, such as cabbage, cauliflower, and Brussels sprouts, should be cooked uncovered to prevent development of unpleasant flavors. To *stir-fry,* cut vegetables diagonally or into small uniform pieces. Heat a small amount of oil in a wok, tilting frypan, or steam-jacketed kettle. Cook and stir until vegetables are coated with oil. A small amount of liquid is usually added and the vegetables cooked, covered, until tender but crisp.

One of the main purposes of cooking vegetables is to change the texture. During the cooking process, however, the color and flavor may be altered and there may be some loss of nutrients. The degree to which these characteristics change determines the quality of the cooked vegetables. Many factors affect cooking time, including the type and maturity of the vegetable, the presence of acids, size of the pieces, and the degree of doneness. Vegetables are considered done when they have reached the desired degree of tenderness. The starch in vegetables also affects texture. Dry starchy foods, such as beans or lentils, must be cooked in enough water so that the starch granules can absorb moisture and soften. Most starchy vegetables, such as potatoes and yams, have enough moisture of their own, but they must still be cooked until the starch granules soften. Color is a major factor in consumer acceptance of vegetables, so methods of cookery that retain color, as well as nutritive value, should be selected. The green pigment chlorophyll is the least stable of food pigments, and considerable attention is given to preserving this color in vegetables. Chlorophyll is affected by acid to produce an unattractive olive-gray color. Vegetables are slightly acidic in reaction, and when cooked, the acid is liberated from the cells into the cooking water. Fortunately, much of the acid is volatile and given off in the first few minutes of cooking. If an open kettle is used for cooking green vegetables, the volatile acids may escape easily, aiding in the retention of the green pigment.

Canned vegetables are heated in a steam-jacketed kettle, stockpot, steamer, or oven. Overheating, as with overcooking of fresh and frozen vegetables, results in further loss of nutrients and a soft-textured, unattractive, and poor-flavored product.

Dried vegetables are soaked before cooking to restore the water content to that of the fresh legume and to shorten the cooking time. Legumes will absorb enough water to approximately double their dry weight, with an attendant increase in volume. The length of the soaking period depends on the temperature of the water, with warm water cutting the soaking time to about half. The vegetable may be covered with boiling water, let stand for 1 hour, then cooked until tender; or they may be covered with cold water and soaked overnight, drained, then cooked.

Small batch or continuous cooking of vegetables throughout the meal service is the most satisfactory way to obtain high-quality products. Quantities of not more than 10-pound lots, and preferably 5-pound batches, should be cooked at intervals as needed. High-speed steamers and small tilting steam-jacketed kettles behind the service line are the most useful kinds of equipment for batch cooking of vegetables.

Salads

PREPARATION OF SALAD INGREDIENTS   Salad greens should be clean, crisp, chilled, and well-drained. Wash in a spray of water or in a large container of water, shake off excess moisture, drain thoroughly, and refrigerate. All ingredients for salads should be chilled thoroughly and drained when necessary.

SALAD ARRANGEMENT   To make salads efficiently, prepare all ingredients and chill. Arrange salad plates or bowls on trays that have been lined up on a worktable. Place a leafy underliner on each plate, then add the body of the salad to the plates. This may be a mixed salad, measured with a dipper or scoop, or it may be a placed salad in which individual ingredients are arranged on the underliner. Chopped lettuce placed in the lettuce cup gives height to the salad. Top garnishes add the final touch of color and flavor contrast. The trays of salads are then refrigerated until service but should not be held more than a few hours or the salads will wilt. Dressings generally are served separately or added just before serving, except for in potato salad and some entrée salads where flavor is improved by standing 2 to 4 hours after mixing.

SALAD BAR   The basic salad bar consists of salad greens with a variety of accompaniments and dressings. Lettuce usually is the main ingredient, but other greens and accompaniments are usually added. In addition to vegetables and fruits, chopped hard-cooked eggs, crumbled crisp bacon, croutons, shredded cheese, cottage cheese, cabbage slaw, pasta salads, molded fruit gelatin, and other prepared salads often appear on salad bars. A variety of dressings is offered. The salad bar should be attractively presented and the salad ingredients kept cold. A logical arrangement places chilled plates or bowls on ice first, near the greens, followed by the accompaniments, the prepared salads and, finally, the dressings. The salad bar offers an opportunity for creativity and can be an effective merchandising tool.

Sandwiches

Sandwiches may be prepared to order in commercial foodservice operations by pantry workers and/or short-order cooks. Fillings are made and refrigerated, margarine or butter softened, lettuce is cleaned and crisped, and other ingredients prepared ready for assembling. Ingredients should be arranged for maximum efficiency, with everything needed within easy reach of both hands.

In large quantity, all sandwiches needed may be made and refrigerated until service or, in cafeteria service, may be assembled a few at a time. Hot sandwiches may be made up and grilled or baked as needed, or for cafeteria service, the fillings may be cooked and the sandwiches assembled on the cafeteria counter. An efficient work station should be set up for making sandwiches and an assembly-line procedure used. Place bread slices on a baking sheet or tray, and brush with margarine, butter, or mayonnaise, then spread or place the filling, according to the type of sandwich being made, on all slices on the tray. Add the top bread slices to all the sandwiches. For grilled sandwiches, brush the top and bottom slices with melted margarine or butter. Measure fillings with a dipper or scoop and portion sliced meat or cheese according to count or weight. The recipes or instruction sheets should include the directions for portioning.

Sanitation is important in the making of cold sandwiches because of the amount of handling involved and because they are not cooked. Mixed fillings containing meat, poultry, fish, eggs, or mayonnaise should be prepared the day they are to be served, and only in such quantities as will be used during one serving period. Fillings should be refrigerated until needed, and if sandwiches are made ahead they, too, should be refrigerated. Lettuce should be omitted from sandwiches to be stored for some time in the refrigerator because the lettuce will wilt and become unappetizing.

Soups

Most soups can be classified as clear or unthickened, and cream or thick. *Clear* or *unthickened* soups are based on a clear, unthickened broth or stock. Vegetables, pasta, rice, meat, or poultry products may be added. *Bouillon* is a clear soup without solid ingredients. *Consommé* is a concentrated flavorful broth or stock that has been clarified to make it clear and transparent. *Broth* or *stock,* the basic ingredient for all clear soups, is made by simmering meat, poultry, seafood, and/or vegetables in water to extract their flavor. Brown stock, made from beef that has been browned before simmering, and white or light stock, made from veal and/or chicken, are the stocks used most often. Because the making of stock is so time-consuming, many foodservice operations use concentrated bases, which are mixed with water to make flavored liquids similar to stocks. Bases vary in quality, with the best products being composed mainly of meat or poultry extracts. These are perishable and must be refrigerated. Many bases have salt as their principal ingredient, so it is important to read the list of ingredients on the label. When using these bases, the salt and other seasonings in the soup recipe may need to be adjusted.

Cream or *thick* soups are made with a thin white sauce combined with mashed, strained, or finely chopped vegetables, chicken, fish, or meat. Chicken stock may be used to replace part of the milk in the sauce to enhance the flavor. *Chowders* are unstrained, thick soups prepared from seafood, poultry, meat, and/or vegetables. *Bisques* are mixtures of chopped shellfish, stock, milk, and seasonings, usually thickened. *Purees* are soups that are naturally thickened by pureeing one or more of their ingredients.

Sauces

Basic to many sauces is a *roux,* which is a cooked mixture of equal parts by weight of fat and flour. A roux may range from white, in which the fat and flour are cooked only for a short time, to brown, cooked until it is light brown in color and has a nutty taste and aroma.

Many meat and vegetable sauces are modifications of basic recipes, such as white sauce, bechamel sauce, and brown sauce. *White sauce* is made with a roux of fat, usually margarine or butter, and flour, with milk as the liquid. White sauce is used as a basis for cream soups, as a sauce for vegetables, and as an ingredient in many casseroles. *Bechamel sauce* and its variations use milk and chicken stock as the liquid and are generally served with seafood, eggs, poultry, or vegetables. *Brown sauce* is made with a well-browned roux and beef stock and is used mainly with meats.

Bakeshop Production

Breads, cakes, cookies, pies, and other desserts may be produced in a separate bakeshop or made in an area of the main kitchen in which ovens, mixers, and other equipment are available. Although some foodservice operations purchase all or some of these items already prepared, others prefer to make these on the premises either from mixes or "from scratch."

The choice of baking mixes influences the finished product and should be made only after testing and comparing more than one brand. Some large foodservices contract with manufacturers to make mixes to their specifications. If mixes are used, the baked product may be individualized by variations in finishing and presentation. For example, a basic white cake may be baked as a sheet cake or made into a layer cake by cutting the sheet cake into two pieces and placing one on top of the other. A variety of icings may be used with a basic plain cake. Many possibilities exist also when making up plain or sweet roll dough.

If mixes are not used for breads and cakes, balanced formulas should be developed and standardized for the pan sizes used in the foodservice. Many variations are possible if good basic recipes are developed for butter, white, and chocolate cakes, and for biscuits, muffins, and rolls. An important factor in successful bakeshop production is the weighing and portioning of batters and doughs. Each recipe should include the size pan to use and the weight of batter for each pan for products such as cakes, coffee cakes, and loaf breads; the weight of each roll or bun; and the size dipper for muffins and drop cookies.

A baking sheet 18 × 26 inches and 1 1/2 inches deep with straight side is used for cakes, cookies, and some quick breads. A half-size baking sheet 12 × 18 inches is often used and is especially good for layer cakes. If a baking pan 12 × 18 inches, or 12 × 20 inches, with 2 1/2- to 3-inch sides is used, special attention must be given to the amount of batter in the pans. Loaf pans for pound cakes and quick breads, and tube pans for foam cakes, vary in size and should be selected according to the size serving desired. Pans should be prepared before mixing of the products begins. Pans for angel food and sponge cakes are not greased; baking powder biscuits and cookies with high fat content are usually placed on ungreased baking sheets. Most other pans are either lightly greased, greased and floured, or covered with a parchment paper liner.

Considerations for Facilities Planning

TABLE B.1.   Restaurant Feasibility Study Resources.

Sources	Available Information
Chamber of commerce, economic development authority, or city planning office	• Population trends (historical and projected) • Age, occupation, income level, ethnic origin, and marital status by census tract • Retail sales, food and beverage sales • Maps • Consumer shopping habits and patterns • Employment and unemployment statistics • Major employers and industries • Planned commercial, residential, and industrial developments • Demographic and socioeconomic trends • Area master plan
Housing and community development	• Residential occupancy and housing • Urban renewal projects • Property values
Building commission	• Building permits data • Planned construction developments
Zoning commission	• Planned uses for zoned areas • Building height, signage, parking, and construction restrictions
Transportation department	• Road traffic patterns and counts • Proposed traffic developments • Types of public transportation and routes
Department of revenue	• Income and other related sales taxes • Real estate assessments
Convention and visitors bureau	• Number of visitors by month and spending habits/statistics • Conventions—size, type, frequency, and duration • Recurring festivals and fairs
Utility companies	• Estimates of gas and/or electric expenses for the proposed restaurant
Local newspapers and magazines	• Restaurant critiques • Dining guides • Planned commercial developments

SOURCE: Courtesy, National Restaurant Association.

The Americans With Disabilities Act—As Related to Foodservice Management

The requirements of the Americans with Disabilities Act (ADA) of 1990 protect the rights of those with disabilities to enjoy and have access to employment, transportation, public accommodation, and communications. It has two main sections, one dealing with employment (see discussion of this part of the act in Chapter 11) and the other with public accommodation. The provisions detailed in the act are voluminous, and anyone wishing to assure compliance must become familiar with them.

The two checklists that follow are provided to alert readers to some of the act's requirements regarding foodservice accommodation. Taking the actions outlined in these checklists will not necessarily ensure compliance with the ADA; however, they can be used as tools to identify and eliminate potential problem areas. The diagrams of space requirements, shown in Chapter 8, Fig. 8.9, help interpret some of the requirements of this act.

REMOVAL OF BARRIERS

(a) *General.* A public accommodation shall remove architectural barriers in existing facilities, including communication barriers that are structural in nature, where such removal is readily achievable (i.e., easily accomplishable and able to be carried out without much difficulty or expense).

(b) *Examples.* Examples of steps to remove barriers include, but are not limited to, the following:

1. installing ramps
2. making curb cuts in sidewalks and entrances
3. lowering shelves
4. rearranging tables, chairs, vending machines, and other furniture
5. lowering telephones
6. installing flashing alarm lights
7. widening doors
8. installing offset hinges to widen doorways
9. eliminating a turnstile or providing an alternative accessible path
10. installing accessible door hardware
11. installing grab bars in toilet stalls
12. rearranging toilet partitions to increase maneuvering space
13. insulating lavatory pipes
14. installing a raised toilet seat
15. installing a full-length bathroom mirror
16. lowering the paper towel dispenser in a bathroom
17. creating a designated accessible parking space
18. removing high pile, low density carpeting

Figure B.1. Compliance with the Americans with Disabilities Act—barriers checklist. (Courtesy, Liberty Northwest Insurance Corporation, Portland, Oregon.)

BARRIERS CHECKLIST

Building Access

1. Are 96″ wide parking spaces designated with a 60″ access aisle?
2. Are parking spaces near main building entrance?
3. Is there a "drop off" zone? a building entrance?
4. Is the gradient from parking to building entrance 1:12 or less?
5. Is the entrance doorway at least 32 inches?
6. Is door handle easy to grasp?
7. Is door handle easy to open (less than 8 lbs pressure)?

Building Corridors

1. Is path of travel free of obstruction and wide enough for a wheelchair?
2. Is floor surface hard and not slippery?
3. Do obstacles (i.e., phones, fountains) protrude no more than 4 inches?

Rest rooms

1. Are rest rooms near building entrance/personnel office?
2. Do doors have lever handles?
3. Are doors at least 32″ wide?
4. Are rest rooms large enough for wheelchair turnaround (51″ minimum)?
5. Are stall doors at least 32″ wide?
6. Are grab bars provided in toilet stalls?
7. Are sinks at least 30″ high with room for a wheelchair to roll under?
8. Are sink handles easily reached and used?
9. Are soap dispensers and towels no more than 48″ from floor?

Figure B.1. (*Continued*)

The following checklist aids in the assessment of the current level of compliance and, in the future, will assist in accessibility issues. Any changes in an establishment must be *readily achievable*—this means that a task must be able to be easily accomplished, that is, carried out without much difficulty or expense.

ADA Compliance Checklist

The following checklist will aid in assessing the current level of compliance and assist in future accessibility issues. Any changes in an establishment must be readily achievable. This means that the task must be easily accomplished and able to be carried out without much difficulty or expense.

Passenger Arrival

- ☐ Adequate space
- ☐ Ramp to entry
- ☐ Proper width of walk
- ☐ Door opening clearance
- ☐ No obstructions

Parking

- ☐ Special stalls
- ☐ Access to building by level path

Walks

- ☐ Minimum 48" wide
- ☐ Firm, nonslip surface
- ☐ Curb cuts at streets, driveways, parking lots
- ☐ 5% maximum grade
- ☐ Free of obstructions
- ☐ Level platforms at doors

Ramps

- ☐ Maximum 8 1/3% grade
- ☐ Free of grates
- ☐ Landings at 32" high, extended 12" beyond ramp
- ☐ Well illuminated
- ☐ Firm, nonslip surface
- ☐ Level approaches
- ☐ Guardrails on walls

Entrances

- ☐ One major entrance for wheelchair
- ☐ Level approach platform

Doors

- ☐ 32" wide clear opening
- ☐ Thresholds flush with walk or floor
- ☐ Vestibules with 6'6" separation
- ☐ Handles maximum 42" high
- ☐ Closers with time delay
- ☐ Closers with 8 lbs maximum pressure
- ☐ Single effort with 8 lbs maximum pressure
- ☐ Kickplates 16" high
- ☐ Vision panels at 36" above floor maximum

Corridors, Public Spaces, Work Areas

- ☐ Corridors minimum 60" wide
- ☐ Floors on common level
- ☐ Nonslip floor materials
- ☐ Recessed doors when opening to corridor
- ☐ Noncarpeted circulation paths

Stairs

- ☐ Minimum 42" wide
- ☐ Nonprojecting nosings
- ☐ Level, differentiated approaches
- ☐ Handrails 18" beyond top/bottom
- ☐ Maximum 7" risers
- ☐ Nonslip treads
- ☐ Handrails 32" high
- ☐ Well illuminated

Figure B.2. Americans with Disabilities Act compliance checklist. (Courtesy, Liberty Northwest Insurance Corporation, Portland, Oregon.)

Foodservice Equipment

Cooking Equipment

Ranges

Simple design, easily cleanable; heavy, well-braced angle iron frame; sturdy riveted or welded construction; body—sheet steel with baked-on black Japan or porcelain enamel smooth finish, or stainless steel; with or without ovens and high backs; heating elements of burners with individual controls; automatic pilot; removable drip trays to prevent spillage under elements or burners; may be mounted on casters or flush-to-wall.

Types: (1) Heavy-duty ranges—durable and well-suited for large volume foodservice operations with constant usage, as in hotels, large restaurants, colleges, hospitals. Approximate sizes of sections: electric—36 inches wide, 36 inches deep, 32 inches high; gas—31 to 34 inches wide, 34 to 42 inches deep, 33 to 34 inches high. (2) Medium weight or restaurant type—lighter in construction than heavy-duty and used where demands are less constant such as short-order cooking or where use is intermittent as in churches and clubs. Complete units, 6, 8, or 10 burners, or combination with fry-top and/or even-heat top; 1 or 2 ovens. Approximate size 35 to 64 inches wide, 27 to 32 inches deep, 34 inches high; ovens, 26 inches wide, 22 inches deep, 15 inches high.

Tops: polished chrome-nickel-iron alloy, high strength and heat absorption qualities; resistant to warping, chipping, and corrosion; accurate thermostats provide controlled heat surfaces as desired.

1. Open or hot plate top—usually associated with short-order preparation. Heat concentrated under kettles; heating elements and grates simple in design, easily removable for cleaning; gas cones elevated so combustion and ventilation can be complete; burners can be turned on and off as needed; instant heat available; high Btu output by means of small blower to force air into burner (Fig. C.1).

Figure C.1.   Open-top range with oven base. (Courtesy, U.S. Range, 14501 South Broadway, Gardena, California 90248.)

2. Closed top—styled for heavy-duty continuous cooking as entire surface area is heated; various burner arrangements. For gas:—*Uniform hot top:* even heat distribution from rows of bar burners set in fire brick under smooth top; depression in brick around edge acts as duct to flue in gas range. *Graduated heat:* by means of concentric ring burners with separate controls; intense heat in center (approximately 1100°F) to low heat at edge (450°F); projections on underneath side of top help direct heat to edges. *Front-fired* (gas): row of burners under front of range top; heat concentrated at front with gradation in degrees of heat intensity toward back (Fig. C.2).

3. Fry- or griddle-top—even heat; solid top with edges raised to prevent overflow of grease; fitted with grease trough and drain to receptacle (Fig. C.3).

Range ovens: even heat distribution, automatic pilot and heat control; high-quality insulation; walls, top, bottom, and removable racks or shelves of smooth, durable, cleanable material or finish; sturdy counterbalanced door with nonbreak-

Figure C.2. Closed-top range with oven base. (Courtesy, U.S. Range, 14501 South Broadway, Gardena, California 90248.)

able hinges, cool handle; door to support at least 200 pounds. Designed so spillage will drain to front for easier cleaning. Approximate size: 26 inches wide, 28 inches deep, 15 inches high (inside measurements).

Legs and feet: simple design; rigid support; adjustable legs; shaped at floor contact to prevent accumulation of dirt or harborage of vermin; sealed hollow sections; minimum clearance of 6 inches between floor and lowest horizontal parts unless mounted on raised masonry island at least 2 inches high and sealed to floor.

Installation: heavy-duty range sections often joined together with other modular units as broilers and fryers to make a complete cooking unit.

Griddles

Separate griddle units to supplement or substitute for range sections; mobile griddles give use where needed, such as kitchen or counter; extra-heavy, highly polished plates to hold heat and recover rapidly; even heat distribution;

Figure C.3.   Griddle-top or fry-top range with oven base. (Courtesy, U.S. Range, 14501 South Broadway, Gardena, California 90248.)

chromium or stainless front and ends; oversized, cool valve handles; sloped to grease drain-off. Sizes from 7 by 14 inches to 36 by 72 inches. Capacity expressed in terms of food that can be cooked at one time.

Two-Sided Cookers

A relative newcomer to the cooking equipment line-up, this type of cooker offers the benefits of both a griddle and a grill (see Fig. C.4). Some models sandwich food between a heated top and bottom plate, or platen. This eliminates the need for turning. Other models utilize a bottom plate and an infrared, noncontact broiler on top. Both gas and electric cookers are available and are constructed of stainless steel, varying in widths from 2 to 6 feet. The platens are made of cast iron, highly polished steel, cold-rolled steel, or a chrome finish.

Figure C.4.   A two-sided cooker, with a griddle on the bottom and a broiler on the top, cuts broiling time in half. (Courtesy, Lang Manufacturing Company, Redmond, Washington.)

Broilers

Sheet steel of 16 gauge or better, with smooth, baked-on black Japan finish, or stainless steel, rigidly reinforced with angle support; warp-resistant heating units with radiant ceramic or alloy materials to give even heat distribution, lining of long-wearing reflective materials; spring-balanced raising or lowering device; right- or left-hand operation; safety stop locks; close-fitting cast-iron grids, removable for easy cleaning, adjustable over distances of 1½ to 8 inches from heat source; removable drip tray; drain to receptacle; size of grid determines capacity.

Types: (1) Unit or heavy-duty broilers—designed for large volume production and fast continuous broiling; grid area varies from 3.3 to 5.0 square feet; may be same height as range section and with high shelf above or integral with an overhead oven, heated by burners in broiler below, or mounted on a conventional range-type oven and with or without overhead warming oven. (2) Combination broiler and griddle units—suitable for small kitchen where space is limited. Fry griddle forms top of broiler and both are heated by the same set of burners but simultaneous use not recommended. (3) Salamander or elevated miniature broiler—mounted above the top of a heavy-duty closed range or over a spreader plate between units of cooking equipment. Features are similar to heavy-duty broiler except for a smaller grid area of only 1.6 to 2.8 square feet. Advantage is that it requires no floor space but may be mounted on separate legs or stand if desired. Used where small amounts of broiled foods are served. (4) Hearth-type or open-top broilers—utilize a heavy cast iron grate horizontally above the heat source. Charcoal or chunks of irregular size ceramic or other refractory material above gas or electric burners, forms the radiant bed of heat. Juice and fat drippings cause smoking and flaming that necessitate an efficient exhaust fan over the broiler. Available in multiple sections of any desired length (Fig. C.5).

Fryers

Chromium-plated steel, stainless steel; automatic temperature control with signal light and timer; quick heat recovery; cool sediment zone; self-draining device; easy removal of sediment and filtering of fat; capacity expressed in pounds of fat or pounds cooked per hour; fuel input used to determine production capacity also; should fry from 1½ to 2 times the weight of fat per hour.

Types: (1) Conventional instant fat fryers—sizes from 11 by 11 to 24 by 24 in. with fat capacities 13 to 130 pounds. Models are available as free-standing, counter, or built-in, single, or multiple units. The bank of deep-fat fryers shown in Fig. C.6 is computer-controlled to automatically control temperature and cooking time by lowering and raising the frying baskets at precisely timed intervals. (2) Pressure fryers—equipped with tightly sealed cover, allowing moisture given off during cooking to build up steam pressure within kettle; cooking accomplished in approximately ⅓ normal time. (3) Semiautomatic—speed production model equipped with conveyer to permit continuous batch cooking and automatic discharge of product as completed. (4) Convection fryers. See Fig. C.7.

Installation: Adequate ventilation necessary, venting into hood recommended; flue venting from fryer to general vent flue not desirable; table or work space adjacent to fryer is necessary.

Tilting Frypan

Versatile piece of equipment—can be used as a frypan, braising pan, griddle, kettle, steamer, thawer, oven, food warmer-server; eliminates most top-of-stove

Figure C.5.   This countertop, underfired charbroiler has a tilting grate to draw off excess grease and to provide variable heat zones on the cooking surface. (Courtesy, U.S. Range, 14501 South Broadway, Gardena, California 90248.)

cooking and provides for one-step preparation of many menu items. All surfaces, interior and exterior heavy-duty stainless steel; contoured pouring spout; one-piece counterbalanced hinged cover; self-locking worm and gear tilt mechanism; even-heat smooth flat bottom (either gas or electric); automatic thermostatic heat controls for wide range of temperatures. Available in several sizes and capacities as floor models mounted on tubular legs with or without casters, wall-mounted, or small electric table-mounted (see Fig. C.8); conserves fuel and labor; quick-connect installation conducive to rapid rearrangement, easy maintenance, and good sanitation. Easy to clean and reduces use of pots and pans and their washing.

Ovens

Two basic designs for ovens: *still-air radiation,* in which heated air circulates around outside of heating chamber and radiates through lining, and *convection,* where heated air from heat source is forced over and around food racks by fans

Figure C.6. A system of computer-controlled fryers. (Courtesy, Dean Industries, a Welbilt Company, Shreveport, Louisiana.)

located on the rear wall of the oven. All welded construction of structural steel for durable rigid frames; inner lining of 18-gauge rustproof sheet metal reinforced to prevent buckling; minimum of 4 inches of nonsagging insulation on all sides, up to 10 inches in large bakery ovens; thermostatic heat control precise between 150° and 550°F; signal lights and timer; level oven floor or deck of steel, tile, or transite (concrete and asbestos combination); well-insulated, counterbalanced doors that open level with bottom of oven to support a minimum of 150-pound weight; nonbreakable hinges; concealed manifolds and wiring; cool handles; system designed to eject vapors and prevent flowback of condensate; light operated from outside oven; steam injector for baking of hard rolls; thermocouple attachments for internal food-temperature record, and glass windows in doors available upon request.

Types: (1) Deck—units stacked to save space; separate heating elements and controls for each unit and good insulation between decks; decks at good working heights; 7 or 8 inches clearance for baking, 12 to 16 inches high for roasting; capacity expressed in number of 18 by 26-inch bun pans per deck; pie, cake, or baking pans should be sizes to fit multiples of that dimension; floor space requirements and inside dimensions vary with types; example of a typical one-section oven of compact design on 23-inch legs:

Figure C.7.   Convection fryer combines convection cooking, continuous fat filtration, and heat exchanger to produce an energy efficient, highly productive piece of equipment. (Courtesy, Hobart Corporation.)

Figure C.8.   An example of a tilting frypan. (Courtesy, Groen Division, Dover Corporation.)

- Floor space requirements   60 ½ inches wide, 39½ inches deep without flue deflector
- Inside dimensions   42 inches wide, 32 inches deep, 7 inches high
- Capacity   Two 18 × 26-inch bun pans; 24 one-pound loaves of bread; 12 ten-inch pies
- Btu/hour   50,000

(2) Convection oven-forced air circulation cabinet, which employs high-speed centrifugal fan to force air circulation and guarantee even-heat distribution by an

air-flow pattern over and around product in a minimum of time or from one-third to three-quarters of time required in a conventional oven. More cooking is accomplished in smaller space as food is placed on multiple racks instead of on a single deck (see Fig. C.9).

Sizes vary with the manufacturers, but a typical convection oven measures 36 inches wide by 33 inches deep or larger models 45 inches wide by 42½ inches deep. Removable rack glides designed to accommodate 8 or 9 trays or baking sheets, 2 inches apart, thus holding more than other ovens that require greater floor space. Units may be stacked to double the output in the relatively small floor space. Convection ovens must be well insulated; may have interiors of stainless steel or vitreous enameled steel. Shelves and shelf supports lift out for easy cleaning; fitted with inside lights, timer, thermostatic heat control, glass doors or window in doors, removable spillage pan. Quick-connect installation and addition of casters made for flexibility in arrangement. Muffle-type seal on doors for roasting and baking reduce shrinkage because of moisture retention and reduced time for cooking.

(3) Revolving tray or reel ovens—flat tray decks suspended between two revolving spiders in a ferris-wheel type of rotation; compact, space saving; welded steel,

Figure C.9.   Filled baking trays placed in an oven-fitted frame can be rolled directly into this convection oven from a specially designed dolly. (Courtesy, The G. S. Blodgett Co., Inc.)

heat-tight construction; all parts highly resistant to heat and corrosion; main bearings and entire tray load supported independently of side walls; trays stabilized to keep level and sway proof; each tray equipped with individual emergency release; heavy-duty motor; smooth roller-chain drive, self-adjusting, automatic controls; example of relative dimensions; four trays, each 96 inches long by 26 inches wide; capacity, twenty 18 by 26-inch bun pans; outside, 10 feet 2 inches wide, 7 feet 4 inches deep, 6 feet 7 inches high. Small units 3½ feet deep and 6-pan units available for small foodservice operations.

(4) Rotary ovens—similar to revolving tray ovens except rotation is on a vertical axis instead of a horizontal one. Both revolving tray and rotary type ovens are most suitable for large volume baking.

(5) Microwave ovens—electromagnetic energy directed into heating cavity by magnetrons producing microwaves that penetrate food, create a magnetic field, and set up friction, causing almost instantaneous cooking of the food; energy produced at given rate is not stored nor does it heat the air surrounding or the dish containing the food (glass, china, plastic, paper); components include heating cavity of stainless steel, radio frequency generator, power supply, usually 220 volts, between 30 and 50 amperes; must pass close inspection to assure safety in use; automatic shut-off before door can be opened. Can be stacked; used extensively for fast reheating of prepared bulk or plated foods, but items can be cooked quickly and served immediately on the same dish.

(6) Combi ovens—combination convection oven, pressureless steamer, proofing cabinet, and cook-and-hold oven in a single compact unit (Fig. C.10a).

(7) Conveyor ovens—programmable for temperature/speed/heat zones, typically use one of three technologies: infrared—a radiant heating process that doesn't heat the air surrounding the food but transfers heat directly to the surfaces it contacts; jet sweep—sometimes called air impingement, hundreds of air ducts under and over the food sweep away cold air, cooking the food uniformly; convection—hot air is circulated by fans in the oven cavity (Fig. C.10b).

(8) Cook-and-hold ovens—food temperature rises until nearly done, then burner turns off and a fan continues to circulate stored heat. Once the hold temperature is reached, the burner and fan cycle to maintain heat.

Steam Equipment

Steam may be supplied from a central heating plant, directly connected to the equipment; or steam may be generated at point of use, which requires water connection and means of heating it to form the steam; pressures vary according to needs, with automatic pressure control and safety valve if supply is above 5 to 8 pounds per square inch (psi); equipment of stainless steel or aluminum for rust resistance; smooth exterior and interior surfaces for easy cleaning and sanitation; timing and automatic shut-off devices; concealed control valves; steam cookers offer fast cooking in two general types: cabinet steamers and steam-jacketed kettles.

(a)

(b)

Figure C.10. (*a*) This combination steamer oven is most suited to a small operation in which space is limited. (Courtesy, Groen Division, Dover Corporation.) (*b*) Air impingement technology is the design for this conveyor oven. (Photo courtesy of Lincoln Food Service Products, Inc.)

Cabinet Cookers

Steam injected into cooking chamber comes in direct contact with food—to ensure that steam is clean, the supply may need to be generated on-premise from a tap water source instead of from the steam system for a group of buildings; door gaskets to seal; doors of full-floating type, with automatic bar-type slide-out shelves linked to doors; timers and automatic shut-off, and safety throttle valve for each compartment so doors cannot be opened until steam pressure is reduced; perforated or solid baskets for food; capacity in terms of number of 12 by 20-inch counter pans side by side each shelf or 10 by 23-inch bulk pans. Counter pans are used both for cooking and serving.

Types: (1) Heavy-duty, direct connected steamers—compartments fabricated to form one-piece body and entire interior of stainless steel; 5 to 8 pounds per square inch with continuous steam inflow and drain-off of condensate; 1 to 4 compartments with adjustable shelves; inside dimensions 28 × 21 inches desirable to accommodate two 12 × 20-inch counter pans on each shelf, and 10 to 16 inches high. (2) Pressure cookers—operate at 15 pounds steam pressure for small-batch speed cooking; reheating frozen meals or thawing and cooking frozen foods; smaller than free-venting cabinets; self-sealing inside door cannot be opened under pressure; 15-pound safety valve and 30-pound gauge; automatic timers and cutoffs. Inside capacities, from 12 to 40 inches wide, 14 to 28 inches high, 18 to 31½ inches deep; 1 to 3 cooking compartments. (3) Self–steam-generating (nonpressure)—intended for installations without direct steam supply; requires water (hot preferred) connection and adequate source of heat supply to produce the steam; steam generators fit below cookers; designs and capacities similar to heavy-duty steamers. (4) Pressure-less forced convection steamers—high-speed steam cookers with convection generators producing turbulent steam, without pressure, in the cooking compartment. Doors may be safely opened at any time during cooking cycle, and cooking is faster than in the conventional pressure cooker.

Installation: heavy-duty steamers of cabinet type may have pedestal support or be equipped with feet and have at least 6-inch clearance from floor, or be wall-mounted to save space; install in drip pan or floor depression with drain; modular units available in many combinations with other steam equipment (Fig. C.11).

Steam-Jacketed Kettles

Two bowl-like sections of drawn, shaped, welded aluminum or stainless steel with air space between for circulation of steam to heat inner shell; food does not come in contact with steam; steam outlet safety valve and pressure gauge; steam pressure inside the jacket determines the kettle's operating temperature (e.g., 50 psi = 298°F); direct-connected or self-generated steam supply; full or two-thirds jacketed; stationary or tilting, open or fitted with no-drip, hinged and balanced cover (note Fig. C.12), mounted on tubular legs, pedestal, wall brackets, or set on table. Power twin-shaft agitator mixer attachment for stirring heavy mixtures while cooking, and electrically operated device to automatically meter water into kettle are available; may have cold water connection to jacket

Figure C.11.   Self–steam-generated jacketed kettles and compartment cooker designed as a single unit for a small operation.

to cool products quickly after cooking; modular design (square jacket) for easy combining with other modular equipment to save space. Basket inserts available for removing and draining vegetables easily (Fig. C.13).

> Types: (1) Deep kettles, fully or two-thirds, jacketed—best for soups, puddings, pie fillings. (2) Shallow kettles, always full-jacketed—suitable for braising and browning meats, stews; prevents crushing of under layers of food as in deep type. (3) Trunnion or tilting kettles—mounted on trunnions with tilting device and pouring lip for easy unloading; either power-driven or manual mechanism; self-locking devices to secure kettle in any position; large floor models, or small units mounted to table to form battery; used on deep or shallow-type kettles. Capacities: from 1 quart to 80 gallons; up to 12-gallon size suitable for table mounting and rotation vegetable cookery. (4) Stationary types for liquids or thin mixtures—tangent outlet for straight-flow drain-off; capacities: from 10 to 500 gallons.
>
> Installation: kettle set for easy draw-off of food; and drip into grated drain in floor or table; mixing swivel faucet over kettle to fill or clean; table models at height convenient for workers; adequate voltage or gas supply for self-generating models.

Figs. C.14 and C.15 show equipment designed to be used in the cook/chill or cook/freeze foodservice systems. As the diagram in Fig. C.14 shows, food is cooked, packaged in a special air- and water-tight plastic casing at or above pasteurization temperature, chilled rapidly in ice water, and stored up to 45 days in 28° to 32°F storage. Pumpable foods are cooked in mixer kettles, pumped into the casings, sealed, and chilled in the tumble chiller. Solid foods, such as

Figure C.12. Steam-jacketed kettle cover actuator assembly. Counter-balanced spring tension (*a*) holds cover securely tight, or (*b*) open in any position for safe, easy use; cover removable for cleaning. Suited for all types of kettles either floor- or wall-mounted, stationary, or tilting. (Courtesy, Groen Division, Dover Corporation.)

roasts, are browned, encased, and vacuum-sealed in casings, and then cooked in the cook/chill tank. In this tank, the product is water bath cooked and then rapidly cooled by circulation of ice water in the same tank. Rethermalization may be accomplished by convection oven, combi oven, a convection steamer, pressure steamer, or steam kettles. Fig. C.15 shows a cook/chill system designed for a small foodservice operation.

Mixers

Bench models for use on tables, counters, back bars, and floor models; 3- or 4-speed transmission, ball-bearing action; timed mixing control with automatic shut-off; action designed for thorough blending, mixing, and aerating of all ingredients in bowl; electrically controlled brake; possible to change speeds while in action on some machines; durable washable finish as stainless steel or anodized aluminum. Bowls: heavily tinned steel, or stainless steel (see Fig. C.16).

(a)

(b)

Figure C.13.   Steam-jacketed kettle showing (*a*) swivel power mixer attachment assembly mounted on extension of back leg of trunnion-type kettle; (*b*) cross-section view of triple basket insert for holding and draining vegetables cooked in kettle. (Courtesy, Groen Division, Dover Corporation.)

RETHERMALIZATION

MIXER KETTLE

SOUPS, SAUCES, STEWS ETC.

METERING STATION, CLIPPER & LABELLER

BAGGED & LABELLED FOOD

TUMBLE CHILLER

CONVECTION OVENS

COMBI OVEN/ STEAMER

PRESSURE CONVECTION STEAMER

SKILLET

SOUPS, SAUCES, STEWS ETC.

FOOD AT 40°F

FOOD BANK
(for storage (30°F)
up to 45 days)

BROWNED & SEARED ROASTS

CONVECTION STEAMERS

VACUUM PACKAGING SYSTEM & LABELLER

BAGGED & LABELLED FOOD

COOK/CHILL TANK

FOOD AT 40°F

KETTLES

Vertical; Sweep & Fold™ Tilting Mixer Kettles

COOK/CHILL MIXER KETTLES are especially designed and equipped for cooking pumpable food products. A sequential microprocessor and time/temperature recorder combined with automatic water cooling and water metering assures that the product is always cooked to your specifications. The infinitely variable scraper speed and adjustable scraper/agitator ratio assures the best possible mixing conditions for any product and proper suspension during pumping.

Horizontal; Stationary, Mixer Kettles

Horizontal agitator, MIXER KETTLES have processed food for years in industrial applications. This system is now also available for the food service industry. The patented, easily removable agitator is ideal for blending thick and heavy products at a gentle speed. The removable, sanitary temperature sensor is connected to the temperature set point controls and chart recorder.

Metering Filling Stations

METERING FILLING STATIONS are designed to pump cooked foods from MIXER KETTLES and TILT SKILLETS and accurately meter into special Cryovac® casings or other containers. A clipper and labeler are mounted conveniently on the cross bar for one or two person operation. The air operated piston pump has infinitely variable volume adjustment and is designed for easy cleaning and long life.

Tumbler Chillers

TUMBLE CHILLERS cool casing packaged products from 180°F to 40°F in 25 to 65 minutes depending on the product. The gentle tumble action in recirculating ice water assures maximum storage life without product damage. Casings are loaded through the entry chute by hand or conveyor. Fully automated controls assure correct chilling prior to removal and 30°F refrigerated storage.

Cook/Chill Tanks

COOK/CHILL TANKS are designed for water bath cooking of packaged meats and other prepared items. Low temperature cooking reduces shrinkage, ensures tenderness while retaining natural juices and flavor. When the desired cooking process is complete, hot water is automatically exchanged for ice water, efficiently reducing food temperature to below 40°F in minimum time.

Ice Builders

ICE BUILDERS are designed to provide a continuous supply of ice water to TUMBLE CHILLERS, COOK/CHILL TANKS and COOK/CHILL MIXER KETTLES. The system economically builds ice up to 24 hours a day and circulates the ice water when required through heat exchangers to maintain sanitary water at the chilling source.

Figure C.14. A cook/chill system and its components. (Courtesy, Cleveland Range, Inc., Cleveland, Ohio.)

Figure C.15. A cook/chill system with (from left to right) a combination tumble chiller cook tank, a fill stand, a horizontal agitator mixer kettle, and a component control center. (Courtesy, Cleveland Range, Inc., Cleveland, Ohio.)

Figure C.16. Mixers are available in many sizes and capacities. Thorough mixing of ingredients is made possible by the planetary action of the beater or whip. (Courtesy, Blakeslee.)

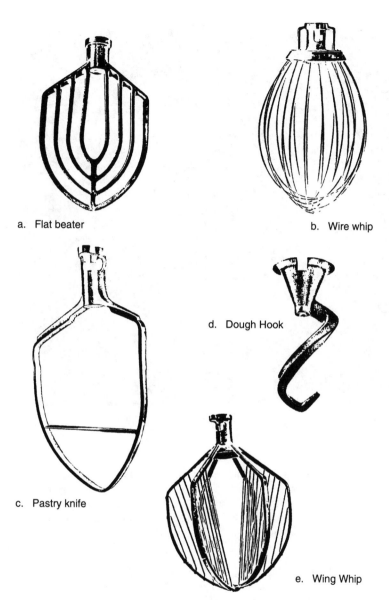

a. Flat beater

b. Wire whip

d. Dough Hook

c. Pastry knife

e. Wing Whip

Figure C.17.   Mixer attachments. (Product of Hobart Corporation, Troy, Ohio.)

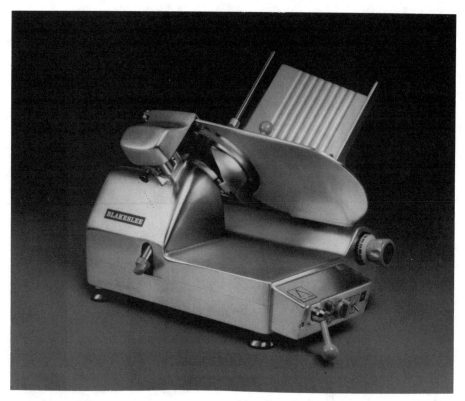

Figure C.18. A slicer with an angle-fed trough. (Courtesy, Blakeslee.)

Standard equipment: one bowl, one flat beater, one wire whip; other attachments available such as bread hook, pastry knife (see Fig. C.17), chopper, slicer, dicer, oil dripper, bowl splash cover, dolly, purchased separately; most models have one or two adapters with smaller bowls, beaters, and whips that may be used on same machine. Capacities: 5 to 200 quarts.

Choppers, Cutters, Slicers

Some foodservices meet their needs for chopping, slicing, and shredding through the use of mixer attachments; others need specialized pieces of equipment in certain work areas. Various sizes and capacities of such machines are available in pedestal or bench models or mounted on portable stands. A typical slicer is shown in Fig. C.18. All should be made of smooth, noncorrosive metals, have encased motors, safety protectors over blades, and parts removable for cleaning and should slice in horizontal or angle-fed troughs. Fig. C.19 illustrates how a slicer and portion control scale may be combined into one piece of equipment.

Figure C.19. Automatic portion control scale slicer is adaptable to operate with most late model gravity feed automatic slicers. It is designed to shut off the slicer when a preset weight of thinly sliced meat drops onto the scale platter. (Courtesy, E. L. Sly Co., Portland, Oregon.)

Vertical Speed Cutter Mixer

High-speed vertical cutter-mixer (Fig. C.20), gray enamel cast iron base, stainless steel or aluminum bowl; blades move at 1,100 to 3,400 rpm giving increased product yield and quality as well as speed over conventional mixing. Mixes, cuts, blends, whips, creams, grates, kneads, chops, emulsifies, and homogenizes. Counterbalanced bowl cover interlocks with motor; easy tilt design for emptying. Mounted on tubular steel frame equipped with casters for portability or permanent installations; variety of cutting blades, shafts, and baffles for specific uses. Capacities: 25, 40, 60, 80, and 130 quarts; 40-quart model handles 80 pounds ingredients in one load. Cuts 40 pounds frozen meat and blends for meat loaf in 40 seconds; 12 heads lettuce in 3 seconds.

Refrigerators

Detailed information in Chapter 8. Central or self-contained units; water- or air-cooled compressors; walk-in, reach-in, pass-through, cabinet convertible

Figure C.20. High-speed cutter-mixer knife blades move at 1,100 to 3,400 revolutions per minute. Prepares foods for cooking or serving in seconds. (Product of Hobart Corporation, Troy, Ohio.)

Figure C.21. Convenient unit refrigerator; exterior surfaced with thermal-bonded vinyl in choice of colors, interior silver-tone white vinyl; doors same as outside finish or sliding glass; 3-inch thick glass fiber insulation; may be fitted with pan slides or shelves and 5-inch swivel casters. (Product of Hobart Corporation, Troy, Ohio.)

temperatures; efficient nonabsorbent insulation; tight-fitting doors, strong no-sag hinges, strong catches; all surfaces and parts cleanable. *Reach-in:* fitted with tray glides to accommodate standard tray sizes, or removable wire or slatted stainless steel shelves (note Fig. C.21). *Walk-in:* portable, sectional, slatted metal shelving. Some reach-in models can be detached from motor unit to provide portable, temporary refrigerated storage.

Counter units: individual compressors for salad, frozen dessert, milk storage areas; self-leveling dispensers for cold or freezer storage and service. *Ice makers:* central and self-contained units; cubes, tubes, flakes, capacity, measured in output per hour; many models and sizes are available. *Water coolers:* glass filler or bubbler faucet; capacity; depends on cooling volume per hour and size of storage tank; designed for convenient storage of clean glasses.

Dish and Utensil Cleaning Equipment

(1) Pot and pan cleaners. *Manually controlled power scrubbing brush,* cleans and polishes; multiple use with accessories, extension cords, scouring brushes, buffers; requires no extra space. *Water agitator attachment for pot soaking sinks;* loosens cooked-on food; can be installed with limited space. Dishwashers, pot and pan washers, glass washers. Stainless steel, welded construction; operation control, manual or automatic. This type of equipment is discussed in detail in Chapters 7 and 8.

Dishwashers: undercounter or floor models; single or multiple tank; semi- or fully automatic operation; rack, rack conveyor or flight style conveyor for continuous racking (see Figs. C.22 a, b, c); doors or curtains; automatically timed conveyor speed; separate temperature controls for rinse, wash, and final rinse; automatic detergent dispenser; parts removable for cleaning; inspection door for easy access to wash and rinse compartments; scrapping, prerinse, and blower-type assemblies available; water—pressure, temperature, hardness, pipe size; waste disposer. Model designed especially to accommodate trays is illustrated in Fig. C.23.

Capacity expressed in number of pieces washed per hour, many sizes from 1-tray bench model, 22 inches long, 23 inches wide up to heavy-duty conveyor machine, approximately 30 feet long. Trend is toward smaller units or circular units to conserve space.

Racks: chrome-plated or stainless steel, plastic-coated, removable, and adaptable dividers; or all-plastic, light-weight, space-saving nesting racks. Open divided racks for cups, glasses; designed for stacking in storage.

Flight-style conveyors: linked metal, plastic, or metal tipped with plastic or nylon projections to hold dishes in inclined position.

Waste Disposers

One system for the disposal of waste may solve the problem in a given situation but, in many cases, it may be feasible to combine two or more of the following methods.

Unit disposers for food waste at vegetable and salad preparation, sinks, and dish scrapping areas eliminate the need for garbage can collections, storage, and outside pickup unless their installation and use are prohibited by environmental controls. All waste paper, cardboard cartons, wood crates, plastics, tin cans, broken china, and glassware (and garbage) might need to be discharged

Figure C.22.   Examples of (*a*) single tank,
(*b*) double tank, and (*c*) flight-type
dishwashers. (Courtesy, Hobart Corporation,
Troy, Ohio.)

(a)

(b)

(c)

Figure C.23.   Machine designed especially for washing trays. (Courtesy, Insinger Machine Company.)

into dumpster bins for pickup if incineration of burnable waste is restricted by antipollution regulations in the community.

Can and bottle crushers are capable of reducing this type of disposable bulk up to 90% and cut labor costs, refuse space, and cost of pickup. Capacities of models vary from 50 cans and bottles per minute to 7,500 per hour. Design of such a crushing mechanism is shown in Fig. C.24.

The use of *compactors* to reduce the volume is a convenient and economical aid to the disposal of all waste in many foodservices. One model with 13,000 pounds of force can compact paper, milk cartons, cans, bottles, and food scraps to a minimum 5-to-1 ratio or as high as 20-to-1, depending on the combination of materials. Discharge of the compacted material, up to 50 pounds, into a polybag or carton on a dolly makes it ready for short-time storage and haulaway. Most machines operate on a 120-volt, 20-ampere outlet, have safety interlocks throughout for operating protection, and a sanitizing-deodorizing spray that may be released at each return stroke of the compaction ram to avoid any objectionable odor from the compacted mass (Fig. C.25).

Figure C.24. Rugged crushing mechanism of can and bottle crusher. Rollers set in "v" design prevent clogging and progressively reduce cans to smallest bulk possible. (Courtesy, Qualheim, Inc.)

The *pulping system* reduces the volume of disposable materials such as food scraps, paper, plastic, and cooked bones up to 85%, depending on the mix. Cans, silverware, and some glass are tolerated, but are automatically ejected from the pulping tank into a trash box. Durable teeth on a rotating disc and cutters pulp the material in the tank. It is then circulated to a powerful waterpress above, reducing the pulp to a semidry form that is forced into a discharge chute to containers for removal as low-volume waste. The water from the press recirculates to the pulping tank. This equipment is available in several sizes. It may be incorporated into the dishwashing system or other area where pulpable waste originates (see Fig. C.26).

Transport Equipment

Usually powered equipment for transport of food and supplies within a foodservice is kept to minimum distances by careful planning of area relationships. A thorough study of the advantages, capabilities, and maintenance factors should precede the selection of a system for a particular situation. Also, automatic and emergency shutoffs, enclosed but easy access to working parts, safety, and cleanability are important features to consider.

Conveyors and Subveyors

Reverse for two-way service; emergency brakes; safety guards; automatic stop and start with removal of tray, or continuous flow. *Conveyors:* horizontal transportation; stationary or mobile units for flexibility of tray or food assembly.

Figure C.25.   This mobile, hydraulic trash compactor can reduce trash to 1/10 of its original size and features a compactor dolly for ease of unloading of the compacted trash. (Courtesy, Precision Metal Products, Inc.)

Figure C.26. Diagram showing how pulpable waste can be reduced in volume and form. (Product of Hobart Corporation, Troy, Ohio.)

Subveyors: vertical conveying, used where space may be limited on a single floor and work or serving units are on different floors.

Monorail and Driverless Vehicles

These require special equipment and installations; reduce labor and hand-pushing of carts; speedy; relatively expensive to install. Monorail requires overhead rail and "Amsco" system, a special electronic track under the floor. Cars of the latter are monitored from a control panel; powered by batteries; directed over the track to locations on the same floor or to a bank of special elevators that automatically open and close on signal and exit on the assigned floor.

Nonmechanical Kitchen Equipment

Tables and Sinks

Often fabricated by specification order to fit space and need; stainless steel, No. 12 or 14 gauge. No. 4 grind; welded and polished joinings; rounded corner construction; seamless stainless steel tubular supports with welded cross rails and braces of same material; adjustable inside threaded stainless steel rounded or pear-shaped feet; worktables may be fitted with ball-bearing rubber-tired casters, 2 swivel and 2 stationary, brakes on 2 casters.

For *tables:* Top of one sheet without seams; edges; integrally finished, rolled edge, raised rolled edge where liquids are used, turned up as flange, or splashback and with rolled edge. Legs and feet: tubular, welded, or seamless metal; adjustable; simple design; provide a minimum of 6 inches of space between bottom of unit and floor; drawers: operate on ball bearings, equipped with stop, removable. Undershelves: stationary bar, slatted, solid, removable sections; sink or bain-marie; note Fig. C.27.

Dimensions: standard, length 48, 60, 72, 84, 96, 108, 120 inches; width 24, 30, 36 inches; height, 34 inches; other dimensions by individual specification.

Types: *Baker's tables*—fitted with drawers; separate storage bins as specified. *Salad tables*—with or without refrigerated work space and storage, sinks. *Sandwich tables*—refrigerated storage for fillings; removable cutting boards. *Dish tables*—well-braced sturdy understructure; 3-inch upturned and rolled edges, higher if joined to wall; scrap block, waste drain, sinks for soaking, over-and-under shelves, rack return, tray rest; adequate space for receiving, soiled dishes, clean dishes, preflush.

For *sinks:* one, two, three compartments; all-welded seamless construction, drainboard and splashback integral from one sheet of metal, rolled edges; corners fully rounded with 1-inch radius, coves spherical in shape at intersection of corners; bottom of each compartment scored and pitched to outlet: outlet recessed 5 inches in diameter, ½-inch deep, fitted with nonclog waste outlet; partitions: two thicknesses formed of one sheet of metal, folded and welded to bottom and sides of sink; provision for overflow; drainboards pitched to drain into sink; drainboards supported by channel braces to sink legs or wall-bracketed, if longer than 42 inches usually supported by two pipe legs at end away from sink; removable strainer at waste outlet; external lever control for outlet valve; stationary or swing faucets.

Dimensions, standard single compartment, 20, 24, 30, 36, 48, 60, 72 inches long, 20, 24, 30 inches wide, 14, 16 inches deep; two-compartment, 36, 42, 48, 54, 60, 72 inches long, 18, 22, 24, 30 inches wide, 14, 16 inches deep. Others by individual specification; 38-inch height convenient for sinks.

Figure C.27. Kitchen worktable. Note simplicity of design, rounded edges and corners of top, smooth joinings of tubular supports, and rounded feet or may be fitted with casters. (Courtesy, S. Blickman, Inc.)

Storage Cabinets, Racks, Carts

Cabinets and racks stationary or portable. Open or closed; shelves: attached, removable, adjustable, tray slides; sturdy construction for use; solid floor; bolted or welded; doors, hinged, or side sliding, side sliding removable, suspension hung. Both stationary or portable types can be heated or refrigerated. Size determined by needs and space.

Scales

Heavy-duty *platform scale* built into floor of receiving room area for weighing in supplies and food; weight indicator should be plainly visible from both front and back. *Exact-weight* floor or table models in storeroom, ingredient room, bakeshop, and where recipes are made up. *Portion scales* for weighing individual servings where needed. All types of scales are now available with electronic (LED) readouts, locking in accurate weight almost instantly on an easy-to-read screen, as in Fig. C.28.

Cooking Utensils

Strong and durable to withstand heavy wear; nontoxic material; resistant to chipping, dents, cracks, acids, alkalis; cleanable; even heat spread; highly polished metal reflects heat, dull metal absorbs and browns food more readily in baking; variety of sizes of sauce pans, sauce pots, stock pots, frypans, roast and bake pans; *aluminum heavy-duty*—double-thick bottoms, extra-thick edge; *semiheavy*—lighter weight, uniform thickness, rolled edge; *stainless steel*—uniform thickness, spot heats over direct fire. Small equipment as pudding pans, pie and cake pans, quart and gallon measures, mixing bowls of lighter weight metals. Pudding and counter pans selected to fit serving table, refrigerator, and mobile racks for flexibility of use: 12 by 20-inch-size recommended. Clamped on lids cut spillage losses in transporting prepared foods.

Cutlery

High-carbon tooled steel or high-carbon chrome-vanadium steel; full tang construction, compression-type nickel-silver rivets; shapes of handles and sizes of items varied to meet needs; handle and blade weight balanced for easy handling.

Model PS10F

Figure C.28.   An electronic portion control food scale gives accurate weight almost immediately on a large lighted electronic display (LED) readout. This model is shown with an AC adaptor and optional foot pedal control. (Courtesy, Pelouze Scale Company.)

Serving Equipment

Counters

Attractive, compact, efficient arrangement designed for specific foodservice; welded and polished in one piece; hot and cold units well insulated; easily cleaned; separate temperature controls for each unit of heated section; counter guard shields for open food display sections; portable or built-in self-leveling dish and tray storage may be desired; adequate tray slide to prevent accidents.

Serving Utensils

Variety of sizes of ladles, long-handled spoons, perforated, slotted, and solid; spatulas; and ice cream dippers; selected to give predetermined portions size. Capacity or size marked on ladle handles and on dippers.

Special counter equipment: Convenient arrangement; easily operated automatic heat controls. Coffee maker—urn or battery vacuum makers with cup storage near; toasters, egg cookers, grills with hoods; temporary storage cabinets for hot cooked foods, rolls—controls for temperature and moisture content; freezer cabinet unit for ice creams; bread dispensers; milk-dispensing machines.

Self-Leveling Dispensers

Counterweighted springs bring platform to uniform level upon removal of item; for foods, dishes, containers; heated, refrigerated, or freezer storage; mobile, stationary, or built-in; open or closed frames of stainless, galvanized, carbon steel or aluminum; noncorrosive springs. Tube type: for plates, saucers, bowls; chassis type; accommodates square or rectangular trays, or racks, empty or filled; adjustable to vary dispensing height (see Fig. C.29).

Coffee Makers

Coffee-making equipment falls into two general types: (1) urns for making large quantities of coffee when many people are served in a short period of time, and (2) small electronic automatic brewing units for a continuous fresh supply of the beverage. Requirements are fairly simple in either case, but important to the making of an acceptable product: glass or stainless steel liners for urns, glass or stainless steel decanters for the automatic brewing machines; fluted paper filters; controlled hot water temperature, coffee and water measurement, infusion time, brewing speed and holding temperatures; easily cleaned. Installation with quick-disconnect utilities outlets provide for easy relocation of equipment (see Fig. C.30). The use of freeze-dried coffee simplifies the process, reduces time and labor, and eliminates the necessity of discarding coffee grounds.

Mobile Food Serving Carts

Specialized equipment for transporting bulk or served food some distance to the consumer; well-insulated, automatic temperature controls; engineered for ease in moving and turning; circumference bumper guards; designed for easy cleaning; may require high voltage outlets; combination heated, nonheated, low temperature, and refrigerated sections; beverage dispensers and other accessories as found on serving counters (see Chapter 6 for details).

Figure C.29.   Mobile self-leveling china dispensers can also be specified with heating mechanisms. (Courtesy, Precision Metal Products, Inc.)

Figure C.30. Coffee dispenser uses brewed liquid coffee concentrate to produce regular and decaffeinated coffee. (Courtesy, Pasco Packing Company.)

The selection of foodservice equipment by any arbitrary rule would be unwise and ill-advised. Each operation must be studied to determine the real needs and purchases made accordingly. *The foregoing statements are suggested as a guide only in helping to recall basic considerations regarding various items of equipment.*

China

TYPES OF CHINA   There are three types of china: vitrified, semivitrified, and pottery. Of these, only vitrified is considered durable enough for use in most foodservices.

Vitrified china, also known as porcelain, is made of excellent quality clay free from iron, with flint and feldspar added. These materials plus water can be shaped and fired to a high temperature for at least 60 hours, which fuses the mixture into a homogeneous body that is durable and virtually nonabsorbent. At this point, the shaped piece is known as "bisque." A notable improvement in making vitrified china was effected by the introduction of a metallic ion "alumina" into the body of the materials. This enabled the industry to make a thinner, whiter, stronger piece of china with greater edge chip resistance, greater impact strength, and smoother body that has faster surface cleanability than china made without alumina.

The U.S. Bureau of Standards has established three standards for vitrified china for institutional use:

1. Thick—5/16 to 3/8 inches thick (which is quite heavy)
2. Hotel—5/23 to 1/4 inches thick, with a rolled underedge
3. Medium-weight—sold on the market as "banquet" weight; thinner than hotel weight and has straight edges

The bureau also tests and sets limits for moisture absorption for each size piece, and tests for durability by use of chipping, impact, and breakage tests under stated conditions. Fig. C.31 shows a resistance-to-breakage test being conducted by one china manufacturer to ensure that government standards are met.

Figure C.31. The resistance to breakage of china can be measured accurately. (Courtesy, Syracuse China Company.)

It is essential that the buyer recognize that weight does not mean strength and long life for china. Durability and strength are far more directly related to the quality of materials used and the methods of manufacture employed than they are to weight.

The thick china is commonly used for lunch counter service or other situations where extra heavy service is demanded of the table appointments. It is clumsy to handle and apt to be unattractive in appearance. All hotel-weight china except cups have a roll under the outer edge that gives the effect of weight and also lessens chipping on the upper side of the plate. This type of china is well-adapted for use in institutions such as hospitals, residence halls, and restaurants. It is highly resistant to shock, easy to handle, and available in many designs and colors. Banquet-weight china is used extensively in exclusive restaurants, clubs, and the private room service of hospitals. It resembles more closely household dinnerware.

Vitrified heat-resistant ware of good quality is nonabsorbent, stainproof, and withstands high temperatures without crazing or breaking. Items are available in a variety of attractive colors and designs and include coffee pots, teapots, casseroles, ramekins, and individual pudding or pie dishes.

Semivitrified china is a good quality earthenware that has been fired insufficiently to obtain vitrification. This treatment results in a soft body, which is, therefore, porous and absorbent. Semivitrified china has been given a glaze that seals and finishes the dish, but the glaze may be sensitive to heat shocks and checks easily. The design may not be permanent as it is applied after the china is glazed and fired in making semivitrified and semiporcelain china.

DECORATION   Three methods are used to put color, designs, and decorations on china:

1. Lining—a line design applied to the edge or rim of the dish by machine; only one color can be used.
2. Printing—any type of design may be applied by this stamping or printing-on process.
3. Decalcomania process is used when two or more colors in the design are desired.

After the colored design has been applied on vitrified china by whatever method, the item is dipped into a glaze and fired at a high temperature. The glaze is a molten glass that is applied as a coating to the shaped, fired, and decorated dish and is fused to it. This process seals the surface of the bisque, covers and protects the design, further strengthens the body, makes the surface smooth, and is then highly resistant to chemicals and to cracking, crazing, or marring by physical shock.

Certain colors such as some blue pigments and the application of gold trim are affected by high temperatures of the firing of the glaze, so may be applied after the glazing process. This design over the glaze is not as satisfactory as under glaze for institutional foodservice use in most situations. The colors and gold that are put on top of the glaze are less durable and wear away faster than those that are put on under the glaze and protected by it.

FACTORS IN SELECTION OF CHINA   The things to consider in selecting china are its weight, the color and design, budget, availability of replacement, shapes, sizes, and capacities. In addition, in purchasing china, "firsts" the most perfect pieces that can be selected from each run of the kiln after the firing process, are the most desirable. They are free from warping, chips, faults in the glaze, thin or uneven glaze, large scars on the underside from the pins on which the china was held during firing, and uneven or poorly applied designs. Other pieces are graded as "seconds" or "thirds," depending on the degree of imperfection. Warped plates are detected by rolling several plates on edge simultaneously. The warped ones show up plainly in the rolling in contrast to the first selection. Close inspection of each piece by experienced workers completes the grading process.

The *color and design* of the china selected should be in harmony with the overall motifs and general atmosphere desired in the dining area. Pigments and processes have been so perfected that at the present time there is practically no limit to the color and design possibilities of china. Conservative but attractive designs enhance the beauty of any dining room and ordinarily do not detract from interest in the food. Colors primarily used for the body of china are white, off-white, or ivory, and buff or tan. These complement natural food colors and serve as a good background for them. Design colors should harmonize. Gaudy and naturalistic designs in the center of plates seem to leave little room for food. Also, such designs may add 5% to 25% of the cost of each plate. In contrast, an inexpensive design may be created with a colored edge for the dominant note.

That the choice of china is influenced by the size of the budget is evident. Not infrequently, the budget limits the choice to the china with the simple border pattern, which may or may not have artistic appeal. Managers need to weigh values of beauty and durability along with cost in the selection of china. Interest in and demand for good design in less expensive china has influenced manufacturers to produce such items.

Another factor that may influence choice is the available designs for which *replacements* can be obtained within a reasonable time period. Stock types of patterns are usually available for immediate shipment. Specially made china, such as that having a monogram or crest, must be ordered weeks in advance. This fact must be considered along with the relatively higher cost of such special china in selecting a pattern for any specific service. Even open-stock types of patterns may be discontinued with limited notice; so when the initial selection is made, the possibility of replacements with identical china or that similar in type should be considered.

Another consideration in selecting china is the *shape* of the pieces because there are many different ones on the market. Plates are available with a wide flat

1 to 1½-inch rim; Econo-Rim, which is ¼ to ⅜-inch rolled under edge, designed to save space on trays and in storage and give extra strength to the edge; and coupe-shape, which is a no-rim design with the body of the plate scooped or slightly concave. Cups are made in a low, wide shape and in a taller, slender shape with a much narrower opening, which holds heat in the beverage longer and stores easier than the more open shape. In addition, mugs of all sizes and shapes, some footed and some not, have become popular in many foodservices and eliminate the need for saucers.

A wide range of *sizes and capacities* of china is available and can vary somewhat from manufacturer to manufacturer. The present trend in purchasing is to limit the number of different size dishes, supplying one size for several uses. For example, instead of buying both 4-inch bread and butter plates and 6-inch salad/dessert plates, a 5-inch plate to satisfy both uses can be purchased. Or, instead of ordering different size bowls for soup, cereals, and similar items, one size is purchased for all. This simplification is advantageous from the standpoint of service, inventory, dishwashing, replacement, and storage.

The size of plates is the measurement from outer rim to outer rim, and that is the size specified when ordering. Cups, bowls, sugar bowls, creamers, and pitchers are specified by capacity in terms of ounces.

AMOUNTS TO PURCHASE   The quantity of dinnerware to be purchased for equipping a foodservice depends on many factors: the seating capacity and total number of people to be served, the length of the serving period, the type of menu and the price of the meal, the kind of service, the dishwashing facilities and whether they are used intermittently or continuously, and the caliber and speed of the employees. Other factors not to be overlooked are the variety of sizes of each item to be stocked and the frequency of use of the piece. For example, if only one size plate is purchased for multiple use as a bread and butter, salad, and underliner, fewer total pieces would be required than if three different-size plates had been selected. Also, a larger number of coffee cups used many times a day must be purchased to provide a margin of safety than would be necessary for bouillon cups that may be used only once or twice a week.

Any listing of quantities must be determined by the needs of a particular institution and not by a set formula. The following suggestions for the number of each item of dinnerware needed per customer in a foodservice using an intermittent dishwashing cycle might be used as a basis for initial planning.

Item	Number Per Customer
Cups	1.25
Saucers	1.25
9-inch plates	1.0
5-inch plates	0.66
Bowls, cereal	0.5
Sauce dishes	0.5

CARE China has a much longer life when handled carefully and cleaned properly. It is believed that most breakage is caused by china hitting against china, and that 75% to 80% of all breakage occurs in the soiled dish and washing area. Careful training and supervision of the personnel do much to prevent breakage and keep dishes looking bright and clean. Procedures to reduce the number of times a piece of china is handled will also assist in this. Examples are to separate and stack soiled dishes into like kinds before taking them to the dishroom for washing, and to store clean cups and glasses in the racks in which they are washed. Rubber plate scrappers and collars on openings in scrapping tables not only decrease noise but help to reduce breakage of dishes. Also helpful are the use of plastic and other synthetic-coated metal dishracks and plastic or nylon pegs on dishmachine conveyors.

Suitable washing compound, proper temperature of wash and rinse waters, in addition to careful attention throughout the scrapping, washing, and stacking and storing of clean dishes contribute to the lifespan of china.

The soiled dishes, scrapped and ready for the machine, are placed on belts or in racks, so that all surfaces are exposed. Sorting and stacking dishes into piles of the same kind and size helps to reduce breakage. The loading of one type of dishes in the racks or on the conveyor belt speeds washing at both the loading and unloading ends of the machine and ensures better wash action, since there is no overlapping of larger dishes to block the spray. After the washing and rinsing, the china is air dried. Plates of like size are stacked carefully so that the bottom rim of one does not mar the surface of the plate beneath it. Cups and glasses are stored in the wash racks, stacked on dollies, and wheeled to the unit where they will be used next. Plates and bowls likewise may be placed directly from the dishmachine into self-leveling mobile units or onto dish storage trucks where they remain until needed. Thus, breakage is lowered through reduced handling, and fewer labor hours are required for this one-time handling as opposed to storing dishes in a cupboard and then having to remove them when needed.

Generally, breakage is highest on small plates, saucers, and fruit dishes; they are often stacked too high and slide off the trays or carts; handles are broken from cups; and the edges of large heavy plates may be chipped if stacked carelessly. As a means of reducing breakage through carelessness, it is advisable to make a frequent inventory of stock in circulation. Thus, the workers become aware that a constant check of breakage is being made. Often a price list of china is posted, so the total loss to the foodservice through breakage is made known to the workers. Supervisors, too, should try to determine how and where breakage is occurring, if it seems unreasonably high, and then include corrective procedures in training sessions held for those workers involved in dish handling.

Replacement of china may be made as breakage demands, or provision may be made for a stockroom supply ample for the probable yearly need. In this case, replacement may be made of the storeroom stock following the annual inventory. Managers should be aware of the supply of dishes in circulation and an ample quantity made available so service is not slowed because of a lack of clean dishes when needed.

Glass Dinnerware

A popular dinnerware made by the Corning Glass Company is a basic glass in which a percentage of the sand used in its manufacture is replaced with aluminum powder. The resulting dinnerware is strong, thin, well-tempered, has a smooth surface, and is highly resistant to stains, heat, scratching, and breakage. It is available in a variety of sizes, shapes, and decorative designs on a white background. The cost is less than that of some high-quality vitrified china dinnerware. The amounts to order and the care of Corning dinnerware is comparable to china.

Plastic Dinnerware

The introduction and availability of synthetic compounds for molded dinnerware has given competition to china and glass for use in some types of institution foodservices. The history of the development of a suitable and highly acceptable product has been a long one.

Celluloid (1868), an early synthetic thermoplastic compound and a forerunner of modern plastics, was made of cellulose nitrate and camphor. Its nonresistance to heat, high inflammability, and camphor odor and flavor made it unsuitable for dishware. In the next period of development (1908), phenol and formaldehyde were incorporated into a thermosetting compound that was capable of being molded under pressure and heat into forms that would retain their shapes under mechanical strains, at well above the temperature of boiling water. This type of compound has had wide and varied usage, but because of its odor and unattractive brownish color, its use in the foodservice industry was limited mainly to counter and serving trays. The substitution of urea for phenol made it possible to produce a white compound of great strength that would take colors well. The basic cost of this material was high; therefore, it was often made into thin dishes suitable only for picnic or limited use and that could be sold for a reasonably low price.

During World War II, it was found that melamine could be combined with formaldehyde to give a tough resin that could withstand the demands on it in high-altitude flying equipment. This type of melamine plastic compound is now used in the production of dinnerware, often called melamine ware.

The first heavy-duty dinnerware made of melamine-formaldehyde compounds contained a chopped cotton cloth filler. The products had a high tensile and impact strength but were unattractive and limited to a low color range. Compounds made by blending long-fiber, high-grade paper stock with melamine resin and colorfast pigments are used in the production of dinnerware at the present time. This material is known as alpha-cellulose–filled, melamine-formaldehyde, thermosetting molding compound, and the products made from it are available in a wide range of colors and designs.

The melamine compound undergoes chemical change in the molding process under pressure of some 3,000 to 3,500 pounds per square inch at 335°F, which gives the dinnerware pieces a smooth lustrous surface, resistant to scratching, chippage, breakage, detergents, and grease. Also, it is not affected by the hot water used in dishwashing. Because the color pigment is thoroughly blended with the compound before molding, there is no fading of the finished product.

The permanent decoration of melamine dinnerware is made possible by opening the press when the material has just been shaped and adding a melamine-impregnated overlay, with the lithographed side placed down onto the dish. The mold is closed and, during the cure, the overlay becomes an integral part of the base material, and the resulting product has a smooth wear-resistant and protective glaze over the design.

FACTORS IN SELECTING PLASTICWARE   The U.S. Department of Commerce has established standards for heavy-duty type of melamine dishes. Foodservices should specify that the ware being purchased complies with Commercial Standards (CS) 173-50 that relate to thickness, resistance to acids, boiling water, dry heat, and the finished product.

Sample pieces of plasticware may be purchased or requested for testing before an order is placed. Special attention should be given to balance and to any marring of the surface by normal cutting and use.

The original cost of plastic dinnerware may be somewhat higher than for medium-weight china, but the replacement costs are estimated to be only about one-tenth of that for china. Differences in shape, density, and balance in design account in some measure for the price range in melamine ware. Competition is keen between the molding companies to produce items from this common basic material that are attractive in color and design and that meet the needs of the food industry. A price quotation from several companies should precede purchase.

The choice between melamine or the long-accepted china dinnerware may pose problems for the prospective buyer. The light weight of melamine, which is about one-third that of ordinary dinnerware, its low breakage, minimum handling noise, and attractive colors make it especially acceptable in many types of foodservice operations, especially in hospitals and other health care facilities, and in school foodservices.

One disadvantage of melamine may be staining and difficulty in cleaning, although improvements in manufacture have reduced this as a major problem. Although melamine products possess low thermal conductivity, thus eliminating the need to preheat them for service, they may present some dishwashing problems. This ware does not air dry quickly and may remain damp for storage. Bacteriological tests on such dishes, however, indicate no cause for concern over this condition.

CARE   The same care in dishwashing as described for china should be followed for plasticware dishes. However, the staining of cups may require the extra step of soaking them to remove the stain. China cups may also require this step.

Many manufacturers of melamine dinnerware have successfully incorporated stain-resistant compounds into the thermosetting resin, which prevents much of the objectionable staining and adds to the life of this type of dinnerware. The development of new washing compounds and closer attention to washing techniques have eliminated the problem somewhat. Alkaline detergents are recommended for washing. Abrasives cannot be used successfully on plastic surfaces; therefore, chemical rinses must be depended on, preferably those without chlorine. Some users believe that frequent cup replacement is the answer and is justly compensated by the high resistance to breaking, chipping, cracking, and crazing under ordinary conditions, the lightness of weight, the low noise level in handling, the attractive coloring and luster, and the relatively low upkeep and replacement costs.

AMOUNTS TO PURCHASE   The initial stock of plastic dinnerware is comparable to that given for china. Sizes of dishes are also comparable. Another guide for amounts of dinnerware to select for the average foodservice would be an allowance of three times the number of dining room seats for items such as bread and butter plates, salad dishes, dinner plates, saucers, fruit and/or cereal dishes, and four times for cups. The amounts of these and other items would depend much on the menu pattern and other conditions mentioned earlier.

Disposable Dinnerware

One-time use items for table service are available in many different materials: paper, plasticized paper, clear or colored thin plastics, styrofoam, and aluminum foil among them. They are available in a wide range of sizes, shapes, colors, and quality by weight. Some are made for use with cold foods only; others withstand considerable heat, making them suitable for oven or microwave use, and for serving hot foods.

The selection of disposable dishware over other types may well be justified, especially for any foodservice using the assembly/serve system, and for fast-food, carry-out businesses.

FACTORS IN SELECTION   Consideration should be given to initial and replacement *costs* of conventional dinnerware, space and equipment for dishwashing, and labor for handling in comparison to the initial and repeat cost of paper or plastic; and its *disposal* and *acceptability* by the persons to be served. In any case, it is well for all foodservices to have ready access to some disposable dishware for times of emergency.

Disposal of large quantities of "disposables" poses problems in some situations. The availability on premises of a large trash compactor is a necessity to handle this waste without undue bulk.

Quantities to purchase are determined by the amount of space to store the large cartons of paper or plastic goods, the relative closeness to a marked supply, and, of course, the number of persons to be served in a given period of time and the menu items offered.

Silver Tableware

SILVERWARE   Quality silverware has been used in discriminating foodservices because of the demands for and interest of the residents or clientele in attractive service. It lends dignity and charm to dining tables, perhaps because of the association of the idea that silver, a precious metal, is found where people know and appreciate gracious, comfortable living. Some knowledge of the manufacture of silverware will help the foodservice manager make a wise decision in the selection of this item.

"Blanks" serve as the basic forms for flatware as well as hollow ware. They are made of 18% nickel-silver, a metal that gives the utensil the needed strength and resistance to bending or twisting to which institutional silverware is often subjected. The design, shape, and thickness or weight of the blanks should be conducive to heavy wear and beauty.

Nine pounds per gross is the standard weight of blanks of ordinary teaspoons sold for public service. The principal weights of blanks used are: heavy, 10½ pounds; regular, 9 pounds; medium, 7½ to 8 pounds. The 9-pound blanks are desirable for hospital tray service, whereas the 10½-pound patterns may be advisable for heavy-duty silverware for certain commercial restaurants and cafeterias. The weight of the blank used influences the price of the silverware.

Flatware blanks are stamped, graded, and rolled until they are the corresponding size of forks or spoons. They are then placed in various presses, and the fork tines or spoon bowls are shaped. In the next step, they are struck with the pattern die, after which the edges are trimmed and smoothed down so that the articles resemble the finished products. Forks should have well-designed tines, durable and heat-treated, to give maximum strength, and both forks and spoons should have heavy reinforced shanks to give the best wearing qualities. After being cleaned and polished, the articles are ready for plating with the silver.

The steps in the manufacture of knives prior to plating differ from those in the making of blanks for forks and spoons. The 18% nickel-silver base was found to produce a blade that bent easily and refused to take an edge sharp enough for practical use in cutlery. Stainless steel has become widely used for knife blades, and noncorrosive alloys have been made that prove satisfactory as the base for solid-handle knives that are to be plated. The popular hollow-handle knife, made with the 18% nickel-silver as the base of the handle, has been largely replaced by the one-piece stainless steel knife with the plate handle. An improvement in the design of knives was the change in style from the long blade, short handle to the short blade, long handle type that permits the user to press down with the forefinger on the back of the handle instead of on the narrow edge of the steel blade.

For better qualities of flatware there is an intervening step between the making of the blank and its plating. Reinforcements of an extra disc of silver are made on blanks at the point of greatest wear: the heel of the bowls of spoons and the base of fork tines (see Fig. C.32). Such treatment is referred to as *overlay*, *sectional plate*, or *reinforced plate*, and increases many times the length of wear.

The plating of silverware is accomplished by electrolysis. Pure silver bars or ingots are placed around the side of a plating tank, and the articles to be plated are hung in the solution in the tank. By means of an electric current, the silver passes from the bars and is deposited on the blanks, the length of time and the strength of the current determining the amount of silver deposited.

After the articles are removed from the plating tank, they are sent to the finishing rooms. Better grades are burnished, or rubbed under pressure with a round pointed steel tool, to harden and smooth out the plate. It is then polished and colored. The better qualities of silverware are given extra burnishing. The various finishes are: butler or dull finish, hotel finish or medium bright, and bright, which are obtained by using different types of buffs and polishing compounds and by carrying the polishing process to different degrees.

The plating of institution silverware is heavier than for the silverware generally used in the home, the most common institution ware being known as *triple plate*, or three times full standard. In triple plate, 6 ounces of pure silver

Figure C.32. Plated silver should be reinforced on the points of greatest wear. (Courtesy, Oneida, Ltd.)

have been applied to 1 gross of teaspoons, with other items in proportion—for example, tablespoons with 12 ounces of silver to the gross. A much lighter plating known as *full standard* carries a deposit of 5 ounces of pure silver to the gross of tablespoons and only 2½ ounces to the gross of teaspoons. *Half standard,* as its name implies, carries half the amount of silver deposit of full standard. Full standard plate quality is the lightest grade recommended for use in institutions.

The leading manufacturers of silver plate generally make, under their own trade name, a better quality of silver plate than those noted above. An example of such silverware is heavy hotel teaspoons, which weigh 11½ to 12 pounds per gross. An extra-heavy plate deposit is used on 10½-pound blanks in their production. Usually the silver overlay on tips and backs of bowls and tines is invisible on any 10½- and 11-pound qualities. The heavy finely finished metal blanks, the heavy plating standard, and the fine finish of this quality of silverware make the initial cost greater than the ordinary commercial grades of plate, but the cost is offset by the long-wearing qualities and satisfactory service of the various items.

HOLLOW WARE   Silver hollow ware items such as serving bowls, platters, sugar bowls, creamers, pitchers, teapots, and coffee pots are made from the same materials as for flatware and are plated in similar manner to varying qualities. The bodies of the various items are die-shaped, and the several pieces for each are assembled and hand soldered by expert craftspeople before plating. The quality of materials and workmanship and the design determines cost.

Features to consider in selecting hollow ware include: sharp corners are to be avoided; short spouts are easier to clean than long ones; simple designs are usually more pleasing than ornate ones and easier to clean. However, plain silverware can become badly scratched with ordinary handling; hence, a pleasing, simple design that breaks the smooth surface may be more practical than plain silver. Simplicity is always the keynote of good taste.

Standard designs and patterns are often made individual by stamping or engraving the name, crest of the organization, or a special decorative motif on the otherwise plain surface. If silverware is to be stamped, the stamping should be done on the back of the item before it is plated. The name of the manufacturer is stamped on the bottom.

Silver hollow ware may seem an extravagance, but when the cost is considered over a period of years, it may be more economical than china or glassware. Furthermore, the satisfaction and prestige gained through its use are not to be discounted.

CARE   The care of silverware has much to do with its appearance and wearing qualities. Careful handling prevents many scratches. The following procedure is suggested for cleaning silverware and keeping it in good condition: sort, then wash in a machine to which has been added the proper cleaning compound, at a temperature of 140° to 150°F, and rinse thoroughly. A final dip in a solution with high-wetting properties prevents spotting of air-dried silver. It is advisable to presoak flatware or wash immediately after use. If washed in flat-bottom racks, the silver should be scattered loosely over the rack surface, sorted after washing, placed into perforated dispensing cylinders, and rewashed to ensure sanitization. If silver is sorted into cylinders before washing, the handles of the utensils are down so that all surfaces of knife blades, fork tines, and bowls of spoons are subjected to the wash and rinse processes. Care must be taken not to overcrowd the containers. The washed silver is left in the cylinders to dry. This system is convenient, especially in self-service units, because clean dispensing cylinders may be inverted over those used in washing, turning the silver upside down so handles are up, and placed on the counter without handling of the clean silver.

Tarnishing of silver occurs readily when exposed to smoke or natural gas, or comes in contact with rubber, certain fiber, or sulphur-containing foods. Detarnishing is accomplished quickly and easily by immersing the silver, placed in a wire basket, into a solution of water plus a cleaning compound containing trisodium phosphate in an aluminum kettle reserved for this purpose.

The tarnish (oxide) forms a salt with the aluminum, and can be removed through a mild electrolytic action. The cleaning compound also cuts and dissolves any grease or dirt on the silver. The silver is left in the solution *only long enough to remove the tarnish*. It is then rinsed in boiling water and dipped in a solution of high wetting qualities. Burnishing machines are used for silver polishing in large foodservices. Care must be taken to see that the machine is not overloaded and that there are enough steel shots of various sizes in the barrel of the machine to be effective in contacting all surfaces to be polished. Also, the right amount of proper detergent must be added to the water in the burnishing machine to produce the required concentration of the solution. There can be no set rule about the frequency of detarnishing and polishing; each foodservice must set up its own standards.

Stainless Steel Tableware

Stainless steel tableware has gained wide acceptance for heavy-duty tableware in many foodservices. The flatware is fairly inexpensive, is highly resistant to heat, scratches, and wear, and will not rust, stain, peel, chip, or tarnish. It stays bright indefinitely with ordinary washing and offers a wide selection of attractive designs from which to choose. Flatware in stainless steel is available in light, standard, and heavy weights. Cheap quality stainless steel utensils have appeared on the market, but they are not really suitable for most establishments. These are made from rolled sheets of the metal and are die-stamped into desired shapes. The resulting pieces are the same thickness throughout and have poor balance, and fork tines and bowls of spoons are too thick to pick up food easily. This quality should be avoided.

Good quality ware is rolled and tapered as needed to give good balance and to be comfortable in the hand. A test for good balance is to place a fork or a spoon at the base of its bowl or tines on an index finger: the utensil should balance equally between handle and bowl or tines. In poor quality, the bowl or tines will overbalance the handle and the utensil will fall off the finger.

Another consideration in selecting stainless steel tableware is the size and shape of the handles. Older persons particularly find it difficult to hold a slim handle and much prefer a wider, easier-to-grasp shape and size.

Water pitchers and individual teapots of stainless steel are considered a lifetime investment, although the initial cost is high in comparison to these items in ordinary glass or pottery. The same methods of sorting, washing, and drying are recommended for stainless steel tableware as for silver.

Amounts of Tableware to Purchase

The menu to be offered determines what items of tableware the foodservice must supply. It is more difficult to calculate the quantities of each piece to stock. As with dinnerware, the trend in use of flatware is toward as few different pieces as possible. For instance, knives and forks of dessert size can be used for many purposes and are usually preferred to knives and forks of dinner size. Dessert spoons may be used for soup and serving spoons as well as for certain desserts.

A good quantity estimate of flatware for cafeterias is twice the seating capacity for all the flatware items required. Should the dishwashing facilities be limited and the turnover of patrons rapid, this quantity might need to be increased to three or even four times the seating capacity. For table or tray service, 3 teaspoons per cover, 3 forks, using a dessert fork for all purposes, and 2 knives per cover usually are sufficient. All other items are estimated on the basis of 1½ per cover, or according to the needs as for banquet or special party service. This may call for limited quantities of specialized items such as oyster or fish forks, bouillon spoons, butter spreaders, or iced tea spoons.

On the basis of total investment in tableware, an estimate found to be about average is that 2½% of the budget for all foodservice equipment is required.

Glassware

Glassware is classed as lead or lime glass, depending on the use of lead or lime oxide in the manufacturing process. Lead glass is of better quality, is clearer, and has more brilliance than lime glass, which is less expensive. Articles of glass are made from a molten compound, formed by blowing them into shape by machine or hand processes or by pressing molten glass into molds by means of a machine. The blowing method is the more expensive and produces a thinner glass of finer texture, higher luster, and clearer ring. Hand-blown lead glass is superior to all other glassware because of its brilliance, light weight, and variety of styles. Lime-blown glassware possesses these characteristics in a lesser degree, is less expensive, and is used extensively in institutions. It is usually machine blown. The style, color, and decoration determine the cost of manufacture of blown-glass articles.

Pressed lime glass is used in many institutions. It is serviceable, and better qualities of it are comparatively free from bubbles and cloudiness. Moreover, it is relatively inexpensive and can be obtained in many styles. A good quality of glassware should be selected for the institution, regardless of whether pressed glass or blown glass is to be used. Desirable characteristics are clearness, luster, medium weight, freedom from such defects as marks and bubbles, and a clear ring. Also, it should be designed so that it is not easily tipped over.

Glassware must pass boiling and shock tests without showing signs of corrosion, chipping, scumming, or cracking in order to meet federal specifications. In making the boiling test, articles are suspended for 6 hours in boiling water in a closed container with vent. The shock test is made by immersing articles in tap water at $18.5°C \pm 2\frac{1}{2}°$ ($65°F \pm 5°$) for a 10-minute period, then suddenly transferring them into boiling water. This procedure is repeated five times. Not all the glassware sold meets federal specifications, and there is no labeling to indicate which, if any, is of that quality.

The sizes of glassware used most commonly in institutions are glasses of 5- or 6-ounce capacity for fruit juice, glasses of 9- or 10-ounce capacity for milk and water, and glasses of 12- or 14-ounce capacity for iced tea. A wide range of sizes and shapes must be stocked for bar service.

Goblets and footed dessert dishes are other items of glass selected for some foodservices. Portion size of specific menu items will determine the capacity size required for these items.

Care of Glassware

Glassware to be washed is sorted and often washed in a separate dishwashing machine from that used for other dishes, or in glasswasher built for that purpose. If glassware must be washed in the same machine used for dishes, it should be segregated and washed first while the water is entirely free from grease and food particles, or left until after the dishes are finished and the soiled water is replaced by clean. In either case, with a rack machine, all items to be washed are placed upside down in racks after they are transported from the dining room and remain in the same racks to wash and drain, and are then loaded onto carts for transport to the point of storage or use without rehandling.

Glassware should be under constant scrutiny to maintain in service only those pieces that are not chipped, cracked, clouded, or scratched in appearance. Filmed glasses may be caused by low rinse pressure and volume, too short rinse cycle, nonaligned spray jets, and a hard water precipitate. Tea stains may be removed by using a chlorinated detergent in the glass washing machine. Water spots may be caused by slow drying or the need for softening the rinse water. The effect of an otherwise attractive dining service may be spoiled by damaged or poorly washed glassware on the tables.

The breakage of glassware in institutions is often high and results from careless handling and storage, choice of improper designs for heavy service wear, use of poor quality of glassware, and subjection to high temperature during washing. The shape of the glass has much to do with the breakage anticipated. Straight side tumblers that can be stacked are a decided breakage hazard, and there are patented shapes available that make it impossible to stack tumblers. Many styles of glassware curve in slightly at the top so that the edges do not touch when they are set down together, the contact coming at a reinforced part away from the edge of the glass. Other styles have reinforced edges at the top, advertised as making them more highly resistant to chipping. This feature is also found around the foot of some stemmed ware.

Amounts to Purchase

The amount and kind of glassware to supply vary as for tableware and dinnerware. Choice is based primarily on the menu, type of service, seating capacity and rate of turnover, dishwashing facilities, skill of persons employed in dish handling, and whether scheduling is continuous or intermittent. However, since glassware is more fragile than other tableware, it is well to have an ample stock on hand of the most frequently used items: tumblers, fruit juice glasses, and sherbet or dessert dishes (if glass ones are used). A suggested rule for quantities to purchase is two pieces for each person to be served; one piece in use and one-half in the dishroom, plus 50% of that total in reserve in the stock room.

Cloth Table Covers

In some localities, tablecloths may be rented from local laundries, thus relieving the foodservice of purchasing and storing this item. However, if cloths are to be purchased, there are many materials from which to choose: pure linen, union, rayon, cotton, cotton mercerized, or linenized damasks, and polyester-cotton blends.

Cotton fibers may be used in combination with linen or rayon in the union damasks to produce durable and satisfactory table coverings and napkins. Rayon and cotton blend table napkins are highly resistant to wear and often superior to all-cotton or all-linen napkins in appearance and breaking strength. Cotton is used alone in plain cotton, mercerized, or linenized fabrics. The last two fabrics are so treated after being woven that a permanent finish is produced to give the cloth characteristics similar to linen. The wearing quality of cotton fabrics is better than that of linen, less loss in strength occurs through laundering, and cotton does not lint. Linen gives satisfaction in use, is attractive, and lintless.

Because of the high initial and maintenance costs of both linen and cotton cloths, those of a 50-50 blend of polyester and cotton with a no-iron finish are rapidly replacing the former in other than the most sophisticated foodservices. Polyester yarns are used in the making of lace cloths as well as the plain woven ones.

Tablecloths may be purchased in white, in colors, or in white with colored borders or designs. Colored linen is popular as place mats and luncheon cloths for breakfast and luncheon services, as well as to help create "atmosphere" in many dining rooms. Fabrics may be purchased by the yard and made up for the specific size tables of the individual establishment, or the cloths may be purchased ready-made.

The size and shape of the tables determines the *sizes* of cloths needed. The cloth should be large enough to hang 7 to 12 inches below the table top at both sides and ends, with allowances made for shrinkage according to the material selected. The usual sizes of tableclothes are 52 by 52 square, 60 by 80 inches, 67 by 90 to 102 inches or longer, depending on the length of banquet tables. Some places use a table-size top over the regular cloth, which allows for frequent changes and reduced laundry costs.

Common sizes for cloth dinner napkins in institutions are 18, 20, or 22 inches square.

Paper Place Mats and Napkins

The range of colors and designs available in paper products is so large that selection of appropriate covers should be relatively easy. Size is dependent upon the size of tray for tray service. For use on table tops, 12 by 18-inch mats provide generously for each cover, although the 11 by 14-inch size is frequently used. Often the name, logo, or design of the foodservice is imprinted on the mat and/or napkin, which serves as good advertising for the establishment.

Glossary

A la carte menu: Menu on which food items are listed and priced separately.

Accident: An unintentional incident that results in injury, loss, or damage of property.

ADA: Americans with Disabilities Act—prohibits discrimination against qualified persons with disabilities in all aspects of employment.

Aesthetics: Having an appreciation for beauty. In foodservice, this applies to food presentation.

Affirmative action: The desire to reach goals to increase the number of women and minorities in specific positions.

AI: Artificial intelligence—information technology that includes robotics, expert systems, and neural networks.

AP: As purchased—refers to weight before trimming or removal of undesired parts.

Assembly/serve system: Also known as the "kitchenless kitchen," fully prepared foods are purchased, stored, assembled, heated, and served.

Banquet: An elaborate, intensive feast in which the service and menu are preset for a given number of people for a specific time of day.

BARS: Behaviorally anchored rating scales—performance appraisal scales that contain specific behaviors identified for each performance level for each job category.

Brand: A particular make of a good or product usually identified by a trademark or label.

Break-even point: Level of activity such as sales volume in which total revenues and total expenses are equal.

Brix: The percentage of sugar by weight in a sugar solution. Expressed as degrees brix and usually applied to canned fruits packed in syrup.

Broker: A wholesaler who does not assume ownership of goods but whose responsibility it is to bring buyers and sellers together.

Budget: A prediction of the amount of money needed for a specific period of time.

Budget variance: The difference between actual expenditures and budgeted amounts.

Budgeting: Fiscal planning, accounting, and controlling.

CAD: Computer-aided design—software programs used to assist in the design and layout of a facility.

Chef de rang: The principle food server in French-style table service, responsible for all table-side preparation.

Chronocyclegraph: A photographic technique to show motion patterns of hands in performing rapid repetitive operations.

Classical theory: A historical theory of management that focuses on tasks, structure, and authority.

Closed shop: Illegal—obligates an employer to hire only union members.

Collective bargaining: An obligation to meet and discuss terms with an open mind.

Commis de rang: An assistant in French-style table service, carries the food to the table and removes dishes as guests complete the courses.

Commissary system: A central production kitchen or food factory with centralized food purchasing and delivery to off-site facilities for final preparation and service.

Conceptual skills: Understanding and integrating all the activities and interests of the organization toward a common objective.

Consideration: Behavior that indicates friendship, mutual trust, respect, and warmth between the leader and the work group.

Contamination: The unintended presence of harmful substances, such as microorganisms in food and water.

Contingency approach: Holds that managerial activities should be adjusted to suit the situation.

Conventional system: Raw foods are purchased, prepared on site, and served soon after preparation.

Coordinating: The functional activity of interrelating the various parts of work for smooth flow.

Cost: The resources expended or sacrificed in order to achieve an objective.

Coved: A curved rather than an angled joining, as at a floor and wall joining.

Critical control points: A food safety and self-inspection system that identifies potentially hazardous foods and proper handling procedures.

Critical incident: Records are kept of critical incidents for each employee to be used for performance appraisal purposes.

Cross-contamination: The transfer of harmful *microorganisms* from one item of food to another via a nonfood surface such as human hands, equipment, or utensils. May also be a direct transfer from a raw to a cooked food item.

Cryogenic: Very low temperature.

Cycle menu: A carefully planned set of menus that is rotated at definite time intervals.

Danger zone: The temperature range between 45 degrees and 140 degrees Fahrenheit in which most bacteria grow and multiply.

Demographics: Dividing or segmenting a market into groups of people based on variables such as age, sex, income, education, religion, and race.

Detergent: Cleaning agents, solvents, or any substances that will remove foreign or soiling material from surface.

Directing: The continuous process of making decisions, conveying them to subordinates, and assuring appropriate actions.

Disseminator role: Transmitting information gathered outside the organization to members inside.

Disturbance handler role: Handling unexpected change.

Du jour menu: Menu of the day.

EEO: Equal Employment Opportunity—the umbrella term that encompasses all laws and regulations prohibiting discrimination and/or requiring affirmative action.

EEOC: Equal Employment Opportunity Commission—provides guidance to management for compliance with EEO statutes.

Entrepreneurial role: Initiating controlled change in the organization to adapt and keep pace with changing conditions in the environment.

EP: Edible portion—weight after trimming, preparation, and cooking.

Ethics: The science of morals in human behavior.

Expectancy theory: Motivation theory, which states that motivation is a function of the person's ability to accomplish the task and his or her desire to do so.

Expert systems: Software products designed to replace specific tasks performed by a specific person.

Extended care facility: An organization concerned with the provision of suitable care for nursing the sick or elderly for long periods of time.

Feedback: Information on how operations worked or failed, or how they should be changed or modified.

FIFO (first-in, first-out):   An inventory method where stock is rotated to assure that items in storage are used in the order in which they are delivered.

Figurehead role: Performing duties of a symbolic, legal, or social nature because of position in the organization.

Flow diagram or chart: A written sketch of the movement of people and/or materials from one step or process to the next, as on a floor plan of a kitchen with arrows drawn to show routes of workers and/or supplies in logical sequence through the facility.

Forecasting: A prediction of food needs for a day or other specific period of time.

Functional principle: Work is divided by specialization.

Garnish: To decorate food, or a decoration used to decorate food.

Geographic segmentation: Dividing a market into different units based on variables such as nations, states, regions, cities, and neighborhoods.

Grade: The rating of quality of meats, poultry, and eggs. Grading is a voluntary service.

Hazard Analysis and Hazard Communication Standards: A standard defined by OSA whereby foodservice operators must inform their employees of potential hazards of all chemicals used in the operation. This communication is done through training programs and proper labeling of chemicals.

Human relations theory: A historical theory of management that views the organization as a social system and recognizes the existence of the informal organization.

Human skills: Understanding and motivating individuals and groups.

Initiating structure: The relationship between the leader and the members of the work group.

Integrated staffing: An orderly plan for moving people into, through, and eventually out of the organization.

Interdependency: A key concept in systems theory that the elements of a system interact with one another.

Interstate commerce: Financial transactions (buying and selling of goods), existing or carried on between states.

Intrastate commerce: Financial transactions (buying and selling of goods), carried on within state boundaries.

Inventory: A detailed and complete list of goods in stock.

Invoice: A list of goods shipped or delivered, including prices and service charges.

Job description: An organized list of duties, skills, and responsibilities required in a specific position.

Job specification: A written statement of the minimum standards that must be met by an applicant for a particular job.

Key result areas: Areas of operation used to quantify quality standards.

Labor-Management Relations Act: Taft-Hartley Act—prevents unions from coercing employees to join, outlaws "union" and "closed" shops, and requires collective bargaining.

Labor-Management Reporting & Disclosure Act: Landrum-Griffin—contains a bill of rights for union members, requires financial disclosures and prescribed union officer election procedures, and provides civil and criminal remedies for financial abuses.

Layout: The arrangement of equipment on a floor plan.

Leader role: Establishing the work atmosphere within the organization and activating subordinates to achieve organizational goals.

Liaison role: Establishing and maintaining contacts outside the organization to obtain information and cooperation.

Line and staff: Support and advisory activities are provided for the main functions of the organization.

Linking processes: Methods used to unify a system.

Local markets: Farmers' markets and minimarkets.

Managerial Grid: A graphical representation of management styles based on the relationship between concern for people and concern for production.

Market: The set of actual or potential customers for a product or service.

Market, local: Suppliers within close proximity to the buyer; includes farmers' markets, nearby supermarkets, and local fish and produce growers.

Market, target: The set of actual or potential customers for a product or service.

Market segment: A group of customers, actual or potential, who behave or react similarly in the marketplace.

Market segmentation: The process of placing customers into groups of like characteristics, such as demographics and geographies.

Marketing: An activity directed at satisfying the needs and wants of customers.

Marketing channel: The food processing and distribution system, beginning with the grower of raw food products and ending at the final customer or point of consumption.

Marketing concept: The management philosophy that holds that determining and satisfying the needs and wants of customers is the primary objective of the organization.

Menu: A detailed list of foods to be served at a meal or, in a broader sense, a total list of items offered by a foodservice.

Menu pattern: An outline of food to be included in each meal, and the extent of choice at each meal.

Merchandising: A marketing term that describes sales promotions. It is a comprehensive managerial function that may include marketing research, product development, advertising, and selling.

Micromotion study: A technique whereby movements of the worker are photographed and recorded permanently on film.

MIS: Management information systems—computerized data processing to facilitate management functions.

Misbranded: A food product whose label either does not include the information mandated by law or the label information is misleading.

Modular: A module is a standard or unit of measure. Modular is that size to which all units, as pieces of equipment, are proportioned; compatible in size to fit together.

Monitor role: Collecting all information relevant to the organization.

National Labor Relations Act: Wagner Act—established the NLRB (National Labor Relations Board), regulates the right of employees to join a union, and requires collective bargaining.

Negotiator role: A person who deals with individuals and other organizations.

Neural networks: Advanced computer technology used predominantly in medical research.

Nonselective menu: A menu that offers no choice of food items.

Open system: A system that interacts with external forces in its environment.

Operations: The work performed to transform inputs.

Organization chart: A graphic representation of the basic groupings and relationships of positions and functions.

Organizing: The function of management that involves the development of the formal structure through which work is divided, defined, and coordinated.

OSHA: Occupational Safety & Health Act—requires employers to furnish employment free from safety hazards.

Path goal theory: Functions of a leader should consist of increasing personal rewards and clarifying pathways for goal attainment for subordinates.

Pathway chart: Flow diagram—a scale drawing of an area on which the path of the worker or movement of material during a given process may be indicated and measured.

Pellet: A preheated metal disc used to maintain the temperature of an individual portion of plated hot food.

Perpetual inventory: A running record of the balance on hand for each item of goods in a storeroom.

Physical inventory: An actual account of items in all storage areas.

Pilferage: To steal in small quantities at a time.

Planning: The function of management that involves developing, in broad outline, the activities required to accomplish organizational objectives and the most effective ways of doing so.

POS terminals: Point-of-sale—cash registers that interact with computers to provide data on items sold.

Primary market: The basic source of food supply, including growing regions and processing plants.

Process chart: Operation chart—a technique for recording and analyzing the breakdown of a job.

Procurement: The process of obtaining. Used synonymously with the term purchasing.

Product: The amount of money charged for a product or service or the total value a customer is willing to exchange for the benefit of a product or service.

Production schedule: A detailed list of food items to be produced for the current day's menu, plus any advanced preparation needed.

Prospectus: A written plan for a building/designing project that details all elements of the situation being planned; used as guide and communication tool for clear understanding by all who are involved in the planning.

Psychographic segmentation: Dividing a market into groups based on variables such as social class, life-style, or personality traits.

Purchase order: Written requests to a vendor to sell goods or services to a facility.

Purchasing: The act of buying.

Quality: In its broadest sense, anything that can be improved.

Quality assurance: Assuring that the quality of the product is satisfactory, reliable, and, yet, economical for the customer.

Quality control: A system of means to economically produce goods or services that satisfy customer requirements.

Quality control circles: A small group that voluntarily performs quality control activities in the workplace.

Quota: An almost always illegal fixed, inflexible percentage or number of positions that an employer decides can be filled only by members of a certain minority group.

Quotation: An amount stated in current price for a desired product or service.

QWL: Quality of Work Life—an approach to management that takes into consideration the quality of human experiences in the workplace.

Ready-prepared system: Also known as cook/chill or cook/freeze, foods are prepared on site, then chilled or frozen, and stored for reheating at a later time.

Receiving: In foodservice, it is the point at which a foodservice operation inspects product and takes legal possession of the product ordered.

Rechaud: A small heater placed on a small table. Used for table-side temperature maintenance of hot foods.

Recommended Daily Allowance (RDA): Levels of intake of essential nutrients considered to be adequate to meet known nutritional needs of practically all healthy persons.

Reporting: Keeping supervisors, managers, and subordinates informed concerning responsibility through records, research, inspection, and other methods.

Requisition: A list of desired products, which generally originates in a department and is submitted to the purchasing department.

Resource allocator: Making decisions concerning priorities for utilization of organizational resources.

Rethermalization: Returning to eating temperature.

Rinsing agent: A compound to remove and flush away soils and cleaners so they are not redeposited on surfaces being washed.

Robotics: Computer-driven devices that are reprogrammable and multifunctional, and designed to perform specific tasks.

Saponify: To turn fats into soap by reaction with an alkali.

Scalar principle: Authority and responsibility flow in a direct line from the top to the bottom of the organization.

Schematic: A scheme or plan in diagrammatic form, such as a rough sketch of a kitchen floor plan and its work units to express ideas, not necessarily to scale.

Scientific management: Popular theory in the early 1900s, concerned primarily with the "best" method and "right" wage for a job.

Secondary market: The physical, functional unit of the marketing system in which products are accepted from the primary markets and distributed to buyers.

Selective menu: A menu that includes two or more food choices in each menu category such as appetizers, entrées, vegetables, salads, and desserts.

Semiselective menu: A menu that includes one or more food choices in at least one menu category.

Sequestering: The isolating of substances, such as a chemical ion, so it cannot react. In foodservice, this is a desired characteristic of polyphosphate detergents to bind lime and magnesium of hard water. Results in clear solution with insoluble precipitates.

Service: An intangible good or product that is offered for sale. A service is intangible and does not result in the ownership of anything.

Sexual harassment: Unwanted sexual advances, or visual, verbal, or physical conduct of a sexual nature.

Single-use menu: A menu specially planned and used only once, usually for a holiday or catered event.

Situational management: Effectiveness of a leader is a function of the individual leader, the subordinate, socioeconomic interests, and situational variables.

Skills matrix system: An organized plan that allows employees to plan their own professional growth within the organization.

Social Security: A federal program of insurance to protect wage earners and their families against loss of income due to old age, disability, and death.

Spokesperson role: Transmitting information from inside the organization to outsiders.

Staffing: The personnel function of employing, training, and maintaining favorable work conditions.

Standard of identity: Defines what a food product must contain to be called a certain name.

Standard of quality: Describes the ingredients that go into a product and apply mainly to canned fruits and vegetables.

Standardized recipe: A recipe that has been carefully tested under controlled conditions. A recipe is considered standardized only when it has been tried and adapted for use by a specific foodservice.

Standards of fill: Regulate the quantity of food in a container.

Static menu: A menu that is used each day, such as a restaurant-style menu.

Subsystems: The interdependent parts of a system.

Subsystems analysis: A method of problem solving or decision making.

Suspension: The action of a cleaning agent required to hold the loosened soil in the washing solution so it can be flushed away and not redeposited.

Synergism: The combined effects of individual units exceeds the sum of the individual effects. This principle is applied to certain types of insulated patient meal trays.

System: A set of interdependent parts that work together to achieve a common goal.

System inputs: The necessary resources for a system to operate.

System outputs: The finished product or services.

Systems management: The application of systems theory to managing.

Systems philosophy: A way of thinking about phenomena in terms of wholes, including parts, components, or subsystems, with emphasis on their interrelationships.

Systems theory: Viewing the organization as a whole made up of interdependent parts.

Table d'hote menu: Menu that offers a complete meal at a fixed price.

Target market: A market segment identified by the seller as having specific wants or needs. Once the segment is identified, the seller develops products to satisfy their wants and needs.

Technical skills: Performing specialized activities.

Theory X: The traditional set of managerial assumptions that employees have an inherent dislike of work and will avoid it if possible.

Theory Y: The attitude held by the emerging manager of the 1960s and 1970s that employees, under the proper conditions, will seek and accept responsibility, be motivated to achieve organizational objectives, and will exercise creativity and imagination in solving organizational problems.

Therbligs: The 17 subdivisions of basic hand movements employed in job performance.

TQM: Total quality management—a management philosophy combining principles of quality assurance, participative management, and QWL.

Union shop: Illegal, requires an employee to become a member of a union in order to keep a job.

Unity of command: Each person should be responsible to only one superior.

Vendor: A seller. A source of supply.

Vermin: Pests that infect foodservice operations, including rodents, insects, and birds.

Wetting: The action of a cleaning agent enabling it to penetrate between particles of soil and between the layers of soil and the surface to which the soil adheres. This action reduces surface tension and makes penetration possible.

Wholesale: The sales of products in large quantities to be retailed or resold by others.

Wholism: The systems theory doctrine that the whole of an entity is more than the sum of its parts.

Work sampling: Random sampling of work to measure the activities and delays of people or machines to determine percentage of productive time.

Work schedule: An outline of work to be performed, procedures to be used, and time schedule for a particular position.

Workmen's compensation insurance: A program administered by the state in which premiums are paid by the employer to cover employee accidents.

Index